A HISTORY OF GENDER IN AMERICA

A HISTORY OF GENDER
IN AMERICA

ESSAYS, DOCUMENTS, AND ARTICLES

Sylvia D. Hoffert

University of North Carolina–Chapel Hill

Upper Saddle River, New Jersey 07458

Library of Congress Cataloging-in-Publication Data

HOFFERT, SYLVIA D.
  A history of gender in America / Sylvia D. Hoffert.
    p. cm.
  Includes bibliographical references.
  ISBN 0-13-012225-4
    1. Sex role—United States—History. 2. Sex role—United States—History—Sources.
3. Masculinity—United States—History. 4. Femininity—United States—History. 5. Gender
identity—United States—History. I. Title.

  HQ1075.5.U6 H64 2003
  305.3'0973—dc21   2002070933

VP, Editorial Director: *Charlyce Jones Owen*
Acquisitions Editor: *Charles Cavaliere*
Editorial/Production Supervision: *Edie Riker*
Prepress and Manufacturing Buyer: *Sherry Lewis*
Marketing Manager: *Claire Rehwinkel*
Cover Art Director: *Jayne Conte*
Cover Designer: *Bruce Kenselaar*
Cover Art: *George Whitefield (1714–1770); Sitting Bull and Buffalo Bill; Women War Workers; all courtesy of Library of Congress.*

This book was set in 10/11 Palatino by Compset, Inc. and was printed and bound by RR Donnelly & Sons Company. The cover was printed by Phoenix Color Corp.

 © 2003 by Pearson Education, Inc.
Upper Saddle River, New Jersey 07458

Printed in the United States of America

10 9 8 7 6 5 4 3 2 1

ISBN 0-13-012225-4

Pearson Education LTD., *London*
Pearson Education Australia PTY, Limited, *Sydney*
Pearson Education Singapore, Pte. Ltd
Pearson Education North Asia Ltd, *Hong Kong*
Pearson Education Canada, Ltd., *Toronto*
Pearson Educación de Mexico, S.A. de C.V.
Pearson Education—Japan, *Tokyo*
Pearson Education Malaysia, Pte. Ltd
Pearson Education, *Upper Saddle River, New Jersey*

CONTENTS

PART ONE
CHRONOLOGICAL HISTORY

CHAPTER FOUR

MASCULINITY IN THE NINETEENTH-CENTURY NORTH (1820–1890)

CHAPTER FIVE

FEMININITY IN THE NINETEENTH-CENTURY NORTH (1820–1890)

CHAPTER SIX

MASCULINITY IN THE NINETEENTH-CENTURY SOUTH (1820–1890)   167

CHAPTER NINE

THE NEW WOMAN AND THE NEW MAN AT THE TURN OF THE CENTURY (1890–1920)

CHAPTER TEN

MASCULINITY IN THE TWENTIETH CENTURY (1920–1975)   320

CHAPTER ELEVEN

FEMININITY IN THE TWENTIETH CENTURY (1920–1975) 360

PART TWO   TOPICAL HISTORY

CHAPTER TWELVE

GENDER, IDENTITY, AND SEXUALITY (1600–1975)   392

Chapter Fifteen

Gender and Work (1600–1975)   523

NOTE TO READERS

The history of gender in America is a relatively new field of inquiry. In 1986, Joan W. Scott published an essay, "Gender: A Useful Category of Historical Analysis," in which she called on historians to add a consideration of the influence of gender on human experience to their repertoire of analytical tools. Since then, ever increasing numbers of historians have begun to systematically study the way that gender has influenced the course of American history. They have attempted to analyze how masculinity and femininity have been constructed and experienced and how ideas about gender have changed over time.

At this point, however, both the quantity and quality of books and articles on the subject are still very uneven. For example, some scholars use the term "gender" as a very specific reference point for analyzing what being a man or a woman meant in various periods in American history. Others use the term as a descriptive rather than an analytical tool, substituting it for the words "man" or "woman" in their histories of human accomplishment. Other problems plague the field as well. Historians have paid more attention to the construction of gender in some periods in American history than in others. There is a substantial body of literature on how gender was constructed and contested during the nineteenth century in various regions of the United States. But historical analysis of how gender was defined and negotiated in the twentieth century is comparatively thin and tends to ignore regional differences. Historians have also paid more attention to the construction of masculinity than they have to the construction of femininity. And until very recently, they have tended to ignore issues of diversity. This is particularly true of historical research on masculinity. Not only does much of it focus on white men, it focuses on those who were middle-class and native-born. Studies on the social construction of femininity are more likely to specifically address the significance of factors such as race, class, and ethnicity. But even so, there is a great deal more information on the gendered identities of white, native-born women than there is on women of other races or ethnic backgrounds. The field of gender studies is developing at a rapid pace. And as it does, new research will give us a clearer and more detailed picture of the influence that gender has had on the lives of various groups of Americans and will fill in the chronological gaps that exist in the literature.

The purpose of this book is to provide college undergraduates with an introduction to the most recent literature on the history of gender in the United States as well as the sources upon which some of this literature is based. Each chapter includes a short introduction explaining the context of the period or subject in question and describing what other scholars have discovered about how femininity and masculinity were defined in that context or period. With the exception of Chapter One, a section of primary documents follows each introduction. These documents are intended to illustrate some of the generalizations discussed in the introductions. Following the documents is an article or articles that illustrate the ways that historians have approached the study of gender. At the end of each chapter, you will find a section that contains suggestions for further reading. This list is not intended to be definitive. Rather, it is a list of books and articles for those who want to pursue a particular topic in more detail. Together, these components are intended to provide the reader with a sense of how gender has been constructed in America and how those constructions have changed over time. They are also intended to provoke questions and prompt discussion about the role that gender has played in the lives of Americans past and present.

This book has two sections. The first is organized chronologically so that students can develop a general understanding of which gender conventions have been most important to the construction of American gender identities, how gender conventions change over time, and which factors have influenced those changes. It covers the period from the onset of English colonization in the early seventeenth century to 1975. The chronological categories that I have used reflect the way that the literature on the history of gender has been presented. The ending date, 1975, is not an altogether arbitrary one. It simply reflects the fact that historians concerned with issues of gender had not shown much interest in systematically studying the last quarter of the twentieth century.

The second section is organized topically in order to provide students with an in-depth analysis of how attitudes toward gender have affected the ways Americans have experienced sexuality, sports, violence, and work. This section builds on the first in the sense that I have assumed in writing the introductory essays for the last four chapters that students have mastered the general outline of how gender conventions have changed over time in American history and that they are sensitive to those factors that cause gender conventions to change. I have included this comparatively short, topical section for three reasons. First, as I did my research for this book, it became apparent that because the literature on these particular topics was so vast, it would be impossible to do justice to it in only a few paragraphs scattered among eleven chronological chapters. My second reason is that the regional distinctions that are so important to many aspects of gender history have less relevance for these topics. And third, I set aside a discrete part of the book for these subjects because it became clear to me that they had special appeal to the students who were taking my gender history classes. For whatever reasons, students feel that these topics are particularly relevant to their lives and spoke to their immediate concerns.

Like most textbooks, this history of gender has no footnotes. In writing the introductions to each chapter I have relied on the original research of hundreds of scholars, most of whom are listed in the "Suggestions for Further Reading" section of each chapter. It is to them and their pioneering work that I dedicate this book.

Before we proceed, a few words about vocabulary are in order. In this text I will be using the terms **manhood**, **manliness**, and **masculinity** interchangeably. I use them to refer to any set of images, values, interests, and activities that a man or group of men hold to be important in the achievement of manhood. I use the terms **womanhood**, **womanliness**, and **femininity** in a similar way.

I will also be using a variety of sociological terms in the introductions to each chapter. The way I use them is defined below.

Sex a word used to describe a person's biological condition; a set of physical/ anatomical characteristics based on chromosomes, hormones, and reproductive capacity.

Gender the cultural meaning given to an individual's sex; a social condition based on anatomical characteristics.

Gender ideal the cluster of characteristics, behavior patterns, and values that members of a group think a man or a woman should have; a set of cultural expectations.

Gender convention the way most people in a particular group express their manliness or womanliness.

Gender construction the process by which individuals both unconsciously and consciously go about defining for themselves what it means to be a man or a woman.

Gender identity the way a person experiences being masculine or feminine.

Sylvia D. Hoffert
Chapel Hill

ACKNOWLEDGMENTS

Like all research projects, this one has benefited from the help of a great number of people. Peter Filene, one of the first historians in the United States to take an interest in the social construction of masculinity and femininity, took time away from his own work to read and comment on every chapter in this book. I appreciate his friendship, generosity, and support more than I can say. Theda Perdue, Doug Stoker, Jim Roark, Sally McMillen, Jan Shipps, Anne Butler, Susan Hartmann, Laurie Maffly-Kipp, Margaret Wiener, Sarah Shields, Chuck Korr, Stephanie Snow, Dick Kohn, Leon Fink, Wendy Gamber, and Cynthia Kierner read and commented on various chapters or parts of chapters. Their insight and expertise were invaluable. The students in my first Gender in American History class at the University of North Carolina along with colleague Roger Lotchin helped me find documents that would be appropriate for this book. I also want to thank the Institute for the Arts and Humanities and the College of Arts and Sciences at the University of North Carolina–Chapel Hill for their financial support.

Sylvia D. Hoffert
Chapel Hill

CHAPTER ONE

GENDER AS A HISTORICAL CATEGORY

WHAT IS SEX? WHAT IS GENDER?

In 1972 *MS* magazine published a short story by Lois Gould entitled "X: A Fabulous Child's Story." In her tale, a group of scientists solicit the cooperation of the parents of a new baby to see what would happen if they failed to train their child to conform to conventional gender expectations. Armed with an *Official Instruction Manual*, the parents name their baby X. They refuse to tell anyone whether X is a boy or a girl. Both of them bounce X, and both of them cuddle it. They expect it to be strong as well as gentle and kind. Sometimes they dress X in boy clothes, and sometimes they dress X in girl clothes. They teach X to catch a ball and to shoot marbles. And they teach X to serve tea and to skip rope. When X is ready to go to school, they dress it in red and white checked overalls that fasten neither on the right nor on the left.

Intellectually, athletically, and artistically gifted, X enjoys school. It excels at both boy and girl activities and has fun doing both. X's teachers are delighted. X's enthusiasm is catching. The other students in X's school begin to follow its example. The boys begin to play with dolls. The girls refuse to wear pink dresses. Their parents are deeply disturbed. They forbid their children to associate with X. But the children are having much too much fun to obey their parents in this matter. So the parents define X as a "disruptive influence." They insist that there is something wrong with X and demand that the Parent's Association meet to discuss "the X problem." They eventually convince school administrators that X needs to be tested by the school psychiatrist. When the psychiatrist concludes that X is the "least mixed-up child" that he has ever examined, they are utterly bewildered.

Their response was in many ways quite predictable. This short piece of fiction illustrates how much we tie our ideas about how people should behave to what we perceive to be their biological characteristics. It shows how much we depend on our understanding of what constitutes masculinity and femininity to make sense of the world we live in. And it testifies to the importance we place on maintaining continuity in our understanding of what is manly and womanly and passing that understanding along to our children. Think how disconcerting it would be, for example, to look through the glass window into a hospital nursery and see little bundles with yellow and green hospital identification tags rather than the more conventional pink and blue. We feel the same kind of momentary unease when we discover that the name Alex designates a girl and that the name Leslie designates a boy. Gould's story exposes in a very dramatic if fanciful way the discomfort, anxiety, hostility, and even anger that we may feel when we are confronted with any sort of gender ambiguity.

We tie our ideas about how people should behave (**gender**) to their biological characteristics (**sex**). There is, as one might expect in any newly emerging field of intellectual inquiry, some debate over the relationship between gender and the body. The problem is a "which comes first, the chicken or the egg?" sort of problem. Or to put it another way, "which comes first—the body or ideas about the body?" This is not the place to try to resolve this problem. So for purposes of this study we will assume the following: **Sex is the word we use to describe a person's biological condition based on perceived physical characteristics as determined by chromosomes, hormones, and reproductive capacity.** Normally, human beings are born with 23 sets of chromosomes. One of these sets determines the person's sex. If that particular chromosome set has two X chromosomes, the person will probably be female. If it has one X and one Y chromosome, the person usually develops into a male. The other biological factor that affects the sex of an individual is hormones. The hormone that is most important for determining sex is androgen. The presence of the Y chromosome usually allows the se-

cretion of androgens that encourage the development of male sex organs and genitalia while the baby is in the womb. The absence of the Y chromosome inhibits such secretion. Without it, the sex organs and genitalia that develop typically are female. Any number of internal and external factors can interfere with this general process. But on the whole, the biological process that determines sex differences is predictable and unchanging.

Our sex may influence our behavior, but it does not necessarily determine it. This is where gender comes in. **Gender is a social condition based on the way any particular group of people interprets anatomical characteristics. It is a label we use to reflect the meaning we attach to perceived sex differences.** Put another way, gender is not just determined by the presence of anatomical differences. It is also determined by the social position of men and women which in turn influences what people think about anatomical differences. If, for example, in a particular society women are considered inferior to men, the possession of a womb is likely to be considered less important than the possession of a penis. Such was the case in ancient Greece where women's subordinate position caused philosophers like Aristotle to argue that women's bodies were not just different from those of men but were inferior to those of men.

Like people in other cultures, we take note of biological sex characteristics and invest them with social significance. Then we teach that social significance to our children. Doing so allows us to organize our understanding of our place in the world. In that sense, manliness and womanliness are social/cultural constructs based on biological difference. They are essentially attitudes and learned behaviors taught to us when we are children by people like our parents, teachers, and ministers. In that sense, they are a product of our socialization. For example, we are socialized to believe that it is not feminine to play football. Similarly, we believe that needlework is not an appropriate activity for boys. So we discourage girls from playing football and boys from embroidering pillowcases. And we do this in any number of ways. We might try shaming them by calling girls who want to play football "tomboys" and boys who are interested in embroidery "sissies." Or we might try to distract them with what we consider to be more gender appropriate activities. The desire to discourage what is considered gender inappropriate behavior is not dictated either by God or by nature. It is simply the way we go about perpetuating and preserving our understanding of biological difference.

It should be pointed out that all societies do not necessarily organize their understanding of sexual difference the same way we do. They may give different meaning to those differences. Early in the twentieth century, Margaret Mead, an anthropologist, went off to the island of New Guinea in the Pacific Ocean to study its inhabitants. There she found three societies whose gender conventions (which simply means the way most people in a group express their masculinity or femininity) were dramatically different from our own. In one, the Arapesh, both men and women tended to be nurturing and relatively passive. In the second, called the Mundugumor, both men and women tended to be extremely competitive and aggressive. The third society was called the Tchambuli. Femininity in that society was defined by the degree to which a woman displayed strength and sexual aggressiveness. Because men were considered to be weaker than women, they were expected to defer to female authority. There was no discernible biological difference among the people in these three groups. Thus, Mead's discussion of the gender conventions in New Guinea clearly illustrates the degree to which ideas about gender are culture specific rather than biologically or divinely determined.

Unlike the Arapesh and the Mundugumor, who make very little distinction between what is manly and what is womanly, our ideas about gender tend to be binary, comparative, and dichotomous. Under normal circumstances, we recognize only two genders (a binary system): male and female, and we view them as being the opposite of one another (dichotomous). Under this system, what

is male is not female. And what is female is not male. We use these binary concepts in a number of ways. Sometimes we divide up work according to gender. For example, we may expect men to do heavy work even if they are physiologically small and women to do lighter work even if they are perfectly capable of lifting heavy objects. We often divide knowledge in much the same way. We automatically expect men to know something about how cars work and are surprised when we find that a woman knows more about them than most men. Traditionally, many aspects of our legal system are based on assumptions of gender differences. Juries, for example, are sometimes more likely to convict men than to convict women for committing violent crimes partly because we consider men to be more aggressive than women. In both the nineteenth and the twentieth centuries, the law authorized the federal government to draft men into military service while women were exempt. Congress and the President clearly assumed not only that men were better suited to being warriors than women but also that it was their duty as citizens to give their lives for their country.

In our society, gender identities are also hierarchical. Or to put it another way, men have usually had more power, prestige, opportunities, rights, and responsibilities than women. What men have done has also been more valued than what women have done. For example, the work men have done has typically been worth more money and has carried with it more access to power and more status than the work done by women. Until the passage of the Equal Pay Act in 1963, it was perfectly acceptable to pay men more for performing the same tasks as their female counterparts. Men have also traditionally had more outlets for their intellectual, artistic, and physical energies. Until recently, women's educational opportunities were limited because of their gender, there was little financial support for their creative endeavors, and they were discouraged from participating in competitive sports. As a result, the way that women have been defined in

American society has acted to deny them access to the resources that would have allowed them to attain equality with men.

It should also be noted that ideas about gender are fluid rather than static. They shift over time as individuals adapt the ideas about gender that they are taught to their own needs. Gender conventions are also dependent upon such factors as social class, race, ethnicity, and age. For example, during the colonial period, the ideal woman, white or black, needed to have a good deal of physical strength and stamina. She was supposed to be industrious, and in a land that was short on labor, her fertility was considered a valuable asset. Her work, whether in the house or in the fields, was recognized as having considerable economic significance. If she was free, she worked with her husband and her children as partners in an economic enterprise that benefited the whole family. If she was a slave, her work contributed to the welfare of her master's family. But by the 1850s definitions of what constituted ideal femininity had changed, particularly for white women in the middle and upper classes. The ideal middle-class woman was now supposed to be physically delicate, economically dependent, and aesthetically decorative. In an increasingly commercial economy, the material well being of her family became more and more dependent upon her husband's income rather than on her domestic skills. While it was her job to conserve and manage the resources of the household, the acknowledged economic value of her domestic work declined. She was also less valued for her fertility since middle-class children, who were not expected to contribute materially to the family unit, became a drain on its resources. These changes did not apply to all women equally. During the same period, physical strength and the ability to bear children continued to be an important asset for farm women, immigrant women, and slave women.

In every period in American history, there has been more than one prevailing masculine and feminine ideal. And each has competed with others for dominance. Those competing gender ideologies provide individuals with the opportunity to choose how they want to express their manliness or womanliness and negotiate the right to do so. For example, a strong, healthy man might choose to develop his intellect rather than his physique despite the fact that those around him judge a man in terms of his physical prowess. Or a woman, interested in pursuing her career, might reject altogether the possibility of having children despite the fact that in her social circle motherhood is a central component of the definition of femininity. In essence, in constructing their gender identity, men and women work within a set of parameters established by the gender ideals and conventions of their particular group. Their range of choices is also influenced by their biological characteristics, their economic condition, their age, and their social status. They work out the way they express their masculinity and femininity either in conformity with gender ideals and conventions or in rebellion against them. In the process, some gender ideals come to dominate their lives, some are marginalized, and some are rejected completely.

Constructing a gender identity is an ongoing, life-long process. Gender ideals for men and women are often age specific. The feminine ideal of fifteen-year-old girls is likely to be very different from the feminine ideal of a woman over sixty. Over time, individual men and women negotiate and then renegotiate what it means to be male or female as their circumstances change. By the time they die, they will have constructed multiple gender identities.

This process of constructing a gender identity is both a conscious and an unconscious process. Children define their gender more or less unconsciously in response to stimuli from those around them. Their parents, teachers, siblings, and friends—even the media—influence how they understand what it means to be a boy or a girl. As people age, their conscious control over their identity increases. They begin to make decisions about whether they will conform to or challenge the gender prescriptions that are presented to them.

Ideas about gender have influenced and continue to influence all aspects of American life. They have determined not only how we as individuals have lived our daily lives and related to those around us but also how we have remembered and recorded our collective past.

WHAT IS GENDERED ABOUT AMERICAN HISTORY?

In chapter 14 of Jane Austen's *Northanger Abbey*, Catherine Morland, a young woman vacationing in the English resort town of Bath, comments casually to a friend about her reading habits. "I can read poetry and plays, and things of that sort," she says, "and do not dislike travels. But history, real solemn history, I cannot be interested in." Her view of history was that it was comprised solely of "the quarrels of popes and kings, with wars and pestilences in every page; the men all so good for nothing, and hardly any women at all." She admitted that she read some history as a "duty." But in the end, she found it "dull" and "very tiresome."

Catherine Morland was not American. And she lived in the nineteenth century. But her observation about what one could expect to read in history books was pretty much true throughout most of the twentieth century in both England and the United States. Before about 1970, American history was written primarily by white men who set about chronicling the public political, economic, social, intellectual, and religious activities of other white men. It was a celebration of American men's efforts to develop and preserve democratic institutions, promote the progress of capitalism, institute a tradition of religious tolerance, and encourage geographic expansion. American history was also characterized by the assumption that white men were the norm and the measure of what humans could accomplish. Therefore, it is not surprising that

historians did not spend much time contemplating the historical significance of anyone who was not white and male. One of the results of that tendency was that they typically failed to concern themselves with the lives, circumstances, and accomplishments of more than half of the population of the United States.

A substantial part of that population was female. Generally, American historians largely ignored women. The fourth edition of Thomas Bailey's *The American Pageant* published in 1971 is a case in point. Trained to define history in terms of male achievement, he devoted only 21 out of 1,000 pages to a consideration of women and their concerns. He mentioned 48 women by name. Of those 48, seven were not American women (Edith Cavell, Catherine the Great, Queen Victoria, Elizabeth I, Queen Isabella, Maria Theresa, and Queen Liliuokalani), six were women whose historical significance was that they were related to men who became Presidents of the United States, and nine were historically significant because they wrote prose or poetry (Emily Dickinson, Edith Wharton, Phillis Wheatley, Edna St. Vincent Millay, Harriet Beecher Stowe, Emma Lazarus, Pearl Buck, Helen Hunt Jackson, and Willa Cather). The most politically active of all the Presidents' wives, Eleanor Roosevelt, was not even mentioned. And women like Margaret Sanger, the founder of the American birth control movement, and Jane Addams, the founder of the field of social work, were also conspicuous in their absence.

When Bailey did mention women and their concerns, his rhetoric and tone were both dismissive and demeaning. For example, when he briefly discussed the women who attempted to challenge male privilege and demanded the right to control their own property, to retain custody of their own children, to educate themselves, to pursue respectable employment, or to vote, he characterized them as a "belligerent bevy of female agitators" and "fiery females," (366) implying that any woman who had the courage to protest her unequal condition was both irrational and hysterical. In this section, he mentioned the number of Elizabeth Cady Stanton's children but failed to acknowledge the legitimacy of the cause of woman's rights and neglected to describe the power and influence of her speeches and writings (366). His discussion of Amelia Bloomer, a newspaper editor who promoted dress reform, ignored the fact that in the mid-nineteenth century the clothing worn by middle- and upper-class women inhibited their movements and posed a real threat to their health. Instead, he pictured Bloomer as a crack pot and focused on the "bawdy ridicule" that resulted from the fact that she advised women to give up their corsets and wear an outfit comprised of pantaloons similar to those worn by the Turks and a short skirted dress that fell loosely from the shoulders (367). In a later section, he depicted Mary Elizabeth Lease, a woman who was a powerful orator and leader of the Populist Party in Kansas, as "the queen of the 'calamity howlers' . . . a tall, mannish woman who was called 'the Kansas Pythoness' " (624). Predictably, he treated male "agitators" with much more generosity. For example, he described the revolutionary Thomas Jefferson as a "brilliant writer" (115) and reform President Woodrow Wilson as a "moving orator" and an "idealist who radiated righteous indignation" (730). Presumably, Lease's indignation about the plight of Kansas farmers was not "righteous" enough to merit notice. It is true that not all historians were as willing as Bailey to ignore or dismiss the achievements of women. But before the 1970s, textbook writers who devoted much space to women were a rare breed.

Historians like Bailey were no more generous to scholars who presumed to write history focusing on women. In 1946 Mary Beard published a book called *Woman as a Force in History*. In it she argued that women had always played important roles as historical actors. In his *New York Times* review of her book, the prominent historian Jack Hexter acknowledged that women had always been a part of society. But, he argued, they did not

deserve much attention from historians because the focus of history was to trace change over time. In his opinion, women had never had the power to bring about significant social, economic, or political change. The people who counted, according to Hexter, were almost exclusively men. Unwilling to leave it at that, he also proceeded to criticize Beard's writing style as tedious, her presentation of evidence as "repetitious," and her tone as "waspish." He charged that the way she organized her material was a "grab-bag" and that her treatment of women's activities was "spotty" and "episodic." All in all, he found her discussion rather on the level which one might expect to find in "our secondary schools." So much for Mary Beard.

Not all historians were as insensitive as Thomas Bailey and Jack Hexter to the degree to which ideas about gender influenced the way people experienced their lives. But until recently, most remained more or less oblivious to the ways in which the concepts of masculinity and femininity affected such things as people's work, their interpersonal relationships, their sexuality, their education, the way they spent their leisure time, and the way the law was applied to them. One of the goals of women's history was to produce a body of scholarship that would be more inclusive.

WHAT IS WOMEN'S HISTORY?

Scholars who developed the field of women's history attempted to make the historical record more complete by including women. Systematic, scholarly interest in the history of women dates from the 1960s. It parallels the rise of what has been called second-wave feminism, a social movement that had two wings. The first was comprised of well-educated, middle-class women who identified with the unhappy, dissatisfied housewives described by Betty Friedan in *The Feminine Mystique*, first published in 1963. Friedan provided them with a critique of their situation, but did not provide them with a plan of action, leaving them feeling somewhat victimized by their circumstances. The second group was composed of young female college students who joined the Civil Rights Movement, the Anti-War Movement, and the Student Movement. Attracted to protest movements partly because of the egalitarian rhetoric that characterized them, these women were outraged when they began to realize that while men welcomed their participation in organizations like Students for a Democratic Society (SDS) or the Student Non-violent Co-ordinating Committee (SNCC), they were often unwilling to treat women as equals, to share leadership positions with them, or to hold their opinions in high regard. These female activists found that when their male colleagues sat down to plan strategy, they sent the women off to the kitchen to make coffee or into the office to type letters. When the women complained, they were ignored. And when they insisted on pressing their complaints, their irritated male associates either insulted them or, perhaps even worse, laughed at them.

The anger and frustration that emerged from these kinds of experiences prompted politically aware women, many of whom taught in colleges and universities, to explore the sources of women's unequal status in American society. Those explorations led to the beginning of what has developed into the field of women's history, a field that focuses on women instead of men, argues that women's experience is as valid a field of inquiry as the experience of men, and assumes that women's historical experience differed from that of men because of their gender.

Since its inception, women's history has gone through a number of distinct yet overlapping stages, a process that is worth recounting in some detail. The earliest stage of women's history could be called "victimization history." It exposed the degree to which women had been sexually, socially, politically, and economically exploited and subjugated by men throughout the course of western civilization. But in defining women as victims, it pictured women as passive and powerless, unwilling or unable to find a way to change the circumstances that they found themselves in.

Given their activist background, it is not surprising that those pursuing the study of women in history were unhappy and dissatisfied with this characterization. So they looked for a different approach, one that would allow them to chronicle the accomplishments of women and the degree to which they were able to overcome the limits placed on them because of their gender. This search led to the second stage of women's history, one that has been called "heroine history" or "contribution history." In this stage, women's historians turned their attention to women who stepped out of their traditional roles and in one way or another competed successfully with men. The women that they concerned themselves with were not passive victims of men, but actors and achievers. They included Margaret Brent who served as Lord Baltimore's lawyer; Mercy Otis Warren who wrote the first history of the American Revolution; Susan B. Anthony who fought for the right to vote; Clara Barton who founded the Red Cross; and Amelia Earhart who flew airplanes. The trouble with focusing on these women, however, was the fact that they were atypical. They were notable because they were exceptional. A second problem was that their place in history was dependent upon what men defined as a "great" person and what activities men categorized as historically significant. Their heroine status was dependent upon their exhibiting characteristics that were considered masculine and doing the things that men did.

The third stage of women's history attempted to broaden the definition of what was historically important. Incorporating the concept that gender was a critical factor in distinguishing the historical experience of men from the historical experience of women, women's historians continued to view women as actors rather than merely passive victims. But instead of using male standards for measuring the significance of human accomplishment and accepting male definitions of who was a "great" person, they began to explore how women functioned on their own terms. In doing so, they shifted the ground upon which history had been based. Taking their cue from other social historians in the 1970s, they turned their attention to groups of women who were for the most part unexceptional. For example, they began to analyze how being a woman affected the personal relationships and work experience of female operatives in the early textile mills in New England. And they also began to study activities and experiences that male historians in the past had ignored totally. They claimed, for example, that female experiences such as childbearing and child nurture were as important to the history of women as male experiences such as engaging in warfare or winning an election were to the history of men. And they argued that such experiences were worthy of historical study and analysis.

In the process of making previously invisible women and their activities and experiences visible, women's historians also questioned the way that written history had traditionally been organized. Because they came at their study of American life from a new perspective, they challenged the way that male historians had divided up their discussion of the American historical experience. When women's historians turned their attention away from political and military affairs, the dates that directed attention to events like the beginning of the American Revolution (1776), the ratification of the Constitution (1789), and the War of 1812 lost their preeminence as important signifiers. Dates that directed attention to the challenge that Anne Hutchinson posed to male authority in colonial Massachusetts (1637) or to reforms benefiting women such as the passage of the New York Married Women's Property Act (1848) or to scientific advances such as the discovery of ether and its application to childbirth (1846) took on new significance because they spoke more directly to the experience of women.

By the 1990s women's historians had entered a fourth stage in their quest to chronicle the gendered experience of women in American history. By this time, they had recovered and written about many of the women wor-thies who had been ignored by earlier historians. And while they were still concerned about the ways that women were oppressed, they acknowledged that women sometimes collaborated in their own oppression either because they did not have the analytical tools to identify those social systems that oppressed them or because they saw some personal advantage in perpetuating those systems.

This fourth stage of women's history was also characterized by the willingness to stress the significance of diversity in the lives of women. Much early women's history was written by women who were white. And it was usually based on those records that were the most easily accessible—prescriptive literature like advice books as well as diaries and letters written by white, native born, middle- and upper-class women who were literate and had the time and energy to leave such documents. Early women's historians tended to present the history of this particular group of women as representative of all women. For example, in 1966 Barbara Welter published an article, "The Cult of True Womanhood, 1800-1860," based on her reading of hundreds of ladies' magazines published in the early nineteenth century. In that article, she argued that these magazines promoted an ideology for "women" that demanded that they be pious, pure, domestic, and submissive. Her approach implied that these ideas applied equally to all American women. In fact, it was a set of ideals that was initially directed to the readers of those magazines, women who were by and large white and middle-to-upper-class. This approach was fairly typical in the first stages of women's history. It assumed that all women were essentially the same and that they experienced historical events in much the same way and at the same time. It overlooked the fact that women's experiences and self-concepts were heavily dependent on a variety of factors such as age, race, class, ethnicity, sexual orientation, marital status, and geographic location. And it failed to acknowledge that while an ideology such as the "cult of true womanhood" was eventually applied to both African-American women and to Native American women, its application in those contexts had a different meaning and consequences.

African-American feminist historians were among the first to argue that the experience of black women was very different from that of white women and that any form of women's history that failed to take this into account was at best distorted. Responses to that criticism have led to the study of the ways in which such things as race and class have influenced the female experience and have resulted in a history of women that is much more complex and nuanced.

WHAT IS GENDER HISTORY?

As we have seen, women's historians have expanded our ideas about who and what were historically significant. They began with the desire to discover what women did and in the process began to address the issue of who women were. Ultimately, they began to study how gender conventions or, to put it another way, how prevailing ideas about femininity or womanhood affected women's lives. History written before the 1970s that focused on the male experience documented the activities and accomplishments of men, but it did not concern itself with the issue of what it meant to be a man. It failed to address the question of how the social construction of masculinity or manhood affected what men did or did not do, and it often ignored how men related to each other and to women in private.

Historians of gender bring to their scholarship an appreciation of the importance of gender conventions and attempt to use gender as an analytical tool to explore how both femininity and masculinity have been defined and how those definitions have affected human relationships. They acknowledge the binary and dichotomous way that we think about men and women. Thus, they assume that men and women are and have been seen as the op-

posite of one another and believe that if you want to study masculinity or femininity, you have to study what they are not and vice versa.

They also assume that men's history and women's history are related to each other and attempt to weave them together. For example, it is clear that for most of American history, men have wielded considerable power over women. That being true, analyzing women's position in American society and evaluating their contributions to American history is dependent upon acknowledging and studying the way they have dealt with the power that men have had over them. At the same time, gender historians are interested in questioning and critically evaluating the degree to which male privilege and power has been a benefit to men. In other words, they do not necessarily accept the premise that male privilege has always worked in men's best interests and are concerned about the degree to which gender conventions have prevented men as well as women from living full and complete lives.

Gender history, then, differs from other forms of history in that it is primarily concerned with variability and fluidity of gendered identity. While gender historians use action to study that identity, they are less concerned with what people did than they are with how manhood and womanhood were constructed, how and why gender constructions changed over time, and what role the process of gender construction played in the lives of both men and women.

WHY IS GENDER HISTORY IMPORTANT?

As we have seen, gender is one of the most fundamental categories that we use to frame our understanding of who we are and of our place in society. Our understanding of what it means to be a man or a woman determines how we behave and how we assess the behavior of others. It affects the way we relate to each other. It affects the way we work and worship and play. It affects the way we are educated. It affects the way we participate in politics and the way we identify and address social problems. It affects the way we express frustration and anger. It complicates the way we deal with the realities of such things as race, ethnicity, and class. And finally, anatomy and the social meaning given to it are linked to the distribution of social, economic, and political power and authority. Therefore, an understanding of gender and the role it plays in society will help us to appreciate the ways in which men and women experience everyday events differently.

Every academic discipline has been affected in the last twenty years by an awareness of the way gender is socially constructed and how that social construction affects the production and transmission of knowledge. History is one of those disciplines. Women's history is now an established field in most college and university history departments. Gender history does not yet have the same status. Just as traditional historians resisted the development of women's history, so have some women's historians resisted the development of gender history. Having only recently earned a relatively secure and respected place for themselves among their male colleagues, they fear that the systematic study of gender will turn attention back to men and that women will again be marginalized and ignored. Others, however, argue that incorporating ideas about both femininity and masculinity into the study of American history will provide us with a deeper and more complex understanding of how what people did was connected to who they thought they were and how who they

thought they were governed their relationships with each other. Such intellectual disagreements are to some degree both predictable and inevitable. They lie at the heart of academic life.

The underlying assumption in this book is that gender history provides us with an important framework for both identifying and understanding the differences between male and female cultures and studying the ways in which they are connected. It gives us new ways of understanding the tensions between those cultures. And it provides us with the tools we need to more carefully analyze how power relations between men and women are shaped, expressed, and contested.

The study of gender history encourages us to seek answers to a number of important questions. How, for example, does gender contribute to the way historical knowledge is organized and presented? What factors have been most important in determining how gender is constructed in any particular period in American history? Whose interests do gender conventions serve? What causes ideas about gender to change? How do these changes take place? What are the results of those changes? What influence do factors such as race, class, ethnicity, sexual preference, and geographical location have on the construction of gender? How do men and women solve problems in their everyday lives using culturally constructed notions of gender? The following text, documents, and articles will attempt to help us formulate answers to those questions. In the process, we will gain a more complex picture not only of how men and women have constructed their personal identities and conducted their lives in the past but also how the power to do so has been negotiated and distributed.

SUGGESTIONS FOR FURTHER READING

CAROL BERKIN, "Clio in Search of Her Daughters/Women in Search of Their Past," *Liberal Education*, 71 (Fall 1985), 205–15.

GISELA BOCK, "Challenging Dichotomies: Perspectives on Women's History," in *Writing Women's History: International Perspectives*, ed. KAREN OFFEN, RUTH ROACH PIERSON, and JANE RENDALL (New York: Macmillan, 1991), 1–23.

GISELA BOCK, "Women's History and Gender History: Aspects of an International Debate," *Gender and History*, I (Spring 1989), 7–30.

HARRY BROD, "The Case for Men's Studies," in *The Making of Masculinities: The New Men's Studies*, ed. HARRY BROD (Boston: Allen & Unwin, 1987), 39–62.

HARRY BROD, "Introduction: Themes and Theses of Men's Studies," in *The Making of Masculinities: The New Men's Studies*, ed. HARRY BROD (Boston: Allen & Unwin, 1987), 1–17.

ELSA BARKLEY BROWN, " 'What Has Happened Here': The Politics of Difference in Women's History and Feminist Politics," *Feminist Studies*, 18 (Summer 1992), 295–312.

KATHLEEN M. BROWN, "Brave New Worlds: Women's and Gender History," *William and Mary Quarterly*, 3rd ser., L (April 1993), 311–28.

JUDITH BUTLER, *Gender Trouble: Feminism and the Subversion of Identity* (New York: Routledge, 1990).

LOIS GOULD, "X: A Fabulous Child's Story," *MS*, I (Dec. 1972), 74–76, 105–107.

J. H. HEXTER, "The Ladies Were There All the Time," *New York Times Book Review*, March 17, 1946, p. 5.

EVELYN BROOKS HIGGINBOTHAM, "African-American Women's History and the Metalanguage of Race," *Signs*, 17 (Winter 1992), 251–74.

EVELYN BROOKS HIGGINBOTHAM, "Beyond the Sound of Silence: African-American Women in History," *Gender and History*, I (Spring 1989), 50–67.

DARLENE CLARK HINE and EARNESTINE JENKINS, "Black Men's History: Toward a Gendered Perspective," in *A Question of Manhood: A Reader in U. S. Black Men's History and Masculinity, Vol. I: "Manhood Rights": The Construction of Black Male History and Manhood, 1750–1870* (Bloomington: Indiana University Press, 1999), 1–58.

LINDA K. KERBER, "Separate Spheres, Female Worlds, Woman's Place: The Rhetoric of Women's History," *Journal of American History*, 75 (June 1988), 9–39.

MICHAEL KIMMEL, "Introduction: Toward a History of Manhood in America," *Manhood in America: A Cultural History* (New York: Free Press, 1996), 1–10.

GERDA LERNER, "Placing Women in History: Definitions and Challenges," *Feminist Studies*, III (Fall 1975), 4–14.

JUDITH LORBER, *Paradoxes of Gender* (New Haven: Yale University Press, 1994).

MARGARET MEAD, *Sex and Temperament in Three Primitive Societies* (New York: W. Morrow & Co., 1935).

ELIZABETH H. PLECK and JOSEPH H. PLECK, "Introduction," *The American Man* (Englewood Cliffs, NJ: Prentice Hall, 1980), 1–49.

DENISE RILEY, "Does a Sex Have a History?" in *"Am I That Name?" Feminism and the Category of "Women" in History* (Minneapolis: University of Minnesota Press, 1988), 1–17.

ANNE FIROR SCOTT, "Woman's Place Is in the History Books," in *Making the Invisible Woman Visible* (Urbana: University of Illinois Press, 1984), 361–70.

JOAN W. SCOTT, "Gender: A Useful Category of Historical Analysis," *American Historical Review*, 91 (Dec. 1986), 1053–75.

HILDA SMITH, "Feminism and the Methodology of Women's History," in *Liberating Women's History: Theoretical and Critical Essays*, ed. BERENICE A. CARROLL (Urbana: University of Illinois Press, 1976), 368–84.

BRYCE TRAISTER, "Academic Viagra: The Rise of American Masculinity Studies," *American Quarterly*, 52 (June 2000), 274–304.

CHAPTER TWO

GENDER IDENTITIES IN THE ENGLISH COLONIES (1600–1760)

GENDER IN A "NEW WORLD"

When the Susan Constant, the Godspeed, and the Discovery sailed into the Chesapeake Bay and then up the James River in the spring of 1607, there were no women on board. The captain, crew, and passengers were all men. Numbering 105 and representing the interests of the investors of a joint stock company, these English adventurers had come to establish an English outpost on a site they would call Virginia. There the colonists hoped to make their fortunes. On a bluff along the James River, they built a stockade in the shape of a triangle, called it Jamestown, and then proceeded to explore and settle the fertile land along the river.

Thirteen years after the founding of Jamestown, a second group of colonists began to settle further north in what became known as New England. Unlike their counterparts in Virginia, this group was composed of both men and women. They had come to the New World to practice their own version of Protestantism in peace. In 1620, the Separatists, better known as the Pilgrims, settled on the rocky coast of Massachusetts in a place they named Plymouth. A second and larger contingent known as the Puritans arrived ten years later in 1630. Sponsored by a group of English business entrepreneurs calling themselves the Massachusetts Bay Company, they chose a site on the Charles River and established the town of Boston, which became the economic and political center of the colony. The investors of the Massachusetts Bay Company were interested in profits, but most early New Englanders were primarily motivated by a desire to escape the spiritual contamination that they associated with the corruption of the Church of England. To avoid God's wrath and to serve as an example to others, the Puritans fled their homes in England in order to establish "a city on a hill" or Bible Commonwealth, an ideal and well-regulated colony of Christian communities in the New World.

Cut off from their mother country by the Atlantic Ocean, both the Virginians and the New Englanders were relatively free to try to establish whatever kind of society they wanted in the New World. Their flight from England provided an unprecedented opportunity for them to re-evaluate their definitions of masculinity and femininity and to adapt those definitions to their new environment.

The English arrived at their destination with a relatively rigid set of ideas about the nature of men and women and their proper relationship to each other. Whether they settled along the fertile coastline of the Chesapeake or on the rocky soil of New England, English settlers brought with them a way of looking at their social world that was extremely hierarchical. At the top of the hierarchy was God. Directly underneath God was the king, and under the king were his male subjects in ranked order. Under man was woman followed by children and servants. Individuals in the hierarchy were expected to defer to the authority of anyone above them.

The colonists believed that men and women were not only fundamentally different but also inherently morally, physically, and intellectually unequal. They were convinced that God in His infinite wisdom had created man in His own image and had given him dominion over the earth and all its inhabitants. He had created woman to be man's companion and helper. The colonists believed that all women were to some degree tainted with Eve's lustfulness, deceitfulness, pride, untrustworthiness, greed, and propensity for insubordination. They believed that because of Eve's sin, God had placed all women under the authority of their fathers, husbands, and masters. Men, then, were responsible for making sure that women were not a source of social disorder. Given woman's presumed weakness and inferiority, men were supposed to provide women with physical protection as well as intellectual and spiritual guidance. And men were also expected to devote their energies toward accumulating enough property to support women economically. At the same time, men were supposed to be loving and considerate toward their wives and daughters and even-handed with their female servants. Indeed, the preservation of social harmony—not to mention their own physical and emotional comfort—was dependent upon being benevolent dictators. But dictators they, nevertheless, had a right to be. Few men or women would have presumed to question the perpetuation of this form of patriarchy as the basis for social order in the new English colonies. Support for the principles of human equality had not yet gained much currency.

Gender relationships in England in the seventeenth century were based on these ideas. The social structure was based on male domination of women. And both the government and the Anglican Church did what it could to keep women in their place. Women had no direct voice in government. When a woman married (and most women did), her legal identity was subsumed under that of her husband. So, under normal circumstances, married women could not own property, sign a contract, sue or be sued, or maintain custody over their children. Moreover, women had no positions of leadership, authority, and power within the hierarchies of the churches.

Woman's subjugation was modified somewhat, however, by the value that was placed on her work. In most cases, marriage was an economic partnership. A man's prosperity depended upon the economic contributions of his wife. Whether they worked on farms in the countryside, in textile manufacturing, in the crafts industry, in city shops and open-air markets, or in their homes, women not only contributed materially to their family's welfare but also reproduced the household labor force by bearing children.

In seventeenth-century England, manliness was measured by the ability to accumulate property, maintain peace and order in the household, and participate in the economic and political world outside the home. Womanliness was measured by a willingness to work hard to help one's husband, nurture one's children, take care of household matters, and defer to male authority. Whether they worked outside it or not, the primary world of women was the world of the home.

While the English intended to re-institute in America the kind of hierarchical social structure that was familiar to them, there were factors that had the potential for modifying somewhat the impact of patriarchal power within the colonial household. For example, their religious doctrines included some egalitarian elements. While they were convinced that women were morally suspect, they were willing to admit that God saved both the descendants of Eve and the descendants of Adam. Women, then, were not without hope for salvation. In that sense at least, they were man's equal.

The second factor that had the potential for moderating their notions about gender was the alternative gender conventions presented to them through their contact with the native population. Comments made by English settlers about their Indian neighbors indicate that the colonists were extremely sensitive to the differences between their gender ideals and those of the Indians. While the economy of coastal Indians in the Northeast was based on hunting and fishing, southern Indians were more dependent upon farming. However they made a living, native relations to the land and to each other stood in sharp contrast to those of the English. Unlike the colonists, Native Americans did not view the land as a commodity to be bought, sold, or owned. They viewed the land as a resource and held it in common, although, admittedly, some had a stronger claim on it than others. In England it was typically men who worked in the fields. In America along the Atlantic coast, native women were in charge of planting and harvesting as well as processing the corn that their families depended on for food. They, and not their husbands, owned the implements necessary to do this. Female control over the food supply was the source of considerable authority for women within each clan group. It gave them influence over tribal decision making, including the selection of leaders and the decision to go to war. In some areas, native women rather than the men built the houses in which their families lived and owned all of the domestic furnishings in those houses. Native men helped to clear the fields for planting, defended their villages from intruders, and supplemented the daily diet of corn with game and fish. But because the English considered hunting and fishing a form of recreation, they viewed Indian men as shiftless and lazy. In the eyes of the colonists, native men contributed little to the material well being of their families and exploited the labor of their wives and daughters. Unlike English society where ancestry was traced through the male line and where men determined where they and their wives would live, native society in many regions of North America including the Southeast tended to be both matrilineal and matrilocal. Ancestry was traced through the mother rather than through the father (matrilineal), and when a man married, he left his home and went to live with his wife's residence group (matrilocal).

Because they considered the indigenous population of the New World to be pagan savages, English contact with the woodland Indians along the Atlantic coast seems only to have confirmed the determination of the leaders of the colonies to preserve the gender values that they brought with them. While they were willing to adopt native crops such as corn and the agricultural techniques required to grow them, most English colonists rejected out of hand any contribution the natives might have made toward the organization of their new societies. Faced with the daunting prospect of building new homes, establishing new communities, and securing their financial future in an alien and unfamiliar environment, they set about establishing social order by imposing the gender conventions that were most familiar to them. In the absence of strong local governments and established churches, they tried to institute a strong patriarchal family structure, hoping that order in their families would lead to order and stability in their new communities. They supported traditional ideas about gender by making land available to male colonists. They transferred to the colonies the British legal system that gave men almost unlimited power over the women in their families. And they established a political system that gave law-abiding, respectable, property-owning men the right to represent their own interests and those of their wives, children, and servants in governmental affairs. They did what they could to assure that women carried out their supportive roles as faithful and deferential helpers and nurturing companions. They rewarded women who were pious, modest, and chaste, passive and dependent, patient and nurturing with high regard and tried to use the power of the church and the state to punish those who were not.

The male leaders of the colonial enterprise seem to have had a fairly clear picture of the kind of gender conventions that were best suited for the social experiment that they were trying to carry out. But their ability to institute those conventions was complicated by a number of factors including gender balance or the lack thereof, patterns of settlement, the strength of their churches, the opportunities available to pursue wealth, and the willingness of the women in their midst to collaborate with their efforts. For that reason, while the gender ideals of the colonists may have been similar all along the coast, gender roles and relations in places like Maryland and Virginia in the Chesapeake and those in Puritan Massachusetts Bay in New England, for example, tended to be different. Because of these differences, let us consider the two areas separately.

GENDER IDENTITIES IN THE CHESAPEAKE IN THE SEVENTEENTH CENTURY

Almost immediately after the original group of male colonists arrived in Virginia, it became clear to the colonial promoters back in England that the men they had sent out to their new colony lacked the self-discipline and work ethic necessary to promote the interests of the company's investors. Competitive, individualistic, prone to violent behavior, contemptuous of authority, and often idle, these adventurers had no reason to pursue any in-

terests other than their own. The mortality rate was extraordinarily high in the Virginia wilderness, which meant that the colonists had little reason to plan for the future. Most of the settlers owned no stock in the company and had no private claim on the land that the company owned. They were merely employees of the Virginia Company. As a result, there was little incentive for them to dedicate their lives to establishing a permanent colony or earning profits for their financial sponsors.

So in an effort to settle them permanently in Virginia and turn them into sober, thrifty, hardworking farmers, colonial promoters decided to give them land and encourage them to marry. They recruited single women who were willing to emigrate and then subsidized their transportation to the colony. We don't know much about the first group of about one hundred women they sent out in 1620. But we do know something about a second group of fifty-seven. These women were widows and orphans related to artisans, tradesmen, and gentlemen from in and around London. Having satisfied the recruiters that they were skilled in the domestic arts and of good character, this shipment of potential brides sailed from the Isle of Wight on the *Marmaduke,* the *Warwick,* and the *Tiger* and arrived in the Virginia wilderness in 1621.

Tobacco planters, who could afford to buy a wife, flocked to Jamestown when the ships carrying the women arrived. Looking for women who were strong, healthy, fertile, and used to hard work, they were relatively unconcerned with establishing strong bonds of affection with them before marriage. Those who found someone who suited them simply paid for the transportation of the woman of their choice by handing over 150 pounds of their best leaf tobacco to the ships' captains. They then took their brides home and set up housekeeping on relatively isolated farms and plantations along Virginia's rivers and streams. There they reared their families, worked together in the fields, and pursued their quest for wealth without much interference or assistance from anyone else. Thus, Virginia developed into a colony of hardworking, independent, self-sufficient farming families, who, in the absence of commercial centers, marketed their tobacco themselves from the wharves that jutted out into the rivers that emptied into the Chesapeake Bay. Every year merchant ships would sail up and down those rivers stopping at the wharves just long enough to pick up their cargo of tobacco and exchange it for manufactured goods that they had brought from England.

Virginia planters were typically geographically isolated from one another. They had little regular contact with government officials, the authority of the Anglican Church was very weak, and they did not usually have neighbors living close by to monitor their behavior and to discipline those who did not conform to traditional gender conventions. In English villages and towns, the behavior of the local drunk or scold could sometimes be modified through the subtle and not so subtle use of social pressure from friends, neighbors, and family members. When such pressure failed to produce behavior patterns that were more socially acceptable, the English could always turn to the church and the courts to punish those who failed to conform. Such social controls were weak in early Virginia. The result was that both male and female colonists were pretty much on their own when it came to establishing and then maintaining their gendered identities and relationships.

Given the circumstances that they found themselves in, men came to define their masculinity in terms of the degree to which they could maintain their personal autonomy and their ability to pursue their own self-interest. Male identity came to be tied to the ownership of land, the exhibition of sexual prowess, and the ability to rule, protect, and provide for the various members of their households. But the ability of men to conform to these ideals was complicated by the relative absence of women and a desperate need for labor. Men in early Virginia needed the labor, companionship, and sexual services that women could provide as well as the labor of the children they could produce. The lack of women in the early years meant that they had to compete with each other for wives. The result was that they were in no position to demand that marriageable women conform in every way to the conventional idea of a perfect wife.

The need for labor on the farms and plantations of the Chesapeake also undermined conventional assumptions about woman's innate physical weakness and the relative importance of her domestic skills. Soon after the colonists arrived, they discovered that fortunes were to be made by growing and selling tobacco. They had the land to grow the crop, but they didn't have the labor force to grow it in great quantities. So, farm wives were often called upon to do the same work as their husbands. They plowed, planted, hoed, and harvested their crop. The strength required by their work belied the notion that women were by nature delicate. And their work as field hands meant that especially during planting and harvesting times they had little time for housework. The result was that Virginia planters often found it necessary to use the cash or credit that they received for their tobacco to purchase many of the products that their wives would otherwise have made in their homes.

These conditions meant that the first few generations of women in the Chesapeake had some freedom to define for themselves what it meant to be feminine and desirable. No doubt, many women did try their best to conform to the English gender roles that they were familiar with. Dependent, dutiful, fertile, and deferential to the men in their lives, they worked hard and reared their children without directing much attention to themselves. But other women publicly challenged traditional gender norms and male authority with conduct so disorderly that they were brought before the courts. Such was the case of Margaret Jones in Virginia who, besides committing adultery, beat and scratched a neighbor while he was gathering peas and hit a passerby with a stalk of tobacco when he tried to interfere. The court sentenced her to be dunked in the river. Having to contend with women who were too outspoken or who engaged in illicit sexual activity meant that it was not easy for men living in the seventeenth-century Chesapeake to establish themselves as model patriarchs.

There is so little information about indentured servants, who provided the bulk of the labor force on the farms and plantations of the Chesapeake, that it is impossible to do anything more than speculate about gender ideals and conventions among them. The indentured servant class was composed of free, white men and women who for one reason or another signed contracts binding them to serve a master for a specific period of time. It also included poor children, convicts, and political prisoners who were transported to the colonies by the English authorities. The indentured were temporarily the legal property of their masters. They could be disposed of in a will. They could be won or lost in a wager. They were subject to whipping and other forms of corporal punishment. And they could marry only with the consent of their masters.

However difficult they might have found their situations, they could, nevertheless, look forward to gaining their freedom. Indenture meant that their bondage was temporary and that, if they survived life in the wilderness, they would eventually become free men and women. Their ability to conform to prevailing English gender ideals was postponed but not totally denied. For men, this meant that after their indenture period was over they could control the fruits of their labor and accumulate property. They could freely marry and assume the manly responsibilities of begetting a family, providing for it, and protecting it. And they had the prospect of eventually being able to participate in public affairs. For female indentured servants, freedom meant that they could trade one form of dependence for another as they shifted from being a servant to being a wife.

The institution of slavery also had a profound impact on both white and black gender conventions and relations. By the end of the seventeenth century, slaves had begun to replace white indentured servants as the primary source of labor in the South. Originally, Africans brought to the New World were treated much like indentured servants and were freed after their period of servitude ended. But as the century came to a close, colonial legislatures passed slave codes that made African servants the property of their masters for life. Cut off from kin relationships that served as the basis for establishing and perpetuating gender conventions in Africa and denied the opportunity to adopt white gender conventions because of their race and legal status, slaves had to create their own definitions of masculinity and femininity.

As in the case of indentured servants, we have very little information on how seventeenth-century slaves constructed their gendered identities. The property of their masters, slave men could not hope to fulfill the prerequisites for attaining manliness as it was defined either in free African society or white colonial society. Slave men did not have freedom of movement. The fact that they could own no property and the fruits of their labor belonged to someone else meant that they had less reason than free men to invest their masculine identities in their work. Their relationships with the women they loved had no basis in law. In colonial society marriage was a contract, and slaves could not sign contracts. Moreover, a slave man's family could be sold away from him at any time on the whim of his master. Such conditions made it next to impossible for most slave men to assume primary responsibility for the welfare of their loved ones.

Yet what little evidence exists suggests that some enslaved men took advantage of whatever opportunities existed to define manliness in terms of their ability to provide and protect those they cared about. They took pride in whatever skills they brought with them from Africa or learned from their masters or other slaves. When they had the time, they supplemented the diet of their families by hunting and fishing. They built furniture for their cabins. Occasionally they were able to negotiate informal agreements with their owners for access to small plots of land or the right to work near the other members of their families. And they helped to educate their children in the strategies of survival in a hostile environment. Assertiveness expressed by stealing, running away, and other acts of rebellion, large and small, helped to establish some sense of personal autonomy and preserve their masculine self-esteem.

Slave women also had to adapt their understanding of womanliness to their new circumstances. Valued in the beginning for their ability to do heavy field work and eventually for their reproductive capacity, slave women, like slave men, were expected to serve the interests of their white masters. They may have had to submit to the authority of their owners, but there was little reason for them to defer to the men with whom they cohabited, who were for the most part relatively powerless to support them or protect them. There was no legal context for their status as wives, and they did not necessarily get to choose their own sexual partners. Given these conditions, slave women had to be as self-reliant as possible. Those who lived on large plantations or in towns and cities could rely on female networks operating out of the slave quarters to provide them with emotional support and material services. But in the end, they had to depend upon their wits to protect their interests and those of their children.

In Virginia, political matters seem to have further complicated ideas about masculinity and femininity. Questions about the relationship between manhood and the state came to a head in that colony as early as the 1670s. In their efforts to obtain land and thereby attain status as independent householders, backwoods farmers were increasingly frustrated by the resistance of the Indians to the movement of white settlers westward and by government officials in Jamestown, who did little to defend those who lived on the frontier. Low tobacco prices threatened their ability to provide for their families. And concern over the payment of taxes and the distribution of tax revenues slowly gnawed away at their willingness to defer to the authority of the small group of well-born planters who governed the colony. All of these frustrations culminated in

what is known as Bacon's Rebellion, a struggle that was in part a conflict between two versions of masculinity. Among the eastern elite, manhood was constructed around property ownership, the maintenance of gentlemanly honor, the ability to maintain social order as representatives of the British crown, and the right to demand deference from those less privileged than themselves. Manliness among independent backwoodsmen was constructed around contempt for authority and a kind of individualism that justified the pursuit of one's own interests and resistance to perceived economic and political injustice at the point of a gun.

The rebellion began in the spring of 1676 when a twenty-nine year old, recent immigrant to Virginia named Nathaniel Bacon led a rag-tag army of backwoods farmers against the seventy-year-old Governor Berkeley and his forces. Bacon soundly defeated Berkeley, invaded Jamestown, and burned it to the ground. Bacon's sudden death, the onset of winter, and royal intervention brought the rebellion to an end.

Women, servants, and slaves all participated in the rebellion. But when the fighting was over, ordinary white men were able to use their political power to pass laws intended to control their potentially disorderly household dependents. Led by those who were in control of the legislature and the courts, they slowly limited the avenues available for women and slaves to challenge their authority. In the seventeenth century, women had been able to influence politics by spreading rumors about those they thought unfit to lead the colony. In the wake of Bacon's Rebellion, the House of Burgesses passed laws that defined politically inflammatory forms of female gossip as libelous speech. Legislators also imposed more control over female sexuality by establishing new and harsher punishments for such crimes as bastardy. At the same time they confirmed their masculine obligation to protect the physical safety and sexual virtue of their wives and daughters by forbidding black men to carry guns or have sex with whomever they wished. By the time the century ended, white, property-owning men and their representatives were well on their way to establishing the basis for patriarchal dominance in both public and domestic life.

GENDER IDENTITIES IN NEW ENGLAND IN THE SEVENTEENTH CENTURY

The original settlement patterns and demographic characteristics of New England were very different from those in the South. As a result, the kinds of gendered relationships that characterized the northern colonies were somewhat distinct. Unlike their southern counterparts, many of the men who originally settled New England brought their wives, children, and servants with them. Sometimes whole church congregations emigrated from England, applied for land grants from colonial governments, and transplanted themselves in a group onto the land that was granted to them. In the towns and villages that they created, both the church and the state were omnipresent sources of social control. So unlike the colonies in the Chesapeake, there was less gender imbalance in New England, and men found it easier to immediately establish their hierarchical control over their dependents.

While there was some opportunity to make a living by fishing or engaging in commerce, most of the early settlers engaged in some form of agriculture or animal husbandry. They lived in close proximity to each other in towns and villages, characterized by the prominence of a meeting house which served their religious and civic needs. The society that they created was one dominated by religious concerns. This is not to say that they were uninterested in the pursuit of wealth. They did, after all, have to find some way to support their families. But for many of the original settlers, such economic concerns were secondary to religious ones.

Because of the importance of community and the power of religion in New England, Puritan ideals of masculinity did not allow for the expression of much individuality or selfishness. Nor were men expected to be particularly self-reliant or autonomous. Theoretically, they could depend on help from their friends and neighbors when they needed it. In charge of the spiritual life of their communities, men living in New England towns and villages were supposed to be pious and churchgoing. Their masculinity was tied up in their ability to support their families and their usefulness to their communities. As a result, the pursuit of wealth was supposed to serve the interests of others as well as themselves.

The case of Robert Keayne illustrates the point. Keayne was born in Windsor, England in 1595. His father was a butcher. When he grew up, he married well, earned the title of "gentleman," and became a successful merchant in London with a reputation for sharp dealing. With his wife, son, and £2000–3000 worth of dry goods and hardware, he left England in 1635 to re-establish his mercantile business in Boston. There, however, his business practices attracted the attention of the magistrates. Three years after his arrival, they hauled him before the colonial court and church. Admonishing him for "selling his wares at excessive rates," they found him guilty of "covetousness and greed" and eventually fined him £80 for what we would call "price gouging." His sentence and punishment were intended to remind him that pursuing his own self-interest at the expense of his neighbors would not be tolerated.

Being a husband was also central to the definition of manliness in colonial New England. Puritan marriages, like those in the Chesapeake, were essentially economic partnerships based on mutual respect if not romantic love. Hierarchically structured with the husband acting as the head of the household and assuming responsibility for the physical, intellectual, and spiritual welfare of its members, they provided a man with the opportunity to construct his manliness around the exercise of power and authority. At the same time, however, a man's self-respect was dependent upon his ability to assure domestic harmony in his home and maintain cordial relations with his neighbors. The man whose wife or children flagrantly disobeyed his orders was subject to public and private ridicule.

From the very beginning, the women of New England had to define themselves within the parameters established by a highly patriarchal social structure. They too were supposed to contribute to the welfare of their families in particular and communities in general by exhibiting those characteristics designed to ensure social harmony, moral uprightness, and economic prosperity. The ideal "goodwife," therefore, was supposed to be hardworking, pious, and deferential to male authority. But imposition of that authority by fathers, husbands, the church, and the state did not necessarily guarantee the co-operation of New England women. Like women in the South, they had any number of ways to challenge gender norms that restricted their lives and the power that men had over them.

Take the cases of Anne Hutchinson, Ann Hopkins, and Anne Bradstreet. Anne Hutchinson arrived in Boston with her husband and eleven children in 1634. Described by John Winthrop, the governor of the colony, as a woman of "ready wit and bold spirit," Hutchinson went about setting up her household, caring for her children, nursing her neighbors through childbirth and illness, and attending church. On the surface she conformed fairly well to the gendered expectations made of her. Like other Puritans, Hutchinson took her religion seriously, but she was unhappy about the way in which her gender inhibited her role in religious life. Following Paul's admonition to the Corinthians and to Timothy that women should keep silent in church, the Puritans did not allow women to preach the Gospel. And they did not believe that God spoke to believers by divine revelation. Instead, they believed that He revealed Himself to them only through the Bible. They were also convinced that God was all-powerful, that human beings were at His mercy, and that there was nothing a person could do to assure his or her own salvation. In their view, God chose a few people to go to heaven, and everyone else was condemned to hell. Through a "covenant of grace," God filled those whom he had chosen to go to heaven with faith. For a minister to suggest to anyone in his congregation that they were not entirely helpless in this matter and that they might go so far as to prepare themselves to receive the gift of faith by being pious or charitable was called preaching the "covenant of works." Implying in any way that individuals could earn their way into heaven by performing good works was, as far as they were concerned, to preach false doctrine. It was over these issues that Anne Hutchinson publicly challenged male authority and attempted to expand her role as a woman in the colony of Massachusetts Bay.

It was a custom in Boston for women to hold religious meetings during the week in their homes where they instructed each other on church doctrine and discussed their ministers' sermons. Like other female church members, Hutchinson held such meetings. Her father had been a minister. So in his household, she had learned the intricacies of Biblical interpretation and theological debate. Hutchinson was apparently a woman of great intellect, strong opinions, and considerable charisma. At some point during her weekly meetings, she began to criticize openly most of the colony's ministers for preaching the "covenant of works" instead of the "covenant of grace." Her charges must have rung true because many in Massachusetts Bay agreed with her.

As her influence spread, it became clear to the ministers and the political leaders of the colony that she posed a serious threat to the patriarchal system and the social order that they had so carefully tried to institute. By charging the ministers with preaching false doctrine, Hutchinson directly challenged male authority on any number of levels. She—a mere woman in their eyes—presumed to interpret scripture and preach the word of God, she publicly insulted most of the ministers in the colony, and she divided the colony into two groups—those who agreed with her and those who did not.

The Puritan leaders of Massachusetts believed that establishing their "city on the hill" depended upon discouraging dissent and fostering co-operation and unity among the colonists. So, in November, 1637, Anne Hutchinson was called before Governor John Winthrop and the other magistrates for behaving in a manner "not tolerable nor comely in the sight of God nor fitting for" one of her sex. For the two days of the trial, she conducted her own defense. She exhibited impressive self-possession considering the fact that she was being questioned by the most important men in the colony, some of whom had been formally trained in law. Much to the frustration of her accusers, she unequivocally denied some of the charges, refused to respond to others, and successfully deflected the rest of them by quoting scripture and engaging in theological debate. But in her enthusiasm, she eventually claimed to have had a divine revelation from God. It took only a few minutes for Winthrop and the other magistrates to find her guilty of heresy and sentence her to banishment.

Allowed to remain in the colony over the winter, she was tried again in the spring by her church. During that trial, Hugh Peter, a minister from Salem, reminded her of the degree to which she had transgressed New England gender conventions. "You," he said, "have stepped out of your place, you have rather been a husband than a wife and a preacher than a hearer; and a magistrate than a subject." For her social transgressions and her religious heresy, she was excommunicated. She and her followers left Massachusetts for Rhode Island shortly thereafter.

Anne Hutchinson refused to conform to some of the Puritan ideals regarding woman's proper place in society. But the magistrates of Massachusetts Bay were able to use the state and the church to prevent her from permanently redefining the meaning of womanhood. Nevertheless, among other things, her case exposed the tenuousness of male power within the Puritan family. Hutchinson's husband appears to have been unable or unwilling to control his wife's behavior or to silence her voice. His failure to do this forced Winthrop and the magistrates to act as surrogate husbands and do it for him. Having moved to Massachusetts at her behest in the first place, William Hutchinson now found himself following her into the Rhode Island wilderness where he would yet again have to establish a new life for himself and his family.

Anne Hutchinson was not the only woman to try to redefine what it meant to be a woman in colonial Massachusetts. Anne Bradstreet, the daughter of one governor and the wife of another, was much more successful in her attempt to critique male power in New England and to expand ideas about what constituted the feminine ideal.

In the seventeenth century, most men had little regard for female intellect. They considered women to be unstable emotionally and intellectually inferior to themselves. John Winthrop, for one, was convinced that a woman who engaged in intellectual activities was likely to come to no good end. In the second volume of his *History of New England*, he chronicled the case of Ann Hopkins, the wife of Governor Edward Hopkins of Hartford, Connecticut. She was, Winthrop wrote, "a godly young woman, and of special parts, who has fallen into a sad infirmity, the loss of her understanding and reason . . . [because of] giving herself wholly to reading and writing, and . . . [for having] written many books." Winthrop felt that her husband was partly to blame for tolerating this activity, implying that Governor Hopkins should have realized what everyone else already knew, that "if she had attended her household affairs and such things as belong to women, and not gone out of her way and calling to meddle in such things as are proper for men, whose minds are stronger, etc., she . . . [would have] kept her wits, and might have improved them usefully and honorably in the place God had set her." Hopkins brought his wife to Boston in 1645, hoping to find someone who could help bring her to her senses. But his efforts were in vain. Presumably, she never recovered from the insanity brought on by stepping outside her sphere.

Winthrop had only to look to his own community for evidence that a female could pursue rigorous intellectual interests and still maintain her sanity, respectability, and womanliness. Anne Bradstreet arrived in Massachusetts on the Arbella with Winthrop in 1630. Married at the age of sixteen, she eventually bore eight children and saw them grow to adulthood. She appears to have conformed to most of her community's gender ideals for women. According to her brother-in-law, she was "honored and esteemed . . . for her gracious demeanor, her eminent parts, her pious conversation, her courteous disposition, her exact diligence in her place, and discreet managing of her family occasions." Apparently a paragon of wifely and domestic virtue, Bradstreet spent what few moments she could spare from her domestic responsibilities and religious obligations writing poems. In 1650, her brother-in-law arranged for their publication in a volume called *The Tenth Muse.*

In her poetry Bradstreet asserted her right to an intellectual life. At the same time, she was able to maintain the respect and goodwill of her friends and neighbors, not to mention those of the colonial authorities. She did this by exploiting Puritan gender ideals rather than trying to challenge them directly. Writing poems filled with affection for her husband, she acknowledged his power over her and articulated her respect for and emotional dependence upon him. In poems about her children, she testified to the depth of a mother's love for her offspring. All the while, she maintained a suitably gendered tone of humility. Bradstreet was not confrontational like Hutchinson. She did not directly challenge the notion of male superiority. Widely admired for what she had created, she was able to establish a feminine persona that included intellectual accomplishment and thereby make a place for herself in the literary life of colonial New England.

THE NATURE OF GENDER RELATIONS IN THE EIGHTEENTH-CENTURY COLONIES

As we have seen, circumstances largely beyond their control helped to determine the ways in which New Englanders and settlers in the Chesapeake implemented their ideas about gender. Those circumstances changed as the colonies matured. As a result, gender ideals as well as gender relations began gradually, almost imperceptibly to change.

By the middle of the eighteenth century there were more colonies along the Atlantic coast, and the colonial population had become religiously and ethnically diverse. Pennsylvania was founded by the Quakers and settled by large numbers of Germans. Maryland served as a haven for Catholics. Scotch-Irish Protestants had settled in the Carolinas. The colony of New York had a large Dutch population. And African slaves continued to be imported to provide both northerners and southerners with labor. Each group of settlers brought with them their own gender ideals and to one degree or other found it necessary to adapt those ideals to their new environment.

Changes in the economy also contributed to changes in gender conventions. To some degree, all of the colonies were established for economic reasons. As they grew and developed, commerce based on agriculture, manufacturing, and the slave trade became increasingly important. While most of the colonies remained primarily rural, some towns grew into cities. Charleston in the South, New York and Philadelphia in the Middle Colonies, and Boston in the North each had its own distinctive urban culture. While some colonists were moving from the farm to the city, others moved westward and gradually formed settlements along the frontier. In each colony, a small group of men, most of whom lived along the eastern seaboard, were able to concentrate wealth and political power into their own hands. As this occurred, social class distinctions increasingly became important in determining how gender ideals were defined and expressed.

In Virginia, for example, the culture of the gentleman began to evolve as propertied men developed a distinctive set of standards for judging manly behavior among their peers. In an effort to distinguish themselves from ordinary tobacco farmers, men who aspired to gentry status flaunted the fact that while they might consider themselves hardworking, they did not normally engage in physical labor and could afford to spend time pursuing such leisure activities as gambling. Betting on horses or cards allowed them to exhibit such manly characteristics as competitiveness, willingness to take risks, and personal independence, which in this case usually meant the right to unilaterally decide how they would spend their money. Since one of the characteristics of the ideal gentleman was skill in the ability to command others, men who aspired to that rank were supposed to maintain peace in their households and tranquility in the slave quarters and to assume leadership roles in the government and the military.

William Byrd II, who lived on a Virginia plantation called Westover, serves as an example of a southern gentleman during this period. Byrd's father, William Byrd I, was a wealthy planter who had made his money trading with the Indians. He sent his young son to England to receive a classical education in 1681. After he finished school, William Byrd II went to London to study law and was eventually admitted to the bar. He returned to Virginia in 1705 and married a year later. We know a great deal about his life because in 1709, he began to keep a diary. In it he recorded his daily activities, attitudes, and aspirations. His daily routine could not have been more regular. He typically awoke at five or six, read Hebrew or Greek, said his prayers, ate breakfast, did his accounts and wrote letters, read a little Latin, ate his midday meal, rode out to visit his friends or stayed home to receive visitors, supervised the work of his overseer and slaves, spent time with his wife, said his prayers, and went to bed. He wrote of his difficulties in trying to "master" his wife and his slaves. He also recorded with pride his activities as commander-in-chief of the local militia and vestryman of his church and wrote of his desire to become governor of the colony. Byrd may or may not have been typical. But from his diary, we know that he tried to exhibit the characteristics he believed that a gentleman should have.

Given the way that he described her, Byrd's wife was what we would call "a handful." She was quarrelsome, had a vicious temper, and did not hesitate to criticize both his manners and the way he conducted plantation business. Nevertheless, she was dependent upon him for support, and every once in a while William did something to remind her of that fact. The kind of power and authority that men like Byrd had over their wives resulted in part from the fact that by the time they married, colonies like Virginia had achieved some degree of gender balance. By the end of the seventeenth century, there were almost as many women living in the Old Dominion as there were men. Men still needed women to gratify their sexual urges, to provide them with domestic services, and to bear their children, but they no longer had to marry any woman who was available. Because it was difficult for a single woman to survive without an economic partner, women who wanted to marry had to be more sensitive to what a man wanted in a wife. So men began to find themselves in a stronger position to expect the women they married to be physically pleasing, modest, and compliant as well as hardworking and domestically skilled.

The expansion of slavery also affected white gender conventions. Once field labor was supplied primarily by slaves, the wives of slave owners could spend less time planting, cultivating, and harvesting and more time in their homes. Their feminine identities became increasingly tied to their domestic duties and maternal responsibilities. Among the upper class, work done by white men and white women became more and more segregated. And while white men continued to take pride in their sexual prowess and to take advantage of their access to Afro-American women, the ability of white women to engage in sexual activity with anyone other than their husbands was increasingly restricted by social custom and by law. As time passed, white, upper-class, southern women were held to a sexual standard that demanded that they be chaste before marriage and faithful after it.

The presence of a potentially rebellious labor force also helped to justify and facilitate the imposition of male authority over women.

In a society that was economically dependent upon the labor of the enslaved and where social status was dependent upon the ownership of those in bondage, it was in the interests of women in slave-owning families to collaborate with their husbands and fathers in establishing a system of deference that would help to assure their economic future and their physical safety. The price they paid for such collaboration was that it became increasingly difficult for them to challenge gender prescriptions or the distribution of power within their households.

It seems clear that southern men tried to impose their patriarchal authority over women during the colonial period. It is hard to tell with any certainty how successful most of them really were. By the eighteenth century, it appears that some upper-class southern men had become less heavy handed in their attempts to establish their patriarchal rights and, within their families at least, had begun to place more emphasis on paternal influence than on patriarchal power. As wealthy male planters began to feel more secure in their social and political positions and less dependent upon the willingness of their wives to work in the fields, they began to openly acknowledge the depth of their emotional dependence on women. The result was that upper-class marriages, while not necessarily always harmonious, were increasingly based on companionship and affection. Wealthy planters socialized their sons to become gentlemen by encouraging them to move about independently, teaching them plantation management skills, encouraging them to expect deference from their social inferiors and obedience from their slaves, and introducing them to the male world of the tavern, cockfight, courthouse, and gaming table. And they collaborated with their wives in the socialization of their daughters by expecting them to remain in the home with their mothers and to concern themselves with domestic matters. Rigid gender roles as well as the ideals of the agrarian patriarch and the companionate marriage were becoming firmly entrenched in upper-class southern culture by the time of the American Revolution.

Change was occurring in New England as well. While patriarchy was gaining strength in the South, the props of male authority were crumbling in New England. The small, homogeneous communities controlled by a religious elite led by a highly regarded minister were beginning to be replaced by towns and cities populated by a wide variety of people, many of whom were more interested in the pursuit of wealth than in matters of the spirit. Disinterest in religion on the part of many and religious disunity on the part of the faithful brought about a decline in the prestige and power of the clergy.

In the seventeenth century in New England, the ideal man was supposed to be community oriented. He was supposed to be a man noted for his personal integrity, moral purity, and religious piety. Many of the original Puritan settlers had tried to conform to those ideals. But their grandchildren and great-grandchildren lived in a different age and had a different view of what constituted ideal manliness. Gradually, a significant number of New Englanders began to behave more like Yankee traders than Godly Puritans and, like their Quaker brethren to the south in Pennsylvania, they began to move the focus of their lives from the meeting house to the counting house and to express their manliness through economic success rather than religious piety. In the process, they increasingly held in high regard men who, while honest and hardworking, exhibited a strong sense of individualism and self-serving ambition. John Winthrop would have been appalled.

Though not a New Englander, Benjamin Franklin of Philadelphia was one of the most influential proponents of this way of measuring manliness. Franklin was the quintessential self-made man. In his youth, he was bound out as an apprentice to a printer. He eventually made his way to Philadelphia where he set up his own printing business and became a wealthy man by the standards of his day. Among the kinds of materials he printed were a series of handbooks called *Poor Richard's Almanack*. The character that Franklin invented to narrate his almanacs was Richard

Saunders, a hen-pecked astrologer. Issued every year, Franklin's almanacs contained all sorts of practical information such as interest tables, calendars, and charts containing the number of hours of daylight and the movement of tides. These were interspersed with advertising and advice. Richard's maxims were the source of such practical wisdom that they have become clichés. It was Richard who pointed out, for example, that "He that lies down with Dogs, shall rise up with fleas" and that "Fish and Visitors stink in three days." In 1758, Franklin published an essay in the Preface to his *Poor Richard Improved* called "The Way to Wealth." In it he discussed those qualities he thought were necessary if a man was to take full advantage of the economic opportunities available to him. Among his observations was that "God helps them that help themselves," "The sleeping Fox catches no Poultry," "Early to Bed, and early to rise, makes a Man healthy, wealthy, and wise," and "The second Vice is Lying, the first is running in Debt."

As male interest in making money increased and concern with religious matters declined, men began to loose their claim to moral leadership in their families and communities. By the early 1700s women began to comprise the majority of church members, and Protestant ministers looked out into a sea of women's faces and heard female voices raised in prayer during services on Sunday mornings. With so many husbands outside the church, women could no longer turn to the men in their family for religious instruction and guidance or depend on them to responsibly carry out their obligations as spiritual leaders of their families. So while women were still subject to the religious influence of their ministers, many found themselves relatively free from the spiritual authority of their husbands and fathers and more and more responsible for the moral training of their children. Mothers were slowly replacing fathers as the link between God, the church, and the family.

Economic expansion and the growth of commercial centers such as Boston and New York also influenced the gendered identities of the wives and daughters of wealthy men. With the availability of a wide variety of imported goods, they could now buy many of the things they needed rather than produce them in their households. They could shop for cloth, for example, rather than spin and weave it. And unlike women who lived on farms and the wives of mechanics and artisans who continued to act as their husband's economic partners, they found themselves increasingly isolated from the business world of their husbands and fathers. Able to hire servants or buy slaves to perform many of their household tasks, they constructed their identities as housewives in part around supervising their servants. They had time on their hands and money to spend. So, they turned their attention to entertaining themselves, cultivating a reputation for gentility, monitoring changes in fashion, and engaging in community service in the form of female benevolence. Eventually, they would claim for themselves a gendered identity that included an important place in the world outside the home.

SUMMARY

Throughout the seventeenth and eighteenth centuries, colonists adapted their gender ideals to the realities of their lives in a constantly changing environment. As they did this, gender relations went through periods of considerable strain as white men sometimes succeeded and sometimes failed to impose their patriarchal authority over women and socially disadvantaged men. By the time of the American Revolution, southern planters were well on their way to establishing a form of agrarian patriarchy. However much it might be contested, the authority they were able to wield over their wives, children, and slaves provided them with a relatively secure basis for their gendered identity. In contrast, the kind of control that men in New England had once been able to exert over women was slowly eroding and their identities as the moral leaders of their communities were weakening.

Changes in gender ideals for white women paralleled these trends. In the early period of colonization, there were more men in the South than there were women. In order to survive and prosper, women needed to work hard and bear children to help clear and farm the land. Their femininity was more or less defined in terms of their ability to do this. As the number of men and women achieved some balance and women began to have to compete for partners, they had to take into consideration male concepts of ideal womanhood in order to attract a husband. This was particularly true among the social elite where wealthy men could pick and choose among a host of young women willing to become their wives. In their households, slaves did most of the manual labor and white plantation mistresses increasingly confined themselves to managing the work of others. In their circles beauty, refinement, and the appearance of physical delicacy began to replace physical strength and stamina as the most desirable feminine attributes. At the same time in the North, women began to replace men as the moral leaders of the family and took advantage of economic changes to begin tentatively to make a larger place for themselves outside the home.

As we have seen, the development of colonies made it necessary for men and women, whether they were native-born, English-born, or African-born, whether they were free, enslaved, or indentured, to reformulate their ideas about gender roles and relations to conform to the circumstances they found themselves in. The ideals and behavior patterns that each of these groups originally established evolved as time passed and circumstances changed. The rebellion against England provided yet another opportunity to reformulate gender ideals and relationships as both white men and women went about redefining what it meant to be a citizen rather than a subject.

DOCUMENT

Excerpts from Anne Bradstreet's *"Prologue" to* The Tenth Muse

As a published poet, Anne Bradstreet excelled at what was considered to be a male activity in the seventeenth century. A well-educated member of an elite Massachusetts Bay family, she was in a particularly advantageous position to observe and comment upon

Source: Anne Bradstreet, *The Poems of Mrs. Anne Bradstreet* (New York: The Duodecimos, 1897), 17–18.

the relations between men and women during the early years of colonization. That she was not censored or disciplined for having stepped out of her sphere may reflect her tact as well as her skill at claiming and maintaining a role for herself as the intellectual and artistic equal of her male peers.

What is Bradstreet's attitude toward her poetry? How does she justify her desire to write it? How do her attitudes toward woman's place reflect the gender conventions that prevailed in colonial New England?

1.
To sing of Wars, of Captaines, and of Kings,
Of Cities founded, Common-wealths begun,
For my mean Pen, are too superiour things,
And how they all, or each, their dates have run:
Let Poets, and Historians set these forth,
My obscure Verse, shal not so dim their
    worth. . . .

3.
From School-boyes tongue, no Rhethorick we
    expect,
Nor yet a sweet Consort, from broken strings,
Nor perfect beauty, where's a maine defect,
My foolish, broken, blemish'd Muse so sings;
And this to mend, alas, no Art is able,
'Cause Nature made it so irreparable.

4.
Nor can I, like that fluent sweet tongu'd
    Greek
Who lisp'd at first, speake afterwards more
    plaine
By Art, he gladly found what he did seeke,
A full requitall of his striving paine:
Art can doe much, but this maxime's most sure,
A weake or wounded braine admits no cure.

5.
I am obnoxious to each carping tongue,
Who sayes, my hand a needle better fits,
A Poets Pen, all scorne, I should thus wrong;
For such despight they cast on female wits:
If what I doe prove well, it wo'nt advance,
They'l say its stolne, or else, it was by
    chance. . . .

7.
Let *Greeks* be *Greeks,* and Women what they are,
Men have precedency, and still excell,
It is but vaine, unjustly to wage war,
Men can doe best, and Women know it well;
Preheminence in each, and all is yours,
Yet grant some small acknowledgement of ours.

8.
And oh, ye high flown quils, that soare the
    skies,
And ever with your prey, still catch your praise,
If e're you daigne these lowly lines, your eyes
Give wholsome Parsley wreath, I aske no
    Bayes:
This meane and unrefined stuffe of mine,
Will make your glistering gold but more to
    shine.

DOCUMENT

About the Duties of Husbands and Wives

Benjamin Wadsworth

This document is an example of advice literature. It does not necessarily describe the way people behaved. Rather, it was intended to outline how they should behave. Written and delivered as a sermon by a Boston minister, Benjamin Wadsworth, it indicates what he considered to be the ideal relationship between a husband and his wife in the early eighteenth century. Notice that it was published at a time when gender roles were clearly changing in New England and the authority of the clergy was declining. Thus, among other things, it may serve as a way of measuring the degree of anxiety that accompanied those changes.

What does Wadsworth think the ideal relationship between a husband and a wife should be? What does his sermon suggest might be possible sources of conflict between husband and wife? Would you be willing to use his sermon as the basis for your wedding vows? Why or why not?

About the Duties of Husbands and Wives

Concerning the duties of this relation we may assert a few things. It is their duty to dwell together with one another. Surely they should dwell together; if one house cannot hold them, surely they are not affected to each other as they should be. They should have a very great and tender love and affection to one another. This is plainly commanded by God. This duty of love is mutual; it should be performed by each, to each of them. When, therefore, they quarrel or disagree, then they do the Devil's work; he is pleased at it, glad of it. But such contention provokes God; it dishonors Him; it is a vile example before inferiors in the family; it tends to prevent family prayer.

As to outward things. If the one is sick, troubled, or distressed, the other should manifest care, tenderness, pity, and compassion, and afford all possible relief and succor. They should likewise unite their prudent counsels and endeavors, comfortably to maintain themselves and the family under their joint care.

Husband and wife should be patient one toward another. If both are truly pious, yet neither of them is perfectly holy, in such cases a patient, forgiving, forbearing spirit is very needful. You, therefore, that are husbands and wives, do not aggravate every error or mistake, every wrong or hasty word, every wry step as though it were a willfully designed intolerable crime; for this would soon break all to pieces. . . .

The husband's government ought to be gentle and easy, and the wife's obedience ready and cheerful. The husband is called the head of the woman. It belongs to the head to rule and govern. Wives are part of the house and family, and ought to be under the husband's government. Yet his government should not be with rigor, haughtiness, harshness, severity, but with the greatest love, gentleness, kindness, tenderness that may be. Though he governs her, he must not treat her as a servant, but as his own flesh; he must love her as himself.

Source: Benjamin Wadsworth, "About the Duties of Husbands and Wives," in *The Well-Ordered Family,* 2nd ed. (Boston: S. Kneeland, 1719), 22–59.

Those husbands are much to blame who do not carry it lovingly and kindly to their wives. O man, if your wife is not so young, beautiful, healthy, well-tempered, and qualified as you would wish; if she did not bring a large estate to you, or cannot do so much for you, as some other women have done for their husbands; yet she is your wife, and the great God commands you to love her, not be bitter, but kind to her. What can be more plain and expressive than that?

Those wives are much to blame who do not carry it lovingly and obediently to their own husbands. O woman, if your husband is not as young, beautiful, healthy, so well-tempered, and qualified as you could wish; if he has not such abilities, riches, honors, as some others have; yet he is your husband, and the great God commands you to love, honor, and obey him. Yea, though possibly you have greater abilities of mind than he has, was of some high birth, and he of a more common birth, or did bring more estate, yet since he is your husband, God has made him your head, and set him above you, and made it your duty to love and revere him.

Parents should act wisely and prudently in the matching of their children. They should endeavor that they may marry someone who is most proper for them, most likely to bring blessings to them.

ARTICLE

Vertuous Women Found: New England Ministerial Literature, 1668–1735

Laurel Thatcher Ulrich

Ministers in the New England colonies made it their business to create and monitor gender ideals in their communities. Some of them did this through sermons. Others wrote about those ideals in eulogies and memorials. In some of those documents, they laid out for their audiences the qualities they believed to be most feminine. In her article, "Vertuous Women Found," Laurel Thatcher Ulrich outlines the characteristics that New England ministers most admired in women, compares them with the qualities that virtuous men were expected to have, and then discusses how ministerial attitudes toward virtue in women changed over time.

Source: Laurel Thatcher Ulrich, "Vertuous Women Found: New England Ministerial Literature, 1668–1735," *American Quarterly,* XXVIII (Spring 1976), 20–40, © The American Studies Association. Reprinted by permission of the Johns Hopkins University Press. Notes omitted.

What characteristics did ministers admire in women? To what degree did they apply different standards to men and women when it came to measuring virtue? What changes in their attitude toward feminine virtue does Ulrich describe? What was occurring in economic, political, and social life that might account for those changes?

Cotton Mather called them "the hidden ones." They never preached or sat in a deacon's bench. Nor did they vote or attend Harvard. Neither, because they were virtuous women, did they question God or the magistrates. They prayed secretly, read the Bible through at least once a year, and went to hear the minister preach even when it snowed. Hoping for an eternal crown, they never asked to be remembered on earth. And they haven't been. Well-behaved women seldom make history; against Antinomians and witches, these pious matrons have had little chance at all. Most historians, considering the domestic by definition irrelevant, have simply assumed the pervasiveness of similar attitudes in the seventeenth century. Others, noting the apologetic tone of Anne Bradstreet and the banishment of Anne Hutchinson, have been satisfied that New England society, while it valued marriage and allowed women limited participation in economic affairs, discouraged their interest in either poetry or theology. For thirty years no one has bothered to question Edmund Morgan's assumption that a Puritan wife was considered "the weaker vessel in both body and mind" and that "her husband ought not to expect too much from her." John Winthrop's famous letter on the insanity of bookish Mistress Hopkins has been the quintessential source: ". . . if she had attended her household affairs, and such things as belong to women, and not gone out of her way and calling to meddle in such things as are proper for men, whose minds are stronger, etc., she had kept her wits."

Yet there is ample evidence in traditional documents to undermine these conclusions, at least for the late seventeenth and early eighteenth centuries. For the years between 1668 and 1735, Evans' *American Bibliography* lists 55 elegies, memorials, and funeral sermons for females plus 15 other works of practical piety

addressed wholly or in part to women. Although historians have looked at such popular works as Cotton Mather's *Ornaments for the Daughters of Zion*, they have ignored the rest. Thus, New England's daughters remain hidden despite the efforts of her publishing ministry. True, a collection of ministerial literature cannot tell us what New England women, even of the more pious variety, were really like. Nor can it describe what "most Puritans" thought of women. It can tell us only what qualities were publicly praised in a specific time by a specific group of men. Yet, in a field which suffers from so little data, there is value in that. A handful of quotations has for too long defined the status of New England's virtuous women. This interesting collection deserves a closer look. . . .

In ministerial literature, as in public records, women became legitimately visible in only three ways: they married, they gave birth, they died. In the written materials, dying is by far the best documented activity. Although a minister might have had a specific woman in mind as he prepared an idealized portrait of the good wife for a wedding or espousal sermon or as he composed a comforting tract for parishioners approaching childbed, it is only in the funeral literature that he is free to name names and praise individual accomplishments. Not that a funeral sermon is ever very specific. Circumlocution, even a certain coyness in referring to "that excellent person now departed from us," is the rule. Still, it is a rare sermon that does not contain a eulogy, however brief. Some append fuller biographical sketches often containing selections from the writings of the deceased. From these materials a composite portrait emerges.

A virtuous woman sought God early. Hannah Meigs, who died in New London at the age of 22, was typical. She began while still a child to pay attention in church, acquiring the habit of reading and praying at night when the rest of her family was asleep. Becoming preoccupied with her own salvation, she bewailed her sinfulness, at last receiving an assurance of God's mercy. In the sickness which eventually claimed her, she submitted her will to God, from her death bed meekly teaching her brothers and sisters and other "Relatives, Acquaintances, & Companions." Praise of early piety was not confined to sermons for young women. In his eulogy for Mary Rock, who died at the age of 80, Cotton Mather devoted considerable space to her early religiosity and the wise education of her parents. The women eulogized typically found God before marriage, having been, in Danforth's phrase, first "Polish'd and Prepar'd" by pious parents.

A virtuous woman prayed and fasted. Jane Colman was said to have lain awake whole nights mourning for sin, calling on God, praying. Mrs. Increase Mather regularly prayed six times a day. After her death her husband wrote a tribute to her from his study, a spot which had become endeared to him when he discovered in some of her private papers that during his four years absence in England she had "spent many whole Days (some Scores of them) alone with God there" in prayer and fasting for his welfare and that of her children. Thomas Foxcroft characterized a praying mother as "One that *stood in the Breach* to turn away wrath" and concluded that the death of such women was a bad omen for the community. Cotton Mather was fond of saying that good mothers travailed twice for their children, once for their physical birth, again for the spiritual.

A virtuous woman loved to go to church. On the day of her death ailing Sarah Leveret went to hear the sermon even though the weather was bitter. When her friends tried to dissuade her, she answered: "If the Ministers can go abroad to Preach, certainly, it becomes the People to go abroad; and hear them." Sarah was not alone among New England's pious matrons. The ministers who preached the funeral sermons for Anne Mason and Jane Steel both commented on the fact that they came to church even when they were ill. Jabez

Fitch said of Mrs. Mary Martin: "The feet of those that brought the glad Tidings of the Gospel, were always beautiful in her Eyes, and it was her great Delight to attend on the Ministry of the Word."

A virtuous woman read. Throughout the eulogies reading is mentioned as often as prayer, and the two activities are occasionally linked as in John Danforth's praise of Hannah Sewall:

> Observing Ladys must keep down their Vail,
> 'Till They're as *Full* of Grace, & *Free* from Gall,
> As *Void* of Pride, as *High* in Vertue Rare
> As *much* in Reading, and as *much* in Prayer.

After her children were grown, Maria Mather took renewed interest in reading the scriptures, more than doubling the prescribed pace by reading the Bible through twice in less than a year. Her daughter Jerusha was a great reader of history and theology as well as scripture, having been given eyesight so excellent she could read in dim light. Katharin Mather, Cotton's daughter, went beyond her grandmother and her aunt. She mastered music, penmanship, needlework, the usual accomplishments of a gentlewoman, "To which she added this, that she became in her childhood a Mistress of the Hebrew Tongue."

A virtuous woman conversed. Mourning for Elizabeth Hatch, Joseph Metcalf lamented nothing so much as the loss of her pious discourse. For John Danforth, Elizabeth Hutchinson's conversation was "sweeter than Hybla's Drops," while for Cotton Mather, the "Fruitfulness" of Mary Rock's "Religious Conferences" made her sick room "A little *Anti-Chamber* of Heaven." James Hillhouse said his mother could converse "on many subjects with the Grandees of the World, and the Masters of Eloquence" yet she was not haughty. "Her incessant and constant Reading, with her good Memory, and clear Judgment, made her expert (even to a degree) in the Bible. Insomuch, that she was capable on many occasions, very seasonably and suitably to apply it, and that with great facility and aptness, to the various Subjects of Discourse, that offered themselves." James Fitch said that if he were to "rehearse the many Spiritual, Weighty, and Narrow Questions & Discourses" he had heard from Anne Mason, "it would fill up a large book." Benjamin Wadsworth praised Bridget Usher for promoting "pious and savoury Discourse." Godly matrons were meant to be heard.

A virtuous woman wrote. A quill as well as a distaff was proper to a lady's hand. Despite eight pregnancies in ten years, Katharin Willard was such a good manager and so industrious that she was "hindred not from the Use of her Pen, as well as of her Needle." One form of writing was simply taking notes in church. Mary Terry wrote down the main points of the preacher's sermon, recalling the whole thing later from her notes, a habit which had apparently become less common by Foxcroft's time, for he commented that aged Bridget Usher and her associates had "practiced (even to the last) the good old way of *writing* after the Minister. They were *swift to hear;* and by this laudable (but not too unfashionable) Method, took care to hear *for the time to come,* as the Prophet Speaks." . . .

A virtuous woman managed well. Increase Mather said his father's greatest affliction was the death of his wife, "Which Affliction was the more grievous, in that she being a Woman of singular Prudence for the Management of Affairs, had taken off from her Husband all Secular Cares, so that he wholly devoted himself to his Study, and to Sacred Imployments." Women were praised in the funeral sermons not only for being godly but for being practical. Even the saintly Jerusha Oliver was not above dabbling in investments. "When she sent (as now and then she did) her Little *Ventures to Sea*, at the return she would be sure to lay aside the *Tenth* of her gain, for Pious Uses." . . .

A virtuous woman submitted to the will of God. Increase Mather told the story of a "Person of Quality" whose only son contracted smallpox. She called in the ministers to pray for him. When they prayed that if by God's will the child should die the mother would have the strength to submit, she interrupted, crying: "If He will Take him away; Nay, He shall then *Tear* him away." The child died. Sometime later the mother became pregnant, but when the time for delivery arrived the child would not come and was consequently "Violently *Torn* from her; so she Died." For the godly woman rebellion was not worth the risks. She learned to submit to God, meekly acquiescing to the deaths of husband and children and ultimately to her own as well. Only one minister suggested that a departed sister was less than patient in her final sickness and Samuel Myles cautioned his reader lest he "Uncharitably, and Unchristianly impute that to the *Person,* which was justly chargeable on the *Disease.*" Cotton Mather's women were typically terrified of death until it approached, then they triumphed over the "King of Terrours." Jerusha Oliver sang for joy and sent a message to her sister in Roxbury telling her not to be afraid to die. Rebeckah Burnet, age 17, expired crying, "Holy, Holy, Holy—Lord Jesus, Come unto Me!" In her illness, Abiel Goodwin heard voices and music and was transported by the tolling of funeral bells. In her quieter moments she exhibited a wry sense of humor, agreeing with a visitor that, given her hydropical condition, she was "A going to Heaven by Water" and might soon sing that song with Jesus.

Read directly, the qualities attributed to these women have little meaning. It is easy to conclude from the lavish praise bestowed upon them that they enjoyed an exalted position in the Puritan ethos. It is even more tempting to conclude the opposite, that the limited nature of their intellectual achievement and their continually lauded meekness and submission document a secondary role. It is helpful, then, to compare this portrait of a virtuous woman with a contemporary portrait of a godly man. Richard Mather, according to the eulogy written by his son Increase, found God early, prayed often, read the scriptures, and though he was learned "was exceeding low and little in his own eyes." Though well-educated, he was careful not to display his learning, and he always preached plainly. He loved to listen to sermons and in his last months continued to attend lectures in neighboring congregations until he was too sick to ride. "Yea and usually even to his old Age (as did Mr. Hildersham) he took notes from those whom he heard, professing that he found profit in it." He was patient in affliction, submitting to the will of God in death. The inference is clear. While a godly woman was expected to act appropriately in all the relations in which she found herself, to be a dutiful daughter, an obedient and faithful wife, a wise parent and mistress, a kind friend, and a charitable neighbor, in her relationship with God she was autonomous. The portrait of Richard Mather, the first spiritual autobiography published in America, is duplicated in miniature in dozens of funeral sermons printed in Boston. But it didn't originate there. It is a pattern of godliness basic to the English reformed tradition. This much should be obvious to anyone familiar with Puritan literature, yet it bears repeating in a time when qualities such as "meekness" and "submissiveness" are presumed to have a sexual reference. In a very real sense there is no such thing as *female* piety in early New England: in preaching sermons for women, the ministers universally used the generic male pronouns in enlarging their themes, even when the text had reference to a scriptural Bathesheba or Mary; the same Christ-like bearing was required of both male and female.

Because dying is an individual rather than a social act, it is in the funeral literature that we see most clearly the equality of men and women before God. It is important, then, to try to determine whether this acknowledged spiritual equality impinged on the prescribed social roles described in the general works of practical piety.

In 1709 there appeared in Boston a reprint of a wedding sermon preached at Sherbourn in Dorsetshire by a nonconformist minister named John Sprint. Called *The Bride-Woman's Counsellor,* it virtually ignored the groom. Marital troubles, the author concluded, were mainly the fault of women anyway. "You women will acknowledge that Men can learn to command, and rule fast enough, which as Husbands they ought to do, but tis very rare to find that Women learn so fast to Submit and obey, which as Wives they ought to do." Like Sarah, women should call their husbands "Lord," never presuming to the familiarity of a Christian name lest they in time usurp his authority and place him under the discipline of an Apron-String. Although women might make light of this instruction to obey, he continued, "I know not of any duty belonging to any Men or Women, in the Whole Book of God, that is urged with more vehemency." Authority had been given to the husband as "absolutely and as peremptorily as unto Christ himself."

This is a remarkable document, all the more remarkable because in the whole corpus of materials printed in Boston there is nothing remotely like it in content or in tone. It makes a useful reference point for looking at three other works printed about the same time: Benjamin Wadsworth's *The Well-Ordered Family,* 1712; William Secker's *A Wedding Ring,* an English pamphlet reprinted in Boston in 1690, 1705, 1750, and 1773; and Samuel Willard's exposition of the fifth commandment in *A Complete Body of Divinity,* 1726.

Wadsworth's treatise must be looked at structurally. Like Sprint he reminded wives to "love, honour and obey," but his entire essay was organized around the notion of mutual responsibility, mutual caring. He listed seven duties of husbands and wives. The first six are reciprocal: to cohabit, to love one another, to be faithful to one another, to help one another, to be patient with one another, to honor one another. It is only with the seventh duty that there is any differentiation at all: the husband is to govern gently, the wife to obey cheerfully. It was thus within an ethic of mutual concern and sharing that Wadsworth developed the obedience theme, and he maintained the parallel structure of the essay even in these paragraphs. Both mates were scolded if they should lift up their hands against the other. A woman who struck her husband usurped not just his authority but that of God. A man who twitted his wife affronted not just a Woman but God. Wadsworth thus undercut the subjection of women to their husbands even as he upheld it.

The same tendency is apparent in Secker. *A Wedding Ring* is a frothy bit of writing, a tiny little book which would have fitted a pocket or pouch. Its intention was not so much instruction as celebration, and it appropriated attractive quotations and metaphors at random, regardless of inconsistency. Although there are traditional proverbs enjoining submission, the great weight of the imagery falls on the side of equality. Eve is a "parallel line drawn equal" with Adam. A husband and wife are like two instruments making music, like two streams in one current, like a pair of oars rowing a boat to heaven (with children and servants as passengers), like two milch kine coupled to carry the Ark of God, two cherubims, two tables of stone on which the law is written.

Willard accepted this two-sided view of the marriage relation and in his short disquisition on the family attempted to harmonize it. "Of all the Orders which are unequals," he wrote, "these do come nearest to an Equality, and in several respects they stand upon even ground. These do make a Pair, which infers so far a Parity. They are in the Word of God called *Yoke-Fellows,* and so are to draw together in the Yoke. Nevertheless, God hath also made an imparity between them, in the Order prescribed in His Word, and for that reason there is a Subordination, and they are ranked among unequals." Yet, referring to the duties of the wife "as inferiour," he cautioned that "the word used there is a general word, and signified to be ordered under another, or to keep Order, being a Metaphor from a Band of Souldiers, or an Army." Further he explained that "the Submission here required, is not to be measured by the Notation or import of the Word itself, but by the Quality of the Relation to which it is applied." The husband-wife relation must never be confused with the master-servant or child-parent relation. A husband ought to be able to back his counsels with the word of God "and lay before her a

sufficient Conviction of her Duty, to comply with him therein; for he hath no Authority or Compulsion." While in any relation it is the duty of inferiors to obey superiors unless a command is contrary to God, "a wife certainly hath greater liberty of debating the Prudence of the thing." Thus, the emphasis throughout is on discussion, on reasoning, on mediation. Wives as well as husbands have the responsibility to counsel and direct. Each should "chuse the fittest Seasons to Reprove each other, for things which their Love and Duty calls for." The command to obedience, for Willard, was primarily a principle of order.

Sprint's sermon, bristling with assertive females and outraged husbands, is an oddity among the ministerial literature. Harmony, not authority, was the common theme. Thus, the marriage discourses support the implication of the funeral literature that women were expected to be rational as well as righteous, capable of independent judgment as well as deference, and as responsible as their spouses for knowing the word of God and for promoting the salvation of the family. A virtuous woman was espoused to Christ before she was espoused to any man.

That few tracts and sermons on childbirth survive is probably evidence in itself of the reluctance of the ministers to stress "feminine" or "masculine" themes over a common Christianity. The limited writing on parturition is worth examining, however, for here if anywhere authors had an opportunity to expound upon the peculiar failings or virtues of the weaker sex.

A pregnant woman in New England's godly community had two preparations to make for the day of her delivery. On the one hand she had to arrange for a midwife, ready a warm and convenient chamber, prepare childbed linen for herself and clothing for her infant, and plan refreshment for the friends invited to attend her. But she knew, even without a ministerial reminder, that these things could prove "miserable comforters." She might "perchance need no other linen shortly but a winding sheet, and have no other chamber but a grave, no neighbors but worms." Her primary duty, then, was preparing to die. Female mortality is the most pervasive theme of the childbirth literature. The elegists loved to exploit the pathos of death in birth—the ship and cargo sunk together, the fruit and tree both felled, the womb became a grave. In his poem for Mary Brown, for example, Nicholas Noyes dwelt at length on the fruitless pangs of her labor: "A BIRTH of *One*, to Both a Death becomes;/ A Breathless Mother the *Dead Child* Entombs." Thus, it was often in a very particular sense that the ministers spoke of the "fearful sex." In stressing the need for a husband's tenderness, for example, Willard had singled out those bodily infirmities associated with the "breeding, bearing, and nursing" of children.

Yet these grim realities had their joyous side. Cotton Mather was fond of saying that though an equal number of both sexes were born, a larger proportion of females were reborn. He wondered why. Perhaps they had more time to spend in godly activities, "although I must confess, tis often otherwise." No, he concluded, it was probably because in childbirth the curse of Eve had turned into a blessing. Given the spiritual equality of men and women, the only possible explanation for a disparity in religious performance had to be physical. Benjamin Colman resolved the same problem in a similar way in a preface to one of his sermons. Writing later in the period than Mather, he could toy with the idea of a "natural Tenderness of Spirit" given to women through the election of God, yet he too focused upon their bodily experience. Pregnancy and childbirth, by turning female thoughts frequently "towards the Gates of Death, by which We all receive our Life," increased women's susceptibility to the comforts of Christ. Pregnancy was superior to regular human ills in this regard, thought Colman, because it continued for months rather than surprising the victim with an acute attack forgotten as soon as it was over.

Even here the ministers were ready to stress similarities between men and women. Though John Oliver urged husbands to be kind to their pregnant wives because of their increased vulnerability to "hysterical vapours," his argument really rested on an analogy, not a contrast, between the sexes. Husbands should be tolerant of their wives, he insisted, because they "desire or expect the like favour to themselves in their own sickness, wherein all men are lyable to many absurdities, and troublesome humours." Eve in her troubles was no more unstable than Adam.

Thus, the ministers were able to acknowledge the reproductive role of women without giving a sexual content to the psyche and soul. They stressed the *experience* of childbirth, rather than the *nature* of the childbearer. It is significant that the one place where they openly referred to the "curse of Eve" (rather than the more generalized "sin of Adam") was in dealing with the issue of birth. In such a context, Eve's curse had a particular and finite meaning, and it could be overcome. Stressing the redemptive power of childbirth, they transformed a traditional badge of weakness into a symbol of strength. Locating the religious responsiveness of women in their bodily experience rather than in their eternal nature, they upheld the spiritual oneness of the sexes. The childbirth literature, though fragmentary, is consistent with the marriage and funeral sermons.

When New England's ministers sat down to write about women, they were all interested in promoting the same asexual qualities: prayerfulness, industry, charity, modesty, serious reading, and godly writing. From 1660 to 1730 the portrait of the virtuous woman did not change. Her piety was the standard Protestant piety; her virtues were those of her brothers. Although childbearing gave her an added incentive to godliness, she possessed no inherently female spiritual qualities, and her deepest reality was unrelated to her sex. Yet an examination of the ministerial literature is not complete without consideration of an important but subtle shift, not in content but in attitude. This begins around the turn of the century in the work of Cotton Mather and continues, though less strikingly, in the sermons of Foxcroft and Colman. Mather's elegy for Mary Brown of Salem, "Eureka the Vertuous Woman Found," marks the tone:

Monopolizing HEE's, pretend no more
Of wit and worth, to hoard up all the store.
The Females too grow wise & Good & Great.

Everything Mather said about Mary Brown had been said before by other ministers about other women. But his open championship of her sex was new. All of the ministers believed in the inherent equality of men and women, but for some reason first Mather, then others, seemed *compelled* to say so.

If we turn to the earliest of the advice literature, Hugh Peter's *A Dying Father's Last Legacy*, written for his daughter in 1660, this subtle shift becomes immediately apparent. The researcher who combs its tightly-packed pages looking for specific comments on women will come away disappointed. Yet the entire work is a profound comment on his attitude toward the subject. That he would write a long and detailed treatise to Elizabeth without reference to her sex is evidence in itself that he considered her basic responsibilities the same as his. Know Christ, he told her. Read the best books. Study the scriptures, using the annotations of divines. Pray constantly. Keep a journal; write of God's dealings with you and of yours with him. Discuss the workings of salvation with able friends. Seek wisdom. Speak truth. Avoid frothy words. Do your own business; work with your own hands. The one explicit reference to feminine meekness is inextricable from the general Christian context: "Oh that you might be God-like, Christ-like, *Moses*-like. *Michael* contesting with the Dragon, maintained his Meekness; and Paul says, it is the Woman's Ornament." For Peter, virtue had no gender. In putting on the woman's ornament, Elizabeth was clothed in the armor of a dragon-fighter as well. In a short paragraph on marriage, he reminded his daughter that while it was the husband's duty to lead, hers

to submit, these duties "need mutual supports." Husbands and wives "need to observe each others Spirits; they need to Pray out, not Quarrel out their first Grablings; They need at first to dwell much in their own duties, before they step into each others." When he told her to stay much at home, he was applying a judgment to his own stormy career and troubled marriage. "For my Spirit it wanted weight, through many tossings, my head that composure others have, credulous, and too careless, but never mischievous nor malicious: I thought my work was to serve others, and so mine own Garden not so well cultivated." Thus, Peter's treatise epitomized the central sermon tradition.

Thirty years later Cotton Mather was promoting the same qualities—but with a difference. Clearly, a contrast between inherent worth and public position was at the heart of his attitude toward women. "There are People, who make no Noise at all in the World, People hardly known to be in the World; Persons of the *Female Sex*, and under all the Covers imaginable. But the world has not many People in it, that are fuller of the Truest Glory." That women made no noise bothered Mather, and he was continually devising metaphorical detours around the Pauline proscriptions. "Yes, those who may not *Speak in the Church*, does our Glorious Lord Employ to *Speak*: to *Speak* to us, and *Speak* by what we *see* in them, such Things as we ought certainly to take much Notice of." He made much of the fact that Abiel Goodwin, a little damsel half his age, had taught him much of salvation, and in her funeral sermon he expressed pleasure that she could finally "without any Disorder" speak in the Church.

But there was a route to worldly honor open to women, one which no epistle denied. "They that might not without *Sin*, lead the Life which old stories ascribe to *Amazons*, have with much Praise done the part of *Scholars* in the World." A long section in *Ornaments for the Daughters of Zion* was devoted to the promotion of female writing. Mather combed the scriptures and the classics for precedents and applauded the efforts of near contemporaries such as Anna Maria Schurman, a Dutch feminist whose tract *The Learned Maid* probably influenced his decision to teach Katharin Hebrew. Schurman's argument, deeply imbedded in traditional piety, would have been congenial to Mather. She excluded from discussion "*Scriptural Theology*, properly so named, as that which without Controversie belongs to all Christians," directing her attention to that wider scholarship commonly denied women. If you say we are weak witted, she wrote, studies will help us. If you say we are not inclined to studies, let us taste their sweetness and you will see. If you say we have no colleges, we can use private teachers. If you say our vocations are narrow, we answer they are merely private; we are not exempt from the universal sentence of Plutarch: "It becomes a perfect Man, to know what is to be Known, and to do what is to be done." She concluded by suggesting that young women be exposed from their infancy to the "encouragement of wise men" and the "examples of illustrious women." In his tracts and in his sermons, Mather enthusiastically provided both.

It is important to understand that we are not dealing with a new concept of women in Mather's work, but a new visibility. Though in 1660 under sentence of death, Peter could hardly have recommended a public role for Elizabeth, there is evidence that he was as ready as Mather to value female scholarship and writing. In 1651 he had contributed a Prefatory letter to a revolutionary tract by Mary Cary, applauding her clear opening of the scriptures and her rejection of "naked Brests, black Patches" and "long Trains" in favor of a pen. He referred to "Two of this Sexe I have met with, very famous for more than their mother-tongue, and for what we call Learning, yet living." One of these women, "the glory of her sexe in Holland," was apparently Anna Maria Schurman, whom Peter may have met in Utrecht.

As important as Mather's promotion of increased intellectual activity for women was the luster he gave to their more traditional roles. In beginning his funeral sermon for his own mother, he exclaimed: "Oh! The Endearments of our God! Beyond all the Endearments of the Tenderest Mother in the World!" Taking for his text Isaiah 49:15, "Can a Woman forget her Sucking Child, that she should not have Compassion on the Son of her Bowels? Yea, They may forget: yet will not I forget thee," he drew out the parallels between the love of God and the love of a mother. "The Disposition which the Glorious God has to provide for the *Comfort* of His People, has Two Resemblances, in *His Two Testaments;* And in both of them, 'tis Resembled unto the Provision which *Female-Parents* make for their Young-ones." Mothers comfort their children through their good instructions, through their good examples, and through their pious prayers. These, however, are temporary comforts. Mothers feed us, but God does more. Mothers clothe us, but God does more. Mothers guide us, but God does more. Mothers keep us out of harm's way, but God does more. Mothers confer ornaments upon us, but God confers upon us the lasting ornament. Thus God is a better mother than our earthly mothers. At this point, Mather drew back somewhat from his metaphor, assuring his audience that God was also our father. "What is the best of Mothers weigh'd in the Ballance with Such a *Father*? Our *Father* is now the Infinite God." But he went on:

> It has been a little Surprising unto me to find That in some of the Primitive Writers, the *Holy Spirit* is called, *The Mother*. Tertullian uses this Denomination for the *Holy Spirit; the Mother,* who is Invocated with the *Father* and the *Son*.

Instead of recoiling from the heresy, Mather explained the reasonableness of the metaphor. It is through the Holy Ghost that we are born again. The Holy Ghost is spoken of in the scriptures as a comforter. Surely nothing is of greater comfort than a good mother.

Mather did not mean to deify women. In finding female as well as male virtues in the Godhead, he was simply reasserting the spiritual equality of men and women and the essentially asexual nature of godliness. But he was doing something else as well. He was openly and generously bolstering the public image of Boston's women.

If a person believes in the inherent equality of the sexes yet notes an inequity in the way they are regarded in society, he can resolve the discrepancy in three ways. He can try to change women, encouraging them to enlarge those activities which might bring them honor and recognition. He can try to change society, urging recognition and praise for the unsung activities women already excel in. Or he can dismiss the whole problem, deny the importance of status altogether, and turn his attention to the spiritual realm. Mather tried all three. In praising the works of Anna Maria Schurman and in teaching his daughter Hebrew, he put himself on the side of enlarged opportunity. In eulogizing his mother, he gave public recognition to a specifically feminine role. But as a good minister he could not commit himself completely to any worldly activity. His real commitment had to be to the glory of God. Paradoxically, then, one of the attractions of women for Mather seems to have been their very lack of status. In praising them, he was not only encouraging their good works, he was demonstrating his own superiority to earthly standards. Thus he withdrew with one hand what he had given with the other.

Mather's work points to a difficulty in reconciling inherent worth and earthly position. For most of the ministers through most of the period this had been no problem. Either they had seen no discrepancy or they were unconcerned with questions of status. The reasons for Mather's position are not entirely clear, although several explanations suggest themselves. On the one hand, he may have been influenced by European feminist thought; in a letter to his sister-in-law, who was living in England, he mentioned not only Anna Maria Schurman but Marie de Gournay. Yet even with an allowance for the Atlantic, the writings of neither were new. Gournay's essays were published in the 1620's, Schurman's in the 1650's. Nor was Schurman unknown to earlier ministers, as the Hugh Peter friendship shows. More probably, Mather was dealing

with changes in his own provincial society. It is a commonplace that by the end of the seventeenth century, New England was becoming more secular as well as more prosperous. The presumed threat of leisure hangs over much of Mather's writing. In his first booklet, he noted that while women often had a great deal to do, "it is as *often* so, that you have little more Worldly Business, that to Spend (I should rather say, to Save) what others *Get*, and to *Dress* and *Feed* (should I not also say, to *Teach*) the Little Birds, which you are *Dams* unto. And those of you, that are *Women of Quality* are Excused from very much of *this* Trouble too." He picked up the same theme in his tract for midwives, urging mothers to suckle their own infants. "Be not such an Ostrich as to Decline it, merely because you would be One of the Careless Women Living at Ease." Clothing and jewels are pervasive metaphors not only in *Ornaments for the Daughters of Zion* but in *Bethiah*, a similar pamphlet written thirty years later. In both, women are told that if they will resist the temptation to worldly adornment they will be "clothed with the sun." Perhaps changes in the provincial lifestyle gave new impetus to the traditional Puritan distrust of leisure. Such an explanation accounts for Mather's injunctions to piety and his warnings against worldliness, but it does not totally explain his preoccupation with status.

Cotton Mather's writings on women point to a much more fundamental problem, a paradox inherent in the ministerial position from the first. This paper began by noting the obvious—that New England's women could not preach, attend Harvard, or participate in the government of the congregation or commonwealth. It went on to argue that this circumscribed social position was not reflected in the spiritual sphere, that New England's ministers continued to uphold the oneness of men and women before God, that in their understanding of the marriage relationship they moved far toward equality, that in all their writings they stressed the dignity, intelligence, strength, and rationality of women even as they acknowledged the physical limitations imposed by their reproductive role. Cotton Mather may not have been fully conscious of this double view, yet all his writings on women are in one way or another a response to it. Such a position requires a balance (if not an otherworldliness) that is very difficult to maintain. In the work of his younger contemporaries, Benjamin Colman and Thomas Foxcroft, this is even more clearly seen.

Colman's daughter Jane was apparently fond of the sermons of Cotton Mather for she composed a tribute to him on his death. Certainly in her own life she exemplified his teaching, spurning balls, black patches, and vain romances for godly scholarship. She had the run of her father's library, which included, in addition to edifying tomes, the poetry of Sir Richard Blackmore and of Waller. At eleven she began composing rhymes of her own and as a young bride she wrote letters to her father in verse which he sometimes answered in kind. Although intensely religious, she began to measure her own writing against a worldly as well as a heavenly scale, a tendency that must have contributed to her own self-doubts and frequent headaches. In a letter to her father, she expressed the hope that she had inherited his gifts. His answer epitomized the possibilities and the limitations of the ministerial position:

> My poor Gift is in thinking and writing with a little Eloquence, and a Poetical turn of Thought. This, in proportion to the Advantages you have had, under the necessary and useful Restraints of your Sex, you enjoy to the full of what I have done before you. With the Advantages of my liberal Education at School & College, I have no reason to think but that your Genious in Writing would have excell'd mine. But there is no great Progress or Improvement ever made in any thing but by Use and Industry and Time. If you diligently improve your stated and some vacant hours every Day or Week to read your Bible and other useful Books, you will insensibly grow in knowledge & Wisdom, fine tho'ts and good Judgment.

Both the "useful Restraints" and the encouragement of study are familiar themes. If Colman saw no possibility for a university

education, neither did he deny her ability to profit by it. Like the other ministers, he made no attempt to extrapolate a different spiritual nature from a contrasting social role. But he fully accepted that role and expected Jane to fulfill it.

In 1735, Jane Colman Turrel died in childbirth. In her father's sermons and in the biography written by her husband, there is little to distinguish her from Katharin Mather or even Jerusha Oliver. But in a poem appended to the sermons, there is a fascinating crack in the portrait. The Reverend John Adams wrote:

> Fair was her Face, but fairer was her Mind,
> Where all the Muses, all the Graces join'd.
> For tender Passions turn'd, and soft to please,
> With all the graceful Negligence of Ease.
> Her Soul was form'd for nicer Arts of Life,
> To show the Friend, but most to grace the Wife.

Negligence, softness, ease! These are concepts alien to the virtuous woman. Jane Colman had been invited into her father's library as an intellectual equal, but to at least one of her male friends she had become only that much more attractive as a drawing-room ornament. It is tempting to conclude that by 1735, even ministers were seducing the Virtuous Woman with worldly standards. But the new prosperity was not entirely to blame. As an instrument of piety, scholarship had its limits. With no other earthly outlet available, dinner-party conversation had to do.

Thomas Foxcroft was either less comfortable with the intellectual role than Mather or Colman or more concerned about its limits. In *Anna the Prophetess* he went to great lengths to deny the implications of his own text, arguing on the one hand that women were worthy of the title of prophet and on the other that they certainly shouldn't be allowed to speak in church. His choice of a text and title were very much in the tradition of Mather, but his handling of it betrayed a discomfort his mentor never acknowledged. When he came to write of motherhood, however, his defense of women blossomed. In his sermon for his own mother, preached in 1721, he described women as the bastions of religion in the home and the community. "At the Gap, which the Death of a wise and good Mother makes, does many times enter a Torrent of Impieties and Vices." Some mothers were simply too good for this world: God might gather them home to prevent them seeing the "Penal Evils" about to befall their children. Foxcroft's praise overlay a more conservative base. He cautioned that the death of a mother might be a punishment for loving her too much as well as for loving her too little. But his own sermon is evidence of where he felt the greater danger lay. "Indeed Children's Love and Regard to their Parents living or dead, commonly needs a Spur, Tho' the Parents too often need a Curb." As a good Puritan, he could not embrace mother love or any other form of human love as an unqualified good, but like Mather he was concerned that Boston's mothers receive the proper respect.

This is a crucial point. In the funeral literature there had been little mention of "motherhood" as opposed to the more generalized concept of "parenthood." Even Colman, who published a baptismal sermon entitled *"Some of the Honours that Religion Does Unto the Fruitful Mothers in Israel,"* was unable to maintain the sex differentiation much beyond the title. If a distinction between mothers and fathers is ever made in the literature, however, it is over the issue of respect. Wadsworth felt that "persons are often more apt to *despise a Mother,* (the weaker vessel, and frequently most indulgent) than a Father." Despite its text, John Flavell's *A Discourse: Shewing that Christ's Tender Care of His Mother is an Excellent Pattern for all Gracious Children* is about parents rather than about mothers specifically. But the one direct comment on women echoes Wadsworth: "[S]he by reason of her blandishments, and fond indulgence is most subject to the irreverence and contempt of children." Thus Boston's ministers showed a concern for neglect of women well before they identified or elaborated any sex-related virtues. Foxcroft built upon this concern, but with a subtle difference. Although his mother's piety was the traditional piety, it

was as a *mother* rather than as a Christian that she was singled out. With a new set of values, a focus upon tenderness and love rather than on godliness and strength, Foxcroft's effusiveness would be indistinguishable from nineteenth-century sentimentality.

Thus, in New England sermons firmly rooted in the reformed tradition of the seventeenth century, we can see developing, as if in embryo, both the "genteel lady" of the eighteenth century and the "tender mother" of the nineteenth. Adams' poem for Jane Turrel shows the short step from Puritan intellectuality to feminine sensibility. Foxcroft's eulogy for his mother demonstrates how praise for a single virtue might obliterate all others. If Puritan piety upheld the oneness of men and women, Puritan polity in large part did not. Nor, we assume, did the increasingly mercantile world of early eighteenth-century Boston. Unwilling or unable to transfer spiritual equality to the earthly sphere, ministers might understandably begin to shift earthly differences to the spiritual sphere, gradually developing sexual definitions of the psyche and soul.

It is important to remember here that the sermon literature deals with a relatively small group of people, that it reveals attitudes not practices. Presumably, few women experienced the conflicts of Jane Turrel. Most housewives in provincial Boston were probably too occupied with the daily round to consider the nature of their position in society. Yet when a minister of the stature of Cotton Mather assumes a defensive tone, telling us that "those *Handmaids of the Lord,* who tho' they ly very much Conceal'd from the World, and may be called *The Hidden Ones,* yet have no little share in the *Beauty* and the *Defence* of the Land," as historians we ought to listen to him. Attitudes are important. Subtle shifts in perception both reflect and affect social practice. Mather's advocacy of women suggests a real tension in early eighteenth century New England between presumed private worth and public position. It demonstrates the need for closer study of the actual functioning of women within congregation and community. But it has ramifications beyond its own time and place. Mather's work shows how discrete and ultimately confining notions of "femininity" might grow out of a genuine concern with equality. Finally, the ministerial literature to which it belongs illustrates the importance of the narrow study, the need to move from static concepts like "patriarchal New England society" to more intricate questions about the interplay of values and practice over time. Zion's daughters have for too long been hidden.

ARTICLE

The Anglo-Algonquian Gender Frontier

Kathleen M. Brown

In her article, Kathleen Brown describes a gender frontier that served as the context for early contact between white, European settlers and Native Americans in seventeenth-century Virginia. That gender frontier existed all along the eastern seaboard. As colonists and colonized tried to adapt to the presence of each other, their societies went through fundamental changes. Among those changes were shifts in the definitions of what constituted masculinity and femininity in the both Native American and Anglo-American communities.

In what way did ideas about gender affect the way that Native Americans and Anglo-Americans related to each other during the early period of contact? What changes in those ideas occurred because of cultural contact between the two groups?

Recent scholarship has improved our understanding of the relationship between English settlers and Indians during the early seventeenth century. We know, for instance, that English expectations about American Indians were conditioned by Spanish conquest litera-

Source: Kathleen M. Brown, "The Anglo-Algonquian Gender Frontier," in *Negotiators of Change: Historical Perspectives on Native American Women*, ed. Nancy Shoemaker (New York: Routledge, 1995), 26–42. Reproduced by permission of Routledge, Inc. part of the Taylor & Francis Group. Notes omitted.

ture, their own contact with the Gaelic Irish, elite perceptions of the lower classes, and obligations to bring Christianity to those they believed to be in darkness.

Largely unacknowledged by historians, gender roles and identities also played an important role in shaping English and Indian interactions. Accompanied by few English women, English male adventurers to Roanoake and Jamestown island confronted Indian men and women in their native land. In this cultural encounter, the gender ways, or what some feminist theorists might call the "performances," of Virginia Algonquians challenged English gentlemen's assumptions about the naturalness of their own gender identities. This interaction brought exchanges, new cultural forms, created sites of commonality, painful deceptions, bitter misunderstandings, and bloody conflicts.

Identities as English or Indian were only partially formed at the beginning of this meeting of cultures; it required the daily presence of an "other" to crystallize self-conscious articulations of group identity. In contrast, maleness and femaleness within each culture provided explicit and deep-rooted foundations for individual identity and the organization of social relations. In both Indian and English societies, differences between men and women were critical to social order. Ethnic identities formed along this "gender frontier," the site of creative and destructive processes resulting from the confrontations of culturally-specific manhoods and womanhoods. In the emerging Anglo-Indian struggle, gender symbols and social relations signified claims to power. Never an absolute barrier, however, the gender frontier also produced sources for new identities and social practices.

In this essay, I explore in two ways the gender frontier that evolved between English settlers and the indigenous peoples of Virginia's tidewater. First, I assess how differences in gender roles shaped the perceptions and interactions of both groups. Second, I analyze the "gendering" of the emerging Anglo-Indian power struggle. While the English depicted themselves as warriors dominating a feminized native population, Indian women and men initially refused to acknowledge claims to military supremacy, treating the foreigners as they would subject peoples, cowards, or servants. When English warrior discourse became unavoidable, however, Indian women and men attempted to exploit what they saw as the warrior's obvious dependence upon others for the agricultural and reproductive services that ensured group survival.

The indigenous peoples who engaged in this struggle were residents of Virginia's coastal plain, a region of fields, forests, and winding rivers that extended from the shores of the Chesapeake Bay to the mountains and waterfalls near present-day Richmond. Many were affiliated with Powhatan, the *werowance* who had consolidated several distinct groups under his influence at the time of contact with the English. Most were Algonquian-speakers whose distant cultural roots in the Northeast distinguished them from peoples further south and west where native economies depended more on agriculture and less on hunting and fishing. Although culturally diverse, tidewater inhabitants shared certain features of social organization, commonalities that may have become more pronounced with Powhatan's ambitious chiefdom-building and the arrival of the English.

Of the various relationships constituting social order in England, those between men and women were among the most contested at the time the English set sail for Virginia in 1607. Accompanied by few women before 1620, male settlers left behind a pamphlet debate about the nature of the sexes and a rising concern about the activities of disorderly women. The gender hierarchy the English viewed as "natural" and "God-given" was in fact fraying at the edges. Male pamphleteers argued vigorously for male dominance over women as crucial to maintaining orderly households and communities. The relationship between men and women provided authors with an accessible metaphor with which to communicate the power inequities of abstract political relationships such as that of the monarch to the people, or that of the gentry to the lower orders. By the late sixteenth century, as English attempts to subdue Ireland became increasingly violent and as hopes for a profitable West African trade dimmed, gender figured increasingly in English colonial discourses.

English gender differences manifested themselves in primary responsibilities and arenas of activity, relationships to property, ideals for conduct, and social identities. Using plow agriculture, rural Englishmen cultivated grain while women oversaw household production, including gardening, dairying, brewing, and spinning. Women also constituted a flexible reserve labor force, performing agricultural work when demand for labor was high, as at harvest time. While Englishmen's property ownership formed the basis of their political existence and identity, most women did not own property until they were no longer subject to a father or husband.

By the early seventeenth century, advice-book authors enjoined English women to concern themselves with the conservation of estates rather than with production. Women were also advised to maintain a modest demeanor. Publicly punishing shrewish and sexually aggressive women, communities enforced this standard of wifely submission as ideal and of wifely domination as intolerable. The sexual activity of poor and unmarried women proved particularly threatening to community order; these "nasty wenches" provided pamphleteers with a foil for the "good wives" female readers were urged to emulate.

How did one know an English good wife when one saw one? Her body and head would be modestly covered. The tools of her work, such as the skimming ladle used in dairying, the distaff of the spinning wheel, and the butter churn reflected her domestic production. When affixed to a man, as in community-initiated shaming rituals, these gender symbols communicated his fall from "natural" dominance and his wife's unnatural authority over him.

Advice-book authors described men's "natural" domain as one of authority derived from his primary economic role. A man's economic assertiveness, mirrored in his authority over wife, child and servant, was emblematized by the plow's penetration of the earth, the master craftsman's ability to shape his raw materials, and the rider's ability to subdue his horse. Although hunting and fishing supplemented the incomes of many Englishmen, formal group hunts—occasions in which associations with manual labor and

economic gain had been carefully erased—remained the preserve of the aristocracy and upper gentry.

The divide between men's and women's activities described by sixteenth- and seventeenth-century authors did not capture the flexibility of gender relations in most English communities. Beliefs in male authority over women and in the primacy of men's economic activities sustained a perception of social order even as women marketed butter, cheese and ale, and cuckolded unlucky husbands.

Gender roles and identities were also important to the Algonquian speakers whom the English encountered along the three major tributaries of the Chesapeake Bay. Like indigenous peoples throughout the Americas, Virginia Algonquians invoked a divine division of labor to explain and justify differences between men's and women's roles on earth. A virile warrior god and a congenial female hostess provided divine examples for the work appropriate to human men and women. Indian women's labor centered on cultivating and processing corn, which provided up to seventy-five percent of the calories consumed by residents of the coastal plain. Women also grew squash, peas, and beans, fashioned bedding, baskets, and domestic tools, and turned animal skins into clothing and household items. They may even have built the houses of semi-permanent summer villages and itinerant winter camps. Bearing and raising children and mourning the dead rounded out the range of female duties. All were spiritually united by life-giving and its association with earth and agricultural production, sexuality and reproduction. Lineage wealth and political power passed through the female line, perhaps because of women's crucial role in producing and maintaining property. Among certain peoples, women may also have had the power to determine the fate of captives, the nugget of truth in the much-embellished tale of Pocahontas's intervention on behalf of Captain John Smith.

Indian women were responsible not only for reproducing the traditional features of their culture, but for much of its adaptive capacity as well. As agriculturalists, women must have had great influence over decisions to move to new grounds, to leave old grounds fallow, and to initiate planting. As producers and consumers of vital household goods and implements, women may have been among the first to feel the impact of new technologies, commodities, and trade. And as accumulators of lineage property, Indian women may have been forced to change strategies as subsistence opportunities shifted.

Indian men assumed a range of responsibilities that complemented those of women. Men cleared new planting grounds by cutting trees and burning stumps. They fished and hunted for game, providing highly valued protein. After the last corn harvest, whole villages traveled with their hunters to provide support services throughout the winter. Men's pursuit of game shaped the rhythms of village life during these cold months, just as women's cultivation of crops determined feasts and the allocation of labor during the late spring and summer. By ritually separating themselves from women through sexual abstinence, hunters periodically became warriors, taking revenge for killings or initiating their own raids. This adult leave-taking rearticulated the *huskanaw*, the coming of age ritual in which young boys left their mothers' homes to become men.

Men's hunting and fighting roles were associated with life-taking, with its ironic relationship to the life-sustaining acts of procreation, protection and provision. Earth and corn symbolized women, but the weapons of the hunt, the trophies taken from the hunted, and the predators of the animal world represented men. The ritual use of *pocones*, a red dye, also reflected this gender division. Women anointed their bodies with *pocones* before sexual encounters and ceremonies celebrating the harvest, while men wore it during hunting, warfare, or at the ritual celebrations of successes in these endeavors.

The exigencies of the winter hunt, the value placed on meat, and intermittent warfare among native peoples may have been the foundation of male dominance in politics and religious matters. Women were not without their bases of power in Algonquian society, however; their important roles as agriculturalists, reproducers of Indian culture, and caretakers of lineage property kept gender relations in rough balance. Indian women's ability to choose spouses motivated men to be "paynefull" in their hunting and fishing. These same men warily avoided female spaces the English labeled "gynaeceum," in which menstruating women may have gathered. By no means equal to men, whose political and religious decisions directed village life, Indian women were perhaps more powerful in their subordination than English women.

Even before the English sailed up the river they renamed the James, however, Indian women's power may have been waning, eroded by Powhatan's chiefdom-building tactics. During the last quarter of the sixteenth century, perhaps as a consequence of early Spanish forays into the region, he began to add to his inherited chiefdom, coercing and manipulating other coastal residents into economic and military alliances. Powhatan also subverted the matrilineal transmission of political power by appointing his kinsmen to be *werowances* of villages recently consolidated into his chiefdom. The central military force under his command created opportunities for male recognition in which acts of bravery, rather than matrilineal property or political inheritance, determined privileges. Traditions of gift-giving to cement alliances became exchanges of tribute for promises of protection or non-aggression. Powhatan thus appropriated corn, the product of women's labor, from the villages he dominated. He also communicated power and wealth through conspicuous displays of young wives. Through marriages to women drawn from villages throughout his chiefdom, Powhatan emblematized his dominance over the margins of his domain and created kinship ties to strengthen his influence over these villages. With the arrival of the English, the value of male warfare and the symbolism of corn as tribute only intensified, further strengthening the patriarchal tendencies of Powhatan's people.

Almost every writer described the land west and south of Chesapeake Bay as an unspoiled "New World." Small plots of cultivated land, burned forest undergrowth, and seasonal residence patterns often escaped the notice of English travelers habituated to landscapes shaped by plow agriculture and permanent settlement. Many writers believed the English had "chanced in a lande, even as God made it," which indigenous peoples had failed to exploit.

Conquest seemed justifiable to many English because Native Americans had failed to tame the wilderness according to English standards. Writers claimed they found "only an idle, improvident, scattered people . . . carelesse of anything but from hand to mouth." Most authors compounded impressions of sparse indigenous populations by listing only numbers of fighting men, whom they derided as impotent for their failure to exploit the virgin resources of the "bowells and womb of their Land." The seasonal migration of native groups and the corresponding shift in diet indicated to the English a lack of mastery over the environment, reminding them of animals. John Smith commented, "It is strange to see how their bodies alter with their diet; even as the deare and wild beastes, they seem fat and leane, strong and weak."

The English derision of Indian dependence on the environment and the comparison to animals, while redolent with allusions to England's own poor and to the hierarchy of God's creation, also contained implicit gender meanings. Women's bodies, for example, showed great alteration during pregnancy from fat to lean, strong to weak. English authors often compared female sexual appetites and insubordination to those of wild animals in need of taming. Implicit in all these commentaries was

a critique of indigenous men for failing to fulfill the responsibility of economic provision with which the English believed all men to be charged. Lacking private property in the English sense, Indian men, like the Gaelic Irish before them, appeared to the English to be feminine and not yet civilized to manliness.

For many English observers, natives' "failure" to develop an agricultural economy or dense population was rooted in their gender division of labor. Women's primary responsibility for agriculture merely confirmed the abdication by men of their proper role and explained the "inferiority" of native economies in a land of plenty. Smith commented that "the land is not populous, for the men be fewe; their far greater number is of women and children," a pattern he attributed to inadequate cultivation. Of the significance of women's work and Indian agriculture, he concluded, "When all their fruits be gathered, little els they plant, and this is done by their women and children; neither doth this long suffice them, for neere 3 parts of the yeare, they only observe times and seasons, and live of what the Country naturally affordeth from hand to mouth." In Smith's convoluted analysis, the "failure" of Indian agriculture, implicitly associated in other parts of his text with the "idleness" of men and the reliance upon female labor, had a gendered consequence; native populations became vulnerable and feminized, consisting of many more women and children than of "able men fitt for their warres."

English commentators reacted with disapproval to seeing women perform work relegated to laboring men in England while Indian men pursued activities associated with the English aristocracy. Indian women, George Percy claimed, "doe all their drugerie. The men takes their pleasure in hunting and their warres, which they are in continually." Observing that the women were heavily burdened and the men only lightly so, John Smith similarly noted "the men bestowe their times in fishing, hunting, wars and such manlike exercises, scorning to be seene in any woman like exercise," while the "women and children do the rest of the worke." Smith's account revealed his discomfort with women's performance of work he considered the most valuable.

The English were hard pressed to explain other Indian behavior without contradicting their own beliefs in the natural and divinely-sanctioned characteristics of men and women. Such was the case with discussions of Indian women's pain during childbirth. In judgements reminiscent of their descriptions of Irish women, many English writers claimed that Indian women gave birth with little or no pain. English readers may have found this observation difficult to reconcile with Christian views of labor pains as the source of maternal love and as punishment for the sins of Eve. Belief in indigenous women's closer proximity to nature—an interpretive stance that required an uncomfortable degree of criticism of civilization—allowed the English to finesse Indian women's seeming exemption from Eve's curse. This is also why the association of Native American gender norms with animals proved so powerful for the English: it left intact the idea of English gender roles as "natural," in the sense of fulfilling God's destiny for civilized peoples, while providing a similarly "natural" explanation for English dominance over indigenous peoples.

The English were both fascinated and disturbed by other aspects of Native American society through which gender identities were communicated, including hairstyle, dress and make-up. The native male fashion of going clean-shaven, for example, clashed with English associations of beards with male maturity, perhaps diminishing Indian men's claims to manhood in the eyes of the English. Upon seeing an Indian with a full "blacke bush beard," Smith concluded that the individual must be the son of a European as "the Salvages seldome hav any at all." It probably did not enhance English respect for Indian manhood that female barbers sheared men's facial hair.

Most English writers found it difficult to distinguish between the sexual behavior of Chesapeake dwellers and what they viewed as sexual potency conveyed through dress and ritual. English male explorers were particularly fascinated by indigenous women's attire, which seemed scanty and immodest compared to English women's multiple layers and wraps. John Smith described an entertainment arranged for him in which "30 young women came naked out of the woods (only covered behind and before with a few greene leaves), their bodies al painted." Several other writers commented that Native Americans "goe altogether naked," or had "scarce to cover their nakednesse." Smith claimed, however, that the women were "alwaies covered about their midles with a skin and very shamefast to be seene bare." Yet he noted, as did several other English travelers, the body adornments, including beads, paintings, and tattoos, that were visible on Indian women's legs, hands, breasts, and faces. Perhaps some of the "shamefastness" reported by Smith resulted from Englishmen's close scrutiny of Indian women's bodies.

For most English writers, Indian manners and customs reinforced an impression of sexual passion. Hospitality that included sexual privileges, for instance sending "a woman fresh painted red with *Pocones* and oile" to be the "bedfellow" of a guest, may have confirmed in the minds of English men the reading of Indian folkways as sexually provocative. Smith's experience with the thirty women, clad in leaves, body paint, and buck's horns and emitting "hellish cries and shouts," undoubtedly strengthened the English association of Indian culture with unbridled passion:

> . . . they solemnly invited Smith to their lodging, but no sooner was hee within the house, but all these Nimphes more tormented him than ever, with crowding, and pressing, and hanging upon him, most tediously crying, *love you not mee.*

These and other Indian gender ways left the English with a vivid impression of unconstrained sexuality that in their own culture could mean only promiscuity.

The stark contrast between Indian military techniques and formal European land stratagems reinforced English judgements that indigenous peoples were animalistic by nature. George Percy's description of one skirmish invoked a comparison to the movement of animals: "At night, when we were going aboard, there came the Savages creeping upon all foure, from the Hills, like Beares, with their Bowes in their mouthes." While writers regaled English readers with tales of Indian men in hasty retreat from English guns, thus reconfirming for the reader the female vulnerability of Indians and the superior weaponry of the English, they also recounted terrifying battle scenes such as the mock war staged for the entertainment of John Smith, which included "horrible shouts and screeches, as though so many infernall helhounds could not have made them more terrible." Englishmen were perhaps most frightened, however, by reports of Caribbean Indians that echoed accounts of Irish cannibalism; George Percy claimed that Carib men scalped their victims, or worse still, that certain tribes "will eate their enemies when they kill them, or any stranger if they take them." Stories like these may have led Smith to believe he was being "fattened" for a sacrifice during his captivity in December 1607.

Although the dominant strand of English discourse about Indian men denounced them for being savage and failed providers, not all Englishmen shared these assessments of the meaning of cultural differences. Throughout the early years of settlement, male laborers deserted military compounds to escape puny rations, disease and harsh discipline, preferring to take their chances with local Indians whom they knew had food aplenty. Young boys like Henry Spelman, moreover, had nearly as much to fear from the English, who used him as a hostage, as he did from his Indian hosts. Spelman witnessed and participated in Indian culture from a very different perspective than most Virginia chroniclers. While George Percy and John Smith described Indian entertainments as horrible antics, Spelman coolly noted that Patawomeck dances bore a remarkable resemblance to the Darbyshire hornpipe.

Even among men more elite and cosmopolitan than Spelman, a lurking and disquieting suspicion that Indian men were like the English disrupted discourses about natural savagery and inferiority. John Smith often explained Indian complexions and resistance to the elements as a result of conditioning and daily practice rather than of nature. Smith also created areas of commonality with Algonquians through exchanges of gifts, shared entertainments, and feasts. Drawn into Indian cultural expressions despite himself, Smith gave gifts when he would have preferred to barter and concocted Indian explanations for English behavior. Despite the flamboyant rhetoric about savage warriors lurking in the forests like animals, Smith soon had Englishmen learning to fight in the woods. He clearly thought his manly English, many of whom could barely shoot a gun, had much to learn from their Indian opponents.

Most English did not dwell on these areas of similarity and exchange, however, but emphasized the "wild" and animalistic qualities of tidewater peoples. English claims to dominance and superiority rested upon constructions of Indian behavior as barbaric. Much as animals fell below humans in the hierarchy of the natural world, so the Indians of English chronicles inhabited a place that was technologically, socially, and morally below the level of the civilized English. Anglo-Indian gender differences similarly provided the English with cultural grist for the mill of conquest. Through depictions of feminized male "naturalls," Englishmen reworked Anglo-Indian relations to fit the "natural" dominance of men in gender relations. In the process, they contributed to an emerging male colonial identity that was deeply rooted in English gender discourses.

The gendering of Anglo-Indian relations in English writing was not without contest and contradiction, however, nor did it lead inevitably to easy conclusions of English dominance. Englishmen incorporated Indian ways into their diets and military tactics, and Indian women into their sexual lives. Some formed close bonds with Indian companions, while others lived to father their own "naturall" progeny. As John Rolfe's anguish over his marriage to Pocahontas attested, colonial domination was a complex process involving sexual intimacy, cultural incorporation and self-scrutiny.

The Englishmen who landed on the shores of Chesapeake Bay and the James River were not then first European men that Virginia Algonquians had seen. During the 1570s, Spanish Jesuits established a short-lived mission near the James River tributary that folded with the murder of the clerics. The Spaniards who revenged the Jesuit deaths left an unfavorable impression upon local Chickahominy, Paspegh, and Kecoughtan Indians. At least one English ship also pre-empted the 1607 arrival of the Jamestown settlers; its captain was long remembered for killing a Rappahanock river *werowance.*

The maleness of English explorers' parties and early settlements undoubtedly raised Indian suspicions of bellicose motives. Interrogating Smith at their first meeting about the purpose of the English voyage, Powhatan was apparently satisfied with Smith's answer that the English presence was temporary. Smith claimed his men sought passage to "the backe Sea," the ever-elusive water route to India which they believed lay beyond the falls of the Chesapeake river system. Quick to exploit native assumptions that they were warriors, Smith also cited revenge against Powhatan's own mortal enemies, the Monacans, for their murder of an Englishman as a reason for their western explorations. The explanation may have initially seemed credible to Powhatan because the English expedition consisted only of men and boys. Frequent English military drills in the woods and the construction of a fort at Jamestown, however, may have aroused his suspicions that the English strangers planned a longer and more violent stay.

Equipped with impressive blasting guns, the English may have found it easy to perpetuate the warrior image from afar; up close was a different matter, however. English men were pale, hairy, and awkward compared to Indian men. They also had the dirty habit of letting facial hair grow so that it obscured the bottom part of their faces where it collected food and other debris. Their clumsy stomping through the woods announced their presence to friends, enemies, and wildlife alike and they were forced, on at least one very public occasion, to ask for Indian assistance when their boats became mired in river ooze. Perhaps worst of all from the perspective of Indian people who valued a warrior's stoicism in the face of death, the Englishmen they captured and killed died screaming and whimpering. William Strachey recorded the mocking song sung by Indian men sometime in 1611, in which they ridiculed "what lamentation our people made when they kild him, namely saying how they [the Englishmen] would cry whe, whe."

Indian assumptions about masculinity may have led Powhatan to overestimate the vulnerability of Smith's men. The gentlemen and artisans who were the first to arrive in Virginia proved to be dismal farmers, remaining wholly dependent upon native corn stores during their first three years and partially dependent thereafter. They tried, futilely, to persuade Indians to grow more corn to meet their needs, but their requests were greeted with scorn by Indian men who found no glory in the "woman-like exercise" of farming. Perhaps believing that the male settlement would always require another population to supply it, Powhatan tried to use the threat of starvation to level the playing field with the English. During trade negotiations with Smith in January 1609, Powhatan held out for guns and swords, claiming disingenuously that corn was more valuable to him than copper trinkets because he could eat it.

When Powhatan and other Indian peoples reminded Smith of his dependence upon Indian food supplies, Smith reacted with anger. In his first account of Virginia, he recalled with bitterness the scorn of the Kecoughtan Indians for "a famished man": they "would in derision offer him a handfull of Corne, a peece of bread." Such treatment signified both indigence and female vulnerability to the English, made worse by the fact that the crops they needed were grown by women. At Kecoughtan, Smith responded by "let[ting] fly his muskets" to provoke a Kecoughtan retreat and then killing several men at close range. The survivors fell back in confusion, allowing the image of their god Okeus to fall into English hands. After this display of force, he found the Kecoughtan "content" to let the English dictate the terms of trade: Kecoughtan corn in exchange for copper, beads, hatchets, and the return of Okeus. The English thus used their superior weaponry to transform themselves from scorned men into respected warriors and to recast the relationship: humble agriculturists became duty-bound to produce for those who spared their lives.

Powhatan's interactions with Englishmen may also have been guided by his assessment of the gender imbalance among them. His provision of women to entertain English male guests was a political gesture whose message seems to have been misunderstood as sexual license by the English. Smith, for example, believed the generosity stemmed from Powhatan's having "as many women as he will," and thereby growing occasionally "weary of his women." By voluntarily sharing his wealth in women and thus communicating his benign intent, Powhatan invoked what he may have believed to be a transcendent male political bond, defined by men's common relationship to women. Powhatan may also have believed that by encouraging English warriors' sexual activity, he might diminish their military potency. It was the fear of this loss of power, after all, that motivated Indian warriors' ritual abstinence before combat. Ultimately, Powhatan may have hoped that intimacy between native women and English men would lead to an integration of the foreigners and a diffusion of the threat they presented. Lacking women with whom to reciprocate and unfettered by matrilineage ties, the English, Powhatan may have reasoned, might be rapidly brought into alliance. Powhatan's gesture, however, only reinforced the English rationale for subjugating the "uncivilized" and offered English men an opportunity to express the Anglo-Indian power relationship sexually with native women.

Indian women were often more successful than Powhatan in manipulating Englishmen's desires for sexual intimacy. At the James River village of Appocant in late 1607, the unfortunate George Cawson met his death when village women "enticed [him] up from the barge into their howses." Oppossunoquonuske, a clever *werowansqua* of another village, similarly led fourteen Englishmen to their demise. Inviting the unwary men to come "up into her Towne, to feast and make Merry," she convinced them to "leave their Armes in their boat, because they said how their women would be afrayd ells of their pieces."

Although both of these accounts are cautionary tales that represent Indians literally as feminine seducers capable of entrapping English men in the web of their own sexual desires, the incidents suggest Indian women's canny assessment of the men who would be colonial conquerors. Exploiting Englishmen's hopes for colonial pleasures, Indian women dangled before them the opportunity for sexual intimacy, turning a female tradition of sexual hospitality into a weapon of war. Acknowledging the capacity of English "pieces" to terrorize Indian women, Oppossunoquonuske tacitly recognized Englishmen's dependence on their guns to construct self-images of bold and masculine conquerors. Her genius lay in convincing them to rely on other masculine "pieces." When she succeeded in getting Englishmen to set aside one colonial masculine identity—the warrior—for another—the lover of native women—the men were easily killed.

Feigned sexual interest in Englishmen was not the only tactic available to Indian women. Some women clearly wanted nothing to do with the English strangers and avoided all contact with them. When John Smith traveled to Tappahannock in late 1607, for example, Indian women fled their homes in fear. Other Indian women treated the English not as revered guests, to be gently wooed into Indian ways or seduced into fatal traps, but as lowly servants. Young Henry Spelman recorded such an incident during his stay at the house of a Patawomeck *werowance.* While the *werowance* was gone, his first wife requested that Spelman travel with her and carry her child on the long journey to her father's house. When Spelman refused, she struck him, provoking the boy to return the blows. A second wife then joined in the fray against Spelman, who continued to refuse to do their bidding. Upon the *werowance*'s return, Spelman related the afternoon's events and was horrified to see the offending wife brutally punished. In this Patawomeck household, women's and men's ideas about the proper treatment of English hostages differed dramatically.

In addition to violence and manipulations of economic dependence and sexual desire, Algonquians tried to maneuver the English into positions of political subordination. Smith's account of his captivity, near-execution, and rescue by Pocahontas was undoubtedly part of an adoption ritual in which Powhatan defined his relationship to Smith as one of patriarchal dominance. Smith became Powhatan's prisoner after warriors easily slew his English companions and then "missed" with nearly all of the twenty or thirty arrows they aimed at Smith himself. Clearly, Powhatan wanted Smith brought to him alive. Smith reported that during his captivity he was offered "life, libertie, land and women," prizes Powhatan must have believed to be very attractive to Englishmen, in exchange for information about how best to capture Jamestown. After ceremonies and consultations with priests, Powhatan brought Smith before an assembly where, according to Smith, Pocahontas risked her own life to prevent him from being clubbed to death by executioners. It seems that Smith understood neither the ritual adoption taking place nor the significance of Powhatan's promise to make him a *werowance* and to "for ever esteeme him as [he did] his son Nantaquoud."

Powhatan subsequently repeated his offer to Smith, urging the adoptive relationship on him. Pronouncing him "a werowance of Powhatan, and that all his subjects should so esteeme us," Powhatan integrated Smith and his men into his chieftancy, declaring that "no man account us strangers nor Paspaheghans, but Powhatans, and that the Corne, weomen and Country, should be to us as to his owne people."

Over the next weeks and months the two men wrangled over the construction of their short-lived alliance and the meaning of Powhatan's promises to supply the English with corn. In a long exchange of bitter words, the two men sidestepped each other's readings of their friendship as distortions and misperceptions. Smith claimed he had "neglected all, to satisfie your desire," to which Powhatan responded with a plain-spoken charge of bad faith: "some doubt I have of your comming hither, that makes me not so kindly seeke to relieve you . . . for many do informe me, your comming is not for trade, but to invade my people and possesse my Country."

Smith and Powhatan continued to do a subtle two-step over the meaning of the corn. Was it tribute coerced by the militarily superior English? Or was it a sign of a father's compassion for a subordinate *werowance* and his hungry people? Powhatan made clear to Smith that he understood the extent of the English dependence upon his people for corn. "What will it availe you, to take that perforce, you may quietly have with love, or to destroy them that provide you food?" he asked Smith. "What can you get by war, when we can hide our provision and flie to the woodes, whereby you must famish by wronging us your friends." He also appreciated the degree to which the English could make him miserable if they did not get what they wanted:

> think you I am so simple not to knowe, it is better to eate good meate, lie well, and sleepe quietly with my women and children, laugh and be merrie with you, have copper, hatchets, or what I want, being your friend; then bee forced to flie from al, to lie cold in the woods, feed upon acorns, roots, and such trash, and be so hunted by you, that I can neither rest, eat, nor sleepe; but my tired men must watch, and if a twig but breake, everie one crie there comes Captaine Smith, then I must flie I knowe not

whether, and thus with miserable feare end my miserable life.

Ultimately, Powhatan attempted to represent his conflict with Smith as the clash of an older, wiser authority with a young upstart. "I knowe the difference of peace and warre, better then any in my Countrie," he reminded Smith, his paternal self-depiction contrasting sharply with what he labeled Smith's youthful and "rash unadvisednesse." Displeased with this rendering of their relationship with its suggestion of childish inexperience, Smith reasserted the English warrior personae with a vengeance. He informed Powhatan that "for your sake only, wee have curbed our thirsting desire of revenge," reminding him that the "advantage we have by our armes" would have allowed the English easily to overpower Powhatan's men "had wee intended you anie hurt."

Although we can never know with any certainty what the all-male band of English settlers signified to indigenous peoples, their own organization of gender roles seems to have shaped their responses to the English. Using sexual hospitality to "disarm" the strangers and exploiting English needs for food, Algonquians were drawn into a female role as suppliers of English sexual and subsistence needs. Although Indian women were occasionally successful in manipulating English desires for sexual intimacy and dominance, the English cast these triumphs as the consequence of female seduction, an interpretation that only reinforced discourses about feminized Algonquians. Dependence upon indigenous peoples for corn was potentially emasculating for the English; they thus redefined corn as tribute or booty resulting from English military dominance.

The encounter of English and Indian peoples wrought changes in the gender relations of both societies. Contact bred trade, political reshuffling, sexual intimacy and warfare. On both sides, male roles intensified in ways that appear to have reinforced the patriarchal tendencies of each culture. The very process of confrontation between two groups with male-dominated political and religious systems may initially have strengthened the value of patriarchy for each.

The rapid change in Indian life and culture had a particularly devastating impact upon women. Many women, whose office it was to bury and mourn the dead, may have been relegated to perpetual grieving. Corn was also uniquely the provenance of women; economically it was the source of female authority, and religiously and symbolically they were identified with it. The wanton burning and pillaging of corn supplies, through which the English transformed their dependence into domination, may have represented to tidewater residents an egregious violation of women. Maneuvering to retain patriarchal dominance over the English and invoking cultural roles in which women exercised power, Algonquian Indians may have presented their best defense against the "feminization" of their relationship to the English. But as in Indian society itself, warriors ultimately had the upper hand over agriculturists.

English dominance in the region ultimately led to the decline of the native population and its way of life. As a consequence of war, nutritional deprivation, and disease, Virginia Indians were reduced in numbers from the approximately 14,000 inhabitants of the Chesapeake Bay and tidewater in 1607 to less than 3,000 by the early eighteenth century. White settlement forced tidewater dwellers further west, rupturing the connections between ritual activity, lineage, and geographic place. Priests lost credibility as traditional medicines failed to cure new diseases while confederacies such as Powhatan's declined and disappeared. Uprooted tidewater peoples also encountered opposition from piedmont inhabitants upon whose territory they encroached. The erosion of traditionally male-dominated Indian political institutions eventually created new opportunities for individual women to assume positions of leadership over tribal remnants.

The English, meanwhile, emerged from these early years of settlement with gender roles more explicitly defined in English, Christian, and "middling order" terms. This core of English identity proved remarkably resiliant, persisting through seventy years of wars with neighboring Indians and continuing to evolve as English settlers imported Africans to work the colony's tobacco fields. Initially serving to legitimate the destruction of traditional Indian ways of life, this concept of Englishness ultimately constituted one of the most powerful legacies of the Anglo-Indian gender frontier.

SUGGESTIONS FOR FURTHER READING

BERNARD BAILYN, "The *Apologia* of Robert Keayne," *William and Mary Quarterly*, 3rd ser., 7 (Oct. 1950), 568–87.

KATHRYN E. HOLLAND BRAUND, "Guardians of Tradition and Handmaidens to Change: Women's Roles in Creek Economic and Social Life during the Eighteenth Century," *American Indian Quarterly*, XIV (Winter 1990), 239–58.

T. H. BREEN, "Horses and Gentlemen: The Cultural Significance of Gambling among the Gentry of Virginia," *William and Mary Quarterly*, 3rd ser., XXXIV (April 1977), 239–57.

T. H. BREEN, "Looking Out for Number One: Conflicting Cultural Values in Early Seventeenth-Century Virginia," *South Atlantic Quarterly*, 78 (Summer 1979), 342–60.

JUDITH K. BROWN, "Economic Organization and the Position of Women among the Iroquois," *Ethnohistory*, 17 (Summer–Fall 1970), 151–67.

KATHLEEN M. BROWN, *Good Wives, Nasty Wenches, and Anxious Patriarchs: Gender, Race, and Power in Colonial Virginia* (Chapel Hill: University of North Carolina Press, 1996).

RICHARD L. BUSHMAN, *From Puritan to Yankee: Character and the Social Order in Connecticut, 1690–1765* (New York: W. W. Norton, 1970).

JOHN DEMOS, *A Little Commonwealth: Family Life in Plymouth Colony* (New York: Oxford University Press, 1970).

ROBERT STEVEN GRUMET, "Sunksquaws, Shamans, and Tradeswomen: Middle Atlantic Coastal Algonkian Women during the Seventeenth and Eighteenth Centuries," in *Women and Colonization: Anthropological Perspectives*, ed. Mona Etienne and Eleanor Leacock (New York: Praeger, 1980), 43–62.

JANE KAMENSKY, "Talk Like a Man: Speech, Power, and Masculinity in Early New England," *Gender and History*, 8 (April 1996), 22–47.

CAROL F. KARLSEN, *The Devil in the Shape of a Woman: Witchcraft in Colonial New England* (New York: W. W. Norton, 1987).

CYNTHIA A. KIERNER, "Hospitality, Sociability, and Gender in the Southern Colonies," *Journal of Southern History*, LXII (Aug. 1996), 449–80.

LYLE KOEHLER, *A Search for Power: The "Weaker Sex" in Seventeenth-Century New England* (Urbana: University of Illinois Press, 1980).

KENNETH A. LOCKRIDGE, *The Diary, and Life of William Byrd II of Virginia, 1674–1744* (Chapel Hill: University of North Carolina Press, 1987).

EDMUND S. MORGAN, *The Puritan Dilemma: The Story of John Winthrop* (Boston: Little Brown, 1958).

EDMUND S. MORGAN, *The Puritan Family: Religion and Domestic Relations in Seventeenth-Century New England* (New York: Harper and Row, 1966).

MARY BETH NORTON, "The Evolution of White Women's Experience in Early America," *American Historical Review*, 89 (June 1984), 593–619.

MARY BETH NORTON, *Founding Mothers and Fathers: Gendered Power and the Forming of American Society* (New York: Vintage, 1997).

ROBERT OLWELL, " 'Loose, Idle, and Disorderly': Slave Women in the Eighteenth-Century Charleston Marketplace," in *More Than Chattel: Black Women and Slavery in the Americas,* ed. David Barry Gaspar and Darlene Clark Hine (Bloomington: Indiana University Press, 1996), 97–110.

ELIZABETH H. PLECK AND JOSEPH H. PLECK, "Introduction," *The American Man* (Upper Saddle River, NJ: Prentice Hall, 1980), 1–49.

AMANDA PORTERFIELD, *Female Piety in Puritan New England: The Emergence of Religious Humanism* (New York: Oxford University Press, 1992).

DAVID R. RANSOME, "Wives for Virginia, 1621," *William and Mary Quarterly,* 3rd ser., 48 (Jan. 1991), 3–18.

JAMES P. RONDA, "Generations of Faith: The Christian Indians of Martha's Vinyard," *William and Mary Quarterly,* 3rd ser., 38 (July 1981), 369–94.

DIANE ROTHENBERG, "The Mothers of the Nation: Seneca Resistance to Quaker Intervention," in *Women and Colonization: Anthropological Perspectives,* ed. Mona Etienne and Eleanor Leacock (New York: Praeger, 1980), 63–87.

CLAUDIO SAUNT, " 'Domestick . . . Quiet being Broke': Gender Conflict among Creek Indians in the Eighteenth Century," in *Contact Points: American Frontiers from the Mohawk Valley to the Mississippi, 1750–1830,* ed. Andrew R. L. Cayton and Fredrika J. Teute (Chapel Hill: University of North Carolina Press, 1998), 151–74.

ABBOT EMERSON SMITH, *Colonists in Bondage: White Servitude and Convict Labor in America, 1607–1776* (New York: W. W. Norton, 1971).

DANIEL BLAKE SMITH, *Inside the Great House: Planter Family Life in Eighteenth-Century Chesapeake Society* (Ithaca, NY: Cornell University Press, 1980).

FREDERICK B. TOLLES, *Meeting House and Counting House: The Quaker Merchants of Colonial Philadelphia, 1682–1763* (New York: W. W. Norton, 1963).

LAUREL THATCHER ULRICH, *Good Wives: Image and Reality in the Lives of Women in Northern New England, 1650–1750* (New York: Oxford University Press, 1983).

ANTHONY F. C. WALLACE, *The Death and Rebirth of the Seneca* (New York: Knopf, 1970), 21–39.

LISA WILSON, *Ye Heart of a Man: The Domestic Life of Men in Colonial New England* (New Haven, CT: Yale University Press, 1999).

CHAPTER THREE

GENDER IDENTITIES IN THE AGE OF REVOLUTION AND THE EARLY REPUBLIC (1760–1820)

AN APPEAL FROM THE LADIES

The act of declaring independence from Britain and the process of writing a constitution uniting the former thirteen colonies under one government were as much stag affairs as the founding of Jamestown. Women were conspicuous by their absence. But that did not mean that they were uninvolved in helping to define what it meant to switch from being a subject of George III to being a citizen of the United States.

In the early spring of 1776, Abigail Adams, the mother of four children, was doing her best to run the Adams farm near Braintree, Massachusetts. Her husband, John, was a delegate to the Second Continental Congress in Philadelphia where he was trying to drum up support for some sort of declaration of independence from Britain. Abigail and John had been happily married for some time, and their relationship was characterized by great mutual affection and respect. Well educated, articulate, and thoughtful, they were in the habit of discussing politics with each other. They both agreed that a revolt against what they considered to be the tyranny of George III was warranted and were astute enough to realize that such a revolt would in all probability have a dramatic impact on the social as well as the political and economic structures of the colonies.

It was, no doubt, with this in mind that Abigail wrote to her husband on March 31, 1776: "I long to hear that you have declared an independency—and by the way in the new Code of Laws which I suppose it will be necessary for you to make I desire you would Remember the Ladies, and be more generous and favourable to them than your ancestors. Do not put such unlimited power into the hands of the Husbands. Remember all Men would be tyrants if they could," she reminded him. "If perticuliar care and attention is not paid to the Laidies we are determined to foment a Rebelion, and will not hold ourselves bound by any Laws in which we have no voice, or Representation," she warned. "That your sex are Naturally tyrannical," she continued, "is a Truth so thoroughly established as to admit of no dispute, but such of you as wish to be happy willingly give up the harsh title of Master for the more tender and endearing one of Friend. Why then," she asked, "not put it out of the power of the vicious and the Lawless to use us with cruelty and indignity with impunity. Men of Sense in all Ages abhor those customs which treat us only as the vassals of your Sex. Regard us then as Beings placed by providence under your protection and in imitation of the Supreme Being make use of that power only for our happiness."

In her letter Abigail Adams succinctly summed up her concern about gender relations as she understood them. In colonial society, husbands had considerable power over their wives. When most women married, they lost the right to own property, sign a contract, draw up a will, or claim custody of their children. They had little recourse if their husbands abused them. Under normal circumstances, a woman and her husband were one in law, and that "one" was him. An unhappily married woman found it almost impossible to get a divorce. As Abigail suggested, women had ways of resisting the power of their husbands. She did not have to remind John that men were dependent for their happiness on the degree to which women were willing to provide for their physical and emotional comfort. Thus, while wives might in theory be subjected to the authority of their husbands, they were not in a position of complete powerlessness in their domestic relations.

Abigail and John Adams were as much companions as they were husband and wife. Their marriage was relatively egalitarian, and in their letters, they frequently addressed each other as "friend." Abigail did not accuse John of abusing his power over her. But while she may have felt comfortable openly demanding more rights for women, she was very much aware that she could do little more than ask for his help. She knew as well as anyone else that women could not change the law on their own and, therefore, had to depend on the good will of powerful men to bring about the kind of legal changes that would liberate women from male authority.

John responded to his wife two weeks later on April 14: "As to your extraordinary Code of Laws, I cannot but laugh," he wrote. "We have been told that our Struggle has loosened the bands of Government every where. That Children and Apprentices were disobedient—that schools and Colledges were grown turbulent—that Indians slighted their Guardians and Negroes grew insolent to their Masters. But your Letter was the first Intimation that another Tribe more numerous and powerfull than all the rest were grown discontented. . . . Depend upon it, We know better than to repeal our Masculine systems. Altho they are in full Force, you know they are little more than Theory. We dare not exert our Power in its full Latitude. We are obliged to go fair, and softly, and in Practice you know We are the subjects. We have only the Name of Masters, and rather than give up this, which would compleatly subject Us to the Despotism of the Peticoat, I hope General Washington, and all our brave Heroes would fight."

John was clearly startled by Abigail's request, but he should not really have been very surprised. The colonies were filled with both men and women who were literate and were reading essays and books written by Enlightenment philosophers such as John Locke and Adam Smith who argued that all men were born with the basic rights of life, liberty, and property, rights that in the Declaration of Independence Thomas Jefferson would call "unalienable." They asserted that the relationship between citizens and the state was contractual rather than based on the "divine right" of kings and that the pursuit of self-interest was not necessarily detrimental to the community as a whole. Whether she actually read the works of Enlightenment philosophers or not, it is clear from her letter that Abigail Adams had her own feminine perspective on the general principles of republicanism as Locke and Smith outlined them, a perspective that differed in fundamental ways from that of John. Abigail seems to have understood that while a revolution might provide the opportunity for men like her husband to redefine their relationship to the state, such a revolution might also allow women to redefine their relationship to the men in their lives.

It is clear from his letter that however much John Adams loved and respected his wife, his male identity was very much tied to the preservation of male prerogatives in the domestic as well as the political realm. While Adams and the other revolutionaries might reject the hierarchical structure upon which the power of the British crown was based, they were not willing to dispense with hierarchy altogether. They used terms like "freedom," "liberty," and "equality" to justify their rebellion against the crown. But they had no desire to give up their positions of power and authority over women let alone children, apprentices, Indians, and Negroes, as John so candidly pointed out. From the point of view of most of the men who led the American Revolution, Enlightenment ideas about liberty and equality were gender, age, class, and race based. They applied to propertied, adult, white men, who presumably had something to lose if social, economic, and political order were not reestablished after the revolution was over. Adams was ready to fight a war to free himself and other Americans from what he considered to be the tyranny of the king. But he was not prepared to replace the king's despotism with what he called the "Despotism of the Peticoat." His dedication to Enlightenment principles had its limits. He could not imagine a world totally devoid of some sort of hierarchy of authority. And he definitely was not committed to supporting a revolution in domestic relations or granting women the same rights as men.

Disappointed in her husband's response to her request, Abigail wrote to John on May 7: "I can not say that I think you very generous to the Ladies, for whilst you are proclaiming peace and good will to Men, emancipating all Nations, you insist upon retaining an absolute power over Wives." She had tried her best to represent the interests of women at a time when change in the law seemed possible and wrote to one of her female friends that she had

"help'd the Sex abundantly." But as it turned out, her efforts were somewhat premature.

John did not pursue this matter any further with his wife in writing. But Abigail's letters apparently prompted him to further consider the state of gender relationships as he speculated about the political implications of the revolution that he was anticipating. On May 26, 1776, John engaged James Sullivan in a discussion about the degree to which government should be based on "the consent of the people." "Shall we say," he wrote, "that every individual of the community . . . must consent, expressly, to every act of legislation? . . . Whence arises the right of the men to govern the women, without their consent?" Adams was not convinced that women as a group were by virtue of their sex either incompetent or unqualified to express their citizenship by participating in public life. Some women, he observed, might be too physically delicate or too concerned with domestic affairs to take an active role in public affairs. But there were also men who, in his opinion, should be excluded from an active role in politics. The kind of government that he hoped to see replace that of the British monarchy required well-educated and articulate citizens who took their civic responsibilities seriously and were capable of making independent decisions. He believed that men who were "destitute of property, . . . too little acquainted with public affairs to form a right judgment, and too dependent upon other men to have a will of their own" had no place in political life. Competence should be the criteria used to determine a citizen's relationship to the state. And he was willing to acknowledge that competence was not necessarily gendered male.

FROM SUBJECT TO CITIZEN

Like the process of colonization, the process of nation building offered both men and women living in what became the United States the opportunity to modify their gender ideals, conventions, and relations to conform to their new civic identities. No longer subjects of the King of England, they were now citizens of a newly formed republic. But it remained to be seen how much the republican ideology of the founding fathers with its theoretical guarantee of equal rights and the formation of a new government based on those principles would actually affect the ways in which masculinity and femininity were constructed in the former English colonies.

The revolution against British authority encouraged men to reassess their relationship to the state and its meaning for their gendered identity. During the colonial period they had been subjects who were to some degree dependent upon the crown for protection and economic prosperity. And while the free, white, and propertied among them could try to influence imperial policy by fighting in the colonial militia and serving in the colonial legislatures or voting for those who did, their ultimate obligation to the king and his representatives in the colonies was to submit to their authority and do what they were told. Until the revolution, few would have suggested that the dependence of a British subject and his willingness to submit to royal authority were in any way demeaning or emasculating.

Women had also been subjects before the revolution. But free, white women were subjugated on two levels rather than just one. Like men, women were expected to defer to the authority of the king and his representatives. But in a society organized around the power of the patriarch, womanhood was defined in terms of domestic subjugation as well. Most Americans considered female dependence on men a permanent, life-long condition. For most colonists, it was simply a part of the natural order of things.

After 1776, women, like men, were no longer English subjects, but it remained unclear what being a "female citizen" meant. As we have seen in the case of John Adams, while male revolutionaries were willing to alter the hierarchical political and social structures of their new nation to accommodate the needs of a republican form of government, they were not willing to dispense with them altogether. Determined to maintain the authority of male government officials as the basis for establishing and maintaining public order, they were no less determined to maintain the authority of husbands as the basis for maintaining order in the family. The result was that women did not achieve equality with men after the war for independence, and the question of what citizenship meant for them remained to be answered.

The period from 1776 to about 1800 was characterized by considerable social and political experimentation as the former colonists went about re-evaluating their relationship to the state and to each other. They had to decide who among them should be granted which privileges and responsibilities of citizenship, what qualities were needed in a citizen in order to secure the well being of the republic, and how citizens should fulfill their civic responsibilities. The result was that the Revolution and the founding of a republican form of government based on the principles of freedom and equality was accompanied by a quite self-conscious reconsideration of what it meant to be a man or a woman.

It seems clear that some Americans were not as actively involved in this process as others. After the revolutionary war was over, many ordinary men and women simply made every effort to return to their prewar existence. They fell in love, married, had children, and earned a living. Busy with the affairs of everyday life, they did not have the time, intellectual training, inclination, or opportunity to consciously reflect upon and participate in a public debate over what it might mean in theory to be a republican man or woman. That did not mean, however, that they were oblivious to the gendered nature of their civic identities. Central to that identity for men was the right to pursue their own economic interests without much interference from the state and the right to participate directly in political life. Along with those rights came the manly obligations of voting, holding office, serving on juries, paying taxes, and defending the country from its enemies. Woman's civic identity was tied to the expectation that she would support her husband in carrying out his civic responsibilities while she took care of his home and reared his children.

THE REPUBLICAN MAN

During the period following the revolutionary war, politicians, intellectuals, and newspaper editors engaged in a debate over what it meant to be a republican citizen, which they usually defined in male terms. The main concern of these writers was how to balance the personal liberty of white, male citizens with the need to establish and maintain social and political order and ensure the success of the republican experiment. They valued individualism and supported the idea that an individual should have the freedom to pursue his own interests. But they also viewed a republican form of government as more fragile than a monarchy and believed that the welfare of a republic depended upon the willingness of its citizens to defer to the authority of the government that they had helped to create and to devote themselves and their material resources to its well being.

It is not surprising, then, that they were in general agreement that the ideal republican citizen should own property. He might be a northern farmer who owned his own land, a skilled artisan who owned his own tools, a merchant who owned his own ships and warehouses, or a southern planter who owned his own work force. The issue was not necessarily how much property he owned but the degree to which possession of property freed him from the influence of others and gave him the kind of economic independence that allowed him to make decisions for himself.

A reputation for personal integrity and honest dealings was a critical component of the definition of what it meant to be a respected businessman in the new republic. Indeed, whether he was a southern slave owner or a Boston shopkeeper, any man who found himself head over heals in debt and unable to

pay off his creditors was likely to think of himself as having been stripped of his manhood. Take Philadelphia's wholesale merchants, for example. Among the city's most wealthy citizens, they conducted business in the highly volatile and risky world of international commerce. Unpredictable markets, poor communication, shipwrecks, privateers, and unscrupulous business associates all had a negative impact on their ability to make money and maintain their reputations as trustworthy and dependable. Because they tended to view business failure as the result of personal inadequacy rather than as the result of larger economic or social forces, they were likely to consider debtors on the verge of bankruptcy as not just unfortunate but treacherous and deceitful. In their business correspondence, they described such individuals in highly gendered terms, characterizing them as predatory, manipulative, and overly influenced by their passions, all negative images often associated with women. In their eyes, a bankrupt, like some women, was untrustworthy, weak, and vulnerable, no longer capable of taking independent action and unworthy of respect. In the world of business, bankruptcy brought in its wake a kind of "servile dependency" that undermined a man's autonomy and claims to manhood. The result was that they tended to think of a bankrupt man either as effeminate or as an ambiguously gendered man-woman.

Those intent on characterizing the kind of man who they felt best represented the ideal republican were fairly specific about the kind of man they had in mind. They defined manhood in terms of morality and industriousness. The true republican worked hard but lived modestly. He neither wore fine clothes nor lived beyond his means. Physically strong and virtuous in both his public and private life, he did not waste his resources by gambling or pose a threat to public order by drinking excessively. If he was not particularly well educated, he at least possessed common sense and was able to base his decisions on reason rather than emotion. He was proud of his autonomy. Empowered by the idea of human equality, he was unlikely to defer indiscriminately to those who were presumptuous enough to assume an air of superiority. He was more likely to address another man as "mister" rather than "sir." It was not that he was unwilling to defer to authority. It was just that in republican circles, the right to deference was no man's birthright. It had to be earned.

What is striking about this model of masculinity is its secular quality. In the seventeenth- and early eighteenth-centuries, the ideal man was a God-fearing man. By the time the Revolution was over, godliness was no longer idealized as an important component of the definition of manliness among many republicans. While there was no objection to a man being a good Christian, most of those who wrote about such matters were much more concerned with the relationship between the individual and the state than they were about the relationship between the individual and God. The founding fathers idealized citizens who were willing to sacrifice their time, their property, and their lives, if necessary, to support the interests of the state. Whether a person thought that doing so was a part of his duty to God was his own business.

The standards for judging who was and who was not an ideal republican citizen were fairly clear. In his romantic comedy, *The Contrast*, performed in New York in 1787, Royall Tyler profiled the ideal republican man in his characterization of his hero, Colonel Manly. Manly was a high-minded ex-Continental soldier, who had very little money but a great deal of personal integrity. Practical in the extreme, unconcerned with fashion, and honest as the day is long, his goal in life was to be of use to others in general and the soldiers who served under him during the revolutionary war in particular.

Writers like Tyler were not sure that American men would live up to the standards of manliness that they had set for them. They exposed their anxieties about this matter by contrasting heroes like Col. Manly with literary villains. Some of these disreputable anti-heroes were disorderly back country farmers or urban artisans who, without concern for the consequences of their actions, pursued their own interests without giving a thought to the welfare of others and spent a considerable amount of time swearing, drinking, and fighting. The behavior of such individuals was not necessarily unmanly, but according to their critics, their thoughtless irresponsibility and lack of self-control led to a neglect of their civic duties and posed a threat to social order. They also portrayed charming, effeminate, self-indulgent libertines as posing a threat to the republic. These dandies did no productive work and spent their time entertaining themselves. In their pursuit of pleasure, they ran up debts by spending money on luxuries. They were rakes who preyed on innocent young women in fashionable drawing rooms. The very epitome of vice, debauchery, and corruption, these men were considered dangerous because they were deceitful, lacking in self-discipline, emotional, extravagant, disorderly, and self-centered. Social critics considered them unmanly because they exhibited negative characteristics that were commonly attributed to women.

DAUGHTERS OF COLUMBIA

While there appears to have been some consensus about the connection between white, property-owning men and citizenship in the early national period, the connection between white women and citizenship was less straightforward. During the colonial period, religious and political authorities idealized the woman who was pious, hardworking, and deferential to authority. But those same authorities were also deeply concerned about women as a potential source of social disorder and did what they could to minimize such threats. By the late eighteenth century, attitudes toward women were changing. Women, as a general rule, were no longer considered morally suspect simply because they were women. And there were some both at home, such as Benjamin Rush, and abroad, such as

Mary Wollstonecraft in England, who argued that women had a capacity for rational thought—a capacity, they argued, that could and should be developed through education. Women's conduct during the revolution had shown that many of them understood the principles upon which the revolution was based and could play an important role in public life. Whether they took up arms, raised money for the war effort, circulated petitions, served as cooks or laundresses for the continental army, or stayed home and ran farms and businesses while their men went off to war, their sense of civic duty was critical to the war effort. By the thousands, they proved that they could be sensible, selfless, self-reliant, competent, and brave.

The ideal male citizen, of course, possessed these virtues. To the degree that women exhibited such qualities, they were theoretically qualified to be considered citizens. But even the most virtuous woman had one disability. If she was married, she was by definition dependent rather than independent. Since most women who lived in the United States were married and were, by law, subject to the authority of their husbands, they were not in a position to have a "will of their own." For that reason, women could not express their citizenship in exactly the same ways that men did.

The right to petition was the only formal political activity that was available to most women during the revolutionary period. By petitioning state officials, they had the opportunity to represent their own interests. But they were also dependent upon the good will of men to give them what they wanted. Take the case of Elizabeth Forbes of Guilford County, North Carolina, for example. Elizabeth was the widow of Col. Arthur Forbes. After her husband died of wounds sustained during the Battle of Guildford Court House in March, 1781, Elizabeth petitioned the state legislature asking for help in supporting her six children. In her petition she wrote with some timidity that "with the help of a Loving and Industrious Husband," she had "lived without being under necessity of troubling your Honorable Body." But she explained that her husband

had sacrificed his life for the revolutionary cause and that she was now in desperate need of economic assistance. The legislature sympathized with her plight and gave her twenty-five barrels of corn to help tide her over.

Women like Elizabeth Forbes were conscious that as female citizens they had the right to assert themselves in pursuit of their own interests in a political setting. But the rhetoric they used in their petitions indicates how aware they were that they were intruding on male political space and that men controlled the resources of the state. The tone of their appeals was feminine in the sense that it reflected both humility and deference to male power and authority.

No one questioned woman's right of petition during the Revolution and the period that followed. But except in the state of New Jersey, the right to vote was a privilege reserved for men. When the male politicians of New Jersey wrote a new constitution during the revolution, they provided that every adult "inhabitant" of the state who owned property and had lived in the state for one year could vote. Adult women who were single could, of course, own property. In that sense, they were relatively independent of male authority. So between 1776 and 1807, single women, who met the suffrage qualifications established by the constitution, attended partisan rallies and demonstrations, participated in political debate, and voted in elections. Not everyone welcomed their participation in male-dominated public life. New Jersey newspaper editors, for example, occasionally questioned the wisdom of allowing women to vote. In 1797 when female voters tried to block the election of a supporter of Jefferson in the town of Elizabeth, the following doggerel appeared in the *Centinel of Freedom*: "Although reinforced by the *petticoat* band/ True *Republican value* they cannot withstand/ And of their disasters in triumph we'll sing/ For the *petticoat faction's* a dangerous thing."

Male citizens in New Jersey may have made female voters the butt of jokes, but they took very seriously the way female voters used the ballot. As time went by, it became increasingly clear to the leaders of both the Federalist and Jeffersonian Republican parties that female voting posed a potential threat to male control over political life in New Jersey. It turned out that when men were evenly divided on a political issue, women who could vote held the political balance of power in their hands. So in 1807, normally contentious male legislators in both parties temporarily united to disenfranchise women, along with any enfranchised free Blacks, aliens, and Native Americans who lived in the state. From that date until the early twentieth century, the definition of what it meant to be a woman did not include the right to vote.

The suitability of women for a larger role in public life was the subject of debate among writers and intellectuals. Judith Sargent Murray, the daughter of a prosperous Massachusetts merchant and the wife of a Universalist minister, was in the forefront among those who argued that woman's role in political life should be expanded. She wrote essays, poems, and plays that addressed a wide variety of contemporary issues including politics and religion as well as gender relations. Murray believed that women's ability to contribute to the welfare of the republic was limited only by the opportunities available to them. She argued that women were not by nature intellectually inferior to men and that they could be educated to understand the principles of republicanism and to willingly carry out their civic responsibilities however they were defined. She maintained that they should be trained to do useful work so that, if necessary, they could be as self-reliant as men. And she politicized woman's maternal role by suggesting that women bore the primary responsibility for inculcating republican values in their sons and daughters. It was mothers, she argued, who were destined to train the next generation of republican citizens to willingly fulfill their obligations to the state. Thus, she sought to assure anyone who would listen that the stability and security of the republic was as dependent upon the support of women as it was on the support of men.

There was much about this sort of ideal republican woman that was familiar. In many ways, she bore a close resemblance to her colonial sister. She was still defined in terms of her relationship to her husband and her function as a wife and mother. And she was still supposed to be chaste, morally upright, and self sacrificing. But after the Revolution, new dimensions to the expression of womanliness emerged because there was now a need to articulate women's relationship to a new sort of government. They, like the men in their lives, were citizens and had a political role to play.

Another way that women could express their womanliness as citizens was to monitor the degree to which men conformed to the manly republican ideals that they had established for themselves. The case of Mercy Otis Warren illustrates the point. Warren's father and her husband were both active in promoting the idea that the colonies should declare their independence from Britain. So she was as much in touch with republican politics as her good friend Abigail Adams. An ardent supporter of the American cause, Warren wrote and published satirical anti-British plays before the revolutionary war. After the war in 1805, she published the first history of the American Revolution. In that history, she publicly criticized the behavior of some of the men who had participated in the revolt against British rule and the process of nation building that followed. Among those men was John Adams. In criticizing male political leadership, she not only added a female voice to the debate over what constituted the ideal republican man but also established herself as a judge of who conformed to the republican ideal and who did not.

Warren did not fault Adams for his activities in bringing about the Declaration of Independence. Nor was she critical of his work during the war. And she testified to his unimpeachable character. It was his inconsistent support of republican principles that she criticized. She suggested that in his effort to stabilize the gains that had been achieved during the Revolution, he had betrayed the republican principles that he has so strongly supported in 1776. He had, she charged, grown conservative and had become "enamored" with monarchy.

When he read her book, Adams was furious. He viewed himself as a paragon of manly republican virtue. He was a loving and considerate husband and father. He had sacrificed his time, energy, and the economic well being of his family to serve the public interest. He felt that he had never taken any public action that was not directed toward the public good. And he was justifiably proud of the contributions he had made to the political life of his country. So, he took up his pen and in a series of letters to Warren, he attempted to defend his reputation and gave her advice on how she might revise her book.

Warren bore his outrage and his long and tedious letters to her with amazing magnanimity. She responded that she had tried "to write with impartiality, to state facts correctly, and to draw characters with truth and candor, whether the friends or foes of my country, or the enemies of myself and family." Throughout the long summer of 1807, she and Adams corresponded. By the end of August, she was thoroughly tired of his complaints and suggestions for revisions. All she had done in her history, she said, was to show that Adams "like all other human beings, was subject to change." Through it all, she never surrendered her right to monitor and make judgments about the degree to which Adams and the other founding fathers upheld the principles of republicanism that she held so dear.

The activities of women like Elizabeth Forbes, Judith Sargent Murray, and Mercy Otis Warren indicate that some American women were quite self-conscious about the privileges and responsibilities that accompanied citizenship in a republic. In her petition, Forbes suggested, at least implicitly, that mothers were so important to the state that state officials should provide her the means to rear her children. Murray argued that gender did not necessarily make women incapable of assuming the responsibilities of citizenship. And Warren assumed the responsibility for monitoring and evaluating the degree to which public figures upheld the standards of republican virtue that they professed.

The rhetoric of republicanism and patriotism had a great impact on the construction of the feminine ideal during the revolutionary war and the period that followed. Popular writers glorified women who were moral, sensible, and self-controlled. At the same time, however, they created an anti-heroine whose image stood as a warning that the behavior of women could seriously undermine the stability of the republic. Their villainess, like the libertine, was completely self-absorbed, lacking in self-discipline, and materialistic. She did not have a serious thought in her head. She neglected her domestic responsibilities and ignored her children. She wasted her time with frivolous pursuits such as gossiping and reading novels. Her concern for fashion drained away the resources of her husband or father and led him down the road to potential bankruptcy. She shirked her civic responsibilities in order to pursue personal pleasure. And she, as much as her male counterpart, posed a potential threat to the economic and political welfare of the state.

It is unclear what impact these literary images had on the conduct of real women. What does seem clear, however, is that during the early national period following the Revolution, the feminine ideal was changing and those changes had profound consequences for the construction of femininity. There was an increasing respect for women's intellectual capacity, for example. And this respect, combined with the need to educate women in the principles of republicanism, resulted in the founding of women's seminaries and academies.

Even attitudes toward motherhood began to change as republican values intruded into private life. During the colonial period, femininity was clearly tied to the willingness and ability to bear children. The economy during that period was based primarily on agriculture. And in that sort of economy, children were an important source of much needed labor. Not surprisingly, then, women who bore seven or eight children were highly regarded.

During that period, it was common to describe a woman who was pregnant as "teeming" or "flourishing" or "great with child." Even the way people referred to childbearing reflected their enthusiasm for the process.

That kind of exuberance regarding pregnancy and childbirth diminished after the Revolution, particularly among those who were middle class and lived in towns and cities. Republican principles emphasized the importance of self-restraint, rationality, and prudent management of resources. And engaging in a republican experiment meant that reproduction was tied not just to producing laborers but also to producing virtuous citizens. In that sense, women's childbearing function was politicized, and there was reason to be more self-conscious about childbearing and child rearing. It is difficult to assess what impact republican principles and rhetoric had on reproductive behavior. What we do know, however, is that during the period following the Revolution, the birth rate began to decline as couples in New England and the mid-Atlantic began to try to control their fertility. Accompanying their efforts in family planning was a change in the way they referred to childbearing. In more refined circles, a pregnant woman no longer "teemed." She was simply described as being "in a family way" or "expecting." As the nineteenth century began and then progressed, femininity in the middle and upper classes was increasingly associated with such good republican virtues as the "prudent management" of emotion and the "restrained expression" of sexuality.

The Gendered Identities of African Americans in the New Republic

Predictably, the way that the American Revolution and the period of nation building that followed it affected the lives of enslaved Africans and African Americans differed significantly from the way they affected the lives of whites. As was true during the colonial period, the gendered identity of slaves depended to some degree on their personal circumstances and the gendered role models that were available to them. If they had originally been free men and women in Africa, they could do what they could to preserve the gender conventions with which they were most familiar. But if they were third or fourth generation American-born, their ability to preserve African gender conventions diminished as time passed. If they lived in a town or city they might have the opportunity to create their gendered identity from among a number of models—that of whites, that of other slaves, and that of free blacks. But if they lived on an isolated plantation or in the household of a small farmer, their lack of contact with the rest of the world reduced the number of options available to them.

The revolution and its aftermath provided the opportunity for some slaves to construct their gender identity around assertiveness and independence. The invasion of British troops during the war meant that masters found it increasingly difficult to inhibit the movement of their slaves. When they found that they could just walk away, many slaves simply sought refuge behind British lines or joined the British army. The war also provided the opportunity for bondsmen to serve in the continental army or state militias and thus construct their masculine identities around the opportunity to fight for the principles of equality and freedom.

The rhetoric of the revolution encouraged some slave owners to question the legitimacy of holding other human beings in bondage. Northerners were not as dependent upon slave labor as southerners and had relatively less capital invested in slaves. So after the war, northern state legislatures passed laws that gradually emancipated the enslaved population within their borders. Ex-slaves now found it possible to adapt their gendered identities to their newly acquired free status, although that freedom was limited by white racism, which was as rampant in the North as it was in the South. Because they were free men and women, their marriages were now legal. And theoretically, they could pursue whatever economic opportunities were open to them. They could live wherever they could find housing and, thus, form their own free black communities. Former slave men could now begin to define themselves in terms of their potential ability to acquire property as well as to support and protect their families. In some states during this period, they could even express their civic identities by voting.

Emancipation also affected the definition of what it meant to be a black woman. Wifehood took on a whole new meaning once marriages between black men and black women were consensual and legal. The same could be said for motherhood once black women no longer had to fear that their children could be taken away from them by force. However free they might have been, however, most black women found it necessary to work for wages in order to help support their families. The fact that they did so meant that they were not completely dependent upon their husbands for support and, as a result, did not necessarily have to defer to the authority of their spouses. Whatever their relationship to each other, ex-slaves could construct their gendered identities around community building and their efforts to establish and maintain their own churches, schools, and benevolent societies.

The southern states depended much more than the North upon the labor of slaves to assure economic prosperity of whites. Some individual slave owners in the South responded to the belief that slavery was inconsistent with the principles of the revolution by freeing their slaves. But most did not. The invention of the cotton gin in the 1790s meant that the economy of the South would continue to be tied to the production of staple crops and the need for a large agrarian labor force. So while communities of freed slaves were established in the South during and after the Revolution, they remained small and relatively isolated from each other. As a result, the gendered identities of most enslaved Afro-Americans in the South continued to be tied to the work that they were forced to do, their relationships with their own and their masters' families,

their own resourcefulness, and their ability to minimize the control that whites exerted over their lives.

THE GENDERED IDENTITIES OF NATIVE AMERICANS IN THE NEW REPUBLIC

The Revolution and the founding of a new republic also influenced gender roles and relations among Native Americans. Before the Revolution, the British crown had attempted to act as mediator between the Indians and American colonists who coveted Indian land. Although there had been some attempts on the part of white colonists to convert the Indians to Christianity and to either assimilate them into white society or isolate them and then impose white gender conventions on them, such efforts were neither widespread nor particularly successful. This is not to say that contact with whites had no impact on Native American culture and the gender conventions that characterized it. The European market for animal skins, for example, meant that the hunting skills of Native American men took on increased economic significance and women spent much of their time processing skins for sale rather than farming. Goods once produced by women could now be purchased with the money they made from the fur trade. Once the role of women as primary providers for the material welfare of their families declined, they became more economically dependent on the men in their families. The propensity of American government officials to negotiate with Native American men when they wanted to arrange the transfer of land to white hands also undercut the political authority of Native American women.

Once the Treaty of Paris ending the Revolution was signed in 1783 and the Americans gained control of all of the land west to the Mississippi River, more and more Indians were subjected to the white assumption that what was best for them was to accept Christianity, give up most of their land, and permanently settle down onto family farms. From the white point of view, the ideal Indian man was one who gave up his role as hunter and warrior to become a farmer, spent his time plowing his fields and looking after his herds, and set himself up as the head of his family. Ideal Indian women were supposed to give up working in the fields, submit to the authority of their husbands, learn to spin and weave, and abdicate their power to influence tribal affairs.

Not surprisingly, these expectations placed a tremendous strain on Native American cultures, particularly those originally characterized by matrilocality (when couples lived with the wife's residence group rather than the husband's) and matriliniality (when kinship is traced through the mother rather than the father), both of which gave considerable power to women. Some Indians began to adjust their gendered identities to conform to these expectations. Some Native American women gave up their work in the fields and began to produce cloth rather than corn or squash. But others continued to farm and demanded that their opinions about the disposition of land be taken into account in negotiations with the representatives of the United States government.

Among those who tried to preserve the political influence of Cherokee women was Nancy Ward. Born in the 1730s in eastern Tennessee, Ward married a warrior of the Deer clan in the early 1750s. Shortly thereafter, she accompanied her husband on a military expedition against the Creeks. During the conflict that ensued, her husband was killed, and she seized his gun and took his place in the struggle until the Creeks fled. By participating directly in the fighting instead of confining her activities to carrying water, gathering firewood, and cooking, she transgressed gender boundaries. Nevertheless, her actions brought her great honor. She became known as "War Woman" and achieved considerable influence in the conduct of tribal affairs. During the American Revolution, she supported the struggle for colonial independence and was received by American officials as a Cherokee diplomat. During the 1780s she spoke at two conferences between Native Americans and U.S. representatives, advocating peaceful relations between the two. Her words indicate that she was very much aware that contact with Anglo-Americans was having a profound effect on the position of women in Native American society. She realized that the influence of women on tribal relations with the representatives of the American government was declining and demanded that women's interests not be ignored in treaty negotiations. "We are your mothers," she told her audience. "Our cry is for peace, let it continue."

But preserving the peace eventually required that the Cherokee give up their land and move farther west. During the removal crisis of 1817–1818, Ward and other Cherokee women met together and then presented petitions to the all-male National Council regarding the disposition of the land that the federal government was trying to obtain. They wrote that "as mothers" it was their duty to address the warriors and chiefs who were assembled, and they asked that the council not part with any more of the land. They argued that it had been given to them by "the Great Spirit above" as their "common right" and that, therefore, they "claimed the right of the soil" and demanded that it be kept for their children. Disregarding the wishes of the petitioning women, the men on the council agreed to transfer large tracts of land in Georgia, Alabama, and Tennessee to the federal government. At the same time, however, they refused to give up common ownership of land in exchange for individual allotments and promised not to cede away any more territory. During Nancy Ward's lifetime, what it meant to be a man and a woman in Cherokee society was undergoing significant change. When she was born, women's work was essential to the economy, men shared influence with women when it came to the conduct of tribal affairs, and neither sex was subordinated to the other. By the 1820s in some segments of the Native American population, gender roles and relationships began to look more and more like those in Anglo-American society.

SUMMARY

The American Revolution and the period of nation building that followed it provided an unprecedented opportunity for Americans to quite self-consciously redefine themselves, their relationship to each other, and their relationship to the state. The result was that new versions of masculinity and femininity slowly emerged among the white, African American, and Native American inhabitants of the United States.

The demands of republican citizenship meant that white, property-owning men had to assume new responsibilities for the welfare of their communities. With more rights came more obligations. And their ideas about what constituted ideal manhood had to be adjusted to accommodate those responsibilities. The demands of citizenship also prompted a reevaluation of the relationship between women and their husbands, their children, and the state. And although in the end, women were still subordinate to men, still expected to serve their interests, and still confined to a role designed to support male institutions, their roles were politicized and the prospect for increased educational opportunities loomed on the horizon. Freed slaves had to determine how emancipation affected their ideas about what constituted manliness and womanliness. And Native Americans had to contend with increasing pressure to make their gendered identities conform to those of whites.

Individual Americans responded in a wide variety of ways to these new opportunities for self-definition. Some tried to adjust their gender identities to accommodate the needs of a republican form of government. Some openly resisted the possibilities available to them. And others appear to have remained oblivious to the need to redefine who they were and how they expressed their gendered identities. For the time being, their idea of what it meant to be a man or a woman did not change in any observable way, and their relationships to each other remained about the same. Still others, especially those who remained in bondage, were not in a position to initiate any major changes in their gender roles and relations despite the change to a republican form of government. Nevertheless, the political, economic, and social changes initiated by the American Revolution would continue to influence definitions of masculinity and femininity well into the nineteenth century.

DOCUMENT

Excerpts from Judith Sargent Murray's "Observations on Female Abilities"

Like Anne Bradstreet, Judith Sargent Murray was aware of the "indifference, not to say contempt, with which female productions are regarded." Nevertheless, after the American Revolution Murray wrote and published plays, poems, stories, and essays under the

Source: Judith Sargent Murray, *The Gleaner* (Schenectady, NY: Union College Press, 1992), 703–705.

pen name of Constantia. In a number of her essays, she attempted to identify the role that white women should play in the new republic. Murray was particularly sensitive to the need for women to be self reliant and well informed so that they could claim the rights of citizenship that were available to many of their male contemporaries. Murray also helped to politicize woman's domestic role by arguing that women could serve the interests of the republic in the home by training their sons to be virtuous, sober, thrifty, self-sacrificing citizens and training their daughters to be good wives and mothers.

Murray had great confidence in what she called "THE SEX." What kind of characteristics did she hope the next generation of women would cultivate? Why is she concerned about promoting those particular characteristics? To what degree were those characteristics gender specific?

I may be accused of enthusiasm; but such is my confidence in THE SEX, that I expect to see our young women forming a new era in female history. They will oppose themselves to every trivial and unworthy monopolizer of time; and it will be apparent, that the adorning their persons is not with them a *primary* object. They will know how to appreciate personal advantages; and, considering them as bestowed by Nature, or Nature's God, they will hold them in due estimation: Yet, conscious that they confer no *intrinsic* excellence on the *temporary* possessor, their admeasurement of *real virtue* will be entirely divested of all those *prepossessing ideas*, which originate in a beautiful exterior. The noble expansion conferred by a liberal education will teach them *humility*; for it will give them a glance of those vast tracts of knowledge which they can never explore, until they are accommodated with far other powers than those at present assigned them; and they will contemplate their removal to a higher order of beings, as a desirable event.

Mild benignity, with all the modest virtues, and every sexual grace—these they will carefully cultivate; for they will have *learned,* that in no character they can so effectually charm, as in that in which nature designed them the *pre-eminence.* They will accustom themselves to reflection; they will investigate accurately, and reason will point their conclusions: Yet they will not be assuming; the characteristic trait will still remain; and retiring sweetness will insure them that consideration and re-

spect, which they do not presume to demand. Thinking justly will not only enlarge their minds, and refine their ideas; but it will correct their dispositions, humanize their feelings, and present them the *friends of their species. The beauteous bosom will no more become a lurking-place for invidious and rancorous passions;* but the mild temperature of the soul will be evinced by the benign and equal tenour of their lives. Their manners will be unembarrassed; and, studious to shun even the *semblance of pedantry,* they will be careful to give to their most systematic arguments and deductions, an unaffected and natural appearance. They will rather *question* than *assert;* and they will make their communications on a supposition, that the point in discussion has rather *escaped the memory* of those with whom they converse, *than that it was never imprinted there.*

It is true, that every faculty of their minds will be occasionally engrossed by the most momentous concerns; but as often as *necessity* or *propriety* shall render it incumbent on them, they will *cheerfully* accommodate themselves to the more *humble duties* which their situation imposes. When their sphere of action is enlarged, when they become wives and mothers, they will fill with honour the parts allotted them. Acquainted, theoretically, with the nature of their species, and experimentally with themselves, they will not expect to meet, in wedlock, with those faultless beings, who so frequently issue, armed at all points, from the teeming brain of the novelist. They will learn

- Women should become educated then
  educate children
- Behave as they know more but are kind about it.

properly to estimate; they will look, with pity's softest eye, on the natural frailties of those whom they elect partners for life; and they will regard their virtues with that sweet complacency, which is ever an attendant on a predilection founded on love, and happily combining esteem. As mothers, they will assume with alacrity their arduous employment, and they will cheerfully bend to its various departments. They will be primarily solicitous to fulfil, in *every instance,* whatever can *justly* be denominated *duty;* and those intervals, which have heretofore been devoted to frivolity, will be appropriated to pursuits, calculated to inform, enlarge, and sublime the soul—to contemplations, which will ameliorate the heart, unfold and illumine the understanding, and gradually render the human being an eligible candidate for the society of angels.

Such, I predict, will be the daughters of Columbia; and my gladdened spirit rejoices in the prospect. A sensible and informed woman—companionable and serious—possessing also a facility of temper, and united to a congenial mind—blest with competency—and rearing to maturity a promising family of children—Surely, the wide globe cannot produce a scene more truly interesting. See! the virtues are embodied—the domestic duties appear in their place, and they are all fulfilled—morality is systematized by religion, and sublimed by devotion—every movement is the offspring of elegance, and their manners have received the highest polish. A reciprocation of good offices, and a mutual desire to please, uniformly distinguishes the individuals of this enchanting society—their conversation, refined and elevated, partakes the fire of genius, while it is pointed by information; and they are ambitious of selecting subjects, which, by throwing around humanity, *in its connexion,* additional lustre, may implant a new motive for gratitude, and teach them to anticipate the rich fruition of that immortality which they boast. Such is the family of reason—of reason, cultivated and adorned by literature.

The idea of the incapability of women, is, we conceive, in this *enlightened age,* totally *inadmissible;* and we have concluded, that establishing the *expediency* of admitting them to share the blessings of equality, will remove every obstacle to their advancement. In proportion as nations have progressed in the arts of civilization, the value of THE SEX hath been understood, their rank in the scale of being ascertained, and their consequence in society acknowledged. But if prejudice still fortifies itself in the bosom of any; if it yet enlisteth its votaries against the said despot and its followers, we produce, instead of arguments, *a number of well attested facts,* which the student of female annals hath carefully compiled. . . .

A Profligate Wife for the Independent Mechanic

The economic changes that accompanied the Revolution not only provided men with more opportunities to make money but also resulted in the availability of an extraordinary variety of consumer goods from all over the world. Housewives could now buy many of the items that they had previously been expected to produce in their homes. This letter to the Independent Mechanic, *a newspaper intended for respectable working class men, not only glorifies the hardworking, thrifty, and sober artisan but also serves as a warning about the hazards of marrying the wrong kind of woman.*

What kind of woman was the author looking for when he began to search for a wife? Why did he think he would make a good husband? In what way did he feel that his choice of a wife was an unfortunate one? Would the author of this letter have agreed with Benjamin Wadsworth (Document in Chapter 2) about what qualities were most desirable in a wife?

The following letter, from a discontented husband, I received a few days since, and which I have no doubt will be acceptable to some of my readers.

Mr. Censor,

I am unfortunately a married man that can not live comfortably with my wife; and our uneasiness is altogether owing to her conduct.

Now, as your paper comes regularly to our house, and is pretty generally read by her, I hope you will be so good as to publish a little wholesome advice in one of your numbers, that may tend to convince *her*, as well as any other woman, who may give their husbands like cause of complaint. That you may be the better able to feel for me, I will give you a fair statement of my case, from the beginning to the present time.

I am a mechanic, and am called a good workman, on which account I am able to keep in constant employ, and earn a good deal of money. While a single man, I was not fond of frolicking, and in about a year and half after I was free, I had saved a pretty good sum. I then began to look about me for a wife, and pitched upon one that seemed to be every way calculated to make a fine companion for a steady mechanic. She appeared good tempered, sufficiently accomplished for a wife for me, *extremely neat* in her person, but without being extravagant in her dress; and to make all complete, she did not seem to be over fond of company-keeping. I accordingly made my addresses to her, and in a short time finally determined to ask her for my wife. I made her fully acquainted with my *then* present circumstances and my future prospects; and entreated her to maturely consider whether she would be content to live in the manner she might expect, if she accepted me for a husband; at the same time assuring her, that nothing should be wanting to make her life happy, that my industry could supply. She accepted the terms, and in a short time we were married.

All went well for about three months, when she began to form a new set of female acquaintances, some in the same circumstances

Source: Anonymous Letter to the *Independent Mechanic*, July 21, 1811.

with herself, but who were enabled, by foolishly squandering their husband's substance, to dress in all the extravagance of every new fashion, give tea parties once or twice a week, resort to the theatre, and, in short, to launch out into every kind of extravagance, unfitting for a mechanic's wife. She no sooner got well acquainted with the *ladies* in question, than she began to be very discontented. Our furniture was become too common. The *rag carpet* was a disgrace to the floor. Mrs. _____ had a fine Turkey carpet, and her husband did not make as much money as I did. Our chairs were not fit a decent person to sit on, because Mrs. _____ had a set of white and gold, with painted *rush bottoms*. Our *calico* curtains ought to be burnt; she was ashamed to look at them, after she had seen Mrs. _____'s white muslin ones, with net fringe and *gilt* cornices. She was quite ashamed to ask a few ladies to tea, after having spent an afternoon at Mrs. _____'s, whose set of china cost *forty dollars*. In short our tables and irons, lookingglass, and every article in the house ought to be sent to vendue, they were a disgrace to a decent family. I endeavoured to reason with her, but in vain; a remonstrance always produced a fit of the *pouts*, which generally lasted until I was forced to give her something which I was truly ashamed to do; further, she would refuse to be seen twice in the same gown or hat; she should be *known* by her clothes, always in the same dress. In short an article was scarcely soiled till it became so horribly old-fashioned that she could not possibly wear it unless it was at least *altered* and *new trimmed*, to give it a change of appearance.

Scarce a week passed, in which the husbands of some of her extravagant friends did not appear in the list of *insolvents*. Mrs. _____'s carpet, Mrs. _____'s china, and Mrs. _____'s curtains, were all sold by the hammer of the auctioneer. These instances I brought as warnings but in vain; and to save myself from a similar fate, I was obliged to lock up my money, and forbid her to run me in debt.

From this time she dashed into another extreme, she discharged our servant girl, declaring that if she could not appear like a Christian (as she termed it) she would not be seen out of the house, and would be completely the mope I wanted her. She now appeared continually in a state always out of humor, and from being ashamed to be seen unless decked out in a manner unbecoming a trademan's wife, she was now so careless of herself, that I was, in truth, ashamed that any one *should* see her. And thus has she continued to the present day. You must think, then, Mr. Censor, that my life is not very agreeably spent. We have a growing family, to make a decent provision for which, I work hard, and it is truly distressing to me, after my day's labour is over, to come home to a house, in which I had been accustomed to meet the smiling face of a sweet tempered wife, and could sit down to my comfortable supper, happy myself, by seeing all contented about me; but which is now so sadly reversed, that I find nothing but frowning ill-humor, and slovenly neglect. Instead of that neatness, which formerly proved my wife was anxious to make herself agreeable to me, I now find a shameful inattention even to common and necessary cleanliness; which fully evinces a total disregard, as well of my good opinion, or happiness, as of the opinion of the world at large.

Your, &c,

A TRADESMAN

Scarce anything tends more to breed discontent between married people, than an avowed indifference, on the part of the females, to cleanliness, and neatness in their persons. Can it be supposed that a man in his senses, could ever give the preference before marriage, to a girl who paid no attention to her appearance, but was always to be seen as if she [was] employed in the kitchen? Everyone will answer—No. And where can there be a greater insult offered to a man, one only excepted, than for his wife to so far deviate from that neatness of habit, which first fixed his attention, as to bring the blush of shame into his face when a friend calls at his house. Is it not a tacit declaration that she values not his love, or his good opinion, that she is joined for life to a man she dislikes, and that in his approbation there is no inducement of sufficient weight to balance the trouble she should have, in rendering herself agreeable. To this, everyone must answer—Yes.

I would recommend to all married ladies to think seriously on this subject, and some, perhaps, may find their own lives rendered more happy, from profiting by the example in the foregoing letter.

ARTICLE

Slave Artisans in Richmond, Virginia, 1780–1810

James Sidbury

James Sidbury turns our attention to the South and to working-class culture. Free, white men who made their living as skilled artisans often thought of themselves as forming the bedrock upon which the new republic was based. They provided services for their neighbors, were respected as masters of their craft, typically owned the tools of their trade, took pride in their independence, and exerted authority over their apprentices and journeymen. All of these characteristics served as the basis for the construction of their manly identities. Given the fact that they did not own themselves, let alone their tools and their labor, slaves were forced to define manliness in different terms. In his article, Sidbury describes what those terms were.

What conditions did Richmond's skilled slaves live under? What qualities do they appear to have used to define what it meant to be a man? What strategies did they employ to develop those qualities?

Skilled slaves fit awkwardly into the existing literature on the history of artisans in America. Virginians had been engaged in large-scale production for distant markets since the 1620s. During the first half of the eighteenth century slaveowners began to have their bondsmen trained to work in crafts that supported the region's staple-crop economy, especially carpentry and cooperage. Relationships between skilled slaves and their masters—a word with far different connotations for historians of slave societies than for historians of free artisans—had long been unequal, paternalistic, and conflict ridden. As the nineteenth century commenced, northern journeymen faced increasingly long odds against their rising to the status of master, but

Source: Howard B. Rock, Paul A. Gilje, and Robert Asher, eds. *American Artisans: Crafting Social Identity, 1750–1850.* pp. 48–60. © 1995. Reprinted by permission of the Johns Hopkins University Press. Notes omitted.

slave artisans had never enjoyed legitimate aspirations to that status or to any public voice. All of these differences have led historians to conclude that slaves sought to increase the social and cultural space that separated them from their masters. . . .

This [essay] analyzes the experiences of slave artisans in Richmond from 1780 to 1810. During those three decades Richmond became Virginia's capital and grew into the largest urban center in the new state. A town of little more than 1,000 people in 1782, it included almost 4,000 in 1790 and almost 6,000 in 1800. By 1810 it contained 9,735 residents, half of whom were black. Three-quarters of these black Richmonders were slaves. During those three decades the town developed a diversified economy that rested on mining coal, making iron, milling grain, and processing tobacco. It was well on its way toward becoming "the most industrialized of southern cities." Thus, of all Virginia cities Richmond probably had the greatest experience with the kinds of changes affecting northern cities during the first decades of the nineteenth century. The city therefore provides a promising opportunity to evaluate the lives of slave artisans in relation to the more extensively documented experiences of free artisans in the North.

Inquiring into the nature of artisanal slaves' lives in early Virginia towns also calls into question the relevance of traditional definitions of artisanship for slave societies. Many Richmond slaves worked in carpentry, brick masonry, blacksmithing, and other trades traditionally deemed artisanal. But the widely accepted definitions according to which artisans were workers who owned their own tools and engaged in petty commodity production would obviously exclude all slaves, for they did not even own themselves. White Virginians did refer to slave craftsmen according to the skills they possessed. But patterns of race relations within Richmond suggest that the most important variable for classifying different occupations held by enslaved urbanites was the degree of personal autonomy the job afforded. Artisanal slaves

used the high demand for their labor to win autonomy. Semiskilled urban slaves who drove carts and drays or worked at the town's warehouses and tobacco factories also escaped some of the burdens of close white supervision and achieved similar levels of autonomy. Thus a taxonomy of slave occupations should group the jobs of several types of worker traditionally labeled semiskilled—carters, draymen, warehousemen, stevedores, sawyers, messengers—with traditional crafts. Some traditionally "white-collar" jobs held by black Richmonders—clerks, storekeepers, and physicians—should also be included. Unlike artisans in free states, enslaved skilled workers could not, of course, lead public movements in defense of their rights; instead, they sought to protect their families and their abilities to work and worship as they chose. In short, they struggled to protect their private lives, not to enhance their public standing.

Demographics and Working Conditions

Before examining the lives of skilled slaves in early Richmond, some might find it helpful to know how many there were, what they did, and the conditions under which they worked. Early Richmond records allow only broad and general approximations of the number of slave craftsmen who worked there. A 1784 city census that listed free residents' occupations indicates that 41 percent of free white men (123 of 302) had skills. Twenty-two artisanal occupations were represented in this census, and households headed by white craftsmen included 34 percent of the small town's enslaved men. Some highly specialized artisans (a goldsmith, two silversmiths, two chairmakers, and two watchmakers) worked in Richmond, but masons, woodworkers, tailors, and shoemakers predominated. Masons, joiners, and carpenters—construction workers who built the rapidly growing town—owned 62 percent (34 of 55) of the adult male slaves possessed by white artisans. Some of the slave men owned by artisans definitely shared their masters' skills, but the census did not list slaves' occupations, so it provides no way to determine how many did so. Attempts to estimate the total number of slave artisans are further complicated because not all slave artisans belonged to free craftsmen: in 1806 George William Smith, a prominent Richmond attorney, offered ten slaves for hire; they included a carpenter, a house servant, a stonemason and road paver, and a boy with experience in a tobacco factory. Clearly, some professionals invested in (or perhaps inherited) skilled slaves whose labor they hired out. Assuming that the skilled slaves owned by non-artisans canceled out many of the unskilled adult male slaves owned by free craftsmen, the total number of slave craftsmen in Richmond might have very roughly approximated three-quarters of the total number of adult male slaves owned by free artisans in 1784. If these assumptions are correct, slaves comprised about 25 percent of Richmond's skilled labor force in 1784. This number would probably be much higher if semiskilled workers such as carters, draymen, and warehousemen were included.

Though the 1784 Richmond City Census allows only crude speculation about the number of slave artisans at work in the city, it permits reasonable inferences about the various strategies chosen by free craftsmen to organize their labor forces and the uses they made of slave artisans. Wealthy building contractors invested in skilled bondsmen and built large work forces on whose expertise they could rely. Dabney Minor, a joiner, headed a household of fourteen adults. Three of them—his wife Anne and two slaves named Amy and Liddea—were women. Of the men, two were white apprentices, and eight were adult male slaves. Presumably Minor could lead a substantial ten-man gang to construction sites, or split up his force to work simultaneously on separate projects. As long as his slaves did not run away, Minor had a large, stable, and presumably skilled labor force. Similarly, the brick mason Henry Anderson's twelve-person household included at least ten people who probably worked at construction sites: An-

derson himself, four white apprentices, a wagoner, and four adult male slaves. Anderson also owned a twelve-year-old slave boy who may well have been an apprentice. The carpenter Anderson Barrett paid personal property taxes on sixteen adult slaves in 1800.

Other craftsmen chose different strategies. The joiner Samuel Ford headed an eleven-member household in 1784. He owned six slaves, but only one was an adult male. Unless his two slave women did carpentry work—and no evidence of female carpenters has survived in the Richmond records—then the five-man crew Ford probably led to construction sites included four white apprentices and his slave Ben. Ford invested far less than Minor in his labor force. Ford was also relatively free of the economic exposure that Minor faced if a valuable slave carpenter ran away or died. Perhaps he also faced fewer difficulties associated with forcing unmotivated laborers to work. On the other hand, his work force, composed predominantly of apprentices, must have been far less skilled than Minor's, and he periodically must have faced the frustration of replacing skilled workers in labor-poor Richmond.

Slaves who lacked craft skills also played important roles in artisanal household production. Some white craftsmen probably invested in slave women to increase their work forces. John Selate, a tailor, probably could not have afforded to invest in four skilled slaves, but he did own a woman named Molley. His household also included a journeyman and at least two, probably three, apprentices. Catey Selate, John's wife, might not have been able to keep up with the demands of a household that included her husband, two young children, and four other males. Molley no doubt contributed greatly to the gardening, spinning, sewing, washing, marketing, and cooking, thus making it possible for the household to include several additional male artisanal workers.

Slaves worked in a wide array of artisanal jobs in early Richmond. In 1784 enslaved men were included in households headed by tradesmen practicing thirteen different crafts.

These crafts ranged from building trades (carpentry and masonry) to metalwork (blacksmithing and goldsmithing) to shoemaking, tailoring, and baking.

As Richmond grew, its economy developed, and the number of crafts practiced in the city increased. In the absence of city directories or censuses that listed occupations there is no way to know exactly how many occupations slaves pursued in the town. The court records and newspapers of Richmond from the period 1780–1810 specifically mention 183 male slaves, who among them practiced thirty-four different skilled occupations. Slaves worked at crafts that ranged from the quite specialized—sailmaking, making hats, and painting carriages—to the more basic (blacksmithing, carpentry, and driving wagons). Many slaves had mastered more than one craft.

Though Richmond slaves practiced a wide variety of crafts around the turn of the nineteenth century, they were not evenly distributed among those crafts. More than half of the identified slave craftsmen worked in the construction trades (carpentry, masonry, and related areas), in transportation (as sailors, wagoners, and draymen), or as coopers. While some slaves may have worked in high-prestige artisanal jobs such as goldsmithing or cabinetmaking, the records of personal property taxes paid by free Richmonders reinforce the data derived from newspapers and local court records. The largest slaveholder in Richmond in 1800 was the James River Canal Company, which paid taxes on thirty-three adult slaves. Many of those slaves may have worked at unskilled jobs, but digging the canal must have required many wagoners to haul dirt, as well as a corresponding number of carpenters to build locks, and wheelwrights and blacksmiths to keep equipment in working order. The next largest Richmond slaveholder was Moses Bates, a building contractor who paid taxes on twenty-nine bondsmen, most of whom surely worked on major building projects. Other large slaveholders included the building contractor Anderson Barrett (who owned sixteen slaves), the miller Joseph Gallego (who owned ten),

and the blacksmith Richard Young (who owned twelve). Men pursuing more specialized crafts generally listed fewer slaves: the coppersmith John Taylor paid taxes on five slaves, the wheelwright Nathaniel Sheppard listed four, and the watchmaker William Richardson listed three. Some of those slaves may have been coppersmiths or watchmakers, but many probably worked as domestic servants. The vast majority of slave artisans in Richmond at the turn of the nineteenth century, like the majority of free artisans, worked in basic construction, transportation, and clothing trades.

Slave artisans' working conditions in early Richmond are almost as obscure as their numbers. The composition of artisanal households recorded in the 1784 census indicates that most slaves working in the building trades worked at racially integrated sites alongside white artisans. Surviving records of early Richmond building sites ratify this finding and indicate that free black artisans worked at the same sites. When John Mayo rebuilt the bridge across the James River in 1800 and 1801, he employed a mixed labor force that included two slave "Masons, Sam and Harry," whom he hired from a Richmond widow; the carpenter "Frank Sheppard the [free] yellow man"; and the white plasterer Frederick Ayton. Mayo's Bridge was an exceptionally large construction project—on one particular day, "70 hands [were] at work"—but integrated labor forces also built the houses and workshops that were the primary project of Richmond's construction industry. In 1801 Anderson Barrett contracted to build a shop for the hatters John and Jacob Fackler. As already noted, Barrett paid taxes on sixteen slaves in 1800, so slaves certainly helped with the "801 feet of shelving" used "in fitting oute a store room" and other jobs. But Barrett's slaves could not do all the work, so he also hired "Mr. [Ninian] Wise," a white craftsman, "for stone work," and the free black "John Sabe for plastering and whitewashing" and "for Iron work." Similarly, in 1805, when the white carpenter Robert Means subcontracted work to the carpenter John P. Gordon, a mixed work force carried out the job. Gordon charged Means for "sawing out a parcel of window frames . . . at my Pit," for his own labor, for cash he paid Solomon "for 3 days work," for one day's "work of Gordon[']s Bob," and for several days' labor by white workers.

Little surviving evidence sheds light on the quality of race relations at these integrated construction sites, but free and slave craftsmen probably worked together relatively harmoniously. Employers sometimes included among their building expenses cash spent on liquor. Slaves, free blacks, and whites often drank together in Richmond's shops, so it seems likely that they shared a few drinks during breaks from their work. Perhaps the most convincing evidence that free workers and slaves coexisted peacefully in Richmond's construction industry is the absence of any record of conflict. In eighteenth-century Charleston, South Carolina, by contrast, a wide assortment of white artisans left a clear record of opposition to slave artisans. White Richmond shoemakers proved similarly willing to oppose the employment of black artisans: during the 1790s the self-styled "Journeymen Cordwainers of the City of Richmond" refused to work "for any person who had negro workmen in [his] employ." In 1802 the journeymen placed an advertisement in the *Virginia Argus* announcing their refusal to work for "John McBride . . . in consequence of his importing Boots, and employing Negroes . . . to the prejudice of our trade."

The cordwainers' complaint may explain why white journeymen in some trades accepted slave co-workers while the shoemakers did not. Their complaint was not, after all, limited to McBride's employment practices. They also charged McBride with importing shoes "of an inferior quality, manufactured in New York." Richmond grew rapidly between 1780 and 1810, and the housing needs of the growing population—combined with public construction projects (including the capital and the state penitentiary), large commercial projects (including Mayo's Bridge and several merchant mills), and the need to rebuild houses that burned in the town's periodic fires—probably created greater demand for building tradesmen than town residents could meet. A similar situation probably prevailed among coopers. Richmond became a major center of Virginia's burgeoning grain trade during the last decades of the eighteenth century. The flour produced at the mills owned by Joseph Gallego and Thomas Rutherfoord had to be shipped in barrels. The demand for barrels was met by shops like that run by Michael Grantland. In 1798 Grantland advertised his desire to "hire . . . six or eight Negro Coopers and four or five Journeymen coopers." Grantland expected slaves and white journeymen to work together in his shop. Doing so may well have been easier because of the brisk demand for barrels. The shoemakers, by contrast, worked in one of the first crafts to be heavily capitalized, and they faced competition from New York and Boston capitalists as well as from slave craftsmen. As the demand for local shoemaking decreased, slave shoemakers became increasingly dangerous competitors, and white journeymen sought to exclude blacks from shoemaking. They also sought to discourage "journeymen from the North or from anywhere else" from moving to Richmond for fear that the "Town . . . [would become] greatly overstocked with Journeymen Shoemakers." Racial antagonism among artisans appears to have hindered on-the-job cooperation between white and slave artisans only when work was scarce. That occurred in few trades around the turn of the nineteenth century, when Richmond was growing rapidly. This pattern suggests that early opposition to integrated artisanal work sites in Richmond grew out of straightforward fears of competition rather than concern that slave (or black) participation in a craft degraded that labor. That pattern would, of course, change during the course of the nineteenth century.

The World View of Slave Artisans

More important than the conditions in which slave artisans worked are the ways in which they perceived the world they inhabited.

Historians of early American labor have argued (or sometimes assumed) that preindustrial artisans identified with their crafts. Northern craftsmen took pride in their skills and in the things they produced. While they were journeymen they perceived themselves to be on a career path that would allow them to accumulate enough capital to open shops and become their own masters. Northern artisans developed an ethic of producerism and a world view that glorified personal independence. Their ideology eventually led them to support Jeffersonian Republicanism.

Few historians have searched for artisanal republicanism in states south of the Potomac. Richmond's free white journeymen probably shared much of their northern brethren's world view. The city census takers in 1784 distinguished among masters, journeymen, and apprentices when listing the occupations of free residents. That contemporaries deemed such distinctions worth noting strongly implies an assumption that craftsmen could progress through the prescribed levels to master status. The "Journeymen Cordwainers of the City of Richmond" provide explicit evidence that at least some town artisans subscribed to the basic tenets of artisanal republicanism. The shoemakers had formed their organization "for the purpose of regulating the prices of work, Board, etc." In 1803 two charter members who had accumulated enough capital to open their own shops tried to hire journeymen at rates that undercut those set by the organization. The journeymen took out an advertisement expressing their disdain for the traitors as "men who have no Object beyond the accumulation of money." These journeymen had a sense of community in their craft; they accused their former co-workers of having betrayed the brotherhood.

There is little reason, however, to suspect that enslaved artisans participated in this vision of artisanal republicanism. Propertied independence and republican citizenship remained beyond their reach. The 1784 Richmond census did not note which slaves worked as journeymen or were training as apprentices, because slaves could not follow the standard progression to master status. Artisanal slaves did, however, gain real advantages from their skills, and at least a few slaves rooted part of their personal identities in their occupations. Dick, a "good carpenter" who ran away from Dabney Minor, took "a band saw, jack and long plane," suggesting that he intended to continue working at his craft when free. Naming practices provide clearer evidence of slaves' construction of personal identity, but they suggest a tenuous link between identity and occupation. Occasionally slaves took last names that reflected their work. One of the leaders of Gabriel's Conspiracy in 1800 was Jack Ditcher, a ditcher by trade. More frequently, however, those slaves who took last names that have survived in the records appear to have taken the names of prominent white or free black families. The scanty surviving evidence strongly suggests that slaves used work skills to gain autonomy from their masters' households. Slave artisans could not head productive households built around artisanal shops. Instead, they used their skills to increase the social distance that separated them from their masters. That distance allowed Richmond-area slave artisans to take advantage of social and cultural opportunities offered in the growing town.

The first object pursued by many enslaved Virginia artisans during the post-Revolutionary era was to move to a growing town. Richmond served as a processing and transportation center for a large agricultural hinterland. The large mills, warehouses, wharves, and tobacco factories that grew up in town became centers for much work that was once done in the countryside. As the town grew, it absorbed many slave artisans from the surrounding countryside. Some of these slave artisans belonged to master craftsmen and had moved to Richmond as part of established households. Others were hired out by rural masters to urbanites who needed skilled workers. Still others won the privilege of self-hire; they got to move to town and find their own housing, food, and work in return for a set weekly wage.

Rural slaves had little control over the economic forces that pushed skilled workers into Virginia's growing towns, but they sought to use those forces for their own benefit. As Richmond grew it developed a great need for carters, wagoners, and draymen to transport goods to and from warehouses and wharves. Obviously, slave wagoners played only an indirect role in creating this need. Nonetheless, Bob, a Goochland County slave who belonged to Thomas Woodson, used the demand for wagoners to his advantage. Bob was, according to Woodson, an "honest and cerfull felow," and "as good a wagoner as any in richmond." In 1800, perhaps after taking some of Woodson's wheat to market, Bob reported to his master that he could "get 6 or 7 Dolers per month" working in town. He would also be able to live with his Richmond wife. Woodson needed money more than he needed Bob's labor on the farm, so he allowed Bob to hire out his own time. This arrangement was illegal, so Woodson asked a Richmond friend to "stand as marster" for Bob; but that only entailed collecting Bob's wages and keeping the slave from "being interupted when at his bisiness." Unfortunately, Bob was not "cerfull" enough: the Richmond authorities caught him, and the Hustings Court ordered that he be sold by the sheriff. As usually happened in these cases, however, the court rescinded the order to sell and "award[ed] the discharge of B[ob]" after he spent a month in jail. Bob's story shows how slaves could make use of the urban demand for transport workers to influence where they were allowed to live, but it also reinforces the fact that skilled slaves remained slaves and subject to white power. Many other slaves from the Richmond area did the same thing as Bob; only a small minority were caught, and the court rarely sold those who were caught.

Artisanal slaves' preference for urban life grew out of the greater opportunities for autonomy that the town offered. Virginia plantations were relatively small, and the number of slaves who lived on a single quarter rarely exceeded twenty or thirty. In Richmond, in 1800, more than two thousand black people lived within a little more than one square mile. Richmond authorities left ample evidence of the unease caused by slaves exploiting the social opportunities created by this demographic concentration. Richmond grand jurors complained of free blacks running disorderly houses, tippling houses, and gambling houses that catered to slaves. They pointed out the "evils" that resulted from "the toleration of such a number of vagrants, beggars, free negroes, and runaway slaves as daily infest[ed]" Richmond's streets. They decried the "negro dances where persons of all colors . . . too often assembled." They sought remedies for the "great disorders" caused by "negroes . . . who behave[d] in a very riotous manner, particularly on the Sabbath day," and for the "numerous collections of negroes and other persons" who gathered "(almost) every Sunday in the Street near such Houses (as we believe) supplies them with Spirits," and "engaged in Gaming, fighting and other disorderly Conduct." By 1799 disorderly people assembling "for the purpose of dancing at night" had "become very common throughout the City." In short, urban life offered slave artisans more excitement and variety than did rural life. This excitement created among Richmond-area rural slaves a "custom to visit" town "every Saturday night."

Implicit in white authorities' complaints about black behavior in Richmond is the assumption that slaves were insufficiently supervised. White authorities' fear of the lack of supervision had two related sources. Historians of slavery have long recognized that plantation slaves and masters struck an implicit bargain that respected the relative autonomy of slaves' communal life in the quarters. On the one hand, slaves' freedom in town was no different from that in the countryside: when not working for their masters, their time was their own. On the other hand, however, town life offered many new opportunities, and masters feared that unoccupied slaves could cause far more trouble in town than they did on the plantation. More important, whites feared the cumulative effect of so many slaves gathering together at night to drink, gamble, and dance. Grand jurors' complaints represent a fear for the maintenance of "proper order," but there is little evidence that the slave property of many masters was threatened by the autonomy of Richmond blacks' night life.

What then, did slave artisans seek to gain when they won the right to move to town? They certainly enjoyed urban social life, but town life offered enslaved urban artisans more than the opportunity to drink, dance, and gamble, as the story of John Russell illustrates. Russell, a slave carpenter, belonged to a New Kent County planter named Armistead Russell. In 1805 and 1806 Armistead Russell hired the slave to Anderson Barrett, the Richmond building contractor. When Barrett returned John Russell to his master on December 25, 1806, the slave ran away. He returned to Richmond ("where he [had] . . . a wife") and sent word to Armistead Russell that he would not willingly live outside of town. Armistead Russell gave in and hired out John Russell to Barrett for a third year. At the end of 1807, John and Armistead Russell played out the same drama once again. Barrett returned John Russell, who promptly ran away. Armistead Russell advertised for his runaway slave. Unfortunately, the outcome of this struggle is unrecorded.

John Russell's story provides a rare glimpse into the inner world of a Richmond slave artisan. He was a carpenter. Given Anderson Barrett's apparent zeal to retain his services, he was probably highly skilled and industrious. But no matter his skill and industry, John Russell could not have risen any further as a carpenter. He used his skill to influence his master's choice of whom he would work for, but he would always work for someone. The opportunity to become an artisan-entrepreneur remained completely beyond the reach of slave craftsmen.

Armistead Russell's advertisements suggest that John Russell focused his ambition toward other kinds of independence. John Russell may well have enjoyed the active urban social life that Richmond offered slaves. Armistead Russell obviously suspected, however, that it was his slave's wife, more than the town's night life, that attracted John Russell. According to the second advertisement,

John Russell's Richmond wife was "a free mulatto woman." John Russell had married a free black woman and presumably had begun to raise a family of free children. Slavery prevented him from becoming the master of an artisanal workshop but perhaps not from becoming the patriarch of a free black family.

Marriages like John Russell's were, of course, extralegal, and there is no way to determine how common they were. Other evidence shows that some Richmond slave artisans used their skills (or good relationships with their masters) to protect and stabilize families in the growing town. Many slaves who won their freedom while manumission was legal in Virginia used the money they earned through their skills to buy family members. Nathaniel Anderson, a freed blacksmith who acquired his son Charles from Thomas Nicolson, set the young man free in 1804 as thanks for "exemplary faithfulness and industry and great good conduct." The free black barber John Kennedy manumitted Sally, a twenty-one-year-old woman, in 1792, and in 1796 the free black blacksmith Thomas Gibson freed Lucy, whom he owned "by virtue of a sale from . . . John Gibbons." Peter Hawkins, a free black man and early Richmond's only dentist, emancipated his "wife Rose . . . and . . . child called Mary" as a token of his "love and regard." That slave artisans who won their freedom placed a high priority on protecting their families is shown by their buying and freeing their spouses and children.

Numerous advertisements seeking the return of runaways illustrate that family and friends were also important to black artisans who remained enslaved. "Bob a black smith by trade" left his Buckingham County master for "Richmond since he has relations there." Ransom, a literate "tailor by trade," ran away to the place where "his father lives." George, "by trade a blacksmith," belonged to Susanna Crenshaw. For several years prior to 1799 he was hired out in Richmond. Crenshaw then hired him out to a Hanover County man, but George ran back to Richmond, where he was "suspected . . . [of] lurking," presumably with his friends. Conversely, town life might have little appeal to slaves forced to leave their families to work in the city: Lewis, a sixteen-year-old barber, ran from Richmond back to his home in King and Queen County, where "he ha[d] a mother."

Some slave artisans, perhaps more ambitious, sought to escape slavery entirely, while others sought to improve their lives as slaves. A few fled from Virginia, usually by water. Richard James expected the "Mulatto Man" Jim Sovall, "a rough carpenter and coarse shoemaker," to "make his escape" from Richmond "by water." Robert Gamble believed that his "BLACK MAN named Jackson, a House Carpenter," planned to use "false papers of freedom" to make "his way to the eastern states." Others planned to pass as free within the state: David Logan felt certain that Robert, "a mulatto man . . . [and] a shoemaker by trade," had "procured a forged pass or free papers." At least one slave blacksmith named Davy rejected the fugitive life of a runaway passing as free; he struck an agreement with a white "villain" with whom he had become "too familiar." Davy ran off with the villain, chose a new master for whom he preferred to work, and allowed himself to be sold.

Advertisements for the return of runaways provide the clearest available evidence of slave artisans' values and goals, but they defy efforts to make simple generalizations. Runaway artisans pursued a wide range of goals; there is no clear distinction between their goals and those pursued by other runaway slaves. In fact, what is most striking about the behavior of artisanal slaves in the Richmond area is the modest degree to which their skills shaped their outlooks.

Urban slave artisans, like other Virginia slaves, appear to have focused principally on family and, if the evidence from Gabriel's Conspiracy provides a key, on religion, rather than on work, when constructing their personal identities. Urban social conditions offered many opportunities that rural slaves lacked; slave craftsmen used their artisanal skills to improve their chances to get to the city and enjoy those opportunities. But skilled slaves remained slaves, and lacking realistic opportunities to pursue advancement through their crafts, they developed an instrumental attitude toward their skills.

This does not mean that slaves failed to develop their skills, or that they took no pride in their work. One need only visit the capitol building in Virginia—a building that the slave carpenters discussed in this essay helped to build—or one of many other eighteenth- and nineteenth-century structures in Richmond to see that enslaved Richmonders displayed great mastery of their work. Nor should one assume that slave craftsmen lacked pride in their work. On the contrary, Richmond artisans were infamous among area whites for their haughtiness: one master explained that "as [his runaway shoemaker was] a proud negro, it is probable he may make for Richmond." Similarly, some slaves derived satisfaction from their work: a runaway named Davy was described as "a very good blacksmith" who would probably seek employment "in that business as he was more fond of that than any other occupation." But even very skilled artisans such as Davy apparently developed competence in several crafts. Slaves mastered as many skills as they could to make themselves as valuable as possible and thus to gain greater bargaining power against their masters. They used that power to win greater autonomy from whites, autonomy they used to pursue their private goals. . . .

SUGGESTIONS FOR FURTHER READING

RUTH H. BLOCH, "American Feminine Ideals in Transition: The Rise of the Moral Mother, 1785–1815," *Feminist Studies*, IV (June 1978), 100–26.

RUTH H. BLOCH, "The Gendered Meanings of Virtue in Revolutionary America," *Signs*, 13 (Autumn 1987), 37–58.

L. H. Butterfield, *The Book of Abigail and John: Selected Letters of the Adams Family, 1762–1784* (Cambridge, MA: Harvard University Press, 1975).

James Taylor Carson, " From Corn Mothers to Cotton Spinners: Continuity in Choctaw Women's Economic Life, A.D. 950–1830," in *Women in the American South: A Multicultural Reader,* ed. Christie Anne Farnham (New York: New York University Press, 1997), 8–25.

Toby L. Ditz, "Shipwrecked; or, Masculinity Imperiled: Mercantile Representations of Failure and the Gendered Self in Eighteenth-Century Philadelphia," *Journal of American History,* 81 (June 1994), 51–80.

Jay Fliegelman, *Prodigals and Pilgrims: The American Revolution against Patriarchal Authority, 1750–1800* (New York: Cambridge University Press, 1982).

Philip Greven, *The Protestant Temperament: Patterns of Child-rearing, Religious Experience, and the Self in Early America* (New York: Knopf, 1977).

Joan R. Gundersen, "Independence, Citizenship, and the American Revolution," *Signs,* 13 (Autumn 1987), 59–77.

Jacqueline Jones, "Race, Sex, and Self-Evident Truths: The Status of Slave Women during the Era of the American Revolution," in *Women in the Age of the American Revolution,* ed. Ronald Hoffman and Peter J. Albert (Charlottesville: University Press of Virginia, 1989), 293–337.

Susan Juster, *Disorderly Women: Sexual Politics and Evangelicalism in Revolutionary New England* (Ithaca, NY: Cornell University Press, 1994).

Mark E. Kann, *The Gendering of American Politics: Founding Mothers, Founding Fathers, and Political Patriarchy* (Westport, CT: Praeger, 1999).

Linda K. Kerber, "Daughters of Columbia: Educating Women for the Republic, 1787–1805," In *The Hofstadter Aegis: A Memorial,* ed. Stanley Elkins and Eric McKitrick (New York: Knopf, 1974), 36–59.

Linda K. Kerber, Nancy F. Cott, Robert Gross, Lynn Hunt, Carroll Smith-Rosenberg, Christine Stansell, "Forum—Beyond Roles, Beyond Spheres: Thinking about Gender in the Early Republic," *William and Mary Quarterly,* 3rd ser., XLVI (July 1989), 565–85.

Linda K. Kerber, "The Republican Mother: Women and the Enlightenment—An American Perspective," *American Quarterly,* 28 (Summer 1976), 187–205.

Linda K. Kerber, *Women of the Republic: Intellect and Ideology in Revolutionary America* (Chapel Hill: University of North Carolina Press, 1980).

Cynthia A. Kierner, *Southern Women in Revolution, 1776–1800: Personal and Political Narratives* (Columbia: University of South Carolina Press, 1998).

Susan E. Klepp, "Revolutionary Bodies: Women and the Fertility Transition in the Mid-Atlantic Region, 1760–1820," *Journal of American History,* 85 (Dec. 1998), 910–45.

Judith Apter Klinghoffer and Lois Elkis, " 'The Petticoat Electors': Women's Suffrage in New Jersey, 1776–1807," *Journal of the Early Republic,* 12 (Summer 1992), 159–93.

Suzanne Lebsock, "Free Black Women and the Question of Matriarchy: Petersburg, Virginia, 1784–1820," *Feminist Studies,* 8 (Summer 1982), 270–92.

Jan Lewis, *The Pursuit of Happiness: Family and Values in Jefferson's Virginia* (New York: Cambridge University Press, 1985).

Jan Lewis, "The Republican Wife: Virtue and Seduction in the Early Republic," *William and Mary Quarterly,* 3rd ser., 44 (Oct. 1987), 689–721.

Cynthia Lynn Lyerly, "Religion, Gender, and Identity: Black Methodist Women in a Slave Society, 1770–1810," in *Discovering the Women in Slavery: Emancipating Perspectives on the American Past,* ed. Patricia Morton (Athens: University of Georgia Press, 1996), 202–26.

Patricia Jewell McAlexander, "The Creation of an American Eve: The Cultural Dialogue on the Nature and Role of Women in Late Eighteenth-Century America," *Early American Literature,* 9 (Winter 1975), 252–66.

MARGARET A. NASH, "Rethinking Republican Motherhood: Benjamin Rush and the Young Ladies' Academy of Philadelphia," *Journal of the Early Republic*, 17 (Summer 1997), 171–91.

MARY BETH NORTON, *Liberty's Daughters: The Revolutionary Experience of American Women, 1750–1800* (Boston: Little, Brown, 1980).

THEDA PERDUE, "Nancy Ward," in *Portraits of American Women: From Settlement to the Present*, eds. G. J. Barker-Benfield and Catherine Clinton (New York: St. Martin's Press, 1991), 83–100.

TERRI L. PREMO, *Winter Friends: Women Growing Old in the New Republic, 1785–1835* (Urbana: University of Illinois Press, 1990).

HOWARD B. ROCK, *Artisans of the New Republic: The Tradesmen of New York City in the Age of Jefferson* (New York: New York University Press, 1979).

LAUREL THATCHER ULRICH, *A Midwife's Tale: The Life of Martha Ballard, Based on Her Diary, 1785–1812* (New York: Vintage, 1991).

JOAN HOFF WILSON, "The Illusion of Change: Women and the American Revolution," in *The American Revolution: Explorations in the History of American Radicalism*, ed. Alfred F. Young (Dekalb, IL: Northern Illinois University Press, 1976), 385–445.

ROSEMARIE ZAGARRI, "Morals, Manners, and the Republican Mother," *American Quarterly*, 44 (June 1992), 192–215.

CHAPTER FOUR

MASCULINITY IN THE NINETEENTH-CENTURY NORTH (1820–1890)

AMERICAN MEN AND THE GOSPEL OF SUCCESS

"Dick's appearance," wrote late nineteenth-century novelist Horatio Alger, "was rather peculiar. His pants were torn in several places, and had apparently belonged in the first instance to a boy two sizes larger than himself. He wore a vest, all the buttons of which were gone except two, out of which peeped a shirt which looked as if it had been worn a month. To complete his costume he wore a coat too long for him, dating back, if one might judge from its general appearance, to a remote antiquity." Ragged Dick, the young hero of Alger's first successful novel, was *not* "dressed for success." But what could you expect from a homeless, shoe shine boy on his own in New York City, who earned ten cents for every pair of shoes he shined and slept outdoors in a box lined with straw?

As it turned out, you could expect a great deal. Indeed, Alger described Dick as having all of the qualities necessary to succeed in life. That did not mean that he was a paragon of virtue. Dick was ignorant and uncouth. He swore and often wasted what little money he had in the pursuit of pleasure. But despite all that, he was enterprising, trustworthy, energetic, shrewd, self-reliant, and personable. And he was fortunate enough to be at the right place at the right time. His first stroke of luck came when a rich businessman, whose nephew he had befriended, gave him a new set of clothes and introduced him to respectable society. Very much impressed, Ragged Dick turned over a new leaf. He opened a savings account, took up residence in a boarding house, and learned to read. In the midst of his self-improvement campaign, he happened to see a child fall into the river. When he saved the little boy, the child's father rewarded him with yet another suit of clothes and a regular job at ten dollars a week. At that point, says Alger, our hero changed his name from Ragged Dick to Richard Hunter and became a "gentleman on the way to fame and fortune."

When he created the character of Ragged Dick just after the Civil War ended, Horatio Alger was largely unknown. By the turn of the century, he was a famous author who turned out three to five enormously popular "rags to riches" novels a year. Alger confirmed what his reading audiences already believed—America was the land of opportunity, and manliness was defined by the degree to which a man was able to exploit his opportunities to achieve social respectability. The character "Ragged Dick" was Alger's prototype for the self-made man.

America had always been viewed as a place where a man could make his fortune. But never had those opportunities seemed so unlimited as in the nineteenth century. The American Revolution had freed Americans from British trade and manufacturing restrictions. They could now trade with whomever they wished. And once they had accumulated enough investment capital, they could engage in manufacturing.

These new opportunities combined with belief in the doctrine of free enterprise helped to create what historians have called the "market economy." By 1830 the bustling harbors of Boston, Philadelphia, New York, Charleston, and New Orleans were crowded with tall-masted ships from all over the world, and some merchants were making great fortunes in the import/export business. Manufacturing was still in its infancy. But wealthy businessmen on the lookout for good investment opportunities combined with an increase in the production of southern cotton prompted the development of a textile industry centered in small New England towns such as Lowell, Massachusetts.

One of the consequences of this economic development was that the identity of the American male became even more closely tied to what he did for a living and how successful he was in making his fortune. Men in the colonial period and the early republic had taken pride in their work, and some had become wealthy, socially prominent, and politically influential in the process. But few had pursued the acquisition of money, status, and power with the vigor and single-mindedness that was characteristic of many men in the nineteenth century. The rotund Benjamin Franklin with his metal-framed spectacles sitting atop his nose had set the standard for defining manliness in terms of economic success in the eighteenth century. But it wasn't until the nineteenth century that the self-made man really came of age.

During the early part of the nineteenth century, the gendered identities of northern men were also constructed around the rhetoric of equality and the influence of evangelical religion. As we have seen, after the American Revolution, masculinity was defined and expressed within the context of a republican ideology of democratic equality. Originally only those men with a certain amount of property had been able to participate in public life by voting or holding office. But by the 1830s, most states had either repealed laws establishing property qualifications for voters or were in the process of doing so. In theory, all men had the right to enjoy the privileges and fulfill the responsibilities of American citizenship. The prevailing assumption, for native-born white men at least, was that no matter what one's vocation, class, or ethnic background, a man had a right to be considered the equal of any other until he did something to prove himself unworthy of high regard. The so-called "Age of the Common Man" was at hand.

Evangelical Christianity also provided a framework for constructing masculinity in the early nineteenth century. During this period revivalists like Charles Grandison Finney supervised the conversion of thousands of Americans by preaching the word of God and promising those in their audiences that any who chose to do so could assure themselves a place in heaven. Gone was the elitism of the old Calvinist message of predestination that argued that only a few would be saved by the grace of God. The evangelical message was that all men stood before God as equals in their sinfulness and as equals in their ability to receive forgiveness for their sins. In return for that forgiveness, they were obliged to live exemplary lives and do what they could to improve the world in anticipation of the second coming of Christ.

While all of these factors had a direct impact on the construction of masculine ideals and identity in the early nineteenth century, they had varying degrees of influence depending on where a man lived, what he did for a living, his rank in the social structure, and his race. In order to illustrate this point, let us analyze how they affected five groups of men—those with great wealth or social prestige sometimes known as patricians, men who worked as farmers and artisans, men of the middling classes including evangelicals, free blacks, and immigrants.

THE PATRICIAN DEFINITION OF MANHOOD

Despite the glorification of the "common man" during the 1830s, not all men defined themselves as common. Prominent ministers, wealthy merchants, successful lawyers, and gentlemen farmers, in fact, considered themselves a cut above most men. They were men whose birth, talent, education, or wealth placed them in an extremely secure position among the social elite where they were free to define their own masculine ideals without much regard for the opinions of those who were less economically and socially privileged than they were.

Many men in this position supported the idea of republican democracy in theory and took their civic responsibilities seriously. But they were suspicious of the suggestion that all men were created equal. Used to being treated with deference by their social and economic inferiors, they resented the presumption of those who took the rhetoric of equality too literally. They often expressed great contempt for "common men" who they considered undisciplined and turned up their nose at those whom they judged to be unrefined. They feared the consequences of common men gathering together. Such opinions seemed justified when the ordinary people, who were invited to Andrew Jackson's inauguration reception in the White House, trampled on the furniture and wrecked havoc on the tables full of refreshments. From the point of view of the social elite, the idea of equality definitely had its down side.

In an age where manliness was often defined within a context of action, conflict, and competition, the patrician man was leisured. He had the wealth and social position to pursue his own interests. Able to avoid strenuous manual labor whenever he wished, the gendered identity of the patrician male was more likely to be vested in intellectual and social skills than in physical strength and stamina. If such a man worked at all, he usually occupied himself with supervising the work of others. The patrician man defined his masculinity by improving himself through reading books and traveling abroad, by seeking public office as a way of serving his country, and by engaging in acts of benevolence designed to improve the lives of those less fortunate than himself. Manliness for men like these was measured by the degree to which their productive use of leisure time, civic virtue, decorous behavior, and appreciation for the finer things in life made them gentlemen.

MANHOOD IN THE AGRARIAN AND ARTISAN TRADITIONS

At the other end of the spectrum were skilled laborers and farmers. They were "common men" with considerably less money and leisure than the patrician. Nevertheless, they considered themselves to be the backbone of the American republic, essential to the economic and political well-being of the nation.

There was a great deal of continuity between the gendered identities of farmers in the colonial period and those in the early nineteenth century. Like their forebears, nineteenth-century farmers took pride in their ownership of the land, the skill, physical strength, and stamina it took to work it, and their ability to pass their estates, no matter how humble, on to the next generation. They did not feel that their manliness was in any way threatened by the fact that they depended upon their wives and children to help them with their work. Nor was their sense of their own masculinity usually tied to their ability to acquire and display a wide range of material possessions. They felt a sense of manly pride in being able to produce enough to adequately feed, clothe, and shelter their families and then sell their surplus on the open market for a profit. Along with the other men in their farming communities, they fulfilled their civic responsibilities by voting, running for public office, and serving on juries, and they shared their resources with their neighbors when circumstances demanded it. They valued their autonomy and self-sufficiency and took orders from no man.

Master craftsmen had a good deal in common with farmers. Their masculine identities were tied to the idea of being propertied and productive. Both had the skill and owned the tools and raw materials needed to produce marketable goods. And both took considerable manly pride in their sense of independence. They set their own work rhythms and could take time off to entertain themselves anytime they wished.

The world of the artisan was typically a world of men, and it was within this context that he defined his masculinity. This is not to say that women were unimportant or totally invisible. Many master craftsmen/tradesmen depended upon their wives and daughters to contribute to the production process or act as salespersons in their shops. But, generally speaking, artisans such as coopers, blacksmiths, carpenters, and printers spent most of their time working with other men. They also spent much of their leisure time outside the home socializing with each other on street corners, drinking with each other in taverns, and associating with each other in all male volunteer organizations like fire companies and lodges. Since the master artisan owned the knowledge, the tools, and the raw materials necessary for production, his apprentices and journeymen were his dependents. But that condition was a temporary one since both

could look forward to eventually deriving their masculine identities from becoming masters in their own right.

The context in which the artisan expressed his manliness began to change in the 1830s when machine manufacturing began to break down the relation of skilled workers to each other and the rhythms of work that they were used to. The result was that master craftsmen slowly began to lose their independence and sense of autonomy. Unable to compete with the speed and efficiency of machines which could produce massive amounts of cheap goods for an expanding world market, they began to move from being independent artisans and tradesmen to wage laborers in factories. In the process, they were increasingly subjected to the control of professional managers. They no longer owned the tools of their trade, and the wide variety of skills that they had spent so many years acquiring gradually became superfluous. They lost their ability to determine where they worked, how many hours they spent working, and the conditions under which they worked. And their lives were increasingly affected by market forces such as periodic recessions and depressions which were beyond their control and understanding.

While some early industrial workers made attempts to form labor unions or to organize politically in order to reclaim some of the autonomy they had once enjoyed, most were left with the sense that they had somehow or other been reduced to a permanent state of dependence. They would have to find another basis for defining their masculine selves and pursuing their masculine interests.

The religious revivals of the 1820s and 1830s provided some of them with the opportunity to do just that. In places like Rochester, New York, Christian evangelists were successful in awakening the religious impulses and social consciousness of local wage earners. Ambitious working men found that they were likely to secure better jobs, earn more money, and establish themselves as good credit risks if they developed reputations for being church-going, sober, self-disciplined, and civicly responsible. In such cases, the masculine identities of members of the artisan class were tied to their spiritual life and their commitment to the ideology of self-improvement and social responsibility.

THE ENTREPRENEURIAL, MIDDLE-CLASS, SELF-MADE MAN

The onset of industrialization did not reduce all artisans to performing wage labor for other men. Some, blessed with the entrepreneurial spirit and money, were able to make the transition from being master craftsmen to being small businessmen and merchants. Often under-capitalized, they suffered periodically from lack of cash and operated on a thin profit margin. But having made the transition, they were still independent, could now pursue the almighty dollar in earnest, and could try to secure their positions as "self-made" men of the middle class.

Accompanying the increasing emphasis within the middle class on proving one's manliness through economic success was the tendency to stress individualism rather than community responsibility and to concern oneself with secular matters rather than religious ones. The ambitious were constantly exposed to the temptation to place their own personal interests before those of others. Many men in the middle class resisted that temptation, and despite their concern with personal achievement, they tried to hold themselves to high standards of moral behavior and continued to take their civic responsibilities seriously. And they derived their manly identities from their reputations as sober family men, their church and volunteer work, and their participation in local politics.

Nevertheless, the gendered identities of middle-class men were very much tied to their work. Working hard to earn a great deal of money in the shortest amount of time possible contributed to their sense of their own masculinity in any number of ways. First, it gave men the opportunity to fulfill their manly responsibilities for supporting their families. In middle-class families, women and children did not work for wages. Both were financially dependent upon men to support them. Women still played an economic role in family life, but that role was increasingly invisible to those outside their homes. These circumstances allowed men to derive their gendered identities from being able to support their families by themselves.

Concentration on work had a number of other implications for the construction of middle-class masculinity. One of those was an increasing concern on the part of men about their bodies and their health. During the colonial period and the early republic, men tended to take their bodies for granted. The work done by farmers, day laborers, and many sorts of artisans, was hard, grueling, and sometimes dangerous. It demanded great energy, strength, and stamina. If they did not develop strength and stamina in the normal course of their daily activities or if they were not able to maintain their good health, they did not typically set about self-consciously to do so. Ill health was a fact of everyday life. The food and drink that ordinary people consumed was not necessarily nutritious. The existence of bacteria and viruses had yet to be discovered. And there were no effective treatments for most serious diseases. So attitudes towards the body and health tended to be relatively fatalistic. The fate of one's body was considered to be largely in the hands of God.

But in the nineteenth century, middle-class men became increasingly concerned about the condition of their bodies. These men expended a great deal of energy working hard and pursuing economic opportunity, but that energy was more likely to be mental than it was physical. It was not unusual for them to spend most of their day sitting in smoky, smelly, drafty offices and counting houses rather than exercising in the fresh air. Given such working conditions and the kind of self-imposed pressure that ambitious men placed on themselves to succeed, it is not surprising that many began to complain of a wide variety of symptoms that were as debilitating as they were mysterious.

At the same time, the fatalism that had once characterized American attitudes towards their bodies was being replaced by the belief that the body could be controlled and cured of disease. Both domestic science and medical science focused attention on the preservation of good health. Domestic science manuals, which had begun to proliferate by mid-century, argued that the success of every member of one's family depended upon the possession of a healthy and vigorous body. They provided concerned and conscientious wives and mothers with information about the importance of personal hygiene and good nutrition and advice about how to fulfill their health care responsibilities. Health reformers such as Sylvester Graham echoed these concerns by suggesting that men could strengthen their bodies by eating health foods such as Graham crackers and by sensibly balancing rest with exercise. And doctors, trying desperately to establish themselves as highly regarded professionals and to make the practice of medicine more lucrative, offered a wide variety of services for those interested in preserving and improving their health. Given these circumstances, it is not surprising that as the nineteenth century neared its end, middle-class men were becoming increasingly self-conscious about their bodies. Such concern eventually evolved into the demand that they compensate for their inactive and sedentary working lives by pursuing strenuous, physical activities in their spare time.

Concentration on work as the source of masculine identity also affected gender relations. Achieving and maintaining middle-class status was dependent upon men establishing themselves as the heads of their households by assuming sole responsibility for the support of dependent wives and children. In theory, a man who acted as sole breadwinner had almost unlimited power within the family. But it didn't quite work out that way. As we have already seen, during the period immediately following the American Revolution, women were beginning to replace their husbands as the spiritual leaders of their families. Now because they were working so hard, middle-class men gradually began to relinquish many of their paternal responsibilities to their wives. For example, while fathers might serve as role models for their sons, pay for their educations, and teach them to manage money, they were not necessarily able to spend much time with them. The result, according to some historians, was that the mother-son bond began to replace the father-son bond. Added to a mother's duties to provide for the physical, emotional, and psychological welfare of her children was the responsibility for preparing her sons to face the world of men outside the home.

To some degree, she was spectacularly unprepared to do this. Middle-class women were expected to remain largely ignorant of the cruel and competitive world of business and politics. They may have been prepared to inculcate in their sons such values as the importance of moral and ethical behavior, love, co-operation, compassion, piety, and generosity. But however useful such values might be in preparing a young man to be a good son, husband, or father, they might turn out to be of little use to a man who hoped to compete and succeed in the rough and tumble and sometimes corrupt worlds of business and politics.

The influence of women had a number of potential consequences for men. One result was that it perpetuated the ambivalence men had traditionally felt towards women. As the moral authority who laid down the rules of acceptable behavior for the household, mothers and wives discouraged the expression of such manly characteristics as autonomy, aggressiveness, and competitiveness. Concessions to women's right to establish acceptable standards of behavior placed a limit on male power and authority. And being manly was in part tied to a man's ability to limit woman's influence over him. Torn between their physical and emotional need for women and their need to express manly independence from female influence and control, men had to find a delicate balance between freely pursing their own manly inclinations and making themselves minimally acceptable to women.

One of the ways that some of them responded to this problem was to equate manliness with not being womanly. Any behavior pattern that conformed too closely to the feminine ideal such as excessive politeness, compassion, or neatness was suspect and, thus, deemed unmanly. Another response was to compartmentalize their lives. In this case, they made an effort to defer to female standards of behavior when they were in the presence of women and more or less ignored those standards when they were alone with one another outside the home. When they conducted business with each other, when they drank and gambled with each other in local taverns or hotels, or when they associated with each other in the conduct of local political affairs, they claimed the right to cultivate a distinctively male environment that, depending on the circumstances, might be characterized by boisterous camaraderie and a tolerance of noise, foul language, and dirt as well as the pursuit of self-indulgent pleasure. When they were by themselves, many of them felt free to indulge in all kinds of behavior that would have been considered inappropriate in the home or in the presence of a lady. In this way, they created working and recreational spaces where they could celebrate manliness in their own way uncensored by women.

Fraternal organizations provided men with such a space. Brotherhoods such as the Freemasons and the Odd Fellows brought men from a wide variety of social and economic backgrounds together to celebrate their manhood in the absence of their mothers, sweethearts, and wives. The rituals of a man's lodge and the opportunities it provided for leadership had the potential for providing a man with the emotional and physical space to celebrate popular notions of manliness with other men. By excluding women, fraternal organizations proclaimed the emotional self-sufficiency of their members and established environments in which they could celebrate male moral autonomy.

EVANGELICAL MANHOOD

While most middle-class men were desperately trying to achieve economic success, there were others who were more concerned with brotherly love, human equality, self-sacrifice, and social usefulness than they were with individualistic competition and the pursuit of wealth. Often the products of a strong religious upbringing or a religious conversion experience, these men were afraid that many of their contemporaries had abdicated their civic and humanitarian responsibilities in the selfish pursuit of wealth and power. And they challenged prevailing gender conventions by rejecting the principles of male domination and instead championed virtues such as cooperativeness, self-sacrifice, and compassion, qualities that were usually considered feminine. Some even went so far as to accept women as their equals on the grounds that the human condition would be improved if women had more public influence. They spent their lives boldly and passionately championing the cause of the unfortunate and oppressed and helped to lead such unpopular social reform movements as temperance, abolition, and women's rights.

Their rhetoric of equality, their censorious attitude towards the consumption of alcohol, and their efforts to improve the condition of women and blacks in American society posed a threat to men whose identities were tied to preserving white male power and privilege. Those whose gendered identities were threatened by the prospect of social change, called male temperance workers, abolitionists, and woman's rights advocates "Aunt Nancy men" and accused them of being weak, impotent, and effeminate. Sensitive to these charges, the reformers argued that manliness was to be found in the physical robustness, aggressiveness, and courage that were required of those who dedicated their lives to the pursuit of social reform.

William Lloyd Garrison typified the evangelical reformer. Born in 1805, Garrison never knew his father, a drunken ne'er-do-well who deserted his family when his children were very young. Reared by his intensely religious mother, Garrison eventually apprenticed as a printer at the age of 13. Without wealth or social status, Garrison was determined to make something of himself and do God's work while he was at it. His apprenticeship completed, he went to Boston and became editor of a temperance newspaper. Once he became interested in the abolition of slavery, he pursued that cause with vigor and evangelical enthusiasm. In 1831 he began publishing an abolitionist newspaper called *The Liberator*. He then helped to found the New England Abolition Society and called for the immediate abolition of slavery. Garrison's unrestrained attacks on anyone who opposed abolition did not make him a popular man. On October 21, 1835, he was captured by a howling mob in Boston and dragged through the streets with a rope tied around his neck. He was saved through the intervention of the mayor, who put him in jail for his own safety. Five years later, Garrison and other American abolitionists including Lucretia Mott attended a World Anti-Slavery Convention in London. There he took a stand against British abolitionists who were determined to deny regularly elected female delegates from America their right to participate in the proceedings of the convention on an equal basis with men. When his female compatriots were relegated to the gallery, Garrison gave up his own seat and joined them there. In 1854, during an anti-slavery rally called to protest the Fugitive Slave Act, he dramatically set fire to a copy of the United States Constitution, denouncing it as "a covenant with death and an agreement with hell." Garrison was unable to prevent a split in the ranks of the abolitionists over such issues as the immediate emancipation of slaves, woman's rights, and participation in political affairs, but he nevertheless became one of the most well-known and provocative leaders of the anti-slavery campaign. His evangelical zeal and courage combined with his willingness to sacrifice himself to the cause of the weak and powerless provided an alternative model for manliness in an age that was increasingly characterized by the pursuit of self-interest.

FREE MEN OF COLOR AND DEFINITIONS OF MANLINESS

In the nineteenth century, most free men of color in the North lived in towns and cities. They derived their gendered identities from the models provided to them by their African heritage and slave backgrounds, those provided to them by white men, the ideals of black manhood prescribed for them by their own ministers, newspaper editors, and other community leaders, and their own personal experiences. For blacks as for whites, manhood was equated with freedom and personal independence. A "real" man had no master. Besides that, manliness was determined by the degree to which a man was strong enough, influential enough, and far-sighted enough to protect himself, his wife, and his children, the degree to which he was economically successful enough to support his family, and the degree to which he was able to establish himself as master in his own home no matter how humble that home might be. In order to achieve these goals it was necessary for free African-American men to be as well educated, skilled, and enterprising as possible and to exhibit such bourgeois attributes as responsibility, industriousness, thrift, and sobriety.

Fulfilling those ideals was complicated by a number of factors. Before the Civil War, there was always the danger, however remote, that a northern free black man could be kidnapped, taken south, and then enslaved. Such was the case with Solomon Northup. Born a free man in New York in 1808, Northup was, besides being a farmer, an accomplished musician. In 1834, he and his wife moved to Saratoga where they lived comfortably. But Northup, now the father of three children, wished to improve his economic circumstances. In an effort to do so, he accepted an offer from two respectable looking men to accompany them to New York City where they agreed to employ him to play his violin. After paying him as they had promised for his performance, they then suggested that he accompany them to Washington where they assured him he would find more work. Shortly after their arrival in the capitol city, they drugged him, placed him in chains, and sold him to a slave dealer. A Louisiana cotton planter eventually bought him. Solomon Northup was held in bondage for twelve years before he was able to smuggle a message north telling his friends and family where he was. He was rescued and returned to New York in 1853.

Even if they were able to preserve their freedom, black men in the North had trouble gaining access to occupational training and then finding jobs with good wages so that they could support their families. Northern employers preferred to hire whites, and northern white laborers saw blacks as competitors. Both did what they could to limit a black man's economic opportunities. In some states laws barred them from certain trades and occupations. Even the most entrepreneurial, honest, and hard working could not get business loans and were turned down when they went to apply for the necessary licenses to conduct their businesses. What that meant was that only a few black men could derive their masculine identities from being the sole support of their families. Most found that if their children were to be adequately housed, fed, and clothed, their wives had to work.

Another factor that complicated black men's ability to express their masculine autonomy was the self-imposed desire to do what they could as individuals and in groups to uplift the less fortunate members of their race. Here again black men found themselves tied to their communities and dependent to some extent on the activities of women, who like their male counterparts participated in social reform movements and carried out benevolent activities designed to help other blacks. Black men and women worked side by side with each other building churches, providing

services and financial assistance to those who were in need of them, and supporting social reform such as abolition of slavery before the Civil War and civil rights after it. But while men generally supported the reform efforts and benevolent activities of black women, they did not necessarily welcome them as their equals. In the area of community activism, their sense of their own masculinity often depended on the degree to which they felt themselves to be in charge of the major organizations in their communities.

Another component of racial uplift that helped to dictate standards for judging manliness were the kinds of behavior patterns that black men were encouraged to exhibit in the effort to overcome racial prejudice. Black journalists and ministers placed a particularly heavy burden on men when they prescribed the kind of appearance and deportment they felt was necessary to refute negative racial stereotypes. They admonished black men to dress and act as much like gentlemen in public as their circumstances would permit, to go about their business freely but as inconspicuously as possible, and to refrain from the sort of drunken and disorderly behavior that was common among some white working-class men.

THE CIVIL WAR AS A TEST OF MANLINESS

The Civil War was only one of four major wars fought by Americans in the nineteenth century, but of the four it was the longest, it involved the most men, and was the most devastating in terms of economic destruction, social dislocation, and loss of life. In that sense, it was the most important. Like other wars, the Civil War was a manly event. It was started by men in 1861. It was fought almost exclusively by men. And it was men who made the peace in 1865. It provided a backdrop for the expression of male initiative, courage, and power and in the armed forces provided an environment conducive to male bonding experiences. Thus, the Civil War, like other wars, provided an opportunity for the individual to test himself against an externally imposed set of standards for judging what it meant to be a man.

For young men, the Civil War was a coming-of-age experience. Many a fresh-faced adolescent found that volunteering to fight in the armed services and donning a uniform suddenly made him inexplicably much more appealing to women. Serving in the military took young men away from home and provided many of them with their first opportunity to pursue such "manly activities" as drinking, gambling, and whoring. Most had never been exposed to life-threatening danger on a regular basis. Combat changed all that. When they went into their first battle, they went in as boys. If they stood their ground, if they attacked, if they resisted the impulse to turn and run in the face of enemy fire, if they survived, they felt that they had earned their claim to manhood.

For older men, the Civil War was an ordeal of manhood. Combat provided them with a particularly dramatic environment in which they could reassure themselves that they were indeed men. War provided them the opportunity to exhibit their willingness to protect their property and their families and sacrifice themselves for the welfare of their country. It encouraged the expression of male aggressiveness and also legitimated the expression of anger and the pursuit of revenge. Serving in the military provided another context in which men could judge themselves by competing with others. Mastering the skills required of a good soldier more quickly than one's comrades could earn a man high regard and enhance his self-esteem. Demonstrating leadership potential could result in a promotion in rank, a bigger paycheck, and the right to exert more power and authority over others. The coarseness of life both in camp and in the field discouraged men from exhibiting such feminine sensibilities as love of comfort and cultural refinement. At the same time, however, the threat of death not only made soldiers dependent upon each other and but also encouraged them, given the right cir-

cumstances, to express love for and tenderness toward their comrades.

Military life and combat put soldiers' manliness to the test. It tested their ability to maintain their sense of personal independence and self-worth while deferring to military discipline. It tested their physical endurance and their emotional and spiritual strength. It tested their ability to stoically withstand the ghastly spectacles of war—the unrelenting butchery, the sea of blood, the heart-rending screams of the wounded, and the deafening thunder of artillery. It tested their self-control by demanding that they take heroic action in the midst of battle without acknowledging fear verging on terror. It demanded that they ignore their desire for self-preservation in order not to appear cowardly. It tested their ability to withstand physical and psychological pain without complaint. And it tested their ability to tolerate the tedium and frustrations of military life without becoming cynical or losing their willingness to fight.

In some ways the wartime experience of black men was the same as their white counterparts. Fighting in the Civil War stood as testimony to their freedom to act on their own behalf and served as the ultimate test of their manliness. In other ways, however, the wartime experience for African Americans was qualitatively different from that of whites. Despite the willingness of black men to fight, northern whites were not enthusiastic about recruiting and arming African Americans. But by 1862 it became clear that the war would be a long one and that the armed forces could use all the help it could get. The official attitude toward incorporating black soldiers into the military began to change, thus opening the way for black enlistments.

The military establishment was a microcosm of the larger white society, so it is not particularly surprising that black soldiers had to contend with as much racism in the army as they had experienced in civilian life. Despite the fact that they offered to make the supreme sacrifice of giving their lives for their country, they found that those lives were not as valued as those of whites. Typically, they were paid half of what white soldiers received for doing the same job. They were harassed, insulted, and discriminated against by white soldiers and officers and by civilians who lived near their encampments. They were denied leadership positions within the army. And they were often ordered to work as common laborers instead of being given the opportunity to participate in combat. In such cases, many found that an experience that was supposed to give deeper meaning to the concept of manliness could be demeaning rather than confirming.

The Civil War toughened all of the men who participated in it in ways that no other experience could. It forced them to reassess their own values, their relationships with others, and their definitions of masculinity. But we know almost nothing about how that experience affected men's ideas about manliness once they returned to civilian life. Some came home with war-related mental and physical disabilities that made them incapable of resuming their normal lives. Unable to move about freely or to work at their usual jobs, they faced the vexing problem of finding alternative ways of expressing their manhood. The more fortunate among them were apparently able successfully to repress their memories of the war and whatever trauma their wartime experiences caused them, adjust to civilian life, and go about the business of making a living and reestablishing themselves as valuable members of society. Respected as veterans by their loved ones, friends, and neighbors, their gendered identity was, for the moment at least, relatively secure.

MANLINESS IN THE GILDED AGE

During the period following the Civil War, known as the Gilded Age, the cultural context for expressing manliness changed. The Civil War brought in its wake the development of technology, the rise of great corporations, and the accumulation of great fortunes. While others were fighting to preserve the Union and end slavery, civilian business entrepreneurs spent their time and energy profiting from the sale of war supplies to the federal government and speculating on risky business ventures. When the war was over, there was capital to invest in industrial and commercial expansion.

The United States had always been rich in natural resources such as coal, oil, and iron. But most of those resources remained largely untapped until after the Civil War when bankers like J. Pierpont Morgan, railroad men like Cornelius Vanderbilt, and industrialists like John D. Rockefeller and Andrew Carnegie were able to exploit them along with the labor of a burgeoning immigrant population to make the United States one of the leading industrial nations of the world. By the 1890s railroads crisscrossed the country, factories belched black smoke into the air, and cities teemed with populations that were distinguished for their racial and ethnic diversity.

The nineteenth century had begun with the assumption that equality should serve as one of the contexts within which manhood was defined. That assumption largely disappeared after the Civil War. During the Gilded Age, men like Herbert Spencer and William Graham Sumner applied Darwin's theory of evolution to human affairs and created an ideology popularly known as Social Darwinism. This ideology, which suggested that progress was determined by the ability of the strong to prevail over the weak, combined with Adam Smith's doctrine of laissez faire, which held that no one should interfere in this natural process, gave those who were in positions of economic and political power the license to ignore those at the bottom of the heap. In some circles, it became acceptable to excuse the abuse of political, economic, and social power on the grounds that such behavior was a natural and predictable part of the competitive process. Those who were poor, socially insignificant, and politically powerless were considered inferior. Belief in the survival of the fittest did not carry with it much compassion for any of them.

Evangelical religion did not continue to exert as much influence over the definition of manliness after the Civil War as it had before.

Men whose gendered identity was expressed in the advocacy of social, economic, and political reform did not disappear. But it could be argued that evangelical masculinity was expressed much more quietly than it had been by men such as Garrison. Without much fanfare, men like O. O. Howard dedicated themselves to promoting the welfare of the freed slaves and others carried out private acts of Christian benevolence designed to relieve the suffering of those less fortunate than themselves. But as we shall see, it was not until the 1890s that Christian men organized in large numbers to promote social reform by forming the Social Gospel Movement which again brought corruption, poverty, and man's inhumanity to man to the attention of the public.

In the late nineteenth century, northern business came to be increasingly dominated by large corporations. As a result, both middle-class and working-class men found their work environment changing. After the Civil War it became increasingly difficult for the small business owners to compete with large corporations. So instead of trying to accumulate enough capital and risking everything they owned so that they could set up their own businesses and work for themselves, many young men went to work for someone else. Entrepreneurship was increasingly reserved for the few and became less important as a primary component of male identity. Employment in big companies managing and supervising the work of others or selling and distributing goods made in factories gave some middle-class white collar workers more predictable incomes as well as job security and more time for leisure. But it also deprived them of a sense of autonomy, independence, and self-reliance. Corporate work was often boring and monotonous. And many found to their chagrin that no matter how hard working and ambitious they were, once they got a job in middle management, it was difficult to go much further up the corporate ladder.

Working in a corporation or large business enterprise also meant that success depended on a different set of values and work practices.

For salaried managers who had once been independent businessmen, team work and cooperation took the place of individualism and competition. Wage laborers found themselves increasingly distanced from their supervisors and increasingly unable as individuals to influence the conditions under which they worked. This did not mean that they were completely powerless. It simply became obvious that if they expected to define their masculinity in terms of their ability to support their families and to maintain their dignity as workers, they would have to take collective action rather than rely on themselves.

The masculine identities of farmers were also influenced by urbanization, industrialization, and the rise of corporations. Some men left the relative isolation of living and working in a rural area to find jobs in the city where they became wage laborers. There they adjusted their definitions of masculinity to conform to those of the working class. But throughout much of the late nineteenth century, farmers continued to measure their manliness by their ability to make a profit running their families' farms and to pass their title to the land on to their sons as their fathers and grandfathers had done before them. Farmers remembered a time when they had derived a great deal of manly pride from the political power they had been able to wield in state and national government. As the century progressed, however, they found their political influence dwindling as more and more people crowded into cities and corporate leaders used their enormous wealth to manipulate politics to serve the interests of big business. Farmers also found themselves becoming increasingly dependent upon the railroads to provide them with storage facilities and to transport their crops to market. Desperate to maintain their competitiveness in a world market, many felt it necessary to increase production. So they used their land as security and borrowed money from the banks to buy more land and purchase expensive farm machinery. Their fate was now in the hands of bankers and the railroads. Under the circumstances, they found it more and more difficult to maintain the sense of competency, self-sufficiency, autonomy, and independence that had once served as the cornerstone for their masculine identities. By the 1880s, farmers were emerging as a beleaguered and disadvantaged group. Unable to hold their own in politics and often facing financial ruin, they found it difficult to maintain the belief that their fathers and grandfathers had handed down to them—that they were the men upon whom the welfare of the republic depended.

THE CHALLENGE OF EXPRESSING IDEALS OF AFRICAN-AMERICAN MANHOOD

The end of the Civil War secured the freedom of all northern blacks and brought with it new economic opportunities. The booming economy allowed African American men in ever increasing numbers to find employment in factories. But they still had to contend with the unwillingness of white laborers to work with them and the lack of enthusiasm of union leaders to represent their interests. Thus their ability to derive a masculine identity from the pursuit of wealth remained elusive.

Those with some access to education and capital were more fortunate. Hardworking, intelligent, ambitious, and filled with entrepreneurial spirit, they were able to establish themselves as small businessmen and professional men. Black men who were teachers, ministers, newspaper editors, grocers, contractors, doctors, lawyers, and bankers derived their gendered identity from their ability to make enough money to support their families without relying on the financial contributions of their wives, buying their own homes, providing for their children's education, and seeking outlets for their own self-improvement by founding literary clubs and fraternal organizations. Dedicated to eradicating the effects of Northern racism and already politically visible because of their participation in the abolition movement, black

men provided leadership for the emerging civil rights movement. And they used their wealth and influence to establish schools, churches, and welfare agencies in order to provide material and financial assistance to those in their communities who were less fortunate than themselves. They often measured their manhood by the degree to which they were able to conform to the gender conventions of the white middle class.

MANHOOD AND THE IMMIGRANT EXPERIENCE

Men from all over the world poured into the United States in the nineteenth century. Because they were the products of widely divergent cultures, it is very difficult to generalize about their attitudes toward gender. Before the Civil War most immigrants came from Germany or Ireland. The Germans tended to settle in the Midwest where they made their living by farming. Their gendered identities were tied to land ownership and their ability to preserve their ethnic distinctiveness. When they could, they settled in groups, formed their own communities, continued to speak in German, and did what they could to perpetuate the patriarchal nature of the German farm family.

The Irish experience was considerably different. Despite the fact that most Irish men had been engaged in agriculture in Ireland, few of them came to the United States with much money. Most did not have the resources necessary to travel to the Midwest and buy land. So they tended to make their homes in the cities along the eastern seaboard where they worked at first as day laborers, on the railroads, or as factory workers. Without the power to prevent their employers from exploiting their labor, they tried with varying degrees of success to fulfill their manly obligation to support their families. And they sought out places where they could express their manly autonomy. Irish men were able to carve out public life separate from their work and their domestic lives. Irish neighborhoods were filled with taverns of one sort or another where Irish men met to socialize, discuss politics, and drink. Their masculine identities centered, then, around their work, whatever authority they were able to claim within their families, their participation in local politics, and their ability to hold their liquor.

Because of their rural backgrounds and the economic realities of life in America, German and Irish men did not invest much of their masculine identities in the middle-class ideal of being sole breadwinners. The economic survival of their families had depended upon the labor of their wives and children in their country of origin. That situation did not change when they came to the United States. So unlike native-born, middle-class men, they did not view dependence on female labor either demeaning or emasculating.

After the Civil War immigration patterns began to change so that by the 1890s most immigrants were coming from southern and eastern Europe. These so-called "new immigrants" were relatively impoverished, uneducated, and unskilled. Settling in cities all across the United States, they lived in ethnic neighborhoods where they tried to balance the comfort of preserving their ethnic identities with the need to adapt themselves to American life. Men from places like Poland, Italy, Greece, and Russia found work wherever they could. Unable to speak English and often without any marketable skill, many of them, like the Irish before them, worked at first as day laborers, in construction, on the railroads, or in the factories. Most at first could not make enough money to support their families by themselves, and, like earlier immigrants, were forced to depend on the wages of their wives and children to make ends meet.

The way that immigrant men responded to that reality depended on their ethnic background. Many newly arrived Jewish men, for example, willingly allowed their daughters to work in shops and factories. As a practical matter, many of their male prerogatives, such as the leisure to study the Torah and participate regularly in religious observances, were dependent upon the labor of women. In that sense, their gendered identity was enhanced rather than threatened by their dependence on female labor. The masculine identity of Italian men, however, was very much tied to their ability to support and protect their female relatives. So when they needed the supplementary wages of their wives and daughters, they preferred to have them work at home or in family businesses. Their manly obligations required that they restrict the ability of their womenfolk to roam the streets unaccompanied and work without the supervision of someone associated with the family.

Because they had often lacked political influence in their country of origin, being able to participate in politics in America was a source of masculine pride for most immigrant men. In the period following the Civil War, however, politics in the cities where most immigrants lived was corrupt. Political bosses were able to buy political support by providing voters with much needed social services such as helping them find jobs. This system meant that while immigrant men could vote, they could not make political decisions independently. They, in effect, traded their votes in return for the good will of the local political bosses. On election day they typically accepted free drinks from their district chairman and voted the way he told them to. Thus, their masculine identities as citizens were identities characterized by dependence.

No matter what their ethnic background, immigrant men came to America hoping to make a better life for themselves and their loved ones. They accepted the idea of the self-made man and struggled sometimes against great odds to earn enough money so that their wives and children would not have to work for wages, so that they could send their children to school, and so that they could buy their own homes, establish their own businesses, and eventually move to more affluent parts of town. Some, like Andrew Carnegie, were spectacularly successful in achieving wealth, social prominence, and power. A Scottish immigrant with no resources other than a brilliant head for business and a willingness to work hard, Carnegie started his working life as a bobbin boy in a factory. By the time he retired, he was a multi-millionaire who controlled most of the steel production in the United States. But many men in that first generation of immigrants were not so successful. Their sense of their own manliness was undermined by the desperate economic circumstances they found themselves in. And their authority in their own households was diminished by the eagerness of their children to reject their ethnic backgrounds and become Americans.

SUMMARY

Whether they were white and native-born, African American, or immigrants, whether they lived on a farm or in a town or city, the masculine identity of northern men in the nineteenth century was very much defined by the degree to which they were able to achieve economic success. But the context within which each man pursued wealth and the social, economic, and political power that accompanied that success changed as the century progressed. One of the legacies of the American Revolution was that in the early part of the century the ideal of the self-made man was carried out within a social and political context that theoretically held that all men were potentially equal. By 1890 that assumption of fundamental equality among men had disappeared in some circles.

Because most men in the nineteenth century derived their masculine identities from the work that they did, industrialization had a dramatic impact on the way they expressed their manliness. Industrialization demanded a great deal more capital investment than that which was required to run small workshops and businesses. Thus, it became difficult for men of limited means to pursue their fortunes as entrepreneurs. If they found it necessary to go to work as wage laborers, they lost control over their time, they became dependent upon the good will of their supervisors, and they found it increasingly difficult to exert much influence over their working conditions. So as the century progressed, more and more men lost the independence and autonomy that had once formed the core of what it meant to be a man.

The role of men in the home also changed in the nineteenth century. And as it did so, their masculine identities became less and less tied to their ability to impose their authority over the various members of their families. The decline in their spiritual leadership had begun in the late eighteenth century. And in the nineteenth century, male domestic authority, particularly among those who lived in the cities, declined as well. Whether they were middle-class businessmen or factory workers, they were increasingly absent from their homes for longer periods of time. The result was that during the 1800s men tried to maintain their patriarchal power in their households while at the same time ceding their moral authority as well as many of their paternal responsibilities to their wives. In the process, while men were increasingly willing to acknowledge the moral superiority of women and to allow them more control over child rearing, they continued to express a great deal of ambivalence toward the female half of the population. They did what they could to limit the influence that women had over them by carving out all-male environments such as lodges and taverns where they could express their manliness without being inhibited by standards of behavior dictated by their wives and mothers.

Male attitudes towards their bodies were also in the process of change. Compared to their forebears, men in the nineteenth century were becoming much more self-conscious about maintaining their physical strength and good health. The wage laborer no less than his employer vested much of his sense of his own masculinity in the relationship between his physical condition and his ability to earn a decent living. The welfare of a workingman's entire family was dependent upon his physical ability to withstand the grueling nature of work on the railroad, or in the factories, or in construction. Succumbing to illness or suffering from the effects of an industrial accident could not only be economically devastating in its impact on the family but also undermine his claim to domestic authority based on his role as primary wage earner. The economic well being of most middle-class men was not so dependent upon their physical strength. It was their intellectual, psychological, and emotional abilities that were tested in the workplace. Yet, it seems clear, as we shall see in Chapter 9, that ill health and lack of physical prowess was of increasing concern to a wide variety of men. Underneath a great deal of bravado was the fear of being or becoming a "ninety pound weakling."

Thus by the 1880s, ideas about manliness were in a state of flux. Most northern men were in the process of coming to terms with the fact that defining manliness in terms of authority, independence, and autonomy was a problem. At the same time, as we will see in the next chapter, definitions of femininity were also in the process of change. And as women began to demand expanded educational and vocational opportunities and political rights, it became increasingly difficult for men to use women as a foil for defining their own masculinity. So at the turn of the century, northern men joined their southern and western counterparts to try to come to some consensus about what it meant to be a real "man."

DOCUMENT

Henry Wadsworth Longfellow's "The Village Blacksmith"

Harvard professor Henry Wadsworth Longfellow was a major American literary figure in the early nineteenth century. His enormously popular poems such as "Evangeline," "The Song of Hiawatha," and "The Courtship of Miles Standish" helped to provide Americans, newly liberated from British domination, with a sense of their own history and culture. A part of that effort included defining what it meant to be an American man. Longfellow was a teacher/scholar/author whose work did not require much strength or endurance. He married the daughter of a prominent Boston merchant and lived in a fine house in Cambridge only a few blocks from Harvard Square. In his poem reprinted below, Longfellow idealizes the skilled artisan by describing for

Source: Henry Wadsworth Longfellow, *The Complete Poetical Works of Henry Wadsworth Longfellow* (Boston: Houghton Mifflin, 1902), 18–19.

his readers the village blacksmith, the sort of man he was, and the kind of life that he led.

What did Longfellow think was particularly manly about the village blacksmith? To what degree were the blacksmith's manly qualities class specific?

THE VILLAGE BLACKSMITH

Under a spreading chestnut-tree
  The village smithy stands;
The smith, a mighty man is he,
  With large and sinewy hands;
And the muscles of his brawny arms
  Are strong as iron bands.

His hair is crisp, and black, and long,
  His face is like the tan;
His brow is wet with honest sweat,
  He earns whate'er he can,
And looks the whole world in the face,
  For he owes not any man.

Week in, week out, from morn till night,
  You can hear his bellows blow;
You can hear him swing his heavy sledge,
  With measured beat and slow,
Like a sexton ringing the village bell,
  When the evening sun is low.

And children coming home from school
  Look in at the open door;
They love to see the flaming forge,
  And hear the bellows roar,
And catch the burning sparks that fly
  Like chaff from a threshing-floor.

He goes on Sunday to the church,
  And sits among his boys;
He hears the parson pray and preach,
  He hears his daughter's voice,
Singing in the village choir,
  And it makes his heart rejoice.

It sounds to him like her mother's voice,
  Singing in Paradise!
He needs must think of her once more,
  How in the grave she lies;
And with his hard, rough hand he wipes
  A tear out of his eyes.

Toiling,—rejoicing,—sorrowing,
  Onward through life he goes;
Each morning sees some task begin,
  Each evening sees it close;
Something attempted, something done,
  Has earned a night's repose.

Thanks, thanks to thee, my worthy friend,
  For the lesson thou hast taught!
Thus at the flaming forge of life
  Our fortunes must be wrought;
Thus on its sounding anvil shaped
  Each burning deed and thought.

Charles Francis Adams, Jr.,
On Being a Soldier

The great-grandson of President John Adams and the grandson of President John Quincy Adams, Charles Frances Adams, Jr., was born in 1835. During his early life, he came into contact with some of the most prominent political figures of his day. He graduated from Harvard in 1856 and then studied law but had no love for the subject and did not enjoy practicing it. Like many other young men his age, he was a member of a volunteer militia when the Civil War broke out in 1861. He was unenthusiastic about going to war, but in October, 1861, he applied for a captaincy in the First Massachusetts Cavalry. Commissioned as a first lieutenant in December, he headed for South Carolina just after Christmas to join his regiment. He left the army in June, 1865 and went on to become an historian and expert on building and managing railroads. In the excerpt from his autobiography reprinted below, Adams describes what serving in the Union Army meant to him and to his sense of what kind of man he was.

What qualities does he suggest were essential for a good officer? Are there any qualities generally considered desirable in a soldier that he does not mention? Why does he say that his experience in the army made a man of him?

Looking back now, fifty years after, were I asked whether I would give up as an experience of subsequent value, both educationally and in the way of reminiscence, my three years at Harvard or my three and a half years in the army, I would have great difficulty in reaching a decision. On the whole, I am inclined to think that my three and a half years of military service and open-air life were educationally of incomparably the greater value of the two. And especially was this so for me, constituted as I was and yet am. It gave me just that robust, virile stimulus to be derived only from a close contact with Nature and a roughing it among men and in the open air, which I especially needed. The experiment was, it is true, a somewhat risky one, and involved not a few hair-breadth escapes; but I

succeeded in getting through without sustaining any lasting personal or physical injury, or any moral injury at all. I never was wounded; and though, when mustered out of the service in the summer of 1865 I was a physical wreck, eighteen months of change and a subsequent temperate and healthy life repaired all waste and injury. Thus, so far as physique is concerned, I from my army experience got nothing but good. I was, and at seventy-seven am, in every way the better for it. Otherwise, that experience was not only picturesque, but of the greatest possible educational value. For two years enjoying it keenly, it, so to speak, made a man of me. . . .

Far from being a born soldier, I was in many respects unfitted for such a career. Not quick, daring or ready-witted, robust but not muscularly agile, I could not take advantage of sudden or unforeseen circumstances. With no personal magnetism, I was rather deficient in presence of mind in time of peril. The most that could be said of me was that, as a

Source: Charles Francis Adams, *An Autobiography* (Boston: Houghton Mifflin, 1916), 129–30, 134–36.

camp officer, I was distinctly above the average. I was conscientious, understood my duties fairly well, and cared anxiously for my men and horses. But I did not understand myself, nor did I take in the situation. Unseeing of my opportunities, I quite failed to realize in any broad way the nature of the occasion. I went into the service with a strong sense of duty, and a desire to see hard work, in no way seeking to save myself. I had no conception of army functions, or of the relative fields of usefulness of the staff and line. In common with most of my friends, I had rather a contempt for the staff positions; we wanted to be where the work and hardship were, and where the knocks were to be looked for. It was in some respects a praiseworthy feeling, and I lived up to it; but living up to it involved much hardship and danger,

besides leaving out of sight, in my own individual case, that, while I had no particular aptitude for line work, I would have made a really valuable staff officer, had I only diligently qualified myself for the position. . . . As it was, I had to learn by hard experience that, in warfare on a large scale, a regimental officer, no matter how high his grade, sees nothing and knows nothing of what is going on. He is a mere minor wheel, when not simply a cog, in a vast and to him in greatest part unintelligible machine, moving on given lines to a possible result; wholly regardless of his comfort or even life. Obedience, self-sacrifice and patient endurance are the qualities most in demand for him; but as for any intelligent comprehension of the game in progress, that for the regimental officer is quite beyond his ken. . . .

DOCUMENT

Excerpts from Russell Conwell's "Acres of Diamonds" Lecture

Born in 1843, Russell Conwell began his professional life as a lawyer but eventually became a Baptist minister in Philadelphia. He was also an itinerate speaker who, beginning in 1873, traveled all over the country delivering a lecture called "Acres of Diamonds." In his speech, Conwell equated wealth with virtue. His purpose was to convince everyone in his audiences that they too could fulfill God's plan that they become wealthy. Conwell did not see the prospect of acquiring great wealth just as an opportunity, he saw it as an obligation that the individual owed to God Almighty. It is clear from his lecture that there were women in his audiences. It is also true, that there were women in the nineteenth century who flourished as entrepreneurial businesswomen. It seems, clear, however, that the kind of attributes that were required to exploit the "acres of diamonds" were usually gendered male.

Source: Russell H. Conwell, *Acres of Diamonds* (New York: Harper & Row, 1905), 17–21.

What characteristics does Conwell equate with manliness? According to Conwell, what is the connection between manliness and the accumulation of money? What is his attitude toward men who are not economically successful?

Now then, I say again that the opportunity to get rich, to attain unto great wealth, is here in Philadelphia now, within the reach of almost every man and woman who hears me speak tonight, and I mean just what I say. I have not come to this platform even under these circumstances to recite something to you. I have come to tell you what in God's sight I believe to be the truth, and if the years of life have been of any value to me in the attainment of common sense, I know I am right; that the men and women sitting here, who found it difficult perhaps to buy a ticket to this lecture or gathering to-night, have within their reach "acres of diamonds," opportunities to get largely wealthy. There never was a place on earth more adapted than the city of Philadelphia to-day, and never in the history of the world did a poor man without capital have such an opportunity to get rich quickly and honestly as he has now in our city. I say it is the truth, and I want you to accept it as such; for if you think I have come to simply recite something, then I would better not be here. I have no time to waste in any such talk, but to say the things I believe, and unless some of you get richer for what I am saying to-night my time is wasted.

I say that you ought to get rich, and it is your duty to get rich. How many of my pious brethren say to me, "Do you, a Christian minister, spend your time going up and down the country advising young people to get rich, to get money?" "Yes, of course I do." They say, "Isn't that awful! Why don't you preach the gospel instead of preaching about man's making money?" "Because to make money honestly is to preach the gospel." That is the reason. The men who get rich may be the most honest men you find in the community.

"Oh," but says some young man here to-night, "I have been told all my life that if a person has money he is very dishonest and dishonorable and mean and contemptible." My friend, that is the reason why you have none, because you have that idea of people. The foundation of your faith is altogether false. Let me say here clearly, and say it briefly, though subject to discussion which I have not time for here, ninety-eight out of one hundred of the rich men of America are honest. That is why they are rich. That is why they are trusted with money. That is why they carry on great enterprises and find plenty of people to work with them. It is because they are honest men. . . .

My friend, you take and drive me—if you furnish the auto—out into the suburbs of Philadelphia, and introduce me to the people who own their homes around this great city, those beautiful homes with gardens and flowers, those magnificent homes so lovely in their art, and I will introduce you to the very best people in character as well as in enterprise in our city, and you know I will. A man is not really a true man until he owns his own home, and they that own their homes are made more honorable and honest and pure, and true and economical and careful, by owning the home.

For a man to have money, even in large sums, is not an inconsistent thing. We preach against covetousness, and you know we do, in the pulpit, and oftentimes preach against it so long and use the terms about "filthy lucre" so extremely that Christians get the idea that when we stand in the pulpit we believe it is wicked for any man to have money—until the collection-basket goes around, and then we almost swear at the people because they don't give more money. Oh, the inconsistency of such doctrines as that!

Money is power, and you ought to be reasonably ambitious to have it. You ought because you can do more good with it than you could without it. Money printed your Bible, money builds your churches, money sends your missionaries, and money pays your preachers, and you would not have many of them, either, if you did not pay them. . . .

I say, then, you ought to have money. If you can honestly attain unto riches in Philadelphia, it is your Christian and godly duty to do so. It is an awful mistake of these pious people to think you must be awfully poor in order to be pious.

Some men say, "Don't you sympathize with the poor people?" Of course I do, or else I would not have been lecturing these years. I won't give in but what I sympathize with the poor, but the number of poor who are to be sympathized with is very small. To sympathize with a man whom God has punished for his sins, thus to help him when God would still continue a just punishment, is to do wrong, no doubt about it, and we do that more than we help those who are deserving. While we should sympathize with God's poor—that is, those who cannot help themselves—let us remember there is not a poor person in the United States who was not made poor by his own shortcomings, or by the shortcomings of some one else. It is all wrong to be poor, anyhow. Let us give in to that argument and pass that to one side. . . .

ARTICLE

Violence, Protest, and Identity: Black Manhood in Antebellum America

James Oliver Horton and Lois E. Horton

After the American Revolution, northern states from New England to the Mid-Atlantic passed legislation gradually abolishing slavery within their borders. The result was that by the mid-1820s, a substantial portion of the black population in the North was free. That did not mean, however, that race became irrelevant to the construction of gender in the black community. Because emancipated men of color were in a position to accept some responsibility for ending slavery where it continued to exist, exhibiting such manly characteristics as aggressiveness had particular immediacy for them. In their article, James Oliver Horton and Lois E. Horton discuss the role that self-assertion played in the construction of northern black manhood. They begin by discussing the problem that assertiveness posed for slaves and slave owners alike and then turn their attention to the specific problems that free northern black men had incorporating aggressiveness into their definition of what it meant to be a man.

Source: Free People of Color: Inside the African American Community edited by James Oliver Horton. pp. 80–96. Copyright © 1993 by the Smithsonian Institution. Used by permission of the publisher. Notes omitted.

What influences contributed to a sense of ambivalence about defining Black manhood in terms of aggressiveness? What role did the attitudes of Whites play in the debate that surrounded the issue?

. . . Although the American man in the nineteenth century could choose from a variety of gender ideals, virtually all the combinations of characteristics, values, and actions constituting each ideal included self-assertion and aggression as key elements. Aggression, and sometimes sanctioned violence, was a common thread in American ideals of manhood. Charles Rosenberg believes that two masculine ideals exemplified the choices open to nineteenth-century men, the *Masculine Achiever* and *Christian Gentleman*. The Masculine Achiever ideal was closely associated with the rapid economic growth of the nineteenth century. As the rise of the market economy disrupted local relationships and tied formerly isolated communities to distant economic affiliations, this ideal provided American men with a dynamic model of behavior. The man of action was unencumbered by sentiment and totally focused on advancement, the quintessential individualist and the self-styled ruthless competitor. He was the rugged individual succeeding in the world of commercial capitalism.

The Christian Gentleman ideal arose in reaction to the Masculine Achiever and threats to traditional values and relationships. Eschewing self-seeking behavior and heartless competition in the commercial world, this gentler ideal stressed communal values, religious principles, and more humanitarian action. It was a natural outgrowth of the religious revival that blossomed under the Second Great Awakening of the early nineteenth century and stressed self-restraint and Christian morality. Christian Gentlemen were not expected to be passive. Dynamic and aggressive action was assumed, but in the name of moral values and self-sacrifice, not personal greed.

E. Anthony Rotundo argues that an additional ideal emerged among northern males in the nineteenth century—the *Masculine Primitive*. This ideal stressed dominance and conquest through harnessing the energy of primitive male instincts and savagery lurking beneath the thin veneer of civilization. This was a more physically aggressive ideal, based on the natural impulses of man's most primitive state, and violence was its confirming feature. Although Rotundo sees this ideal as influential among northern men by the middle of the nineteenth century, southern historians have found a strikingly similar ideal in the South throughout the eighteenth and nineteenth centuries. Bertram Wyatt-Brown and Grady McWhiney describe the violence in defense of honor sanctioned by even the most genteel southerners. Elizabeth Fox-Genovese notes the simultaneous existence of gentility and savagery: "Southern conventions of masculinity never abandoned the element of force or even brutality . . . This toleration of male violence responded to the perceived exigencies of governing a troublesome people . . ." The behaviors believed necessary for managing the slave system were incorporated into the gender ideals for all southern white men.

Black men growing up as slaves in southern society had an especially complex gender socialization. The gender ideals of white southern society overlaid the foundations of African cultural expectations and the intentional socialization imposed on slaves. The dual and contradictory genteel and savage images applied to southern white manhood paralleled characteristics whites imagined black men possessed. The happy, contented Sambo stereotype slaveholders wanted to believe existed was placed alongside the brute, savage Negro they feared. Slaveholders tried to cultivate a slave approximation of the Christian Gentlemen ideal, typified by Harriet Beecher Stowe's Uncle Tom, all the while dreading the emergence of the barbaric Masculine Primitive. Thomas R. Dew argued in 1832 that Africans were by nature savage and that it was only the civilizing influence of slavery that restrained their brutish nature. According to William Drayton, another nineteenth-century apologist for slavery, only slavery checked the "wild frenzy of revenge, and the savage lust for blood" natural to the African and dramatically apparent in the Haitian Revolution. In 1858 Thomas R. R. Cobb alleged that once removed from the domesticating influence of slavery, Haitian blacks "relapsed into barbarism."

Ever watchful for any outward signs of rebellion, white southerners went to great lengths to suppress black aggression and assertiveness. As one former slave recalled, "Every man [was] called boy till he [was] very old, then the more respectable slaveholder call[ed] him uncle." Actions expected of white men were condemned in black men. No black man could defend his family from a white attacker, "let him be ever so drunk or crazy," without fear of drastic reprisal. Yet a black man under the orders of white authority could legitimately use his strength against a white person. A slave directed by his overseer could strike a white man for "beating said overseer's pig."

"A slave can't be a man," proclaimed former slave Lewis Clarke. Slavery was designed to make it impossible for a man to freely express his opinions and make his own decisions. Yet many slave men asserted aspects of manhood even under the most difficult circumstances. William Davis refused to be whipped by his overseer. When the white man realized he could not administer the beating alone, he ordered three "athletic fellows" to assist him, but Davis served notice that he would not be taken easily. "Boys, I am only a poor boy and you are grown men, but if either of you touch me, I'll kill one of you . . . ," he warned. Davis was not whipped.

Slave men found many ways to assert themselves. Even the threat of self-assertion could be effective. One man reported that he avoided being sold at auction by meeting the gaze of prospective buyers directly as they inspected him, an obvious sign of a hard-to-handle slave. Another stopped his master from beating slave

children by standing beside them, glaring at the master as he began punishment. Among the slaves, men who refused to submit to the master's authority were accorded respect. Those who submitted too easily to the master's authority lost respect. "Them as won't fight," reported Lewis Clarke, "is called Poke-easy." How could a man be both manly and a slave? A central theme in the abolitionists' attacks on slavery was that it robbed men of their manhood. The widely used antislavery emblem was a manacled slave kneeling in the supplication, "Am I not a man and brother?"

David Walker, a free black North Carolinian who migrated to Boston, gained national attention and raised southern fears by urging slaves to prove their manhood, to rise up and take their freedom by force if necessary. His call to arms was issued in partial answer to Thomas Jefferson's suggestions that African Americans were an inferior species and could not be granted freedom. Walker asserted that the African American could not be domesticated like an animal and could never be held in slavery against his will. He goaded black men to action by rhetorically wondering how so many could be enslaved: "Are we Men!! How we could be so submissive to a gang of men, whom we cannot tell whether they are as good as ourselves or not, I never could conceive." Blacks, he wrote, must not wait for either God or slaveholders to end slavery. "The man who would not fight . . . to be delivered from the most wretched, abject and servile slavery, that ever a people was afflicted with since the foundation of the world . . . ought to be kept with all his children or family, in slavery or in chains to be butchered by his cruel enemies."

In his *Appeal* David Walker called upon the memory of the successful Haitian Revolution in 1804 as proof of the power of unity and manliness. "One thing which gives me joy," he wrote of the Haitians, "is, that they are men who would be cut off to a man before they would yield to the combined forces of the whole world." Black men demonstrated in Haiti, Walker contended, that "a groveling, servile and abject submission to the lash of tyrants" is not the African man's natural state.

Walker believed that slaves could transform themselves into men through aggressive action. "If ever we become men," he said, "we must assert ourselves to the full."

In his call to action, Walker claimed the physical superiority of black men. "I do declare," he wrote, "that one good black can put to death six white men." The assertion that slaves were stronger and better in combat than their masters was not new. It became part of the racial folklore of the period and was often cited in conjunction with rumors of slave uprisings. Yet this declaration posed problems for African Americans. The use of violence to assert manhood tended to reinforce white stereotypes of the "brutish African nature" only restrained by slavery.

Despite David Walker's mysterious death in 1831, his advocacy of the use of violence as an acceptable tactic for the acquisition of freedom and equality, what were increasingly referred to as *manhood rights,* remained an important position among blacks throughout the antebellum period. At the time that Walker wrote his *Appeal,* the American imagination was captured by Greek revolutionaries seeking independence from Turkey, by rising Polish discontent with their Russian masters, and the revolutions in Latin America that, in 1826, brought the abolition of slavery to the former Spanish colonies. Thus he drew on more than the distant models of the American Revolution and the revolt in Haiti. He was undoubtedly aware that freedom was being sought through violence abroad and that revolutionary armies in Latin America included black soldiers bearing arms supplied by the Haitian government.

Walker was not alone in using international illustrations to attack slavery or in considering the prospect of slave revolt. In 1825 in his commencement address at Bowdoin College, John Russwurm, one of the first African Americans to graduate from an American college, assailed the institution, taking as his paradigm the establishment of Haitian independence. Later, as coeditor of *Freedom's Journal,* Russwurm speculated that if the federal government would stop providing protection for

slaveholders, slaves might very well settle the question of slavery themselves. Ohio judge Benjamin Tappan shocked an acquaintance by inquiring rhetorically "whether the slave has not a resort to the most violent measures, if necessary, in order to maintain his liberty? And if he has the least chance of success, are we not, as rational and consistent men, bound to justify him?" Historian Merton Dillon asserts that most antislavery proponents of the time accepted the right of slaves to strike for their liberty.

The 1830s brought a new, more forceful critique of violent means in the fight against slavery as William Lloyd Garrison began publishing his newspaper, the *Liberator,* in Boston. His commitment to immediate emancipation for slaves and civil rights for free blacks was popular among African Americans who had worked toward these ends for decades with only marginal assistance from white reformers. Garrison was a nonresister—a pacifist opposed to cooperating with any government built on slavery and compromise with slaveholders. His pacifism led him to oppose government that forced citizens to participate directly or indirectly in violence, through, for example, war, imprisonment, or capital punishment. He opposed voting or participating in politics, and condemned the use of violence even to achieve freedom. The route to manhood, he believed, was through strength of character and principled action. In the pages of the *Liberator* he rejected Walker's call for slave revolt, and although he praised Walker personally, Garrison made clear that "we do not preach rebellion—no, but submission and peace." His stand on the use of violence by slaves was complex. He considered slaves "more than any people on the face of the earth" justified in the use of force and compared slave revolt to the American Revolution in the justice of its cause, but a just cause, Garrison believed, was no justification for violence.

Garrison's strong commitment to nonviolence and his philosophy of nonresistance entered the continuing debate within black society over violent and nonviolent means for the abolition of slavery. African Americans had been influenced by arguments for nonviolence early in the colonial era. Quakers, some of their first allies, were pacifists. Blacks who became Friends often wrestled with the question of the practicality of nonviolence for a people violently deprived of their rights. Yet blacks were obliged to "become convinced of [Quaker] principles" in order to be accepted into the society. During the War of 1812, black Quaker David Mapps of Little Egg Harbor, New Jersey, demonstrated his pacifist principles and refused to transport cannon balls aboard his schooner, explaining, "I cannot carry thy devil's pills that were made to kill people."

Although black Quakers were strongly committed to nonviolence, most African Americans expressed a great deal more ambivalence on this issue. At the opposite extreme from the Quakers, many continued to agree with David Walker that violence was the surest route to freedom and manhood. Some opposed the use of violence on practical grounds, others wrestled with moral issues and searched for alternative ways to assert themselves and to achieve dignity without the use of force. Garrison and his philosophy had become the center of this debate by the 1830s, but the debate was over means, not ends. All blacks agreed that freedom and equality were the goals, and most continued to equate these with manhood.

Speaking to a gathering of black Bostonians in 1831, black activist Maria W. Stewart echoed Walker's call to black men to assert their manhood: "O ye fearful ones, throw off your fearfulness . . . If you are men, convince [whites] that you possess the spirit of men." Yet hers was not a call to violence. She called forth the "sons of Africa" to show their bravery, their intelligence, and their commitment to serving their community. "But give the man of color an equal opportunity . . . from the cradle to manhood, and from manhood to grave, and you would discover a dignified statesman, the man of science, and the philosopher."

Maria Stewart urged a version of the *Masculine Achiever* ideal of manhood that incorporated achievement, autonomy, and "intensive competition for success in the marketplace." Her ideal, however, was not completely individualistic. The object of success in the masculine competition was to prove black men the equals of other men. It was also important, according to Stewart, that successful men become assets to the black community and contribute to the struggle of black people. Even though Stewart was a friend and co-worker of Garrison, her appeal was not incontrovertibly nonviolent. The heroes she called upon to inspire black men to the competition included the black soldiers of the American Revolution and the War of 1812—and David Walker.

Garrison agreed that bondage and discrimination denied human dignity and pledged his efforts to combat these destructive forces. He was a pacifist, but his philosophy and style was neither passive nor apologetic. As he began the *Liberator*, Garrison promised to speak clearly and forcefully in words that could not be misunderstood. He was unequivocal in his opposition to slavery, but he also believed he had a responsibility to free blacks in the North. He dedicated himself and his paper to work for their "moral and intellectual elevation, the advancement of [their] rights, and the defense of [their] character." Less than two months after beginning publication, Garrison felt his venture had already met with success. He reported: "Upon the colored population in the free states, it has operated like a trumpet call. They have risen in their hopes and feelings to the perfect stature of men . . ."

Garrison's conception of manhood, characterized by intellectual achievement, personal dignity, and moral responsibility, was shared by many abolitionists, whose underlying antislavery motivation was religious. It had particular appeal for black abolitionists, who felt they carried the added burden of disproving the claims of black inferiority advanced by Jefferson and the proslavery interests. Yet even among black Garrisonians there was some ambivalence regarding total reliance on the pacific means of moral suasion. A widely circulated poem composed by the intellectual black abolitionist Charles L. Reason illustrates this ambivalence. Reason's poem, entitled "The Spirit Voice: or Liberty Calls to the Disfranchised," is filled with martial images but comes to a decidedly nonviolent conclusion. He wrote:

> Come! rouse ye brothers, rouse! a peal now
>   breaks,
> From lowest island to our gallant lakes,
> 'Tis summoning you, who long in bonds
>   have lain,
> To stand up manful on the battle plain,
> Each as a warrior, with his armor bright,
> Prepared to battle in a bloodless fight.

Respect for Garrison and his work kept many black abolitionists from openly questioning reliance on moral suasion, even when they harbored doubts about its effectiveness. Some Garrisonians, of course, were committed to nonviolence on principle; others saw it as a practical strategy. Throughout the 1830s and early 1840s, the small band of antislavery crusaders was continually under attack. Mobs broke up their meetings, attacked them in the streets, and occasionally set fire to their lecture halls and homes. Slaveholders posted rewards for the most notorious abolitionists, dead or alive. In the face of such opposition, taking the principled stance of moral suasion had the additional practical benefit of attracting adherents while avoiding inflaming even more violent reactions.

Yet some continued to proclaim the right of slaves to take their freedom "like men." One of the most radical and elaborate schemes for the forcible abolition of slavery came from a white sixty-year-old politician, Jabez Delano Hammond, a jurist and former U.S. congressman from Cherry Valley, New York. In 1839 Hammond proposed that abolitionists sponsor military academies in Canada and Mexico that would train blacks in military arts and sabotage. The trainees would then be set loose in the South to commit terrorist acts and to encourage and lead slave rebellions. Referring to these infiltrators as potentially "the most

successful Southern missionaries," Hammond explained that such steps were necessary because "the only way in which slavery at the South can be abolished is by force."

Many black reformers were also growing impatient with moral suasion as the primary weapon against slavery and moral elevation as the surest route to progress for free blacks. Peter Paul Simons spoke for a growing minority in 1839 when he challenged the efficacy of moral reform. Instead of lessening the hold of slavery and prejudice on blacks, he believed, it had encouraged timidity and self-doubt. African Americans do not suffer from lack of moral elevation, he argued. "There is no nation of people under the canopy of heaven, who are given more to good morals and piety than we are." He contended that blacks suffered from a lack of direct "physical and political" action. They lacked confidence in one another, he said, and were thus likely to depend on the leadership of whites, a not-so-subtle reference to the willingness of many blacks to follow Garrison's lead. His argument continued, charging that black children learned passive acceptance not manly action and leadership from parental examples. Action must be the watchword: "This we must physically practice, and we will be in truth an independent people."

Although Simons stopped short of endorsing a David Walker–style call for violence in this pursuit of self-confident independence, his statements did signal the move toward a more aggressive posture. He was not alone. Many who worked most closely with fugitive slaves or on behalf of free blacks kidnapped into slavery were among those least able to accept the doctrine of nonviolence. Black abolitionist David Ruggles, an officer of the New York Committee of Vigilance, had never been totally committed to nonresistance. As early as 1836 he wrote that in dealing with slave hunters and kidnappers, "Self-defense is the first law of nature." Gradually Ruggles grew more impatient with the slow pace of antislavery and civil rights progress. In the summer of 1841, he addressed a meeting of the American Reform Board of Disfranchised

Commissioners, a New York protest group of which he was a founding member. In strident tones he rallied the group to action and explained that "in our cause" words alone would not suffice. "Rise brethren rise!" he urged the distant slaves. "Strike for freedom or die slaves!"

Two years later at the Buffalo meeting of the National Negro Convention, twenty-seven-year-old black abolitionist minister Henry Highland Garnet echoed David Walker's exhortation, urging black men to act like men. Addressing himself to the slaves, he used provocative and incendiary language. "It is sinful in the extreme," he admonished, "for you to make voluntary submission." As Walker had accepted the necessity for a man to use violence in the assertion of his manhood, so Garnet concluded that "there is not much hope of Redemption without the shedding of blood." Black men must not shrink from bloody confrontation—there was no escape. A mass exodus was not an option for African Americans, he argued. The solution must be found in America, and it might well be violent. "If you must bleed, let it come at once, rather, die freemen than live to be slaves." Garnet did not urge a revolution. "Your numbers are too small," he observed. But all slaves should immediately "cease to labor for tyrants who will not remunerate you." He assumed, however, that violence would be the inevitable result of this tactic. And when it came, he instructed, "Remember that you are THREE MILLIONS."

As Maria Stewart had done a decade earlier, Garnet used black heroes as a standard for manhood, and he found contemporary black men wanting. Questioning the commitment of his fellows to the assertion of manhood, Garnet cut to the heart of masculine pride. "You act as though your daughters were born to pamper the lusts of your masters and overseers," he charged. Garnet continued forcefully: "And worst of all, you timidly submit while your lords tear your wives from your embraces and defile them before your eyes. In the name of God, we ask, are you men? Where is the blood of your fathers? Has it all run out of your veins?" Here

Garnet drew upon one of the most powerful justifications for the link between physical prowess and masculinity in American gender ideals—the responsibility of men to protect their families. This responsibility was an important part of all male ideals in the society. Even those most committed to the Christian Gentleman ideal, even the most fervent black nonresisters had great difficulty arguing that nonviolence was the only recourse when one's family was in physical danger. Garnet's charge to the slaves forcefully affected the black and white abolitionists and observers in his audience as he evoked the universal images of manhood.

Garnet's speech split the convention; debate was heated. Ardent Garrisonians Frederick Douglass and Charles Lenox Remond spoke against endorsing his sentiments. They pointed to the bloody retribution slaves and free blacks, especially those in the border states, might suffer should the convention support such a radical call to violence. Although there was substantial support for Garnet's message, by a narrow margin the convention refused to endorse his words. For the time being the black Garrisonians remained convinced and had successfully blocked the open embrace of violent means.

A commitment to nonviolence and a sense of the dangers the relatively powerless slaves faced continued to prevent most blacks from urging slaves to gain their freedom through physical force. Many black abolitionists had been slaves and were intimately familiar with the dangers involved. Even Frederick Douglass, who recounted the story of attaining his manhood through physical confrontation, was aware of the risks and continued to be reluctant to sanction calls for slave rebellion. A news story he printed in his paper in the late 1840s illustrated the horrors of slavery and made the point that resistance could be deadly:

Wm. A. Andrews, an overseer of J. W. Perkins, Mississippi attempted to chastise one of the negro boys who seized a stick and prepared to do battle. The overseer told the boy to lay the stick down or he would shoot him; he refused, and the overseer then fired his pistol, and shot the boy in the face, killing him instantly. The jury of inquest found the verdict, "that the said Wm. A. Andrews committed the killing in self-defense."

In the 1840s Garrisonian nonresistance came under fire from many quarters. There was a split in the abolition movement at the start of the decade, and many of those committed to political antislavery cast their lot with the newly formed Liberty party. Among white abolitionists there was also growing intolerance of what some saw as Garrison's unreasoned radicalism, not only attacking slavery but also condemning the Constitution, the entire federal government, and the national political system. Further, some criticized his support of women's rights as an unnecessary complication that made abolition even less palatable to the general public and threatened to blunt the central thrust of the movement. This fear was reinforced when feminist Abby Kelley was elected to be the first female member of the business committee of the Garrisonian-dominated American Anti-Slavery Society. Opposition groups sprang up to challenge this and other Garrisonian organizations.

This debate between those who favored political participation and those who opposed it split the black abolitionist ranks. Despite their ambivalence, most black Bostonians remained personally loyal to Garrison. New York's *Colored American* attempted to remain neutral, but many black New Yorkers sided with the political abolitionists. Blacks in several northern states faced the curtailment or loss of their voting rights. The vote was an instrument of males' political power, and blacks viewed disenfranchisement as symbolic emasculation. Garrison himself conceded that where rights were in jeopardy, black voters should vote in self-defense.

The debate was short lived among blacks, and even Boston blacks openly took part in electoral politics by the mid-1840s. There were Liberty party announcements inserted in the pages of the *Liberator,* and by 1848 the paper reported on meetings at which African Americans in Boston discussed the formation of an auxiliary to the Liberty party. William Cooper Nell, one of the most loyal of the black Garrisonians, allowed his name to be put into nomination as Free-Soil party candidate for the 1850 Massachusetts legislature.

By the mid-nineteenth century, Garrisonians were also reassessing their stand on nonviolence. Among African Americans almost all reservations about the appropriateness of violence in the struggle against slavery were wiped away by the passage of the federal Fugitive Slave Law of 1850. This measure, which made it easier for fugitives to be captured and for free blacks to be kidnapped into slavery, was seen as a direct blow against all African Americans. It generated a strongly militant reaction even among those who had favored nonviolence. Charles Lenox Remond, who had opposed Garnet's call to arms in the early 1840s, a decade later demanded defiance of the law, protection of all fugitives, and the withholding of federal troops should the southern slaves rise against their masters.

Douglass, who had joined Remond in voting against Garnet, published a novella in 1853 in which slaves killed the captain of a slave ship and a slave owner. In an editorial entitled "Is It Right and Wise to Kill a Kidnapper?" published in *Frederick Douglass' Paper* a year later, he was even more forthright. Violence, even deadly violence, was justifiable when used to protect oneself, one's family, or one's community. At a community meeting in Boston, Nell cautioned African Americans to be watchful for kidnappers. If confronted, he urged them to defend themselves.

The defection from nonviolence was not limited to African Americans. Boston journalist Benjamin Drew suggested that when the government supported oppression, violence against the state might be reasonable. Pacifist minister Samuel J. May and five fugitive slaves stood before an antislavery convention in Syracuse. In surprising tones for the longtime Garrisonian, May asked, "Will you defend [these fugitives] with your lives?" The audience threw back the answer: "Yes!"

Most plans of action were far less offensive. New vigilance committees were formed to protect the safety of fugitives, and already established committees redoubled their efforts, publicly vowing that no slave would be taken. This was a manly pursuit it was said, for every "slave-hunter who meets a bloody death in his infernal business, is an argument in favor of the manhood of our race." Yet not all blacks viewed violent confrontation with slave catchers as the route to manliness. Former slave Philip Younger, who sought refuge in Canada in the 1850s, wrote that even more than in the free states, Canada offered a black man self-respect and dignity. "It was a hardship at first," he reported, "but I feel better here—more like a man—I know I am—than in the States."

Some reformers, such as New York's Gerrit Smith, were critical of men who protected themselves and their families by escaping to Canada, viewing this as a cowardly act. Black abolitionist William Whipper took offense when Smith published such criticism, considering it a slur on the bravery of all black men. Whipper offered a combative reply, saying that he could not understand Smith's attack, considering that African Americans were leaving "a country whose crushing influence . . . aims at the extinction of [their] manhood." Reactions to the Fugitive Slave Law of 1850 ranged from flight to confrontation—different, but each an assertion of personal dignity.

The rising anger at the attack by the "slave power" through its influence over the federal government went beyond militancy to an interest in military preparedness. The Negro Convention in Rochester in 1853 called for the removal of all restrictions on black enlistment in state militia. Sixty-five Massachusetts blacks petitioned their state legislature, demanding that a black military company be chartered. The right to bear arms for their state, they contended, was part of their "rights as men." Their petition was rejected, but a black military company called the Massasoit Guard was formed in Boston in 1854. The unit took its name, their second choice, from a powerful seventeenth-century Indian chief. Most would have preferred the name Attucks, in honor of the black revolutionary hero Crispus Attucks, but the name had already been taken by two other black military companies, the Attucks Guards of New York and the Attucks Blues of Cincinnati. Before the decade ended, there were several black military units in northern cities. Binghamton, New York, named its company after black abolitionist Jermain Loguen, an associate of John Brown, and Harrisburg, Pennsylvania, formed the Henry Highland Garnet Guards. Thus during the 1850s, black men armed themselves, poised to strike against slavery and to reaffirm their manhood through military action.

The opinion in the Dred Scott decision in 1857, which declared that African Americans were not citizens of the United States, further inflamed antigovernment sentiment, as it placed African Americans in an even more perilous position. Increasing militancy and the continuing formation of black military companies led white abolitionist John Brown to believe that substantial numbers of northern free blacks might join a military attack on slavery. He was wrong; in 1859 only five blacks and sixteen whites (three of whom were Brown's sons) joined his attack on the federal arsenal at Harpers Ferry, Virginia. Despite the depth of their antislavery feeling, anger, and frustration, African Americans were not ready to join a private venture that seemed doomed to failure.

Within two years Brown's private war assumed national proportions. Although Lincoln firmly proclaimed preservation of the Union as his sole Civil War aim, northern blacks were convinced that abolition would be its outcome. Their immediate offer of service was refused, even though more than eighty-five hundred men had joined black militia units by the fall of 1861. Two years later, however, with U.S. casualties mounting and the nation bogged down in a protracted war, the government reversed itself and began active recruitment of African American troops. Black abolitionists became energetic recruiters. Jermain Loguen, William Wells Brown, Martin R. Delany, Garnet, and Douglass were among those who encouraged black men to provide their services to the forces of the United States. Victories in the abolition and civil rights struggles during the antebellum period had enhanced their self-image, and most viewed the war as another opportunity to prove themselves to a skeptical white populace. "The eyes of the whole world are upon you, civilized man everywhere waits to see if you will prove yourselves . . . Will you vindicate your manhood?" challenged the *Weekly Anglo-African* in 1863. African Americans hoped that the war would do more than end slavery. Dignity awaited the black man who would "get an eagle on his button, a musket on his shoulder, and the star-spangled banner over his head." Black men marched off to win freedom for slaves and respect and equality for those already free. War was the culmination of the aggressiveness emphasized in much of the resistance to slavery. It celebrated the instincts necessary for survival and reinforced the violence of the *Masculine Primitive* ideal.

Given the realities of life for African Americans under slavery or in freedom during the antebellum period, the irony of using the term *manhood* to apply to the assertion of dignity or the acquisition of freedom is striking. All black people were aware that such action respected no lines of gender. Yet both black men and women used the term. Maria Stewart, David Walker, and Henry Highland Garnet used appeals to manhood to incite blacks to action, but it was not clear whether black women were included. Did calls for slave resistance include women? Were they expected to be "manly"?

Black women's resistance to slavery paralleled black men's, running the gamut from trickery and feigning illness to escape and physical confrontation. Women's physical prowess was acknowledged and often admired within the slave community. Silvia Dubois was proud of the strength that enabled her to run a ferryboat better than any man on the Susquehanna River. As a child she endured her mistress' brutality, but when grown to five feet ten inches tall and weighing more than two hundred pounds, Silvia finally exacted her retribution by severely beating her mistress. After intimidating white spectators who might have subdued her, she picked up her child and made her escape from slavery.

Woman's rights advocate and abolitionist Sojourner Truth often spoke with pride of her ability while a slave to do the work of any man. She did not find her strength or her six-foot frame incompatible with being a woman. Nor did Frederick Douglass question the appropriateness of one slave woman's refusal to be beaten and her physical ability to stand her ground against any disbelieving master. When Douglass was resisting Covey, a slave woman named Caroline was ordered to help restrain him. Had she done so, Douglass believed her intervention would have been decisive, because "she was a powerful woman and could have mastered me easily . . ." Thus only because a woman defied her master was Douglass able to assert his manhood.

For black women no less than black men, freedom and dignity were tied to assertiveness, even to the point of violence. Slavery blurred distinctions between the gender expectations in black society and reinforced the broader economic and political roles provided to black women by their African heritage. Slavery attempted to dehumanize the slave without regard to gender. Both men and women resisted in concert with others and through the force of their individual personalities; dignity and respect could be achieved by remarkable individuals of both sexes. In freedom, black women protected themselves and their families from slave catchers and kidnappers. They were also aggressive wage earners, providing substantial portions of their household income. Scholars have described the independence and economic autonomy of women in precolonial West and Central Africa. As women's spheres and traits became increasingly differentiated from men's in nineteenth-century America, the experience and traditions of black women led them to depart from American gender expectations.

There was no ideal in American society encompassing the experience or honoring the heritage of black women. Perhaps the closest was the notion identified by Ronald W.

Hogeland as *Radical Womanhood,* which allowed women a public role. But even this most extreme norm was not sufficient. It accepted the separation of feminine and masculine capabilities, granting moral superiority to women but reserving intellectual and physical power to men.

Accepting masculine traits as the opposite of feminine traits was one of many ways black men sought to establish and define themselves as men in the face of assaults by slavery and racial discrimination. Gender comparisons in Western society were carefully controlled to favor men, limiting women's sphere. Here black people participated in the ongoing effort in nineteenth-century America to construct gender roles in what Hogeland argued was a male-initiated attempt "not conceived of essentially to improve the lot of women, but [implemented] for the betterment of men." The argument set forth by black minister J. W. C. Pennington in opposition to the ordination of women into the African Methodist Episcopal Church illustrates this point. Pennington contended that women were unsuited for "all the learned professions, where mighty thought and laborious investigation are needed," because as "the weaker sex" they were "incapacitated for [them] both physically and mentally."

The force of prevailing gender conventions outside the black community led some to promote gender expectations totally inappropriate for black women's lives. In the face of solid evidence to the contrary, several blacks, such as abolitionist Charles B. Ray, argued that the proper place for women was in the home, as "daughters are destined to be wives and mothers—they should, therefore, be taught to . . . manage a house, and govern and instruct children." Even Douglass, who spoke at the Seneca Falls Convention in 1848 in favor of women's right to vote, asserted in that same year that "a knowledge of domestic affairs, in all their relations is desirable—nay, essential, to the complete education of every female . . . A well regulated household, in every station of society, is one of woman's brightest ornaments—a source of happiness to her and to those who are dependent upon her labors of love for the attractions of home and its endearments." Although this may have been an appropriate ideal for many white middle- and upper-class women of the time, it was unrealistic for white working women, and even more unrealistic for black women. Most black women did become wives and mothers, but for many their knowledge of domestic affairs was necessarily applied in someone else's home in exchange for wages to help support their families.

Of all the techniques for bolstering black manhood, this was the most internally destructive. It demanded that women affirm their own inferiority in order to uphold the superiority of their men. Not that every African American accepted these gender images, many did not, but they nevertheless became touchstones for gender conventions within black society. Moreover, women faced sanctions for disregarding them, for to do so was viewed as furthering the aims and continuing the effects of slavery, depriving black men of their manhood.

There were women who recognized the dangerous consequences of counterpoising male and female traits, but only the boldest voices were raised in opposition. One of those voices was Sojourner Truth's. In the aftermath of the Civil War, when Congress debated the Fifteenth Amendment and related legislation providing the franchise to black men but not to women, she warned of the dangers inherent in such a move: "I feel that I have a right to have just as much as a man. . . . if colored men get their rights and not colored women theirs, the colored men will be masters over the women, and it will be just as bad as before."

ARTICLE

Manhood Is Everything: The Masculinization and Democratization of Success

Judy Hilkey

During the period after the Civil War known as the Gilded Age, the American book market was flooded with large, leather bound volumes that offered advice to men who wanted to be regarded as successful. Written by ministers, educators, and literary figures and addressed to ambitious young men of modest means, these success manuals were marketed in small towns and rural areas all across America. In this excerpt from Character Is Capital: Success Manuals and Manhood in Gilded Age America, *Judy Hilkey explores the ways in which the content and rhetoric of those books linked the idea of manhood with the pursuit of success.*

How did the authors of these books define manhood? What was their definition of success? What did they say was the connection between manliness and success? In what ways, if any, did their definition of success differ from men like Russell Conwell?

In a "dog-eat-dog" world, character needed buttressing by a motive force—some power akin to the engine of the industrial age. Furthermore, character alone was not powerful enough to unite the poor-but-honest with the great capitalists in a common definition of success. Success writers found the unifying concept in the notion of success. Success writers found the unifying concept in the notion of "manhood," reinforced by what they described as the most manly of all traits, "will-power." These advisors masculinized "success" by defining manhood and manliness as the ultimate necessity for individual achievement. Success, they agreed, was the reward not simply of those of character but of those who combined character with manliness. They democratized success when they insisted that true manhood, like character, was a goal within the reach of the poor as well as the rich, the humble as well as the great.

A focus on manliness and manhood was not unique to success manuals. Historians of nineteenth-century America have noted the manhood theme in many aspects of the popular culture of the period—including medical advice literature, fraternal initiation rituals, and the popularity of bare-knuckle prizefighting—and in the writing and oratory published in American books and magazines, from the tales of Davy Crockett to the essays of Ralph Waldo Emerson, from the beginning of the western genre with Owen Wister's *The Virginian* to Theodore Roosevelt's call for a "muscular Christianity." The preoccupation with manhood in the second half of the nineteenth century in part reflected the fact that ideas about what it meant to be a man were in flux. Changes in the relations of work, home, and family brought about by industrialization and urbanization narrowed and redefined men's roles as well as women's. Traditional male identities as providers, protectors, and patriarchs were either diminished or transformed. The dominant male ideal that emerged in the Gilded Age was increasingly one-dimensional and focused on entrepreneurship and money-making. The much celebrated "Napoleons of the Mart" and "captains of industry" were fast becoming new American heroes.

But there was a problem with the entrepreneurial model of manhood; for most it was as unattainable as it was compelling. Tough economic times, the trend toward business concentration and large-scale enterprise, and the monopolistic practices of those who got there first all conspired against independent proprietorship. Even the American farmer— proud symbol of economic independence who thought of himself as a small-scale entrepreneur—was chastened by the impact of falling farm prices, high interest rates, and farm foreclosures. It was wage and salaried employment, not entrepreneurship, that would account for the way more and more Americans would make their livings. Furthermore, the conditions of the new industrial workplace generated a competing model of manhood among workers. Labor's notion of manhood was based on solidarity rather than individuality, and it posed a direct challenge to the entrepreneurial ideal of manliness and to the entrepreneur himself. This ideal of manhood was characterized by a fraternal recognition of group or class interest, especially as expressed at the workplace by a mutualistic "one for all and all for one" ethic and by a code of behavior that called for a "manly bearing" toward the boss. It was this idea of manhood that Eugene Debs had in mind when he described the American Railway Union's successful strike of the Great Northern Railroad in 1894. He attributed the victory to the unity of the workers who, as he put it, "stood up as one man and asserted their manhood."

Success writers eschewed this militant model of manhood and celebrated the lives and the achievements of the great American captains of industry. Yet ultimately they defined both manhood and success in ways that had no necessary association with wealth, fame, or power. Success writers offered a notion of manliness that built upon the contemporary crisis about male identity, but went beyond it. Within the pages of the success manual "manhood" took on special meaning; "manhood" became an indispensable aspect of the American ideology of success. The ways in which success writers defined and equated manhood and success had far-reaching implications for how men might see themselves, how they might view their chances for success, and how they might regard the new industrial order that was the backdrop against which they would play out their own struggles with success and failure. Finally, the linkage of manhood and success had implications for how womanhood and the feminine would be defined. Indeed, the equation of manhood and success was built in part on the equation of the feminine with failure.

Wanted—A Man

The words "manhood," "manliness," and "manly" recurred with frequency in success manuals. Authors rhapsodized about "manly qualities," "manly vigor," "manly character," "manly self-assertion," and that "layer of metal that makes manhood." Success writers sometimes capitalized or italicized the letters of the word "man" or "manhood" for even further emphasis. The importance of manhood was evident even in the titles of certain success manuals, such as William Owen's *Success in Life, and How to Secure It: or Elements of Manhood and Their Culture* and Reverend Alexander Lewis's *Manhood-Making: Studies in the Elemental Principles of Success.*

In the world of the success manual, manhood meant far more than male adulthood. True manhood, like true success, was "self-made." Manhood, like character, was forged in the battle of life. In order to succeed in life, success writers urged readers to develop the "grandest possible manhood," the "stamina of manhood," or a "magnificent manhood." According to these manuals, "manhood" was a quality everywhere in demand in a fast-moving, ever-changing, new age. Marden's *Rising in the World* began with the following announcement: "The world has a standing advertisement over the door of every profession; every occupation; every calling: 'Wanted—A Man.'" In *Masters of the Situation,* William James Tilley wrote that the "real object of all training and all education should be to develop the best type of manhood." Marden recounted the story of President James Garfield who, when asked in his youth what he planned to be, reportedly said: "First of all, I must make myself a man; if I do not succeed in that, I can succeed in nothing." Owen wrote: "It is the man who makes the business, and if any undertaking has no *man* behind it, of how frail a texture it is! Broidered [sic] gold and lace cannot compensate for such a lack." And Tilley concluded: "The world is looking for men, and the success of all business enterprise depends on the character of those who manage them."

What exactly did it take to be a man? Sterling character and personal virtue were always central in the success manuals' definition of manhood, just as they were in the advice to young men of the antebellum period. In some cases, success writers presented the terms "manhood" and "character" as practically interchangeable. When Marden advised readers about selecting a vocation, he suggested a "clean, useful, honorable occupation," remarking, "You may not make quite so much money, but you will be more of a man, and manhood is above all riches, overtops all titles, and character is greater than any career." Bates embellished this thesis in a chapter entitled, "Business Traits, Qualities and Habits":

The highest object of life we take to be to form a manly character, and to work out the best development possible, of body and spirit—of mind, conscience, heart and soul. Accordingly, that is not the most successful life in which man gets the most pleasure, the most money, the most power of place, honor or fame; but that in which a man gets the most manhood, and performs the greatest amount of useful work and human duty. Money is power after a sort, it is true, but intelligence, public spirit and moral virtue are powers, too, and far nobler ones.

Dale exhorted readers to have the "manliness to plead for the right," insisting that the "most manly men" were the most "godly," while Edward Hale announced in *What Career?*: "The central truth is proclaimed, that manliness is a moral quality,—that it belongs to spirit and the empire of spirit."

But success writers agreed that in the rush and roar of the late nineteenth century, character alone did not make the man. The battle of life required that virtue be reinforced with some special power, some source of strength and energy suited to rugged times. In the individualistic world of the success manual, this power could come only from within. Thus the final element in the formula for success and the crowning glory of manhood was the power of individual will. Success writers described *will* as that "mysterious form of mental energy which makes the difference between the great and the insignificant." Aggressiveness, determination, perseverance, decisiveness, self-assertion, and self-motivation were the hallmarks of the strong-willed man. Success writers presented "will" as a driving power within the man himself—a corollary to the machine power of the industrial age. According to Mathews, "will" was the "driving wheel" and the "spring of motive Power." In a chapter entitled "The Will and the Way," Marden confided: "Were I called upon to express in a word the secret of so many failures among those who started out in life with high hopes, I should say unhesitatingly, they lacked will-power. They could not half will. What is a man without a will? He is like an engine without steam, a mere sport of chance, to be tossed about hither and thither, always at the mercy of those who have wills." Smiles claimed that "energy of will" was the "central power of character in a man,—in a word, it

[was] the *Man* himself. It [gave] impulse to every action, and soul to every effort." In short, he wrote, "it is *will*,—force of purpose,—that enables a man to do or be whatever he sets his mind on being or doing." These advisors attributed an incalculable power to "will." In Tilley's words, "Nothing [is] impossible to a man who can will. This is the only law of success." And Harry Lewis insisted, "Whether a man is conditioned high or low; in the city or on the farm: 'If he will; he will.'" One writer admitted that willpower could not perform miracles, yet he assured readers that all history proved that it was "almost omnipotent." And another concurred, claiming that "there are few circumstances over which a strong will has no control." One writer suggested "banishing from the dictionary" the word "impossible," and another said of the man who sought success, "He must become a pugilist, knocking the 'I' out of 'If's.'" Success manuals immortalized a number of still-familiar maxims, such as "Where there's a will there's a way," "Wishes fail, but wills prevail," "Strong men have wills; weak ones wishes," and "They can—who *think* they can." The last is reminiscent of the children's story about the little locomotive who made it up a steep hill by saying "I think I can, I think I can," a story that may have originated in the American popular culture of this period.

But much of the rhetoric about willpower had a more aggressive tone, evoking a do-or-die struggle of man against man. A "vacillating man," observed Mathews, "no matter what his abilities, is invariably pushed aside in the race of life by the man of determined will." The conditions of modern life called for a new forcefulness. Marden wrote that "in this electronic age, where everything is pusher or pushed, he who would succeed must hold his ground and push hard." In a chapter entitled "The Man of Push," George R. Hewitt proclaimed: "Push paves the way. . . . Today the thoroughfares of life are crowded; if a man would win a place in the ranks of professional or mercantile life, he must push for it. Push brings men of mediocrity to the front, and enables them to stay there. . . . Push is the passport to success." True men, then, were a special breed of the male species, much in demand in a challenging new age. Successful men combined virtue and force, character and willpower.

Where There's a Will There's a Way

Success writers presented the power of will as not only the most aggressive element in the formula for success but as the most specifically masculine. It was especially in describing the power of will that success was not only masculinized but sexualized. In language rich in sexual innuendo, success writers linked symbolically the drive to achieve in the economic sphere with male libido and conquest in combat. In its milder forms, the qualities needed to succeed in business were likened to those needed to succeed in romantic or marital relations: "Know your business in all its details. Marry it. Take it with you wherever you go . . . devotion will tell on the profit side of the ledger." Mathews advised, "No man ever need fear refusal from any lady, if he only gives his heart to getting her; and the same is true of success." According to Marden, "A bank never becomes very successful . . . until it gets a president who takes it to bed with him." But more extraordinary was the symbolic language in accounts of successful combat in the battle of life. Success writers portrayed what might be called a "phallocentric" world of battle, which celebrated self-made men for their virility, their "potent spirits" and "erect and constant character." William Owen recounted Henry Clay's confrontation with coworkers in his early career as a Richmond store clerk in just such language: Young Clay, mocked by the "city boys," finally counterattacked with repartee "like a scorpion's sting."

> That night he slept better than he had for weeks, and from that day forward he carried his sword unsheathed. He soon came to be recognized as the leader of the company. . . . While he was too

generous to make war upon those who persecuted him in the days of his weakness, he was too much of a general to pause at the parrying of a thrust. He never stopped until he had disarmed his enemy.

In explaining the virtue of decisiveness, Owen wrote that "men must be soldier like, and rest on their arms ready to spring up and fire on the instant. . . . It is a curious condition of mind that this requires. It is like sleeping with your pistol under your pillow, and the pistol on full cock; a moment lost, and all may be lost." By combining phallic symbolism and military metaphor—these quotes likened both sexual prowess and combat readiness to the qualities needed to achieve success in the world of business and industry. Taken literally, they describe an intensely competitive and individualistic world fraught with danger, a world in which a "moment lost, and all may be lost," a dilemma in which one either conquers the competitor or risks being conquered by him.

The battle of life called not only for overt force but for a kind of secret readiness— "reserve" and "self-possession" that again had subtle and not-so-subtle sexual overtones. "Self-control is only courage under another form," advised William Makepeace Thayer in *Onward to Fame and Fortune,* while Tilley mixed images of military might and industrial power in his description of the power of "reserve":

Reticence and reserve seems to have an influence like that of the sides of a cannon, giving an added impetus to one's purpose and sending one straight to the mark. The great motive power which drives the engine is unseen, and held fast within the strong ribs of the boiler—when once seen, the steam has wasted its force and is useless. That brilliant electric flash but shows that a mysterious power has disappeared.

Jerome Bates counseled:

[K]eep cool, have your resources well in hand, and reserve your strength until the proper time arrives to exert it. There is hardly any trait of character or faculty of intellect more valuable

than the power of self-possession, or presence of mind. The man who is always "going off" unexpectedly, like an old rusty firearm, who is easily fluttered and discomposed at the appearance of some unforeseen emergency; who has no control over himself or his powers, is just the one who is always in trouble and never successful or happy.

"Going off unexpectedly" could be understood not only as an analogy for failure in coping with the "unforeseen emergencies" in the outside world of business but also as a veiled reference to premature ejaculation. Furthermore, the phallic reference to an "old rusty firearm," an eminently untrustworthy device, suggests that a man's sexuality was potentially dangerous. In order to achieve success, writers advised readers to control themselves and their sexuality—the valuable yet dangerous faculty.

The belief that reining in sexuality was a necessary precondition for achieving success in business was not unique to the success manuals. Medical and sexual advice literature articulated what Ben Barker-Benfield called a "spermatic economy." This doctrine held that sperm was the vital force of energy in the well-balanced economy of the male body. The imprudent loss of sperm could mean the loss of will and order, incapacitating a man for both marriage and business. The same consideration is reflected in the fact that in the nineteenth century, when success depended on capital accumulation (saving not spending), the vernacular for male orgasm was "spend." Success writers couched much of their advice about how to succeed in terms of the accumulation, reserve, and expenditure of "fluid" resources. Mathews warned readers to "guard jealously against the little leaks in expenditures," explaining that "men fail of success from early exhaustion, from a lack of accumulated force, whether physical, mental or spiritual, which only can qualify them to meet any unexpected draught upon their power." In a chapter entitled "Expenditures of Resources," Bates claimed that "if a man 'uses himself up' at every effort he makes in trying to build his imperial highway to fortune, that way will never be finished, nor the fortune secured." The most successful men in life's race, he went on, were those who kept themselves "well in hand" and kept "in reserve some extra power or ability, with which to meet emergencies and eclipse competing rivals." The power of reserve depended on the ability to accumulate resources.

> When old Dr. Bellamy was asked by a young clergyman for advice about the composition of his sermons, he replied: "Fill up the cask! Fill up the cask!, and then if you tap it anywhere you will get a good stream. But if you put in but a little, it will dribble, dribble, dribble, and you must tap, tap, tap, and then you get but a small stream, after all."

The only solution to this dilemma in which man was expected to "sleep with his pistol under his pillow on full cock," "keep his resources well in hand," and avoid "going off unexpectedly like a rusty firearm," was to deploy that most masculine of all virtues, the power of will. In a chapter entitled "Will-Power," Owen lamented, "some of the most potent spirits that ever peered through flesh have been rendered effete and useless for lack of this one element." In another chapter entitled "Decision," he observed: "Unless man can erect himself above himself, how poor a thing is man." Bates advised readers to "be firm" and cautioned that "without will, a man would be like the soft, flabby, nerveless mollusk or shell-fish in the ocean." He elaborated:

> The will, considered without regard to direction, is simple constancy, firmness; and therefore, it will be obvious that everything depends upon right direction and motive. Directed toward the enjoyment of the senses, the strong will may be a demon, and the intellect merely its debased slave, but directed toward good, the strong will is king and the intellect is then minister of man's well being.

Here, *will* symbolized the possibilities and dangers of masculine force and the male sexual drive—"constancy, firmness," a "demon"

when "directed toward the enjoyment of the senses" and "king" when directed toward good. *Willpower* symbolized a man's ability to contain and direct an inner masculine force in productive ways; it represented the proper combination of potency and self-control. The doctrine of sexual reserve power, a corollary to economic reserve power, transformed a constraining ideology of male sexual repression into an ideology of male potency and opportunity. Only the virile could succeed, and then only by holding their inner powers in reserve for use at just the right moment of conquest.

Success, then, demanded a special kind of man—he who possessed great sexual powers as well as the willpower to reserve these vital energies for expenditure in the battle of life. Success in the outside world was possible only for those who first won the battle within and conquered themselves and their unacceptable impulses and emotions. "Surely the world knows not always, indeed seldom imagines the struggles within, or the heroic discipline which at length confers upon man that greatest of all triumphs, the mastery of himself." In the success manual, manhood was not only a symbol of man's mastery in the world, but just as important, manhood stood for self-mastery, mastery of the world within.

On one level, the sexual metaphor of the success manual may have at least subliminally expressed and addressed concerns and interests that were in fact quite literally about sex and sexuality. Victorian middle-class sexual culture confronted men with an especially difficult challenge. At the same time that sex and sexuality were deemed more important and opportunities for illicit sex were more plentiful, admonitions against almost all forms of sexual expression, from masturbation to overexpenditure in sexual intercourse within marriage, became more intense. In such an environment, advice literature addressed to young men that was couched in sexual innuendo and masculine self-aggrandizement must have had special poignancy. It would be a mistake to overlook the possibility that part of the success manual's appeal was the covert eroticism of advice laced with sexual references—heteroeroticism, homoeroticism, and especially autoeroticism. Note, for example, the pervasiveness of sexually oriented self-referential language insisting that men keep their reserve power "well in hand," etc. Paradoxically, success manuals' endless preaching about the importance of self-control and self-restraint may have provided a safe, unacknowledged forum for the celebration of male libido. Far from denying male sexuality, success writers covertly, perhaps unwittingly, acknowledged it and built it into their prescription for success. Here and elsewhere, success writers' ability to address, even subliminally, real concerns of their audience helps explain the appeal of success manuals and helps account for their popularity.

Though the sexualized language in success manuals may have gotten some men's attention by subtly teasing prurient interests, the overt message was, of course, just the opposite. The sexualizing of success in a doctrine of self-control was a way to encourage sexual sublimation—redirecting potentially disruptive sexual energy into economically productive activity. More importantly, by emphasizing body and mind, potency and control, these sexualized prescriptions for success focused readers' attention on the self. The power of "will"—with or without its sexual implications—was unequivocally about the individual man and his capacity for self-control. The sexualized language added a new level of intensity to an already intensely individualistic ideology of success, and in a striking way, it made the call for self-discipline both personal and immediate. Titillating words that called on a man to "erect himself above himself" both dramatized and aggrandized what might otherwise be seen as a somewhat uninspiring duty—the obligation to exercise self-restraint, to work hard, to be sober, prudent, frugal, and industrious. Put another way, the admonition to establish exacting control over body and mind in order to succeed in life was a way to press home the requirement that the individual internalize the rules and the discipline of the new economic order. The sexualization of success, the celebration of willpower, and the presentation of self-mastery as the precondition for mastery in the world can be understood as one of the latter-day strategies in the ongoing nineteenth-century endeavor to "educate the character" and "instruct the conscience" of the nation's young men, to discipline themselves and internalize authority in a society in which the authority formerly vested in church and community had all but disappeared. In the absence of outside authority, success manuals as well as other types of advice literature called on individual conscience to play the role of task master. In the world of the success manual, willpower in the form of self-discipline was the most manly of traits, and the most essential in the battle for success. If a man was going to succeed in the new industrial order, he must voluntarily accept and live by its rules.

A Magnificent Manhood—Greater Than Wealth, Grander Than Fame

Manhood had yet another meaning in the world the success manual created—a significance that went beyond the search for masculine identity, beyond the call for self-control, and beyond the notion that manly qualities were the necessary means to achieving success in life. By insisting that "character was capital" and concluding that "manhood was everything," success writers raised the personal achievement of a truly manly character above the pecuniary gain and individual advancement that otherwise seemed to be the goal of most of their advice. According to this logic, manhood and the character and willpower upon which it was built were not only the means but also the end in the search for success; the achievement of a magnificent manhood was itself success. Success writers never claimed that all men could become millionaires. In *The Way to Win*, Dale explained that "when there is one millionaire, there must of necessity be thousands of men of moderate circumstances." Success manuals offered consolation in the form of a higher type of success to those whose lives might not replicate the rags-to-riches saga. Crafts proclaimed that it was "better to be a man than merely a millionaire." Marden reassured readers that manhood was "greater than wealth, grander than fame." If manhood was higher than wealth, power, and position, what did it matter if all could not succeed by reaching the pinnacle of their profession? William Mathews claimed that some "have been successful as men, though they may have failed as lawyers, doctors, and merchants." Owen concluded a discussion of occupations by remarking, "Let them labor with the hand or the head but busy themselves in the cultivation of manhood." Marden quoted Rousseau in a chapter entitled "What Career": "Let him first be a man. Fortune may remove him from one rank to another as she pleases; he will be always found in his place." Similarly, though Bates wrote under the rubric of "The Highway to Fortune and Success in Business Life," he too claimed that there was something higher than business success: the formation of a "manly character," in his words, was the "highest object of life." And Haines and Yaggy urged the young man discouraged by failure not to despair, observing: "If he can make nothing by any work that presents itself now, he can at least make himself."

Given that every man could not expect to achieve fame, power, or fortune and given success writers' determination to offer the promise of *success* to all men of character and willpower, Haines was suggesting the only logical conclusion: he consoled the discouraged with the prospects of "making themselves" by cultivating their manhood. Accordingly, the definition of the self-made man might be broadened. It could include not only those who, like the great industrialists, were alleged to have built their fortunes entirely by their own efforts but also those who had built a "magnificent manhood" entirely by their own efforts. For many, this may have been the only true meaning of the success manual maxim, "self-made if ever made."

"Manhood," then, could be seen as a nonmaterialistic alternative to a notion of success that focused narrowly on "getting ahead," and a rather exalted alternative at that. To anyone anxious about his prospects in the new industrial order, this "higher" idea of success had three definite advantages.

First, manhood, unlike wealth, represented a kind of success that was unlimited. If success meant wealth, fame, and position, only a few could succeed. This was the problem with the strictly entrepreneurial model of manhood. But if success meant the achievement of a noble manhood, potentially all who were willing to cultivate the character and willpower that made up manliness—all *men* that is—could become successful. Defining "success" in terms of "manhood" democratized success; just as in politics, any man could participate in the process if only he would.

Secondly, by this definition, each man was the sole judge of his own success. Wealth was quantifiable, manliness was not. Fame, fortune, and power often constituted the public measure of a man; manhood was a private matter—measurable only by the man himself. Manhood was a matter of self-esteem. If success was the achievement of a magnificent manhood, the embodiment of sterling character, even the man of modest means might define himself as a success. Thus a man determined his own status in the world—not only by his actions—but by self-definition or identity.

Thirdly, designating "manhood" as the definition of true success provided a common ground on which the haves and have-nots might unite. If the meaning of success was not wealth or position but personal virtue—as conveyed by the idea that "character is capital" and "manhood is everything"—then economic differences among men and places could be minimized. In this view, the worthy—be they rich or poor, capitalists or laborers, great or small—might be joined together in a shared set of ideas about what it meant to be a man and about what it meant to be a success. The manly man was distinct not only from the feminine but from the lazy and profligate complainers who would not struggle, from the demagogues and critics of American society who wanted only to "fire cities and deprecate capital," and from the pretentious, dissipated rich who live by inherited wealth. True men, by this logic, be they the virtuous poor or the self-made millionaires, shared a harmony of beliefs that transcended a disharmony of interests. The true man did not complain of lack of opportunity or capital. He believed that there was no failure for the man who invested character in every enterprise; he created opportunities out of difficulties; he was the one who knew that all men were "self-made if ever made." In the last analysis, true men sought not after wealth, power, and place; rather they were motivated by the desire to perform the "greatest amount of useful work and human duty." In the world of the success manual, as in the world of the Puritan forefathers, fame and fortune were welcome but nonessential signs of a higher state of grace. In the modern instance, that state of grace took the form of the achievement of a magnificent manhood.

In a literature devoted to "getting on in life," this may seem like an odd conclusion and a strange definition of success. But from the perspective of the authors—and perhaps the readers—there was beauty in a book that at first glance seemed focused on advice about how to get rich but which ultimately insisted that true success was not necessarily wealth, but something higher, a type of manhood that could be won by those who may have failed utterly in business. The beauty was that these books offered a magnificent loophole in the otherwise unworkable theory that all could achieve success and live what later would be called "the American dream." The promise of this nonpecuniary version of success, after all, was much easier to deliver than the rags-to-riches scenario.

This broadly inclusive definition of success may have been very practical for success writers who were looking to achieve success of their own—presumably of the pecuniary sort—through the sale of success manuals. In this regard, it might be useful to note that success manuals had something in common with another product that was marketed in the same period by these same methods—namely patent medicine. Both were peddled door-to-door by traveling agents, in small towns and rural areas across the nation. The families that these salesmen canvassed were not likely to have had the spare cash to spend on either many books or many different medicines. The best patent medicine, therefore, promised to cure everything from syphilis to rheumatism and, likewise, the best success manual promised success to all customers—all male customers, that is—who were willing to follow the prescription carefully. In an anxious age, success manuals offered to the spirit what patent medicine offered to the body—an antidote for a multitude of ills.

Finally, by defining success and manliness in terms of personal virtues—especially duty to one's calling, willpower, self-control, and self-discipline—success writers did more than reassure worried readers and obscure class fissures. They laid the ideological foundation for a new model of manhood that paradoxically lacked both the fierce individualism of the entrepreneurial model of manhood and the militance and solidarity of labor's notion of manhood. This new economic man would work hard and contribute to the new industrial order while not demanding too much from it. He would identify his interests with the dominant social and economic order and voluntarily conduct himself in ways that were consistent with its triumph in the hopes of sharing some of its bounty. He could identify with the successes of the entrepreneur kings without having his manhood depend on achieving the same for himself. Here were the antecedents of the twentieth-century corporate "organization man." The heirs of this generation and of this way of seeing the world would become members of what C. Wright Mills called the "new middle class" of economically dependent, politically passive, white-collar workers.

If, under the harsh light of the twentieth century, this model of manhood appears as a self-effacing capitulation to the powers that be, it must be remembered that success writers presented it to late-nineteenth-century readers as something very different. Success manuals flourished in a period of great economic and social upheaval and crisis. In trying times, success writers offered readers a view of the world—a way of thinking about and understanding the new social order and their place in it—that was more palatable and more hopeful than the apocalyptic predictions of Gilded Age radicals, dissenters, and critics. By making an exalted but achievable form of manhood the measure of success in a frightening yet promising new era, success writers offered those who feared they were being left behind a way to overcome their anxieties and uncertainty and to identify with the optimism and achievement of those at the pinnacle of the new industrial order. In offering men a way to rationalize their new and sometimes unwelcome circumstances, success writers helped to legitimize the new industrial order. And for those who could not muster that kind of enthusiasm about what the new order might bring, at the very least the ideology of manhood and success provided a graceful and respectable way to accommodate themselves to things they lacked the power to change. The success manual was an invitation to the ideological mainstream; the success ideology was the ultimate big tent—it welcomed all believers in the legitimacy of the new industrial order. In this light, the success manual provides evidence not of consensus about the efficacy of the new industrial order but rather a glimpse at the subtle ideological process whereby the *appearance* of consensus—or hegemony—was created.

Suggestions for Further Reading

Mark C. Carnes, *Secret Ritual and Manhood in Victorian America* (New Haven, CT: Yale University Press, 1989).

Mark C. Carnes and Clyde Griffin, eds., *Meanings for Manhood: Constructions of Masculinity in Victorian America* (Chicago: University of Chicago Press, 1990).

Mary Ann Clawson, *Constructing Brotherhood: Class, Gender, and Fraternalism* (Princeton: Princeton University Press, 1989).

Jim Cullen, " 'I's a Man Now': Gender and African American Men," in *Divided Houses: Gender and the Civil War,* ed. Catherine Clinton and Nina Silber (New York: Oxford University Press, 1992), 76–91.

Stephen M. Frank, *Life with Father: Parenthood and Masculinity in the Nineteenth-Century American North* (Baltimore, MD: The Johns Hopkins University Press, 1998).

Robert L. Griswold, "Divorce and the Legal Redefinition of Victorian Manhood," in *Meanings for Manhood: Constructions of Masculinity in Victorian America,* ed. Mark C. Carnes and Clyde Griffin (Chicago: University of Chicago Press, 1990), 96–110.

Robert L. Griswold, *Fatherhood in America: A History* (New York: Basic Books, 1993).

Kristin Hoganson, "Garrisonian Abolitionists and the Rhetoric of Gender, 1850–1860," *American Quarterly,* 45 (Dec. 1993), 558–95.

James Oliver Horton, *Free People of Color: Inside the African American Community* (Washington, DC: Smithsonian Institution Press, 1993).

James Oliver Horton, "Freedom's Yoke: Gender Conventions among Antebellum Free Blacks," *Feminist Studies,* 12 (Spring 1986), 51–76.

James Oliver Horton and Lois E. Horton, *Black Bostonians: Family Life and Community Struggle in the Antebellum North* (New York: Holmes and Meier, 1979).

Paul E. Johnson, *A Shopkeeper's Millennium: Society and Revivals in Rochester, New York, 1815–1837* (New York: Hill and Wang, 1978).

Michael Kimmel, *Manhood in America: A Cultural History* (New York: Free Press, 1996).

BRUCE LAURIE, " 'Nothing on Compulsion': Life Styles of Philadelphia Artisans, 1820–1850," *Labor History,* 15 (Summer 1974), 337–66.

DAVID LEVERENZ, *Manhood and the American Renaissance* (Ithaca, NY: Cornell University Press, 1989).

GERALD F. LINDERMAN, *Embattled Courage: The Experience of Combat in the American Civil War* (New York: The Free Press, 1987).

J. A. MANGAN AND JAMES WALVIN, eds., *Manliness and Morality: Middle-Class Masculinity in Britain and America* (New York: St. Martin's Press, 1987).

REID MITCHELL, "Soldiering, Manhood, and Coming of Age: A Northern Volunteer," in *Divided Houses: Gender and the Civil War,* ed. Catherine Clinton and Nina Silber (New York: Oxford University Press, 1992), 43–54.

DAVID G. PUGH, *Sons of Liberty: The Masculine Mind in Nineteenth-Century America* (Westport, CT: Greenwood Press, 1983).

STACEY M. ROBERTSON, " 'Aunt Nancy Men': Parker Pillsbury, Masculinity, and Women's Rights Activism in the Nineteenth-Century United States," *American Studies,* 37 (Fall 1996), 33–60.

E. ANTHONY ROTUNDO, *American Manhood: Transformations in Masculinity from the Revolution to the Modern Era* (New York: Basic Books, 1993).

E. ANTHONY ROTUNDO, "Body and Soul: Changing Ideals of American Middle-Class Manhood, 1770–1920," *Journal of Social History,* 16 (Summer 1983), 23–38.

E. ANTHONY ROTUNDO, "Patriarchs and Participants: A Historical Perspective on Fatherhood in the United States," in *Beyond Patriarchy: Essays by Men on Pleasure, Power, and Change,* ed. Michael Kaufman (New York: Oxford University Press, 1987), 64–80.

SYLVIA STRAUSS, *"Traitors to the Masculine Cause": The Men's Campaigns for Women's Rights* (Westport, CT: Greenwood Press, 1982).

TAMARA PLAKINS THORNTON, *Cultivating Gentlemen: The Meaning of Country Life among the Boston Elite, 1785–1860* (New Haven, CT: Yale University Press, 1989).

MAURICE WALLACE, " 'Are We Men?': Prince Hall, Martin Delaney, and the Masculine Ideal in Black Freemasonry, 1775–1865," *American Literary History,* 9 (Fall 1997), 396–424.

BERTRAM WYATT-BROWN, "The Abolitionist Controversy: Men of Blood, Men of God," in *Men, Women, and Issues in American History,* eds. Howard H. Quint and Milton Cantor, Vol. 1 (Homewood, IL: Dorsey Press, 1975), 215–33.

DONALD YACOVONE, "Abolitionists and the 'Language of Fraternal Love,' " in *Meanings for Manhood: Constructions of Masculinity in Victorian America,* ed. Mark C. Carnes and Clyde Griffin (Chicago: University of Chicago Press, 1990), 85–95.

DONALD YACOVONE, " 'Surpassing the Love of Women': Victorian Manhood and the Language of Fraternal Love," in *A Shared Experience: Men, Women, and the History of Gender,* ed. Laura McCall and Donald Yacovone (New York: New York University Press, 1998), 195–221.

CHAPTER FIVE

FEMININITY IN THE NINETEENTH-CENTURY NORTH (1820–1890)

AMERICAN WOMEN AND THE CULT OF DOMESTICITY

One of America's most beloved novels is Louisa May Alcott's *Little Women.* Published in 1868, Alcott's story revolves around the lives of the respectable but impoverished Marsh family. When the story begins, Mr. Marsh is absent. So it is a particularly female world that we are invited to enter. Alcott introduces us to five main characters whose personal attributes together create a composite of the possibilities that were available for expressing womanliness in the American middle class in the nineteenth century. Marmee is a competent and skilled housewife who is able to manage on the meager resources available to her, and who, in the absence of her husband, provides the family with moral and intellectual leadership. She is the epitome of a perfect mother—warm, loving, and self-sacrificing. Jo is high spirited and distressingly independent. Much to the dismay of her sis-

ters, she is careless about her appearance and often unladylike in her behavior. She is simply much too boisterous, intellectual, and creative for her own good. Meg is the most conventional of the sisters. She is attractive and interested in the finer things in life, but lacks imagination or ambition. Amy is pretty and well mannered, but she is also vain, competitive, flirtatious, and self-centered. Beth is too good to be true. She is patient, gentle, compassionate, and kind. She has musical talent, but she is so painfully shy that she shuns the limelight and refuses to play for anyone except her family and close friends. Physically delicate, she is the most dependent of the sisters and requires a great deal of care from the other members of her family.

The Marshes were not yet affected by the expansion of commerce, the development of industry, the massive immigration, and the growth of cities that characterized the period following the Civil War. Their world is the world of the small town and the home. There were, of course, conflicts in the Marsh household. And the Marsh sisters were as concerned with "self making" as any American man. In the process, however, they tried with varying degrees of success to conform to the demands of what historians have called the "cult of true womanhood."

Male and female authors along with ministers, teachers, and doctors all took part in the effort to establish a feminine ideal in the nineteenth century. The rise of literacy and advances in printing technology meant that they could disseminate their message through advice manuals, ladies' magazines, and novels such as *Little Women*. In their opinion, an ideal or "true" woman was supposed to be domestic and submissive, self-sacrificing, clingingly dependent, sexually pure, religiously pious, and benevolent. She was supposed to marry and then willingly submit herself to her husband's authority, defer to him in all matters, and concern herself with his physical, emotional, and spiritual well-being in return for his financial support. According to the model, it was a woman's responsibility to preserve and perpetuate her husband's family name by bearing his children and assuming primary responsibility for rearing them. She was supposed to keep the house neat and clean and conserve whatever material resources her husband made available to her. She was expected to serve her husband's business or professional interests and her children's marital prospects by acting as a gracious hostess, by spending a considerable amount of time paying and receiving social calls, and by purchasing, arranging, and displaying material symbols of her spouse's economic success in the public spaces of their home such as the foyer, the parlor, and the dining room. The ideal woman was supposed to be active, but her activity was generally directed toward being of service to others.

In the nineteenth century, it was considered a woman's duty to preserve her family's claim to respectability and gentility. To do that she was expected to remain primarily in the domestic sphere. In theory at least, her public life was confined to attending church and performing acts of Christian charity. It was said that a lady's name should appear only three times in public—when she was born, when she married, and when she died. A lady did not intrude upon the male world of politics and business, and she certainly did not work for wages outside her home.

There was some continuity between the cult of true womanhood and the ideology of republican motherhood that was discussed in Chapter 3. Both stressed the importance of piety and purity among women. Both defined women in terms of their domestic and maternal roles. Both required that women fulfill their civic responsibilities by providing assistance to those less fortunate than themselves. But perhaps the biggest difference between the two was that the ideal of the republican mother was not really class based. Poor women and rich women alike could potentially fulfill its prescriptions and dedicate themselves to bearing and rearing children who would help to preserve the republic. But the cult of true womanhood was a distinctly middle-class ideology. So it was very difficult for any woman who was not a member of that social class to construct her identity in conformity with its prescriptions.

THE FEMININE IDENTITIES OF MIDDLE-CLASS HOUSEWIVES

One of the most significant changes in ideas about what constituted femininity during this period was the change in popular attitudes toward woman's bodies and health. During the colonial and revolutionary periods, strength, stamina, and robust good health were highly regarded in women. But in the nineteenth century, middle-class women were increasingly viewed as being physically delicate by nature. Indeed, Catharine Beecher, a prominent nineteenth-century educator, reported that few of her friends or acquaintances considered themselves to be completely healthy. They suffered from a wide variety of ailments ranging from headaches, backaches, nervousness, and anemia to serious cases of indigestion.

Given their lifetstyles, this is not too surprising. Besides dressing themselves in corsets and clothes that constricted their bodies and made it difficult for them to breathe and to move about freely, many women spent their time in houses with poor ventilation. They lived in towns and cities with inadequate sanitation facilities, and they were profoundly ignorant of their bodies. Despite the fact that they had the money to pay for it, they did not usually receive what we would consider to be adequate medical care. A sense of feminine modesty often prevented them from seeking the help of male doctors, and when they did, they were hesitant to allow their physicians to examine them. To make matters worse, doctors proved to be appallingly ignorant about the female body. The result was that femininity was increasingly equated with physical debility. By the 1850s it had become positively fashionable to suffer from various and sundry physical ailments. A pale skin and languid demeanor were thought to testify to a woman's femininity since they made her even more dependent on a strong man and in need of his care and protection.

In truth, of course, a middle-class housewife had to be physically strong in order effectively to carry out her domestic responsibilities competently. The "true woman" in fact performed a great deal of physical labor. Doing laundry, for example, meant carrying heavy pails of water, bending over a wash tub, lifting heavy, wet garments and household linens, hanging them up to dry, and standing for endless hours before the stove or fireplace doing the ironing. Even in affluent households with servants, a mistress had to be able to show her servants how she wanted them to perform their domestic duties. A housewife worked in the privacy of her home rather than in a factory or a shop, and she was not paid a wage. Her work was considered feminine as long as it had no publicly acknowledged economic worth, as long as it was invisible to those outside the household, and as long as the skill, strength, and stamina required to do it could be ignored.

The cult of true womanhood idealized women who were intelligent but did not necessarily encourage them to develop their intellects. It held that a woman should be literate and familiar enough with arithmetic to manage her household accounts competently and to supervise the education of her children. But in most social circles, a learned woman was considered somewhat masculine and could be an embarrassment to her family. Most men did not welcome the opportunity to engage in serious intellectual conversations with women. And most women were unlikely to choose as their friends those who were more interested in discussing Plato and Aristotle than in sharing recipes and child care concerns. It was quite acceptable for a woman to dabble in drawing and painting during her leisure time, to sing prettily, or to play piano for her family and friends. It was not acceptable for her to take her talents too seriously or to seek acclaim by exhibiting her accomplishments in public.

The gendered identity of middle-class women also revolved around the assumption that they were morally superior to most men. As we saw in Chapters 2 and 3, women had not always been regarded as particularly virtuous. But shortly after the American Revolution, strong moral fiber became a hallmark of the "true woman." During the revivals of the Second Great Awakening, vast numbers of women experienced conversion. In some churches, they outnumbered men three to one. In the words of one historian, "piety had become female property," and women assumed the moral leadership of their communities even if they could not preach or hold office in their churches.

A part of a true woman's reputation for being virtuous also lay in the assumption that before she married she would guard herself against temptations of the flesh in order to protect her virginity. As we shall see in Chapter 12, there was considerable anxiety about the way women expressed their sexuality during this period. But it was generally accepted in the middle class that after a woman married, she would follow her husband's lead in sexual matters, make herself available to him whenever he demanded it, and bear as many children as God deemed appropriate.

A part of the duty of the morally upright was to concern themselves with the well being of the poor. This traditional Christian duty was made more imperative by the evangelical revivalists of the Second Great Awakening, who preached that the converted Christian was obliged to pursue benevolent activities and try to reform society in order to prepare for the second coming of Christ. Acts of Christian benevolence like organizing Sunday Schools were considered particularly feminine because they were obvious extensions of women's domestic, care taking role. These sorts of activities posed little or no threat to the social, economic, and political status quo.

A great many women in the United States did their best to conform to the prescriptions set down in the cult of true womanhood. They perpetuated the myth of female delicacy by carrying parasols and wearing bonnets in order to protect their skin from the sun. They remained virgins until they married. Constructing their lives around the demands of domesticity, they deferred to their husbands' authority. They bore children and did their best to rear them to be responsible citizens and good Christians. They read their Bibles, led their families in prayer, attended church regularly, and spent time tending to the needs of the poor. While they may have been interested in political matters, they did not express a desire to vote or hold public office. And it was unnecessary for them to leave their homes to support their families. Their letters and diaries are full of the mundane things in life—housekeeping, childbearing and child care, visiting friends and relatives, gardening, cooking, and sewing. In return for their conformity to the cult of true womanhood, they felt justified in expecting their husbands to love and support them and their communities to honor them.

At the same time, however, there were some women who felt unfulfilled and dissatisfied by the lives they were expected to lead as middle-class housewives and mothers. They struggled to subvert the prescriptions of the true womanhood ideology and to expand the possibilities for expressing their femininity.

IDEALS OF MIDDLE-CLASS FEMININITY AND THEIR CONSEQUENCES

We have already seen that physical delicacy was important to definitions of femininity in the nineteenth century. While such notions belied the realities of the lives of middle-class housewives and the stamina it took to fulfill their duties, they also had the potential for helping women to subvert the ideology of true womanhood in a number of ways. First, poor health was an effective way for a woman to regulate her sex life. A woman who was unwell could use her illness to refuse to have sexual intercourse with her husband. And a woman who was ill and listless could be excused from housekeeping duties she did not enjoy and social obligations that she found tedious. Claiming to suffer from poor health allowed some women to use their femininity to mask resentment and hostility and could easily serve as either a conscious or unconscious form of passive rebellion against the restrictions that the cult of true womanhood placed on her life.

The femininity of a woman in the nineteenth century was also defined in terms of her concern about ameliorating the conditions of the poor and unfortunate. Most female acts of benevolence posed little threat to the perpetuation of conventional gender roles and relationships. But others were not so benign. Interest in philanthropy and concern about such social problems as drunkenness and prostitution encouraged women to criticize men and to demand a larger place for themselves in public life. And as some women began to take on increasingly active roles in social reform, they began to reject passivity and deference to male authority as ideal feminine attributes.

Female participation in the abolition movement serves as a good example of how social activism could lead to questioning conventional ideas about what constituted womanliness. Male anti-slavery advocates welcomed the help of women in their attempts to free the slaves, but most did not consider women their equals. Nor were they willing to give women leadership roles in the movement. Despite the abolitionist rhetoric about freedom and equality, some male abolitionists found it extremely difficult to apply those principles to the condition of women. They were perfectly willing to encourage women to organize auxiliaries to their own organizations, but they were not willing to welcome women into their own ranks. It was male resistance to the idea of female equality that helped to prompt the rise of the woman's rights movement.

If you recall from the last chapter, the issue of what role women should play in the abolition movement came up at the 1840 World Anti-Slavery Convention held in London. British delegates led the move to exclude female delegates like Lucretia Mott from the proceedings, and William Lloyd Garrison gave up his seat in protest. Mott was furious about her exclusion. But not until 1848 was she able to organize a protest to respond publicly to the treatment she had received in London.

In that year, Mott and four other women, including Elizabeth Cady Stanton, decided to call a woman's rights convention in Seneca Falls, New York. A few days before the convention, they met to draw up a list of their grievances and a call for action. That document, called the "Declaration of Sentiments," was modeled on the Declaration of Independence. In it, the women declared that "all men and women" were created equal and that they like their fathers, husbands, brothers, and sons had been endowed by their creator with the right to life, liberty, and the pursuit of happiness. They claimed the right to "refuse allegiance" to any government that deprived them of those rights. The despotism of men, they claimed, deprived them of equal opportunity in employment and education. They blamed men for supporting a double standard of morality. "Moral delinquencies which exclude women from society, are not only tolerated but deemed of little account in man," they wrote. They objected to the fact that they were excluded from the Christian ministry and that as married women they were deprived of their property and the custody of their children. The most controversial of their demands was that women be granted the right to vote. They ended their declaration by laying claim to "all of the rights and privileges" that belonged to "citizens of the United States."

Only a little over one hundred people attended the Seneca Falls Woman's Rights Convention. And public response to the "Declaration of Sentiments" was largely negative, indicating the degree to which those who lived in the nineteenth century organized their understanding of the world around gender distinctions rather than gender equality. Most men and women could not conceive of a world in which women and men had the same privileges and responsibilities. Their gendered identities were too vested in the belief that men and women were inherently different for them to tolerate a muting of the distinctions between what was considered masculine and what was considered feminine. And their conception of gender was too hierarchical to allow them to imagine a woman who had exactly the same rights as men. They were convinced that any woman who demanded those rights abdicated her feminine identity. James Gordon Bennett, one of the most important newspaper editors in the country, for example, wrote an editorial in his paper in which he asked rhetorically, "Who are these women?" His answer was that woman's rights advocates were "hens that crow." At one time or another between the Seneca Falls Convention and the Civil War, he called those who supported the Declaration of Sentiments "mannish women" and "hybrids," whose sex was "not accurately defined by exterior developments." In his opinion, they were nothing more than "viragos" and "Amazons" who reversed "the law of nature."

The anger and vituperation that were directed against women who demanded the same rights and privileges as men continued throughout the nineteenth century. Woman's rights advocates threatened to disrupt the gendered basis for the organization of American society. The changes that they demanded had the potential for undermining the power relationship between men and women. They suggested that it was time to redefine what it meant to be male and female. And the prospect of such a redefinition terrified a great many people.

Other factors also threatened to disrupt traditional gender identities and relationships in the nineteenth century. Motherhood, for example, had always played a role in defining what it meant to be a woman. In the seventeenth and eighteenth centuries, motherhood had an economic component. The labor of children was crucial to the economic well being of the family. But in the nineteenth century among the middle and upper classes, children were no longer expected to work. In fact, since they needed to be fed, clothed, sheltered, and educated, they became a drain on family resources. One response to this reality was to idealize and romanticize motherhood in order to perpetuate the idea that children were important to family life. According to some, bearing and rearing children were necessary to fulfill a woman's feminine destiny. A "true" woman was supposed to want, above all else, to be a mother and to fulfill her social and civic obligations by centering her life around her children and dedicating herself to their care. Any woman who failed to bear children, no matter what the reason, was considered incomplete.

And yet there is evidence to suggest that as the century progressed, an increasing number of middle- and upper-class women resorted to various forms of birth control or abortion to limit the size of their families. Often with the consent and collaboration of their husbands, they privately rejected the imperative that they bear and rear as many children as they were able to conceive. When the birth rate in middle- and upper-class families fell, doctors, legislators, and social critics accused women of rejecting their maternal roles and behaving in a most unfeminine manner. They viewed any woman who could not bear a child as unfortunate and to be pitied. But they accused any fertile woman who refused to

bear a child of being unnatural, selfish, and unwomanly. In 1873 Congress passed the Comstock law which forbade the distribution of birth control and abortion information through the mail on the grounds that such information was "obscene." In this way, male legislators tried to prevent women from separating womanhood from motherhood.

Access to education also helped to undermine traditional definitions of feminine dependence. By the 1890s, there were hundreds of small women's colleges in the North. Theoretically, an education was supposed to prepare a young woman to fulfill her conventional role as a wife and mother. But educating women had unintended consequences. It introduced them to ideas and critical thinking skills that led some to question their subordinate position in society. And it helped to prepare women to support themselves, thus providing them with unprecedented opportunities for economic independence. As a result, some educated women decided to postpone or forgo marriage and motherhood. They did not need to depend upon a man to provide them with food, clothing, and shelter. And they found it possible to tie their feminine identities to their work instead of to maternity and other domestic responsibilities. As the century progressed, an increasing number of educated women began to claim for themselves the kind of autonomy and independence that had traditionally been reserved for wage-earning men.

There were, of course, those who did what they could to discourage this development. Public response to well-educated women who married late or not at all indicates how strongly femininity was tied to domesticity in the public imagination. Guardians of the gender hierarchy began to express real ambivalence about the role of education in the lives of women. Doctor Edward Clarke of Harvard University wrote, for example, that education for women could pose a danger to them and to society as a whole. Too much intellectual exertion, he argued, could undermine a woman's ability to bear healthy children by draining away her energy and destroying her reproductive system. Too much book learning, he believed, could promote nervous exhaustion and endanger a woman's physical health. The message seemed to be that it was better for a woman to remain ignorant than for her to endanger her ability to fulfill her feminine destiny to marry and bear children.

The problems that married women faced in real life also helped to undermine the emphasis that the cult of true womanhood placed on female dependence. It was in some ways quite unrealistic for women in the nineteenth century to assume that they could spend their entire married lives depending upon their husbands to support them. Sometimes husbands died. Other times they became ill or were injured and unable to work. Some turned out to be alcoholics, gambled away their salaries, or lost their jobs. And sometimes even the most conscientious, hardworking, and successful of husbands went bankrupt. Under such circumstances, a married woman had to be resourceful and self-reliant. So beginning in the 1840s some authors began to shift from picturing the ideal woman as a clinging vine to describing her as a sturdy oak. They advised unmarried women to prepare for marriage not only by making themselves attractive to men but also by engaging in some sort of vocational training that would make it possible for them to support themselves and their children as clerks, bookkeepers, printers, or dressmakers if the need should arise. And they suggested that it was in woman's best interest to ignore capricious shifts in fashion and wear sensible clothing, attend school as long as possible, eat wholesome and nutritious meals, and exercise frequently in the fresh air so that they could serve as heads of their own households if fate or bad luck made it necessary. Ideals of middle-class womanhood were clearly undergoing a significant shift. For some, womanliness was beginning to be equated with intellectual development, physical fitness, and economic self-sufficiency.

THE FEMININE IDENTITIES OF SINGLE WOMEN IN THE MIDDLE CLASS

Single women in the middle class found it virtually impossible to construct their femininity within the parameters established by the cult of true womanhood. They did not marry; they did not sacrifice themselves for their husbands and children; and they often had to work for wages to support themselves. Yet in some ways being a spinster in the nineteenth century was easier than it had been in the colonial period. In the seventeenth century, unmarried women were considered sinful because they failed to fulfill their social obligation to marry and have children. Attitudes toward them began to shift in the eighteenth century. Viewed as pathetic and often scorned or belittled, they were no longer considered sinful, but they were certainly viewed at the very least as inadequate if not defective women. This was the legacy that single women in the nineteenth century had to deal with when they tried to construct their feminine identities outside the bounds of married domesticity.

Women chose to remain single for any number of reasons ranging from personal choice to lack of opportunity. But those who explained their reasons usually couched them in terms of a self-conscious desire to construct their gendered identities around celibacy, economic self-sufficiency, the opportunity to establish their own households, and the ability to pursue their own interests without having to take the needs and desires of others into account. To do this was not easy. They often found that their parents, brothers, and sisters expected them to stay at home and spend their lives providing them with companionship as well as free housekeeping, childcare, and nursing services. Given such family claims, it was not easy to maintain their independence even if they could find ways to adequately support themselves. In their attempts to construct their feminine identities as single women, they tried to convince anyone who would listen that they had made an honorable choice and that their position was a dignified and useful one.

Fairly typical of the independent, self-sufficient, single woman was Catharine Beecher. Beecher was the daughter of Lyman Beecher, a highly regarded and very influential evangelical minister, and the sister of Harriet Beecher Stowe, the author of *Uncle Tom's Cabin*. She intended to marry, but after her fiance was tragically lost at sea, she dedicated her life to the education of women. She supported herself by establishing schools for girls in Connecticut and Ohio and by publishing what we would call home economics manuals. Despite the fact that she remained single, she glorified woman's role as mother and housewife. She believed that woman's power lay in her influence over her husband and children and dedicated her *The American Woman's Home* to the "Women of America, in whose hands rest the real destinies of the republic." Through her manuals, she hoped to regularize housekeeping in America and to provide the American housewife with expertise in everything from interior design and ventilation to cooking, the supervision of servants, and childcare.

Beecher was well-educated, single, and relatively independent and autonomous. But she was careful not to encourage women to challenge the principles of femininity established by the cult of true womanhood. Other women in similar circumstances were much more critical of woman's status in nineteenth-century society and much less satisfied with idealization of women as dependent and domestic. Susan B. Anthony illustrates the point. Anthony was a Quaker who originally earned her living as a teacher. Enraged when she discovered that female teachers were not paid at the same rate as male teachers, she began to advocate equal pay for equal work. She eventually became active in the temperance movement. In 1851 she met Elizabeth Cady Stanton, and they became very close friends. The rest, as they say, is history. Until they died, Stanton and Anthony worked together in the woman's rights movement to improve woman's economic, social, and political position in American society and to provide women with the opportunity to enlarge their definition of what constituted femininity.

THE CONSTRUCTION OF FEMININITY AMONG WORKING-CLASS WOMEN

It was just as difficult for working-class women to construct their feminine identities around the prescriptions of the cult of true womanhood as it was for single, middle-class women to do so. Economic circumstances made it impossible for them to depend on their fathers and husbands to support them. Working-class women worked for wages because they had to. The money that they made went to help feed, clothe, and house themselves and sometimes their families. That fact alone tended to exclude them from the middle class. It is true that those who were well-educated could maintain a tenuous claim to middle-class respectability by teaching school or by writing poems, essays, short stories, or novels for publication. But most wage-earning women were not well-educated. Some tried to mask their economic need by taking in sewing or laundry or renting out rooms in their houses to other working-class folk rather than going out to work in a shop or a factory. But ultimately their need to make money at least threatened if it did not completely undermine any claim they might have to middle-class ladyhood.

In contrast to middle-class women, wage-earning women could not afford to indulge themselves in the belief that they were "by nature" physically delicate. Whether black or white, whether native born or foreign born, they simply could not afford to be fashionably sick. Their ability to help put food on the table and a roof over their heads depended on their physical strength and stamina. Since strength and the maintenance of good health were critical to their survival, they formed an important component of working women's feminine identities.

Like their middle-class sisters, wage-earning women had domestic responsibilities. But domesticity did not form the core of working-class feminine identity. Working women did not typically spend much time "keeping house" because they didn't have much house to keep. They often lived in small, cramped rooms with very little furniture. They had other things to do besides trying to keep their living quarters clean. They sometimes spent more time and energy getting food to eat than they did cooking it. And since they had only a few pieces of clothing, they did not have to spend much time washing and ironing.

Motherhood only complicated their situation. Bearing and rearing children did not have the same resonance for working-class women as it did for middle-class women. Pregnancy, childbirth, and lactation only hampered their efforts to make money and to care for their other children. And unless they were able to earn money in their homes, they were unable to invest much time and effort in child rearing. This is not to say that they did not love their children and want to take care of them. It was just that if they worked outside their homes, they had to delegate many of their childcare responsibilities to someone else. And if no one else was available, they had to let their children roam the streets. Thus, their circumstances made it very difficult for them to equate mothering with femininity to the degree that was possible for women in the middle class. Women who worked long hours outside the home had little energy to focus on providing a warm and nurturing environment for their children. Many of them simply lacked the physical and material resources to invest much of their gendered identities in motherhood.

Unlike middle-class women, wage-earning women could not confine themselves to "woman's sphere." While middle-class ladies were supposed to avoid public notice at all costs, their less affluent sisters had a very public presence. They had no maids to send out to do the shopping. And they often appeared on the street unaccompanied by a man to protect them. Indeed, unlike their middle-class con-temporaries, they spent a great deal of time outside their homes. They walked up and down the streets alone or in groups as they went about their daily business. They frequented taverns and dancehalls. And when the weather was good, they congregated outside on the stoops of their tenements to gossip and socialize.

In setting standards for public behavior, some working-class women went to great lengths to distinguish themselves from middle-class ladies. This was particularly true of the Bowery Girls. The Bowery was a working-class neighborhood on the east side of New York City. In the 1840s and 1850s, it was also the center of the youth culture. It was there that young, working-class men and women paraded up and down the streets after work and on Saturday nights and frequented bawdy houses, saloons, and theaters. According to Christine Stansell, Bowery Girls "were distinguished by their self-conscious 'airs,' a style of dress and manner which was a studied departure from ladyhood." Bowery girls did nothing to deflect attention from themselves when they walked down the street looking for a little fun on a Saturday night. They boldly looked other pedestrians in the eye. And they dressed in brightly-colored and provocative clothing which testified to their economic independence and their right to define for themselves what was fashionable. They were high-spirited and loud. Even the way they walked and held their bodies suggested that they were perfectly capable of taking care of themselves.

Whether a Bowery Girl could really take care of herself was a different matter altogether. The possibility of rape and other forms of sexual abuse was ever present partly because Bowery Girls did not necessarily define their femininity in terms of preserving their virginity. That did not mean that they were prostitutes, but it did suggest that they might be willing to engage in sexual activity in return for the food, drink, and entertainment that their male companions provided for them. The ambiguity of their attitude toward premarital sex, their opportunity to meet and associate with strange men, and the potentially commercial nature of their casual relationships all combined to make them more sexually vulnerable than their middle-class sisters.

Not all working-class girls posed such a direct challenge to middle-class standards of femininity. Except for the fact that they worked for money, the young farm girls who went to work for the New England textile manufacturers in the 1820s and 1830s generally conformed to patterns of feminine behavior associated with the middle class. Known as the "Lowell girls" because they worked in Lowell, Massachusetts, these young women worked all day tending their spinning machines and lived together in company-supported boardinghouses supervised by matrons who were supposed to serve as surrogate mothers. Lowell Girls were expected to attend church regularly, restrain their sexual impulses, and submit to the authority of their employers. They were encouraged to read literature of redeeming social value, and their employers encouraged them to express themselves in poetry and prose by providing them with a newspaper of their own called the *Lowell Offering*. It is clear from what they wrote that Lowell girls derived considerable self-esteem from the fact that they earned their own money and autonomy from the fact that they lived away from home. Most of them maintained close ties with their families and many sent a substantial portion of their earnings back home to their parents. But others felt free to spend their wages on fashionable new dresses, ribbons for their hair, or bonnets to wear to church on Sunday. Working in the mills provided some young women with unprecedented opportunities to develop feelings of self-respect and independence that became an integral part of their definition of what it meant to be a woman.

The Lowell girls did not usually dedicate their entire lives to working outside the home, however. For many, working in the mills was merely an interesting and profitable way to spend the interlude between childhood and marriage. Most considered their employment temporary and eventually left their jobs in the factories to set up households of their own. They may have valued the independence and autonomy they enjoyed as single, wage-earning women, but in the long term they constructed their feminine identities around married life, housekeeping, and child bearing.

Because women in the working classes were such a diverse group, it is difficult to generalize about the impact that the cult of true womanhood had on their lives. As we have seen, some wage-earning women ignored middle-class definitions of femininity when it came to constructing their gendered identities. But others could not afford to do so, particularly if they were the objects of middle-class philanthropy. Middle-class ladies interested in helping those less fortunate than themselves typically tried to assess whether or not the poor really "deserved" their help. In their effort to do this, they tended to impose middle-class standards of behavior on working-class women who were in need of money or services. If those in need kept their houses and children clean, if they attended church regularly, if they abstained from the consumption of alcohol, and if they were suitably deferential to their genteel guests, they probably qualified for aid and assistance.

A perfect example of attempts on the part of middle-class women to impose their own standards of behavior on poor women is to be found in the records of the New York Asylum for Lying-in Women founded in New York City in 1823. The hospital was organized to provide obstetric services for women in need. But admission to the hospital depended on whether or not the woman applying for help had a marriage certificate in her possession. The good ladies of New York were willing to help an abandoned wife. But they had no intention of providing medical care for a woman who engaged in premarital sex and was unlucky enough to be pregnant with an illegitimate child. As a result of that policy, they refused to admit a woman named Burley to their asylum in January, 1826, because they were not certain that she was a woman of virtue. All alone and penniless, Burley took shelter in an unheated garret where, unattended, she gave birth to a baby girl. The next day, two workmen discovered her there with the infant frozen to her clothing. The demand that working-class women accept middle-class values and conform to middle-class standards of behavior did not always have such tragic consequences. But this incident does illustrate the risks involved when poor women ignored the prescriptions of the cult of true womanhood as they went about constructing their own feminine identities.

Not all working-class women felt it necessary to depend upon middle-class philanthropic efforts to improve the quality of their lives. Proud and assertive, they organized to protect their own interests. In doing so, they began to construct their gender identity around protest and public activism. When wages for textile workers declined and conditions in the factories and mill boarding houses began to deteriorate in the 1830s, for example, the "Lowell girls" went out on strike. Unable to preserve the living and working standards that had originally been so appealing, they eventually lost their jobs to immigrants who were willing to accept lower wages. So it wasn't until after the Civil War that large numbers of wage-earning women began to assert themselves in terms of union activism. The Knights of Labor opened its membership to women in 1881. It welcomed both skilled and unskilled workers, supported the idea of equal pay for equal work, and advocated both temperance and woman's suffrage. While the ladies' locals organized by Knights of Labor were proud to represent the interests of women who were willing and able to earn wages and were dedicated to public activism on behalf of female workers, they also tried to adapt many of the prescriptions of the cult of true womanhood to the realities of their lives. Motherhood, wifehood, and domestic virtue were as important to them as it was to their middle-class contemporaries.

THE FEMININE IDENTITIES OF FARM WOMEN

It was, perhaps, easier for farm women to conform to the prescriptions of the cult of true womanhood than it was for single or working-class women. Typically they considered piety, purity, and domesticity to be ideal feminine attributes. Farm women tended to be very much involved with the spiritual life of their communities. They had a low tolerance for sexual indiscretions. And generally speaking, farm women willingly accepted primary responsibility for nurturing their children and maintaining their households. But they did construct their feminine identities around ideas that were in some ways fundamentally different from those of women in the urban middle class. For example, farm women did not generally subscribe to the belief that men and women should necessarily inhabit separate spheres. As Nancy Osterud has pointed out, farming women tended to define themselves in terms of their relationship with men rather than their difference from men. Unlike middle-class women who lived in towns and cities, farm women worked on a daily basis side by side with the men in their lives. Their work was visible. And unlike that of middle-class women, it was quite productive.

It is certainly true that much of the work on a farm was divided into gender specific tasks. Generally speaking, men were responsible for planting, cultivating, and harvesting the crops. They built and maintained the barn, the house, and the outbuildings. They provided fuel for cooking and heating, and they assumed responsibility for repairing farm and household equipment. Women typically tended the garden, raised poultry, processed food, and prepared the meals. They cleaned house and did the sewing and laundry. But farming men and women also performed many tasks together and were flexible in their allocation of the work that needed to be done. Sometimes women hoed, and sometimes men churned butter. And certainly in cases of emergency, they both did whatever needed to be done to save their crops and herds and, thereby, protect the viability of their agrarian enterprise.

As the nineteenth century progressed, farming became more and more integrated into the market economy and subjected to market forces beyond the control of the individual farmer. In order to compete for access to world markets, American farmers tended to overproduce, thus driving prices for grain and livestock down, a situation that threatened a great many of them with bankruptcy. But on an individual basis, farm families remained much more self-sufficient than those who lived in the cities. Farm wives in the late nineteenth century no longer spent their time spinning and weaving, but they did continue to produce much of what the family needed to sustain itself. They made their own clothes, raised their own poultry, and grew their own fruits and vegetables. And the pride they took in such feminine accomplishments was evident to anyone who saw them competing with each other to win blue ribbons at fairs and local fund raisers for the quality and beauty of their pies, cakes, quilts and canned goods.

Despite their contributions to the farm economy, farm women did not achieve any degree of autonomy during the nineteenth century. It was extremely difficult for women to support themselves outside the farm household. And since they were not regarded by their male relatives as independent economic agents, they usually didn't inherit the family farm. Unless they left their communities and went to the city, unmarried farm women generally remained an integral part of their families and simply continued to contribute to the family economy. They were no more autonomous than their married sisters.

While there was considerable continuity between the gendered identity of farm women in the seventeenth and eighteenth centuries and those in the nineteenth century, farm women in the later period found it possible to quite self-consciously modify and to some extent expand their definition of what it meant to be a woman. For example, they began to re-

assess the connection between their feminine identities and the number of children that they bore. Motherhood was extremely important to farm women. In farming families, children provided much needed labor and a degree of social security for their parents. Children also established ties to other farming families in the community through their marriages. Nevertheless as the century progressed, farm women, like women who lived in towns and cities, began to take steps to limit the size of their families.

By the 1890s, they also attempted to carve out a place for themselves as social and political activists. Farm women participated in the various reform activities including the temperance movement and the Grange Movement. The Grange, also known as the Patrons of Husbandry, was started in the 1860s to relieve the isolation of farm life. Grange organizations had an egalitarian attitude toward gender which is not surprising since farming men and women ideally acted as partners in both domestic life and the production of agricultural products. The Grange reserved ritual offices for women and provided them with the opportunity to fill leadership positions. It is true that women were not treated as equals, but it is also true that they were not necessarily relegated to just providing refreshments for the men who attended Grange meetings. They were free to participate in Grange affairs, they could preside over meetings, and they could express their opinions openly before mixed audiences.

Thus in the nineteenth century, the feminine identities of farming women, like their middle-class contemporaries, centered around their reproductive capacity and their domestic duties. But their economic contributions to the well-being of their families and their role in the public life of their small, rural communities gave them the opportunity to establish a feminine identity that was distinct. They could not claim that they were man's equal since they usually did not own the land and for most of the nineteenth century, none of them could vote or hold political office. But throughout the period, they, like other women who worked for a living, came as close to establishing their claim to equality as was possible under the circumstances.

FEMININITY AND THE IMMIGRANT WOMAN

During the nineteenth century, women immigrated to the United States from all over the world. And they all brought with them ethnically specific ideas about what was feminine and what was not. Since it is impossible, given the space available, to generalize about how all of these women constructed their gendered identities, let's concentrate on one group: women from Ireland.

The immigration of Irish women to America began very early in the history of this country. But the largest number of "Erin's daughters" came to the United States in the nineteenth century. The potato famine of the 1840s, the starvation that accompanied it, and the land policy changes that followed it produced a situation that made it difficult for women to find either a husband or employment in Ireland. So hundreds of thousands of young, single Irish women left their homes and came to America.

They arrived with a specific set of ideas about what it meant to be a woman. First, they equated femininity with self-sufficiency. Typically, they made their own decisions to leave Ireland. They came by themselves rather than with their parents. And after they arrived, they made their own arrangements for housing and employment. Some of them found work in factories or as seamstresses, but most of them took jobs as domestic servants. The work was familiar, they received room and board, and the pay was relatively good.

Domestic service meant that they had to defer or forgo marriage. But this was nothing new. After the famine, the opportunity for a young Irish maid to marry was increasingly determined by whether or not she had a dowry. And most Irish women did not. Thus when they arrived in America, being married was not an important component of their def-

inition of femininity. That is not to say that they rejected the idea of marriage. They simply did not define a single woman as unfeminine, and, since most were perfectly capable of supporting themselves, they were not necessarily in a hurry to find husbands.

Many of them, of course, did eventually marry. And central to their identity as married women was their role as mothers. They made little effort to control their fertility, and their homes tended to be mother-centered. Society in Ireland was generally segregated by gender in the nineteenth century. Women dominated the home and the church and men spent their leisure time with other men, enjoying each other's company, talking politics, and drinking in pubs. The result was that women had particularly strong ties to family. When they immigrated, they tended to replicate those patterns. Single Irish women often sent a part of their wages back to Ireland so that other members of their families could follow them to America. Many married women found that while their husbands were willing to work to support their families, they were likely to abdicate responsibility for family affairs, financial and otherwise. However irresponsible this tendency might have appeared to observers, such an arrangement gave Irish women considerable authority in the domestic sphere. Typically they were the ones who literally put food on the table, settled family disputes, monitored the education of their children, and supervised the observance of religion. And if their families eventually achieved middle-class respectability, it was as much a result of their efforts as it was of their husbands'.

Irish women who did not marry typically embraced opportunities to get an education and eventually became nurses, teachers, and clerks. Others worked hard, saved their money, bought real estate, and opened boarding houses or small shops. Their feminine identities were tied to being economically self-sufficient and upwardly mobile.

Irish women did not come to America to redefine what it meant to be a woman. They came to America to find a place where they could express what were to them traditionally feminine characteristics. In that, they seem to have succeeded. Irish culture had always encouraged women to work and to exhibit a certain degree of assertiveness in an economic context. In America, Irish women continued that tradition by playing an active role in the labor movement. But while it is true that they participated in labor union activities and demanded higher wages, shorter hours, and better working conditions for themselves and others, they took little interest in politics and typically were not among those who enthusiastically supported the woman suffrage movement. They accepted and apparently valued the separation of spheres between men and women that characterized politics both in Ireland and in America.

Women who immigrated to the United States from Ireland typically came alone. They based their feminine identities on their resourcefulness and economic self-sufficiency and seem to have been in no hurry to marry. They were in these ways somewhat atypical. Most immigrant women came because their husbands or fathers decided that leaving their homeland was the best thing to do. Most worked for wages because they realized that their families would starve if they didn't. But whatever their ethnic background, they eventually found it necessary to adapt their ideas about what constituted womanliness to their new environment.

SUMMARY

The cult of true womanhood with its glorification of sexual purity, married domesticity, female moral superiority, and submissiveness provided American women in the nineteenth century with guidelines around which they could construct their feminine identities. An extension of republican motherhood, it was a distinctively middle-class ideology in an age when the influence of the middle class was extremely powerful. As a result, even if they could not conform to all of its prescriptions, women who were not white, those who were

not native born, and those who were not middle class had to take account of its tenets. They could reject or modify its prescriptions and devise their own definitions of femininity to conform to their personal circumstances. But at some point they had to deal with the consequences of having done so.

Many middle-class women who remained single throughout their adult life, for example, felt compelled to justify the fact that they were unmarried and had failed to conform to the expectation that they would devote their lives to caring for husbands and children. Working-class women, excluded from the middle class by virtue of their need to work for wages, often found themselves torn between upholding middle-class standards of domesticity and fulfilling their obligations as workers. Whether they were white or black, immigrant or native born, their competence as mothers and housewives was judged by standards set by middle-class women who were in a position to provide them with social services that many of them desperately needed. Farm women had a similar problem. While they could present themselves as respectable and God-fearing, they were not always able to carve out an exclusively domestic niche for themselves. In terms of gender, farm life tended to be well integrated. When push came to shove, farm women who valued resourcefulness and hard work over refinement and gentility, did not hesitate to hitch up their long skirts, put on work boots, and help to build fences, slaughter animals, or do field work. Separate gender spheres were hard to maintain on farms where work needed to be done, and no one was particularly interested in whether it was a man or a woman who did it.

It is perhaps because the cult of true womanhood had such a powerful influence among those in the middle class that it was women from that social class who took the lead in fomenting a public campaign to reject many of its prescriptions and to quite self-consciously set about redefining what it meant to be female. At the Seneca Falls Convention in 1848, Elizabeth Cady Stanton argued that women should have the same political rights as men. She and the others who attended the convention signed their names to a Declaration of Sentiments that demanded more educational and vocational opportunities for women. Those who joined with her in the campaign for woman's rights refused to equate femininity with intellectual inferiority, passive submission to the authority of men, and economic dependence. They had no problem constructing an ideology of femininity within the parameters of piety, purity, and concern for the welfare of others. And most did not quarrel with the desire of some women to marry and bear children. But they did argue that a true woman should have the opportunity to pursue her own interests and be as independent and self-sufficient as any man if that is what she wanted. As we shall see, their attempts to create a new definition of femininity in the nineteenth century continued to cause controversy in the twentieth.

<u>DOCUMENT</u>

Caricatures of Woman's Rights Advocates

In 1848, those who attended the first woman's rights convention at Seneca Falls, New York, demanded equal rights for women. Three years later, woman's rights advocates such as Elizabeth Cady Stanton and Susan B. Anthony began wearing what became known as the Bloomer costume. Their purpose was to take a first step toward equality by freeing themselves from the restrictions that conventional women's clothes imposed on them. The Bloomer costume combined pantaloons such as those worn by the Turks with a short-skirted dress drawn in loosely at the waist. Since those who wore Bloomers did not have to wear a corset, the costume was much more comfortable than conventional dress. A woman wearing Bloomers could move about freely. And since her dress did not sweep the ground, it stayed relatively clean. The outfit was such a dramatic departure from what was considered fashionable that it attracted considerable attention and almost immediately became associated with the woman's rights movement. Caricatures of woman's rights advocates and the kind of clothing they wore illustrate the anxiety and confusion that the demand for equal rights and opportunities for women produced in the society at large.

What kind of gender stereotypes do these illustrations present? What role does clothing play in these presentations? What threat do these cartoons suggest that supporters of woman's rights posed to conventional gender roles?

Source: Harper's New Monthly Magazine, January, 1852, p. 286 and June, 1853, p. 141; *Frank Leslie's Illustrated Newspaper,* Jan. 15, 1859, p. 110.

STRONG-MINDED "BLOOMER."—"Now, do, Alfred, put down that foolish Novel, and do something rational, and play something You never practice, now you're married."

Harper's New Monthly Magazine, January 1852, p. 286. (Courtesy of the Library of Congress)

LADY PRACTICE IN PHYSIC.

Mr. SMITHERS being sick, sends for a Lady Doctress to attend upon him professionally. Being a singularly bashful young man, Mr. SMITHERS' pulse is greatly accelerated on being manipulated by the delicate fingers of the Lady Practitioner, whereupon she naturally imagines him to be in a high fever, and incontinently physics him for the same.

Harper's New Monthly Magazine, June 1853, p. 141. (Courtesy of the Library of Congress)

Frank Leslie's Illustrated Newspaper, January 15, 1859, p. 110. (Courtesy of the Library of Congress)

Lucy Larcom's "Unwedded"

Lucy Larcom was born in the seaport town of Beverly, Massachusetts in 1824. After her father died, her mother moved to Lowell, Massachusetts where she opened a boarding house for female mill workers. Lucy worked in the mills from 1835 to 1846. Still unmarried in 1846, she went to Illinois where she supported herself as a teacher. Larcom enjoyed writing but found that teaching did not leave her much time for literary pursuits. So she left teaching for good in 1864 to become the editor of a literary magazine called Our Young Folks. *Larcom never married. She did not object to the institution of marriage, but she simply could not bring herself to give up her independence and subject herself to the authority of someone else. She valued her freedom, regarded the single life as an honorable one, and found life as a writer and editor very satisfying.*

In the poem reprinted below Larcom defends a woman's decision not to marry. What kind of life does the woman in "Unwedded" have? How does it compare to the lives of most married women? According to Larcom, how can a woman fulfill her feminine role if she remains single?

UNWEDDED

Behold her there in the evening sun,
  That kindles the Indian Summer trees
To a separate burning bush, one by one,
  Wherein the Glory Divine she sees!

Mate and nestlings she never had:
  Kith and kindred have passed away;
Yet the sunset is not more gently glad,
  That follows her shadow, and fain would stay.

For out of her life goes a breath of bliss,
  And a sunlike charm from her cheerful eye,
That the cloud and the loitering breeze
    would miss;
  A balm that refreshes the passer-by.

"Did she choose it, this single life?"—
  Gossip, she saith not, and who can tell?
But many a mother, and many a wife,
  Draws a lot more lonely, we all know well.

Doubtless she had her romantic dream,
  Like other maidens, in May-time sweet,
That flushes the air with a lingering gleam,

And goldens the grass beneath her feet:—

A dream unmoulded to visible form,
  That keeps the world rosy with mists of youth,
And holds her in loyalty close and warm,
  To her grand ideal of manly truth.

"But is she happy, a woman, alone?"—
  Gossip, alone in this crowded earth,
With a voice to quiet its hourly moan,
  And a smile to heighten its rare mirth?

There are ends more worthy than happiness:
  Who seeks it, is digging joy's grave, we know.
The blessed are they who but live to bless;
  She found out that mystery, long ago.

To her motherly, sheltering atmosphere,
  The children hasten from icy homes:
The outcast is welcome to share her cheer;
  And the saint with a fervent benison comes.

For the heart of woman is large as man's;
  God gave her His orphaned world to hold,
And whispered through her His deeper plans
  To save it alive from the outer cold.

And here is a woman who understood
  Herself, her work, and God's will with her,
To gather and scatter His sheaves of good,
  And was meekly thankful, though men
    demur.

Source: Lucy Larcom, *The Poetical Works of Lucy Larcom* (Boston: Houghton, Mifflin and Company, 1884), 26–28.

Would she have walked more nobly, think,
    With a man beside her, to point the way,
Hand joining hand in the marriage-link?
    Possibly, Yes: it is likelier, Nay.

For all men have not wisdom and might:
    Love's eyes are tender, and blur the map;
And a wife will follow by faith, not sight,
    In the chosen footprint, at any hap.

Having the whole, she covets no part:
    Hers is the bliss of all blessed things.
The tears that unto her eyelids start,
    Are those which a generous pity brings;

Or the sympathy of heroic faith
    With a holy purpose, achieved or lost.
To stifle the truth is to stop her breath,
    For she rates a lie at its deadly cost.

Her friends are good women and faithful men,
    Who seek for the True, and uphold the Right;
And who shall proclaim her the weaker, when
    Her very presence puts sin to flight?

"And dreads she never the coming years?"—
    Gossip, what are the years to her?
All winds are fair, and the harbor nears,
    And every breeze a delight will stir.

Transfigured under the sunset trees,
    That wreathe her with shadowy gold and red,
She looks away to the purple seas,
    Whereon her shallop will soon be sped.

She reads the hereafter by the here:
    A beautiful Now, and a better To Be:
In life is all sweetness, in death no fear:—
    You waste your pity on such as she.

<u>DOCUMENT</u>

Excerpt from Bradwell v. Illinois

Myra Bradwell of Chicago was married to a lawyer. She was educated in the law and met all of the qualifications necessary to practice law in the state of Illinois except one. She was a not a man. So when she applied for admission to the Illinois bar, she was refused. Bradwell was furious, so she appealed the decision to the Illinois courts and eventually to the United States Supreme Court, who heard the case in 1872. In their decision, all of the justices except Chief Justice Salmon P. Chase supported the right of the state Illinois to deny female citizens the opportunity to earn their living as lawyers. The following is an excerpt from that decision.

Why do Justice Joseph P. Bradley and his colleagues think being female makes women unfit to practice law? What anxieties about gender does their decision expose?

Mr. Justice BRADLEY:

I concur in the judgment of the court in this case, by which the judgment of the Supreme Court of Illinois is affirmed, but not for the reasons specified in the opinion just read.

The claim of the plaintiff, who is a married woman, to be admitted to practice as an attorney and counsellor-at-law, is based upon the supposed right of every person, man or woman, to engage in any lawful employment for a livelihood. The Supreme Court of Illinois denied the application on the ground that, by

Source: John William Wallace, *Cases Argued and Adjudged in the Supreme Court of the United States, December Term, 1872*, Vol. XVI (Washington, DC: W. H. & O. H. Morrison, 1873), 139–42.

the common law, which is the basis of the laws of Illinois, only men were admitted to the bar, and the legislature had not made any change in this respect, but had simply provided that no person should be admitted to practice as attorney or counsellor without having previously obtained a license for that purpose from two justices of the Supreme Court, and that no person should receive a license without first obtaining a certificate from the court of some county of his good moral character. In other respects it was left to the discretion of the court to establish the rules by which admission to the profession should be determined. The court, however, regarded itself as bound by at least two limitations. One was that it should establish such terms of admission as would promote the proper administration of justice, and the other that it should not admit any persons, or class of persons, not intended by the legislature to be admitted, even though not expressly excluded by statute. In view of this latter limitation the court felt compelled to deny the application of females to be admitted as members of the bar. Being contrary to the rules of the common law and the usages of Westminster Hall from time immemorial, it could not be supposed that the legislature had intended to adopt any different rule.

The claim that, under the fourteenth amendment of the Constitution, which declares that no State shall make or enforce any law which shall abridge the privileges and immunities of citizens of the United States, the statute law of Illinois, or the common law prevailing in that State, can no longer be set up as a barrier against the right of females to pursue any lawful employment for a livelihood (the practice of law included), assumes that it is one of the privileges and immunities of women as citizens to engage in any and every profession, occupation, or employment in civil life.

It certainly cannot be affirmed, as an historical fact, that this has ever been established as one of the fundamental privileges and immunities of the sex. On the contrary, the civil law, as well as nature herself, has always recognized a wide difference in the respective spheres and destinies of man and woman. Man is, or should be, woman's protector and defender. The natural and proper timidity and delicacy which belongs to the female sex evidently unfits it for many of the occupations of civil life. The constitution of the family organization, which is founded in the divine ordinance, as well as in the nature of things, indicates the domestic sphere as that which properly belongs to the domain and functions of womanhood. The harmony, not to say identity, of interests and views which belong, or should belong, to the family institution is repugnant to the idea of a woman adopting a distinct and independent career from that of her husband. So firmly fixed was this sentiment in the founders of the common law that it became a maxim of that system of jurisprudence that a woman had no legal existence separate from her husband, who was regarded as her head and representative in the social state; and, notwithstanding some recent modifications of this civil status, many of the special rules of law flowing from and dependent upon this cardinal principle still exist in full force in most States. One of these is, that a married woman is incapable, without her husband's consent, of making contracts which shall be binding on her or him. This very incapacity was one circumstance which the Supreme Court of Illinois deemed important in rendering a married woman incompetent fully to perform the duties and trusts that belong to the office of an attorney and counsellor.

It is true that many women are unmarried and not affected by any of the duties, complications, and incapacities arising out of the married state, but these are exceptions to the general rule. The paramount destiny and mission of woman are to fulfil the noble and benign offices of wife and mother. This is the law of the Creator. And the rules of civil society must be adapted to the general constitution of things, and cannot be based upon exceptional cases.

The humane movements of modern society, which have for their object the multiplication of avenues for woman's advancement, and of occupations adapted to her condition and sex, have my heartiest concurrence. But I am not prepared to say that it is one of her fundamental rights and privileges to be admitted into every office and position, including those which require highly special qualifications and demanding special responsibilities. In the nature of things it is not every citizen of every age, sex, and condition that is qualified for every calling and position. It is the prerogative of the legislator to prescribe regulations founded on nature, reason, and experience for the due admission of qualified persons to professions and callings demanding special skill and confidence. This fairly belongs to the police power of the State; and, in my opinion, in view of the peculiar characteristics, destiny, and mission of woman, it is within the province of the legislature to ordain what offices, positions, and callings shall be filled and discharged by men, and shall receive the benefit of those energies and responsibilities, and that decision and firmness which are presumed to predominate in the sterner sex.

For these reasons I think that the laws of Illinois now complained of are not obnoxious to the charge of abridging any of the privileges and immunities of citizens of the United States.

ARTICLE

At War with Herself: Harriet Beecher Stowe As Woman in Conflict within the Home

Mary Kelley

In her article on Harriet Beecher Stowe, Mary Kelley calls Stowe and other nineteenth-century writers of domestic fiction "sentimentalists." Like Louisa May Alcott, Harriet Beecher Stowe framed middle-class femininity within the parameters of the cult of true womanhood in her novels. But Stowe found it difficult to successfully construct her own feminine identity around being a wife and a mother and the kind of self-sacrificing feminine ideal that she glorified in her fiction. Kelley uses information found in Stowe's personal papers to document the tensions that this problem created in her efforts to balance her belief that true femininity was based on meeting the needs of others and her desire for personal autonomy and control over her fertility.

What were the sources of tension between Stowe's ideal woman as depicted in her fiction and her own version of womanhood? How did she resolve it?

Source: Mary Kelley, "At War with Herself: Harriet Beecher Stowe As Woman in Conflict within the Home," *American Studies,* XIX (Fall 1978), 23–37. Reprinted with the permission of Cambridge University Press. Notes omitted.

Like other nineteenth-century sentimentalists, Harriet Beecher Stowe sought a place and purpose for woman in an America being transformed by modernization. The place was the home, the family the unit for the dissemination of values, and woman the spiritual and moral overseer. Likening the home to the church in *The Minister's Wooing*, Stowe compared woman's role to the minister's. Home, she stated, was the "appointed sphere for woman, more holy than cloister, more saintly and pure than church and altar. . . . Priestess, wife, and mother there she ministers daily in holy works of household peace." The wife and mother was portrayed as the exemplar and inculcator of the pre-eminent value of service to others, the inspirer and reformer of man, and the educator of children, all within the confines of domesticity. The home was assigned a dual function. Not only was it rhapsodized as a peaceful, joyful retreat, but also it was christened as the hallowed ground for the dissemination of a selflessness that would purify the larger society.

Concurrent with their attempt to idealize woman's role as wife and mother, the sentimentalists sought to glorify the marital relationship. Addressing themselves to the bonds uniting wife and husband, they alternately presented frothy, beribboned, love letters and sacred intonements. Stowe assured the readers of *We and Our Neighbors* that the true tale of a wife's and husband's union was an intense, egalitarian devotion. "Intimate friendship—what the French call *camaraderie*," she proclaimed, was "the healthiest and best cement." At the same time, the bond, as a sacred responsibility, implied more than earthly intimacy and delight. Writing in the introduction to *My Wife and I*, Stowe described marriage as "the oldest and most venerable form of Christian union on record." Her chosen title, "My Wife and I," Stowe stressed, was to be construed as the "sign and symbol of more than any earthly partnership," as, instead, "something sacred as religion, indissoluble as the soul, endless as eternity—the symbol chosen by Almighty Love to represent his redeeming eternal union with the soul of man." Underlying these sentiments was the anticipation that wife and husband would perform in perfect harmony their respective duties within designated spheres. The superior, selfless woman set an example for her husband and nurtured her children, while the strong, reliable male absented himself from the family on a daily basis in order to provide for its support.

Seeking to promote the image of women as superior beings and wedded to their domestic dream, Stowe and the other sentimentalists openly presented models of correct behavior along with instances of idyllic family life. Stowe's preface to *Pink and White Tyranny* is typical of a group of writers who were anxious to instruct as well as entertain a readership that numbered in the hundreds of thousands and was largely female. Stowe did not hesitate to inform her audience that hers was "a story with a moral." Concerned that her message might elude obtuse readers, she took them by the hand and explained her none too subtle approach. Her readers were told that she had decided upon "the plan of the painter who wrote under his pictures 'this is a bear,' and 'this is a turtledove.'" For those who needed additional guidance there was yet her assurance that "We shall tell you in the proper time succinctly just what the moral is, and send you off edified as if you had been hearing a sermon." At other times, Stowe and her literary cohorts were less obvious, but there was no doubting their presence. Maneuvering behind the scenes, manipulating characters, and concocting incongruous endings, their presence was plain and their intent obvious.

The sentimentalists were directing their novels and stories to women not only because there was a vast, commercial, female market waiting for their fiction, but also because they had a message. As moralists they sought to prescribe standards of behavior for an entire society. Their demand for selfless behavior extended to everyone regardless of gender. But they presented and promoted woman as a distinct being, and charged her with the mission to reform society, both because they believed in her superiority and felt the need for a reformation of values, and because they found man inferior and wanting, just as wanting as the values they sought to change.

The heroine's self-discipline, her self-denial for the benefit of others, is proclaimed the behavior necessary to redeem society. Self-sacrifice and service to others were the dominant values. Man is the central, predatory villain in the fiction because he is perceived as the primary transgressor of these values. That all men in the novels and short stories are not evil incarnate tells us that the writers were not motivated by a vengeful hatred of men. Quite often it is the male who dispenses accolades to the sterling character of the heroine. In *Poganuc People,* Stowe's Dolly Cushing receives just such an accolade from her suitor, Alfred Dunbar: " 'She impresses me as having, behind an air of softness and timidity, a very positive and decided character.' " That character, that " 'sort of reserved force,' " is apparent in Dolly's defense of " 'everything high and noble.' " Nor did the sentimentalists think that every erring, sinning man was hopeless. The great encampment of reformed men confirms that conclusion; male tributes to women point to the source of reformation. Stowe's Mary Scudder is offered the typical paean by her fiance, James Marvyn, who proclaims, " 'It is only in your presence, Mary, that I feel that I am bad and low and shallow and mean, because you represent to me a sphere higher and holier than any in which I have moved, and stir up a sort of sighing and longing in my heart to come toward it.' " Reformed or not, however, man can never be woman's equal. Lest inferior man forget that fact, superior woman reminds him of it, as Stowe's Mara Lincoln in *The Pearl of Orr's Island* reminds her repentant lover, Moses Pennel, on her death bed, saying, " 'I have felt in all that was deepest and dearest to me, I was alone. You do not come near to me nor touch me where I feel most deeply.' "

Although the sentimentalists wanted to glorify woman's role as wife and mother, wanted to idealize marriage, indeed, sanctify the bond between husband and wife, they were touched with glimmerings of doubt about woman's place in the home and her relationship with her mate. Their skepticism, however, was seldom and imperfectly conceptualized, and never totally embraced. It is clear, too, that their doubts stemmed from what they observed and what they experienced concerning woman's situation in nineteenth-century America. Note, for example, Stowe's bewailing in *We and Our Neighbors* "that a large proportion of marriages have been contracted without any advised or rational effort." She was even more dismayed at "The wail, and woe, and struggle to undo marriage bonds, in our day. . . ." And, elsewhere, she alluded to man's shortcomings and his failure to fulfill the husband's responsibilities in the marital relationship. In querulous tones, she commented in *My Wife and I* that "In our days we have heard much said of the importance of training women to be wives. Is there not something to be said on the importance of training men to be husbands?" Her most despairing and poignant observation was a private one. "Women," she said in a letter to her brother, Henry Ward Beecher, "hold the faith in the world. [It is] the wives and mothers who suffer and must suffer to the end of time to bear the sins of the beloved in their own bodies."

Despite the sentimentalists' thousands of readers, despite their fiction's immense popularity, it is difficult to assess the fiction's actual impact upon that readership. It is critically important for historians to attempt to link prescription with behavior, but it is frequently impossible to develop correlations with any great precision. Historians can speculate, interpret, surmise, and arrive at fairly sound judgments. And, as has already been done, they can point to the importance of roles and family structure in determining the content and character of life for nineteenth-century women. But, as Daniel Scott Smith has aptly noted, "It is easier, for example, to describe historical attitudes toward women's proper role than to determine what the roles were at any given time." Smith himself has suggested a number of sources by which women's lives might be explored; those cited by him include manuscript lists, local history, and personal documents.

Particularly illuminating is the last approach. When available, letters, diaries, and journals offer the possibility of a sustained, intimate, recounting of actual experience as well as responses to that experience. Equally important, the examination of women's documents represents, as has been suggested by Gerda Lerner, a needed "shift from a male-oriented to a female-oriented consciousness." Not only does such an analysis reveal women's perception of reality but it also discloses how and why these perceptions differed from those of male contemporaries.

In the case of the sentimentalists, it is possible to go beyond an exploration of their fiction, if not to the lives of the readers, to the lives of the writers, themselves. Fortunately, several of the writers left a substantial body of personal papers. By examining their papers, we can gain insight into the crucial and complex relationship between socially accepted prescription and social behavior. The sentimentalists' personal opinions and ideas as well as moments of recorded behavior reveal the extent to which they internalized their own prescriptions and how they managed, if at all, to resolve the discrepancies and contradictions apparent in the fiction. Such an examination also provides a means for investigation and analysis of women's consciousness. Women can thereby be presented as they actually were: active, involved human beings coping, sometimes successfully, sometimes less so, with a rapidly changing nineteenth-century world; human beings striving to find a sense of identity within roles deemed appropriate for them and a familial institution increasingly isolated from the world beyond the four walls of the home.

Like the other sentimentalists, Harriet Beecher Stowe differed from most of her peers in that she achieved great success in a profession traditionally dominated by men—and achieved that success while publicizing women as superior to men. Involved in a demanding and lucrative career that required stepping beyond the doors of her home, Stowe provided a receptive audience with a seemingly endless stream of prose glorifying woman and the family. Nevertheless, as a woman, as a wife and mother, her own life frequently diverged from the ideal presented in her fiction. There was alternately ambivalence and tentativeness, confusion and conflict in her life, as there is in the lives of the heroines she paraded before her adoring public. Stowe's life symbolized the tension between an ideal to which the sentimentalists subscribed and a reality which they as women experienced. Stowe's own experiences were fraught with anxiety and uncertainty. At times, she maintained a relatively satisfying marriage, but signs of discord and friction are apparent in her relationship with her husband, and in her open admission concerning the heavy burden associated with the rearing of her children.

Stowe's relationship with her husband, Calvin, was marred by strain and doubt. In part, the difficulties stemmed from the frequent and lengthy separations that characterized the early years of a marriage that spanned more than half a century. From time to time, Stowe herself left the family for visits with various brothers and sisters. Much more frequently, Calvin, a teacher at Lyman Beecher's Lane Theological Seminary for half of his career, left Stowe and the children in order to recruit students, raise funds, and purchase books for the seminary. At different times, each of them spent at least a year at a water cure in Brattleboro, Vermont. Yet, the friction between them was rooted to a greater extent in disparate needs and conceptions of their relationship. Their correspondence tells a tale of longing in a double sense of the word. There, of course, was the longing for each other during the separations, but just as significantly, there was the longing for an unattainable relationship during their times together.

Just as Stowe was unable to sustain an ideal relationship with Calvin, so her attempt to create an idealized home met with frustration. The transfer of the Edenic, the perfect, home from the pages of her fiction to the reality of her life in the nineteenth century proved to be impossible. Try as she might Stowe could not create the idyllic home in which the serene and contented wife and mother presided over a refuge from a restless, transitory, society.

Ironically, she found such a home only as a visitor. Writing to Calvin during a short visit to her brother, Henry Ward Beecher, she described the Beecher's home as the "calm, placid quiet retreat I have been longing for. . . ." (Of course, she probably found her home ideal simply because someone else was meeting the demands of wifehood and motherhood.) Her own home mirrored the more unsettled, disrupted society; control of her own sphere remained elusive. To Calvin she fretted: "You have no idea of the commotion that I have lived in since you left." The endless litany of household duties to be performed and children to be cared for echoed through her letters. Always there was "the cleaning—the children's clothes, and the baby." The burdens on her, the tensions and apprehensions that tortured her, were equally apparent in Stowe's anguished dirge that everything in her home "often seemed to press on my mind all at once. Sometimes it [seemed] as if anxious thoughts [had] become a disease with me from which I could not be free."

Certainly as much as any of the sentimentalists, Stowe approximated the stereotype of woman as set forth in the fiction. She married, bore seven children, and considered her duties as a wife and mother more important than the demands imposed upon her as a writer. Invariably, Stowe gave a higher priority to guiding and restraining a husband who was a self-admitted "creature of impulse," and to rearing and supporting children who received "all [her] life and strength and almost [her] separate consciousness." Considered a means to an end rather than an end in itself, she envisaged her literary activity as yet another opportunity to serve her family and contribute to its welfare. In a letter written to one of her sisters at the beginning of her career as a writer, she expressed convictions that were to govern the rest of her life. Noting that she had received forty dollars for a "piece," she related that, "Mr. Stowe says he shall leave me to use [it] for my personal gratification." That she should do so she thought ludicrous—"as if a wife and mother had any gratification apart from her family interests."

Before she wrote *Uncle Tom's Cabin*, Stowe's literary endeavors were restricted to occasional short stories submitted to newspapers and magazines. So peripheral was her writing to her major involvement with wifehood and motherhood that she was surprised by Sarah Josepha Hale's request for biographical material to be used in *Woman's Record* and actually doubted that she ought "to rank among 'distinguished women.'" Appropriately, Stowe read Hale's letter "to my tribe of little folks assembled around the evening table to let them know what an unexpected honour had befallen their Mama." Her reply to Hale's request indicates the choices made and the proportionate energies expended. Reminding Hale of the "retired and domestic" life she had chosen, she told her that she was devoted to her family rather than to her writing: "I have been a mother to seven children—six of whom are now living—and . . . the greater portion of my time and strength has been spent in the necessary but unpoetic duties of my family."

Stowe's career as a writer changed radically with the publication of *Uncle Tom's Cabin*. Abraham Lincoln's witticism that she was "the little lady who made this big war" was a fitting characterization in the eyes of many. She quickly became a prominent figure. Her literary production increased and included nine additional novels along with innumerable essays. But her perspective on the importance of being a wife and mother remained the same. Despite her newly acquired prominence, the demands of her family still came first—sometimes to the extent that she was forced to curtail her writing. At one point she wrote to her publisher's wife, Annie Adams Fields, that she had temporarily ceased writing; in fact, she had "not been able to write a word, except to my own children." Writing metaphorically, she stressed that the varying needs of her children required that she "write chapters which would otherwise go into my novel." Yet another time her writing was restricted by the care given her husband during the long illnesses that preceded his death. That she considered his need legitimate and did not resent its impact upon her literary activities is revealed in a letter to their doctor: "I have him in my room nights and watch over him as one time in our life he used to watch over me. 'Turn about is fair play' you know."

Whatever earnings Stowe derived from her writings were used to meet the monetary demands of her family, and, as familial circumstances changed, those earnings became more crucial. Only a supplement prior to the early 1850s, her royalties provided major support for the family after the publication of *Uncle Tom's Cabin.* As early as 1853, Stowe's husband, Calvin, informed her that "Money matters are entirely in your hands, and no money is spent except in accordance with your judgment and that saves me a great deal of torment and anxiety." Having relieved himself of the obligation to manage the family's resources, Calvin had no qualms about transferring the duty to support the family. Throughout the 1850s, he reminded his wife to "think of your responsibilities— an old man and six children." Although it would have been equally superfluous, he could have added that she was also obliged to contribute to the support of her father and his third wife. Stowe's earnings became even more critical from the mid-1860s onward. Calvin retired from teaching in 1864 and became completely dependent upon his wife. With the exception of Georgiana, all of their children who survived to adulthood continued to rely upon their mother for support. The twins, Hattie and Eliza, who remained unmarried, lived at home; Fred who became an alcoholic required institutionalization and then support during his unsuccessful attempts at rehabilitation; and Charley who entered the ministry needed substantial aid after beginning his career.

Stowe's correspondence with various members of her family reveals her continuing need to juggle the private and public, the domestic and literary, to accommodate the needs of her family. Never questioning the legitimacy of their demands, her letters indicate her unwavering commitment to serve them—and they indicate, as well, the cost of that commitment. Stowe's letters to Calvin are replete with allusions to her dual responsibilities and with admonitions to him: "You must not expect very much writing of me for it drinks up all my strength to care for and provide for all this family—to try to cure the faults of all— harmonize all." She also pleaded with him "to *try* to be considerate and consider how great a burden I stagger under."

Alternating between sentimental effusions of affection and graphic descriptions of her financial difficulties, Stowe's letters to her children document her attempt to fulfill both roles simultaneously. Beginning one letter with the comment, "Let me tell you first how heavy is the weight which lies upon me," she hastened to inform Hattie and Eliza that she was providing daily income from her writing and also attempting to arrange the family's finances in order to secure "a higher income from our property so that we may have a solid and certain basis of two *thousand* a year to go on." That these were wearying challenges was obvious, but they seemed insignificant before the threatening prospect that "if my health fails all will fail." A later letter to the twins bemoans the fact that illness had interfered with her attempts to provide needed income from writing. Fully recognizing that "*all* the income that supports the family comes from my ability to labor at my pen," she found it particularly frustrating to be suffering from poor health when she was "beset with offers" for her fiction: "Mr. Ford who has sent me 300 for two stories in the South's Companion wants me to promise him another for the same sum. The Western Home sent a cheque for 100 and begs for an article—In short you see that my health just now is gold for my family." Just as Stowe dedicated herself to her daughters, she expected and received whatever aid they could offer. Together Hattie and Eliza became her housekeeper, secretary and amenuensis.

Stowe's obligations extended beyond those children who continued to share a home with her. Hoping that Fred's stay in an institution would end his alcoholism, she willingly bore the expenses. That failed attempt notwithstanding, she then proceeded to arrange various positions for her son. Investing $10,000 in Florida's Laurel Grove Plantation, she insured that Fred would be made overseer of the thousand acres devoted to the production of cotton. But she could not guarantee the cure of a son whose drunkenness remained habitual. Her final and equally unsuccessful effort involved an arrangement in which Fred helped in the management of her own orange groves in Mandarin, Florida. Stowe's unswerving commitment to her son, her continuing attempts to aid him were testimony to her devotion; her son's failure to rehabilitate himself was the most enduring sorrow of her life. Stowe also helped her son, Charley, and his wife, Susy, establish themselves in Charley's first parsonage in Presque Isle, Maine. When Charley considered moving for financial reasons, she offered to send them "$500, rather than have you make any change—or try any other place—I will back you up." Even after Charley had taken another position in Saco, Maine, Stowe advised them that "you may count on $300 a year from me a sum I calculate equal to houserent and fuel." At a later date, she gave them the $7,000 necessary for the purchase of a parsonage after they had settled permanently near Stowe's own home in Hartford, Connecticut. In contrast to Fred, Stowe's other son, Charley, was able not only to return her devotion but also to fulfill her desire that at least one son enter the same profession as her father, husband and seven brothers.

Through prescription and protest, Stowe, as a writer, performed in the service of improving woman's self-and-social image, and yet, as an individual, she was less a professional writer than she was a woman in the nineteenth century. Stowe did come to provide the primary financial support for her family, but her career as a writer remained secondary to her role as a wife and mother. Her family always came first, her fiction second. In fact, her struggle to succeed as a writer became part of a larger struggle to succeed with a marriage that

brought alternating suffering and satisfaction. Unlike the majority of her female contemporaries, she assisted her husband in his prescribed obligation to support the family. Her success in this endeavor was obvious. But Stowe's needs and expectations made her less successful in meeting the responsibilities of her role as a wife and mother. Calvin's demands came into conflict with her own desire to protect her sexual and emotional autonomy, and she found it necessary to deny her husband physically and emotionally. Her attempt to provide a model for her seven children, to mold and control human development, met with equally mixed success. Her efforts acquainted her as much with failure as with achievement, with grief as with joy. This is not to say that Stowe lacked sincerity and conviction in her attempt to promote the role of wife and mother as the ideal for woman. The zealous tone and didactic thrust of her prescriptions speak to that. It is to say that Stowe internalized her prescriptions, only too well.

Separated during nearly a third of the first fifteen years of marriage, Stowe's and Calvin's correspondence tells a story of a relationship continually beset with crisis. The separations themselves were a relatively minor part of the crisis—and at times proved to be beneficial. More important was the fact that each brought differing expectations to the marriage. Stowe was not content merely to achieve a satisfactory relationship with a husband. What she sought was an idyllic one in which both husband and wife shared intimately but acted autonomously. Unfortunately, she achieved far less. In contrast, Calvin, who had been left a childless widower little more than a year before his marriage to Stowe, sought to fulfill much more specific, more pragmatic needs. Initially drawn to Stowe because she had been the closest friend of his first wife, Calvin hoped that she would provide an end to his desperate loneliness, satisfy his sexual and emotional needs, and give him the children denied him in his first marriage. Rooted in disparate needs and desires, exacerbated by differing temperaments, their conflicts were inevitable. Stowe wanted to actualize the ideal relationships portrayed in the pages of her fiction, but Calvin's sexual and emotional demands were so intense and unremitting that her own autonomy was continually threatened. Again and again, she found herself hoping that the end of each separation would find him "indeed renewed in spirit," yet she wrote that she feared "that may not be so, and that we may again draw each other earthward." Letter after letter of Calvin's points to the impossible demands that would dash Stowe's hopes. Writing to her prior to their marriage, he foretold the immensity of his demands: "I will react upon all you have given me thus far, I will keep asking for more as long as I live (the fountain of that which I want is in you inexhaustible)."

The problem, of course, was that Stowe's reserves were *not* inexhaustible. To try to meet Calvin's physical demands meant not only disregarding the need to protect her health but also yielding her desire to control her reproductive function. To attempt to fulfill Calvin's emotional demands involved the risk of setting her own self adrift in the turbulence of Calvin's continually vacillating, volatile temperament. The problem, too, was that Calvin found it practically impossible to curb his demands. His loud and angry complaints reverberated through their correspondence, his emotional demands continued unabated. Faced off as if soldiers in combat they struggled to maintain both their own position *and* their marriage.

Calvin's letters harp upon his sexual needs. An extremely sensual person, Calvin repeatedly lamented that "my arms and bosom are hungry, hungry even to starvation." He recalled the times that he had "lain on the same pillow with you, your face pressed to mine, and our bare bosoms together," and practically cursed the celibacy enforced by their separations. His desire to "just step into your bedroom . . . and take that place in your arms to which I alone of all men in the world ever had a right or ever received admission," nearly drove him into a frenzy. A devoted but markedly more restrained Stowe did not respond with the same passion. Determined to control the number and spacing of her chil-

dren, Stowe saw their separations from a different perspective. Certainly she was sincere in writing that "I have thought of you with much love lately—a deep tender love—and I long to see you again." But she was also aware that the most effective method for controlling fertility, abstinence, was inherent in separation.

Stowe's and Calvin's differing perspectives, their conflicting needs and desires, were brought into sharpest relief during their times together. Calvin was not willing to deny himself in his own bedroom, while Stowe remained bent upon serving her own interest through restriction of their sexual involvement. Their sexual relationship provides a means for the examination of various hypotheses concerning the decline in fertility during the nineteenth century. These hypotheses have pointed to either the female or the male as the primary determinants. Daniel Scott Smith has argued that the female tended to be the controlling party. Women, as Smith has termed it, were practicing "domestic feminism" and thereby exercising significant power and autonomy within the family. In contrast, Gerda Lerner has noted that the lowered birth rates can be attributed just as easily to the male's desire, motivated by economic considerations, to limit the number of children in his family.

The evidence from Stowe's and Calvin's correspondence suggests not only the complexity of sexual relationships but also the tenuousness of broad generalizations about the most intimate of human experiences. In their unabating sexual tug-of-war, neither Stowe nor Calvin emerged unscathed, or victorious. Clearly, Stowe wanted to engage in domestic feminism. But just as clearly her struggle to control her fertility was only partially successful: she gave birth to seven children and suffered at least two miscarriages. The cost was great for both of them. Theirs was an irresolvable conflict in an age in which sexual relations were always shadowed by the threat of pregnancy. Sexual denial limited intimacy; sexual gratification led to child after child. For them at least the conflict heightened the tensions between them—and not only fueled Calvin's resentment and anger but was also an important factor in Stowe's decision to escape from him (and the hostility) by spending an entire year away from her family.

Stowe's decision to try the water cure in Brattleboro, Vermont, in the mid-1840s, was determined by a growing invalidism. Her sickliness was hardly unique. The high incidence and variety of female invalidism in the nineteenth century has led a number of historians, Kathryn Kish Sklar and Carroll Smith-Rosenberg, in particular, to interpret sickliness as a response, albeit a negative one, to the role of wife and mother. The woman who became an invalid effectively shed a role that demanded unremitting concern for others. In turn, she became the center of attention. Her individual needs became dominant. Simultaneously, she made herself unavailable sexually. She no longer had to act to restrict her sexual relationship or bear the responsibility for that act.

Stowe's invalidism was fed from manifold sources, physical and psychological. She no doubt sought to rest a body battered by at least two miscarriages, drained and worn by the demands of family chores. Her journey away also promised a retreat from the tension engendered by psychological conflict, as well as sexual, by the psychological demands associated with bearing and rearing children. And it offered the opportunity to contemplate in relative repose unfulfilled ideals. Most certainly, Stowe would have agreed with her husband that their conflicting needs were "Bringing us both to the grave by the most lingering and painful process." Recalling that Stowe had been "so feeble, and the prospect of permanent paralysis [had been] so threatening" during the winter prior to her departure for Vermont, Calvin admitted that he was resigned to their separation. Nevertheless, he informed her that he himself had fallen into a species of invalidism, had been in "a sad state physically and mentally" that winter, but the cure he proposed for himself meant the end of their separation and promised a recurrence of Stowe's invalidism: "If your health were so far restored that you could take me again to your *bed and board*, that would be the surest

and safest, and indeed the only infallible way." In the end, they could not help each other: one's needs clashed with the other's; one's cure brought the other's illness.

Inevitably, the separation had a different effect upon each of them. Stowe had sought the water cure only after her condition had worsened. She could therefore envision absence from husband and children not as abandonment but as separation necessary for her eventual restoration to them. She could rationalize that she was continuing to serve them rather than herself. Her psychological conflicts resolved, the water cure brought relief from the burdens of domesticity, a supportive environment that was predominantly female, and physicians sympathetic to her maladies. It also brought a welcome respite from Calvin's demands. The separation intensified rather than assuaged Calvin's sexual longings, and it re-introduced loneliness. Letter after letter written by Calvin refers to their sexual relationship and his desire for her. Brimming with anger and frustration, he recounted the one week that he had joined her in Vermont. Their separation had made him all the more eager to see her; yet he still had to deny himself during this interlude. He had enjoyed their visit, had been satisfied to "see that you do love me after all." But that satisfaction had been severely limited by the "mean business of sleeping in another bed, another room, and even another house, and being with you as if you were a withered up old maid sister instead of the wife of my bosom." He concluded that "of all contemptible things the most unutterably intolerable is *having the love of marriage and denying the power thereof.*"

Other letters indicate that Calvin almost preferred separation to the practice of abstinence when with his wife. In one letter written after Stowe had been away for ten months, he told her that "much as I suffer from your absence, I should suffer still more from your presence, unless you can be in a better condition than you have been for a year past." Why would the presence of someone to whom he was devoted bring pain and frustration? Calvin bluntly reminded his wife that "It is now a full year since your last miscarriage, and you well know what has been the state of things both in regard to yourself and me ever since." A few months later he had changed his mind and stated emphatically "I want you to come home." Why the reversal? What would he expect with her return? A sentence or two later he revealed his hope that her return would bring an end to his celibacy: "It is almost in fact eighteen months since I have had a wife to sleep with me. It is enough to kill any man, especially such a man as I am."

Stowe did return shortly. She would write to Calvin that she was "better but not well." She would compare herself to "a broken pitcher that has been boiled in milk, that needs very careful handling, or it will come to pieces again." Inevitably, the conflict between them would continue. Calvin no doubt continued to lament any restrictions on their sexual relationship. And Stowe, her devotion to her sons and daughters notwithstanding, must have had some misgivings about the two children that crowded the end of her childbearing years.

Forced to curb his sexual demands, Calvin openly advanced others. Freely admitting that "my good feelings are quiet and silent and my ill ones urgent and obtrusive," Calvin's temperament alternated between an irritating excitability and an equally trying despondency. He relied upon Stowe to help him achieve a more stable, calmer state. Her absences made him "go bamboosing about like a hen with her head cut off, because you are not here to be a balance wheel to my emotions." That Stowe found it difficult to cope with Calvin's mercurial temperament is obvious from her letters to him. Pointing to his "hypochondriac morbid instability" in letter after letter, she anguished about the unhappiness he caused her and begged him to try to relieve this source of strain in their marriage. Calvin might not be able to control either his moodiness or its toll upon his wife but his absences did provide at least temporary relief. Unlike Calvin, Stowe admitted to a certain ambivalence about the end of their separations. Her description of the typical reconciliation made that ambiva-

lence understandable: "You will love me very much at first when you come home and then, will it be as before all passed off into months of cold indifference [?]"

Stowe was also very conscious of the pain, suffering and burdens entailed in the rearing of children. She freely gave of herself and suffered much as a consequence of her attachments. Her approach to Hattie and Eliza, was both affectionate—and efficient. Perceiving herself as a model, she did not hesitate to advise and instruct them in a self-confident manner exuding strength and expecting the same from them. They would never know, she wrote, how much she loved them "*till* you love someone as I do you—you have educated me quite as much as I you—you have taught me the love of God—by awakening such in me." The devotion of parents was "all giving—the child can neither understand nor return it—but the parent is learning by it to understand God." Yet she was also conscious of the trials of parenthood. Writing to Calvin, she noted that Hattie's and Eliza's "tempers are very trying to me." She and Calvin "must bear with all the impatiences, excrescencies and disproportions." Of course, Calvin's frequent, lengthy absences while engaged in professional activities meant that Stowe bore most of the burden herself.

There was as much love and pain involved in the raising of her sons. Despite a distaste for liquor inherited from a father who had been a prominent agitator for temperance, Fred's alcoholism elicited a deep and tolerant sympathy in his mother. Replying to their criticisms of Fred, Stowe wrote to Hattie and Eliza, "If God had not meant us to pass through exactly this form of trial there were many ways for him to prevent it—but *just this and no other is our cross*." Instead, she urged her daughters to adopt the more heroic, demanding posture, prescribed in the pages of her novels and short stories: Hattie and Eliza "should remember how young men are tempted and tried [and] feel that instead of casting them off you who lead pure and sheltered lives ought to try to rouse their noble natures and influence them to good." Henry

Ellis' death at the age of nineteen led her to write that "between him and me there was a sympathy of nature a perfect union of mutual understanding." He was "the *lamb of my flock* [and she] *rested* on him as on no other." His death also reminded her that she loved her children "with such an *overwhelming* love."

Written a few days before their eleventh wedding anniversary, a letter of Stowe's to Calvin is indicative of her marital experiences, symbolic of her hopes and disappointments. Recognizing that she was "a very different being" at the outset of their marriage, she recalled her total desire "to live in love, absorbing passionate devotion to one person." The first time she and Calvin were separated was her "first trial." Comfort came with the prospect of motherhood: "No creature ever so longed to see the face of a little one or had such a heart full of love to bestow." That experience, however, proved to be agonizing: "Here came in trial again sickness, pain, constant discouragement—wearing, wasting days and nights . . ." In all of Stowe's marital experiences there was much disappointment, much agony. She noted retrospectively that hers and Calvin's very different characters made "painful friction inevitable." After eleven years, the damage had been done and the cost counted in Stowe's admission that, "I do not love and never can love with the blind and unwise love with which I married." Stowe's love was blind because it knew little of human inadequacy; unwise because it asked too much. Had she the choice of a mate to make again she would choose the same, but she would love "far more wisely." Hers was the comment of a matured, chastened individual who had come to recognize the disparate needs and expectations brought to the marriage by each of them. Stowe's attitude toward motherhood suggested greater regret. She had wished for much, but felt she had received little: "Ah, how little comfort I had in being a mother—how all that I proposed met and crossed and my way ever hedged up!" In despair, she was even brought to thank God for teaching her "that I should make no family be my chief good and portion." Neverthe-less, for the remaining half century of her life her family remained her primary and fundamental concern.

Not only does Stowe herself serve as a case study of the tension engendered between an ideal and a less felicitous reality, but her experience sheds light upon important questions concerning women in the nineteenth century. For example, in addressing themselves to the implications of the nineteenth century's glorification of woman's nature and role, historians have sought to determine not only the benefits women might have derived from being considered different from men in more than a biological sense, but also what difficulties they might have encountered in striving to fulfill the role as the creator of a family utopia.

Stowe located the idea of female distinctiveness in the context of self-sacrifice. In a woman's selflessness was her superiority and means for her fulfillment. In *Pink and White Tyranny*, Stowe told her female readers that, "Love, my dear ladies, is self-sacrifice; it is a life out of self and in another. Its very essence is the preferring of the comfort, the ease, the wishes of another to one's own for the love we bear them. Love is giving, not receiving." The efficacy of such a doctrine was obvious. As the major practitioner of self-sacrifice, woman was the logical candidate for spiritual and moral leadership. The embodiment of selflessness, she should be its primary teacher. In one sense, the doctrine served Stowe well. It rationalized her denial of self for husband and children and gave her a sense of purpose. That she perceived her role as a writer as secondary and supportive is thoroughly documented in her writings and reflected in her own life. She firmly believed that it was the duty of woman to devote herself to her husband and children, and she was gratified that she could meet their monetary as well as emotional demands. Simply, the role of wife and mother provided the focus for her life. Envisioning herself as a model, she strove to actualize the selflessness preached in the pages of her fiction. The members of her family were the primary beneficiaries.

But while Stowe subscribed to the ideal set forth in the sentimentalists' fiction, and to a certain extent fulfilled that ideal in her life, her personal papers indicate that her own experience as a wife and mother was riddled with the same tensions, ambiguities, and conflicts that characterize the negative strains in the novels and stories. Her commitment to wifehood and motherhood made her captive to an ideal that in many respects she was unable to realize in her own life. Her hopes that Calvin would become an ideal partner were doomed to disappointment. Her children were as much a burden as a source of satisfaction. Neither Calvin nor the children were transformed into models of selflessness. And the family together struggled not so much for perfection as survival. Stowe also confronted the limitations inherent in her doctrine of self-sacrifice. If she wished to stand as a model of selflessness, she simultaneously wanted to act as an autonomous individual. But frequently she had to place the needs and desires of her husband and children first, rather than her own. Rather than develop an autonomous identity she had to merge hers with theirs. In this dilemma, too, she symbolized the plight of nineteenth-century womanhood.

ARTICLE

Benevolence and Antislavery Activity among African American Women in New York and Boston, 1820–1840

Anne M. Boylan

The cult of true womanhood, a white, middle-class, feminine ideal, was not originally meant to apply to women of color. That did not mean, however, that black women were unaffected by its prescriptions. During the nineteenth century, Afro-American women in cities like New York and Boston banded together whenever they could to establish benevolent and self-help societies and to try to reform society. In her article, Anne Boylan describes the activities of these women, compares and contrasts their efforts with those of white women, and assesses how participation in the activities of benevolent and reform

Source: Reprinted from Anne M. Boylan, "Benevolence and Antislavery Activity among African American Women in New York and Boston, 1820–1840" in *The Abolitionist Sisterhood: Women's Political Culture in Antebellum America*, edited by Jean Fagan Yellin and John C. Van Home. Copyright © 1994 by the Library Company of Philadelphia. Used by permission of the publisher, Cornell University Press. Notes omitted.

organizations contributed to the construction of a black feminine ideal in the 1820s and 1830s.

How did gender influence the benevolent activities of these women? In what way did race and class affect their definition of femininity?

The formation of women's antislavery societies in the 1830s brought black and white women together in an unprecedented fashion. Although white women's benevolent groups had existed since the 1790s, almost none accepted African Americans as clients, let alone as members. Instead, white women generally restricted their organizations to serving "the virtuous poor" of their own race and religion. When free black women organized independent associations, beginning in the 1820s, the realities of white racial exclusivity and desperate need among the black poor guaranteed that they would have neither white clients nor white members. Interracial antislavery societies represented a new departure in the history of both black and white women's organizing.

The ideal of cross-racial cooperation to end slavery often proved elusive, and attempts to achieve it were extremely controversial. Occasionally, they evoked violent reactions among northern whites, such as the 1835 mobbing of the Boston Female Anti-Slavery Society and the burning of Pennsylvania Hall during the Anti-Slavery Convention of American Women in 1838. What enraged the rioters in these instances was the behavior of white female abolitionists, not black. When white female abolitionists engaged in public agitation and figuratively embraced free black women, their opponents conceived images of racial "amalgamation" and presumed their loss of all claims to feminine virtue. Although some women's societies, such as the Ladies' New York City Anti-Slavery Society, tried to sidestep controversy by choosing only white officers, most women's antislavery groups defied public opinion on this matter. African American women were active members and leaders of many female antislavery societies and of the three antislavery conventions of American women held between 1837 and 1839.

Nevertheless, ideals of feminine respectability were very powerful in the antebellum North, and they took a toll on black women. Unlike white women, who enjoyed the presumption that they were "virtuous" until proven otherwise, free black women were uniformly slandered as "degraded" (that is, sexually promiscuous) because of their race. By forming their own organizations African American women could challenge the slander and also create an autonomous organizational tradition. Yet such activity also exposed them to the scrutiny of whites and heightened the expectations of African American men that women could do much to uplift the entire race. The organizational experiences of free black women in New York and Boston during the 1820s and 1830s illustrate their enormous resourcefulness in meeting family and community needs and their vulnerability in the face of white racial attitudes and gender conventions. Even within mixed-race groups such as female antislavery societies, their participation was constrained by attitudes and conventions that they had little power to control.

African Americans began to organize for mutual assistance and benevolent purposes immediately after the first emancipations in the Northeast. (In Boston, emancipation came overnight, as a 1783 judicial decision ended slavery in Massachusetts; in New York, it was a long, slow process that began in 1799 but was not completed until 1827.) Migration patterns, together with the end of slavery, brought increased numbers of free blacks into urban areas, creating the bases for the formation of separate black churches and institutions. By 1841, when a survey counted some thirty-three black benevolent societies, New York had a free black population of over sixteen thousand. Boston's considerably smaller African American population (about two thousand in 1840) supported at least three churches and a coterie of organizations. Free black women initially devoted themselves to aiding the fledgling churches that relied on their work and fund-raising abilities and to supporting the masonic orders and mutual aid societies that free black men had begun to create in the 1780s and 1790s. By the 1820s, however, separate women's groups had begun to multiply.

These organizations resembled the myriad societies formed by other Americans, black and white, female and male. Their organizers wrote constitutions and bylaws, chose officers, met regularly, raised funds, and established programs. But the proliferation of such groups in the 1820s and 1830s suggests that black women, like white women, experienced a consciousness of gender that made separate organizations seem desirable. African American women's groups fell into the same broad categories of benevolence and reform as white women's (although, as we shall see, the distinction between benevolent and reform activity often evaporated quickly). Benevolent societies concentrated on the needs of black women and children, particularly widows and orphans, or did fund-raising for religious purposes. New York's Female Branch of Zion, attached to the African Methodist Episcopal Zion Church, aided sick church members, buried the dead, and helped support the orphaned children of deceased members. A second Zion Church group, the United Daughters of Conference, raised money to support the ministry, as did the Female Education Society at the First Colored Presbyterian Church. Reform organizations, such as temperance and antislavery groups, sought broad social change.

But most black women's benevolent organizations addressed the needs of members and their families as well as those of the church and other community institutions, thus differing from comparable white women's groups. Literary and educational societies were important sources for self-education and self-improvement, although some also raised funds for children's education or promoted the training of young black men as ministers. Members

of Boston's Afric-American Female Intelligence Society, for example, met to discuss literature or their own essays, thus improving their reading, writing, and speaking abilities. That the group's president, Elizabeth Riley, signed legal documents with a mark, not a signature, suggests how resourceful and how needy some organizers of literary societies could be. The society also collected books for a library and brought in guest lecturers for the members' edification. Mutual aid societies, by far the most common organizations of free black women, united individuals who contributed small sums on a regular basis in return for sickness or death benefits. The payment of seventy-five cents every three months entitled members of New York's Abyssinian Benevolent Daughters of Esther Association to two dollars per week sick benefits for up to six months. Offering a small measure of insurance against illness or other personal catastrophe, mutual benefit societies were far more numerous among black than among white women. By creating such groups, African American women expressed a belief that they alone could meet certain needs, particularly women's needs, and they also showed faith in their collective ability to address the enormous problems faced by all free blacks.

Such beliefs fit the dominant gender conventions of northern free blacks in the early nineteenth century. As James Oliver Horton has noted, these conventions emphasized differences between the sexes, not similarities. Newspapers, sermons, and organizations, the major sources of prescriptive attitudes, propounded the message that women were, in Horton's words, "the gentler sex, naturally more moral, more loving, more caring than men." Yet the admonitions to free black women—to guide but not nag men, to take a secondary role in family and community life, and to be nurturing and submissive—resonated differently from similar warnings directed to white women, because black men's ability to be providers and patriarchs was severely compromised by racial discrimination. Except in menial occupations or in a few trades where black men had a foothold, jobs were hard to come by. For women, the range of occupations was even narrower; in addition, they faced uneven sex ratios (women outnumbered men in both cities) and high rates of widowhood. Education was no guarantee of occupational success, and hard-won economic prosperity could be wiped out overnight, as New York's African Americans discovered in 1834 when white mobs who descended upon their neighborhoods made property holders specific targets of their fury. Unable to take women's dependence upon men as a given, free black women had to assume multiple roles as wage earners, educators, and community builders. At the same time, they believed it necessary to bolster black men's tenuous claims to social power whenever possible.

To be sure, some black women's organizations bowed to gender conventions. A few groups owed their existence to men's sponsorship, as did some white women's missionary societies. New York's African Dorcas Association, formed in January 1828 to provide clothing for pupils in the city's African schools, developed at the prompting of the Manumission Society, a white men's group that sponsored the schools. A black minister chaired the African Dorcas Association's initial meeting, and Charles C. Andrews, a white teacher in the African boys' school, presented the women with a written constitution for their approval. Although the female members elected their own officers and met weekly to sew at the home of their president, Margaret Francis, seven black ministers, one from each African church in the city, formed an advisory committee that scrutinized their activities. The advisory committee (with the aid of three white businessmen) not only received all donations for the Dorcas Association but had the authority to call annual meetings as well. Boston women also observed convention when they met with male temperance advocates in 1833. After an address from a male speaker, "the ladies retired to the School Room for the purpose of forming a Temperance Society," reported the *Liberator,* "and the gentlemen remained in the House for the same purpose."

Both these women's groups followed accepted practices for mixed-sex audiences. Similarly, when New York's Female Assistant Benefit Society met in 1838, its officers and members merely sat in the audience while the featured speaker, a young Henry Highland Garnet (later to be famous as a black nationalist orator), delivered a speech. Sharing the podium with Garnet were three other African American men: Henry Watson, who chaired the meeting, the Rev. J. D. Richardson, who offered the prayer, and F. Reynolds, who read the group's constitution. (It was the women, though, who had raised $360 that year and made 765 charitable visits.) Using the services of male "advisors," as the African Dorcas Association did, was also a common practice among white women's benevolent groups; many institutionalized the practice by appointing formal "Committees of Gentlemen" during the 1830s, 1840s, and 1850s.

Gender conventions and ritual practices aside, however, the deferential posture evident in these examples was unusual. More often, black women defied stereotypes of female behavior and the pronouncements of powerful men about how to channel female humanitarianism. Among white women, only reform group members such as antislavery and antiprostitution crusaders, whose numbers were small compared with the mass of organized women, exhibited similar defiance. (And even some of those women submitted to such critiques of female public speaking and political activity as that of the Congregational Association in 1837.) In black women's circles, however, inviting women to speak or hosting both male and female speakers was accepted practice. The 1832 anniversary orator of the recently organized Afric-American Female Intelligence Society was Maria W. Stewart. The following year, the group heard from the Congregationalist minister Amos A. Phelps, whose wife, Charlotte Brown Phelps, was the first president of BFASS. In announcing their fifth annual gathering, New York's Daughters of Abyssinia specified that "the meeting will be addressed by several distinguished speakers, both male and female."

This pointed announcement came in September 1837 on the heels of the Congregational Association's critique of women's public speaking and four months after the group's participation in the first Anti-Slavery Convention of American Women. These women clearly did not intend to be constrained by white ministerial rules. Black women's benevolence, unlike white women's, often blended seamlessly with reformist work aimed at ending slavery. In yet another challenge to established rules, at least one organization, the Boston Mutual Lyceum, organized in 1833, had a mixed-sex membership. In this literary society, one of the two vice-presidents and two of the five managers were women.

Black women's own visions for their organizations can be viewed most clearly through the names they chose, the programs they pursued, and the rules they established. Given the importance of naming in African and African American cultures, we can assume that organizational names were not chosen lightly. Like black men, free black women commonly selected "African" for association titles (African Dorcas Association, Afric-American Female Intelligence Society), although "colored" (as in Colored Female Charitable Society) came into more frequent use in the 1830s among both women and men as a protest against efforts to colonize slaves and free blacks in Africa. The term "African" expressed racial pride, "Afric-American" proclaimed an American identity in the face of colonization efforts, and "Abyssinian" (as in Abyssinian Benevolent Daughters of Esther Association) harked back to a glorious past while also echoing the name of New York's premier black Baptist church, Abyssinian Baptist.

Unlike black men, who favored classical names for their groups, such as New York's Phoenix Society, New York's and Boston's Philomathean societies, or Boston's Adelphic Union, black women chose gender-conscious titles. Many contained allusions to the Old Testament (for example, New York's Daughters of Israel), reflecting the singular importance of the story of Israel's captivity and deliverance in black Christianity. Others infused a specifically female element into black Christianity by recalling the notable women of the Old Testament. The Abyssinian Benevolent Daughters of Esther Association in New York had a name calculated to bring to mind the courageous actions of Esther (also called Hadassah in the Book of Esther), who in saving the Jews from annihilation became a symbol of heroic resistance against persecution. Such names conveyed an image of black womanhood that was strong and redemptive.

Only occasionally did black women choose New Testament names or names without distinctive racial content. The title of the African Dorcas Association recalled the woman described in the New Testament as "full of good works and acts of charity," whose name white women also employed for sewing societies. It is likely, however, that the men who created this group, not the women themselves, chose its name. Boston's Garrison Society, a literary group, and New York's Juvenile Daughters of Rush, an African Methodist Episcopal Zion Church organization, honored individual men by their titles: William Lloyd Garrison, the white abolitionist, and Christopher Rush, the black Zion Church supervisor. New York's Female Mite Society and Female Assistant Benefit Society carried names that might just as well have belonged to white women's organizations, as did the Female Literary Society. But even without racial markers, black women's groups were usually easy to distinguish from white women's groups. A title such as "Society for Employing the Female Poor" or "Association for the Relief of Respectable, Aged, Indigent Females" invariably designated a white women's organization. Black women did not use organizational titles to set themselves off from potential clients (although they were not averse, as we shall see, to establishing morality tests for membership). Instead, black women's associations blended benevolence, mutual aid, self-improvement, community service, and social reform in ways that defied easy categorization. As a result, black women's benevolence reflected their special situation as women within highly vulnerable free black communities.

Even groups that on the surface appeared to be strictly benevolent in focus sustained this unique character. The African Dorcas Association, with its Wednesday sewing meetings and numerical accountings of garments distributed, looked for all the world like any other "fragment" society, dispensing aid to people of a different social class. But the association's benevolence was directed toward the members' neighbors and friends and toward their children's schoolmates, not toward an abstract category of "the poor." Maria De Grasse, one of the association's managers in 1828, undoubtedly could afford to clothe her fifteen-year-old son Isaiah for classes at the African Free School. Her husband, George De Grasse, ran a provisioning business on Orange Street, and Maria, like most women in the free black community, probably did remunerative work too. Her labor for the association aided those of Isaiah's classmates who could not afford decent clothing. But Maria never knew when she might need help herself; she had a three-year-old son, John, who would soon attend the African Free School and might some day need clothing. Economic security was often evanescent for families like the De Grasses; endemic racial discrimination and a volatile economy meant that running a business or even owning property seldom offered protection from destitution. Maria De Grasse's work for the African Dorcas Association could be termed "benevolent," but among women whose middle-class status was extremely tenuous, benevolence often resembled mutual assistance. The resemblance existed in other benevolent organizations as well, such as New York's Female Mite Society and Female Assistant Benefit Society, or Boston's Colored Female Union Society and Colored Female Charitable Society.

Black women's literary societies combined not only benevolence and mutual aid but also abolitionism and self-improvement. In addition to buying books for a library and engaging lecturers like Maria W. Stewart, Boston's Afric-American Female Intelligence Society made provisions to aid members experiencing "any unforeseen and afflictive event" by agreeing to visit them when sick and furnish monetary assistance ("one dollar a week out of the funds of the Society as long as consistent with the means of the institution"). Members of New York's Ladies Literary Society, while seeking to "acquir[e] literary and scientific knowledge" for individual and collective advancement, used their resources to raise funds for the New York Vigilance Committee, a men's group that assisted runaway slaves. At the 1837 Anti-Slavery Convention of American Women in New York, the society pledged five dollars to support a petition campaign directed at the abolition of slavery in Washington, D.C. The women of Boston's Garrison Society, a literary group, made sure that African American girls learned their multiple responsibilities early. By sponsoring a Garrison Juvenile Society, the women encouraged schoolchildren to do useful sewing, save (in the words of a sympathetic white observer) "the money they would otherwise have spent for candy, &c.," and promote "the 'improvement of the mind' and the cultivation of the virtues of industry, fidelity, frugality, self-respect, propriety of deportment, &c., &c." To do so, the women knew, was to counteract negative stereotypes of free blacks and aid the cause of emancipation, because self-improvement promoted the welfare of all African Americans. Indeed by the late 1830s even church fund-raising groups connected their efforts to the attack on slavery by carefully advertising that all items sold at church fairs would be "the product of FREE LABOR."

The intertwined concern with self-improvement, mutual aid, and abolitionism so typical of literary societies was also evident in the lives of individual members. Henrietta Green Regulus Ray, president of the New York Ladies Literary Society from its inception until her death in 1836 at the age of 28, had also served as secretary of the African Dorcas Association; several members, including Maria W. Stewart, who joined after her arrival from Boston, and Matilda and Sarah Jennings, were also active in abolitionist causes. In Boston, the lives of Jane Putnam, Margaret Scarlett, Susan Paul, and Lavinia Hilton exhibited similar patterns of involvement. They all were officers in a women's temperance society founded in 1833; Putnam and Hilton also served as officers of the Garrison Society and lent support to abolitionist activities, and Scarlett and Paul helped lead BFASS. Indeed, during her brief life (she died of tuberculosis at age 32), Susan Paul pursued a teaching career (including managing a well-known African American children's choir) helped support her deceased sister's four children, and held offices in the women's temperance group, BFASS, and the 1838 Anti-Slavery Convention of American Women. She also assumed personal responsibility for combatting racial prejudice by, for example, publicly reporting her humiliation at the hands of a white coach attendant who refused to take her as a passenger. Jane Putnam and Margaret Scarlett opposed discrimination, as well, by signing a petition protesting segregated schooling in Boston.

Both in naming their organizations and in undertaking specific organizational programs, African American women behaved differently from their white counterparts. Black benevolent societies, unlike white, provided services to family, friends, and neighbors, as well as to strangers. Well aware that this month's dispenser of aid might be next month's recipient, black women's groups did not, like middle-class white women's organizations, assume that those who gave and those who received would come from different social classes. And because self-help could not be separated from the advancement of their race, members of black mutual aid societies did not, like the working-class white women who formed such societies, restrict themselves primarily to mutual assistance.

Yet in their membership rules and practices, African American women were neither inclusive nor democratic. Many groups adopted exclusionary practices that reinforced existing status distinctions within the free black community. Requiring high dues was one such practice. Members of Boston's Afric-American Female Intelligence Society were assessed twelve and a half cents per month,

or one dollar and fifty cents per year, an amount well beyond the pocketbooks of most free black women. Moreover, missing a monthly meeting brought a fine of six and a quarter cents. New York's Abyssinian Benevolent Daughters of Esther Association levied dues of seventy-five cents per quarter, or three dollars per year, an amount comparable to the annual subscription fee for most white women's groups. Dues were necessary, of course, if the organizations were to have any funds to dispense, but those charging high dues clearly limited their membership to the more affluent women in the community. In this way, such groups, although taking a less hierarchical approach to benevolence than white women's organizations, still established class standing as a precondition for joining.

Why they did so must be understood in the context of other forms of exclusion practiced by the organizations. Most common were ritual announcements that members must be "of good moral character," but some societies were very specific in their strictures. New York's Abyssinian Benevolent Daughters of Esther Association excluded from membership "any person addicted to inebriety or having a plurality of husbands," and refused to provide aid to members who became ill as a result of "immoral conduct." Nor could pregnancy be used to claim any benefits. In a similar fashion, Boston's Afric-American Female Intelligence Society warned that sick benefits would be denied to members "who shall rashly sacrifice their own health." Such scrutiny of other women's characters and personal circumstances also existed in middle-class white women's groups, but it was characteristically applied to an organizaton's clients, not its members.

These regulations revealed a focus on propriety and appearances in the thinking of organizational leaders, as well as very practical concerns about guaranteeing the solidarity and financial stability of the organization. Because free African American women leaders, like their male counterparts, usually had some access to property and education, they felt the need to protect scarce resources amid desperate poverty. They therefore developed criteria to measure their own and others' social class standing. By clarifying the attributes potential members would need in order to join the organization, group regulations defined middle-class behavior, including monogamy, education, temperance, religion, and self-control. Middle-class white women stipulated such detailed standards only for potential clients. For example, white widows expecting assistance from the New York Society for the Relief of Poor Widows with Small Children were required to be "of fair character" (a quality determined by a home visit from one of the society's managers), to put children over ten years of age out to service, to abstain from liquor, and to avoid "vicious habits." Only working-class white women who formed temperance mutual aid societies in the 1840s imposed similar standards of conduct on their own members; they hoped to protect their organizations from economic disaster and to promote female unity.

But there were other reasons why organized black women felt they had to be extremely careful about appearances and behavior. They knew that racist stereotypes made them, like their slave sisters, vulnerable to sexual and moral debasement. How could they counteract white stereotypes except by careful attention to their own dress, language, and behavior, and by policing the behavior of their sons, brothers, and husbands? "Sensible of the gross ignorances under which we have too long labored," commented the founders of Boston's Afric-American Female Intelligence Society, the group would work "for the diffusion of knowledge, the suppression of vice and immorality, and for cherishing such virtues as will render us happy and useful to society." Prescriptive literature written by black men (themselves people of education and property) reinforced the expectation that women would explode negative white stereotypes of free African Americans. "We are all . . . branded with the epithets of vicious, degraded, and worthless," wrote an editorialist in the first issue of the New York *Weekly Advocate;* it was up to women to "exert all their power to dis-

abuse the public mind of the misrepresentations made of our character." That they should do so by adopting certain standards of public behavior was clear from the praise and scorn handed out to two groups by the editors of New York's *Freedom's Journal* in 1829. Commending the African Dorcas Association, Samuel Cornish and John Russwurm noted that "they have no annual processions; they have no blazing banners, pharisee-like to proclaim to the world the nature of their work." Unlike the Daughters of Israel, a mutual relief organization that evoked the ire of Cornish and Russwurm for organizing "a female procession, dressed in the full costume of their order," the African Dorcas Association conducted its business in an unobtrusive and decorous fashion.

Concern about public perceptions shaped the exclusionary rules that some organizations adopted. Intended for the gaze of outside observers as well as for potential members, behavioral rules might deflect the prying white eyes that were ever ready to judge, evaluate, and condemn black actions. But as women, organization members also faced potential hostility from within their own community, as Maria W. Stewart discovered when she spoke in public on religious subjects. Despite the long tradition of "women preaching and mixing themselves in controversies," she conceded, she was wearied by the "prejudice," "opposition," and "contempt" she had encountered from her own people. Because they assumed responsibility for racial "uplift" and community maintenance, members of black women's organizations felt pressure to prove their respectability, both from white racial hostility and from black gender conventions. Unlike white women, especially of the middle class, black women could not presume that they would be seen as "virtuous" simply because they were women. Unlike black men, they had no special claim on leadership roles among their own people.

The experiences of these free black women illuminate the complex ways in which race and gender intertwined to shape their autonomous organizations. On the one hand, African American women flouted the conventions of feminine respectability that so often restricted white women: by speaking in public, forming mixed-sex organizations, or combining benevolent and reform activities. Just as they assumed multiple roles in family and community life, free black women created organizations that were more multi-faceted than comparable white groups. Both Margaret Scarlett, for example, who belonged to Boston's black women's temperance society and to the Boston Female Anti-Slavery Society, and Hester Lane, former slave, manager of the African Dorcas Association, and nominee for the Executive Committee of the American Anti-Slavery Society, readily combined benevolence with reform work. But in their dealings with whites, these same women often had to prove the respectability of their characters; in their dealings with African American men, they sometimes had to accept subordinate roles. In 1838, for example, the all-male New England Temperance Society of Colored Americans refused to consider admitting women to membership because the society's president, John T. Hilton, whose wife Lavinia was treasurer of a Boston women's temperance group, opposed the proposal.

When black women's organizational activities intersected with white women's, the power of both racial prejudice and ideals of feminine respectability became clear. In New York, white women ran Sunday schools and infant schools for black children, as well as the Colored Orphan Asylum and the Ladies' New York City Anti-Slavery Society. Despite the financial support provided to the orphanage and to the 1837 Anti-Slavery Convention of American Women by individuals and by black women's church groups, the leadership of both the Association for the Benefit of Colored Orphans and the women's antislavery society remained in white hands. Indeed, as Amy Swerdlow has noted, LNYCASS was so hostile to black involvement that Angelina Grimké privately condemned its "sinful prejudice" in having "hardly any colored members . . . [and not admitting] any such in the working S[ociet]y" and publicly alluded to

the society's color prejudice in her *Appeal to the Women of the Nominally Free States*. Grimké considered "forming an Anti Slavery Society [*sic*] among our colord sisters & getting them to invite their white friends to join them"; eventually, black women pursued precisely that course, forming the Manhattan Abolition Society in 1840. In Boston, by contrast, African American women were active as members, officers, and fund-raisers for the female anti-slavery society and the Samaritan Asylum for Colored Children. The differences between Boston and New York are explicable not by external factors such as antiabolitionist mobs, which existed in both cities, but by the attitudes of white women abolitionists. Where the white leaders of female antislavery societies cultivated the involvement of black women (as in Boston and Philadelphia), black women abolitionists participated; where white women abolitionists were fearful of or hostile to black involvement (as in New York), black women were excluded. Either way, African American women's participation depended in part on white sufferance.

Even white abolitionists who were very supportive could be judgmental of their black co-workers. Anne Warren Weston's comment that Susan Paul had been chosen to represent BFASS at the first Anti-Slavery Convention of American Women because she was "a favorable specimen of the coloured race" revealed Weston's class and color prejudices. On occasion, African American women themselves made similar judgments, arguing that the most "worthy," "industrious," "respectable," or "wealthy" among them suffered the most from racism. Rather than challenge critics who classed all black women as degraded, both white and black women sometimes tacitly accepted their critics' terms by attempting to prove their virtue.

Issues of gender, race, and social class shaped the work of all women's organizations in the early nineteenth century. In varying ways, black and white women's organizations confronted questions of how much they could do, whom they would assist, and whom they would accept as members. African American women's decisions molded multifaceted instruments of benevolence, mutual assistance, self-help, and social reform that differed materially from the single-focus groups of white women. Excluded by virtue of their race from white conventions of feminine respectability, African American women were more adventurous in speaking out on public issues, combining abolitionism with community uplift, and challenging the pronouncements of male leaders. Nevertheless, in their relations with African American men and in their interactions with white women abolitionists, black women activists encountered barriers of gender, class, and color that also affected their organizations. African American women never endorsed standards of feminine respectability as fully as did white women. But insofar as they adopted those standards in order to establish their claim to feminine virtue, they found themselves constrained by narrow definitions of appropriate behavior.

Suggestions for Further Reading

Jeanie Attie, "Warwork and the Crisis of Domesticity in the North," in *Divided Houses: Gender and the Civil War,* ed. Catherine Clinton and Nina Silber (New York: Oxford University Press, 1992), 247–59.

Linda J. Borish, " 'Another Domestic Beast of Burden': New England Farm Women's Work and Well-Being in the Nineteenth Century," *Journal of American Culture,* 18 (Fall 1995), 83–100.

Jeanne Boydston, *Home and Work: Household, Wages, and the Ideology of Labor in the Early Republic* (New York: Oxford University Press, 1990).

Lee Virginia Chambers-Schiller, *Liberty, a Better Husband: Single Women in America, The Generations of 1780–1840* (New Haven, CT: Yale University Press, 1984).

Frances Cogan, *All-American Girl: The Ideal of Real Womanhood in Mid-Nineteenth-Century America* (Athens: University of Georgia Press, 1989).

Nancy F. Cott, *The Bonds of Womanhood: "Woman's Sphere" in New England, 1780–1835* (New Haven, CT: Yale University Press, 1977).

Nancy F. Cott, "Young Women in the Second Great Awakening in New England," *Feminist Studies,* 3 (Fall 1975), 15–29.

Hasia R. Diner, *Erin's Daughters in America: Irish Immigrant Women in the Nineteenth Century* (Baltimore, MD: The Johns Hopkins University Press, 1983).

Ann Douglas, *The Feminization of American Culture* (New York: Avon, 1977).

Blanche Glassman Hersh, "The 'True Woman' and the 'New Woman' in Nineteenth-Century America: Feminist-Abolitionists and a New Concept of True Womanhood," in *Woman's Being, Woman's Place: Female Identity and Vocation in American History,* ed. Mary Kelley (Boston: G. K. Hall, 1979), 271–82.

Ronald W. Hogeland, " 'The Female Appendage': Feminine Life-Styles in America, 1820–1860," *Civil War History,* 17 (June 1971), 101–14.

James Oliver Horton, "Freedom's Yoke: Gender Conventions among Antebellum Free Blacks," *Feminist Studies,* 12 (Spring 1986), 51–76.

Joan M. Jensen, *Loosening the Bonds: Mid-Atlantic Farm Women, 1750–1850* (New Haven, CT: Yale University Press, 1986).

Mary Kelley, *Private Woman, Public Stage: Literary Domesticity in Nineteenth-Century America* (New York: Oxford University Press, 1984).

Susan Levine, "Labor's True Woman: Domesticity and Equal Rights in the Knights of Labor," *Journal of American History,* 70 (Sept. 1983), 323–39.

JANET A. NOLAN, *Ourselves Alone: Women's Emigration from Ireland, 1885–1920* (Lexington: University Press of Kentucky, 1989).

NANCY GREY OSTERUD, *Bonds of Community: The Lives of Farm Women in Nineteenth-Century New York* (Ithaca, NY: Cornell University Press, 1991).

MARY P. RYAN, *Cradle of the Middle Class: The Family in Oneida County, New York, 1790–1865* (New York: Cambridge University Press, 1981).

CARROLL SMITH-ROSENBERG AND CHARLES ROSENBERG, "The Female Animal: Medical and Biological Views of Woman and Her Role in Nineteenth-Century America," *Journal of American History*, 60 (Sept. 1973), 332–56.

CHRISTINE STANSELL, *City of Women: Sex and Class in New York, 1789–1860* (Urbana: University of Illinois Press, 1987).

BARBARA WELTER, "The Cult of True Womanhood, 1800–1860," *American Quarterly*, 18 (Summer 1966), 151–74.

SHIRLEY J. YEE, *Black Woman Abolitionists: A Study in Activism, 1828–1860* (Knoxville: University of Tennessee Press, 1992).

CHAPTER SIX

MASCULINITY IN THE NINETEENTH-CENTURY SOUTH (1820–1890)

MANHOOD IN THE AMERICAN SOUTH

In public spaces all over the former Confederacy, there are images of southern white men carved in stone or cast in bronze, standing on pedestals or astride horses. On the campus of the University of North Carolina in Chapel Hill, "Silent Sam," a figure quite literally bigger than life, looks out onto Franklin Street over the heads of passersby. Twenty or so miles away in Raleigh, a similar figure, no less impressive in size and demeanor, dominates a space on the lawn in front of the state capitol building. These figures are of indeterminate age; they are uniformed; and they are armed. They stand straight and tall, heads held high, chins up, shoulders thrown back, and feet solidly on the ground. Those they represent marched off to war for many reasons. Some of them wanted to preserve slavery. Others wanted to protect the rights of their state against the intrusive power of the federal government. Some fought to protect their families and their property from the depredations of invading federal troops. And still others were bored and simply sought adventure. Whatever their "cause," they all fought under the Confederate flag because to one degree or another they thought it was the honorable, "manly" thing to do under the circumstances.

The men who fought for the Confederate cause came from every walk of life. Some of them were shopkeepers and others were skilled artisans. But most of them were farmers of one sort or another. Some of them grew rice, indigo, tobacco, or grain. Others raised livestock. But the crop that was the most profitable was cotton. Once there was a gin to remove the tiny seeds that were deeply embedded in the fluffy, white bolls of short staple cotton, fortunes were just waiting to be made. And southern men, as concerned as their northern brethren with making their fortunes, proceeded to make cotton "king."

Largely missing from the landscape of the South are memorials to African-American and

Native-American men. They were also tied to the land. And some of them also grew cotton. But their ability to express their manhood in their own way was inhibited by the dominance of the white men in their midst.

Throughout the nineteenth century, manhood in the South was defined by race. Native Americans expressed their manliness in a cultural context that made them increasingly dependent upon the willingness of white men to respect their claim to the land as provided for in federal treaties. African Americans, whether they were free or slave, expressed their manly identities in a cultural context characterized by a legal system of bondage. And the masculine identities of white southerners, no matter what their social class, were defined by their ability to control those who were not white. Thus, the gendered identities of all southern men were inextricably intertwined.

SOUTHERN PLANTERS AND THE MASCULINE IDEAL

When we think of southern planters we tend to think of gentlemen of taste and refinement who owned vast amounts of land, exploited the labor of large numbers of slaves, depended upon overseers to actually run their plantations, and lived in gracious splendor in large pillared mansions. But in reality, most southern planters were relatively uneducated and sometimes crude and boorish, had modest holdings of real estate, owned as few as twenty slaves, managed their own plantations, and had little leisure time. But whether a man owned a grand estate or was a planter of more limited means, his white skin combined with his ownership of land and slaves served as the basis for his manly identity, authority, and power.

Planters were as preoccupied as their northern brethren with making money. But their view of work and leisure differed both from men who lived in the North and from yeoman farmers who were their neighbors. Among the southern elite, manliness was measured by the degree to which a man could avoid physical labor. It is true that small planters worked from dawn to dusk along side their slaves in the fields. But the need to perform physical labor was considered demeaning by those who could hire overseers to run their plantations or use one of their slaves as a driver. The work of a large planter was largely supervisory. Thus, his manliness was measured in his ability to make sure that some one else carried out his orders. The bottom line, then, was that manliness among planters was defined by a man's ability to effectively exploit slave labor, grow crops of high quality, and time the sale of those crops on a world market in order to maximize profits.

Central to the construction of masculinity among white men in the South was the concept of honor. The southern code of honor demanded that a man be willing to sacrifice his life, if necessary, to defend his reputation or that of his family and community. The shame and humiliation that accompanied the failure to do this was considered emasculating. A man's identity under such circumstances was dependent upon and confirmed by the good opinion of others. The result was that southern men in general and southern planters in particular were extremely sensitive to what was said to them and about them.

In order to conform to the demands of the code of honor, men on occasion had to respond to real or perceived insults by demanding "satisfaction" either in the form of an acceptable apology or in the form of a duel. The conflict between Andrew Jackson and Charles Dickinson helped to set the pattern for conducting affairs of honor during the period between the American Revolution and the Civil War.

The duel between these two men began with a horse race. Jackson liked to brag about the speed of his stallion Truxton. So in the fall of 1805, he and Joseph Ervin arranged for Truxton to race Ervin's Plowboy. The stakes were high—$2000 payable on the day of the race and $800 forfeit if either of them canceled. One day before the race, Plowboy went lame. So Ervin paid the forfeit fee in bank notes.

Shortly thereafter, one of Jackson's friends claimed that Jackson had accused Ervin of trying to pay his forfeit in notes of questionable value. Ervin's son-in-law Charles Dickinson heard the allegations and, determined to protect the honor of his wife's family in general and that of his father-in-law in particular, took exception to them. During the winter of 1805–1806, Jackson and Dickinson sent letters back and forth discussing the alleged insult and the Nashville *Impartial Review* published statements regarding the controversy. In May, Dickinson angrily published a statement calling Jackson "a worthless scoundrel" and "a coward." Jackson issued a challenge, and the two men met to fight it out. Dickinson, reputedly one of the best shots in Tennessee, wounded Jackson but did not kill him. Jackson, bleeding but still standing, cocked his gun and shot a bullet straight through Dickinson's body. The twenty-seven-year-old Dickinson died a short time later.

The extended ritual of letter writing that Jackson and Dickinson engaged in while trying to clarify precisely what had been said and by whom usually resulted in the acceptance of an apology. Most matters of honor never came to blows. But however affairs of honor were resolved, southern men considered them critical to preserving their manly self-esteem, dignity, and public reputations.

Another important dimension to the expression of manliness among planters was their ability to preserve their authority as heads of their households. Being able to control every member of his household was critical for perpetuating the system of slavery upon which a planter's identity rested. If a man could not demand and elicit the obedience of his wife and children, it was unlikely that he would be able to control his potentially rebellious work force. Whether he ruled his home with an iron hand or a velvet glove, planters knew how difficult it was to establish domestic authority.

Southern planters were no less ambivalent about women than men who lived in the North. Their manly identities were tied to their ability to successfully court a woman, marry her, set up housekeeping with her, and sire children with her. In short, men needed women. At the same time they were aware that however much a woman might need a man to support her, she could humiliate him by publicly rejecting his advances, exposing him as sexually inadequate, squandering his resources, ignoring his wishes, and disobeying his orders. The power of women was, then, very much connected to the southern code of honor. It lay in their ability to shame men. One male response to this reality was to reduce their sense of dependence on women by treating them as ornaments or decorative figures on pedestals, thus trivializing them. Another was to engage in sexually promiscuous behavior as testimony to male independence. Any planter who owned female slaves had both the power and ample opportunity to force his attentions on any one of them any time he chose. Indeed, the southern diarist Mary Boykin Chesnut noted that "Like the patriarchs of old, our men live all in one house with their wives and their concubines; and the mulattoes one sees in every family partly resemble the white children. Any lady is ready to tell you who is the father of all the mulatto children in everybody's household but her own. Those, she seems to think, drop from the clouds."

Rich southern planters liked to think of themselves as gentlemen. But the degree to which they could lay claim to gentility varied. The standards for judging that claim lay not so much in how much property a planter owned but how he behaved. Gentility demanded a man hold himself to high moral standards and ethical behavior, at least in public. It took a smattering of education, including an acquaintance with the classics, to qualify a man as a southern gentleman. Whether he was seated at the dining table, drinking in a tavern, or betting around a gaming table, at a cock fight, or at a horse race, a southern gentleman's geniality, generosity, and conversation set him apart from other men in his midst.

Planters regarded themselves as natural political leaders. And when they decided to run for political office, they expected to be elected.

They dominated the practice of law and took for granted their political significance. Thus, the manliness of southern planters was as much tied to their political power as it was to their wealth and social status.

MANLINESS AMONG THE PLAIN FOLK OF THE SOUTH

It is difficult to say anything very definitive about the way southern yeoman farmers and herdsmen viewed themselves as men. Few left the kind of introspective records, such as diaries and letters, upon which historians depend. Many of them were illiterate. Even a rudimentary education was hard to come by in the antebellum South since there was no public school system comparable to that in the North. So our understanding of their masculine ideals derives more from our knowledge of their circumstances and behavior than from what they might have thought about the matter.

Yeoman farmers were not slave owners and had no direct financial interest in preserving slavery. But slavery was as much a social system as it was an economic one, and non-slave owners did have a vested interest in preserving a social system that defined whiteness as the ideal and privileged whites over those who were not.

Yeoman farmers, like planters and northern farmers, tied their identity as men to ownership of land and the sense of self-sufficiency and autonomy that land ownership gave them. The difference between them and slave-owning planters was that they worked the land themselves with the help of their wives and children. Physical labor in no way undermined their sense of manliness. Like farmers in the North, they took pride in their strength and stamina and in the knowledge and skill it took to run their farms and produce food to feed their families and a surplus to sell in the marketplace.

Yeoman farmers also derived status and manly self-esteem from their relationships with the planting elite. In many cases, they were re-lated by marriage. Planters and yeoman farmers were also economically dependent upon one another. Yeoman farmers sold planters surplus food and homespun made by their wives. And they sometimes rented out the use of their wagons or mules during harvest time. Planters ginned the yeoman farmers' cotton and occasionally rented out their slaves to them. When farmers met planters at the local general store, they spent time socializing—discussing the weather, crops, and politics. And when they both gathered for Fourth of July celebrations and militia musters, they drank with each other as they went about their business. A yeoman knew that whatever the differences in wealth or status that might separate him from the big planters in his county or parish, planters could not afford to take their farming neighbors for granted. Indeed, yeoman farmers felt that they held in the palms of their hands the careers of planters who aspired to become politicians. Both the planter and the yeoman farmer felt it was in their interest to protect the sanctity of property, to maintain social order by controlling the slave population, and to prevent the government from intruding on their lives. So while the southern yeoman recognized that he was not the equal of the local planters, his manly identity was based on his belief that, at the very least, he was entitled to their respect.

Given this situation it is not surprising that men in the yeoman farming class, like the planting elite, based their identities on their conformity to the demands of the southern code of honor. They were no less sensitive to insult and no less likely to demand satisfaction when they felt that their honor had been impugned. But they were somewhat less disciplined in expressing their anger than planters, whose masculinity was in part measured by the degree to which they could restrain themselves long enough to accommodate the requirements of the code duello. Yeomen were far more likely to demand instant satisfaction than they were to engage in the kind of lengthy negotiations that usually preceded a duel between two gentlemen.

There were, of course, men in the yeoman class who eschewed the violence that characterized the expression of manliness in the South. Those who underwent conversions during the revivals of the Second Great Awakening, like northern evangelicals, were more likely to equate manliness with moral uprightness, piety, sobriety, and simple living than they were to concern themselves with matters of honor. From their point of view, it was more God's judgment than the opinion of their neighbors that was important to a man.

Evangelical religion also legitimized the domestic authority of southern white men, yeoman and planter alike. The church may have welcomed everyone to join in what one minister called "the household of faith," but that household was both hierarchical and patriarchal. Even though in some areas female church members outnumbered male church members two to one, men reserved for themselves the right to run church affairs. Whether they were Methodist, Baptist, or Presbyterian, they typically chose their ministers, admitted new members, and disciplined old ones. Religious support for the maintenance of male power carried over to the domestic realm. Evangelicals admonished men to assert themselves as heads of their households and expected male church members to assume responsibility for the moral lapses of their dependents. Despite the fact that yeomen did not own slaves, they were masters over women and children and were free to exploit their labor. It was that mastery and the power and authority that accompanied it that helped to make them "men."

Backcountry herdsmen, sometimes known as "Crackers," tended their cattle or hogs on the unsettled land found in the southern sand hills, piney woods, or mountains. Unlike farmers, they did not have to perform very much manual labor and generally did not own land. All that was necessary to put food on the table and a roof over their heads was to go fishing or hunting or to mark their livestock, set it loose, then round it up, and sell it. They rarely bothered to build barns to shelter their animals and expected their livestock to forage for food. Their days were characterized by leisure and the pursuit of pleasure. They had plenty of time to train their hunting dogs, drink with their friends, and place wagers on cockfights or horse races. They spent their time sitting on their front porches, visiting their neighbors, chewing tobacco, playing music, talking for hours on end, and fighting for the fun of it. Their masculine identities were not tied to industriousness, the accumulation of wealth, or self-improvement. Instead, they took manly pride in their independence and self-sufficiency as well as their knowledge of the land, woods, and rivers and their skill in the use of weapons.

MANLINESS AND FREE MEN OF COLOR

Free black men were an anomaly in the antebellum South. As we have seen, some masters freed their slaves after the Revolution because they were unwilling to live with the tensions and intellectual inconsistency of espousing freedom and human equality on one hand and living off the labor of slaves on the other. As the nineteenth century progressed, white Southerners became more and more fearful of potential slave rebellions, and state legislatures made it more and more difficult to free slaves. Nevertheless, there were enclaves of free blacks all over the South. In such communities, black men were theoretically able to choose their own occupation, could expect to be paid for their services, and could marry and rear families as they wished. But despite their freedom, there were a number of restrictions on their ability to define themselves as men within that context. Because of the hostility of whites toward them, free black men found their civil rights limited. In many places they could not testify in court, own a gun, gather together except to worship God, or move about freely. It was also difficult for them to make a decent living. Whites were often unwilling to sell land to free blacks. And without their own land, they sometimes had to work side by side with slaves. Freedom meant that they could form permanent relationships with free black women. But if they were unlucky enough to fall in love with an enslaved woman, their emotional wellbeing was in the hands of her owner, and their children were her owner's property. White women were, of course, completely off limits as objects of their affections. A free black man was also limited in his ability to protect his wife and family. Ultimately, his liberty was tenuously dependent upon the willingness of whites to respect and protect it. The threat of being sold back into slavery was an ever-present one. A black man's ability to maintain his freedom might well depend upon the support of a white sponsor who was willing to testify to his good reputation. Under such circumstances, it was virtually impossible for a free black man to base his manliness on the principles of independence and autonomy.

There were a few black men, however, who did manage to make a good life for themselves. One of the most notable and the one about whom we have the most information is William Ellison. Ellison was certainly not a typical free black man, but his story serves as a example of how an exceptionally skilled, hardworking, and resourceful free black man in the antebellum South created his masculine identity within the limits imposed on him by a fundamentally hostile environment.

Ellison was born a slave in 1790 in South Carolina. Having been instructed in the construction and repair of cotton gins, he was an extremely valuable skilled laborer. He was able to purchase his freedom at the age of 26. Once he was a free man, he went to court to change his name from the name given him as a slave, which was April, to a name of his own choice, William. He moved to Stateburg, S. C., where he set himself up in business as a gin repairman. Honest, reliable, and deferential to whites, he prospered and accumulated enough money to buy and free his wife and one of his children. He eventually set up his own gin manufacturing business, bought his own slaves, invested in land, and purchased a fine home.

He never forgot, however, the tenuousness of his hold on freedom and the degree to which it was dependent upon the good will of whites and their need for his services. Despite the fact that he belonged to a black elite, he was subjected to special taxes and unending humiliations because of the color of his skin. Demanding payment for services that he performed for whites was a delicate matter, for example, and he approached those who owed him money with great trepidation. Self-disciplined, shrewd, and resourceful, he and other members of the black elite not only preserved their freedom, but also flourished partly because they were few in number and partly because they exhibited qualities such as piety, honesty, sobriety, and deference—qualities that reassured whites that they posed no serious threat to racial relations.

Despite his wealth and the fact that he was a free man, Ellison was forced to define his manliness within parameters determined by his race. He was more autonomous as a free man than he had been as a slave, but when his white customers decided not to pay their bills he was not in a position to do much about it. And his deference to his white neighbors may have been based more on his fear of them than on his respect for them. During the antebellum period, white men had almost complete control over their wives and children not only because they controlled their families' material resources but also because asserting one's power as the head of the household was considered essential in a culture determined to preserve a system of slavery. Ellison was the head of his household because he was able to support his family. He could base his manliness on the ownership of both real estate and slaves. But because he was a black man, he did not have the same kind of legal remedies for protecting his property or his wife and children that his white neighbors had. Charging a white man with theft or suing a white man for non-payment of debt was risky business for a black man. Even more difficult was trying to protect his wife and daughters from the unwanted sexual advances of white men.

Like all free black men in the South, Ellison had to create his gendered identity within a context characterized both by freedom that confirmed his masculinity and powerlessness that undermined it.

MANLINESS IN THE SLAVE QUARTERS

We have already discussed the degree to which enslavement was an emasculating experience (see chapters 2 and 3). The whole point of slavery was to deprive enslaved men of their humanity and, thus, their ability to define manliness in their own way. Nevertheless, male bondsmen did what they could to formulate their own definition of what it meant to be a man. They participated in such activities as gambling, trafficking in stolen goods, and competing for the affections of women. They took pride in their work even though they did not benefit directly from it. They spent their free time fishing or trapping in order to provide food for their families. They built furniture or contrived household implements to make their homes more comfortable and domestic work easier. They valued the idea that men should support and protect the members of their families even if their condition as slaves made fulfilling that obligation difficult if not impossible. Some asserted their right to express their individualism by plaiting their hair or wearing distinctive clothing. Others accepted their master's wish that they convert to Christianity but adapted it to their own needs and expressed their religiosity in distinctive ways. Religion provided slave men with the opportunity to preach and, therefore, to assert themselves as leaders in the slave quarters. The position of preacher was an honored one and carried with it great prestige and authority. Still others resisted the control that white masters and overseers had over them by working slowly, breaking their tools, feigning illness, running away, or appropriating the property of their masters.

For every long suffering "Uncle Tom" willing to forgive his tormentors, there were others who insisted on asserting their manhood by trying to control their lives and exhibiting aggressive behavior toward anyone who attempted to limit that control. Some men were physically intimidating enough to refuse to be disciplined or whipped. Others, both desperate and courageous, participated in open rebellion.

Nat Turner was one such man. Born a slave in 1800, Turner was an intelligent child who somehow managed to teach himself to read the Bible. Eventually able to convince other slaves that he had been chosen by God as a prophet whose destiny it was to end slavery and usher in the millennium, he led a slave revolt in Southampton County, Virginia, in August, 1831. The rebellious slaves killed about sixty white men, women, and children before they were captured and executed. Nat Turner's expression of manly aggression was prompted by a specific set of religious beliefs. But there were other black men who did not need authorization from God to resort to violence in order to confirm their manliness. Enslaved men had few ways to exhibit manly courage publicly. But open rebellion was one of them.

Because they viewed their slaves as property rather than as human beings, white planters would never have acknowledged that their bondsmen had a sense of honor. But the actions of Nat Turner and all of the other slaves who in one way or another resisted the physical, psychological, and emotional abuse heaped upon them by their condition of servitude belie that notion. Slaves developed their own set of standards to judge what did and did not constitute honorable behavior. Lying to one's master or stealing from the supply room, for example, were not necessarily dishonorable acts from a slave's point of view. Indeed, such acts could enhance their reputations in the slave community because they allowed slave men to better fulfill their manly obligation to protect and provide for themselves and their families. It is true that slavery inhibited a man's opportunity to defend his honor and preserve his self-esteem. But the gendered identity of an enslaved man was as much tied to the desire to avoid shame and humiliation as that of his master. It was only the context within which he did so that was different.

MANLINESS AMONG NATIVE AMERICANS

As we have seen in the previous chapters, as white settlers continually pressed westward, Native American men found it increasingly difficult to preserve their traditional definitions of manliness. By the nineteenth century, experience had shown that Native attempts to resist white settlement usually resulted, at the very least, in the loss of their land. Nevertheless, some Native American men attempted to preserve their masculine identities and their traditional way of life by doing just that. Taking pride in their skill as warriors, they attempted, unsuccessfully as it turned out, to stem the tide of white migration. Others moved their families ever westward in an effort to avoid having to associate with whites. Yet another alternative was to assimilate, a process that demanded that native men accept definitions of manliness that were often inconsistent with their traditional gender conventions.

Among those who tried this last alternative were Native American men who lived in the Southeast. Many of them gave up their roles as hunters and warriors, signed peace treaties with the federal government, and made a concerted effort to accommodate white culture and "civilize" themselves. The Cherokees were perhaps the most successful in this effort. By the 1820s Cherokee men had established a form of constitutional government on their reservation. They had created a written language, invited Christian missionaries to educate them and their families, and begun to cultivate private farms sometimes with the labor of African-American slaves. Those who did so defined their manliness not so much by their skill in hunting or their bravery as warriors but by their success as hardworking

farmers. This required a considerable shift in what constituted masculinity since farm work in Cherokee society had traditionally been done by women. A few Cherokee men, like John Ross, accumulated vast fortunes and built beautiful homes. They spoke English, dressed in fashionable clothing, attended Christian churches, and presided over households that were arranged very much like those of white southern planters. Most of those who assimilated, however, were yeomen farmers whose masculine identities were tied to land ownership, their ability to provide food, clothing, and shelter for their families, and participation in the political life of the reservation.

Unfortunately, adapting native ideals of masculinity to conform to white standards did not bring them the peace they had hoped. When white settlers began to encroach on the Cherokee reservation, the state of Georgia refused to protect Indian land claims. And when these "civilized" Indians, behaving like "civilized" men, turned to the courts to protect their right to the land, President Andrew Jackson refused to honor the Supreme Court's decision in favor of the Cherokee. He ordered federal troops onto Indian reservations to round up the inhabitants, shackle them together, and physically remove them to territories further West. In what the Indians eventually called the "Trail of Tears," thousands of Cherokee men, women, and children died on the march to their new reservations in the 1830s. There the quest of a great many Native American men for a gendered identity consistent with their new circumstances continued far from their ancestral homes.

THE CIVIL WAR AND DEFINITIONS OF MASCULINITY IN THE SOUTH

The Civil War was a defining historical moment for the construction of masculinity among southern men, both black and white. The war and the period of reconstruction that followed it were humiliating experiences for white men no matter what their social class.

The opposite was true for black men. Between 1861 and 1877, those who had been slaves were able to define and express their manliness within an exhilarating and unfamiliar context of freedom protected by the presence of federal troops.

After the firing on Fort Sumter in Charleston in 1861, ordinary white southern men rushed to enlist in the Confederate army in order to prove their manliness on the field of battle. Those in the planting elite applied for commissions as officers, went to their tailors to have their uniforms made, cleaned their guns, outfitted their horses, and recruited others to join in the fighting. Some white southern men, of course, stayed at home to serve the Confederacy in other ways. They formed a home guard to protect the property of their neighbors and control the slave population, and they shifted from the production of cotton to the production of supplies for the army. But however they chose to fulfill their obligations to the Confederacy, they were convinced that the war would be a short one and that southern men, trained from childhood to handle weapons and ride horses, could easily defeat the Union army. The southern definition of manliness was tailor made for warfare.

The Civil War tested confederate soldiers in much the same way that it tested those who served the Union. For young southerners, it was a coming-of-age experience. It provided them the opportunity to leave home and initiated them into a world of men largely devoid of female influence. Those who unflinchingly faced the enemy and emerged from battle unscathed claimed the right to consider themselves "men." More mature southern men, like their northern counterparts, experienced the war as an ordeal of manhood. Military life and combat tested their skill in the use of weapons and their physical, psychological, and emotional strength. But in the end, only victory could really affirm their self-esteem and sense of honor.

Victory was elusive on both the civilian and the military level, however. Those who remained on the land found it increasingly difficult to confirm their manliness by rais-

ing money for the confederacy, sending the army supplies, and controlling the movement of slaves. When the war began they lost the market for their cotton in the North. And the Union blockade cut off their access to overseas markets. To make matters worse, the Confederate government increasingly interfered with the way they ran their plantations by telling them what to produce and whom to sell it to. As the war progressed, planters began to lose their social and political influence over non-slaveholders, who were becoming increasingly resentful about the sacrifices they were expected to make to protect the slave property of their more affluent neighbors. Planters also found it increasingly difficult to discipline their slaves and prevent them from running off. When their slaves did escape, they had to roll up their shirt sleeves, get their hands dirty, and work the land themselves with the help of their wives and children. As the war progressed, the leisure, autonomy, authority, and power that had once served as the basis for the masculine identities of southern planters slowly eroded.

The war was an even more humiliating experience for those who served in the Confederate military. Four years after the war began, with vast numbers of their comrades lying dead and buried, they had to admit defeat and surrender to an enemy they had once held in complete contempt. They returned home having failed to defend their homes and preserve the Confederacy to find their families barely scraping by. Their fields were neglected. Some of their homes had been burned to the ground. Planters found their wealth gone and their slaves free. Most of them still had their land, but they had no one to help them tend their crops. Relative poverty undermined their domestic authority, deprived them of whatever leisure that they had previously enjoyed, and made extending hospitality to their friends and neighbors problematical. Defeated on the field of battle, they had to stand by helplessly watching occupying federal troops reestablish public order. By 1865, the context within which white men of the South had once constructed their manly identities had changed dramatically. They would spend the post-war period trying to adjust their ideas about what constituted manliness to conform to their new circumstances.

During the period after the war known as Reconstruction, southern white men found it increasingly difficult to express their manliness in traditional ways. The Radical Republicans in Congress tried to deny men who had participated in the rebellion the right to vote or hold office and passed laws giving the federal government the right to confiscate the land of those who had rebelled. At the same time, Congress passed the thirteenth, fourteenth, and fifteenth amendments to the Constitution guaranteeing freedom, citizenship, and voting rights to ex-slaves. Many former confederates found themselves at least temporarily deprived of political power, economically disadvantaged, and unable to exert much control over freed blacks. So between 1865 and 1890, white men in the South tried to reconstruct their sense of manliness by regaining their political influence, by stabilizing their work force, and by reestablishing a social system that would confirm their sense of racial superiority.

The Civil War and the period of reconstruction that followed it were also defining experiences for southern black men since they broadened the parameters within which black men could express their manhood. Slaves did not wait until they were formally emancipated to test the limits of their enslavement. As federal troops began invading the South, masters and mistresses began complaining that their slaves had become insolent and disrespectful. And as more and more men left to serve in the army, slaves began slipping away from plantations. Some sought refuge behind Union lines and became as dependent upon the good will and generosity of the federal government as they had once been on their masters and mistresses. Others enlisted in the Union army, took up arms, and fought to liberate their enslaved brethren or worked for wages in the army as blacksmiths, stevedores, teamsters, or

guides. Still others simply walked away from their plantations and fended for themselves, finding food, shelter, and employment where ever they could. But whatever they did, they did it by choice rather than by compulsion. For the first time in their lives, they were able to experience freedom of movement and the sense of manly independence and autonomy that accompanied it.

The Emancipation Proclamation, which freed some of the slaves, and the thirteenth amendment, which freed all of them, increased opportunities for black men to make choices about where they would live, whom they would live with, what their relationship to those people would be, and what they would do for a living. Like most white men, ex-slaves equated manliness with land ownership. Many freedmen hoped that the federal government would provide them with forty acres and a mule so that they could become self-sufficient and self-respecting yeoman farmers. But that hope never materialized. Some freedmen were able to accumulate enough money to buy land of their own. Others moved west to places like Kansas where land was available for little or nothing. But most simply did not have the resources to move, so they remained in the South. Whether they remained or not, they based their manly identities on the belief that a man had the right to work or not as he chose and to demand payment for whatever labor he performed.

Before the war, the political identity of black men derived largely from their status as property. In what was called the Three Fifths Compromise, the framers of the U. S. Constitution had originally arranged to count a slave as three-fifths of a person for purposes of allocating congressional representation in the various states. After the war, the leaders of the Republican Party tried to secure a political identity for blacks as citizens. The Republicans made this effort not necessarily because they were committed to human rights and the equality of all men, but because it was politically expedient to do so. They were afraid that once the war was over, the northern and southern wings of the Democratic Party would reunite and vote them out of office. Desperate to preserve their power, the Republicans did what they could to guarantee black men the right to vote and then stationed federal troops in the former Confederacy to protect them when they tried to exercise their newly acquired political power. Black men in the South responded by organizing themselves, setting their own political agendas, and running for local, state, and national office.

Black men also used emancipation as an opportunity to regularize their personal relationships and establish their own social identities. Some, who were living with women they loved, legalized their marriages and tried to establish themselves as heads of their households. Others searched all over the South to find wives and children who had been sold away from them. And still others used emancipation as an excuse to annul relationships they found unsatisfactory. Many of them asserted their manhood by discarding the names given to them by their masters. Like William Ellison, they chose names of their own. Thus, for many southern black men, the period between the end of the Civil War in 1865 and the end of Reconstruction in 1877, when federal troops pulled out of the South for good, was characterized by the increasing ability to conform to a manly ideal which included the power to move about freely, the right to own land, the expectation that they would be paid for the work they did, the right to vote and hold office, and the right to marry whoever they pleased and live wherever they liked.

Needless to say, the efforts of black men to express their manliness in these ways posed a real challenge to white men in the process of reconstructing their own male identities within a social, political, and economic context that left them relatively powerless. As black men began to assert their independence of movement and their political power and to claim a kind of manhood that had been virtually unimaginable before the Civil War, white men all over the South did what they could reassert their manliness by trying to thwart those ef-

forts. When they found that freed slaves were unwilling to work in gangs, they hired them as tenant farmers and sharecroppers and then loaned them money to buy seed, farming implements, and food and clothes to tide them over until their crops were harvested. The process of establishing this system was a gendered affair that largely excluded women. Typically a white, male landowner prepared a contract which male ex-slaves signed. Each had a legal obligation. The landowner permitted the sharecropper or tenant farmer to farm his land. In return, the farmer agreed to pay rent on the land or share part of the crop with the landowner.

Tenant farming and sharecropping allowed black farmers to manage the production process and the sale of their crops. But in the process, it made debtors of them and allowed white landowners and furnishing merchants to institute a system of forced labor that resembled slavery. The so called "debt peonage" that resulted from loaning farmers the money to buy the supplies they needed to tide them over until harvest time limited their freedom of movement since by law they were required to stay put until they paid off their debts. This system guaranteed that whites would have the labor to work their land and re-established a social context that demanded deference and compliance from newly freed slaves.

Having established some degree of economic control over black men and their families, whites also took steps to restrict the ability of black men to assert their manhood politically. The Ku Klux Klan and other secret white fraternities provided a perfect mechanism for doing so. The Klan was organized in 1866 by six young Confederate veterans from Pulaski, Tennessee, who were in search of some excitement. Calling themselves the Ku Klux Klan, they recruited their friends as members, held secret initiation ceremonies, and took great pleasure in parading around town disguised in sheets. Seeing members of this secret organization mounted on horses and galloping through town was at the very least startling if not terrifying to many recently freed slaves. It was only a short step from youthful high jinks to something more serious once members of the Klan realized that the fear they elicited from blacks could be used as a form of social control. Interest in the group spread, and white men in other southern states began forming their own Klan organizations. The warnings, beatings, and murders perpetrated on ex-slaves, southerners who collaborated with the Yankee occupiers, and northerners who came south to buy land or to run freedmen's schools spread terror all over the South. Humiliated by military defeat and occupation, by their loss of their political power, and by the poverty that made it difficult for them to support their families, southern white men found in the Klan a means to reconstruct their manly identities and redeem themselves. Their disguises gave them courage, and their acts of vigilantism gave them power. The rural nature of southern life, the isolation that accompanied it, and the unpredictable and random nature of white terrorism and intimidation made it difficult to organize resistance to the Klan and for potential victims to protect their families and friends from Klan violence.

Through no fault of their own, many ex-slaves found their newly acquired freedoms diminished and their claim to manhood denied. Not that they didn't resist. Despite the risks involved, black men housed white Yankee schoolteachers and superintendents in their homes. They refused to sign contracts that they couldn't read and took them to someone who could explain what they said. They took their grievances against whites to the Freedman's Bureau and federal officials, and they put their lives and those of their wives and children on the line by continuing to vote and run for office. But in the end, white southern men were able to use secrecy and intimidation to begin to reestablish their dominance over those who had once been slaves.

By the mid-1870s, Reconstruction was coming to an end. Federal troops were slowly pulling out of the South, leaving blacks unprotected. When Reconstruction ended, white men gradually regained the right to vote and

hold office. They used their power in their state legislatures to whittle away at the political rights guaranteed to black men by the fourteenth and fifteenth amendments. In the 1890s they were able to pass laws that for all intents and purposes disenfranchised most black men. And they passed so-called "Jim Crow laws," which effectively segregated blacks from whites by denying them access to public facilities ranging from schools and hospitals to drinking fountains, restaurants, railroad cars, and hotels.

During the period following the Civil War, both black men and white men struggled to define their respective masculine identities and then assert their manliness in a context that was both the same and different from that which had existed before the Civil War. The postbellum South was a land characterized by both poverty and virulent racism. It did not recover quickly from the devastation of war. The low price of cotton during the post-war period combined with a continuing failure to diversify the economy and natural disasters such as infestations of boll weevils meant that even those white planters who had been able to hang on to vast amounts of land and had access to the labor to work it found it difficult, if not impossible, to rebuild their fortunes. After the Civil War, northern cities grew rapidly as commerce and industry flourished. But by and large, in terms of landscape and race relations, the South in 1890 looked remarkably similar to the way it had looked before the war. It is true that slavery was gone, but the economy remained based in agriculture, commerce was sluggish, and industrial development was in its infancy. By the 1890s, white men were in the process of arranging the social, political, and economic landscape to serve their own interests. They once again based their expression of manliness, in part, on their ability to control the black population in their midst. Once more, they found themselves in a position to assert their manliness by thwarting the free expression of black masculinity.

Southern black men, systematically deprived by white men of economic opportunity, social equality, and political power, had to look for ways to express their manliness within the narrower context of their own communities. Most tried to support their families as well as they could. And they fulfilled their civic responsibilities by sponsoring and supporting black schools and by establishing and running black churches.

SUMMARY

In the nineteenth-century South, concern about race and racial dominance established the context in which white men, black men, and Native American men expressed their gendered identities. Manhood for white men during the antebellum period was based on freedom of movement, the right to own property, the ability to control white women and children and the black population in their midst, access to political power, and dedication to a code of honor that held a man responsible for preserving his personal reputation and that of his family and community. Most white men viewed making money as a manly pursuit. But while farmers may have regarded a certain degree of industriousness as a desirable and manly quality, most planters derived their social status and political power from the fact that they did not have to personally perform much physical labor. For them, working hard was what slaves were supposed to do.

The Civil War was a humiliating experience for all white men in the South. They returned from war having failed to defend the Confederacy and having put the lives of their wives and children at risk. They had to watch as federal troops occupied their land. They lost their political power. So in the period that followed reconstruction, white southern men did what they could to redeem their masculine identities by regaining control over southern politics, by socially segregating blacks, and by attempting to stabilize the southern workforce through tenant farming and sharecropping.

Black men in the South spent much of the nineteenth century trying to establish their masculine identities within a context that was very much dictated by white men. Whether they were able to completely fulfill its prescriptions or not, slaves and free black men defined masculinity in terms of supporting and protecting their loved ones, the ability to move about freely, the opportunity to own property, and the right to be paid for their work. After the Civil War, they found it possible to construct their masculine identities around the right to vote and hold office. But their claim on political rights was tenuous. By the 1890s they were largely disfranchised.

Native American men responded in any number of ways to the encroachment of white settlement. Some tried to maintain their manly identities by removing themselves from contact with whites or by aggressively resisting the advance of white civilization. Thus, they continued to construct their manliness around their skill as hunters and their bravery as warriors. Others, like some among the Cherokee, changed their definition of what constituted manliness as they assimilated. Increasingly, their masculine ideal took the form of a law-abiding farmer. No longer did they view agricultural labor as a feminine pursuit. For them, it was now the manly thing to do.

Excerpts from John Lyde Wilson's "The Code of Honor"

Dueling was not necessarily common among upper-class southern men before the Civil War, but it did occasionally occur. It was a ritual designed to preserve a gentleman's honor, an important component of his gendered identity. Before the Civil War John Lyde Wilson, a former governor of South Carolina, published a pamphlet entitled "The Code of Honor; or, Rules for the Government of Principals and Seconds in Duelling." Wilson was not trying to encourage the practice of dueling. But he was convinced that it was unrealistic to expect men whose reputations had been besmirched by others to turn the other cheek.

What did creating a set of rules for duelers have to do with manliness? What kind of manly characteristics are these rules for dueling intended to encourage or allow men to demonstrate?

CHAPTER I

The Person Insulted, Before Challenge Sent

1. Whenever you believe you are insulted, if the insult be in public, and by words or behavior, never resent it there, if you have self-command enough to avoid noticing it. If resented there, you offer an indignity to the company, which you should not.

2. If the insult be by blows or any personal indignity, it may be resented at the moment, for the insult to the company did not originate with you. But although resented at the moment, yet you are bound still to have satisfaction, and must therefore make the demand.

3. When you believe yourself aggrieved, be silent on the subject, speak to no one about the matter, and see your friend who is to act for you, as soon as possible.

4. Never send a challenge in the first instance, for that precludes all negotiation. Let

your note be in the language of a gentleman, and let the subject matter of complaint be truly and fairly set forth, cautiously avoiding attributing to the adverse party any improper motive.

5. When your second is in full possession of the facts, leave the whole matter to his judgment, and avoid any consultation with him unless he seeks it. He has the custody of your honor, and by obeying him you cannot be compromitted.

6. Let the time of demand upon your adversary after the insult be as short as possible, for he has the right to double that time in replying to you, unless you give some good reason for your delay. Each party is entitled to reasonable time to make the necessary domestic arrangements, by will or otherwise before fighting.

7. To a written communication you are entitled to a written reply, and it is the business of your friend to require it.

Second's Duty Before Challenge Sent

1. Whenever you are applied to by a friend to act as his second, before you agree to do so, state distinctly to your principal that you will be governed only by your own judgment, that *he* will not be consulted after you are in full

Source: John Lyde Wilson, "The Code of Honor: or, Rules for the Government of Principals and Seconds in Duelling" (Charleston, SC: James Phinney, 1858), 11–15, 21–22, 24–26.

possession of the facts, unless it becomes necessary to make or accept the *amende* honorable, or send a challenge. You are supposed to be cool and collected, and your friend's feelings are more or less irritated.

2. Use every effort to soothe and tranquilize your principal, do not see things in the same aggravated light in which he views them, extenuate the conduct of his adversary whenever you see clearly an opportunity to do so, without doing violence to your friend's irritated mind. Endeavor to persuade him that there must have been some misunderstanding in the matter. Check him if he uses opprobrious epithet towards his adversary, and never permit improper or insulting words in the note you carry.

3. To the note you carry in writing to the party complained of, you are entitled to a written answer, which will be directed to your principal, and will be delivered to you by his adversary's friend. If this note be not written in the style of a gentleman, refuse to receive it, and assign your reason for such refusal. If there be a question made as to the character of the note, require the second presenting it to you, who considers it respectful, to endorse upon it these words: "I consider the note of my friend respectful, and would not have been the bearer of it, if I believed otherwise."

4. If the party called on refuses to receive the note you bear, you are entitled to demand a reason for such refusal.—If he refuses to give you any reason, and persists in such refusal, he treats, not only your friend, but yourself with indignity, and you must then make yourself the actor, by sending a respectful note, requiring a proper explanation of the course he has pursued towards you and your friend; and if he still adheres to his determination, you are to challenge or post him. . . .

CHAPTER III

Duty of Challengee and His Second Before Fighting

1. After all efforts for a reconciliation are over, the party aggrieved sends a challenge to his adversary, which is delivered to his second.

2. Upon the acceptance of the challenge, the seconds make the necessary arrangements for the meeting, in which each party is entitled to a perfect equality. The old notion that the party challenged was authorized to name the time, place, distance and weapon, has been long since exploded, nor would a man of chivalric honor use such a right if he possessed it. The time must be as soon as practicable, the place such as had ordinarily been used where the parties are, the distance usual, and the weapons that which is most generally used, which in this State is the pistol.

3. If the challengee insist upon what is not usual in time, place, distance and weapon, do not yield the point, and tender in writing what is usual in each, and if he refuses to give satisfaction, then your friend may post him.

4. If your friend be determined to fight and not post, you have the right to withdraw. But if you continue to act, and the challengee name a distance and weapon not usual and more fatal than the ordinary distance and weapon, you have the right to tender a still more deadly distance and weapon, and he must accept.

5. The usual distance is from ten to twenty paces, as may be agreed on, and the seconds in measuring the ground usually step three feet. . . .

CHAPTER V

Duty of Principals and Seconds on the Ground

1. The principals are to be respectful in meeting, and neither by look or expression irritate each other. They are to be wholly passive, being entirely under the guidance of their seconds.

2. When once posted, they are not to quit their positions under any circumstances, without leave or direction of their seconds.

3. When the principals are posted, the second giving the word, must tell them to stand firm until he repeats the giving of the word, in the manner it will be given when the parties are at liberty to fire.

4. Each second has a loaded pistol, in order to enforce a fair combat according to the rules agreed on; and if a principal fires before the word or time agreed on, he is at liberty to fire at him, and if such second's principal fall, it is his duty to do so.

5. If after a fire either party be touched, the duel is to end; and no second is excusable who permits a wounded friend to fight, nor no second who knows his duty will permit his friend to fight a man already hit. I am aware there have been many instances where a contest has continued, not only after slight, but severe wounds had been received. In all such cases I think the seconds are blameable.

6. If after an exchange of shots, neither party be hit, it is the duty of the second of the challengee to approach the second of the challenger and say: "Our friends have exchanged shots, are you satisfied, or is there any cause why the contest should be continued?" If the meeting be of no serious cause of complaint, where the party complaining had in no way been deeply injured, or grossly insulted, the second of the party challenging should reply: "The point of honor being settled, there can, I conceive, be no objection to a reconciliation, and I propose that our principals meet on middle ground, shake hands and be friends." If this be acceded to by the second of the challengee, the second of the party challenging says: "We have agreed that the present duel shall cease—the honor of each of you is preserved, and you will meet on middle ground, shake hands and be reconciled."

7. If the insult be of a serious character, it will be the duty of the second of the challenger to say in reply to the second of the challengee: "We have been deeply wronged, and if you are not disposed to repair the injury, the contest must continue." And if the challengee offers nothing by way of reparation, the fight continues until one or the other of the principals is hit. . . .

DOCUMENT

Excerpt from Frederick Douglass' Autobiography

Frederick Augustus Washington Bailey was born a slave in Maryland in 1818. In 1838, he escaped and settled in New Bedford, Massachusetts, chose to call himself Frederick Douglass, married Anna Murray, and made his living as a day laborer and ship's caulker. By the time he published his autobiography in 1845, he was a prominent and accomplished abolitionist speaker. Douglass's autobiography describes his life as a slave in

Source: Frederick Douglass, *Narrative of the Life of Frederick Douglass, an American Slave. Written by Himself,* 3rd. English Edition (Wortley, Eng.: J. Barker, 1846), 65–73. Notes omitted.

graphic detail. One incident in particular has bearing on our discussion of how manliness was defined by both black and white men in the antebellum South.

In 1832 Frederick Douglass' master, Thomas Auld, leased him to a man named Edward Covey. Douglass began serving his new master on January 1, 1833. Covey was neither a gentleman nor a man of leisure. He rented 150 acres of land and worked side by side with his hands in the fields. A demanding and abusive master, Covey did not hesitate to whip his slaves when they failed to do exactly as he wished. Douglass describes himself as "broken in body, soul, and spirit" by such treatment. In the excerpt below, Douglass recounts a particularly dramatic confrontation with Covey, which he claims made a man of him.

What was Douglass' criteria for judging manhood? Why did he think he was in some way lacking that status before his confrontation with Covey? What was it about the confrontation that he believed made him a man?

I have already intimated that my condition was much worse, during the first six months of my stay at Mr. Covey's, than in the last six. The circumstances leading to the change in Mr. Covey's course toward me form an epoch in my humble history. You have seen how a man was made a slave; you shall see how a slave was made a man. On one of the hottest days of the month of August, 1833, Bill Smith, William Hughes, a slave named Eli, and myself, were engaged in fanning wheat. Hughes was clearing the fanned wheat from before the fan, Eli was turning, Smith was feeding, and I was carrying wheat to the fan. The work was simple, requiring strength rather than intellect; yet, to one entirely unused to such work, it came very hard. About three o'clock of that day, I broke down; my strength failed me; I was seized with a violent aching of the head, attended with extreme dizziness; I trembled in every limb. Finding what was coming, I nerved myself up, feeling it would never do to stop work. I stood as long as I could stagger to the hopper with grain. When I could stand no longer, I fell, and felt as if held down by an immense weight. The fan of course stopped; every one had his own work to do; and no one could do the work of the other, and have his own go on at the same time.

Mr. Covey was at the house, about one hundred yards from the treading-yard where we were fanning. On hearing the fan stop, he left immediately, and came to the spot where we were. He hastily inquired what the matter was. Bill answered that I was sick, and there was no one to bring wheat to the fan. I had by this time crawled away under the side of the post and rail-fence by which the yard was enclosed, hoping to find relief by getting out of the sun. He then asked where I was. He was told by one of the hands. He came to the spot, and, after looking at me awhile, asked me what was the matter. I told him as well as I could, for I scarce had strength to speak. He then gave me a savage kick in the side, and told me to get up. I tried to do so, but fell back in the attempt. He gave me another kick, and again told me to rise. I again tried, and succeeded in gaining my feet; but, stooping to get the tub with which I was feeding the fan, I again staggered and fell. While down in this situation, Mr. Covey took up the hickory slat with which Hughes had been striking off the half-bushel measure, and with it gave me a heavy blow upon the head, making a large wound, and the blood ran freely; and with this again told me to get up. I made no effort to comply, having now made up my mind to let him do his worst. In a short time after receiving this blow, my head grew better. Mr. Covey had now left me to my fate. At this moment I resolved, for the first time, to go to my master, enter a complaint, and ask his protection. In order to [do] this, I must that afternoon walk seven miles; and this, under the circumstances, was truly a severe undertaking. I was exceedingly feeble; made so as much by the kicks and blows which I received, as by the severe fit of sickness to which I had been subjected. I, however, watched my chance, while Covey was looking in an opposite direction, and started for

St. Michael's. I succeeded in getting a considerable distance on my way to the woods, when Covey discovered me, and called after me to come back, threatening what he would do if I did not come. I disregarded both his calls and his threats, and made my way to the woods as fast as my feeble state would allow; and thinking I might be overhauled by him if I kept the road, I walked through the woods, keeping far enough from the road to avoid detection, and near enough to prevent losing my way. I had not gone far before my little strength again failed me. I could go no farther. I fell down, and lay for a considerable time. The blood was yet oozing from the wound on my head. For a time I thought I should bleed to death; and think now that I should have done so, but that the blood so matted my hair as to stop the wound. After lying there about three quarters of an hour, I nerved myself up again, and started on my way, through bogs and briers, barefooted and bareheaded, tearing my feet sometimes at nearly every step; and after a journey of about seven miles, occupying some five hours to perform it, I arrived at master's store. I then presented an appearance enough to affect any but a heart of iron. From the crown of my head to my feet, I was covered with blood. My hair was all clotted with dust and blood; my shirt was stiff with blood. My legs and feet were torn in sundry places with briers and thorns, and were also covered with blood. I suppose I looked like a man who had escaped a den of wild beasts, and barely escaped them. In this state I appeared before my master, humbly entreating him to interpose his authority for my protection. I told him all the circumstances as well as I could, and it seemed, as I spoke, at times to affect him. He would then walk the floor, and seek to justify Covey by saying he expected I deserved it. He asked me what I wanted. I told him, to let me get a new home; that as sure as I lived with Mr. Covey again, I should live with but to die with him; that Covey would surely kill me; he was in a fair way for it. Master Thomas ridiculed the idea that there was any danger of Mr. Covey's killing me, and said that he knew Mr. Covey; that he was a good man, and that he could not think of taking me from him; that, should he do so, he would lose the whole year's wages; that I belonged to Mr. Covey for one year, and that I must go back to him, come what might; and that I must not trouble him with any more stories, or that he would himself *get hold of me*. After threatening me thus, he gave me a very large dose of salts, telling me that I might remain in St. Michael's that night, (it being quite late,) but that I must be off back to Mr. Covey's early in the morning; and that if I did not, he would *get hold of me*, which meant that he would whip me. I remained all night, and, according to his orders, I started off to Covey's in the morning, (Saturday morning,) wearied in body and broken in spirit. I got no supper that night, or breakfast that morning. I reached Covey's about nine o'clock; and just as I was getting over the fence that divided Mrs. Kemp's fields from ours, out ran Covey with his cowskin, to give me another whipping. Before he could reach me, I succeeded in getting to the cornfield; and as the corn was very high, it afforded me the means of hiding. He seemed very angry, and searched for me a long time. My behavior was altogether unaccountable. He finally gave up the chase, thinking, I suppose, that I must come home for something to eat; he would give himself no further trouble in looking for me. I spent that day mostly in the woods, having the alternative before me,—to go home and be whipped to death, or stay in the woods and be starved to death. That night, I fell in with Sandy Jenkins, a slave with whom I was somewhat acquainted. Sandy had a free wife who lived about four miles from Mr. Covey's; and it being Saturday, he was on his way to see her. I told him my circumstances, and he very kindly invited me to go home with him. I went home with him, and talked this whole matter over, and got his advice as to what course it was best for me to pursue. I found Sandy an old adviser. He told me, with great solemnity, I must go back to Covey; but that before I went, I must go with him into another part of the woods, where there was a certain *root*, which, if I would take some of it with me, carrying it *always on my right side*, would render it impossible for Mr. Covey, or any other white man, to whip me. He said he had carried it for years; and since he had done so, he had never received a blow, and never expected to while he carried it. I at first rejected the idea, that the simple carrying of a root in my pocket would have any such effect as he had said, and was not disposed to take it; but Sandy impressed the necessity with much earnestness, telling me it could do no harm, if it did no good. To please him, I at length took the root, and, according to his direction, carried it upon my right side. This was Sunday morning. I immediately started for home; and upon entering the yard gate, out came Mr. Covey on his way to meeting. He spoke to me very kindly, made me drive the pigs from a lot near by, and passed on towards the church. Now, this singular conduct of Mr. Covey really made me begin to think that there was something in the *root* which Sandy had given me; and had it been on any other day than Sunday, I could have attributed the conduct to no other cause than the influence of that root; and as it was, I was half inclined to think the *root* to be something more than I at first had taken it to be. All went well till Monday morning. On this morning, the virtue of the *root* was fully tested. Long before daylight, I was called to go and rub, curry, and feed, the horses. I obeyed, and was glad to obey. But whilst thus engaged, whilst in the act of throwing down some blades from the loft, Mr. Covey entered the stable with a long rope; and just as I was half out of the loft, he caught hold of my legs, and was about tying me. As soon as I found what he was up to, I gave a sudden spring, and as I did so, he holding to my legs, I was brought sprawling on the stable floor. Mr. Covey seemed now to think he had me, and could do what he pleased; but at this moment—from whence came the spirit I don't know—I resolved to fight; and, suiting my action to the resolution, I seized Covey hard by the throat; and as I did so, I rose. He held on to me, and I to him. My resistance was so entirely unexpected, that Covey seemed taken all aback. He trembled like a leaf. This gave me assurance, and I held him uneasy, causing the blood to run where I touched him with the ends of my fingers. Mr. Covey soon called out to Hughes for help. Hughes came, and, while Covey held me, attempting to tie my right hand. While he was in the act of doing so, I watched my chance, and gave him a heavy kick close under the ribs. This kick fairly sickened Hughes, so that he left me

in the hands of Mr. Covey. This kick had the effect of not only weakening Hughes, but Covey also. When he saw Hughes bending over with pain, his courage quailed. He asked me if I meant to persist in my resistance. I told him I did, come what might; that he had used me like a brute for six months, and that I was determined to be used so no longer. With that, he strove to drag me to a stick that was lying just out of the stable door. He meant to knock me down. But just as he was leaning over to get the stick, I seized him with both hands by his collar, and brought him by a sudden snatch to the ground. By this time, Bill came. Covey called upon him for assistance. Bill wanted to know what he could do. Covey said, "Take hold of him, take hold of him!" Bill said his master hired him out to work, and not to help to whip me; so he left Covey and myself to fight our own battle out. We were at it for nearly two hours. Covey at length let me go, puffing and blowing at a great rate, saying that if I had not resisted, he would not have whipped me half so much. The truth was, that he had not whipped me at all. I considered him as getting entirely the worst end of the bargain; for he had drawn no blood from me, but I had from him. The whole six months afterwards, that I spent with Mr. Covey, he never laid the weight of his finger upon me in anger. He would occasionally say, he didn't want to get hold of me again. "No," thought I, "you need not; for you will come off worse than you did before."

This battle with Mr. Covey was the turning-point in my career as a slave. It rekindled the few expiring embers of freedom, and revived within me a sense of my own manhood. It recalled the departed self-confidence, and inspired me again with a determination to be free. The gratification afforded by the triumph was a full compensation for whatever else might follow, even death itself. He only can understand the deep satisfaction which I experienced, who has himself repelled by force the bloody arm of slavery. I felt as I never felt before. It was a glorious resurrection, from the tomb of slavery, to the heaven of freedom. My long-crushed spirit rose, cowardice departed, bold defiance took its place; and I now resolved that, however long I might remain a slave in form, the day had passed forever when I could be a slave in fact. I did not hesitate to let it be known of me, that the white man who expected to succeed in whipping, must also succeed in killing me.

From this time I was never again what might be called fairly whipped, though I remained a slave four years afterwards. I had several fights, but was never whipped.

It was for a long time a matter of surprise to me why Mr. Covey did not immediately have me taken by the constable to the whipping-post, and there regularly whipped for the crime of raising my hand against a white man in defence of myself. And the only explanation I can now think of does not entirely satisfy me; but such as it is, I will give it. Mr. Covey enjoyed the most unbounded reputation for being a first-rate overseer and negro-breaker. It was of considerable importance to him. That reputation was at stake; and had he sent me—a boy about sixteen years old—to the public whipping-post, his reputation would have been lost; so, to save his reputation, he suffered me to go unpunished. . . .

DOCUMENT

Images of a Feminized Confederate President

On April 2, 1865, Jefferson Davis, the President of the Confederate States of America, heeding the advice of his generals, ordered the evacuation of the Confederate capitol, Richmond, Virginia. With his family, he headed south through North Carolina and into Georgia to escape the advancing federal soldiers. On May 10, just short of the Florida border, union troops caught up with him. As he tried to escape, he threw a long, waterproof coat around his shoulders, and his wife draped a shawl over his head. One of the union soldiers recognized him and placed him under arrest.

Almost immediately after Davis' capture, northern artists began drawing cartoons depicting Davis in the clothes of a woman. Sometimes he was wearing a coat or a dress, but most often they pictured him in a hoop skirt. Davis was a proud southerner and a gentleman, a man of honor. By portraying Davis as they did, these cartoons illustrate the degree to which northerners understood that losing the war undermined the gendered identity of southern men.

What kinds of gender characteristics do these cartoons attribute to Davis? What do these cartoons have to say about the relationship between gender identity and clothes? Why would picturing Davis in women's clothes be considered particularly humiliating?

Source: "The Head of the Confederacy on a New Base," Hilton and Company, New York, 1865 and "Finding the Lost Ditch," Oscar H. Harpel, Cincinnati, 1865.

THE HEAD OF THE CONFEDERACY ON A NEW BASE.

Hilton and Company, New York, 1865. (Courtesy of The Lincoln Museum, Fort Wayne, IN [#3585].)

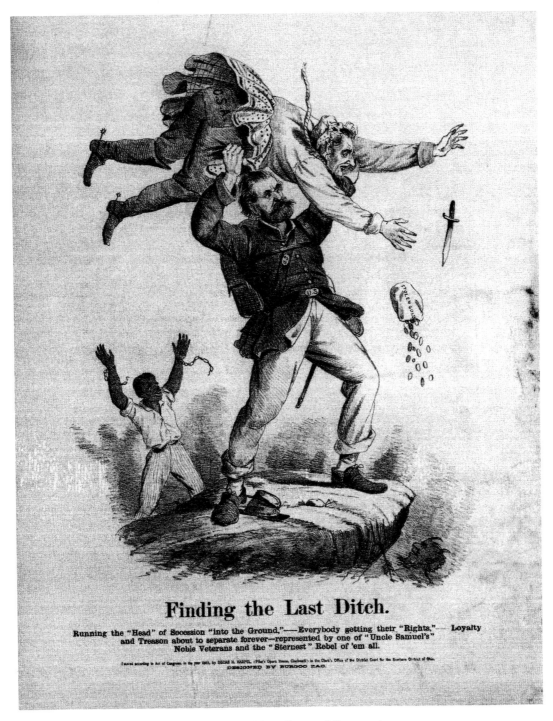

Finding the Last Ditch.

Running the "Head" of Secession "into the Ground,"——Everybody getting their "Rights,"—— Loyalty
and Treason about to separate forever—represented by one of "Uncle Samuel's"
Noble Veterans and the "Sternest" Rebel of 'em all.

Entered according to Act of Congress, in the year 1865, by OSCAR H. HARPEL, (Pike's Opera House, Cincinnati,) in the Clerk's Office of the District Court for the Southern District of Ohio.
DESIGNED BY BURGOO ZAC.

Oscar H. Harpel, Cincinnati, 1865 (Courtesy of the Library of Congress).

ARTICLE

"Some Go Up and Some Go Down": The Animal Trickster [and the Construction of African American Manliness in the Antebellum South]

Lawrence W. Levine

As slaves, African American men found it difficult to construct their gendered identity around the same ideals as white men. Male slaves were not powerful or autonomous. Their masters controlled where they lived, who they married, and what work they did. They could not protect their wives and children. Nor were they expected to be bread-winners. In this excerpt from Black Culture and Black Consciousness, *Lawrence Levine suggests that animal trickster stories were part of the folklore of Africa that African Americans adapted to meet their own needs.*

How did animal trickster stories contribute to the construction of gender identity among enslaved African American men in the South before the Civil War? Were the qualities they glorified the same or different from the manly qualities that white men held in high regard?

. . . [The original trickster stories of African Americans were a means by] which psychic relief from arbitrary authority could be secured, symbolic assaults upon the powerful could be waged, and important lessons about authority relationships could be imparted. Afro-Americans in the United States were to make extended use of this mechanism throughout their years of servitude.

In its simplest form the slaves' animal trickster tale was a cleanly delineated story free of ambiguity. The strong assault the weak,

Source: From *Black Culture and Black Consciousness: Afro-American Folk Thought from Slavery to Freedom* by Lawrence W. Levine, pp. 105–114, copyright © 1977 by Oxford University Press, Inc. Used by permission of Oxford University Press. Notes omitted.

who fight back with any weapons they have. The animals in these tales have an almost instinctive understanding of each other's habits and foibles. Knowing Rabbit's curiosity and vanity, Wolf constructs a tar-baby and leaves it by the side of the road. At first fascinated by this stranger and then progressively infuriated at its refusal to respond to his friendly salutations, Rabbit strikes at it with his hands, kicks it with his feet, butts it with his head, and becomes thoroughly enmeshed. In the end, however, it is Rabbit whose understanding of his adversary proves to be more profound. Realizing that Wolf will do exactly what he thinks his victim least desires, Rabbit convinces him that of all the ways to die the one he is most afraid of is being thrown into the briar patch, which of course is exactly what Wolf promptly does, allowing Rabbit to escape.

This situation is repeated in tale after tale: the strong attempt to trap the weak but are tricked by them instead. Fox entreats Rooster to come down from his perch, since all the animals have signed a peace treaty and there is no longer any danger: "I don' eat you, you don' boder wid me. Come down! Le's make peace!" Almost convinced by this good news, Rooster is about to descend when he thinks better of it and tests Fox by pretending to see a man and a dog coming down the road. "Don' min' fo' comin' down den," Fox calls out as he runs away. "Dawg ain't got no sense, yer know, an' de man got er gun." Spotting a goat lying on a rock, Lion is about to surprise and kill him when he notices that Goat keeps chewing and chewing although there is nothing there but bare stone. Lion reveals himself and asks Goat what he is eating. Overcoming the momentary paralysis which afflicts most of the weak animals in these tales when they realize they are trapped, Goat saves himself by saying in his most terrifying voice: "Me duh chaw dis rock, an ef you dont leff, wen me done . . . me guine eat you."

At its most elemental, then, the trickster tale consists of a confrontation in which the weak use their wits to evade the strong. Mere escape, however, does not prove to be victory enough, and in a significant number of these tales the weak learn the brutal ways of the more powerful. Fox, taking advantage of Pig's sympathetic nature, gains entrance to his house during a storm by pleading that he is freezing to death. After warming himself by the fire, he acts exactly as Pig's instincts warned him he would. Spotting a pot of peas cooking on the stove, he begins to sing:

Fox and peas are very good,
But Pig and peas are better.

Recovering from his initial terror, Pig pretends to hear a pack of hounds, helps Fox hide in a meal barrel, and pours the peas in, scalding Fox to death.

In one tale after another the trickster proves to be as merciless as his stronger opponent. Wolf traps Rabbit in a hollow tree and sets it on fire, but Rabbit escapes through a hole in the back and reappears, thanking Wolf for an excellent meal, explaining that the tree was filled with honey which melted from the heat. Wolf, in his eagerness to enjoy a similar feast, allows himself to be sealed into a tree which has no other opening, and is burned to death. "While eh duh bun, Buh Wolf bague an pray Buh Rabbit fuh leh um come out, but Buh Rabbit wouldnt yeddy [hear] um." The brutality of the trickster in these tales was sometimes troubling ("Buh Rabbit . . . hab er bad heart," the narrator of the last story concluded), but more often it was mitigated by the fact that the strong were the initial aggressors and the weak really had no choice. The characteristic spirit of these tales was one not of moral judgment but of vicarious triumph. Storytellers allowed their audience to share the heartening spectacle of a lion running in terror from a goat or a fox fleeing a rooster; to experience the mocking joy of Brer Rabbit as he scampers away through the briar patch calling back to Wolf, "Dis de place me mammy fotch me up,—dis de place me mammy fotch me up"; to feel the joyful relief of Pig as he turns Fox's song upside down and chants:

Pigs and peas are very good,
But Fox and peas are better.

Had self-preservation been the only motive driving the animals in these stories, the trickster tale need never have varied from the forms just considered. But Brer Rabbit and his fellow creatures were too humanized to be content with mere survival. Their needs included all the prizes human beings crave and strive for: wealth, success, prestige, honor, sexual prowess. Brer Rabbit himself summed it up best in the tale for which this section is named:

De rabbit is de slickest o' all de animals de Lawd ever made. He ain't de biggest, an' he ain't de loudest but he sho' am de slickest. If he gits in trouble he gits out by gittin' somebody else in. Once he fell down a deep well an' did he holler and cry? No siree. He set up a mighty mighty whistling and a singin', an' when de wolf passes by he heard him an' he stuck his head over an' de rabbit say, "Git 'long 'way f'om here. Dere ain't room fur two. Hit's mighty hot up dere and nice an' cool down here. Don' you git in dat bucket an' come down here." Dat made de wolf all de mo' onrestless and he jumped into de bucket an' as he went down de rabbit come up, an' as dey passed de rabbit he laughed an' he say, "Dis am life; some go up and some go down."

There could be no mistaking the direction in which Rabbit was determined to head. It was in his inexorable drive upward that Rabbit emerged not only as an incomparable defender but also as a supreme manipulator, a role that complicated the simple contours of the tales already referred to.

In the ubiquitous tales of amoral manipulation, the trickster could still be pictured as much on the defensive as he was in the stories which had him battling for his very life against stronger creatures. The significant difference is that now the panoply of his victims included the weak as well as the powerful. Trapped by Mr. Man and hung from a sweet gum tree until he can be cooked, Rabbit is buffeted to and fro by the wind and left to contemplate his bleak future until Brer Squirrel happens along. "This yer my cool air swing," Rabbit informs him. "I taking a fine swing this morning." Squirrel begs a turn and finds his friend surprisingly gracious: "Certainly, Brer Squirrel, you do me proud. Come up here, Brer Squirrel, and give me a hand with this knot." Tying the grateful squirrel securely in the tree, Rabbit leaves him to his pleasure— and his fate. When Mr. Man returns, "he take Brer Squirrel home and cook him for dinner."

It was primarily advancement not preservation that led to the trickster's manipulations, however. Among a slave population whose daily rations were at best rather stark fare and quite often a barely minimal diet, it is not surprising that food proved to be the most common symbol of enhanced status and power. In his never-ending quest for food the trickster was not content with mere acquisition, which he was perfectly capable of on his own; he needed to procure the food through guile from some stronger animal. Easily the most popular tale of this type pictures Rabbit and Wolf as partners in farming a field. They have laid aside a tub of butter for winter provisions, but Rabbit proves unable to wait or to share. Pretending to hear a voice calling him, he leaves his chores and begins to eat the butter. When he returns to the field he informs his partner that his sister has just had a baby and wanted him to name it. "Well, w'at you name um?" Wolf asks innocently. "Oh, I name um Buh Start-um," Rabbit replies. Subsequent calls provide the chance for additional assaults on the butter and additional names for the nonexistent babies: "Buh Half-um," "Buh Done-um." After work, Wolf discovers the empty tub and accuses Rabbit, who indignantly denies the theft. Wolf proposes that they both lie in the sun, which will cause the butter to run out of the guilty party. Rabbit agrees readily, and when grease begins to appear on his own face he rubs it onto that of the sleeping wolf. "Look, Buh Wolf," he cries, waking his partner, "de buttah melt out on you. Dat prove you eat um." "I guess you been right," Wolf agrees docilely, "I eat um fo' true." In some versions the animals propose a more hazardous ordeal by fire to discover the guilty party. Rabbit successfully jumps over the flames but some innocent animal— Possum, Terrapin, Bear—falls in and perishes for Rabbit's crime.

In most of these tales the aggrieved animal, realizing he has been tricked, desperately tries to avenge himself by setting careful plans to trap Rabbit, but to no avail. Unable to outwit Rabbit, his adversaries attempt to learn from him, but here too they fail. Seeing Rabbit carrying a string of fish, Fox asks him where they came from. Rabbit confesses that he stole them from Man by pretending to be ill and begging Man to take him home in his cart which was filled with fish. While riding along, Rabbit explains, he threw the load of fish into the woods and then jumped off to retrieve them. He encourages Fox to try the same tactic, and Fox is beaten to death, as Rabbit knew he would be, since Man is too shrewd to be taken in the same way twice.

And so it goes in story after story. Rabbit cheats Brer Wolf out of his rightful portion of a cow and a hog they kill together. He tricks Brer Fox out of his part of their joint crop year after year "until he starved the fox to death. Then he had all the crop, and all the land too." He leisurely watches all the other animals build a house in which they store their winter provisions and then sneaks in, eats the food, and scares the others, including Lion, away by pretending to be a spirit and calling through a horn in a ghostly voice that he is a "better man den ebber bin yuh befo." He convinces Wolf that they ought to sell their own grandparents for a tub of butter, arranges for his grandparents to escape so that only Wolf's remain to be sold, and once they are bartered for the butter he steals that as well.

The many tales of which these are typical make it clear that what Rabbit craves is not possession but power, and this he acquires not simply by obtaining food but by obtaining it through the manipulation and deprivation of others. It is not often that he meets his match, and then generally at the hands of an animal as weak as himself. Refusing to allow Rabbit to cheat him out of his share of the meat they have just purchased, Partridge samples a small piece of liver and cries out, "Br'er Rabbit, de meat bitter! Oh, 'e bitter, bitter! bitter, bitter! You better not eat de meat," and tricks Rabbit into revealing where he had hidden the rest of the meat. "You is a damn sha'p feller," Partridge tells him. "But I get even wid you." Angry at Frog for inviting all the animals in the forest but him to a fish dinner, Rabbit frightens the guests away and eats all the fish himself. Frog gives another dinner, but this time he is prepared and tricks Rabbit into the water. "You is my master many a day on land, Brer Rabbit," Frog tells him just before killing and eating him, "but I is you master in the water."

It is significant that when these defeats do come, most often it is not brute force but even greater trickery that triumphs. Normally, however, the trickster has more than his share of the food. And of the women as well, for sexual prowess is the other basic sign of prestige in the slaves' tales. Although the primary trickster was occasionally depicted as a female—Ol' Molly Hare in Virginia, Aunt Nancy or Ann Nancy in the few surviving spider stories—in general women played a small role in slave tales. They were not actors in their own right so much as attractive possessions to be fought over. That the women for whom the animals compete are frequently the daughters of the most powerful creatures in the forest makes it evident that the contests are for status as well as pleasure. When Brer Bear promises his daughter to the best whistler in the forest, Rabbit offers to help his only serious competitor, Brer Dog, whistle more sweetly by slitting the corners of his mouth, which in reality makes him incapable of whistling at all. If Rabbit renders his adversaries figuratively impotent in their quest for women, they often retaliate in kind. In the story just related, Dog chases Rabbit, bites off his tail, and nothing more is said about who wins the woman.

More often than not, though, Rabbit is successful. In a Georgia tale illustrating the futility of mere hard work, Brer Wolf offers his attractive daughter to the animal that shucks the most corn. Rabbit has his heart set on winning Miss Wolf but realizes he has no chance of beating Brer Coon at shucking corn. Instead, he spends all of his time during the contest singing, dancing, and charming Miss Wolf. At the end he sits down next to Coon and claims that he has shucked the great pile of corn. Confused, Wolf leaves the decision up to his daughter:

> Now Miss Wolf she been favoring Brer Rabbit all the evening. Brer Rabbit dancing and singing plum turned Miss Wolf's head, so Miss Wolf she say, "It most surely are Brer Rabbit's pile." Miss Wolf she say she "plum 'stonished how Brer Coon can story so." Brer Rabbit he take the gal and go off home clipity, lipity. Poor old Brer Coon he take hisself off home, he so tired he can scarcely hold hisself together.

In another Georgia tale the contest for the woman seems to be symbolically equated with freedom. Fox promises his daughter to any animal who can pound dust out of a rock.

> Then Brer Rabbit, he feel might set down on, 'cause he know all the chaps can swing the stone hammer to beat hisself, and he go off sorrowful like and set on the sand bank. He set a while and look east, and then he turn and set a while and look west, but may be you don't know, sah, Brer Rabbit sense never come to hisself 'cepting when he look north.

Thus inspired, Rabbit conceives of a strategy allowing him to defeat his more powerful opponents and carry off the woman.

In the best known and most symbolically interesting courting tale, Rabbit and Wolf vie for the favors of a woman who is pictured as either equally torn between her two suitors or leaning toward Wolf. Rabbit alters the contest by professing surprise that she could be interested in Wolf, since he is merely Rabbit's riding horse. Hearing of this, Wolf confronts Rabbit, who denies ever saying it and promises to go to the woman and personally refute the libel as soon as he is well enough. Wolf insists he go at once, and the characteristic combination of Rabbit's deceit and Wolf's seemingly endless trust and gullibility allows Rabbit to convince his adversary that he is too sick to go with him unless he can ride on Wolf's back with a saddle and bridle for support. The rest of the story is inevitable. Approaching the woman's house Rabbit tightens the reins, digs a pair of spurs into Wolf, and trots him around crying, "Look here, girl! what I told you? Didn't I say I had Brother Wolf for my riding-horse?" It was in many ways the ultimate secular triumph in slave tales. The weak doesn't merely kill his enemy: he mounts him, humiliates him, reduces him to servility, steals his woman, and, in effect, takes his place.

Mastery through possessing the two paramount symbols of power—food and women—did not prove to be sufficient for Rabbit. He craved something more. Going to God himself, Rabbit begs for enhanced potency in the form of a larger tail, greater wisdom, bigger eyes. In each case God imposes a number of tasks upon Rabbit before his wishes are fulfilled. Rabbit must bring God a bag full of blackbirds, the teeth of a rattlesnake or alligator, a swarm of yellowjackets, the "eyewater" (tears) of a deer. Rabbit accomplishes each task by exploiting the animals' vanity. He tells the blackbirds that they cannot fill the bag and when they immediately prove they can, he traps them. He taunts the snake, "dis pole *swear* say you ain't long as him." When Rattlesnake insists he is, Rabbit ties him to the stick, ostensibly to measure him, kills him, and takes his teeth. Invariably Rabbit does what is asked of him but finds God less than pleased. In some tales he is chased out of Heaven. In others God counsels him, "Why Rabbit, ef I was to gi' you long tail aint you see you'd 'stroyed up de whol worl'? Nobawdy couldn' do nuttin wid you!" Most commonly God seemingly complies with Rabbit's request and gives him a bag which he is to open when he returns home. But Rabbit cannot wait, and when he opens the bag prematurely "thirty bull-dawg run out de box, an' bit off Ber Rabbit tail again. An' dis give him a short tail again."

The rabbit, like the slaves who wove tales about him, was forced to make do with what he had. His small tail, his natural portion of intellect—these would have to suffice, and to make them do he resorted to any means at his disposal—means which may have made him morally tainted but which allowed him to survive and even to conquer. In this respect there was a direct relationship between Rabbit and the slaves, a relationship which the earliest collectors and interpreters of these stories understood well. Joel Chandler Harris, as blind as he could be to some of the deeper implications of the tales he heard and retold, was always aware of their utter seriousness. "Well, I tell you dis," Harris had Uncle Remus say, "ef deze yer tales wuz des fun, fun, fun, en giggle, giggle, giggle, I let you know I'd a-done drapt um long ago." From the beginning Harris insisted that the animal fables he was collecting were "thoroughly characteristic of the negro," and commented that "it needs no scientific investigation to show why he selects as his hero the weakest and most harmless of all animals, and brings him out victorious in contests with the bear, the wolf, and the fox."

Harris' interpretations were typical. Abigail Christensen noted in the preface to her important 1892 collection of black tales: "It must be remembered that the Rabbit represents the colored man. He is not as large nor as strong, as swift, as wise, nor as handsome as the elephant, the alligator, the bear, the deer, the serpent, the fox, but he is 'de mos' cunnin' man dat go on fo' leg' and by this cunning he gains success. So the negro, without education or wealth, could only hope to succeed by stratagem." That she was aware of the implications of these strategies was made evident when she remarked of her own collection: "If we believe that the tales of our nurseries are as important factors in forming the characters of our children as the theological dogmas of maturer years, we of the New South cannot wish our children to pore long over these pages, which certainly could not have been approved by Froebel." In the same year Octave Thanet, in an article on Arkansas folklore, concluded, "Br'er Rabbit, indeed, personifies the obscure ideals of the negro race. . . . Ever since the world began, the weak have been trying to outwit the strong; Br'er Rabbit typifies the revolt of his race. His successes are just the kind of successes that his race have craved."

These analyses of the animal trickster tales have remained standard down to our own day. They have been advanced not merely by interpreters of the tales but by their narrators as well. Prince Baskin, one of Mrs. Christensen's informants, was quite explicit in describing the model for many of his actions:

You see, Missus, I is small man myself; but I aint nebber 'low no one for to git head o' me. I allers use my sense for help me 'long jes' like Brer Rabbit. 'Fo de wah ol' Marse Heywood mek me he driber on he place, an' so I aint hab for work so

hard as de res'; same time I git mo' ration ebery mont' an' mo' shoe when dey share out de cloes at Chris'mus time. Well, dat come from usin' my sense. An' den, when I ben a-courtin' I nebber 'lowed no man to git de benefit ob me in dat. I allers carry off de purties' gal, 'cause, you see, Missus, I know how to play de fiddle an' allers had to go to ebery dance to play de fiddle for dem.

More than half a century later, William Willis Greenleaf of Texas echoed Baskin's admiration: "De kinda tales dat allus suits mah fancy de mo'es' am de tales de ole folks used to tell 'bout de ca'iens on of Brothuh Rabbit. In de early days Ah heerd many an' many a tale 'bout ole Brothuh Rabbit what woke me to de fac' dat hit tecks dis, dat an' t'othuh to figguh life out—dat you hafto use yo' haid fo mo'n a hat rack lack ole Brothuh Rabbit do. Ole Brothuh Rabbit de smaa'tes' thing Ah done evuh run 'crost in mah whole bawn life."

This testimony—and there is a great deal of it—documents the enduring identification between black storytellers and the central trickster figure of their tales. Brer Rabbit's victories became the victories of the slave. This symbolism in slave tales allowed them to outlive slavery itself. So long as the perilous situation and psychic needs of the slave continued to characterize large numbers of freedmen as well, the imagery of the old slave tales remained both aesthetically and functionally satisfying. By ascribing actions to semi-mythical actors, Negroes were able to overcome the external and internal censorship that their hostile surroundings imposed upon them. The white master could believe that the rabbit stories his slaves told were mere figments of a childish imagination, that they were primarily humorous anecdotes depicting the "roaring comedy of animal life." Blacks knew better. The trickster's exploits, which overturned the neat hierarchy of the world in which he was forced to live, became their exploits; the justice he achieved, their justice; the strategies he employed, their strategies. From his adventures they obtained relief; from his triumphs they learned hope. . . .

ARTICLE

The "Touchiness" of the Gentleman Planter: The Sense of Esteem and Continuity in the Ante-Bellum South

Steven M. Stowe

No one would dispute the idea that manliness among elite, southern planters was to some degree based on the power that they were able to exercise over their social inferiors—women, children, poor whites, and slaves. Masculinity, as well as social status, was defined in terms of a man's ability to dominate economic, political, and social life in the South. In his article, Steven Stowe explores the relationship between the personal qualities that southern gentlemen were taught to hold in high regard and their definition of what it meant to be a man. He suggests that despite their power and privilege, planters were anything but secure in their sense of their own manliness.

According to Stowe, what caused the tension between self-confidence and self-doubt among southern planters? Was there a difference between how "character" was defined in the South and how it was defined in the North during this period? (See Judy Hilkey's article in Chapter 4.) Did northern men and southern men use different methods in their efforts to develop "character"?

Planter Temperament: Leadership and Doubt

Observers of the ante-bellum South have long been attentive to the temperament of the planter elite. Historians and contemporary witnesses, hostile or admiring, have commented on the showy, elaborate, and often contradictory behavior of the men who dominated the social and political life of the South. Writing in the 1840s a young traveler remarked of the "Southerner" that "He is liberal in his feelings, high minded, a warm and generous friend but a malignant and bitter enemy. . . . He is generous to a fault with his property. . . ." Eugene Genovese has similarly noted of the planters that "They were tough, proud, and arrogant; liberal-spirited in all that did not touch their honor; gracious and courteous; generous and kind; quick to anger and extraordinarily cruel;. . . they were not men to be taken lightly."

Although vivid and apt, this characterization is limited in two respects. First, it is an abstract, "ideal-typical" description of behavior with no systematic link to the subjective perceptions of the people whose intense behavior is thus described. Historians have relied, properly enough, on travelers' accounts, planters' memoirs, and like sources to reveal planter temperament. But careful evaluation and cross-checking aside, most historians have not fully taken into account the essentially random and idiosyncratic nature of this

Source: Steven M. Stowe, "The 'Touchiness' of the Gentleman Planter: The Sense of Esteem and Continuity in the Ante-Bellum South," *Psychohistory Review,* VIII (Winter 1979), 6–15. Used by permission of the author. Notes omitted.

kind of evidence, which is often not rooted in the subjective reporting of experience. Historians have in addition attempted to infer temperament from the planter's objective social situation as a means of corroborating observers' accounts. Thus, the curious mixture of courtesy and arrogance has been seen as a consequence of the need to balance the Christian "cavalier" ethos and the brutal mastery of slaves. But a social situation does not simply "cause" temperament. Social relationships are supported by particular ideologies and moralities; they foster certain emotional and intellectual approaches to the world, but not in automatic or reflexive ways. The interpretation of planter temperament needs to be re-evaluated and deepened in terms of the planters' own subjective assessments of what they did, and why. This entails a consideration of the wishes, fears, and other emotional exchanges that helped shape and sustain a sense of self-esteem, continuity, and moral rectitude indispensable to their leadership and control.

Second, the typical characterization of planter temperament misses what seems to have been a crucial emotional experience for many of the planter elite: pervasive and recurrent feelings of self-doubt that created a tension with an equally pervasive sense of personal worth and power. In part, the implications of this tension have been ignored by most historians because they seem inconsistent with the traditional picture of the powerful and masterful planter. In part, the tension has been overlooked because it was expressed in personal correspondence—typically viewed by historians as a less "reliable" form of evidence than relatively unambiguous public statements. Thus, for example, historians have referred to James H. Hammond's infamous "mudsill" speech—notable for its defiant, seamless assertion of planter class interests—to characterize his ideas and motives rather than referring to the tangled ruminations of his diary.

For historians who increasingly have focused on the oppressive and exploitative real-

ities of planter class power, a consideration of self-doubt seems at best superfluous and at worst exculpatory. Nevertheless, planter self-doubt needs examination because it was an important and recurrent self-assessment of their experience. Reputation and vanity, knowledge and ignorance, work and self-indulgence, were pivots on which the self-image of the planters turned. An aged Edmund Ruffin, alone with his diary, lamented his many "acts of folly, or weakness, or violations of moral duties" which he ascribed to "my vanity and love of notoriety, my simple credulity. . . ." He tended to see his failings as particularly Southern in content. A young planter confided to his diary, "I am astonished at my ignorance. . . . I have gained a reputation for talents and information and yet there is perhaps no one subject that I understand throughout. . . . Do not men, especially in this country [i.e., South Carolina], pretend to everything without knowing anything. . . . [?]"

The tension between self-confidence and self-doubt was crucial to the planter sense of identity because it constantly called into question the legitimacy of their domination. At the same time, the planters developed and participated in social forms that were intended to bolster their self-esteem. The connection between self-esteem and social forms is especially important in the study of the planter elite, since the power of the planters permitted them to shape a wide range of social practices informed by their own values.

The planter sense of self-esteem is best examined in terms of what they called "character" and the affective relationships that centered on the preservation and disruption of good character. Character was an almost tangible *sine qua non* of political, and therefore social, pre-eminence. The power of money, property, and family name was limited unless one also manifested good character. A man's honor, the badge of his character, was a public sign of his inner worth. Evidenced by honor, a man's character gave structure to a field of cognitive and moral experiences, and it provided a focus, shared with other men, of wish and aspiration. Thus, the notion of character is a good beginning from which to examine self-esteem, social forms, and the need for legitimacy of leadership.

Expecting to Lead: The Political Style

"Reputation is everything," James H. Hammond wrote. "Everything with me," observed Nathaniel Beverley Tucker, "depends upon the estimation in which I am held." Reputation, honor, esteem, the criteria of character, were established specifically in the male world of politics. Women and others might note or comment on a man's reputation, but only other men could confirm it. The political world, full of excitement, risk, and comradeship, provided the context in which self-esteem and social meaning jointly were defined. In view of the planters' economic dependence on agriculture, it is remarkable how seldom they reflected on planting in their most deeply felt expressions of hope and value. They were emotionally aroused by political adventure, law, and various politically linked kinds of speculation in land and railroads, not by plantation routine and the income derived from farming.

As children, planter class males were deliberately socialized, first by example and then also by instruction, to value a life based on personal honor, public display of authority, and an elaborate expressiveness. Before they were formally schooled, young planter males observed how these values were given concrete, personal force in their family relationships. Other values, other styles and definitions of manliness, were relatively less available in the typical social isolation of the plantation than they were to young Northern elites. When a planter male began his formal education, he continued to learn that *men* were the preceptors of character. Authoritative moral prescriptions came from fathers, uncles, and older brothers. A Virginia planter wrote to his younger brother, typically, that

"the foundation of all your present and prospective happiness as well as usefulness and standing in society" depended on "a deportment regulated by principles of honor, of virtue, truth. . . ." He warned against being "seduced" by the allurements of the world, as men heir to so much social and political power could be.

Although upper class Northern fathers probably gave generally similar advice, Southern planters seem to have emphasized honor as a desirable social attribute outweighing worldly acumen or even piety. This regional difference in emphasis was well-recognized at the time. Moreover, it seems to have been particularly Southern to stress an awareness of a man's *public* image, his "standing" in a social hierarchy rather than his worth measured by income or by purity of spirit and motive. Young Southern gentlemen were exhorted to seize every occasion for making themselves known to other men, not only in terms of learning or skill, but also in terms of the intricate expressive style which denoted a gentleman. One planter advised his fledgling lawyer son to use even a losing lawsuit as an opportunity "for displaying your eloquence. Let all of your pleadings be full of allusions, trophes, figures, and abound in general knowledge. . . ." The daybooks and diaries of young men reveal, graphically, their attempts to internalize what might be called the aesthetic style of the gentleman; young men did this long before they actually shared in the political power reserved for their sex and class. Academy education and patterns of child-rearing deserve more study in this regard; yet it seems appropriate to observe that even as most young men were trained and otherwise socialized into expectations of social preeminence, they were sheltered from an exact knowledge of what leadership would demand of them. Young men expressed doubt about what awaited them in the "outside" political world; many of them were tempted to forgo political risk and competition. One graduating student, writing to a friend, remarked upon his approaching manhood: "We are thrown upon the performance of the solemn duties of *thinking* and *acting* for ourselves. Boyish trifles are to yield to substantive materials which are to determine the character of our histories. . . ."

For most men of this class, youthful doubts notwithstanding, the "substantive materials" were political. Questions of character and morality inevitably were cast in terms of political behavior. Even after men began to assume their share of power as adults, tensions centering on the nature of legitimate leadership persisted. One such tension concerned the struggle to sort out excellence from ambition, which usually entailed balancing a desire for individual distinction with the need for friends. Hammond thought that these imperatives cut across class lines: "In whatsoever situation a man is placed, from the highest to the lowest, his general desire is to excel. To distinguish himself is the chief end of all his wishes. To become a little more thought of is what he toils for. . . ." In pursuing this goal, he added, a gentleman must not fall into demeaning ambition. Yet when "excellence" depended so much on the opinions of other men with whom one competed, it was difficult to avoid appearing self-centered or even ruthless.

In addition to the tension between ambition and "proper" distinction, the events of a political life often seemed to confuse work with play. Men constantly assessed their political labors as both drudgery and celebration. Planter-politicians were supremely representative of a personal, anti-institutional brand of politics that flourished in the early 19th century. Social issues were translated into personal questions among a network of political elites and then re-inflated with social significance. As Drew Faust has noted, the planter networks were "a particularly striking illustration of the social significance of friendship."

In one sense, political maneuvering required hard work and an almost obsessive attention to nuance. Friends helped a man grasp his relative standing in the political world. Thousands of letters were exchanged among planters; fortunes rode on elaborate expressions of sentiment and the slow mails. Factions were courted in hopes of ending faction; pseudonyms dotted the pages of "newspapers" which were completely dominated by politics; men committed themselves to long hours drafting "felicitous" or "telling" prose. "The publication of your correspondence concerning our Harbor has been of great benefit to you, personally, in this City," one planter wrote to another. "You will . . . receive . . . some marked tribute of respect from our Citizens of *all parties*. Rely upon it, they all feel kindly to you and now is your day to *work, work* and *keep working*."

In another sense, however, the political experience of these men was perceived as a form of self-indulgence. Given a certain amount of success, men delighted to "travel backwards and forwards together, make money, race blooded horses, . . . 'multiply and replenish the earth' and do all such other things as become good citizens . . . ," in the words of one planter. A Congressman from Georgia wrote to his wife that he had been detained "by the disposition of all parties here [in Savannah] to toast . . . my humble self." On another occasion, giving an account of a speech he delivered in Brooklyn, N.Y., the same Congressman said he was "carried to a most splendid entertainment where about one hundred gentlemen . . . made speeches, drank toasts and sang songs until 1 a.m." Expressions similar to these run throughout planter correspondence, testifying to the gratification possible to the ruling male elite. In the company of other men, in a rush of celebration and good-will, even the otherwise sobering concerns of public life could be gaily cast aside. "I am in a humor to be ambitious," stated a prominent planter who usually worried about concealing his ambitions. He added playfully: ". . . What can a man do subject to these fits? Heigho!"

Although sketchily presented here, these characteristic experiences of Southern elite men provided the context in which self-esteem either was maintained or lost. To summarize briefly: men looked to other men as the "significant others" in matters bearing on leadership; the social context of leadership, and thus of manhood, was political; the lexicon of manhood was shaped by moral expressions regarding character and honor; the moral ideals and expressive style internalized by men often were problematic, even paradoxical, because distinctions between (approved) excellence and hard work and (proscribed) "ambition" and self-indulgence were difficult to make. Indeed, the distinctions often seemed not to be there at all, thus calling into doubt not only aspirations and morality, as will be seen, but also significant cognitive orientations.

Obviously, many aspects of these experiences could be further mined for evidence about the relationship of Southern political ideology to morality and emotional life. However, the scope of this article must narrow to a closer examination of a single feature of male relationships that bears upon self-esteem and leadership. I will focus on certain conventions of deference having to do with speech and written expression. I hope to show how gentlemen tried to use these deferential expressions to resolve the tensions characterized above and maintain self-esteem. I will also explore disruptions of deference for what they reveal about the nature of identity and leadership. It is my intention in thus narrowing the scope of evidence and interpretation to show more precisely the affective meaning of the expansive, yet controlled, political style of the planters.

Attaining Esteem: Deferential Language

Planters placed great stock in all kinds of letters. Children in school were judged by parents and teachers in their ability to write graceful, informative, and "presentable" letters as much as they were evaluated for their music-making or grammar. Courtship letters, too, were carefully written and re-written to carry the proper emotional freight. Of interest here are the letters gentlemen wrote to each other in which their status as men of character was addressed carefully. Each type of letter had its own rhetorical conventions that seem excessively "formal" to modern eyes: elaborate forms of address, full-name signatures—even on letters between immediate family members—and literary allusions all were common features of most personal letters.

The formal importance of letters should not be surprising, although historians generally have not been attentive to the ways in which rhetorical conventions reflect social realities. It is easy to overlook the fact that aside from face-to-face encounters, people in the early 19th century had no way of communicating without involving a third-party messenger. Even the upper classes could not command a faster, more reliable, or more private means of delivering written communication much before 1845; the most urgent messages were tied to the speed and misadventures of horseback and steamboat. Personal and other kinds of "news" transmitted by letter always was late, and therefore potentially useless, inappropriate, or even grotesque.

Doubtless the mishaps that could befall a letter contributed somewhat to their formality and expressive weightiness. Too, the conventions of personal letters were related to other kinds of significant written documents, such as legal briefs and contracts, and borrowed certain expressive styles from them and from oratory. Finally, the formal nature of personal letters was a ritual exchange between writer and recipient; as in many rituals, the formalities were probably more noticed in the breach than in the observance, and as in all rituals, were a way of giving vent to problematic or contradictory needs.

These features of written expression in the planter class, and their significance regarding male social values and self-esteem, are apparent in the routine letters between gentlemen in which minor favors were requested. The elaborate courtesy that invariably marked letters of this type combined a graceful verbal style with a deliberate distancing. One such letter, written by the prominent South Carolina lawyer William Henry Trescot, began:

"Dear Sir, I can scarcely hope that you recollect as I do the introduction with which I was favored when in Washington some three winters ago. Should you have forgotten it you must allow your public character to apologize for this liberty."

The letter is typical of the genre in many ways. The "liberty" referred to was Trescot's letter itself; its purpose was to request from the recipient a copy of a speech. Viewing such unsolicited letters as "liberties" was common; the importance of this should not be ignored. A letter, if unasked for and unexpected, could infringe upon a man's honor and be cause for offense. Honor was an expansive possession, but one not intruded upon without permission. Trescot had met the recipient before, yet only obliquely referred to this in a most deferential way ("The introduction with which I was favored") after a self-deprecating disclaimer ("I can scarcely hope that you recollect as I do"). The self-effacement becomes more striking when it is understood that all Trescot desired was a favor that would have been viewed as a flattering request by most gentlemen. Moreover, Trescot was older and more widely known and respected than the recipient.

The latter, Thomas Butler King, a US Congressman from Georgia, doubtless was aware of these distinctions, and may very well have skipped somewhat absently over the ritual deference. Yet the significance of the ritual is not diminished. Trescot testified to King's honor by acknowledging him as a man of "public character" and thus of worth. But in a curious way, Trescot's deferential manner, never quite collapsing into humility, was a sign that he was equal to the man he elevated. Trescot showed that he knew that such a letter was a "liberty" and that "public character" could be an excuse for unsolicited address. Only another gentleman would so acknowledge this. Too, it can be surmised that Trescot knew that his name would be familiar to King, and thus the deference underscored Trescot's own reputation. Deference was a way of displaying the esteem of both men. At the same time, deference served

to confirm their mutual moral legitimacy as members of the ruling elite, enhancing their class's power by the repetition of a subtle, constant ritual.

Another of many similar letters will serve as a further example of the meaning of this deferential rhetoric. James Robertson, a Philadelphia merchant, wrote to William Gaston, a North Carolina jurist and planter: "As I have no claims on your attention, I ought to apologize to you for taking this liberty, or giving you any trouble; but the impressions I received of your character . . . encourages [sic] me to believe that you will excuse me for making this application." Again, the words "apology" and "liberty" stand out, as does the convention of referring to the letter by some qualifying term, in this case "application." Robertson desired only a copy of one of Gaston's speeches to university law students, yet there is a sense that such a request might be an offensive "claim." And once again, the recipient's character, that is, his reputation as a leader among men and as an honorable man himself, was used as justification for the intrusion.

Moreover, the recipient's character could be used by the writer as a hedge against possible insult; a claim could be made against the recipient even in the act of denying the claim. "I have received, however, too much disinterested kindness at your hands to permit the slightest doubt of your continued disposition to oblige me," one gentleman wrote to another. This put the burden of response on the recipient by using his own seemingly inviolable character against him. Sometimes a man's family name could be so used: "[T]hough we are strangers to each other," began one such letter, "yet I feel assured that one descended, as you are, from a family notable for so many noble qualities, will not hesitate to give me the information so anxiously desired."

So deliberate an assumption of deference by the writer implied, in a sense, a right to place a burden on the recipient. A proud man's deference demanded deference in return; thus did rhetorical convention mirror the crucial need for a public acknowledgment of equality between gentlemen. What one man risked losing through self-effacement was compensated for by the other man's attention and compliance. Relationships between men thus apparently turned, in part, on each man placing his honor temporarily in the hands of the other. The risk to character, and the implied challenge to leadership, was shared equally, and both men were confirmed in their social position.

The assertion of equality among gentlemen was central to their relationships and to their self-esteem as individuals. Any single gentleman at any given time could not expect to match all others in terms of political influence, economic security, or personal charisma. But any gentleman could expect equal treatment in terms of his honor. If a man participated or was invited to share in rituals of deference he could assure himself of his elite standing. He knew, consciously, that in making himself available, even vulnerable, to other gentlemen he was displaying the self-confidence that anchored the planters' rule over their many and disparate dependents. The elaborate and compelling nature of these rituals is evidence of the affective intensity with which social power was maintained by the elite. So small in number were the ruling planters that elaborate display was necessary to convince themselves as well as others of the rightness of their power.

The forms of deference were not only a way to testify to the actual status and power of the planter, but also acted as a check on their potential for "ambitious" self-aggrandizement. Despite their small number and growing sense of a common cause, the ante-bellum planters knew that the ambition of some could wrench from others more than a fair share of power. The mannered good behavior and gracefulness with which deferent gentlemen addressed each other was a way of emphasizing excellence and deterring ambition. Only the ambitious man would deny himself to his fellows; availability of one gentleman to another served as a check on the full and exclusive pursuit of the social power they had acquired.

The use of deferential modes also reveals a shared wish for a more perfect community of gentlemen who would refuse the petty tactics of competition. The deferential rituals were used at times to turn even political controversy into a single stream of agreement and agreeableness, as when one office seeker wrote to a possible opponent asking whether the latter was planning a contest: "by [your] giving me an early intimation of your [plans] . . . I shall be able to check my friends and save myself probably from the mortification of a defeat, and you the mortification of being the cause of it." A "mortifying" blow to reputation could be suffered even by a victor when equals competed. The ideal was to transcend the trials of ambition and competition; yet equality lay in such delicate balance that inequality was almost a certainty.

Denying Esteem: The Duel

Conflict was inevitable in relationships in which men strove for equal standing yet demanded and received the deference due superiors. Like the relationships themselves, these conflicts need much more study before the connections between social structure and personality in the ante-bellum planter class can be made systematically useful to the history of the South. But in pursuing the start made here, it is important now to turn attention to the disruption of deferential relationships in order to deepen our understanding of the meaning of self-esteem in this society.

The most drastic disruption involved the duel, or the "affair of honor," as it was so aptly called. When historians have considered Southern duelling at all, it has often been in terms of the "quaintness" of the practice, or in terms that emphasize both its significance and its silliness. Indeed, the latter was noted throughout the ante-bellum period as well. But the almost comically swollen egos, and the elaborate care sometimes taken to avoid a duel while saving honor, need not blind us to the basic significance of a duel: it was a dramatic, class-bound ritual, often with serious consequences, that further illuminates what men wanted from themselves and from each other.

Before looking closely at duels as a disruption of personal continuity and social equilibrium, it is important to emphasize two major features of all duels. First, as dueling manuals and duelists themselves made clear, affairs of honor by nature could not be adjudicated at law. Numerous contemporary pleas, to stop the practice usually conceded that a lawsuit was not the stuff of honor. Obviously, the practice would not have persisted so long in the face of moral disapproval and legal proscription had it not been in the service of nonrational needs. Second, dueling was an exclusively male activity. Women played a passive role in clashes of honor, although they sometimes acted to sooth tempers. But, in general, a woman was expected to "not permit [herself] even to allude to [a duel], much less to speak about it," as one planter wrote to his young daughter.

The fact that many duels arose in a political context again underscores the crucial importance politics held for self-esteem and a sense of social wholeness. An affair of honor could develop over an insult to a man's family or his physical courage. But even if such incitements were not explicitly political, a duel was likely to stem from their being used politically, or used casually in a public forum. Given the risky, speculative, and actually competitive nature of the political world, a man's honor was most exposed to attack there.

However, not all reverses or oppositions intruded upon his honor. Men could, and did, refuse to duel or even to take offense at certain types of remarks or opponents. James H. Hammond, embedded in a scandal with the Hamptons, chose not to fight a "lickspittle of the Hamptons" whom he chanced to meet in New York City. Although the two men spoke, and Hammond wrote that "I might with propriety have taken offense and knocked him down," he felt nothing but "pity and contempt" and thus decided not to "notice" him. Hammond apparently defined the man as not an equal, and probably did not feel sufficiently backed into a corner of his own character to resort to a challenge.

Even so, men had difficulty at times determining when words or incidents went too far. Honor and transgressions of it often were elusive. Letters among three brothers of the Townes family of South Carolina in 1831 illustrate some of the difficulties. Henry Townes took offense at some remarks by a man named Perry; at once the other Townes brothers became intimately involved. While condemning Perry's "low and vulger abuse" of Henry, Samuel Townes also was concerned about how George Townes should "act towards the damned puppy." Samuel advised George to "not touch him" because "it would enlist the sympathies of the public perhaps on his behalf and he would immediately raise the cry of persecution, that he had a whole family on him, etc. . . ." Yet Samuel told George that should the latter feel driven to attack Perry, "don't think of doing so without a good and trusty stick."

Henry Townes, the principal whose life would be threatened, seems to have had two major considerations. First, he, too, was concerned, as he wrote his brother George, that their family have confidence in his judgment and courage "and know I will do nothing but what is right and proper. . . ." Second, he was intent on controlling the timing of the dispute. Although he said he wanted "to post P----at once and in that way make him fight" he also acknowledged that friends "advised me to wait a decent time, say about four weeks" before publishing Perry "as a *coward* and a base *caluminator*. . . ." Dueling in defense of honor thus involved the necessity for both passionate anger and close attention to "decent" behavior.

Almost a month later, the principals still were publishing insulting handbills; but the flash point had not been reached. Samuel still was advising George "to keep your hands off Perry unless he should have the impudence to speak of it (designedly) in an unbecoming manner in your presence. . . ." He implied throughout that George, not the insulted Henry, was the man most likely to do something rash. This letter indicates the subtle boundaries of language that could be crossed or not crossed: not only had impudence to be determined, but it must be "designed" and "unbecoming" impudence.

The crisis turned into a prolonged wrangle. Nearly two months after the original insult to himself, Henry Townes found reason to comment on "the absurdity of P's positions" rather than on their baseness. Conflict between equals was dissolving, in Henry's view, to one honorable man being harassed by a fool. Yet he could still comment, "I would very much like to shoot him, and if he was to challenge me and my friends would let me I would certainly do it." Apparently, Perry ultimately relied on medical reasons—wounds from a previous duel—as an honorable way out of the dispute. In any event, Henry did not have to stand and fire in order to keep his honor. Samuel wrote, however, that he would rather see his brother "a helpless corpse than to have this matter settled in a way which is not perfectly honorable to himself." There is no reason to doubt that he was serious, and that had words or events turned in a different way, a duel would have occurred.

The Townes-Perry affair reveals two features of dueling that seem particularly important. These two features would bear more study, but can be briefly elaborated on here. First, honor and the breach of honor rested on whether language was used with "personal" intent. Much of the ritual behavior of duelists and their seconds concerned itself with language and the precise interpretation of it. One planter, writing a disclaimer to William Gaston, took pains to emphasize that his speech in the legislature was not intended to be "very personal" even though it had been highly critical of Gaston's stand on the Nat Turner rebellion. The planter went on to reveal what constituted "personal" language by asserting that he "did not entertain . . . a sentiment unkind or offensive to you, nor mean, nor intend to offer, the least violence to your feelings, nor impute any improper motive to your actions." "Personal" language, the language in which duels were rooted, was language that cast a man's motives, his intentions, and hence his character and leadership position into public doubt.

Language could mend a man's self-esteem as well. In one duel, settled on paper after the firing of two shots, the participants signed a statement which established that "no personal insult . . . was intended." Another duel was avoided when the two men agreed that a challenge to one's impartiality did not touch honor, whereas a challenge to one's veracity did. The impassioned and often rough-and-tumble political style, of course, made both challenges inevitable and easily confused. It is important to note that distinctions such as this one allowed men to accuse each other of self-interest, but not to the point where ambition could be said to affect character. The linguistic distinctions allow us to see where, in some cases, the line between excellence and ambition was drawn.

The second significant feature of dueling was its public nature, marked by the involvement of friends. Friends could goad men into fighting through appeals to their esteem, but they also could bring about a settlement. Formal, published agreements attest to the latter. One South Carolina planter spoke typically when he announced that an "unpleasant dispute" between two men, a "source of great uneasiness to me," was settled "by great industry and effort on the part of friends of both parties. . . ." Written statements by friends were of critical importance. A North Carolina planter wrote a lengthy, eyewitness account of a legislative argument addressed to one of the disputants with the expressed purpose "that if any difficulties exist, they may be adjusted and mischief prevented" by publication of the account. Another legislator, asking that his disclaimer of insult be accepted, said that he hoped his offended colleague would "put it in my power to say to my relatives and friends that I have not been 'very personal and offensive' to you."

In a tactical sense, of course, a man's friends were relied upon to extricate him, if possible, from a dangerous dispute. Failing this, they were counted upon to support and materially aid him. But in a deeper sense, the involvement of friends is further evidence of the shared importance of self-esteem among elite men, and of the techniques they developed to maintain uninterrupted social control. A man's honor was too important to be left as a private matter. All men had an interest in the way honor was defined and protected. Honor accrued to all men when a dispute was publically resolved by either a duel or a settlement. This was not the case in most lawsuits, where only persons immediately interested and the attorneys benefited. Duels communally aired grievances and distributed the burden of honor equally to all gentlemen, binding them into a sense of legitimate hegemony.

The importance of language and friends to dueling is clearly apparent in the near-contest between Milledge Luke Bonham and Preston Brooks in 1849. A brief look at the events of their dispute through their own letters will conclude this view of honor in the social world of men. It appears that the affair began when Brooks alluded to an incident in the Mexican War in which Bonham had shot himself in the foot and had been relieved of his command of the 12th Regiment, US Infantry. Bonham's courage had been questioned and Bonham himself had requested the board of inquiry which cleared him of charges of cowardice. Brooks' mention of the incident came at a Fourth of July celebration at which Bonham was given a military honor. Brooks remarked in public that he felt neglected; after all *he* had not been talked about as Bonham had.

It is not clear how Bonham heard of Brooks' comments, but he wrote Brooks a letter asking, rather curtly, for clarification. Brooks' reply was conciliatory, saying that "nothing was further from my purpose or desire than to injure you," but he chided Bonham for writing: ". . . had you *spoken* to me . . . I would have removed even a shadow of displeasure." The implication seems to have been that Bonham was being rather aggressive himself in writing a formal letter of inquiry; or perhaps Brooks wanted to suggest that Bonham's language verged on the insulting. In any case, Brooks asserted that he did *not* say that the charges of cowardice against Bonham were true, only that they had been made.

Bonham replied two days later that Brooks' letter was "unsatisfactory" in its expressions despite "the friendly tone of the concluding paragraph." Then Bonham spelled out his position: he objected to Brooks' using the incident of the self-inflicted wound in conversation regardless of whether it was intended to injure Bonham's reputation. Mention of even false charges could injure a man, Bonham wrote. Brooks replied the following day, in effect agreeing with Bonham's last point, but adding that such past injuries to reputation were facts of life, regrettable but true. Brooks showed his growing appreciation of the seriousness of this exchange of letters by stating his position carefully:

> I meant this and *nothing* more, viz., 'that a soldier's honor is as delicate as a woman's' and that any imputation upon it, however false or malicious, was an injury—that this injury you had sustained, though . . . wrongfully and undeservedly, and that I had been more fortunate than yourself, having sustained no such injury and therefore objected [in my July 4 remarks] to being placed on the same footing [with you].

Bonham quickly took issue with the latter remark, saying that if Brooks did not declare them to be equals he would consider Brooks to be impinging on "my standing as a man of honor and courage." Still not quite charging Brooks with being willfully insulting, Bonham nevertheless asked him to disavow any imputation of inequality between them and to "withdraw the offensive language." Brooks' stance was to insist that his "opinion" about past damage to Bonham's honor was itself not an insult; he disavowed impinging Bonham's standing as a courageous man, but refrained from declaring them equals.

At this point in the exchange, two things appear to have happened. First, both men seem to have realized that they were deeply locked into issues of language that would lead them into a duel and perhaps death or injury. Bonham's letter of July 19 takes note of Brooks' expressions of regret and says pointedly that if the latter will only state that Bonham's courage and honor are equal to his then "I accept the explanation." Second, the exchange of letters became daily, indicating that friends of the two men were actively involved in shuttling the correspondence and advising on the issues.

Brooks, in a July 19 response, again denied any intent of insult to Bonham; he reiterated his position that his "opinion" regarding Bonham's "standing" was not meant to "cast . . . imputation upon you." It was clear by this point, however, that Brooks would not say that the two were equals. Bonham, therefore, issued a formal challenge to meet Brooks on the 25th "for the purpose of continuing our correspondence," an expression which may have been euphemism or may have been exact. The site he proposed was by the Savannah River, at noon, a traditional arrangement for duels. Here it is clear that friends intervened. The man chosen as Bonham's second returned with the challenge undelivered, saying that he had "forgotten" that Brooks had joined his own friends on a fishing trip. Clearly, everyone was playing for time. Bonham, however, insisted that the meeting take place as planned and declared that he would write Brooks no more letters.

A final resolution, however, demanded a formal statement. Since Bonham refused to write, James H. Hammond drafted both a letter to Brooks and a suggested reply. Bonham finally agreed to copy the letter in his own hand and it was sent to Brooks. The letter expressed Bonham's willingness to listen to "a mutual friend," presumably Hammond, who convinced him to give "mature reflection" to the conflict. Then Bonham asked simply whether Brooks intended finally to deny them equal standing. The next day, for exact reasons that cannot be known, Brooks responded that "I regard you as a man of honor and courage and of course equal to myself. . . ." Bonham found this satisfactory and so the correspondence and the affair ended.

Sharing Honor: Language and Society

Bonham and Brooks, like many other members of the Southern elite, were prepared to risk death rather than allow their honor to be mis-defined or treated carelessly. The fact that the two men never exchanged shots should not suggest that they were not in dead earnest; nor should the specific rhetoric be passed over as insignificant. Men trafficked in their own honor, and in the honor of their fellows, through the medium of language. When conventions of honor became disrupted, men relied on linguistic agreement to restore reciprocity. Bonham's insistence that Brooks use the word "equal" indicates not only the importance of the concept of equality, but also the importance of uttering the restorative word. This heavy reliance on exact language is related to the planters' cognitive dependence on the supposed preciseness of legal forms and to their affective indulgence in the aesthetics of oratory.

The significance attached to written forms of language, in this case personal letters, was due in part to the planters' need to maintain *intimate* communication across geographical distances that threatened to distort meaning and weaken their class control. Letters were the only way to meet this need. In this sense letters were important regardless of their exact language; but in a deeper sense the language of letters carried currents of personal esteem and social meaning crucial to the equilibrium of this elite. Language—the "right" language—represented one of the less tangible social supports that these men knew were indispensable to their self-esteem and their dominance.

Language and correspondence were important, too, because they allowed the thoughts, fears, and wishes of individuals to take on a public dimension. One's language could be manipulated by one's friends; as the Bonham-Brooks affair shows, a friend could in fact become one's spokesman and scribe. Language and written forms thus engaged men in a shared action that defined and maintained their leadership. The energy devoted to furthering and resolving an affair of honor was not misplaced; honor was the flag of moral leadership. And in this severely stratified social system where a tiny minority of white males exercised control over millions of restive and bitterly exploited dependents, honor became the internalized measure of social stability. In keeping their honor safe, yet "manfully" at risk in the political world, men validated their right to rule. Because they conceived of social processes as a mixture of personal achievement, God-given worth, and shrewd management of dependents, these men created the notion of honor as a most important social barometer by which to maintain their personal balance and measure their fortunes and their future. The honor of one man thus became of considerable importance to all, and the disruption of social relationships between men became centered on the mandates of honor and their preservation.

Redescribing these subjective experiences calls for a measured tentativeness. Historical understanding of the rituals and language that gave elites a sense of esteem and continuity is just beginning to assume a shape of its own. In regard to Southern planters, attention should be given to social events, in addition to the duel, in which male self-esteem was maintained or disrupted. An entire range of subjective experiences, and their relation to the social and political power of men, awaits study. And because men located part of their sense of self-esteem in their family lives, a study of the domestic world, too, should augment our understanding of ante-bellum social control and continuity. Courtship rituals, for example, far from being frivolous occasions, were crucial to the esteem and identity of both men and women in the planter class; these and other conventional experiences should be made central to the study of planter values and power.

It bears repeating that most planters, most of the time, were able to master, at least cognitively, the tensions raised by doubt and the threats to self-esteem examined in this article. Even so, the typical characterization of planter temperament must take into account the subjective assessments by the planters of their often paradoxical experience precisely because the interplay of confidence and doubt shaped their sense of the world and the social structures they created. James H. Hammond revealed something vividly significant when he wrote in 1836, "Life without honor is the deepest damnation. Not to do your duty is dishonor. To do your duty wins honor, [but] destroys health and makes life a burden.... The world works in a circle." Hammond sensed a kind of entrapment in the deepest reaches of planter values. Perhaps he feared that the cyclical tensions in his life contained the code of social collapse. The possibility of such a message could neither be entertained nor ignored by an elite absorbed in balancing their ability to lead with their power to bind and coerce.

SUGGESTIONS FOR FURTHER READING

EDWARD L. AYERS, *Vengeance and Justice: Crime and Punishment in the 19th-Century American South* (New York: Oxford University Press, 1984).

DANIEL P. BLACK, *Dismantling Black Manhood: An Historical and Literary Analysis of the Legacy of Slavery* (New York: Garland, 1997).

JANE TURNER CENSER, *North Carolina Planters and Their Children: 1800–1860* (Baton Rouge: Louisiana State University Press, 1984).

JIM CULLEN, " 'I's a Man Now': Gender and African American Men," in *Divided Houses: Gender and the Civil War,* ed. Catherine Clinton and Nina Silber (New York: Oxford University Press, 1992), 76–91.

DAVID HERBERT DONALD, "A Generation of Defeat," in *From the Old South to the New: Essays on the Transitional South,* ed. Walter J. Fraser, Jr. and Winfred B. Moore, Jr. (Westport, CT: Greenwood Press, 1981), 3–20.

LAURA F. EDWARDS, *Gendered Strife & Confusion: The Political Culture of Reconstruction* (Urbana: University of Illinois Press, 1997).

GEORGE M. FREDRICKSON, "Masters and Mudsills: The Role of Race in the Planter Ideology of South Carolina," *South Atlantic Urban Studies,* II (1978), 34–48.

EUGENE D. GENOVESE, *Roll Jordon Roll: The World the Slaves Made* (New York: Vintage, 1976).

KENNETH S. GREENBERG, *Honor & Slavery* (Princeton: Princeton University Press, 1996).

HERBERT G. GUTMAN, *The Black Family in Slavery and Freedom, 1750–1925* (New York: Pantheon, 1976).

JOHN STARRETT HUGHES, "The Madness of Separate Spheres: Insanity and Masculinity in Victorian Alabama," in *Meanings for Manhood: Constructions of Masculinity in Victorian America,* ed. Mark C. Carnes and Clyde Griffin (Chicago: University of Chicago Press, 1990), 53–66.

MICHAEL P. JOHNSON, "Planters and Patriarchy: Charleston, 1800–1860," *Journal of Southern History,* 46 (Feb. 1980), 45–72.

MICHAEL P. JOHNSON AND JAMES L. ROARK, *Black Masters: A Free Family of Color in the Old South* (New York: W. W. Norton, 1984).

LEON LITWACK, *Been in the Storm So Long: The Aftermath of Slavery* (New York: Knopf, 1979).

STEPHANIE MCCURRY, *Masters of Small Worlds: Yeoman Households, Gender Relations, and the Political Culture of the Antebellum South Carolina Low Country* (New York: Oxford University Press, 1995).

GRADY MCWHINEY, *Cracker Culture: Celtic Ways in the Old South* (Tuscaloosa: University of Alabama Press, 1988).

TED OWNBY, "The Defeated Generation at Work: White Farmers in the Deep South, 1865–1890," *Southern Studies,* 23 (Winter 1984), 325–47.

JAMES L. ROARK, *Masters Without Slaves: Southern Planters in the Civil War and Reconstruction* (New York: W. W. Norton, 1977).

LOREN SCHWENINGER, *Black Property Owners in the South, 1790–1915* (Urbana: University of Illinois Press, 1990).

NINA SILBER, "Intemperate Men, Spiteful Women, and Jefferson Davis," in *Divided Houses: Gender and the Civil War,* ed. Catherine Clinton and Nina Silber (New York: Oxford University Press, 1992), 283–305.

STEVEN M. STOWE, *Intimacy and Power in the Old South: Ritual in the Lives of the Planters* (Baltimore, MD: Johns Hopkins University Press, 1987).

THOMAS L. WEBBER, *Deep Like the Rivers: Education in the Slave Quarter Community, 1831–1865* (New York: W. W. Norton, 1978).

LEEANN WHITES, *The Civil War as a Crisis in Gender: Augusta, Georgia, 1860–1890* (Athens: University of Georgia Press, 1995).

BERTRAM WYATT-BROWN, "The Mask of Obedience: Male Slave Psychology in the Old South," *American Historical Review,* 93 (December 1988), 1228–1252.

BERTRAM WYATT-BROWN, *Southern Honor: Ethics and Behavior in the Old South* (New York: Oxford University Press, 1982).

CHAPTER SEVEN

FEMININITY IN THE NINETEENTH-CENTURY SOUTH (1820–1890)

THE SOUTHERN WOMAN IN MYTH AND LEGEND

It has been Hollywood rather than history books that has given us our most vivid images of what it meant to be a woman in the nineteenth-century South. Directors of such films as "Gone with the Wind," "Roots," and "The North and the South," have fed us romanticized versions of sometimes spirited but always beautiful and charming plantation wives and daughters, tightly laced into dresses with voluminous, swaying skirts. Privileged, soft-spoken, and physically delicate, they gracefully flit across the screen through the spacious rooms of their stately plantation mansions, willing to depend upon the good will of the men in their lives and the labor of their slaves to guarantee them lives of leisure and pleasure.

The Hollywood portrayal of black women has been no less stereotypical. Dominating the scene is the good-humored, asexual Mammy.

She is a surrogate mother, who loves her white charges as much as she loves her own children and who serves as the ultimate source of comfort and wisdom for everyone in the plantation community. Hollywood has also given us the less benign figure of the flirtatious Jezebel lurking in the shadows. She uses her sexual allure to gain whatever personal advantage there might be in satisfying the lust of her white master or his friends. Jezebel is joined by a third, black, female image. She is the docile but sexually vulnerable housemaid or field hand, who minds her own business, works hard, and does what she can to avoid attracting unwanted attention from whites in general and lecherous white men in particular.

Scriptwriters, directors, and producers have provided us with visual images that perpetuate myths about southern life. Their portrayals of southern women rarely reflect the complex ways in which femininity was constructed and negotiated both before and after the Civil War. Nor do they reflect the variability of feminine social roles. They have largely ignored the presence of yeoman farm wives, women living in urban rather than rural settings, free black women, and Native American women. And only a few have presented us with films that explore the ways in which military defeat in the Civil War affected the feminine identities of southern women. The war, as presented in "Gone with the Wind," may have provided Scarlett O'Hara with an opportunity to give full rein to her resourcefulness and her propensity to pursue her own interests no matter what the cost to others. But those in the film industry have shown little interest in exploring the kinds of adjustments less flamboyant women had to make in their concept of femininity in response to changes brought about by war.

During the nineteenth century, white, black, and native women living in the South were forced by circumstances largely beyond their control to reconsider what it meant to be a woman. The Civil War was the defining event for black and white southerners. For Native American women the defining event was the determination of the federal government to "civilize" them and then forcibly remove them from their ancestral lands. Some women, no doubt, found the process of recreating themselves a liberating experience. But as we shall see, it was clearly a difficult, painful, and unwelcome one for others.

THE FEMININE IDENTITIES OF PLANTATION MISTRESSES

Whatever the number of slaves or the size of their husband's real estate holdings, southern plantation mistresses had to construct their ideas about femininity around a series of contradictions. On one hand, their womanliness was derived from the degree to which they appeared to be helpless and dependent on men. On the other, they were supposed to be highly responsible and competent household managers and childrearers who were capable of making independent decisions about do-

mestic matters. They were expected to earn their living by marrying and then to contribute to the plantation economy by maintaining the household, supervising household production, and caring for their husbands, children, and slaves. In other words, while their image was one of the leisured lady, in reality they had to work very hard. And in an age in which many idealized women as "naturally" delicate, asexual beings, southern plantation mistresses needed robust good health, physical strength, and stamina in order to fulfill their womanly responsibilities which included the more or less unrestricted bearing of children.

The cult of true womanhood was just as important for the construction of womanhood in the South as it was in the North. But in the South, complex and distinctly regional gender, race, and class systems established the context within which women expressed piety, maintained their sexual purity, submitted to male authority, and carried out their domestic responsibilities. For example, female submission was crucial to the maintenance of discipline on the plantation. A man who could not control his wife was unlikely to be able to control his slaves. The dependence of women was also an important component of the idea of manly honor. Only if women allowed men to believe that they were dependent upon them for the necessities of life, their social identity, and for protection against insult and injury could southern gentlemen feel secure in their manliness. The question of maintaining female sexual purity was also a component of the southern code of honor, since it required that men defend the reputations of their female relatives.

Most southern women of the slaveholding elite did what they could to conform to the demands that the ideology of domesticity placed on them. They took comfort in the thought that they were morally superior to the men in their families; they tried to be good wives and mothers; they made every effort to run their households as efficiently as possible; and they observed social conventions designed to preserve their claim to gentility.

Given the fact that women in planter families were dependent upon men for their social identities and economic status, it is not surprising that one of the defining moments in a southern woman's life was the day she married. In becoming a wife, she transferred responsibility for her well being from her father to her husband. It was considered the duty of a woman to marry, and failure to do so reflected on her claim to womanliness. Spinsters may have been able to carve out some social space for themselves in the North, but in the South they were not held in very high regard.

Marriage could be, however, an extremely risky business. Once a woman married, there was little she could do but put up with whatever shortcomings her husband might have. Most planter families lived in relative isolation from their neighbors. And the wife of a planter could not necessarily count on friends or family members to intercede on her behalf if her husband turned out to be neglectful, or even worse—a drunk, a gambler, a philanderer, or a wife abuser. The general attitude seemed to be that what a man did in his own home was his business, and few were prepared to interfere. For a woman, the possibility of getting a divorce was minimal even if she were willing to risk the social ostracism that was likely to accompany it. So while it was perfectly acceptable for a woman to tie her feminine identity to her role as a wife, tying it to wifely happiness in that role was problematical. One disillusioned southern woman commented that "Marriages are said to be made in Heaven." But she went on to point out that they got extremely "jumbled" in the construction process. She was convinced that successful and emotionally satisfying marriages were pretty hard to come by.

Whatever ambivalence women of the planter elite may have felt about marriage did not carry over to their role as mothers. It was common for wives of planters to construct their feminine identities around bearing and rearing children. "I imagine nothing, no relation in life [that] makes one feel so differently as that of being a Mother," wrote one Virginia woman shortly before the Civil War. "To woman, I have always heard it said, the gift of a child was a joy. . . ."

Unlike women in the North, plantation mistresses showed little interest in birth control before the Civil War. Southern families welcomed children, despite the fact that childbearing was both dangerous and debilitating. Southern men considered a large number of children as testimony to their virility. There were no economic reasons for a woman to restrict her fertility, and the wives of slave owners had servants to relieve them of some of the more distasteful aspects of childcare. The diaries and letters of plantation mistresses indicate that they placed a high value on motherhood and focused a good deal of their energy trying to provide for the physical, emotional, and spiritual wellbeing of their children.

Another important component of the definition of femininity among those in the planter class was skill in managing large households. The more slaves there were on the plantation, the more time-consuming and complicated was the job of a plantation mistress. It simply made good business sense for plantations to be as self-sustaining as possible. So usually a plantation mistress was in charge of household manufacturing as well as maintenance and was responsible for arranging to feed and clothe all of the slaves that her husband owned. Typically, she was expected to supervise the dairy and the gardening as well as the making of soap and candles. If her husband was unable or unwilling to buy inexpensive cloth so that she could make shifts and pants for the slaves, the production of homespun was her responsibility. As a result, she had to spend hours supervising her servants as they sat at their spinning wheels and looms. Added to these responsibilities was that of providing health care for everyone on the plantation. After working all day, she could still be called upon to spend the night delivering a baby or nursing someone who was ill either in her own household or out in the slave quarters.

A woman who was able to run a large household efficiently and make it look easy was considered to have mastered skills that were defined as womanly. This was no simple task. It is true that she had help in fulfilling her domestic responsibilities, but she needed great patience and highly developed diplomatic skills in order to cajole her slaves to do what she asked of them.

Intellectual accomplishment was not an attribute that was highly prized among most women in the social elite. Rich planters, like successful businessmen in the North, were willing to spend the money to send their daughters off to academies and female colleges. And some young women flourished in an academic environment and received a rigorous education. But southern belles in general had no reason to place great value on advanced education. Since it had very little practical utility for them, only a few took their studies seriously. In the South, college attendance for women was important primarily as an indicator of social class. The result was that feminine ideals were more likely to include the possession of physical grace, sociability, personal charm, politeness, modesty, a sense of moral purpose, and generosity of spirit than the possession of a well-developed intellect.

The extent to which plantation mistresses constructed their identities around politics before the Civil War is unclear. The source of their political identities lay in their patriotism and their willingness to accept responsibility for inculcating republican principles in their children. They could not vote or hold office, but we know from their diaries and letters that many of them were interested in the outcome of elections and the political debates that preceded them. By 1860 support for states rights and the possibility of secession dominated southern politics. Discussions of these issues provided women with increased opportunities to equate femininity with the right to express one's political opinions. As the Civil War approached, women of all ages became politicized. School girls expressed their loyalty to the South by delivering speeches to their classmates while their mothers wore secession cockades in their bonnets.

Although some southern women expanded the meaning of femininity to include political action before the Civil War, they did not embrace the cause of woman's rights. By the 1850s, they may have been unhappy about the way the men in their families abused their power and privilege. But there was simply too much at stake for them to advocate a revolution in gender roles and relations and to make an effort to undermine a social system that provided them with so much wealth and privilege. So they remained disdainful of efforts on the part of northern woman's rights advocates to try to expand the social, economic, and political role of women in American society.

THE FEMININE IDENTITIES OF YEOMAN FARM WOMEN

Our knowledge about how yeoman farm women expressed their femininity is limited. Even if they were literate (and many of them were not), few had the time or the inclination to write diaries and letters. As with their fathers and husbands, we have to depend on our knowledge of their circumstances and the behavior patterns that brought them to public attention in order to understand the role that gender played in their lives.

Yeoman farm women worked as partners in an agrarian enterprise. Because their husbands owned no slaves, many of them lived lives of unremitting toil. They may have been church-going and respectable, but, generally speaking, they understood their class position and made no claim to being "ladies." That did not mean, however, that they were not held to an externally imposed feminine ideal. Evangelical Christianity had a strong influence on the yeoman class in the South. Baptist and Methodist churches held farm women to high standards of morality and expected them to submit to the authority of their husbands. Moreover, the authors of prescriptive literature found in farm journals like the *Southern Cultivator* admonished literate women in the yeoman class to take their domestic responsibilities seriously. The ideal farm wife was at her most womanly, they argued, when she was a sensible, industrious, and practical housekeeper and when she devoted herself to nurturing her own children and caring for her husband, even if that meant helping him with the field work.

Because of their economic circumstances, farm women expressed their femininity in ways that were different from women in the planting class. Most of them spent a considerable amount of time working out of doors. So there was no point in trying to conform to standards of beauty held by their social superiors. Even when they were careful to wear a sunbonnet, their skin was likely to be dry and unfashionably tanned. They had neither the time, the money, nor the opportunity to concern themselves with the latest fashion. They might have a best dress to wear to church, but other than that their clothes were more likely to be functional than aesthetically pleasing.

These women were the mistresses of "make do." They could turn old, ragged pieces of clothing into quilts and braided rugs, and they could make a squirrel stew last for more than one meal. Like poor women in the North, many did not invest much of their feminine identities in their performance of housekeeping skills. Trying to clean a small, two-room cabin with dirt floors was often pointless. They did not have much furniture, often cooked their food in one pot, and the few clothes that they had did not take much time to maintain. What they did have, of course, was children. Motherhood was an important component of their feminine identities, not only because of the emotional satisfaction they derived from their nurturing responsibilities but also because they needed the labor that their children could provide.

The Feminine Identities of Free Women of Color before General Emancipation

In August, 1823, Amelia Galle placed an advertisement in the Petersburg *Republican*. "Health Purchased Cheap," it read. Galle was the owner of a Petersburg, Virginia, bath-house. Her newspaper ad claimed that potential customers would make a much wiser investment in their health if they spent a mere 25 cents on a bath than if they spent their hard-earned money on medicine. There was nothing unusual about a resourceful entrepreneur advertising the availability of a service in a local newspaper. What was unusual about the ad was that the advertiser was a free black woman.

While volumes have been written about slave women, we don't know much about the lives of free black women in the South before the Civil War. The census provides information about where they lived and with whom; tax records give us some idea about how much property they owned; court records indicate the degree to which they were or were not law-abiding; and advertisements testify to their entrepreneurial spirit. But beyond that, what we can say about how they constructed their ideas about gender is fairly tentative.

The most systematic studies of ordinary freed women in the antebellum South concern those who lived in Virginia. Most of them were poor. Most were gainfully employed. And they were more likely than white women to be the heads of their households. It is not clear whether they remained unmarried because of circumstance or because of choice. Certainly their opportunities to marry were limited. In Petersburg, they outnumbered free black men. No matter where they lived, it was legally impossible for them to marry white men. And marrying slave men was socially and legally complicated. It may have been that some of them simply preferred to remain single for economic reasons. The laws of Virginia provided that when a woman married, she had to turn her property over to her husband if he was a free man. That meant that she had to give him control over the wages she made as a laundress, or seamstress, or domestic servant or the profits she made as a small businesswoman. Moreover, since racism made it difficult, if not impossible, for black men to protect their families and fulfill the role of sole breadwinner, free black women did not have the same incentives to marry as white women did. It may have been for these reasons that free black women in Virginia were less likely than their white counterparts to fashion their feminine identities around the concept of wifely dependence.

Some free women did, of course, marry. And what evidence exists suggests that those marriages were more egalitarian than those of whites. A woman might expect her husband to provide her with companionship, sexual gratification, and help in rearing her children, but there was little reason for a hardworking black woman to defer to his authority. Whether she was single or married, a black woman was best served if she constructed her feminine identity around what whites would have considered masculine qualities—physical and emotional strength, ambition, resourcefulness, and self-sufficiency.

Having said all this, it is difficult to determine how typical the freed women of Virginia were. It is reasonable to assume that life for free black women in Virginia was somewhat different from that of those who lived in Tennessee, Mississippi, or Texas. It is equally reasonable to assume that there was a difference between women who lived in southern towns and cities and those who lived in the countryside. But until more research is done, we will have to generalize from the experience of this small group.

THE CONSTRUCTION OF FEMININITY IN THE SLAVE QUARTERS

Slave narratives are the best source for any inquiry into the way that bondswomen defined femininity. What they reveal is that the most obvious constraint slave women faced in trying to construct their gendered identities was the fact that they were the property of whites, whose influence over their lives was tremendous.

Work for slaves was usually gendered. But it tended to be more gendered on large plantations than it was on small ones. On a small plantation, for example, it was impractical for

a planter to pay much attention to whether men or women did the work that needed to be done. If he needed to clear new land, he was likely to order whoever was available to fell trees and clear away brush. A plantation owner who owned many slaves, however, could afford to use more discretion in his work assignments. Even if he was sensitive to issues of gender, he probably would not excuse a woman from having to harness a mule and plow the fields. But he might exempt her from having to perform the most physically demanding jobs such as hauling wood. And if she were pregnant, he might consider it to be in his best business interests to lighten her workload in order to protect her health and that of her unborn child.

Being a woman could be advantageous when a master divided labor by gender and exempted his female slaves from particularly heavy work. But it could also work to her disadvantage in the sense that, except under the most unusual circumstances, it would never have occurred to most masters to place a female slave in a position of authority over a gang of field workers. The opportunity for a woman to become a driver or overseer was virtually nonexistent. Nor was it common for bondswomen to work as craftsmen doing carpentry, laying bricks, or making barrels. If they received any special training at all, it was almost always in some domestic capacity, such a cooking, sewing, or midwifery.

Labor in the slave quarters was equally gendered. When slave women finished their work as field hands or domestic servants, they were usually free to return home to their cabins. On those plantations where slaves were expected to do their own cooking, sewing, or laundry, it was generally the women who performed those duties.

Working in the "big house" placed slave women in daily contact with the various members of the white family who owned or leased them. Having house servants provided mistresses with the opportunity to monitor and try to dictate what comprised acceptable female behavior in their slaves. Because servants were in a sense on display, particularly when guests were around, it was in a mistress's best interest to be concerned about the dress, appearance, and deportment of her house slaves. As a result, bondswomen who worked in close proximity to white women on a regular basis were more likely than women who worked in the fields to include neatness, cleanliness, and a politely deferential manner in their definition of what constituted womanliness.

Constructing their feminine identities around being wives was problematic for many female slaves. First of all, slave marriages were not legal. Slave owners might hold marriage ceremonies on their plantations where the bride and groom jumped over a broom. Or they might even ask a minister to perform a religious service in honor of a betrothed couple. But in American law, marriage was considered a contract, and slaves could not sign contracts.

A second problem for a slave woman was that her options for choosing a spouse were limited. Her master might force her to cohabit with a man of his rather than her choice. Or he could insist on reserving her for himself. If she lived on a small plantation, there might be no available or desirable men around. And falling in love with a man from another plantation made marriage complicated unless her master was willing to buy the object of her desire or make arrangements that allowed them to see each other.

Finally, a slave woman's relationship with her husband was only as permanent as her master allowed it to be. He could sell either of them anytime he wished. Realistically, she had to be prepared to fend for herself if she needed to supplement the minimal amount of food, clothing, and shelter that her master provided. So she might cultivate vegetables in the patch of dirt beside her cabin. And if she worked as a house servant, she might scavenge food and look for opportunities to collect hand-me-down clothing. Added to the limits that slavery placed on her husband's role as provider was the fact that he could do little or nothing to protect her from being raped, beaten, or forcibly separated from her

children. Under such circumstances, a woman might love and respect her spouse, but she had little reason to defer to him. The result seems to be that the marriages of enslaved men and women, like those of free blacks, were more egalitarian than those between white men and women.

Motherhood was an important component of a slave woman's definition of womanliness. But the power of the slave owner distorted her ability to carry out her role as a mother. Because he controlled her body, her owner controlled her reproductive capacity. By controlling her time, he controlled the degree to which she could care for her children. And because her children were as much his property as she was, he controlled their destiny.

There is some debate among historians concerning the degree to which slave owners systematically bred their slaves. Whether they did or not, it is certainly clear that since the legal condition of a child was determined by that of its mother, it was to the economic advantage of a slave owner to encourage female slaves of childbearing age to reproduce. Bondswomen who had proven their fecundity by having borne children were worth more to him than those who had not. Every child born on his plantation was his property and had the potential for enhancing his wealth.

From the master's point of view, however, slave women were at least as important as workers as they were as breeders. The kind of demands that masters and mistresses placed on the time of female slaves made it difficult for them to concentrate on the care and nurture of their children. That is not to say that they did not take care of their children. Nor is it to say that they were unimportant as the primary socialization agents for their sons and daughters. But since they often worked from dawn to dusk, they had to leave much of the day-to-day care of their children to others. Moments spent with their children while they were supposed to be working were stolen moments. When push came to shove, they might be willing to lie, cheat, and steal to provide for and protect their children. But in the end, even if they were willing to risk their lives to do so, there was little they could do to prevent their master or mistress from physically and psychologically abusing their children or selling them to someone else. Under such conditions, motherhood took on a whole new dimension. Slave women may have considered childbearing and child rearing as much a testimony to their femininity as it was for white women. But the experience of mothering for many of them was worlds removed from that which the cult of true womanhood glorified.

Slave women also constructed their feminine identities around resistance to the worst aspects of enslavement. Gender was important in determining how individuals experienced slavery. It was also important in determining how they resisted it. The case of Harriet Jacobs illustrates the point. Born in Edenton, North Carolina, in about 1813, Jacobs was orphaned as a child and eventually bequeathed to the daughter of Dr. James Norcom. When Jacobs was about fifteen, Norcom refused to allow her to marry a free black man and put pressure on her to become his concubine. "My master met me at every turn," Jacobs wrote in her memoir, "reminding me that I belonged to him, and swearing by heaven and earth that he would compel me to submit to him." She was able to resist his advances, but she lived in constant terror that he would force her to have sexual relations with him. When it eventually became clear that a white neighbor named Samuel Tredwell Sawyer also wanted her for his mistress, she agreed, explaining, "to be an object of interest to a man who is not married, and who is not her master, is agreeable to the pride and feelings of a slave. . . . It seems less degrading to give one's self, than to submit to compulsion. There is something akin to freedom in having a lover who has no control over you, except that which he gains by kindness and attachment." Her association with Sawyer was also motivated by her desire to do anything she could to humiliate Norcom. "I knew nothing would enrage [him] so much as to know I favored another; and it was something to triumph over my tyrant even in that small way." Jacobs eventually bore Sawyer a son and a daughter. In 1842, she escaped from the South, found employment in the North, and became an abolitionist.

Jacobs admitted that in bearing Sawyer's children she betrayed her belief that a "true woman" was a chaste one. But she felt that she had chosen between the lesser of two evils. She cared for Sawyer and took pleasure in her rejection of Norcom. Since the possibility of being sexually exploited was greater for women than it was for men, bondsmen rarely had to make the kind of choices that Jacobs did. Even though slave women found it difficult to express their womanliness in terms of self-sovereignty, it was, nevertheless, integral to the gendered identities of many. Some bondswomen resisted the demands of their masters and mistresses by feigning sickness, malingering, or breaking tools. Others, like Jacobs, insisted on deciding for themselves who did and did not have access to their bodies.

THE FEMININE IDENTITIES OF NATIVE AMERICAN WOMEN

Between the arrival of English settlers in the seventeenth century and the Civil War, what it meant to be a woman in Native American culture underwent significant change. As we saw in chapter 2, ideas about gender in Native American culture differed substantially from those of Anglo-Americans. Among the Cherokee in the Southeast, for example, women had a great deal of personal autonomy, economic power, and political influence. Cherokee women were free to engage in premarital sexual activities any time they wanted with whomever they wanted as long as they observed incest, menstrual, and pregnancy taboos. When a woman married, she did not move into her husband's household. Instead, Cherokee culture was matrilocal, which means that her husband took up residence with her family. Marriage was very much a partnership of equals. Men and women each had their roles to play in sustaining their families, and each was dependent upon the other. That kind of dependence did not, however, prevent them from ending a marital relationship that proved unsatisfactory. Divorce was easy and socially condoned.

Cherokee women also had a great deal of autonomy in their role as mothers. The Cherokee traced kinship matrilineally, that is, through mothers rather than fathers. Children knew their fathers, of course, but they grew up in the households of their mothers, who along with their mother's male relatives served as the primary socializing agents. In that sense, mothers were more important as parents than biological fathers.

Labor among the Cherokee tended to be divided by gender. Men helped to clear the land and harvest the crops, but other than that they spent most of their time hunting and fishing as well as protecting the clan and representing tribal interests in negotiations with whites and other Indians. Cherokee women assumed primary responsibility for farming, cooking, childcare, and sewing. Their most important economic role was as food producers. In Cherokee culture, it was the women who farmed the land held in common by their clan. They decided what to plant, when to plant, how much to plant, and where to plant it. They sowed the seeds, cultivated their crops, and directed harvest activities. Their connection to the land and their control over the production of food, along with matrilineal kinship, gave them influence in tribal affairs. Cherokee women were allowed to speak in tribal council, had the right to decide the fate of war captives, and could on occasion even go to war themselves.

In the eastern portion of the United States, gender roles and relations in Native American culture changed gradually between the end of the seventeenth century and 1850. Women's power was diminished by trade with whites. Originally trade between the Indians and whites involved the barter of animal skins for such items as plows and metal pots, which began to replace the baskets and pottery that native women had traditionally

made. Typically, Indian men hunted the animals, and women processed the skins. But it was men who negotiated the terms of the trade. Once women came to value manufactured goods that made it easier for them to carry out their traditional agrarian and domestic responsibilities, they became less self-sufficient and more dependent upon the negotiating skills of their husbands and fathers. The result was that the relationship between native men and women became less egalitarian.

The way treaties were negotiated also undermined the power of women. By the 1830s diplomatic relationships between Native Americans and representatives of the federal government were carried out exclusively by men. Native women were simply left out of the process and gradually lost their ability to influence the conduct of war and the transfer of land.

Another factor that led to profound changes in the gendered identities of Native American women was the attempt on the part of Protestant missionaries and the federal government to "civilize" the Indians. The goal of missionaries was to save the souls of their converts and to transform Native American culture through education. The model that they sought to impose on southern Indians as well as those in other parts of the country was that of the white, male-dominated, Christian household. For the federal government, the goal was to make farmers out of Indian men so that their former hunting grounds would be available for white settlement and to make housewives out of Indian women so that they could provide domestic services for their farming husbands. As we saw in the last chapter, the missionaries, in collaboration with the federal government, were most successful among the Cherokee.

After the War of 1812, evangelical Christians began to open schools on Indian land where they attempted to modify Cherokee behavior patterns and values. Teachers in mission schools taught young Indian women to conform to white feminine ideals by combining religious training and lessons in reading, writing, spelling, and arithmetic with those in house cleaning, cooking, sewing, and laundry. They praised and rewarded young Cherokee women who developed a proficiency in knitting, spinning, weaving, and fancy needlework. At the same time, they tried to discourage what they considered to be the promiscuity of their students by emphasizing the importance of piety and pre-marital chastity. They encouraged female students to be attentive to their appearance, to deport themselves with modesty, and to submit to male authority.

At the same time, the American government did what it could to encourage a shift away from female control over agriculture. Through the Bureau of Indian Affairs, it provided carding implements, spinning wheels, and looms to Cherokee women and plows and farm implements to Cherokee men. The government also attempted to undermine the relationship between Cherokee women and the land by encouraging the Indians to adopt a system of private land ownership. The result of these efforts was that political and economic life among the Cherokee slowly began to change as emphasis on pursuit of individual self-interest began to undermine the traditional emphasis that Cherokee culture had placed on cooperation.

When this happened, the political power and economic significance of women declined, and their role in their families shifted. Men began to assume responsibility for farming and expected women to acknowledge them as the heads of their households. Many women gradually abdicated their control over agriculture and accepted their position as helpmates and housewives. At the same time, men not only assumed sole responsibility for conducting and monitoring tribal relations with the federal government but also established a constitutional government on their reservations which excluded women from the political process altogether. Without regard for tradition, they disfranchised women, passed laws that diminished female autonomy, and made judicial decisions that weakened the matrilineal kinship system by allowing inheritance of property through the male line.

Of course, not all Cherokee women were influenced by these changes to the same degree. Only a select few went to mission schools, and those who did tended to come from families of the tribal elite. Despite the attempts of Protestant missionaries and Indian agents to impose a white, feminine ideal on Indian women, it is likely that many Cherokee women remained relatively oblivious to those efforts. They continued to define their femininity in terms of their traditional relationship to the land, skills as farmers, and roles in their families.

Their ability to do so ended when the federal government forcibly removed the Cherokee from Georgia and the Carolinas in the 1830s. A remnant of the tribe remained. But most were forced off of their ancestral land, and, in the process, clan relationships were disrupted. The result was that the matrilocal and matrilineal practices that had once provided Cherokee women with considerable personal autonomy, economic power, and political influence became difficult to maintain. During their removal, about 4,000 Cherokees died on what became known as the "Trail of Tears." Those who survived had to recreate their gendered identities in a context only remotely resembling the one they had left behind.

THE IMPACT OF THE CIVIL WAR ON THE CONSTRUCTION OF SOUTHERN WOMANHOOD

The Civil War had a profound effect on how femininity was defined in the South. War made it impossible for plantation mistresses to remain complacent about their role in southern society. Some may have had reservations about the benefits that they derived from slavery or the wisdom of seceding from the Union, but when the men in their lives marched off to war, most women in the planting elite supported them. On one level, they expressed that support in traditionally feminine terms reminiscent of the revolutionary era. They formed ladies' associations dedicated to sewing uniforms, knitting socks, and providing nurses to serve in military hospitals. And they tried to increase home manufacturing so that they could boycott consumer goods that had been produced in the North. To wear a ball gown made out of homespun was to make a political statement.

On quite another level, however, they had to adjust their definition of femininity to accommodate the absence of men. Once the men in their families left to join their regiments, plantation mistresses became the heads of their families for all practical purposes. As such, they found themselves in the unfamiliar position of having to run both their households and their plantations, managing field hands as well as house servants, buying supplies, marketing their crop, negotiating bank loans, and paying taxes. For many of them, life without a man around was a new and terrifying experience, and the changes that the war brought to their lives were largely undesired and certainly unwelcome. Where they had once been able to construct their femininity around the idea of female dependence and helplessness, they now had to quite self-consciously fashion a new identity around whatever reserves of emotional strength, physical stamina, resilience, and resourcefulness they could find within themselves. Take the case of Mary Jones of Georgia. When her husband, a retired Presbyterian minister, joined the Confederate army, he left her in charge of running their plantation. In June, 1863, she wrote to her son that she had successfully arranged to sell some cattle. But she complained that she was lonely and was not used to being so isolated. "Not a white female of my acquaintance nearer than eight or ten miles, and not a white person nearer than the depot!" she wrote. She desperately missed her husband. "For thirty-two years I have had a strong arm to lean upon—a wise head to guide, a heart all love and tenderness to bless me and make me happy." Alone she had to contend with the Yankee soldiers who came and went throughout the winter of 1864–1865. Time and

time again, they searched the house looking for food, money, and whiskey. After they had taken her horses and mules, she reported that they ordered the slaves to "bring up the oxen and carts, and took off all the chickens and turkeys they could find. They carried off all the syrup from the smokehouse. We had one small pig, which was all the meat we had left; they took the whole of it." All she could do was grit her teeth and watch while they took the chain off the well bucket and rode off with it, leaving her without the ability to draw water. No wonder that some women wrote despairingly in their diaries that they wished they were men, who they assumed were better suited to dealing with such catastrophes.

Despite the extraordinary efforts of women to carry out their newly acquired manly responsibilities in support of the Confederate cause, the South lost the war. In the process, the Yankees invaded and occupied the land and freed the slaves. By the time the war ended, the southern economy was devastated. Thousands of southern men never returned from the war. And many of those who did make it home were physically and psychologically disabled. It was within this context that planters' wives had to reconstruct their ideas about what it meant to be a woman.

Given the casualties of war, it was difficult for southern women in general and elite women in particular to continue to focus their ideas about femininity on their ability to marry or to equate womanliness with being a mother. There were simply not enough men to go around. The absence of men also meant that a great many women had to find some way to support themselves.

There was a great deal of stress involved in trying to adjust the definition of femininity to these realities. Many women who had lived lives of relative ease before the war found themselves in the position of having to do farm work or work for wages. Job opportunities for white women were virtually nonexistent in the countryside, so many women moved into town. There, if they were lucky and educated, they found employment as school teachers. A few became newspaper editors. Others took in sewing or used what little money they had to rent a house so that they could take in boarders. What was clear, under the circumstances, was that earning money could no longer be considered unfeminine.

The concentration of more women in southern towns and cities also provided the opportunity for women to organize self-improvement societies, such as ladies' literary guilds, to participate to a greater degree in the affairs of their churches, and to take an interest in such reforms as temperance. Such activities helped them develop more confidence in their administrative abilities and their right to participate in public affairs. This in turn led some of them to take an interest in woman suffrage. By the 1870s and 1880s, a few southern women began to reconsider their earlier opposition to giving women the right to vote. In 1870, for example, Cornelia Phillips Spencer wrote in the *North Carolina Presbyterian*, "I confess to being so blind and bigoted that only lately has it occurred to me that there might be some good on the other side of Woman's Rights. Only lately have I looked at it dispassionately and find to my inexpressible surprise and disgust that the female reformers out yonder in Wyoming, Chicago, New York and whatnot, except down South, really have an argument or two on their side." The woman's rights movement was not a popular cause in the South in the 1870s, and Spencer was clearly still somewhat ambivalent about the issues raised by its advocates. But she was finally willing to consider them with a more open mind.

The Civil War produced economic and social conditions that made it necessary for upper-class southern women to acknowledge the importance of female self-sufficiency and reconsider their ideas about what was and was not acceptable female behavior. Many did what they could to preserve their old way of life after the war was over. But eventually a new kind of southern woman emerged—one who was better educated, less dependent upon men, and more self-consciously assertive than her mother and grandmother.

The Civil War meant real deprivation for farm women in both the North and the South who had to try to run their farms without the help of their husbands and sons. But southern farm women experienced the war in ways that were different from their northern counterparts. Slavery and the fact that federal troops invaded the South meant that they had to deal with a unique set of problems as they tried to protect their property and provide for themselves and their children. As a result, they became politicized in ways that would have been unimaginable during the antebellum period. It is unclear how much interest farm women took in politics before the war. But after their sons and husbands left to fight for the Confederate cause, some found it necessary to write to state officials demanding that they do something to protect them from speculators as well as runaway slaves and deserters who threatened their safety and stole their property. As the war dragged on, they pleaded with state officials to allow their men to return home to help them run their farms. These women were used to carrying out their feminine roles as caretakers, housekeepers, and agricultural workers. But like plantation mistresses, they now found themselves in the unfamiliar position of having to assume primary responsibility for running their farms, marketing their crops, and buying supplies. These were manly responsibilities, and most women did not welcome having to carry them out. They had no vested interest in the preservation of slavery and were not willing to suffer deprivations so that the men in their families could fight to protect the property of planters. So some of them armed themselves. Others criticized local political leaders, participated in food riots, or encouraged men to desert from the Confederate army. They responded to their situation by exhibiting assertiveness rather than timidity and aggressive hostility rather than deference. As one anonymous poet put it in a letter to Governor Zebulon Vance of North Carolina, such behavior may have been unladylike, but under the circumstances it was considered admirable.

The Civil War provided farm women as well as plantation mistresses with the opportunity to expand their activities into the realm of politics and commerce. But just as it was in the case of elite women, yeoman farm wives did not push for the redefinition of woman as voter or officeholder. Out of necessity, they may have accepted the idea that, during an emergency, women could act as political beings and could serve as heads of their households. But there is nothing to indicate that they regarded those shifts in definitions of femininity to be permanent. When the war was over, most women in the yeoman class tended to revert back to their previous way of life. Husbands who returned from war reassumed their normal position as head of household. And wives accepted the need to continue to work in both their homes and the fields just as they had done before. Given the desperate economic plight of most southern farming families during the period following the war, the fact that women were denied the right to vote and hold office was the least of their concerns.

That did not mean that they were uninterested in political matters, however. In the 1870s, some of them joined the Grange, an organization designed to promote the social, economic, and political interests of farmers. And in the 1880s, southern farm women became active in the Alliance system, which tried to expand the work of the Grange. The Alliances, whose motto was "Equal rights for all, special privilege to none," welcomed women's participation in their activities. They supported the idea of women's education, encouraged women to become economically self-sufficient, and provided opportunities for women to deliver lectures before audiences composed of both men and women. Participation in Alliance activities prepared them to take an active role in the affairs of the Populist Party, when it was organized in the 1890s.

The Civil War provided slave women the opportunity to do more than just try to subvert the system that oppressed them. When white men went off to war, some bondswomen slipped off their plantations to find refuge behind Union lines. There they were considered contraband and became dependent upon the largesse of the federal government to provide them with food and shelter. Others went in search of loved ones. Some were unwilling or unable to leave a life that was so familiar to them and remained where they were. But whatever they did, they increasingly did so by choice.

With the ratification of the thirteenth amendment to the United States Constitution at the end of the war, slavery was abolished. Freedom provided a new opportunity for former slaves to reassess their ideas about what it meant to be a woman. In many ways, freedom meant the same thing for African American women as it did for African American men. It meant that they were free to move about, choose their own partners and form legal unions, and earn wages for the work they performed. And it meant that their children could not be sold. Being free meant that they could now own property and bequeath it to someone else. And emancipation meant that they had the legal right to learn to read and write and do what was necessary to provide their children with the education that most of them had been denied.

Even though slavery was dead, black women continued to be sexually vulnerable to the unwelcome advances of white men. The rape of a black woman was not considered a serious offense by most white law enforcement officers. And if a white man was prosecuted for attacking a black woman, he could count on being acquitted by the friends and neighbors who sat on all-white juries. Thus, even after they were emancipated, it continued to be difficult for black women to construct their femininity around their right to choose for themselves how, when, and with whom they would express their sexuality.

Emancipation also made little difference in the political identities of black women. Like black men, their political significance was no longer tied to the fact that they were property. But unlike black men, they did not receive the right to vote and hold office as a result of the ratification of the fifteenth amendment to the U. S. Constitution. Freed women could and did take an interest in political affairs after the Civil War. A few were exceptionally well informed, participated in political discussions, and developed clear ideas about how their interests could best be represented. But in the end, they, like white women, had to depend on the men to represent their interests in the years immediately following the Civil War. And like white women, they had to express their political identities informally through their work as community activists. Instead of voting, they served their communities by organizing schools and mutual aid societies.

After the Civil War, poverty remained a fact of life for most freed blacks. Thus, femininity for black women continued to be constructed around their need to work. Some continued to work for white women, who paid them to be domestic servants. But others remained tied to the land.

Ex-slaves were disappointed that the federal government did not give them land so that they could support themselves. Instead, southern landowners made land available to blacks (as well as propertyless whites) by establishing a system of tenant farming and sharecropping based on a contractual agreement between white landowners and prospective farmers, both of whom were usually male. Absent from most contracts was any explicit consideration of the role that women might play in fulfilling its terms.

Both white landowners and black men typically expected women to work so that the terms of the contract could be met. The significance of that expectation, however, is unclear. Working under a tenant farming or sharecropping arrangement usually removed women from the supervision of predatory white men. It also offered some women, particularly those with able-bodied husbands, the opportunity to spend more time taking care of their children and homes rather than working in the fields. But there was a price to pay for constructing their femininity around domesticity since they became more dependent upon their husbands to support them. In such cases, ex-slave women found out what white women already knew—that dependence on a male breadwinner did little to foster egalitarianism within a marriage. When men assumed primary responsibility for supporting their families, they often began to think of themselves as the "heads" of their families. Dependence also made women more vulnerable to spousal exploitation and abuse. Under slavery, domestic quarrels in the slave quarters could sometimes be mediated by the slave owner. Under freedom, the availability of a mediator was less predictable. Poverty and cramped living conditions, combined with the desire for domestic power and authority on the part of men and the culture of violence that continued to prevail in the South, established a context for the abuse and exploitation of wives and children in white and black families alike.

After the Civil War, freed blacks were theoretically free to live wherever they wanted. Many black women sought a better life by flocking to southern cities like Savannah, New Orleans, and Memphis. There they found employment as cooks, laundresses, or domestic servants. Working-class life in southern cities allowed black women various opportunities to redefine what it meant to be feminine. Some single women, like the Bowery Girls before them, helped to create an urban, working-class culture that rejected middle-class notions about what constituted acceptable female behavior. In their subculture, it was acceptable for women to wear provocative clothing and loiter around saloons and dance halls in their free time, drinking and flirting openly with men they did not know.

Other black working women fashioned ideas about what constituted femininity around their roles as church members, wives, mothers, and housekeepers. They may have been desperately poor, but they valued respectability and worked hard to improve the quality of life in their communities by sponsoring picnics and fairs to raise money for schools, to pay off mortgages on their churches, and to take care of the aged and infirm.

Educated black women were able to find employment as teachers and to make a place for themselves in the growing black middle class. Some of them married economically successful and politically influential men. As the wives of merchants, doctors, lawyers, and bankers, they established standards of femininity that conformed to that which was prescribed by the cult of true womanhood. Except for the color of their skins, their sensitivity to racism, and their dedication to the welfare of their people, women in what were called the "better classes" expressed their femininity in ways that were similar to the behavior patterns of white middle- and upper-class women. They constructed their gendered identities around domesticity rather than wage work. They held themselves to high standards of Christian morality, attended church regularly, and assumed responsibility for the religious training of their children. And they valued education, were concerned with self-improvement, and worked hard to help those less fortunate than themselves by establishing day nurseries, orphanages, scholarship funds, and benevolent associations.

SUMMARY

Race, class, and politics were important for establishing the context within which women in the nineteenth-century South constructed their feminine identities.

White plantation mistresses were privileged both by the wealth of their families and by the color of their skin. They constructed their female identities around their legal and social dependence on men, their work as household managers, and their roles as wives and mothers. The main differences between them and the wives of ordinary farmers were that because of the presence of slaves for whom they were responsible, the size of their households was larger and their domestic responsibilities were more complicated. They also were expected to conform to standards of gentility that most farm wives did not have to contend with and to remain more exclusively in the domestic sphere.

There were many similarities between the way free black women and those who were enslaved constructed their gendered identities. In both cases, their lives were centered on their work. Both were subjected to violence and sexual exploitation at the hands of whites. Whether they were slave or free, they both had difficulty finding desirable mates. Neither could assume that if they married, their husbands would be able to support or protect them. The result was that they had to be self-reliant and resourceful, and motherhood was more likely than wifehood to serve as an important component of their gendered identity.

The Civil War produced a context within which both white and black women could and often did readjust their ideas about what constituted femininity. The war made it necessary for many white women to become more self-sufficient. After the war was over, many elite women had to find ways to support themselves and their families. This change in their economic status brought them out of their homes and into the public sphere where a few began to consider the need for more political power.

Like the wives of planters, farm women had to assume manly responsibilities during the Civil War. Their response to the sacrifices they were required to make politicized them to an unprecedented degree during the war. But after it was over, most of them tried to refocus their attention on their housekeeping duties and their role as helpmates. By the 1880s, however, a good number of them became involved in efforts to improve the political position of farmers.

The Civil War brought freedom to all black women. Once their marriages were legal, wifehood took on a new meaning. By constructing their feminine identities around a domestic model which allowed them to spend more time rearing their children and taking care of their homes, some of them became more dependent upon their husbands. In some ways, however, freedom made little difference in their lives on a day-to-day basis. They continued to construct their identities around motherhood. They still had to worry about fending off the unwanted advances of white men. And although they may have preferred to dedicate more time to their domestic duties, many still had to work either as partners in a sharecropping or tenant farming arrangement or as wage earners.

Ideas about what constituted femininity among Native American women in general and Cherokee women in particular were transformed in the nineteenth century. As a result of the campaign by the federal government and Christian missionaries to "civilize" the Indians, many native women in the Southeast began to relinquish their responsibilities as food producers and to accept a more domestic model around which to construct their womanhood. As they traded their hoes and plows for spinning wheels and looms, they lost the authority they had once had in tribal councils and found themselves increasingly subjected to the authority of men. Their forced removal from their ancestral lands made it almost impossible for them to preserve the autonomy their forebears had enjoyed.

<u>DOCUMENT</u>

Excerpts from Louisa S. McCord's "Woman and Her Needs"

Louisa S. McCord was a southern intellectual who supported slavery and secession. Born into a wealthy and politically prominent South Carolina family on December 3, 1810, she spent much of her youth in Philadelphia, where her father served as President of the Bank of the United States. There she received an extraordinarily good education. In 1840 she married David James McCord, a South Carolina politician, planter, banker, and former newspaper editor. When she wasn't managing the plantation that she had inherited, she wrote essays on the subjects of economics and social relations which she published in southern literary magazines like the Southern Quarterly Review *and* De Bow's Review.

The excerpts below come from a review that McCord wrote of Elizabeth Oakes Smith's Woman and Her Needs, *published in New York in 1852. Smith's book was a compilation of a series of essays she had written for Horace Greeley's* New York Tribune. *In those essays, Smith described the condition of women in the United States and argued that women should have the same rights as men. McCord agreed that women had cause for complaint about the way that men treated them, but she felt that woman's rights advocates like Elizabeth Cady Stanton, Susan B. Anthony, and Elizabeth Oakes Smith were misguided in their attempts to redefine what it meant to be a woman.*

Source: De Bow's Review, 13 (Sept. 1852), 271–91.
Notes omitted.

What characteristics does McCord's ideal woman have? Are they significantly different from those idealized in the North during this period? Why does McCord oppose the woman's rights movement?

. . . Our authoress complains of the degradation of woman in society: that she is out of her place, unappreciated, having her talents and powers not only hidden under a bushel, but absolutely thrown away, while she becomes either the slave or the toy of man. Now this is all true of some women—many women—perhaps, we must even confess, of a majority of women. . . . Yet we will not allow the universality nor the necessity of such an effect, from the operation of the actual laws of existing society. It is not woman, as a class, who is thus degraded, but only so many individual women, each one of whom is separately, and from causes quite extraneous from her position as woman, so degraded. Many, noble (and we believe increasing in proportionate numbers with the advance of civilization) are the examples of high, self-relying, heaven-depending, duty-fulfilling women in every position of life, who, by a noble self-abnegation, and a faithful adherence to the laws of God and nature, are daily showing that woman is not inherently, either in her nature or her position, what our authoress would wish to prove her. Many women . . . are degraded, not because they have submitted themselves to the position which nature assigns them, but because, like Mrs. Smith, they cannot be content with the exercise of the duties and virtues called forth by that, and in that, position. . . . Woman was made for *duty*, not for *fame*; and so soon as she forgets this great law of her being, which consigns her to a life of heroism if she will—but quiet, unobtrusive heroism—she throws herself from her position, and thus, of necessity, degrades herself. This mistaken hungering for the forbidden fruit, this grasping at the notoriety belonging (if indeed it properly belongs to any) by nature to man, is at the root of all her debasement. . . .

It is this same misguided love for notoriety which now misleads women to insist upon political rights, as they word their demand—that is to say, admission to the struggle for political distinction. And what is this that they ask? What, but that like the half-barbarous, half-heroic Spartan maid they may be permitted to strip themselves to the strife, and wrestle in the public arena? Can civilized, Christianized woman covet such a right? They pretend, or they mislead themselves to the belief, that they are actuated by a pure desire to ennoble the sex. Let them look honestly and calmly to the bottom of the question, and they will see that it is but notoriety, not elevation, which they seek. In all derelictions from the right, the just, the holy, and the true, woman is responsible for her own degradation, inasmuch as it entirely proceeds from her own act, in casting herself out from her true position. She is herself, we repeat, the sole cause of it; and we wish to lay a stress upon this, because we maintain her to be a responsible, reasoning being, and not man's puppet. It is no excuse for her that man tempts her into folly. Man is unfortunately ready enough to tempt woman to err, and does not always stop to calculate the possible evil resulting from his pleasures and amusements. It amuses him to see the performances of the circus-clown or the monkey-man. It pleases him to have woman for his toy. He will pay the former with his money, the latter with his flattery, and thus tempt to degradation, but he cannot degrade. The degradation can be accomplished only by the consent of the degraded. The accessory to murder cannot be held guiltless because tempted by his principal. No reasoning being can be made an accessory but by his own consent. We may pity the weakness that falls by temptation, but cannot receive it as exculpation from the crime, except by acknowledging, in so far as it is thus received (as in the cases of infants or maniacs), a defect or inferiority in the reasoning powers of the person misled. We allow no such defect or inferiority to woman, and therefore hold her fully responsible for her own course. Seeking notoriety and applause, if (as too often she does) she stoops to conquer, she stoops with her own free will. Man's wishes cannot degrade her. She degrades herself to man's wishes. Let her feel her duty as a woman, avoiding alike an undue valuation of man's applause, and an unworthy grappling with him for notoriety, and there is no shadow of degradation in her position. There may be no publicity, no far-spread reputation, no fame; but certainly there is no degradation in the holy, full, conscientious, and unguerdoned fulfilment of duty. . . .

In conclusion, let us remark, for those of the masculine gender who (if there be any such) may perchance think our authority worth quoting against womandom, that we beg not to be misunderstood. . . . If we have endeavored to lay upon woman the burden of her own sin, as a reasonable, responsible being, and to prove to her how necessary is the exercise of her own inward strength for the performance of life's duties, and how doubly necessary it becomes to her, through physical weakness, that she should guard herself in the position where God and nature have placed her—we have endeavored to be the more forcible in so doing, because we consider her danger doubled through man's constant thoughtless and often heartless oppression. She must guard not only against her own folly and her own weakness, but also against his. If we have pointed out her aberrations from duty, and blamed or ridiculed her short-comings, it is not that we would make her the butt of man's ridicule, who has sinned both with her and against her, but because we consider her as more than him disinterested, more than him swayable by the purer instincts, and more than him exalted above the passions of our common nature. . . .

DOCUMENT

Excerpt from Elizabeth Keckley's Autobiography

Elizabeth Keckley was born on the Burwell plantation near Dinwiddie Court House, Virginia, around 1818. She published her autobiography just after the Civil War in 1868. In it she describes her life as a slave, her opportunity to buy her freedom, her success as a dressmaker in Washington, D.C., and her close relationship with Mary Todd Lincoln. Her memoir provides valuable insights into the contexts within which slave women and free women of color constructed their gendered identities.

Like many female slaves, Keckley was subjected to both physical and sexual abuse. When she was 14, she was loaned to one of her master's sons. A Presbyterian minister, he took her with him when he and his wife moved to North Carolina. In the excerpt from

Source: Elizabeth Keckley, *Behind the Scenes, or, Thirty Years a Slave, and Four Years in the White House* (New York: G. W. Carleton & Co., 1868), 32–39.

her autobiography reprinted below, she describes the beatings she received from a local school master and the determination of another white man to exploit her sexually.

What did being abused mean to Keckley as a woman? Are her feelings about it any different from those of Frederick Douglass?

. . . I was nearly eighteen when we removed from Virginia to Hillsboro', North Carolina, where young Mr. Burwell took charge of a church. The salary was small, and we still had to practise the closest economy. Mr. Bingham, a hard, cruel man, the village schoolmaster, was a member of my young master's church, and he was a frequent visitor to the parsonage. She whom I called mistress seemed to be desirous to wreak vengeance on me for something, and Bingham became her ready tool. During this time my master was unusually kind to me; he was naturally a good-hearted man, but was influenced by his wife. It was Saturday evening, and while I was bending over the bed, watching the baby that I had just hushed into slumber, Mr. Bingham came to the door and asked me to go with him to his study. Wondering what he meant by his strange request, I followed him, and when we had entered the study he closed the door, and in his blunt way remarked: "Lizzie, I am going to flog you." I was thunderstruck, and tried to think if I had been remiss in anything. I could not recollect of doing anything to deserve punishment, and with surprise exclaimed: "Whip me, Mr. Bingham! what for?"

"No matter," he replied, "I am going to whip you, so take down your dress this instant."

Recollect, I was eighteen years of age, was a woman fully developed, and yet this man coolly bade me take down my dress. I drew myself up proudly, firmly, and said: "No, Mr. Bingham, I shall not take down my dress before you. Moreover, you shall not whip me unless you prove the stronger. Nobody has a right to whip me but my own master, and nobody shall do so if I can prevent it."

My words seemed to exasperate him. He seized a rope, caught me roughly, and tried to tie me. I resisted with all my strength, but he was the stronger of the two, and after a hard struggle succeeded in binding my hands and tearing my dress from my back. Then he picked up a rawhide, and began to ply it freely over my shoulders. With steady hand and practised eye he would raise the instrument of torture, nerve himself for a blow, and with fearful force the rawhide descended upon the quivering flesh. It cut the skin, raised great welts, and the warm blood trickled down my back. Oh God! I can feel the torture now—the terrible, excruciating agony of those moments. I did not scream; I was too proud to let my tormentor know what I was suffering. I closed my lips firmly, that not even a groan might escape from them, and I stood like a statue while the keen lash cut keep into my flesh. As soon as I was released, stunned with pain, bruised and bleeding, I went home and rushed into the presence of the pastor and his wife, wildly exclaiming: "Master Robert, why did you let Mr. Bingham flog me? What have I done that I should be so punished?"

"Go away," he gruffly answered, "do not bother me."

I would not be put off thus. "What *have* I done? I *will* know why I have been flogged."

I saw his cheeks flush with anger, but I did not move. He rose to his feet, and on my refusing to go without an explanation, seized a chair, struck me, and felled me to the floor. I rose, bewildered, almost dead with pain, crept to my room, dressed my bruised arms and back as best I could, and then lay down, but not to sleep. . . . It seems that Mr. Bingham had pledged himself to Mrs. Burwell to subdue what he called my "stubborn pride." On Friday following the Saturday on which I was so savagely beaten, Mr. Bingham again directed me to come to his study. I went, but with the determination to offer resistance should he attempt to flog me again. On entering the room I found him prepared with a new rope and a new cowhide. I told him that I was ready to die, but that he could not conquer me. In struggling with him I bit his finger severely, when he seized a heavy stick and beat me with it in a shameful manner. Again I went home sore and bleeding, but with pride as strong and defiant as ever. The following Thursday Mr. Bingham again tried to conquer me, but in vain. We struggled, and he struck me many savage blows. As I stood bleeding before him, nearly exhausted with his efforts, he burst into tears, and declared that it would be a sin to beat me any more. My suffering at last subdued his hard heart: he asked my forgiveness, and afterwards was an altered man. . . .

The savage efforts to subdue my pride were not the only things that brought me suffering and deep mortification during my residence at Hillsboro'. I was regarded as fair-looking for one of my race, and for four years a white man—I spare the world his name—had base designs upon me. I do not care to dwell upon this subject, for it is one that is fraught with pain. Suffice it to say, that he persecuted me for four years, and I—I—became a mother. The child of which he was the father was the only child that I ever brought into the world. If my poor boy ever suffered any humiliating pangs on account of birth, he could not blame his mother, for God knows that she did not wish to give him life; he must blame the edicts of that society which deemed it no crime to undermine the virtue of girls in my then position. . . .

DOCUMENT

Characteristics of a Southern Lady

Cornelia Phillips Spencer was born in Harlem, New York on May 20, 1825. The next year her father accepted a position as a mathematics professor at the University of North Carolina in Chapel Hill. She married a former Carolina student in 1855 and moved with him to Alabama. When he died in 1861, she moved back to Chapel Hill. In an effort to support herself and her daughter after the Civil War she wrote a weekly column for young women and an occasional article for the North Carolina Presbyterian *published in Fayetteville, North Carolina. Concerned about the effect of the war on southern society, she championed the founding of common schools and better education for women.*

In the essay reprinted below, Spencer describes what she considers to be the characteristics of "a real lady." According to Spencer, what is it that distinguishes a "lady" from other women? Is there anything particularly southern about the qualities she describes?

A REAL LADY

Once I saw a lady. A real lady. Ladies so-called are not scarce. Old ladies and young ladies—here I stop short; I was going to say, and middle-aged ladies, but I find we never use the word in that connection. We say middle-aged women; and we also say beautiful women, smart women, clever women, agreeable women. We say pretty girls, amiable girls, fast girls, good girls. We say charitable women, pious women, fashionable

Source: Cornelia Phillips Spencer, "A Real Lady," *North Carolina Presbyterian,* June 28, 1871.

women, but so sure as you apply either of the above epithets to the word lady, you set yourself down as provincial or worse. For a lady is presumed to be all these by right of her title; it is gilding refined gold to say an agreeable lady. The very word suggests the highest style of woman and should not be used lightly, for real ladies are not as plenty as blackberries.

The common notion of a lady is of one gently born and bred, who moves softly and speaks with a grace derived partly from culture, refinement and goodness, and partly from hereditary tendencies and good company. These gracious traits are indeed the distinguishing mark of the favored few, but fortunately for mankind, there can be ladies without them, for to be a real lady demands something that a baby duchess with eleven great-grandfathers in direct descent may not have bestowed upon her in her cradle, and may never be able to get hold of, but which an untaught peasant may be born with: something that can no more be bought or assumed than the perfume of a flower, and is as much the gift of Dame Nature, and therefore the wild flower may be as much distinguished by it as the conservatory darling.

A very plain and may-be rough exterior may veil the real lady, as a fair and fine one may disguise the sham lady for awhile, but let the test of circumstances be applied, like Ithuriel's spear, and out they start, each in their true colors.

This is how I came to see a real lady.

It is a good many years ago. When I was young and short, I lived in a village where it was the custom for the country people to take their produce from house to house, wearily walking with baskets of eggs or fruit, or with string of chickens, or buckets of butter till they could find a purchaser. One hot summer day it happened that many such callers—not all of them ladies—had been at my door. Nobody knows but "who've tried it" how wearing a succession of such visitors is, especially on a hot day. Sometimes you want the things they offer, and sometimes you don't. Either way the interruption jars, and it is vexatious to have to get up half a dozen times from your

drawing or sewing or writing and descend literally and metaphorically into the lower regions, weighing and measuring and discussing prices, and settling change, and very often you can't make the change. I am not apologizing for myself beforehand, for I settled long ago in my own mind that I am not a lady, and I don't mind confessing it here; not one of my ladies at any rate. And not being a lady of course I acted "as sich."

The dozenth caller with eggs and chickens that morning walking in upon me, for our country people seldom waste time knocking, was a comely kind-faced woman of about thirty, with the conventional N. C. calico sunbonnet and white woolen mittens. (Our country women all take care of their hands and their complexions up to a certain age.) She looked weary and flushed, with a basket on either arm. Did I ask her to sit down, or compassionating her fatigue, did I offer her a drink, or a fan, or even speak gently as I refused to buy? I did none of these things. I had been civil to eleven that morning and to the twelfth I was uncivil. I remember her dress to this day, and I remember the tired patient glance she gave me as she left the room silently.

Two months after that I was one of a crowd of young folks going to a camp-meeting six miles in the country. Between the services we strolled about the spring and among the tents as towns-folk will do on such occasions. Presently some of us found ourselves at the door of a neat and comfortable tent, whose mistress came smiling out and invited us in. I recognized her and her calico dress at once, and longed to sink away out of sight. But she recognized me too, and coming up to me with a composed and easy air, addressed me by name, though I knew not hers, and made me welcome with a courtesy and a genuine cordiality there was no mistaking. And there was no mistaking that she marked me out for especial notice and kindness. That July morning, two months or more previous, was in both our minds. Its effect on her was to make her redouble her simple and generous attentions. Nothing that camp-meeting hospitality could provide was too good for the strangers, nothing was good enough for me the sinner. I endured it all, revolving many things in my altered mind, and when we parted I went up to her and took her hand and said, "Come and see me." "I will," she answered with a hearty grip, and a lady-like smile that said, "Don't you ever think of that July morning again."

But I have never forgotten it, and I have never seen her since.

ARTICLE

"I Am My Own Woman and Will Do as I Please": Gender Roles in Poor African-American and Common White Households

Laura F. Edwards

Economic, political, and social life in the South was seriously disrupted during the period of Reconstruction that followed the Civil War. During that time newly freed slaves had the opportunity to formalize their marriages and to redefine the relationship between men and women in their communities. Freedom allowed them to construct their gender identities within a whole new set of parameters. In this excerpt from Gendered Strife & Confusion, *Laura Edwards discusses the differences between elite, white definitions of womanhood and those of ex-slaves and poor whites who lived in rural North Carolina during the period immediately following the Civil War. The evidence that she presents illustrates the importance that race and class had on attitudes toward gender in the South.*

How did attitudes about what was feminine among African Americans and common whites differ from those of elite white women? How did they differ from each other?

. . . Dink Watkins . . . chose her words carefully. Discovered by her former husband in liaison with another man, she dismissed

Source: Laura F. Edwards, *Gendered Strife & Confusion: The Political Culture of Reconstruction.* (Urbana: University of Illinois Press, 1997) pp. 145–161. Copyright 1997 by Board of Trustees of the University of Illinois Press. Used with permission of the University of Illinois Press. Notes omitted.

him in no uncertain terms. "I am my own woman," Watkins claimed, "and will do as I please." . . . Watkins considered herself her "own woman" not because she assumed this kind of independence within marriage but because she believed the marriage had ended. Her distinctive phrasing also reveals a great deal about her own sense of womanhood. Combining race, class, and gender in her identity as a woman, Watkins drew implicit contrasts between herself and elite white women. She insisted on doing as she pleased, instead of bowing to the standards of elite white womanhood. In fact, Watkins still claimed the term "woman" for herself, although local guardians of domestic propriety would have disputed her claim. To be sure, many poor African Americans and whites would have condemned her behavior as well, if only because she chose the lot of a black Baptist church for her rendezvous. But to some extent, Watkins still worked within her community's guidelines concerning male-female relations. She also accepted gender difference, asserting her rights as a woman and rejecting only her husband, not male authority generally. . . .

Other poor blacks and common whites agreed with these basic points. They fashioned their own definitions of manhood and womanhood to fit the needs and realities of their lives. Instead of revolving around a husband and wife whose complementary roles satisfied the needs of the family, the households of the poor of both races included an array of kin who all contributed to the family's welfare. In this context, men's and women's roles overlapped considerably. The poor did not limit women's labor to domestic work within their homes, just as they did not expect men to provide for their wives and children solely through their own labor. Women led much more public lives than their elite white neighbors—although generally not quite as public as that of Dink Watkins. Poor African Americans and common whites considered women's forays into public space necessary contributions to their families' welfare and, as such, a central component of their role as women. They simply could not afford fine distinctions between public and private spaces or rigidly segregated men's and women's roles. Elite whites, however, blanched. Looking into the households and communities of the poor through the lens of their own gender conventions, they saw evidence of personal depravity and social backwardness.

These gender constructions had a public dimension as well. Poor African Americans and common whites rooted their ideas about manhood and womanhood within a social context that acknowledged the oppressive legacies of slavery and class privilege. Racial and class difference thus played a central role in defining personal and community identities, just as they did for elite whites. But the script, stage, and supporting actors were so different that the implications were worlds apart. Where conservative elite whites excluded people on the basis of race and class, common whites and poor African Americans incorporated racial and class differences into the very substance of their definitions of manhood and womanhood. By allowing for a more inclusive universal man and universal woman, these alternative constructions also opened the possibility for greater equality outside the private household. Despite racial and class differences, all women could stand together on equal footing and all men could do the same.

Yet race and gender hierarchies also lay behind the common rhetoric and the similarities in the ways common whites and poor African Americans defined men's and women's roles. Common whites did not always extend their vision of manhood and womanhood to African Americans, just as African Americans did not include those whites who were hostile to their own political goals. Both groups, moreover, relied on gender difference to describe their identity as men and women, their rights, and the social order generally. While this construction of gender difference did not match that of elite whites, it still translated into hierarchy with implications not just for men and women within individual households but for social and political relations outside those borders as well.

Although men and women accepted the presence of a certain level of inequality, they still clashed regularly over the relative distribution of power and the substance of their responsibilities as husbands and wives. Poor African-American and common white women made "private" conflicts a matter of "public" debate, bringing in the community and some-times the state to adjudicate their disputes. Placing limits on male authority within their households and their communities, they also called into question legal precedents that sub-ordinated wives to their husbands and left them isolated within a domestic sphere. These conflicts form yet another strand in the debate over the construction of men's and women's roles both within and outside households, one that reveals the importance of women's voices in a public discourse that so often denied their presence in its near exclusive focus on male prerogatives.

Emancipation presented African-American women with the opportunity to act on their ideas of womanhood in new ways. They with-drew from full-time waged labor to work in their own homes, although many subse-quently went back to the fields or to other paid employment. Nonetheless, claiming the right to place their own families' interests first represented freedom for women who had been compelled to tend to their masters' families for so long. Freedwomen appropri-ated other privileges of elite white wom-anhood as well. Some donned their former mistresses' clothing, wearing veiled hats, gloves, and brightly colored stylish dresses. Others confiscated household goods. In 1866, for instance, Granville County's William Lyon accused Edith Dalby, one of his former slaves, of stealing "one water pail, one iron pot, one tea kettle, one pair pot hooks, and one yard of white cotton cloth." Clearly, all these things would be useful as Dalby set up her own kitchen in her own household. Beyond their practicality, the items spoke volumes about Dalby's sense of freedom. In liberating the kitchen utensils she had used for so long as a slave in another woman's kitchen, she became her own mistress.

Poor African-American women like Edith Dalby infused these symbols of womanhood and domesticity with their own meanings. So did poor white women. They did not tie their lives to a domesticity centered on consumer items and sentimentalized ideals of mother-hood. Instead, they cast their notions of wom-anhood more broadly to encompass whatever was required to contribute to their families' welfare.

For most African Americans and many whites, economic insecurity was as much a part of life as sunshine and rain. Conse-quently, women expected that they would make significant economic contributions to their households. In addition to tobacco, Granville County farm families grew a range of food crops, including corn, potatoes, and other vegetables. Not everyone could afford milk cows, but chickens and pigs roamed around even the poorest yards. Women per-formed much, if not most, of the labor in-volved in food production: they tended the garden and preserved its bounty; they col-lected eggs, made butter, and sold them to local merchants; they butchered hogs and prepared the meat for the smokehouse; they shooed cows, chickens, pigs, and other hun-gry interlopers out of the fields; they hoed rows of corn; and, just as fall began to fade into winter, they dug potatoes. When they could grab a spare moment, they also wove cloth and sewed their families' clothes and linens. In all these ways, women contributed directly to their families' cash and credit re-serves. Producing food and clothing at home eased dependence on the tobacco market, the instability of which could wreak havoc on a family's fortunes, particularly if its members were already living on the margin. In good years, families could then put aside the pro-ceeds from the tobacco crop to purchase land or items not produced at home—a milk cow, mules, a sewing machine, farm implements, or a child's education. In bad years, tobacco money purchased necessities to get the family through the winter. Yet, despite the impor-tance placed on staple-crop production by contemporaries and later historians, it formed only one piece in a successful strategy of household production. Without a full larder, a good tobacco crop was only so much smoke.

In poorer families, moreover, tobacco production would have been impossible without women's labor. The demands of this crop made back-breaking field work a regular chore for poor women of both races. Certain jobs, such as hauling wood, plowing, harvesting, and curing, may have been designated as "men's work," but that did not keep women from these tasks. Women participated in virtually every stage of the production process. The tobacco-growing season began in the winter, when farm families carefully selected land for their seedbeds and sowed the tiny tobacco seeds. The men then headed to the uncleared land to cut and haul wood for curing in the fall. As spring drew near, families cleared their fields and transplanted the delicate seedlings by hand. All other household work came to an abrupt halt at planting time. As one experienced laborer described it, the process defied distinctions between housework and field work by bringing all family members and even household items into the fields: "We took biscuit pans, wash pans, and all other pans on the plantation and with a spoon we dug the plants up and placed them in pans, carrying them in small numbers to the field." After waiting a week or so for the root systems to develop, family members made their way between the rows with plows or hoes to loosen the soil, a process they repeated several times before the plants matured.

Tobacco, unlike cotton, then required careful tending through the summer and well into fall. Farm families "topped" the plants to eliminate the flowery heads that stunted primary leaf growth, "primed" them to remove the useless bottom leaves, and "suckered" them to cut back secondary growth that interfered with the primary leaves. Throughout the summer, men, women, and children also picked off the tobacco hornworms by hand. The work load only increased during harvest and curing time. Men usually worked in the fields, while women readied the plants for curing in specially designed barns. After curing, as winter's chill set in, family members gathered to sort the tobacco according to grade. In poorer households, families simply piled the tobacco in the central room of the house so the work would be close at hand. Once again, field work and housework merged.

The poorer the family, the more women's work expanded beyond the borders of their houses into the fields and off the farms' boundaries altogether. Before the war, many white yeoman women regularly worked in the fields and women of landless families often worked for wages outside their homes as well. After the war, African-American women took on even more economic responsibilities than common white women because of the way race increased the precariousness of their economic position. In rural areas like Granville County, field work often marked racial and class differences among women. Even though women from the wealthiest families could not escape the demands of tobacco production entirely, they generally stayed out of the fields. So did those, both white and black, who aspired to elite status. Their absence from the fields distinguished them from those women who did labor alongside their menfolk. . . .

Women who worked in the fields did not necessarily share this view. Far from an "unwomanly" symbol of degradation, field work formed a central component of their identity. Many women enjoyed it. . . .

Poor African-American and common white women also took great pride in their ability to keep up with the men in the fields. . . .

Embracing a standard in which "men's work" was more valuable than "women's work," these women affirmed a gender hierarchy in which female subordination was the general rule. But they simultaneously rejected a hierarchy among women. Poor African-American and common white women may have worked like men, but they insisted that this did not exclude them from the category "woman." In fact, they boasted about their abilities and used them to measure their own womanhood. Although eighty-one at the time of her WPA interview, Mary Barbour still placed a great deal of emphasis on her capacity for hard labor, maintaining that she was still spry enough to outwork her daughter or, for that matter, any other black woman. The women's menfolk applied a similar standard. Charlie Crump, for instance, bragged about his mother's ability to plow with a particularly ornery donkey. "My mammy had more grit dan any gal I now knows of has in her craw," he noted with discernible pride. Clearly, it was his mother's "grit" that moved her near the top of Crump's scale of womanhood.

Waged work was also a regular component of many women's domestic responsibilities. Some had to work to put food on the table, as the census figures suggest. In Oxford Township 40 percent of all black women age twelve and older worked for wages or headed their own households in 1870. In Dutchville Township, the figure was 14 percent for the same group. By 1880, the figures had dropped in Oxford to 27 percent, but had risen to 21 percent in Dutchville. Waged work was a necessary presence in the lives of many white women as well. Of white women age twelve and older in 1870, 12 percent worked for wages or headed households in Oxford and 7 percent in Dutchville. The percentages inched down to 10 percent in Oxford and up to 12 percent in Dutchville by 1880. The census, moreover, grossly underestimates the number of wage-earning women. Most performed occasional waged work—such as ironing, washing, mending, sewing, or a few days' work in the fields—that went unrecorded in the returns. When the census takers made their rounds, they did not recognize women who engaged in work of this kind as wage workers, nor did the women themselves necessarily identify themselves as such.

Elite whites expected African-American women to work as paid laborers, but they had a certain kind of female worker in mind. Their expectations found expression in the image of the self-sacrificing "Mammy," whose family was the white family of her employer. The *Oxford Torchlight*'s obituary for "Old Aunt Hannah, a colored woman, aged about seventy years, formerly the property of J. C.

Cooper" could have been for Mammy herself: "She was a faithful servant and stuck by her 'master and mistress,' as she called them, after the slaves were free, evincing no change in her manners towards them." Like Mammy, "Old Aunt Hannah" came to life only through her relationship to her "master and mistress." She had no life of her own, at least not one that her white employers needed to know about.

Many black women, unlike "Old Aunt Hannah," did "evince" a significant change in their manners following emancipation. Elite whites found these female laborers deeply troubling, even though they enthusiastically endorsed the abstract concept of waged work for black women. African-American women workers forced their employers to confront the unsettling possibility that they knew virtually nothing about those who cooked, cleaned, cared for their families, and worked in their fields for generations. Wages only added to the growing doubts of white employers, because money gave poor African-American women the means to pursue their own interests. Caroline Hart, for instance, found cash compelling for precisely this reason. Denying accusations that she had stolen one hundred dollars from her employer, this African-American laborer could not resist adding that if she did have the money she "would buy her a hundred dollar dress and another pair of shoes." Not all female wage workers would have made the same choice, but ambitions like Caroline Hart's disturbed elite whites precisely because they were her own.

Poor black women who lived outside male-headed families upset elite white sensibilities even more. The reaction to Dicey Smith and Jennie Bass is suggestive. Smith and Bass lived together with Smith's four children in their own house, where they boarded men who worked nearby on the railroad. They also maintained a high profile in the neighborhood, hosting many popular gatherings. During one, a "quilting" party in 1890, a fight broke out. In the confusion, a shot ricocheted across the room and left one guest dead. By all accounts, Dicey Smith and Jennie Bass had nothing to do with the fight and were never considered suspects in the murder. Nonetheless, the authorities made the women's living arrangements central to their investigation, certain that the explanation for the shooting could be found there. Doubtful that Smith and Bass were operating just a boarding house, they demanded to know if the women had sexual relations with their male renters. They also asked about the paternity of Smith's children, perhaps hoping to uncover a spurned lover amidst the group of men present that night. Smith answered their questions simply: "I have four children living, one dead, I have never been married." In all likelihood, her response confirmed the suspicions of these white officials who took a dim view of her private life. All their questions pointed to an unstated assumption: if the women had lived in the appropriate domestic setting, either as subordinate servants to white families or as wives of properly deferential black men, the shooting never would have occurred.

If Dicey Smith's and Jennie Bass's parties were unique, their living arrangements were not. Poor black women often pooled their resources and their labor to provide material and emotional support for each other. Of course, these women acted under the constraints of poverty, which significantly limited their choices. Yet, however poor, they still controlled their time in a way that other women did not. As Fanny Lathom described her morning schedule: "I don't know what time we ate breakfast. I don't know how high the sun was we sleep late. I know we sleep late. Sometime [the] sun is two hours high when we get up." That same day, Lathom's friend Francis Amis spent the morning fishing for her dinner. According to one of Amis's roommates, "She goes fishing often." Most African-American women chose different life paths. But even if they did not sleep late, fish for their dinners, host "quilting" parties, board strange men in their homes, and live outside male-headed households, they still had one thing in common with Francis Amis, Fannie Lathom, Jennie Bass, and Dicey Smith: a desire to re-move themselves from the control of elite whites. On this scale, the flamboyant independence of this small handful of women becomes one of degree. Like them, other black women dropped the facade of servitude to go about their own business without asking permission or offering apologies. That alone was often sufficient to irritate many elite whites.

Common white women did not labor under the same constraints as black women. But they were supposed to maintain a properly deferential stance toward their betters and to subordinate themselves as faithful wives, mothers, and daughters. If they asserted their own interests outside a male-headed family, they too fell under suspicion. In June 1868, for instance, James T. Gill, a white man, went to the local magistrate with a "case of urgent emergency." The object of Gill's fear was Martha O'Mary, a propertyless, widowed white woman who had lived in a house on the lands Gill was now renting. He accused her of setting fire to "an unoccupied dwelling house" and being "engaged in an attempt to poison himself and family." But that was not all. According to the statement of Harriet Jones: "A short time before [G]ill had moved she saw Martha Omary get a bottle which was hung up in an apple tree (a snuff bottle) and put it down in the hearth and put some nails some small roots and some water (urine) in the bottle and covered it over and placed the rock over it and poured some water on the rock and made some cross marks with another root and said that Gill would go the way that water went and said that she did that to make Gill and his family sick and dissatisfied that they would leave there so she could come back next faul." In other words, James Gill believed himself to be the victim of Martha O'Mary's conjuring. Other white men filed similar charges. Like him, they complained about economically marginal women, who also may have had a history of confronting or criticizing their neighbors too often and too openly.

In court, O'Mary denied the charges, insisting that she had "put the bottle under the hearth . . . to keep people from poisoning her hogs and her." In fact, her intentions were unclear. Her conjuring may have been nothing more than an effort to keep her hogs and herself from harm, but it is equally probable that she meant to scare, if not destroy, the Gill family. Gill and O'Mary had lived in the same neighborhood for years. Perhaps their conflict predated the war, when Gill tilled his own land and O'Mary lived with her husband, a landless shoemaker. If so, the Civil War could only have heated up the feud by sharpening their economic differences. A fifty-three-year-old widow with few economic options in 1868, O'Mary must have struggled to keep from sliding into the poorhouse. Although stripped of his land by war's end, Gill's economic prospects were far brighter; at least bright enough for O'Mary's landlord to evict her and give the house to Gill instead. Whether she conjured against Gill or not, O'Mary did swear to use whatever means necessary to defend her own interests and remain in her home. Indeed, O'Mary's defiant words seem to have guided the community's interpretation of the "evidence." Suddenly, the small, dirty bottle Gill found hidden in his hearth acquired ominous meanings. The local magistrate never doubted its message either. Leaping to the same conclusion as Gill, he charged O'Mary with both arson and "poisoning."

Many poor African-American and common white women led very public lives, even when they lived in male-headed households. They traveled alone to visit neighbors and relatives, to market goods, to go to work, to deliver the wash and sewing they had done, and to purchase supplies. Francis Amis, last seen fishing on a weekday morning, once stopped a teamster for a ride into town. Although the teamster refused Amis a ride, he did pick up another woman that same day, ignoring his employer's orders forbidding him to carry passengers. Apparently this type of "hitch-hiking" was common. From the perspective of many elite whites, unaccompanied travel opened women to the potentially dangerous world that existed outside the protected con-

fines of their homes. Soliciting rides from complete strangers openly tempted disaster. Poorer women and their menfolk, however, viewed the situation from a very different vantage point because they did not draw such a firm line between public and private spaces. To them, such journeys formed a necessary part of life. If women could find a ride and rest their weary feet, it was a risk they were willing to take.

Even if they never traveled the countryside on their own, poor women rarely confined their lives to the four walls of their houses. Both poor African Americans and common whites resolved their problems in the open air of their neighborhoods, and women were no exception to the rule. Many court cases of minor violence involved women who either initiated conflicts or aggressively defended themselves. The fight between Margaret Hughie and Mary Jane Williams, two white women, was not unusual. In 1870, the two became embroiled in a verbal exchange that quickly escalated to physical threats. After Hughie repeatedly threatened to kill Williams with a large rock, Williams finally retreated and took her complaint to the local justice of the peace. In court, Hughie self-righteously defended herself on the grounds that Williams was trespassing and that she had every right to guard her family's land. Not only did she readily acknowledge her part in the dispute but she also gave no indication that she thought her behavior exceptional. Neither did Williams. Although she clearly disagreed with Hughie's position and the way she made her point, Mary Jane Williams never suggested that Margaret Hughie had violated the code of proper feminine conduct.

Isabella Thorp, an African-American woman, shared this perspective. Believing that Ellick Green and Susan Mayho had cheated her out of some money, she swore vengeance. After threatening to kill the two in front of several witnesses, Thorp confronted Susan Mayho at her house. Mayho wisely kept the door closed, but to no avail. Far too angry for a simple piece of wood to get in the way, Thorp broke in. Mayho described the ensuing struggle in her testimony: "[Thorp said] I am in the house now I will do and say what I please and I [Mayho] told her she would not do and say what you please while I am in there and . . . [Thorp said] if you fool along with me I'll cut your guts out with this knife. . . . Then she took a piece of rail and hit me with it on my head and it knocked me out of my senses." Thorp felt cheated and she acted. When she did, she displayed a distinctly "unladylike" affinity for physical violence.

Within their own communities, the public stands of Isabella Thorp, Mary Jane Williams, and Margaret Hughie were extreme examples of accepted patterns of behavior. They, like other poor African-American and common white women, often had to defend themselves because there was no one else around who could. But even if there had been, poor women of both races did not always shrink from confrontations, even potentially violent ones. Isabella Thorp's words, "I will do and say what I please," suggest why. The phrase virtually duplicates the one used by Dink Watkins, whose story opened this chapter. Though the circumstances were very different, neither woman considered her behavior a compromise to her womanhood. The delicate flower of southern womanhood could not survive the harsh conditions that common white and poor African-American women endured. Even the resourceful Sarah A. Elliott would have found it difficult to adapt. Common white and poor African-American women needed a particular kind of resiliency and strength. On occasion, that might mean picking up a large rock, a pine rail, or a good sharp knife.

There was no room for such behavior in elite white standards of womanhood. Measured against them, poor women hopelessly blurred gender boundaries with their public lives and outspoken ways. But even though women's lives overlapped considerably with those of their menfolk, poor African Americans and common whites still accepted the basic notion of gender difference. They just worked from their own understanding of it,

one more like colonial good wives than the "true women" of the nineteenth century. Distinctions between men's and women's roles actually centered around reproductive labor. Poor African-American and common white women assumed primary responsibility for child rearing, cooking, and housework. While they also took on "men's work," poor African-American and common white men did not expand their role to help with "women's work."

Although housework devolved on women as a group, not all women approached it in the same way. . . .

Poor African-American and common white women could not afford to sentimentalize housework. . . . It is unlikely that they measured their success as women in terms of the bleached damask tablecloths or rows of plates stacked neatly on decoratively papered shelves as Sarah A. Elliott and the *Oxford Torchlight* urged them to do. For them, simply putting food on the table was what mattered.

In contrast to housework, motherhood occupied a far more central place in the identity of poor women, although they defined the essence of a "good mother" in their own way. The complaints in the *Oxford Torchlight* about children running unsupervised through the streets actually say a great deal about mothers. Women with husbands whose incomes supported the material needs of their families and with servants who performed the most burdensome household chores could devote a larger portion of their time to child rearing. To poorer women, motherhood meant feeding their children, putting clothes on their backs, and keeping a roof over their heads. Beyond that, they hoped to better their children's lot in life. For instance, Mary Burwell, an African-American mother with six children, worked as a farm laborer so that her children would not have to. Three of her children attended school. The younger ones stayed at home, safe from the demands of a white employer. In fact, the Burwell children may well have been among those running unsupervised through Oxford's streets. If so, their mother had paid for their freedom with her own sweat.

Even if they had the resources to do so, many poor women would not have wanted to emulate the elite ideal of motherhood. Given the size of their houses, common white and poor African-American women would have been hard pressed to raise their children in domestic privacy. But the idea may never have occurred to them anyway, because they did not think of their dwellings as private retreats. Instead, domestic life occupied public space, like the laundry that hung in the yard. With open doors and windows, the houses of the poor physically mingled with the world outside. Even inside, houses were not neatly divided into private and public space. Most contained only one or two rooms, where family members slept, ate, visited, and entertained. During North Carolina's miserable summer nights, poor people abandoned their stuffy interiors altogether in favor of their front porches or yards. Just as women moved between housework and field work, the fields moved indoors during grading time, when tobacco covered virtually every inch of the house. And African-American women who worked as domestic servants turned the distinction between work and home completely on its head. In this context, where domesticity looked outward, not inward, there was no particular reason for children to remain inside. If they ran through the streets it was not because of their mothers' negligence; it was simply what children were supposed to do.

A few women, like Dicey Smith and Jennie Bass, created a space for themselves outside a male-headed household. But they were the exception, not the rule. Even then, their existence was precarious. Far more typical were the poverty and insecurity of Martha O'Mary. Beyond witchcraft, women like O'Mary had very few economic options. Within their own households, common whites and African Americans held women's labor in high regard. Outside, its value fell precipitously. White employers generally paid women about half as much as men. Behind these wage rates were the assumptions that women lived in households headed by men and thus their wages constituted a secondary contribution to the household's income. These rates also reveal the relative importance most white employers placed on women's work. Women did not always perform the same labor as men, even when they worked in the tobacco fields and factories. But it was not necessarily true that women always contributed less to the final product than men. In the minds of their white employers, however, they did.

As a result, wage-earning women barely made enough to support themselves. Single women with young children found it nearly impossible to support their families, especially if their children were too young to work. The experience of Philis Clark, whose story appeared in chapter 1, was not unusual. During the war, Clark's master sent her to Granville County from eastern North Carolina, so that she would not escape or fall into the hands of federal troops. Afterwards, she found herself in desperate economic straits. Clark managed to secure a house from C. W. Raney, a white planter, but "soon found that she could not maintain her children" and pay the rent. Raney then agreed to hire Clark in return for room and board. By 1868, Raney declared himself financially unable to continue the arrangement: "I make nothing by keeping her; the rent of the house and provision they consume would hire two man hands, and I have sent her out repeatedly to find a home, but no one is willing to feed her children for her services. She is a very deserving woman, works hard and should be assisted. . . . I dislike to turn her out to live in the woods, but will be compelled to do so unless I am assisted." As Raney's words reveal, neither men nor women could support their families on one wage. Women with children had even fewer options than men. Philis Clark's dwindled to two: the woods or the poorhouse. If anything, Clark thought the woods more attractive. According to Raney, she said "she will die first" before going to the poorhouse.

Infanticide cases also convey women's economic marginality with vivid clarity. In 1867, for instance, Harriett Jordan, an African-American tobacco factory worker, was charged with burying her baby alive. When asked why, she responded that "she did not know what else to do with it." Her remark seems cold, but the image of a nurturing mother and her innocent children depended on a certain economic position. Lacking this kind of security, Jordan saw her own and her baby's future in very different terms. Christina Thorp also found herself torn between the love for her children and the reality of poverty. When she and her husband divorced in 1879, the court refused to give her custody of her children because the judge believed that she could not support them on her own. Three years later, after she had remarried, Thorp pulled a knife on her ex-husband, grabbed her daughter, ran off with her, and then refused to give her back. Thorp clearly cared for her children and wanted them with her. But the fact that she tried to regain custody only after she remarried suggests that economic considerations

shaped her own outlook just as surely as they determined the court's custody decision.

Economic insecurity ultimately propelled women into the orbit of male-headed households, if not as wives, then as daughters, aunts, sisters, and grandmothers. Of course, common white and poor African-American women strongly identified with their kin, both male and female. In these ties they found not only support and companionship but also a sense of communal solidarity. Yet the lack of economic alternatives also shaped women's vision of social change. Given their vulnerability in the world outside their families and communities, most poor African-American and common white women worked to improve their lot within male-headed households, rather than trying to dismantle the entire structure of gender hierarchy. . . .

Suggestions for Further Reading

Kathleen C. Berkeley, "'Colored Ladies Also Contributed': Black Women's Activities from Benevolence to Social Welfare, 1866–1896," in *The Web of Southern Social Relations: Women, Family, and Education,* ed. Walter J. Fraser, Jr., R. Frank Saunders, Jr., and Jon L. Wakelyn (Athens: University of Georgia Press, 1985), 181–203.

Victoria E. Bynum, *Unruly Women: The Politics of Social and Sexual Control in the Old South* (Chapel Hill: University of North Carolina Press, 1992).

Catherine Clinton, *The Plantation Mistress: Woman's World in the Old South* (New York: Pantheon, 1982).

Christie Anne Farnham, *The Education of the Southern Belle: Higher Education and Student Socialization in the Antebellum South* (New York: New York University Press, 1994).

Drew Gilpin Faust, *Mothers of Invention: Women of the Slaveholding South in the American Civil War* (Chapel Hill: University of North Carolina Press, 1996).

Elizabeth Fox-Genovese, *Within the Plantation Household: Black and White Women of the Old South* (Chapel Hill: University of North Carolina Press, 1988).

Jean E. Friedman, *The Enclosed Garden: Women and Community in the Evangelical South, 1830–1900* (Chapel Hill: University of North Carolina Press, 1985).

D. Harland Hagler, "The Ideal Woman in the Antebellum South: Lady or Farm Wife?" *Journal of Southern History,* 46 (Aug. 1980), 405–418.

Tera W. Hunter, *To 'Joy My Freedom: Southern Black Women's Lives and Labors after the Civil War* (Cambridge, MA: Harvard University Press, 1997).

Harriet A. Jacobs, *Incidents in the Life of a Slave Girl Written By Herself,* ed. Jean Fagan Yellin (Cambridge, MA: Harvard University Press, 1987).

Julie Roy Jeffrey, "Women in the Southern Farmers' Alliance: A Reconsideration of the Role and Status of Women in the Late Nineteenth-Century South," *Feminist Studies,* 3 (Fall 1975), 72–91.

Thelma Jennings, "'Us Colored Women Had to Go Through a Plenty': Sexual Exploitation of African-American Slave Women," *Journal of Women's History,* I (Winter 1990), 45–74.

JACQUELINE JONES, *Labor of Love, Labor of Sorrow: Black Women, Work, and the Family from Slavery to the Present* (New York: Vintage Books, 1985).

SUZANNE LEBSOCK, *The Free Women of Petersburg: Status and Culture in a Southern Town, 1784–1860* (New York: W. W. Norton, 1985).

SALLY G. MCMILLEN, *Motherhood in the Old South: Pregnancy, Childbirth, and Infant Rearing* (Baton Rouge: Louisiana State University Press, 1990).

SUSAN A. MANN, "Slavery, Sharecropping, and Sexual Inequality," *Signs,* 14 (Summer 1989), 774–798.

ROBERT MANSON MYERS, *The Children of Pride: A True Story of Georgia and the Civil War* (New Haven, CT: Yale University Press, 1972).

THEDA PERDUE, *Cherokee Women: Gender and Culture Change, 1700–1835* (Lincoln: University of Nebraska Press, 1998).

THEDA PERDUE, "Southern Indians and the Cult of True Womanhood," in *The Web of Southern Social Relations: Women, Family, and Education,* ed. Walter J. Fraser, Jr., R. Frank Saunders, Jr., and Jon L. Wakelyn (Athens: University of Georgia Press, 1985), 35–51.

GEORGE C. RABLE, *Civil Wars: Women and the Crisis of Southern Nationalism* (Urbana: University of Illinois Press, 1989).

LESLIE A. SCHWALM, *A Hard Fight for We : Women's Transition from Slavery to Freedom in South Carolina* (Urbana: University of Illinois Press, 1997).

ANNE FIROR SCOTT, *The Southern Lady: From Pedestal to Politics, 1830–1930* (Chicago: University of Chicago Press, 1970).

ANNE FIROR SCOTT, "Women's Perspective on the Patriarchy in the 1850s," *Journal of American History,* 61 (June 1974), 52–64.

BRENDA E. STEVENSON, "Gender Convention, Ideals, and Identity among Antebellum Virginia Slave Women," in *More Than Chattel: Black Women and Slavery in the Americas,* ed. David Barry Gaspar and Darlene Clark Hine (Bloomington: Indiana University Press, 1996), 169–90.

BRENDA E. STEVENSON, *Life in Black and White: Family and Community in the Slave South* (New York: Oxford University Press, 1996).

ALICE TAYLOR-COLBERT, "Cherokee Women and Cultural Change," in *Women of the American South: A Multicultural Reader,* ed. Christie Anne Farnham (New York: New York University Press, 1997), 43–55.

CHERYL THURBER, "The Development of the Mammy Image and Mythology" in *Southern Women: Histories and Identities,* ed. Virginia Bernhard, Betty Brandon, Elizabeth Fox-Genovese, and Theda Perdue (Columbia: University of Missouri Press, 1992), 87–108.

ELIZABETH R. VARON, *We Mean to Be Counted: White Women & Politics in Antebellum Virginia* (Chapel Hill: University of North Carolina Press, 1998).

MARLI F. WEINER, *Mistresses and Slaves: Plantation Women in South Carolina, 1830–1880* (Urbana: University of Illinois Press, 1998).

DEBORAH GRAY WHITE, *Ar'n't I a Woman? Female Slaves in the Plantation South* (New York: W. W. Norton, 1985).

LEEANN WHITES, *The Civil War as a Crisis in Gender: Augusta, Georgia, 1860–1890* (Athens: University of Georgia Press, 1995).

MARY E. YOUNG, "Women, Civilization, and the Indian Question," in *Clio Was a Woman: Studies in the History of American Women,* ed. Mabel E. Deutrich and Virginia C. Purdy (Washington, DC: Howard University Press, 1980), 98–110.

CHAPTER EIGHT

GENDER IDENTITIES IN THE TRANS-MISSISSIPPI WEST (1820–1890)

The lyrics to the song that accompanied an immensely popular Disney film released in 1955 described Davy Crockett as a bigger-than-life folk hero who killed a bear in the backwoods of Tennessee when he was three years old and then grew up to be the "king of the wild frontier." The song went on to remind small Crockett fans how their hero risked his life fighting in the Creek Indian War and served in Congress in order to protect American liberty. When Davy heard that pioneers were beginning to move further westward, the lyricists claimed that he loaded up his gear, threw his gun over his shoulder, and "lit out a grinnin to follow the sun." The song ends with Davy Crockett leading the pioneers to their new homes. The story of Davy Crockett was so popular that millions of baby boomers can probably to this day still picture Fess Parker, the star of both the movie and the televison series, in his fringed pants and shirt and coon-skin hat marching across the screen in search of adventure.

Crockett—frontiersman, congressman, and defender of the Alamo—was only one of a variety of western male prototypes which have populated the twentieth-century popular imagination. There was also Wild Bill Hickock, lawman; Buffalo Bill, hunter; Kit Carson, scout; Jesse James, outlaw; and Geronimo, Apache warrior not to mention Cochise, Crazy Horse, and Sitting Bull. In terms of popular culture, for white men, "the frontier" was a place of freedom, adventure, and economic opportunity. It was a place where a man could escape from his dependence on kin, the restraints they placed on his actions, and the demands of civilization in general. Theoretically, there was little in the West to inhibit the newcomer's ability to express his individuality and manliness in any way he liked. He was free to indulge in the most disorderly of male behavior patterns such as swearing, drinking, whoring, gambling, and fighting. There he could give free reign to his competitiveness and aggressiveness in order to tame the land and its inhabitants. He could test his manliness against other men as well as against the forces of nature.

While pre-adolescent boys were running around their back yards wearing fake coonskin hats and looking for imaginary bears to subdue, their sisters were reading stories written by Laura Ingalls Wilder about family life on the prairie. Wilder's stories of homesteading, which were also turned into a television series, were not devoid of adventure. But they tended to focus on individual efforts to restructure home life and personal relationships as well as the process of community building. The context within which Ma and Pa Ingalls tried to rear their four daughters and struggled to make a living on the great plains was one in which attempts to establish schools and churches as well as law and order were central. In that sense, Wilder's picture of the West illustrates the degree to which settling the frontier could be a highly gendered experience. For many Anglo-American men, the idea of moving west stood as a symbol of freedom and opportunity. It is true that some women went west in search of adventure. But for many married women with children, the move was more likely to symbolize the loss of the kind of social restraints that provided a nurturing environment for stable family life. Their job was not to subdue the environment but to re-organize it, domesticate it, and re-establish restraints on the uninhibited expression of masculinity.

Historians have only just begun to pay attention to the gendered nature of the frontier experience. To date, the focus of their interest has been on Anglo-Americans who tended to view the land west of the Mississippi as uninhabited and free for the taking. Certainly the passage of the Homestead Act during the Civil War, which was intended to provide free land to anyone willing to register a claim to it and build a house on it, contributed to such an attitude. But the "West" was inhabited by a wide variety of people. Its native population was large and culturally diverse. The Spanish and Mexicans had settled the land long before the Anglos crossed the Mississippi and headed west across the plains and the mountains into the lush river valleys of the Oregon and California territories. The trans-Mississippi West, then, was an area in which various groups of men and women attempted to preserve their own definitions of masculinity and femininity in a social context in which such factors as imbalanced sex ratios, religious ideology, and the introduction of alternative ideas about gender challenged their ideas about what it meant to be a man or a woman.

Anglo settlement of the land west of the Mississippi had a profound influence on the construction of gender identities for all of the groups who lived there. Whether they were Anglos who came from the East or other ethnic groups who came from abroad, emigrants found it necessary to adapt their ideas about gender to a new environment that was very different from the one they had left. And as emigrants pushed westward, Mexicans and Native Americans were placed under great pressure to modify their ideas about gender, gender roles, and gender relations to accommodate the incursion of those whose ideas about such matters differed widely from their own.

GENDER IDENTITIES AMONG ANGLO-AMERICANS IN THE TRANS-MISSISSIPPI WEST

Between the 1840s and the late 1860s anywhere from a quarter of a million to half a million people from mostly midwestern farming families headed west. Some were looking for gold, but most were looking for better land. They were not poor people. It took from $500 to $1000 to outfit a wagon, buy mules or oxen, and purchase enough supplies to make the trip of up to 2,000 miles, a trip that could take as long as eight months to complete. Those who were single were more likely to be male than female. But most were part of a family.

For them, it was from within a gendered family context that the work involved in preparing for the harrowing journey across the plains took place.

Generally speaking, men made the decision to move westward with or without the consultation and approval or enthusiastic support of their wives. Typically, they were the ones who sold their farms and whatever family possessions they were not willing to cart across the country. They also negotiated the purchase of mules, oxen, a wagon, and supplies and ultimately chose the route that was to be followed as they left their homes and headed westward. Unless they were particularly adventurous or they went west to be teachers or missionaries, women were unlikely to initiate the idea that they should join the massive migration that was occurring. What seems apparent from the diaries and letters of pioneer women was that most were much less enthusiastic about migration than men. Unless a woman had enough property or the skills to support herself, she had little choice but to acquiesce to the decision to move west. She could try to convince her husband to postpone emigration, but in the end she either had to accompany him or be left behind. So there was little for most women to do once their husbands made the decision to migrate but begin to organize their households around what could fit into a wagon and prepare food, clothing, and medical supplies for the long journey ahead.

ANGLO MEN AND WOMEN ON THE TRAIL LEADING WEST

Diaries and letters written on the overland trail illustrate the degree to which the concerns and behavior patterns of the emigrants were gendered. Women, for example, were more likely than men to express anxiety in their personal writings. Since women tended to judge their womanliness in terms of their appearance, homemaking skills, and maternal responsibilities, they expressed concern about their ability to maintain their femininity, their ability to carry out their domestic responsibilities, and the physical welfare of their families on the long journey westward. This, added to the distress they felt about having to leave family and friends behind, meant that the trip across the plains was often a lonely and isolating experience. Men were more likely to talk about the trip as an exciting adventure and view life on the trail as an opportunity to affirm their masculinity by allowing them to test themselves against other men and the natural environment. They tested their skill with firearms on hunting expeditions. They tested their strength and endurance on the trail. Confrontation with hostile Indians provided them with the opportunity to exhibit aggressiveness and courage. And they were able to test their skill in managing livestock when it came time to ford rivers or cross the mountains. They looked at their duties on the trail as a way of fulfilling their manly roles as achievers and men of action and to exhibit and confirm their ability to provide for and protect their families.

The way that men and women responded to the dangers and difficulties inherent in making a long trip across country under primitive circumstances also illustrates the degree to which gender affected their experience. The gender conventions that many of them were familiar with made it acceptable for women to respond to potential danger by admitting their anxiety and fear. Gender conventions for men made such admission less acceptable. Men were supposed to be strong, self-assured, and courageous. So whatever they might have felt, men rarely acknowledged their fears in their diaries. While women might break down in tears when they were frustrated or tense, men were more likely to swear, drink, or pick a fight.

The extraordinarily primitive conditions that they found themselves in as they crossed the plains on their way to building new homes required that men and women be more flexible regarding gender roles and relationships than they might have been had they remained at home. Both men and women had to be hardy and resourceful and to some degree self-sufficient simply to survive the trip. A woman whose husband died on the trail far away from any sort of settlement, for example, often had little choice but to continue on. Men and women were inclined to divide their labor according to the gendered work patterns that they were most familiar with. Men were in charge of the wagons and oxen, hunted for game, and stood guard duty to protect the settlers and the livestock from predators and Indians. Women were in charge of food preparation, childcare, and laundry. Yet partly because of circumstances and partly because it was common in farming families, both men and women were willing to do the work of the other if they needed to. Men cooked, did the laundry, and assumed responsibility for their children when their wives were sick. Women yoked the oxen and drove the wagons when their husbands had to tend to other responsibilities.

Life on the trail dissipated but did not necessarily destroy women's ability to maintain their gendered identities as pious, pure, domestic, and submissive. In some cases, they found it difficult if not impossible to assert their moral authority over those with whom they traveled. They could, for example, demand that the wagon train stop on Sunday to observe the Sabbath. But in doing so, they pitted women's obligations against the prerogative of men to decide what was best for the group, which might include deciding to continue to travel on the Lord's day.

Men and women also related to the Indians in different ways according to their gender. Men, feeling responsible for protecting their families and their property, went west to seize the land that the Indians inhabited. As a result, they often saw relationships with the native inhabitants of the West as potentially adversarial. Assuming that women were unable to protect themselves, they tended to view the potential for engaging in combat with the Indians as an opportunity to exhibit manly courage and military skill as well as a way to affirm their physical prowess.

Although women often expressed some fear about coming into contact with the Indians and were perfectly capable of taking up arms against them if they thought they or their children were in danger, they did not necessarily view the Indians as enemies. In that sense, women's attitudes toward the native population were somewhat different from men. Once they realized that the biggest threat to their safety on the trail came from disease and accidents, they were more likely to approach contact with the Indians with curiosity rather than hostility. Some white women viewed the Indians as unfortunate and disadvantaged and saw themselves as moral missionaries whose responsibility it was to "civilize" the Indians. Others assumed that whites and Indians could be of mutual assistance to each other in times of need such as childbirth or hard times when sharing provisions might come in handy.

Life on the trail made it difficult for women to maintain traditional standards of femininity, particularly when it came to personal hygiene and appearance. Much of their concern about loss of femininity focussed on clothing and appearance. Sunbonnets were designed to shield the eyes and protect the skin from the drying effects of the sun. But exposure to the elements made it difficult if not impossible to preserve the kind of pale and delicate skin that was held in such high regard by white women in the nineteenth century. Travelling across country also took its toll on clothes. Doing laundry was difficult and depended upon the opportunity to camp near a river or stream long enough to wash the clothes and lay them out to dry. Many women ended their journey with their clothes filthy and patched or in tatters. Moreover, the long skirts and petticoats not to mention the corsets that women typically wore were totally impractical for getting in and out of a wagon and for doing the kind of heavy work that was required when they got to their destinations. Despite these considerations, however, many hesitated to adapt their clothes to their situation. A few resorted to wearing wash dresses that had shorter skirts than regular dresses. Fewer still appeared in a kind of bloomer costume that allowed them much greater freedom of movement. But most continued to wear conventional female clothing. When they approached a town or a fort, they may have made the men stop so that they could put a ribbon in their hair or don a clean apron that had been kept in a trunk for just such occasions. But what most of them found was that frontier living made it almost impossible to uphold middle-class standards of femininity when it came to appearance.

GENDER ROLES AND RELATIONS ON FARMS AND RANCHES

Life on farms and ranches illustrates the degree to which settlers were willing to modify gender conventions when the need arose. During the first stages of settlement, farms and ranches were widely separated. For those used to living near friends and family and travelling in groups, life could be incredibly lonely with no one to talk to or turn to in the case of need or an emergency. What that meant was that both men and women had to be even more physically and emotionally strong and self-reliant than may have been the case had they remained in the East. Farm wives, who had been able to confine their work to that of the home and barnyard, now found themselves called upon to work the land along side their husbands. They might even find it necessary to help build their own houses out of sod or tar paper or dig them out of the side of a hill. The wives and daughters of ranchers might find it necessary to learn to ride, rope, shoot, and herd cattle, but since early cowboy culture was a homosocial and hypermasculine one, doing so required that they transgress fairly well delineated gender boundaries and sacrifice their claim to womanhood in the eyes of some. Women living on farms or ranches had to manage in their husband's absence. Under such circumstances, skill, stamina, and physical strength were more useful to a woman than her appearance. It was not unusual for women who lived on ranches to exchange their petticoats, long dresses, and sunbonnets for split-skirts or

pants and wide-brimmed hats. Men might find it necessary to do what in the East would have been considered woman's work and, in the absence of a doctor, midwife, or neighbor, might even be called upon to deliver their own children. And many men found their identities as providers challenged by a whole host of physical phenomena such as droughts, floods, high winds, extreme temperatures, and plagues of grasshoppers.

After the first few years of isolation, more settlers arrived and claimed land. Small towns began to develop. The standard of living began to rise, and settlers began to feel less isolated. Living in or near a town provided women with the opportunity to express their femininity by involving themselves in the same kind of benevolent and social service activities that had characterized many of their lives before emigration. Working with their husbands, who typically controlled the political and economic life in their communities, they initiated efforts to establish schools, churches, and libraries, organize cultural events, and tend to the needs of the poor.

While men generally supported civic improvement projects, some were less enthusiastic about female efforts to eliminate gambling, prostitution, and drinking. Temperance and vice reform posed a threat to the uninhibited expression of manliness. And community leaders were sensitive to the degree to which brothels and saloons helped to keep the economy of their towns booming. So when men were slow to respond to the call to close down saloons and bars, western women joined such organizations as the Women's Christian Temperance Union. No one was more infamous for her attacks on the liquor interests than Carry Nation, who—with hatchet in hand—strode into saloons in the small towns that dotted the landscape in rural Kansas and tried to smash every glass object she could find. Temperance activities such as making speeches and organizing petition drives as well as participation in the protest activities of the Grange and Farmers' Alliances enhanced women's awareness of themselves as political agents. Acquiring the right to vote in Wyoming in 1869 and in Utah in 1870 confirmed their political identity and made it more secure.

GENDER ROLES AND RELATIONS IN MINING TOWNS

If you had walked through the mining towns of Virginia City, Nevada, Cripple Creek, Colorado, or Helena, Montana, during their boom years, you probably would have seen three men for every one woman. The populations of mining towns during the early years of mining were comprised largely of young men with widely diverse backgrounds. Some were Anglo-American or African American, but many came from as far away as China and Europe. Rootless and hedonistic, they were less interested in forming stable communities than in getting rich quick and enjoying the wealth that they extracted from the earth. The highly masculinized society that they created tended to be lawless and disorderly, characterized by the prevalence of prostitution, drunkenness, gambling, street brawls, and shootings.

The first men to prospect in the mountains defined their masculinity in terms of self-sufficiency, physical strength, and skill in wilderness survival. Those who flocked to California in search of gold went off into the mountains in small groups. There they panned for gold nuggets or hacked away at the rock with a pickaxe in order to find a vein of ore near the surface. Their work consisted of digging, carrying, and washing the ore that they found, an enterprise that was both exhausting and tedious. In the absence of women, they shared such domestic responsibilities as cooking and cleaning up. When they ran out of food or found what they had been looking for, they returned to the nearest town to replenish their supplies or stake their claim and take their ore to the assay office to have it weighed and measured. In town, they spent their time drinking, fighting, and whoring—not necessarily in that order—until they ran out of money or wanted to return to the mountains.

The men and women who lived in mining towns expressed their gendered identities in terms that were no less entrepreneurial or survival-oriented than those of the miners. They provided miners with the services they required—pans and pickaxes, food, clean beds, baths, liquor, and sex. And they were the ones who had to deal with the consequences of the violence and disorder that plagued their streets. Such conditions may have provided economic opportunities for single women, but they were not conducive for stable family life. So, most men who emigrated to mining towns went alone and promised to send for their sweethearts or wives when they had made their fortunes. In the early years, the role of women in mining culture was to provide services for single men. And while there were laundresses, boarding housekeepers, and saloon owners among them, many of the women to be found in mining towns were prostitutes whose feminine identities were expressed through their ability to use male lust and sexual allure to make money.

Some prostitutes were spectacularly successful during the boom years. Chicago Joe, a prostitute in Helena, Montana, in the 1870s and 1880s, not only owned a brothel but also a vaudeville theater and other buildings whose construction costs alone amounted to over $30,000. But most of those who worked in brothels, dance halls, and saloons or those who carried out their activities in the dilapidated shacks that lined the alleyways or stood just outside of town barely scraped by. They were subject to violence at the hands of drunken customers or other prostitutes and danger from venereal disease. Prone to drug addiction, alcoholism, and suicide, they led a hand-to-mouth existence. Upholding standards of middle-class femininity was impossible for them even if they were interested in trying to do so. Engaging in prostitution meant that they could lay no claim to social respectability. Although a few of them were able to find husbands, a prostitute had little reason to expect that a man would ask her to become his wife and then provide her with the resources to run her own household. And since motherhood posed a real threat to their ability to support themselves, prostitutes had little reason to construct their feminine identities around childbearing and routinely practiced both birth control and abortion.

Because they chose to sell access to their bodies as a means of supporting themselves, prostitutes' definition of what it meant to be a woman stood in stark contrast to women who settled in mining towns with their husbands after the boom period ended and mining companies took over the job of extracting ore from the mountains. When this happened, the failure of mining town prostitutes to fulfill the prescriptions of middle-class femininity meant that they were sometimes barred from public functions such as community dances and forced to sit in segregated sections of local theaters.

The advent of corporate mining meant that ideas about what constituted masculinity began to change. In this later stage of development, miners lost the kind of independence they had enjoyed as entrepreneurs. Instead a man's identity began to focus on his ability to get and keep his job, his skill in avoiding the dangers inherent in working deep within the earth in mining shafts, his right to vote and hold office, and his ability to organize collectively to protect the economic interests of his co-workers and family. Cave-ins posed a constant danger to both the miners who extracted the ore and carpenters whose job it was to install supports in the mine shafts. And teamsters who drove the wagons pulled by as many as thirty or forty horses at one time constantly faced the prospect of trying to control a runaway team. By the turn of the century, miners began to unionize. Under the influence of union organizers, the willingness to cooperate rather than compete with other miners came to be considered an ideal masculine attribute. As one miner put it, to be an active unionist was to be "a man—not a makeshift." For him, the claim to manhood was based on

the kind of group assertiveness encouraged by union leaders.

The ability of women in mining towns to express their femininity according to the prescriptions of the cult of true womanhood also increased as towns grew and mining corporations took over. Mining companies encouraged their male employees to marry or to bring their wives west. Respectable married women and their daughters constructed their gender identities and activities around the privacy of their homes. Without many options for employment, they were generally supportive of their husbands' efforts to assume the role of sole breadwinner. When that was the case, they tended to define their femininity partly in terms of their economic dependence and partly in terms of their success in imposing a genteel veneer over the rough and tumble world of mining. They set standards of deportment and appearance for those who wished to enjoy their company. And if they were not successful in closing down saloons and bawdy houses, they were at least able to isolate them from their own neighborhoods. They also took the lead in overseeing the cultural life of the town by supporting theatrical, operatic, and musical entertainments.

Marriages in mining towns tended to be patriarchal but the degree to which such circumstances imposed legal disabilities on women depended upon where they lived. The state of Nevada, for example, gave husbands control over their wives' property. And wife beating was common and often went unpunished in places like Virginia City. But other states allowed a woman to register her own personal property, real estate, or livestock with local government clerks. In that way, she was able to protect herself against a wide variety of financial reverses such as her husband's unemployment or his inability to handle money.

The political identities of women in mining towns, like those in farming communities, were defined by their claim to moral superiority and the theoretical disinterestedness of their public service. In places like Helena,

Montana, women ran the early social welfare system. And women in most mining communities were active in church related activities, disaster relief, and reform activities.

GENDER ROLES AND RELATIONS AMONG THE MORMONS

The members of the Church of Jesus Christ of Latter-day Saints, who settled in Utah and the surrounding areas, established a subculture with its own distinctive way of constructing gender. Most Anglo-Europeans went west in search of wealth. But the motive of the Latter-day Saints, more commonly known as Mormons, was more religious than it was secular, and their purpose was not to achieve economic success as individuals but rather to establish a godly community in the desert. The Mormons tended to settle in communities rather than on isolated homesteads. And Mormon society was organized from the very beginning around the church and the family. Self-sacrifice and cooperativeness rather than the pursuit of individual interests and competition on the part of both men and women were regarded as virtues in Mormon culture. To a great degree, the gendered identities of Mormon men and women were bound up in their ideas about God and what he expected of them.

Mormon society was strongly patriarchal. But the idea of patriarchy among the Latter-day Saints focused less on the power relationship between men and women than it did on the belief that they were God's chosen people and were directly descended from the patriarchs of the Old Testament. Mormon doctrine held that neither men nor women could be exalted in the hereafter if they remained unmarried. The church also taught that one of the primary obligations of Mormon couples was to build God's kingdom on earth. They were to do this by working to convert non-Mormons to their faith and by bearing as many children as possible. The practice of plural marriage or polygamy, a system practiced by Abraham, Isaac, and

Jacob in the Bible, fit into this system by, among other things, maximizing a Mormon's ability to fulfill this second obligation.

Men controlled and governed the Mormon Church. Established by Joseph Smith in upstate New York in the 1830s and led by Brigham Young after Smith's death, it provided every man, no matter what his social or economic station in life, with a place of honor and authority. The church also tried to provide every settler with land and the means to support a family and expected him to be sober and industrious. Thus, masculinity in Mormon culture was expressed by a man's willingness to serve God by carrying out his obligations to the church and its missionary goals. In the process, he was expected to marry, sire as many children as possible, work hard to try to provide for his family, and act as the head of his household(s).

Ideals concerning femininity in Mormon communities combined religious doctrine with practical considerations. It is true that being a wife and mother was crucial to a woman's identity. But femininity in Mormon society was defined as much by a woman's self-reliance and productivity as it was by her domestic and maternal duties. Mormon men frequently spent a great deal of time away from home. In some cases their absences were precipitated by a call from the church to pursue missionary activities among the Gentiles (non-Mormons). In others, it resulted from the practice of plural marriage. Although the Mormon Church openly supported the idea of polygamy after 1852, some women opposed the practice, and most Mormon men did not have the economic means to support more than one family. Those men who did practice polygamy often had families in more than one location, which meant they were absent for long stretches of time. Moreover, after the federal government passed stringent anti-polygamy legislation in 1877, polygamists found it necessary to hide out in order to avoid prosecution. Consequently, Mormon women often had to find some means to support themselves and their children. Besides maintaining and managing their households and caring for their children during their husbands' absences, they also had to be able and willing to do such things as clear land, run businesses and farms, and perform such public services as constructing fences and digging canals.

The public identities of Mormon men and women focussed on preserving the integrity of their communities and protecting them from the influence of outsiders. Like women in Gentile society, Mormons expressed their femininity through charity work, but the objects of their charity tended to be other Mormons who were in need of aid and assistance. The most important female organization in nineteenth-century Mormon society was the Female Relief Society. One of its purposes was to encourage Mormon women to perform domestic manufacturing in their homes in order to assure that Mormon families were as self-sufficient as possible and did not become dependent upon Gentiles for supplies, manufactured goods, and services. Participation in the Relief Society provided Mormon women with opportunities to develop leadership skills, the chance to express their religiosity in a single-sex context, and the power to influence the affairs of the Mormon Church as a whole.

The anti-polygamy campaign of the U. S. government helped to encourage Mormon women to develop a political identity. Whether or not they were partners in polygamous relationships, they organized mass meetings and petition drives to oppose the efforts of non-Mormons to interfere with the practice of plural marriage. Their political identities were further enhanced when the leaders of the Mormon Church, already worried about the anti-polygamy campaign of the federal government, became concerned about the political influence of non-Mormons who had begun to settle in Utah. One response to that unwelcome migration was to grant women the vote so that they could assure that Mormons would continue to control the political life of the state. So, settlement patterns, the insular nature of Mormon society, and persecution afforded women the opportunity to expand the definition of femininity to include economic self-sufficiency and direct political action despite the patriarchal nature of Mormon life.

GENDER IDENTITIES AMONG NATIVE AMERICANS IN THE TRANS-MISSISSIPPI WEST

One of the problems of generalizing about gender conventions and identities among the various native tribes who lived west of the Mississippi is that the tribes who lived there were so diverse. Some of them were matrilineal (where descent was traced through the mother) and matrilocal (where a man left his own residence group and went to live with that of his wife). Others were patrilineal and patrilocal. In some, the status of men and the status of women were fairly equal. In others, this was not the case. Some equated femininity and masculinity with the relatively relaxed expression of sexuality and condoned adolescent sexual experimentation, polygamy, adultery, or easy divorce. Others were much more rigid in their attitudes toward such matters.

Two examples illustrate the variety of social arrangements and gender conventions that existed. Among the nomadic buffalo hunting Indians of the Great Plains such as the Lakota Sioux, men derived their sense of manliness from their roles as hunters and warriors. They provided for their families by hunting buffalo and other game, protected their villages from those who posed a danger to it, and raided the villages of other Indians to steal horses. Thus, their gender identities centered on their physical and emotional stamina, their hunting skills, their competitiveness, their aggressiveness, and their courage. And their stature in their tribes as well as their manliness was measured by their ability to influence the decisions of tribal councils, willingness to go to war, and possession of large herds of horses.

The ideal Lakota woman was chaste, industrious, hospitable, generous, and physically strong. Female gender identity centered on a woman's ability to process the buffalo that her husband provided for her. It was a woman's job to provide her family with a tipi, to furnish it with buffalo robes, to fashion clothes from buffalo skins, to collect buffalo chips for fuel, to cook the food, and to take care of young children. Since household goods were her property, she was responsible for moving all of them from place to place as the tribe followed the herds of buffalo across the plains.

The Navajo, who lived in and around New Mexico, led a more sedentary life than buffalo hunting Indians. Herding sheep, farming, and textile manufacturing provided them with food and clothing. Navajo society was matrilineal and matrilocal. A woman and her husband usually lived in a residence group which was organized around her mother or grandmother, herds of sheep, land that by custom could be used for grazing, and cultivated fields. Although a Navajo man was perfectly capable of taking up arms to defend his residence group, being a brave warrior or skilled hunter was not central to his identity. Manliness was more likely to be defined by the number of sheep that he owned and the quality of care he provided for them. And since what little political structure there was centered on the female head of the residence group, Navajo men did not have much of a political identity. It is true that when it came time to deal with outsiders, the residence group representative was usually a man, but all decisions within the group were expected to be unanimous.

Gender identity for women centered on her housekeeping, child rearing, and textile manufacturing skills. Women ground corn for food, processed wool, made clothes, and wove blankets. Like men, they could own sheep. And if they were unhappy with their husbands, they were free to divorce. Thus, gender roles among the Navajo were complementary. Neither men nor women had much power over the other.

Navajo society was both communal and individualistic. On one hand, cooperation rather than competition and aggression character-

ized interpersonal relationships. Land was held in common, and while sheep in the herd were individually owned, the herd as a whole was supposed to provide food and clothing for everyone in the residence group. On the other hand, both men and women were allowed to speak for themselves and pursue their own interests. Generally speaking, they were free to do whatever they wanted. They were expected rather than coerced both to live in harmony with each other and to fulfill their obligations to each other.

The way Native Americans constructed gender was not only varied, it was also flexible. Unlike Anglo-Americans, Indians were relatively tolerant of individuals whose gendered identities were ambiguous or who adopted identities that combined both masculine and feminine attributes. What that meant was that it was possible for men and women to literally redefine themselves in terms of gender. Consider, for example, the case of a "manly hearted" woman known as Woman Chief of the Crows. Born into the Gros Ventre tribe, she was captured by the Crow when she was a child. When she exhibited interest in hunting, riding, and shooting, the Crow warrior who adopted her allowed her to pursue those activities. She became an expert horsewoman and a crack shot. She spent most of her time killing game, butchering it, and carrying it back to camp. And when the Blackfoot attacked her village, she killed three warriors single-handedly, thus proving her courage. As she grew older and became renowned for her bravery in battle, she was able to gather warriors around her and go on raids. Together they scalped their enemy and stole their horses. It was in this way that Woman Chief of the Crows became wealthy and influential. She was able to build up a large herd of horses and eventually sat on the tribal council. Despite the fact that she was taller and stronger than most women, she continued to wear women's clothes, unlike other "manly hearted" women. She eventually took four wives. In 1854, she was trapped and killed by the Gros Ventre, who resented her raids against them. She and other "manly hearted" women occupied positions of prestige and power within their tribes and were known and respected for their aggressiveness, independence, boldness, ambition, and sexual freedom.

Woman Chief of the Crows chose to distinguish herself as a man by redefining what it meant to be a woman. The same cannot be said of the berdache, or what some call "two spirit" people. Neither male nor female, they comprised a third gender in many Native American societies. Found among a wide variety of tribes including the Zuni, Navajo, Shoshoni, and Cheyenne, these individuals were androgynous and occupied a distinct place in their societies. Young men who became berdache usually showed indications of their distinctive gender identity at an early age. As small children they preferred associating with women and helping them cook, clean, sew, grind corn, and engage in the production of textiles, beadwork, baskets, and pottery. Non-competitive and gentle, they resisted participation in the rough, physically demanding, competitive games of the other boys.

Native Americans were able to accommodate such gender ambiguity partly because of their religious attitudes. They believed that if the spirits had taken particular care to create someone clearly different from the rest, that person must be especially close to the spirits and, therefore, sacred. Moreover, it was not unusual for a young man to be guided into being a berdache through visions, thus relieving him of any personal responsibility for his gendered transformation.

Berdaches were noted for being extremely hardworking and for taking great pride in their skill in performing traditionally female tasks. As they grew older, some of them adopted female dress or certain aspects of female dress. They often served as spiritual leaders in their villages, assumed responsibility for caring for the wounded during periods of war, and helped to perform burial and mourning rituals. While some engaged in sexual relations with women, most engaged in sexual activities with other men, and marriage between a berdache and another man was commonplace.

Massive immigration of Anglo-Europeans during the second half of the nineteenth century threatened the ability of Native Americans to preserve their traditional attitudes towards gender, gender roles, and gender relationships. As whites demanded more and more land, the U.S. government signed treaties with the Indians that forced them onto reservations. After the Civil War, the U.S. army concentrated on assuring that the Indians posed no threat to white settlers.

Native response to U.S. policy took a number of forms. Some Indians emigrated to Canada where they continued to live their lives as they had done before. Others, of course, resisted. Unwilling to submit to the inevitable destruction of their culture, men like Sitting Bull and Crazy Horse declared war on the United States and fought to preserve the only way of life they knew. Their cause was a hopeless one, not because they were deficient in determination or bravery but because they were outmanned as well as outgunned and because whites indiscriminately slaughtered the buffalo leaving the plains Indians without adequate food, clothing, and shelter. By 1890, the Indian Wars were for all intents and purposes over. The Natives who signed treaties with the federal government gave up their right to roam across the open range at will and settled on reservations where they depended on the Bureau of Indian Affairs to provide them with housing, food, clothing, medical care, and education. Under those circumstances, they searched for new ways to express their gendered identities.

On the reservations, whites continued their attempts to "civilize" the Indians by turning Native men into farmers and Native women into model housewives. To achieve that goal, the federal government and eastern missionary societies sponsored day schools and boarding schools intended to Christianize Indian children and teach them Anglo moral codes, work practices, and gender conventions. Working under the assumption that Indian women, like white women, would have the moral authority to control the behavior of their husbands and would pass what they had learned in school about gender identity and behavior on to their children, teachers and school superintendents placed special emphasis on training Native American girls. They spent much less time on training them academically than they did trying to instill in them the desire to be virtuous Christians, accomplished housekeepers, and model mothers. To the boys, they taught farming and ranching skills so that they would be able to express their manliness by supporting themselves and their families.

The Dawes Act passed by Congress in 1887 further undermined the gender roles of Native Americans. Traditionally the Indians had held land in common, which meant that women had as much claim to the land as men. The Dawes Act gave each male head of household ownership over a specific tract of land called an allotment, thus dispossessing women. If a woman divorced her husband or her husband died, she was left without land, especially if she had married according to Native American custom rather than under American law.

The Indians responded to the attempts of whites to impose Anglo ideas about gender upon them in a variety of ways. Some parents sent their children to day schools, but most were hesitant to send them to boarding schools because they understood that in doing so they were forfeiting their control over their children's cultural life, not to mention their physical and emotional wellbeing. As far as the students were concerned, some were willing to accept the white work ethic and dress codes because they hoped that doing so might help them to compete in the marketplace. But those who intended to become self-sufficient, independent farmers often failed to make a decent living either because the farms allocated to them by the federal government were too small or because the land was infertile. So in an effort to assume the role of breadwinner, native men sometimes found it necessary to work as hired hands for someone else. Similarly, Indian women found it difficult to express their femininity through a farm-wife version of middle-class domesticity. In order

to make ends meet, they also had to find jobs, often working as domestic servants. In the end, whether they lived off the fruits of their own labor or the largesse of the federal government, Native men and women had to construct their gendered identities around a state of semi-dependence.

GENDER IDENTITIES AND RELATIONS AMONG IMMIGRANTS IN THE TRANS-MISSISSIPPI WEST

After the passage of the Homestead Act in 1862, which offered 160 acres of land to anyone willing to go west and settle, land-hungry immigrants from all over the world flooded onto the plains to stake their claims to farms and ranches or settle in frontier towns. Others headed to the mountains hoping to discover gold or silver and get rich quick. Each group had its own ideas about what was feminine and what was masculine. Since it would be impossible, given the space available, to explore the gender conventions of each of these various immigrant groups, let us confine ourselves to a discussion of the Chinese who settled in San Francisco.

Chinese men who immigrated to the west, like men with other ethnic identities, generally did so for economic reasons. The earliest of them came to help build the transcontinental railroad, the first of which was completed in 1869. Many of them eventually settled in the Bay area where they lived clustered together in what became a Chinese ghetto in the city of San Francisco. There they made their living as merchants, established small businesses, or worked for low wages as industrial or service workers.

In terms of gender distribution, Chinatown looked like mining towns. There were not many women to be seen. According to the California state census, there were only nineteen Chinese women living among 2,954 men in San Francisco in 1852. The ratio had only slightly improved by the 1890s. This kind of gender imbalance was not necessarily due to the fact that most Chinese men were single but rather to a number of other factors. Some of those who were married left their wives at home in China. They returned home periodically in order to visit their wives, assure that their family lines continued through the birth of children, and tend to their other family obligations. Those who were single often deferred to the expectation of their families that they return to China to marry. And finally, the passage of the Chinese Exclusion Act of 1882 made it difficult, if not impossible, for Chinese men to bring their wives into the United States. As a result, there were few families in Chinatown in the early period of settlement, and from the Anglo point of view, Chinese men failed to uphold conventional standards of manhood that demanded that men establish themselves as the heads of households.

This lack of women encouraged Chinese entrepreneurs operating from the west coast to begin importing women from China. The vast majority of the women who immigrated from China during the second half of the nineteenth century came as a kind of indentured servant whose job it was to serve the sexual needs of Chinese men. Such a system was considered both desirable and culturally acceptable since it allowed Chinese men to satisfy their sexual urges with women from their own ethnic group and thus avoid the possibility of forming permanent relationships with women who were not Chinese. In this way, they were able to preserve the integrity of the Chinese family.

The system worked like this. Procurers in China enticed, kidnapped, or purchased young women between the ages of 16 and 25 from poor peasant families and shipped them off to San Francisco where brothel owners purchased them and set them to work as prostitutes. Some ended up as concubines to wealthy Chinese merchants who set them up in their own homes. Some worked in brothels or parlor houses at night and during the day did contract work such as sewing or shoemaking. Others worked in shacks called "cribs" and served the sexual needs of sailors and poor laborers. After four or five years, if they were still healthy, they became domestic servants, laundresses, or garment workers.

This was all possible because of the way the Chinese family was structured, the low regard with which women were held in Chinese society, and the extreme poverty that characterized the lives of so many peasants in China. The Chinese family was patriarchal. Sons were preferred over daughters because sons were expected to stay in the family and carry on the family line as well as assume responsibility for preserving the family's honor and prosperity and for fulfilling the obligations involved in ancestor worship. Daughters were expected to marry into someone else's family where their labor was exploited to benefit their in-laws. These factors, combined with the indebtedness of many peasant families, meant that girls were seen as burdens rather than assets. Some parents avoided the need to support their daughters by killing them as infants or abandoning them. Others sold them or put them to work to help pay off their family's debts. A daughter was expected to acquiesce to being sold or indentured because it was considered to be her duty. So Chinese prostitutes were not necessarily stigmatized as "fallen" women. Instead of being regarded as morally depraved, they could be regarded as good daughters who were willing to fulfill their family obligations by obeying the wishes of their parents. Chinese women who worked as prostitutes may have been unfortunate, but the nature of their employment did not necessarily dishonor them in the eyes of those in their own community.

What this meant was that, unlike prostitutes from other ethnic backgrounds, some of those who worked in Chinatown might realistically expect to escape from the world of sexual commerce by marrying. Some prostitutes wed their customers. Others were assisted in their efforts to marry by white, middle-class Methodist or Presbyterian women who established houses of refuge for Chinese prostitutes in the early 1870s. Intent on protecting runaway prostitutes from the exploitation of Chinese men, the women who ran these homes provided a cloistered environment for the prostitutes who sought their assistance. Their efforts to "save" the prostitutes who came to them were similar to the efforts of those who were trying to "civilize" the Indians on the reservations. They tried to teach Chinese women to appreciate such middle-class values as piety and purity, provided them with vocational training so that they could support themselves if necessary, and taught them housekeeping skills so that when they married they could establish Christian households. Once this was accomplished, marriages were arranged for them from among the Chinese men who applied and could convince the directors of the rescue homes that they were "Christian gentlemen."

Once former prostitutes married, they could construct their feminine identities around being wives and mothers. The wealth of their husbands determined the degree to which their gendered identities were characterized by economic and social dependence. Those who married rich merchants found themselves totally dependent upon their husbands for financial support and socially isolated inside their home. They rarely if ever ventured out onto the street and spent their days entertaining close family members, giving orders to their servants, and supervising the care of their children. Since working-class men usually worked in low-skilled, low-paid jobs, it was difficult for them to assume the role of sole support in their families. So the wives of wage earning men often found it necessary to supplement their husband's earnings by working as laundresses, seamstresses, shop girls, domestic servants, or boardinghouse keepers. But whatever feelings of self-sufficiency or independence they may have garnered from their role as wage earners was minimized by the degree to which they were expected to defer to the authority of their husbands. According to an old Chinese proverb, "A woman married is like a horse sold; you can ride them or flog them as you like."

GENDER IDENTITIES AND RELATIONS IN MEXICAN AMERICAN COMMUNITIES

The United States took over that part of the Southwest called New Mexico and California after the Mexicans signed the Treaty of Guadalupe Hidalgo ending the Mexican War in 1848. But it wasn't until the 1880s that Anglo-American settlers began to arrive in large numbers. What they found was a culture and gender system based on communal values and male authority combined with a surprising degree of female autonomy.

Communal villages were a fundamental part of Mexican-American culture. Original grants of land from the Mexican government had been issued not to individuals but to groups of Mexican settlers who established an agricultural economy based on farming and herding. The culture that they developed did not encourage individualism or competitiveness. Mexican men typically owned small lots, a house, and the land surrounding the house. But pastures and water were held in common by the village as a whole and were managed by elected boards, which assigned grazing rights and maintenance work.

The structure of Mexican families was patriarchal. And male identity, particularly among the upper class, was not only constructed around a man's ability to support and protect his family but also to control his wife and children in order to assure that the honor of his family was not besmirched. Men based their sense of honor on personal integrity, honesty, and loyalty, and willingness to protect the reputations of their female relatives. Women were honorable if they were modest, shy in the presence of men, virginal before marriage, and faithful afterwards. In other words, the honor of an upper-class, Mexican-American family lay as much in the hands of its women as in the hands of its men, just as it did in the antebellum South. Concern about the willingness of young women to uphold their part of the bargain manifested itself in the practice of forbidding them to go out in public without a chaperone.

Children needed the permission of their father to marry. And among those with great status and wealth, marriages tended to be arranged in the interests of property and family ties rather than romantic love. But once they were married it is unclear what kind of authority a husband had over his wife. As one historian has pointed out, beating one's wife was considered cause for divorce. Further research needs to be done to determine just how many divorces were granted on these grounds. What is clear is that women had the potential for some degree of economic independence. Mexican law provided that women could inherit property and then control it themselves, although they were more likely to inherit livestock, furniture, and household goods that they were to inherit land.

The gendered identities of Hispanic men and women focused on their role as parents. The need for labor and the influence of the Catholic Church discouraged the practice of birth control and abortion. Children were welcomed into Mexican-American families. Extended families often played an active role in rearing children both because of the communal way that Mexican-American villages were organized and because fathers were frequently absent from the home tending their herds or working outside the community for wages.

Work on the land and in the home was divided by gender. Men built the houses, selected the crops to be planted in the fields, herded sheep, and supervised the butchering and distribution of meat. Women controlled what was planted in the garden and processed what they grew. Thus each helped to produce food to sustain the family. Women were responsible for plastering their houses every year, but since most homes had very little furniture, housekeeping was relatively uncomplicated. Mats on the floor served as beds, and during the daytime, they were rolled up against the wall to provide seating. Women also cooked, cleaned, and assumed primary responsibility for the religious, intellectual, physical, and emotional wellbeing of children. Because their men were away from home with the herds so much of the time, women dominated village life. They often had to take over responsibility for irrigating the fields and to make decisions that affected both their family and their village.

The arrival of the Anglo-Americans in the latter part of the nineteenth century imposed changes on Mexican-American culture that had gendered implications. The U. S. government declared Mexican-American grazing land to be public domain. It then allowed white settlers to farm it, gave it to the railroads, or made it available to mining companies, making it increasingly difficult for Mexican-American men to support themselves by herding. The kind of economic development that accompanied white settlement was also a disruptive influence in Hispanic village culture. It provided new markets for local goods, thus placing new demands on productivity, and offered new opportunities for both men and women to find employment outside their own villages on the railroads or mines in the case of the men, or as seamstresses, laundresses, cooks, or servants in the case of the women.

By the late nineteenth century, Protestant missionaries were trying to "Americanize" Mexican-Americans as well as Chinese prostitutes and American Indians. Because men were often absent, the missionaries were more likely to try to influence village women than they were village men. Mexican-American women resisted attempts to convert them to Protestantism. And they were quite selective in the ways they were willing to change their lives in order to conform to the white, middle-class expectations. Those who were receptive to the efforts of missionaries tended to adapt middle-class ideas about privacy, deportment, and appearance to their own circumstances. But as a general rule, the cultural borrowing that went on was relatively superficial and centered around their role as housekeepers. Mexican-American housewives were much more likely to adopt the use of iron beds, glazed windows, steel kitchen ranges, and sewing machines than they were to change the way they worshiped God, organized the lives of their families, or related to members of the opposite sex.

SUMMARY

Like other places in the United States, the trans-Mississippi West was a place where ideas about gender were contested. Between about 1840 and 1890, four distinctly different categories of people—(1) Anglo-Americans including the Mormons, (2) immigrants including the Chinese, (3) Native Americans, and (4) people of Spanish-Mexican descent—came into direct contact with each other in an environment where they had to interact and accommodate each other's presence. Each group was intent on maintaining a certain degree of cultural integrity and continuity. And as a part of their effort to do this, they tried to preserve traditional gender conventions. Many, however, found themselves in the position of having to adapt their understanding of how masculinity and femininity should be expressed to frontier conditions and the presence of others.

Anglo-Americans had more economic, legal, and military power and, therefore, more cultural authority over such matters than those in other groups. The result was that they were in the strongest position to direct changes in how gender was expressed in the West.

Response to their efforts was mixed. Some immigrants, Native Americans, and Mexican Americans accepted white, middle-class ideas about gender as a part of their efforts to assimilate successfully. But others were able to resist some of the pressure placed on them to change the way they constructed their understanding of gender and expressed their gendered identities. They simply preserved those cultural attitudes toward gender that had the most meaning for them and selectively adapted Anglo-American gender conventions to their own circumstances as the need arose. Native American men, for example, had always expressed their masculinity in terms of their ability to provide for their families. But by 1890, the context in which most of them did so had changed dramatically. Life on a reservation, combined with the destruction of the buffalo, meant that they could no longer express their manliness through their efforts to provide the raw materials necessary to feed, clothe, and house their families. Instead they had to farm or try to find work as wage laborers and depend on the federal government to provide them with subsistence if they failed in their efforts. Mexican-American men were in a similar situation. They had traditionally supported their families through farming and animal husbandry. But once the U.S. government imposed American law over their territory, Mexican villages lost control over grazing land. The result was that men began to find it necessary to supplement their incomes from meat and wool production with wage labor. This, in turn, sometimes meant that they often had to leave their villages in search of work, leaving their wives and children behind. Village life became even more feminized than it had been before, and women had to accept more and more responsibility for the conduct of village affairs.

The ability of Anglo-Americans to impose their own definitions of femininity on immigrants, Indians, and Mexican-American women was limited in similar ways. Women in these three groups had traditionally expressed their femininity around marriage and domesticity. And they continued to do so, adapting themselves and the way they carried out their domestic duties to the circumstances they found themselves in. Instead of constructing clothes out of buffalo hides, for example, Native American women simply substituted cloth and stitched it together with a sewing machine. And instead of processing buffalo meat for food, they cooked food that they had purchased or that which was supplied to them by the federal government. In the case of Mexican-American women, most refused to give up Catholicism. But they were willing to adopt Anglo technology and house-keeping techniques to make their homes more comfortable and their lives easier. They used the money they or their husbands made as wage laborers to buy iron bedsteads and mat-tresses. After a good nights' sleep, they made beds rather than rolling up the sleeping mats and then cooked breakfast on a stove rather than in a fireplace as their mothers and grand-mothers had done.

DOCUMENT

Excerpts from the Memoir of a Cowboy

Born in 1860, Edward C. Abbott immigrated from England with his parents, who set-tled on a homestead just outside Lincoln, Nebraska in 1871. His father was well educated and hardworking but a very poor businessman. From his son's point of view, he was also "overbearing and tyrannical." So young Teddy spent as little time at home as he could and found refuge associating with the cowboys who had driven cattle up from Texas. By the time he was 14, he was a cowboy himself. "I was a man from the time I was twelve years old—doing a man's work, living with men, having men's ideas," he told Helena Huntington Smith who interviewed him in 1937.

During the 1870s and 1880s, he drove cattle from Texas to Montana. In 1889 he gave up the free and easy life of a cowboy to marry his boss's pretty daughter and settle down. He spent the rest of his life ranching in Montana and died in 1939.

How does Abbott characterize himself and the men with whom he associated? What did being a man mean to him? What was his attitude toward women? What did he think characterized womanliness?

In person the cowboys were mostly medium-sized men, as a heavy man was hard on horses, quick and wiry, and as a rule very good-natured; in fact it did not pay to be any-thing else. In character their like never was or will be again. They were intensely loyal to the outfit they were working for and would fight to the death for it. They would follow their wagon boss through hell and never complain. I have seen them ride into camp after two days and nights on herd, lay down on their saddle blankets in the rain, and sleep like dead men, then get up laughing and joking about some good time they had had in Ogallala or Dodge City. Living that kind of a life, they were bound to be wild and brave. In fact there was only two things the old-time cowpuncher was afraid of, a decent woman and being set afoot. . . .

About this time, 1876, when I had that picture taken, the one with the cigar in my

Source: E. C. Abbott ("Teddy Blue") and Helena Huntington Smith, *We Pointed Them North: Recol-lections of a Cowpuncher* (Norman: University of Oklahoma Press, 1955), 7–8, 25, 35–36, 89, 100–102, 108–09.

mouth. I had a bottle of whisky in the other hand, but it doesn't show, because I had a fight with the other fellow in the picture and tore off his half of it. I was drunk when the picture was made, and I guess I wanted the world to know it. I was sixteen then and dead tough. Oh, God, I was tough. I had a terrible reputation, and I was sure proud of it. I'll never forget the time I walked home with a nice girl. Her people were English, some of those cart-horse-bred English that my father looked down on, and she had walked up to our house to visit with the girls and stayed to supper. I took her home afterwards. It was only about half a mile. Her family just tore her to pieces. They saw to it she never went out with me again. . . .

That trip up the trail in '79 was my second, but in a way it was the first that counted, because I was only a button the other time. I wasn't nineteen years old when I come up the trail with the Olive herd, but don't let that fool you. I was a man in my own estimation and a man in fact. I was no kid with the outfit but a top cowhand, doing a top hand's work, and there is nothing so wonderful about that. All I'd ever thought about was being a good cowhand. I'd been listening to these Texas men and watching them and studying the disposition of cattle ever since I was eleven years old.

Even in years I was no younger than a lot of them. The average age of cowboys then, I suppose, was twenty-three or four. Except for some of the bosses there was very few thirty-year-old men on the trail. I heard a story once about a school teacher who asked one of these old Texas cow dogs to tell her all about how he punched cows on the trail. She said: "Oh, Mister So-and-So, didn't the boys used to have a lot of fun riding their ponies?"

He said: "Madam, there wasn't any boys or ponies. They was all horses and men."

Well, they had to be, to stand the life they led. Look at the chances they took and the kind of riding they done, all the time, over rough country. Even in the daytime those deep coulees could open up all at once in front of you, before you had a chance to see where

you were going, and at night it was something awful if you'd stop to think about it, which none of them ever did. If a storm come and the cattle started running—you'd hear that low rumbling noise along the ground and the men on herd wouldn't need to come in and tell you, you'd know—then you'd jump for your horse and get out there in the lead, trying to head them and get them into a mill before they scattered to hell and gone. It was riding at a dead run in the dark, with cut banks and prairie dog holes all around you, not knowing if the next jump would land you in a shallow grave. . . .

I can never forget Miles City in '84. As far as fun went, I think I had more of it then than any other year of my life, much more fun than when I was a kid, because when I was a kid I was too much on the fight all the time. It was that same old foolishness of worrying about personal courage. When I was eighteen or nineteen I was so full of that shooting business I couldn't be free to enjoy myself, anyway not like I did later. But by the time I was twenty-three I had got over the worst of it and oh, boy, but life was good. . . .

There was a saloon man in Miles City named Charlie Brown. He had the Cottage Saloon and he kept a big bowl of Mulligan stew standing on the stove all the time, and he would say, "Just help yourself." If they wanted to, they could take their blankets and bed down on the floor, and in the morning he would give them a free drink. He figured that when they got a hundred dollars they would blow it right over his bar, and they did.

A cowpuncher would never hang around town after he run out of money. He would get on his horse and drift back out to the ranch. Oh, there was exceptions once in a great while, when a fellow got a mash on a girl. I know of one case where a cowpuncher went in town and gave his sweetheart a hundred dollars, which was all he had in the world, and she kept him all winter. She lived in kind of a little crib behind a saloon, a log shack with just a bedroom and kitchen. He moved in there, and when she had company he slept in the kitchen or in the saloon. But I guess that is what you would call an old story.

Cowpunchers and buffalo hunters didn't mix much, and never would have even if the buffalo hunters hadn't went out of the picture when they did. The buffalo hunters was a rough class—they had to be, to lead the life they led. That buffalo slaughter was a dirty business. . . .

The buffalo hunters didn't wash, and looked like animals. They dressed in strong, heavy, warm clothes and never changed them. You would see three or four of them walk up to a bar, reach down inside their clothes and see who could catch the first louse for the drinks. They were lousy and proud of it.

The cowpunchers was a totally different class from these other fellows on the frontier. We was the salt of the earth, anyway in our own estimation, and we had the pride that went with it. That was why Miles City changed so much after the trail herds got there; even the women changed. Because buffalo hunters and that kind of people would sleep with women that cowpunchers wouldn't even look at, and it was on our account that they started bringing in girls from eastern cities, young girls and pretty ones. Those girls followed us up, like I told you, and we would meet old pals in new places. . . .

That shows you how we were about those things. As Mag Burns used to say, the cowpunchers treated them sporting women better than some men treat their wives.

Well, they were women. We didn't know any others. And any man that would abuse one of them was a son of a gun. I remember one time when a P.I. beat up on his girl for not coming through with enough money or something like that, and a fellow I knew jumped on him and half-killed him. The man hadn't done nothing to him. It was none of his business. It was just the idea of mistreating a woman. . . .

DOCUMENT

Folk Songs about Life in the Trans-Mississippi West

Folk songs that are passed down from generation to generation provide a window on the way that ordinary people define themselves as men and women. They also give us some idea about their attitudes toward each other. The first song refers to the Texas Rangers. Highly mobile, excellent horsemen, and crack shots, these men spent their lives trying to guard American settlers in Texas from being harassed by Mexican outlaws and Indians. It was said that "to belong to the Texas Rangers, a man had to be able to 'ride like a Mexican, trail like an Indian, shoot like a Tennessean, and fight like the very devil.' "

Source: Alan Lomax, *The Folk Songs of North America in the English Language* (Garden City, NY: Doubleday & Co., 1960), 331–32, 335–36, 397–98.

The context for the second song, "Sweet Betsy," is the gold rush that began in 1849 after gold was discovered in California. It describes the trek westward and what happens when Sweet Betsy and her boyfriend Ike reach the gold fields.

The third song refers to life on the plains where the absence of trees made it necessary for settlers to build their houses out of pieces of sod, dirt bricks that were essentially held together by the roots of prairie grass. Some had windows to let the light in, but others did not. Such houses were impossible to keep clean. Dirt and straw from the grass inevitably dropped from the ceiling onto everything on the floor below. There was also a real danger from rain, which could soak through the dirt roof and cause it to fall in. In this song a bachelor describes his life on the prairie and his need for a woman to take care of him.

What do these three songs tell us about gender identity and gender roles in the West? To what degree were those identities and roles different from those one might have found in the eastern part of the United States during the same period?

THE TEXAS RANGERS

Come all you Texas Rangers, wherever you
    may be,
I hope you'll pay attention and listen unto me,
My name is nothing extry, the truth to you
    I'll tell,
I am a roving Ranger and I'm sure I wish
    you well.

'Twas at the age of sixteen I joined this jolly
    band,
We marched from San Antonio unto the Rio
    Grande,
Our captain, he informed us, perhaps he
    thought it right,
'Before you reach the station, boys, I'm sure
    you'll have to fight.'

I saw the Injuns coming, I heard them give a
    yell,
My feelings at this moment no human tongue
    can tell,
I saw their glittering lances and their arrows
    round me flew,
And all my strength it left me and all my
    courage, too.

We fought full nine hours before the strife
    was o'er,
The like of dead and wounded I never saw
    before,
And when the sun was rising and the Indians
    they had fled,
We loaded up our rifles and counted up our
    dead.

Now all of us were wounded, our noble captain
    slain,
The sun was shining sadly across the bloody
    plain,
Sixteen brave Rangers as ever roamed the West,
Were buried by their comrades with arrows in
    their breast.

'Twas then I thought of mother, who to me in
    tears did say,
'To you they are all strangers, with me you'd
    better stay.'
I thought that she was childish and that she
    did not know,
My mind was fixed on ranging and I was
    bound to go.

I have seen the fruits of rambling, I know its
    hardships well,
I have crossed the Rocky Mountains, rode
    down the streets of Hell,
I have been in the great Southwest, where
    wild Apaches roam,
And I tell you from experience, you'd better
    stay at home.

SWEET BETSY

Did you ever hear tell of Sweet Betsy from Pike,
Who crossed the wide mountains with her
    lover Ike,
With two yoke of cattle and one spotted hog,
A tall Shanghai rooster and an old yellow dog.

CHORUS:
Hoodle dang fol-de di-do, hoodle dang fol-de day.

They swam the wide rivers and climbed the tall peaks
And camped on the prairies for weeks upon weeks,
Starvation and cholera, hard work and slaughter,
They reached California spite of hell and high water. (CHO.)

The Injuns come down in a wild yelling horde,
And Betsy got skeered they would scalp her adored,
So behind the front wagon-wheel Betsy did crawl,
And fought off the Injuns with musket and ball. (CHO.)

They camped on the prairie one bright, starry night,
They broke out the whisky and Betsy got tight,
She sang and she shouted and romped o'er the plain
And showed her bare bum to the whole wagon train. (CHO.)

The wagon tipped over with a terrible crash
And out on the prairie rolled all sorts of trash,
A few little baby clothes, done up with care,
Looked rather suspicious, but 'twas all on the square. (CHO.)

Sweet Betsy got up with a great deal of pain
And declared she'd go back to Pike County again,
Then Ike heaved a sigh and they fondly embraced,
And she travelled along with his arm round her waist. (CHO.)

They passed the Sierras through mountains of snow,
Till old California was sighted below.
Sweet Betsy she hollered, and Ike gave a cheer,
'Saying, Betsy, my darlin', I'm a made mil-lioneer.' (CHO.)

A miner said, 'Betsy, will you dance with me?'
'I will that, old hoss, if you don't make too free.
But don't dance me hard, do you want to know why?
Doggon ye, I'm chock full of strong alkali.' (CHO.)

Long Ike and Sweet Betsy got married, of course,
But Ike, who was jealous, obtained a divorce,
And Betsy, well satisfied, said with a smile,
'I've six good men waitin' within half a mile.' (CHO.)

THE LITTLE OLD SOD SHANTY

I am looking rather seedy now while holding down my claim,
And my victuals are not always of the best;
And the mice play shyly round me as I nestle down to rest,
In my little old sod shanty in the West.
The hinges are of leather and the windows have no glass,
While the board roof lets the howling blizzards in,
And I hear the hungry coyote as he slinks up through the grass,
Round my little old sod shanty on my claim.

Yet I rather like the novelty of living in this way,
Though my bill of fare is always rather tame,
But I'm happy as a clam on the land of Uncle Sam
In the little old sod shanty on my claim.
But when I left my eastern home, a bachelor so gay,
To try and win my way to wealth and fame,
I little thought I'd come down to burning twisted hay
In the little old sod shanty on my claim.

My clothes are plastered o'er with dough, I'm looking like a fright,
And everything is scattered round the room,
But I wouldn't give the freedom that I have out in the West
For the table of the eastern man's old home.
Still I wish some tender woman would pity on me take,
And relieve me from the mess that I am in;
The angel, how I'd bless her, if this her home she'd make
In the little old sod shanty on my claim.

And we would make our fortunes on the prairies of the West,
Just as happy as two lovers we'd remain;
We'd forget the trials and troubles we endured at the first,

In the little old sod shanty on my claim.
And if fate should bless us with now and then
   an heir,
To cheer our hearts with honest pride of fame,

O then we'd be contented for the toil that we
   had spent
In the little old sod shanty on our claim.

<small></small>

DOCUMENT

Excerpts from Richard Henry Dana's Memoir

Born in Cambridge, Massachusetts in 1815, Richard Henry Dana was from a socially prominent family. He entered Harvard in 1831, but in the summer of 1833 he contracted the measles and was unable to return to school. Bored and looking for something interesting to do, he decided to go on a sea voyage. Most young men from his social class would have gone to Europe. Instead, he got a job as an ordinary seaman on the Pilgrim *which was headed around Cape Horn to California. Dana's adventure lasted from 1834 to 1836. In 1840 he published a record of his exploits in a book called* Two Years Before the Mast. *In the excerpts that follow, Dana describes life among the inhabitants of California, which was then owned by Mexico.*

What does he have to say about the gendered behavior of the Californios and the Indians? How did it differ from that of that of middle-class Americans? What judgments did he make about what he saw?

The government of the country is an arbitrary democracy, having no common law, and nothing that we should call a judiciary. Their only laws are made and unmade at the caprice of the legislature, and are as variable as the legislature itself. . . .

Revolutions are matters of frequent occurrence in California. They are got up by men who are at the foot of the ladder and in desperate circumstances, just as a new political organisation may be started by such men in our own country. The only object, of course, is the loaves and fishes; and instead of *caucusing*, paragraphing, libelling, feasting, promising, and lying, they take muskets and bayonets, and, seizing upon the presidio and custom-house, divide the spoils, and declare a new dynasty. As for justice, they know little law but will and fear. . . .

In their domestic relations these people are not better than in their public. The men are thriftless, proud, extravagant, and very much given to gaming; and the women have but little education, and a good deal of beauty, and their morality, of course, is none of the best; yet the instances of infidelity are much less frequent than one would at first suppose. In

Source: Richard Henry Dana, *Two Years Before the Mast. A Personal Narrative of Life at Sea* (New York: Harper & Bros., 1840), 211–12, 214–16.

fact, one vice is set over against another; and thus something like a balance is obtained. If the women have but little virtue, the jealousy of their husbands is extreme, and their revenge deadly and almost certain. A few inches of cold steel have been the punishment of many an unwary man, who has been guilty, perhaps, of nothing more than indiscretion. The difficulties of the attempt are numerous, and the consequences of discovery fatal, in the better classes. With the unmarried women, too, great watchfulness is used. The main object of the parents is to marry their daughters well, and to this a fair name is necessary. The sharp eyes of a duena, and the ready weapons of a father or brother, are a protection which the characters of most of them—men and women—render by no means useless; for the very men who would lay down their lives to avenge the dishonour of their own family would risk the same lives to complete the dishonour of another.

Of the poor Indians very little care is taken. The priests, indeed, at the missions, are said to keep them very strictly, and some rules are usually made by the alcaldes to punish their misconduct; yet it all amounts to but little. Indeed, to show the entire want of any sense of morality or domestic duty among them, I have frequently known an Indian to bring his wife, to whom he was lawfully married in the church, down to the beach, and carry her back again, dividing with her the money which she had got from the sailors. If any of the girls were discovered by the alcalde to be open evil livers, they were whipped, and kept at work sweeping the square of the presidio, and carrying mud and bricks for the buildings; yet a few reals would generally buy them off. Intemperance, too, is a common vice among the Indians. The Mexicans, on the contrary, are abstemious, and I do not remember ever having seen a Mexican intoxicated.

Such are the people who inhabit a country embracing four or five hundred miles of sea-coast, with several good harbours, with fine forests in the north; the waters filled with fish, and the plains covered with thousands of herds of cattle; blessed with a climate, than which there can be no better in the world; free from all manner of diseases, whether epidemic or endemic; and with a soil in which corn yields from seventy to eighty-fold. In the hands of an enterprising people, what a country this might be! we are ready to say. Yet how long would a people remain so, in such a country? The Americans (as those from the United States are called) and Englishmen, who are fast filling up the principal towns, and getting the trade into their hands, are indeed more industrious and effective than the Mexicans; yet their children are brought up Mexicans in most respects, and if the "California fever" (laziness) spares the first generation, it is likely to attack the second.

ARTICLE

Jane Grey Swisshelm and the Negotiation of Gender Roles on the Minnesota Frontier

Sylvia D. Hoffert

The frontier environment provided men and women with unprecedented opportunities to transgress gender boundaries. Jane Grey Swisshelm, a feminist, abolitionist newspaper editor from Pittsburgh, Pennsylvania, took advantage of those opportunities to make a place for herself in the political life of her adopted community, St. Cloud, Minnesota. During the almost six years of her residence on the Minnesota frontier, she claimed the kind of cultural authority and political power that was generally reserved for men. Her success in doing so illustrates the degree to which frontier life could lead to a blurring of traditional gender roles, place a strain on gender relations, and allow individuals to renegotiate what it meant to be a woman or a man.

In what way did Swisshelm challenge gender conventions? How did she use them to her advantage? How was she able to negotiate a place for herself in the male-dominated world of frontier journalism and politics?

Sometime during the night of March 24–25, 1858, vigilantes broke into the printing office of the *St. Cloud Visiter* in St. Cloud, Minnesota. They destroyed the press, threw the type into the Mississippi River and onto the road, and left the editor, the feisty and contentious Jane Grey Swisshelm, a note referring to her paper as a nuisance and to her as little better than a prostitute. They warned her that if she persisted in challenging the power of the Democratic leaders of Stearns County she would pay an even "more serious penalty" than the destruction of her press. Violence against the press was not a particularly unusual phenomenon during the antebellum period. In-

deed, historian John C. Nerone has chronicled a long and inglorious history of antipress violence, which he argues was "systemic rather than episodic" and "an integral part of the culture of public expression in the United States." There were two aspects of this incident that were atypical, however. One was that the victim of this attack was female. And the second was that the dispute that prompted the attack was as much a struggle over who would define the proper role of women in St. Cloud as it was over the distribution of political power in Stearns County.

Jane Grey Cannon Swisshelm left Pennsylvania in 1857 determined to make a new life for herself on the Minnesota frontier. By the time she left Minnesota in 1863, she had established herself as a prominent and respected citizen of St. Cloud, an outspoken and influential social arbiter, and a leader of the Republican Party in Minnesota. Except for the fact that she could neither vote nor hold office,

Source: Sylvia D. Hoffert, "Jane Grey Swisshelm and the Negotiation of Gender Roles on the Minnesota Frontier," *Frontiers: A Journal of Women Studies* Vol. 18, Winter 1997, pp. 17–35. Copyright © 1997 by Frontiers Editorial Collective. Notes omitted.

her political life was as rich and active as that of Minnesota's most prominent politicians.

To accomplish all of this, she had to thwart a set of gender conventions based upon what historians have called the doctrine of separate spheres. Ideally, respectable and genteel middle- and upper-class white women were expected to occupy and influence the private world of home and family, where as wives and mothers they were to work selflessly to establish the basis for social and political stability by caring for their husbands and teaching their children to become the hardworking, sober, thrifty, civic-minded citizens that the republic needed to prosper. Because they were expected to be socially and economically dependent on their husbands, their participation in public life was largely confined to those activities connected with benevolence and moral reform. Men were expected to support their families financially and to represent their interests through active participation in the political process. Both men and women contributed to the establishment of these guidelines, and both benefited to some degree from them. As a result, members of both sexes could be expected to view deviance from these roles as a threat to social, economic, and political stability and to look upon it with considerable consternation and alarm.

Settling the West exacerbated the problems of maintaining conventional definitions of femininity and masculinity for white emigrants. . . .

Typically, most men and women tried to replicate the spheres of influence that they had left behind. Women carried the domestic ideal with them and tried to implement it, despite the environment that they found themselves in. They worked hard to reestablish their households. Their public lives tended to center around serving as the moral arbiters of social life and, thus, they led campaigns against prostitution and drunkenness. And they helped to establish public institutions like schools, churches, and libraries. Like their white sisters in the East, they had a public life, but it focused on community action as an extension of women's family roles. The market

economy along with political life remained a largely male preserve.

. . . [G]ender roles were less rigid on the trail and in the early stages of white community building than they were in the more settled parts of the country. Conditions in the West often led to a blurring of gender distinctions. As much as most eastern emigrants might have wanted to recreate social, economic, and political patterns that were familiar and provided them with a sense of comfort and continuity, they also had the opportunity to challenge existing gender conventions. . . . The economy was not well regulated and was starved for services and labor. Distance from traditional sources of social authority allowed for "cultural innovation." As a result, opportunities for women to participate more fully in public life expanded because their communities had immediate need for their services. Thus, more often than not, expediency rather than convention was the determining factor in what women could do in developing communities like St. Cloud.

White frontier settlers were likely, therefore, to find themselves in an environment filled with tension between attempts on the part of some to preserve gender conventions and efforts on the part of others to challenge them. Whether as individuals or in groups, whether consciously or unconsciously, pioneer men and women were integrally involved in the process of redefining and articulating what "masculinity" and "femininity" were supposed to mean. They also had to deal with the threat to power relationships between the sexes that the process of redefinition brought with it.

Thus, while the process of community building provided women like Swisshelm with unprecedented opportunities to claim the right to participate in public life on an equal basis with men, those opportunities were framed by parameters set by friends and neighbors who, on one hand, sought comfort in the familiar and, on the other, realized that their economic security and political future might depend on innovation. White settlers lived in an environment filled with confusing contradictions. And it was those contradictions that provided the framework within which Jane Grey Swisshelm proceeded to shape her life in St. Cloud. Her strategy was as expedient as it was successful. She used and thereby confirmed traditional gender conventions while she simultaneously evaded or subverted them.

Born in Pittsburgh in 1815, a Covenantor Presbyterian of Scotch-Irish descent, Swisshelm was the daughter of a chair maker. Her father died when she was young, and the need to help support her family interrupted her schooling. She married a farmer in 1836; it was a marriage fraught with conflict. Between 1848 and 1854 she edited a four-page reform newspaper in Pittsburgh called the *Pittsburgh Saturday Visiter* in which she advocated, among other things, abolition and woman's rights. . . . More interested in writing than she was in bookkeeping, she eventually found herself in financial difficulty and was able to convince Robert Riddle of the *Pittsburgh Commercial Journal* to take over the *Visiter*. For the next three years, her contribution to journalism consisted of writing columns for both the *Family Journal and Visiter*. . . .

From the moment she arrived in Minnesota in March 1857, Swisshelm's behavior posed a direct challenge to conventional ideas about the role of women in society. Unlike most married women, she did not reluctantly follow her husband West. Instead, she initiated her own emigration despite his resistance. Tied to his mother and their farm, Swissvale, in Pennsylvania, James Swisshelm was determined to remain in the East and refused to accompany his wife to Minnesota. So she abandoned her husband, took her daughter Zo, and traveled alone from Pittsburgh to St. Cloud to live with her sister's family on the frontier. There she began publishing the *St. Cloud Visiter*, using her power as an editor to negotiate a central place for herself in the economic and political life of her adopted community. . . .

Many businessmen in St. Cloud supported her enterprise and placed advertising in her paper. But Sylvanus Lowry, the leader of the Stearns County Democratic Party, held out. In her autobiography, she wrote that Lowry offered to support her paper financially if she would agree to support the Buchanan administration. This was a fairly predictable request since it was common for newspapers, including Swisshelm's own *Pittsburgh Saturday Visiter*, to be affiliated with one political party or the other and to run the names of party favorites on or near their mastheads during elections. As a public advocate of abolition, Swisshelm was not predisposed to support the party of southern slaveowners. But seeing Lowry's offer as an opportunity to attack slavery and any Democrat who supported it and at the same time make a fool out of the party's leader, she agreed.

In order to fulfill her side of the bargain, she published a four-column editorial on the front page stating her support of the Democrats in general and the Buchanan administration in particular, whose objectives, she wrote, were to guarantee that every working person in America be offered the opportunity to become a slave and thus enjoy the benefits of that condition. With a heavy dose of irony, she invited the farmers and workers of Minnesota to embrace slavery and to vote themselves "a pair of handcuffs." Lowry was outraged because he had been outwitted and sent someone to tell her to stop. But she continued to uphold her part of the bargain by expressing her support of Buchanan and the opportunities for servitude that he offered to the voters.

Frustrated, Lowry and his friends devised a plan intended to silence her. On March 10, 1858, James Shepley, Lowry's lawyer, gave a public lecture entitled "Woman." In his speech he described four classes of objectionable women—"coquettes, flirts, old maids," and "utterly depraved" woman's rights advocates. Jane attended the lecture. Outraged, she published a review of it in the next edition of her paper on March 18. She summarized the content of his speech and with cool calculation suggested that Shepley had overlooked a fifth kind of woman—"the large, thick-skinned, coarse, sensual featured, loud-mouthed, double-fisted dames, whose entrance into a room appears to take one's breath, whose conversational tones are audible at the furthest side of the next square, whose guffaws resound across a mile wide river, and who talk with an energy which makes the saliva fly like showers of melted pearls." Such women, she continued "deck their portly persons in coarse prints, of bedspread patterns and rainbow hues . . . as they stand to perform their office as high priestess at the shrine of Euchre." Not even the need to nurse their children could keep them from making themselves "agreeable to companies of unmarried gentlemen and the husbands of other women" at the card table.

Shepley took offense at her review and claimed that Swisshelm was describing his wife, Mary. The little we know about Mary comes from census data. Born in Maine like her husband, she was twenty-eight in 1857 and the mother of a two-year-old daughter who had been born after the Shepleys settled in the territory. We can assume from James Shepley's response to Swisshelm's review of his lecture that Mary played cards and did not completely meet the standards of gentility and social refinement that were held in high regard in the urban East.

Whatever Mary's habits and attributes, it was Swisshelm's description of this fifth kind of woman as much as her intrusion into the male world of politics that prompted Lowry, Shepley, and Dr. B. R. Palmer to break into her office and destroy her press. Her challenge to Shepley's right to establish standards for judging female propriety combined with her public humiliation of Lowry provoked them beyond endurance. So they attempted to silence her.

Her relatives, friends, and supporters—both male and female—were outraged by the attack and called for a public meeting to be held at the Stearns House the following evening. Swisshelm, determined to testify in her own behalf, drew up her will, arranged

for a friend from Pennsylvania to serve as her bodyguard, and then went to the Stearns House and delivered her lecture in which she named Lowry and Shepley as the men who had destroyed her press.

At that meeting, twenty-nine of her supporters, including brothers-in-law from both sides of her family, formed the St. Cloud Printing Company to reestablish her newspaper and sent to Chicago for a new press and type; despite renewed threats from Lowry and his friends, Swisshelm resumed publication of the *Visiter* on May 13. The first issue was filled with indignant descriptions of the attack on her press from her pen and those clipped and reprinted from other newspapers all over the country.

Jane had gone too far. Infuriated, James and Mary Shepley instituted a libel suit on June 8 against the printing company, demanding damages of ten thousand dollars. . . .

Jane's investors settled out of court, guaranteeing under bond that she would publish a statement assuring her readers that the attack on the *Visiter* was not politically motivated and agreeing "never again to discuss or refer to the destruction" of her office in her paper. In order to protect the property of her supporters, Jane agreed, and the bond was executed. She published the statement without comment, and then closed down the *Visiter*. Her investors dissolved the printing company and turned its assets over to her. Immediately thereafter, on August 5, she began publishing the *St. Cloud Democrat* as the editor and sole proprietor, and she later wrote, "Into the first editorial column I copied verbatim, with a prominent heading, the article from the *Visiter* on which the libel suit was founded, and gave notice that I alone was pecuniarily responsible for all the injury that could possibly be done to the characters of all the men who might feel themselves aggrieved thereby." "It seems strange," she wrote in her memoir, "that those lawyers should have been so stupid, or should have accredited me with such amazing stupidity when they drew up that bond; but so it was, and the tables were completely turned."

The controversy that erupted over Swisshelm's challenge to James Shepley's social authority and Sylvanus Lowry's political power reveals in a particularly dramatic way the strains inherent in the process of gender role negotiation on the upper-midwestern frontier. The inhabitants of St. Cloud were being asked to resolve the question of who would establish standards by which genteel femininity would be judged in their community. They were also being asked to determine who would control and dominate political life in Stearns County.

In his lecture "Woman," James Shepley assumed the role of social arbiter by asserting his right to define the meaning of true womanhood and to establish the standards by which those aspiring to genteel and respectable femininity might be judged. Prevailing ideas about femininity at midcentury had a number of components. Among them was the belief that the truly feminine woman was modest, gentle, soft-spoken, even-tempered, nurturing, skilled in the domestic arts, and morally superior to most men. Also incorporated into the rubric of femininity was a denial of woman's carnality. Whether or not they enjoyed sex in reality, they often were viewed as without passion.

Surprisingly, the categories of womanhood presented by Shepley in his lecture on the subject of woman defined women in terms not of their morality, appearance, manners, or skills, but of their sexual nature. In choosing to approach the topic in this way, Shepley violated accepted standards of public discourse. His first two categories (coquettes and flirts) presented women who used their sexuality to expose male emotional vulnerability and sexual inadequacy. Young and physically attractive, they dallied with men. They trifled with men's feelings. They teased and aroused men's sexual fantasies. But in the end, these alluring creatures rejected the physical advances of their admirers and withheld their sexual favors. Such women victimized men by flaunting their female sexuality. They used their power to manipulate male emotions and to expose the affective side of masculine natures.

Old maids were women who, whether by chance or by choice, also denied men the use of their bodies. Some were women doomed to remain single because their appearance, personality, or habits failed to exhibit those characteristics deemed desirable by men. They were viewed as women without charm or attraction, sexual or otherwise. Others simply refused or neglected to marry because they valued their own personal autonomy. In either case, spinsterhood was equated with celibacy, and they were therefore inaccessible to men. Their sexual nature was, by definition, suppressed.

Shepley's final group was composed of "women's rights advocates" who were "utterly depraved." These women were deemed the most dangerous of all; their sexuality was perverted. Shepley's use of all of these categories, but particularly this last one, and their resonance with his audience need to be understood in the context of the newly emerging woman's rights movement of which Swisshelm claimed to be a part. Beginning in 1848 at the Seneca Falls Convention, women in the Northeast began to demand not only more educational and vocational opportunities but also the right to participate on a equal basis with men in the political life of the country. One form of public response to their demands was to call their sexuality into question by labeling them Amazons or hermaphrodites, women who had little if any need for men.

When Shepley introduced these categories into his lecture, he played to an audience already plagued by anxiety about the role of women not just on the frontier but in American society as a whole. To allude to female sexuality in this context was to refer to the extraordinary opportunities available—in newly established frontier communities in general and St. Cloud in particular—for women to resist efforts on the part of men to define and control their very nature as well as their social roles and to create their own feminine ideal, an ideal that could easily neglect to take male interests into account.

In all of the categories identified by Shepley were women who controlled their bodies and their own sexuality and, by extension, their own lives. For one reason or another, all of them by reputation or action denied men access to their most private selves. They were women who had claimed for themselves the power to define what it meant to be female without reference to male ideals, prescriptions, or desires. His demeaning references to them were designed to strip them of that power and to preserve the power of men to define what constituted true womanhood.

Swisshelm was determined to undercut Shepley's social authority and thus challenge his attempt to create a feminine ideal for St. Cloud and establish the standards for judging what was and was not appropriate female behavior. She did this by accepting the terms of the discourse he had established, confirming women's right to their own bodies and their right to determine when and where to make themselves available to men. This was not a surprising response from a woman who, for all intents and purposes, had less than a year before denied herself to her husband by deserting him and who at this point clearly intended to make a somewhat unconventional place for herself in the public life of her adopted community.

At the same time, however, she challenged Shepley's right to dictate the basis for establishing standards for measuring female respectability. In order to do this, she offered an alternative model of utter depravity, one that, from his point of view at least, was closer to home. She identified the self-centered and truly vulgar woman, a woman who was loud and unrefined and without taste in clothes, a woman of leisure who preferred the card table and the company of strange men to her own hearth and children. She did not deny the right of woman to appropriate public space. She simply reserved for herself the right to judge which public spaces were appropriate. She allowed her reading audience to envision such a woman playing cards in the male preserves of saloon and brothel and left it to them to imagine the degree to which she might encourage and accommodate the sexual advances of men. This kind of woman, she

implied, was the true threat to the growth, stability, and moral order of the community. By self-indulgently neglecting her domestic duties, by abdicating her responsibilities to her children and larger community, by ignoring the standards of genteel respectability in dress and speech, and by consorting with men at the card table, the kind of woman described in Swisshelm's review of Shepley's speech made flirts and old maids appear relatively harmless in comparison. By criticizing Mary Shepley's appearance and behavior without directly naming her, Swisshelm attempted to undermine James Shepley's authority and credibility as a judge of what constituted "utter depravity" and to claim that authority for herself. In doing so, she was acting on her belief that newspaper editors should be "reliable teachers of public opinion" and that one of her primary responsibilities was "to organize society."

Swisshelm rejected Shepley's suggestion that she exhibited anything other than those qualities generally accepted as desirable in a respectable woman of modest means. Her friends and neighbors knew her to be a small, delicate wife and mother who dressed modestly; a responsible, self-reliant woman who worked hard to use her scant resources to support herself and her only child; a woman whose strong voice could be counted on to uphold the moral imperatives of justice, equality, and fair play. All were characteristics that fulfilled rather than flouted the conventional precepts of "true womanhood." In her demeanor and behavior, she sought to reassure the reading public that she was willing to acknowledge and uphold their most dearly held definitions of femininity. At the same time, however, she, like other female reformers, prepared her audience to expect that she would use her claim to respectability and moral superiority as the basis both for publicly expressing outrage at social injustice and for legitimately expanding woman's right to participate in both the economic and political life of her community. She claimed for women the right to set and maintain their own standards of socially acceptable female behavior, and in the name of public service, to claim their own place in public life. She appears to have succeeded. There is no evidence to suggest that anyone subsequently challenged her expanded definition of femininity or her position as social arbiter.

Her success in the realm of politics is more surprising. . . .

Men dominated political life on the frontier just as they did in the more settled parts of the country. Don Doyle and Merle Curti have noted the importance of local politics for helping to stabilize and integrate what in most newly established frontier communities was a highly heterogeneous and often transient population. But whatever the role of politics in the development of these communities, women were largely excluded. It was considered the prerogative of men to talk politics and define what was important politically. It was their voices that were heard and their concerns that became political issues. Such prerogatives placed men on a basis of equality no matter what their social or economic condition. This helped to stabilize their young communities and tied them together in networks that helped to establish the basis for economic growth. The result was that men cared what other men thought about political candidates and affairs. When men considered women at all, they considered them political spectators—at best. Swisshelm's public participation in the early political life of St. Cloud illustrates, among other things, how female participation in public affairs magnified the tensions inherent in attempts to define gender roles in emerging frontier communities and what techniques the inhabitants of those communities used to try to resolve them.

As the editor of the *St. Cloud Visiter*, Swisshelm had unprecedented social and political power because, unlike most women, she had a public voice that could not be ignored. She controlled the press and therefore could determine what was news and what was not. She had the power to define or ignore political issues and to report (or not report) and interpret (or misinterpret) political events. She understood perfectly the implications of her position

and took her responsibilities seriously. She claimed that editors had at least as much if not more public influence than ministers and therefore had a responsibility to their communities to expose corruption and the abuse of power by those she called "political hucksters and wire-pullers," those who pursued their own self-interest while pretending to represent the interests of the people. In her view, the press in general and her newspaper in particular should be the arbiter of both political and social affairs in the community.

From the moment she issued the first edition of the *St. Cloud Visiter*, Swisshelm acted upon those principles and, in the process, imposed herself on male-dominated political life. Her intrusion began when she published her "Prospectus," which announced that she would be independent in her editorial policy. She was originally determined that her paper "not be the organ of any party or sect," an unusual position given the fact that, as we have seen, most newspapers were indeed partisan in editorial policy. A few weeks later, she explained that she had a generally low regard for the pretensions to superiority of most men, considered herself to be in "mutual antagonism" to many of them, and warned that she did not intend to mince words in discussing the activities of those who failed to represent the public interest. "When any of our public men appear to require notice of us, or the public good to require that we should call attention to them, we shall say exactly what we believe to be true," she wrote.

Political life in St. Cloud in 1857 centered on a struggle over economic power based on land development and over political power in a territory that was just becoming a state. Swisshelm's presence as the editor of the local newspaper added a complicating gender dimension to a struggle already going on between the male Democratic leadership of the county under Lowry and the politically ambitious like Stephen Miller who sought to displace him and preempt his influence. Her intrusion complicated their struggle and intensified and made more immediate the problem of defining the role of women in the life of the community.

Like many politicians, Lowry exerted control over political life in Stearns County based upon his personal reputation for being able to deliver votes for the Democratic party, to control political appointments, to grant favors, and to persuade the railroads to lay their tracks along routes that would serve the interests of Stearns County businessmen and farmers. His continuing political influence depended upon his ability to reach out to newcomers and incorporate them into the political process. By definition, he and his cronies were the very sort of "wire-pullers" whose machinations Swisshelm was suspicious of and determined to expose. The existence of an independent press was not in their best interests. What they needed was a local newspaper that depended upon their patronage, enhanced their political reputations, and promoted their political/economic agendas, not one whose editorial policy was unpredictable, held them accountable to high standards of public service, and provided the reading public with alternatives to their leadership.

Under normal circumstances, men like Lowry could have ignored and thus discounted the political opinions of the women in their community. But as editor of the local newspaper, Swisshelm could not be ignored; therefore, she needed to be controlled. In order to preserve the political sphere as the exclusive territory of men and confirm the private role of women that made them dependent and politically invisible, Lowry and his clique needed to avoid publicly acknowledging that Swisshelm was politically important. They had to deny and, if possible, destroy her power to impose her personal political opinions upon her readers and discount the public role she insisted on playing in Stearns County politics without publicly recognizing either that she had a right to express those opinions or that she had that role.

Thus, they looked for a quiet way of dealing with the problem. Again under normal circumstances, the Lowry clique could have been expected to handle this matter privately by turning first to her husband, as the person re-sponsible for her actions, and, if that failed, to her employer to arrange for her silence. Unfortunately, James Swisshelm was in Pennsylvania and George Brott was out of town on business. So, Lowry and his friends privately arranged to support her paper in return for the right to dictate what she printed in it. Swisshelm's acquiescence to their demands must have reassured them. By agreeing to support Buchanan and the Democratic Party, she ostensibly sacrificed her independence. If they had not succeeded in silencing her and moving her back into the domestic sphere, they had at least assured themselves that her political opinions would be subordinated to theirs and that her relationship to them had been regularized to conform to the generally accepted political position of women. Public evidence of her dependence and deference would at the very least confirm male dominance over the political life of the community. No doubt they felt confident both that they would again be able to define political issues for themselves and control the surrounding debate and that they had reduced her to the traditional political role for women, that of little more than an observer.

Swisshelm was poor and politically disfranchised, and her marital status was ambiguous, but she was not without resources. She was surrounded by family and friends from Pennsylvania. She was bright, ambitious, self-assured, self-righteous, and energetic as well as being an experienced journalist who was a master of sarcasm and satire. She was also a member of a community whose members had brought with them views about the character of women and men and their place in society. While those views ordinarily denied women direct access to political power, they could also be manipulated in such a way as to serve as advantages rather than disadvantages. For example, she could reasonably assume that because she was a woman, many in her community would be inclined to view her as morally superior to men, untainted by the kind of self-interest that characterized the struggle for money and power among male politicians and businessmen. Therefore, when she took the moral high ground in any conflict, she would have more credibility than her male opponents even though she had to be aware that in the process her moral authority might be tainted by her political activity. It was reasonable for her to hope that if her willingness to sacrifice herself to protect the interests and preserve the civic virtue of the citizenry of St. Cloud placed her in danger, there would be those whose sense of male honor combined with kinship obligations would compel them to try to protect her. And finally, she could assume that male arrogance would lead her opponents to underestimate her intelligence and her political savvy.

She could safely make other assumptions as well. She could be relatively sure that there were men in her community who had political aspirations and were shut out of the Lowry clique who would be willing to take advantage of any opportunity to challenge Lowry's political hegemony. Similarly, she could count on those same people to support the idea of freedom of the press, especially when it could be used for their own personal economic and political advantage.

Swisshelm, of course, never intended to give up her agency as a political figure in St. Cloud. In the name of public service, she was determined to maintain her public presence and to force the Democratic leaders of the county to acknowledge and defer to her political power. In order to do this, she subverted Lowry's attempt to control her editorial policy in the February 18, 1858, edition of her paper by deferring to his demand that she support Buchanan but ridiculing the Democrats, their leaders, and their platform in the process. In so doing, she established her reputation not only for being smarter than Lowry and his political cronies but also for being incorruptible. She was able to demonstrate the lengths to which she would go to avoid being anyone's lackey in order to preserve her editorial independence and thereby fulfill her public obligations to her community.

Having thus been exposed, the Democratic leadership no longer had any reason to deal with Swisshelm privately, and the struggle that ensued took on a more public dimension.

From the lectern and in an act of vigilante justice, Shepley attempted to intimidate and humiliate her, destroy her reputation as a respectable woman, and thereby undercut and trivialize her role in community life. He alleged that she was no lady and that her presence was a public nuisance as a way of undermining her moral authority, thus rendering her socially and politically impotent. His willingness to do such a thing testifies to the degree to which he and Lowry perceived Swisshelm to be a threat to them. By responding so dramatically to her challenge, Shepley inadvertently acknowledged her influence and publicly incorporated her into the political process. . . .

[The attack on Swisshelm's press] was meant to render her impotent on more than one level. First, it took away her ability to participate in the market economy. By taking away the means by which she supported herself and her daughter, the vigilantes deprived her of economic independence. They placed her in the position in which most women found themselves: dependent upon the generosity of their husbands or their male friends and relatives. They also deprived her of a public voice, leaving her with only her private (feminine) one. The platform that provided her the opportunity to challenge the social and political hegemony of men was gone. Finally, by destroying her paper, Lowry and his friends destroyed her usefulness to the community as a booster. She could no longer serve the economic interests of her friends and neighbors through the press. From their point of view, economic independence, a public voice, and an active role in establishing the economic and political foundations of frontier communities were male functions. Lowry, Shepley, and their cronies were not only determined to dominate economic and political life in St. Cloud, but they also claimed the right to suppress attempts to change gender roles on the Minnesota frontier. After the destruction of her press, they initiated a debate over whether or not the conflict between Swisshelm and their clique was political in nature. Shepley sent a letter to the editors of the *St. Paul Pioneer and*

Democrat arguing that the affair was a strictly personal one. The entire settlement of Shepley's suit consisted of her publishing a statement that defined the controversy as private/personal rather than public/political. But Stephen Miller, one of Swisshelm's supporters, countered by publishing a letter arguing that this was not the case.

Why was it so important to the Lowry clique that the community believe the conflict between themselves and Swisshelm was private rather than political? One explanation is that by this time there was no way to ignore the fact that Swisshelm could not be excluded from public participation in politics. By arguing that the conflict between Swisshelm and the leaders of the Democratic Party in Stearns County was a personal quarrel, they could reduce it (and her along with it) to public insignificance, something unworthy of public attention and discussion, and thus deny the legitimacy of her political voice while at the same time reclaiming their exclusive right to define what was political and what was not.

Further evidence to substantiate this interpretation lies in the fact that when Shepley filed the lawsuit over the libel of his wife, he virtually discounted Swisshelm's responsibility for the affair. Instead of suing the editor who wrote and then published the libel, he sued the male investors in the printing company. He named Swisshelm's actions but not her person in the suit.

It could be argued that such a strategy was economically motivated. It had to have been clear to everyone in St. Cloud, as well as anyone who read her paper, that Swisshelm had little or no property. She began her life in St. Cloud living with her sister and brother-in-law and their children. She frequently did not have the resources to publish her paper regularly. Notices that appeared in her paper indicated that she would be willing to be paid in kind for subscriptions because she was in need of such things as firewood. And originally she did not own the office where her paper was published nor the press that printed it. Her supporters, on the other hand, owned not only the press and type but also

substantial amounts of other property, some of it liquid, some of it not. Shepley was lawyer enough to know that if you want to gain a moral victory and collect damages in the process, you sue people who have assets enough to pay them. But there was another dimension to his actions. By suggesting that Swisshelm's supporters could be held morally and financially responsible for her behavior, he figuratively made them into surrogate husbands, reaffirming the traditional, common-law principles upon which the doctrine of femme covert was based and denying her the right to independent action necessary to support her claims to political prerogatives.

Swisshelm's supporters, on the other hand, were willing to argue that the conflict between her and Lowry and his political allies was "political." It was in their interest to support the idea that this particular woman had the right to a political voice. That voice gave balance to political life in a community that before her arrival had been characterized by what they considered to be Lowry's demagoguery. Her voice helped them to challenge Lowry's political power and to compete with him on a level playing field for political leadership in the county. As in other aspects of frontier life, they were willing to support Swisshelm in a nontraditional role because they needed her. She gave them a political leverage that was too good to give up. And it paid off. She helped to found the Republican Party in Minnesota and negotiated a place for herself in its inner circles. With her help, the control that Lowry and his political cronies had exerted over Stearns County politics declined. When they ran for office, she used their role in the destruction of her press to help defeat them at the polls. In 1859 Lowry was defeated by Swisshelm's candidate, Ignatius Donnelly. Soon thereafter, Stephen Miller, one of Swisshelm's staunchest supporters, became governor.

Following the Sioux uprising in Minnesota in the fall of 1862, Swisshelm decided to use whatever political leverage she had as a leader of the Minnesota Republican Party to convince Lincoln to authorize the hanging of more Indians and the internment of the rest for the duration of the war in order to secure the safety of frontier communities like St. Cloud. Leaving the *St. Cloud Democrat* in the hands of her nephew, she moved to Washington. She failed in her mission but remained there until the end of the war.

Sylvanus Lowry continued to live and work in St. Cloud after the uproar over the destruction of Swisshelm's press and the Shepley lawsuit. But by the spring of 1862, he began to exhibit signs of mental instability, a condition that had apparently plagued him periodically since adolescence. At the end of May, his family sent him to an insane asylum in Cincinnati. He returned to St. Cloud after he was released. In the summer of 1864, he had a relapse, tried to kill his sister, and was arrested. He was released after posting a three hundred dollar bond to keep the peace. He died of a heart attack just before Christmas in 1865.

James Shepley moved back to Maine in 1859. Fourteen years later, he migrated to Fresno County, California, where he worked as a sheep rancher. He was reportedly murdered there in 1874.

Jane Grey Swisshelm's experience in St. Cloud illustrates the degree to which the process of frontier community building provided unprecedented opportunities for women to negotiate a significant place for themselves in both the public and the private spheres. Her tendency to both utilize and subvert many of the attitudes that her friends and neighbors had brought with them concerning the distinctions between women and men, private and public, personal and political was her most effective weapon. Swisshelm's simultaneous confirmation of and challenge to contemporary gender conventions helps to explain both their persistence and her achievements. When it suited her purposes, she used deference to established and familiar ideas about the proper roles of men and women to mask the discomfort and anxiety produced by the potentially revolutionary implications of her words and actions. In the process, she confirmed the ideas and beliefs that sustained those traditional roles and thus helped to perpetuate them.

The strategy that Swisshelm used to establish a public role for herself on a local and state level was a duplicitous one. It enabled her to manipulate what it meant to be a "true woman" in a frontier environment and allowed her to achieve a public prominence that would have been inconceivable had she remained in Pittsburgh, where standards for judging social refinement were already clearly defined and male politicos did not need to collaborate with women. . . .

ARTICLE

The Independent Women of Hispanic New Mexico, 1821–1846

Janet Lecompte

Janet Lecompte provides a portrait of gender roles and relations in Hispanic New Mexico before the United States acquired that territory as a result of the Mexican War (1846–1848). Using travelers' accounts and local court records, she argues that the way the inhabitants of New Mexico defined femininity during this period was very different from the way that Anglo-Americans defined it. She also suggests that when Anglo-American settlers arrived in large numbers, the kind of independence enjoyed by Hispanic women declined.

How was femininity defined in Hispanic culture in the territory of New Mexico during the first half of the nineteenth century? In what way did the law serve as the basis for female independence?

The culture of New Mexicans, and especially of New Mexican women, was distinct in many aspects from that of central Mexico or other Mexican frontier territories. In costume, language, religion, government, and legal rights of women, the people of New Mexico kept strong ties to sixteenth-century Spain. Their ancestors had marched boldly through deserts infested with hostile Indians to found a Spanish colony in New Mexico in 1598. From that time until 1821 the deserts and Indians, as well as Spanish policy prohibiting foreign commerce, kept New Mexico more or less isolated. New Mexicans developed traditions in response to this isolation, to climate and terrain, and to their sedentary Pueblo Indian neighbors and the nomadic tribes with whom they alternately fought and traded. In 1821 Mexico declared independence of Spain, became a republic, and opened its borders to foreign commerce. Henceforth foreign trappers, traders, and travelers further altered the lives of New Mexicans with the introduction of new materials, new skills, and attitudes. . . .

The first American woman to see New Mexico was young Susan Magoffin, who accompanied her trader-husband to New Mexico in 1846. Susan's delightful diary portrayed New Mexican women in terms that told as much about her own culture as theirs. In Las Vegas Susan was startled to see women dressed only in chemises and petticoats, which American women wore as undergarments. Around the heads and arms of these women were *rebosos*, or large shawls, under which some of them had their babies, "I shant say at what business," wrote Susan. As the traders' wagons passed villages, Susan saw children running about naked and women pulling their skirts up over their knees and paddling across creeks like ducks. "It is truly shocking," wrote Susan; "I am constrained to keep my veil drawn closely over my face all the time to protect my blushes." No sooner had Susan become accustomed to the bare legs and bosoms of New Mexican women

Source: Janet Lecompte, "The Independent Women of Hispanic New Mexico, 1821–1846," *Western Historical Quarterly*, XII (Jan. 1981), 17–35. Reprinted by permission. Notes omitted.

than she was exposed to their repugnant views on marriage. One old lady was amazed that Susan had left her home and parents "just for a husband" and laughed heartily at Susan's assertion that a husband was the whole world to his wife. Another New Mexican woman suggested slyly that Susan's husband might at that moment be off with "his other senorita," which distressed Susan to the point of tears. Susan was appalled at women smoking cigarettes, gambling, shopping, and paying visits on the Sabbath. But as the New Mexican women came to her carriage to shake hands, bring her gifts of food, and call her "pretty little girl," Susan succumbed to their warmth and kindness and described them in her diary as "decidedly polite, easy in their manners, perfectly free."

Several Americans called this freedom of demeanor "boldness" and contrasted it unfavorably with the modesty of American women. In the emerging industrial United States of the early nineteenth century, the American woman lost her economic importance. Her influence became limited to moral and cultural spheres, and her position in society was subordinate to men. A married woman lost almost all legal rights, and her property and wages belonged to her husband. She was believed to have no sexual urges, from which arose a double standard of behavior that allowed a man to exercise his sexual needs, but not a woman. She was expected to be pious, chaste, and self-sacrificing, and her place was in the home.

In contrast, a New Mexican woman retained her property, legal rights, wages, and maiden name after marriage, like her Spanish ancestors. As we shall see, she was measured by no such ideals of character or double standard of sexual behavior, nor was she assumed to be subordinate to men, except by Americans who carried to New Mexico their image of true American womanhood and judged New Mexican women by it. . . .

W. H. H. Davis described New Mexican women as healthy, graceful, and athletic. They wore loose, low-cut blouses and full short skirts; in this easy costume they did their work, much of it outdoors. Their diet was full of nutrients. They baked bread with unbolted flour containing both husk and germ of the grain; they dried fruits, vegetables, and strips of meat in the sun for later use; and included in nearly every meal fresh or dried chili peppers—high in vitamins—and fresh and dried beans—high in protein. Their adobe houses, with thick walls and high ceilings, were cool in summer and warm in winter, and easy to clean. Their rooms had little corner fireplaces for cooking and heating, but were almost barren of furniture. Ordinary families slept on thin mattresses which they rolled against the walls during the day to serve as sofas. Only the rich had kitchens, beds and bedrooms, imported carpets, draperies, silver table service, and servants to maintain these luxuries.

"A woman's work is never done" was a popular phrase describing the housewifery of American women, but it did not apply in New Mexico. Some Americans regarded New Mexican women as idle, which in the Anglo-Saxon work ethic was a form of sin. "They work but little," wrote one American; "the fandango and siesta form the diversion of time." Another said that women were taught only to "grind corn on a rock, make tortillas and dance." But American accounts show women at many other tasks, often in cheerful groups: "maidens with merry faces" in the vineyard with flat baskets of purple grape clusters on their heads, girls chatting as they filled their Indian water jars at the spring or passed in dignified procession balancing the huge jars on their heads, women wading in the river as they laundered clothes, or watching intently as they washed placer gold from sand in wooden platters or goat horns. One woman was seen outdoors spinning yarn on an upright stick at the same time she suckled her child.

New Mexican women were likely to have other occupations besides caring for home and children. The censuses of New Mexico employ no single word for housewife, unless it was the frequent designation *costurera* or seamstress, perhaps referring not only to women who made clothes or produced elegant embroidery but also to those whose work was primarily in the home. Many paid occupations for women were listed in the censuses—servants, bakers, weavers, gold-panners, shepherds, laundresses, stocking-knitters, healers, midwives, ironers, and prostitutes. Women were often in the town plaza selling products of their domestic animals or gardens, or vending whiskey and traders' goods in stalls along the main streets, or dealing cards in gambling games. Vending was not despised: Doña Barbara Baca kept a stall in Santa Fe and went to court about a fifteen-peso debt, which turned out to be an error in her own ledgers; a sister of Governor Manuel Armijo sold whiskey to American soldiers out of an old coffee pot on a street in Albuquerque; the widow of another governor owned the only billiard table in Santa Fe, which she rented to gamblers for five to six pesos a week.

Nor were women and children barred from men's work. In 1807 Zebulon Pike passed along the Río Grande near Albuquerque as irrigating ditches were being opened and saw men, women, and children "at the joyful labor . . . the cultivation of the fields was now commencing and everything appeared to give life and gaiety to the surrounding scenery." Forty years later, Lieutenant William Emory described the high glee of men, women, and children as they see-sawed on the lever of a molasses press. Yet women apparently did not do the heavy work of farming, and crops were not sown when men were off on campaigns against wild Indians. . . .

As Americans noticed, a New Mexican woman's life was not a weary round of endless chores. The simplicity of her costume, food, and dwelling left her time to take siestas at mid-day and enough energy to enjoy frequent dance parties, called *fandangos,* where she appeared radiant, powdered, perfumed, and jingling with necklaces and earrings. Foreigners were amazed at the democratic aspect of these affairs. Everybody was welcome, from the priest to the criminal released from

jail for the evening; everybody danced—the lady with the ragged peon, the old man with the little girl. On political or religious holidays fiestas involved people of all ages in races, cock-pulls, cock-fights, folk dramas, and *fandangos,* or in watching puppeteers, traveling players, tumblers, and fireworks. They sang, danced, and gambled at *chusa,* or monte, far into the night, the women gambling with as much abandon as the men. Most fiestas were festivals of the Roman Catholic church, to which all native New Mexicans belonged. American observers deplored the desecration of the Sabbath. In church, as the priest recited his service at the altar, women would chat and giggle; as the same musicians of last night's *fandango* struck up the same tunes in church, women would toss their heads and count their beads in time to the music. After church everybody mingled in the plaza—shopping, dancing, gambling.

Many Americans would have agreed with George W. Kendall that New Mexican women were "joyous, sociable, kind-hearted creatures, easy and graceful in their manners." Kendall enjoyed the warmth of the close embrace with which both sexes greeted each other, in contrast to the restraint imposed upon Anglo-Saxons by "cold, conventional rules." The hospitality of New Mexican women did not always stop at a warm embrace. Visitors from the land of the double standard blamed New Mexicans' sexual freedom entirely on the women: "The standard of female chastity is deplorably low," wrote W. H. H. Davis; "the women deem chastity no virtue," wrote Alfred Waugh. Jacob Fowler described an attempted seduction of his negro servant by a Taos wife, and James O. Pattie told of the friendliness of New Mexican ladies they had met at a dance, who expected the Americans to escort them home and spend the night.

Marriage in New Mexico, according to Josiah Gregg, was "a convenient cloak for irregularities." W. H. H. Davis wrote that three-quarters of the married population of New Mexico had lovers, "and the feelings of society are in no manner outraged by it," which was not quite true, as our examination of court records will show. Concubinage, a Spanish tradition, was more common than marriage and was generally accepted. Americans remarked on the priests of New Mexico who had concubines and families, and many American traders took concubines from respectable New Mexican families. Foreigners usually blamed concubinage on high marriage fees charged by priests, for there was no alternative civil marriage in New Mexico. Bearing children out of wedlock was common among all classes; birth records show a high percentage of babies given their mothers' names, their fathers being recorded as "unknown."

Josiah Gregg assumed that all marriages were "forced and ill assorted, and without the least deference to the wishes or inclinations of the young lady." In fact, betrothals arranged by parents were investigated by the priest to ensure that the bride was acquainted with the groom and wished to marry him. W. H. H. Davis assumed that "a young girl can hardly put her nose outside the door without an old duena [sic] tagging after her," but the term *dueña* scarcely appears in the records. In fact, New Mexican girls would hardly have needed a *dueña*, for they were married or living with men as early as twelve years old.

In general, American accounts show an unawareness of Mexican customs, particularly the social and legal rights of women. What these rights were and how they were exercised is illustrated by cases from the records of the alcalde courts. An alcalde combined the civil duties of mayor with the judicial duties of judge. His court was meant to provide inexpensive and prompt legal remedy for most civil complaints, as well as initiatory stages of ecclesiastical and criminal proceedings. In most civil cases plaintiff and defendant appeared before the alcalde, called *juez* in his judicial capacity, for an attempt at conciliation. If the *juez* could not reconcile the parties, each named an arbitrator, or *hombre bueno*, whose opinion the *juez* considered before pronouncing his judgment of conciliation. If plaintiff and defendant did not agree with the judgment, the case was dropped, or the plaintiff

made a formal charge whereupon witnesses were called, testimony taken, and the proceedings sent to the governor for a verdict. Appeal from the governor's verdict was to the superior tribunal at Guadalajara (later at Chihuahua), a slow and costly process.

Alcalde courts were not ruled strictly by national law. Laws promised by the republican constitution of 1824 for the governance of New Mexico had never been promulgated, and national laws in force sometimes did not serve this remote territory because of differences in customs. Furthermore, New Mexico had no native lawyers. Serving occasionally as attorneys were a handful of former deputies sent to the national Congress, where they picked up a little legal lore and returned to annoy the alcaldes in their courts. With this questionable legal assistance and an occasional opinion of lawyers from "below," the *juez* (who was often nearly illiterate) attempted to provide judgments based on what law he knew, but more on common sense and compassion.

A New Mexican woman could own, inherit, loan, convey, or pawn property, as records of the alcalde courts show. Suits involving women's property were many and diverse— over a woman's fat hog or half-interest in a burro inherited from her mother, over a pawned cloak or a pledged gun, over rooms in a house which one woman sold another with stipulation as to use, over a nugget of gold found by a woman in a borrowed placer basin, of which she was allowed half the value. Property suits often concerned the most seemingly trivial things, but New Mexicans were chronically short of clothing, hard money, metal objects, and trinkets commonplace elsewhere. A list of items stolen from Doña María Manuela Martínez of Taos indicates what was worth stealing: a *túnica* (European-style gown) of fine cotton, a multi-colored blanket, a linen mantle, two cigarette boxes decorated with mock pearls and spangles, a spangled suit, a yellow-metal rosary, a man's muslin shirt, a serape, a pair of white canvas stools, and a bordered kerchief. Money was so scarce that when Doña Peregrina Domínguez demanded that Felix García pay his hundred-peso debt to her in hard money, the court gave him a month to collect it.

A few wealthy women of New Mexico used the courts frequently. Doña Ursula Chávez was the wife of Don Antonio Sandoval of Las Padillas, one of the richest men in New Mexico, but she too was wealthy, and although illiterate, she managed her own property. In 1815 she brought suit against her neighbor, Don Pedro Bautista Pino, for two hundred pesos she had loaned him. In 1818 she sued José Sánchez, another neighbor, for the value of 351 sheep. In 1832 the same José Sánchez, now city councilman of Las Padillas, declared a conflict of interest in a suit Doña Ursula had brought against another neighbor, because his livelihood depended on a partido contract with Doña Ursula (meaning that he managed her sheep for a percentage of the annual lamb crop). With her wealth came a measure of concern for the commonweal: in 1835 she complained to the governor that the alcalde of Valencia had appropriated funds belonging to the church. Her complaint was promptly investigated. . . .

Women occasionally stated, according to Mexican custom, that their appearance in court was with permission of their husbands, but in New Mexico their deference was merely courtesy, as is indicated by the many cases in which the wife appeared not only without her husband's permission but with a complaint against him. Permission or lack of it was often on the other side, as in the suit brought by Doña Gregoria Quintana against her husband Jesús Martínez for selling her grain mill without her consent. The *juez* and *hombres buenos* proposed that the new owner of the mill grind twelve fanegas of grain for Doña Gregoria every year until her death and pay the fee for a certificate of cleanliness; the new owner agreed to do so. In another case, the wife of José Sandoval took her husband to court for gambling away her burro to another man. The court ordered the burro returned to the wife and fined the men two pesos each for gambling. . . .

If Mexican law was disregarded in New Mexican courts, the common law of the United States was entirely ignored. In the United States, widows were liable for their husband's debts; not so in New Mexico, as some Americans discovered in trying to collect a debt owed by the estate of Alexander Branch from Branch's widow, Paula Luna. The Americans seized the widow's house and evicted her and her ten dependents, including her own children and six Indian *criados*, aged five to fifteen. The widow appealed to the governor, who ordered her house restored to her since she was not a partner in her husband's business and therefore did not assume his debts. The Americans then managed to have the widow jailed for debt. Again the governor rescued her, ordering that she be freed immediately "because no one in New Mexico could be jailed for lack of property."

A married woman of New Mexico was protected by the Spanish law providing that property acquired before marriage became jointly owned after marriage. A wife could not make donation of her noncommunity property to her husband, nor demand a share of his, unless he was squandering hers. This principle was lucidly explained to the local *juez* by Padre Antonio José Martínez, a former deputy, during a suit brought by the padre's niece against her husband, whose gambling debts had exhausted all the income and part of the principal of her inheritance. As her attorney, Padre Martínez wrote that the husband's attorney, former deputy Juan Bautista Vigil, had attempted to destroy the inventory of her inheritance and had threatened her life if she refused to donate the property to her husband. On Padre Martínez's petition, the governor ordered the husband jailed and the property put in the hands of a trustee. At this threat the husband ended the litigation by dismissing his attorney and agreeing to pay his wife all he owed her. . . .

Alcaldes were charged with protection of public morals and issued edicts against women who walked the streets at night, men who violated the marriage bed of women of the house where *fandangos* were held, and habitual adulterers or fornication of either sex. In 1832 the *juez* of Pecos was ordered by the *juez* of Santa Fe to identify men and women living "the bad life," whether married or not and whether or not husbands were aware of the bad life their wives were leading with other men. "The bad life" described the relationship of the soldier Rosario Gabaldón with Gertrudis Valencia, who had been confined in a private home for her immorality. When Gabaldón asked the alcalde to release Gertrudis to him on bond, the official was outraged, fulminating in the record that the soldier had a nerve asking that the woman be released, as though the alcalde were his pimp! In 1842 Ana María Rendón and another woman living in her house were evicted for their bad life as *amasias* (concubines), although this relationship was rarely cause for court action. This particular judgment may have had a hidden instigator, for La Rendón had accused the powerful La Tules of illegal cohabitation some years earlier.

Because of early maturation of New Mexican girls and lack of shame surrounding sexual activity, girls were frequently living in concubinage or indulging in illicit relations at early puberty. Juan de Jesús Archuleta brought proceedings against a young man for cutting his daughter's face with a razor at ten in the morning because the youth had found the girl in "bad circumstances" with a soldier. The girl denied involvement with the soldier, stating instead she had had sexual relations with the defendant and afterwards told him she did not love him, which caused his anger. This girl was single, living with her parents, and fourteen years old.

Alcaldes were not the only defenders of public morality. Rosalia Sandoval and her daughter, both servants of Governor Armijo, were outside the governor's palace when Manuel Leyva came by and cut off the daughter's braids with his sword because both mother and daughter had had illicit relations with men. The braid-snipper was banished to San Miguel del Bado for three months, and the Sandoval women were ordered to court to defend their virtue.

In the absence of lawyers and marriage counselors, alcalde courts served as the first resort in marital difficulties. Many married couples appeared in the courts seeking reconciliation, looking to the *juez* and *hombres buenos* for advice and guidance as well as legal means of assuring better treatment from their spouses. One jealous wife persuaded the court to order her rival to stop following her husband around or be punished by law and the husband to cease scolding his wife or suffer three months in prison. Doña Rafaela Sánchez, wife of Don Juan Bautista Vigil, withdrew her divorce suit when the court ordered her husband to give bond for her satisfaction with his behavior. The court was not always successful in achieving conciliation. Doña Simona Pineda, sixty-year-old wife of Don José María Alarid, complained of her husband's "maltreatment with words" and asked the court to order her husband out of the house. The husband refused to go, on grounds that her complaints were insufficient cause to disrupt his life. The court agreed with him, but Doña Simona did not agree to conciliation. Another husband whose "maltreatment with words" included a threat of death was banished to Galisteo until he could prove his good intentions toward his wife. Two persons, one in Galisteo and one in Santa Fe, were named to watch over the conduct of this couple....

Men and women were often punished equally for adultery. For example, Doña Francisca Romero brought Doña Rosaria Domínguez to court for adultery with her husband, and both lovers were put in prison. Later the husband was released upon petition of his wife, but Doña Rosaria remained in jail. Adultery did not necessarily lead to divorce, as in the case of Don José Francisco Baca y Pino, who had suspected for five years that his wife Doña Dolores Ortiz was having an affair with José Tenorio. Don José put up with the situation until his suffering became so acute that he feared he might kill his wife or Tenorio, and he appealed to the governor to have Tenorio banished. The governor ordered that the guilty couple should suffer fines and punishment the first and second times they were caught. The third time would mean banishment for Tenorio because he was a bachelor without occupation or fortune and would not be harmed by living elsewhere. The third time occurred one evening when Don José found them bedded down in a neighbor's kitchen. Tenorio was banished to Albuquerque for a year and five months; then he returned to Santa Fe and was jailed for a time and released. The lovers were warned that if they succumbed again to their passion they would both be put in jail until the supreme tribunal should determine their fate, which could take years. . . .

Not only adultery but also toleration of it was illegal. Bautista Espinosa deserted his wife and family to live with Rafaela Rael. When the deserted wife made a complaint, Rafaela's relative Luis Rael was put in jail along with the lovers for tolerating their adultery. In similar cases a man was punished for not reporting the adultery of his wife, and a mother was accused of consenting to her daughter's "bad life."

Court records seem to show that standards of behavior were essentially the same for both sexes, as was the behavior. Men were hauled into court for gossip and slander against women, and women for physical assault on men. During a quarrel, Doña Antonia Suárez called Don Rafael Pacheco "old and ruptured," to which he responded, in front of her children, that she was a "whore, thief, pimp and vagabond." The court ordered both to beg the other's pardon and to cease quarreling or be treated as criminals. Mariano Ortiz brought Franklin Brown to court for reviling the honor of his daughter in accusing her of living "the bad life" with Luis Anaya for two years. Brown brought in two American friends to support the truth of his accusation and to testify that Brown had been drinking whiskey at the time. Neither the truth nor Brown's drunkenness served to mitigate the insult. Brown apologized and retracted the offending words, but he was sent to jail for eight days anyway.

As men were sued for slander, so women were sued for attacks on men. One woman beat a soldier so badly that he was seriously injured; another was accused with her lover of murdering her husband. The power of a woman in the courts is apparent in the case of María de la Cruz Barela, whose personal rights were respected above a man's property, even when the man was wealthy and even when her own actions were not above reproach. María de la Cruz did her laundry in the river and spread it to dry on the nearby adobe wall of Don Miguel Sena. Don Miguel was tired of having to repair his wall after laundresses put their wet clothes on it, so he told her to stop. Shouting improper words, she picked up a rock to attack him. He took her by the shoulder and pushed her to the ground. She took Don Miguel to court, where it was determined that he was at fault in throwing her to the ground and should choose a different course of action in the future. . . .

Lest the reader conclude that New Mexican women were *viragos*, it might be well to cite a murder case that portrays the life of poor women in New Mexico more typically than many of the examples above. Rafael Montoya and his wife set out from Belén on a journey and stopped for the night at a house in Corrales. In the middle of the night the couple went outside to make water in the road, and there Montoya stabbed his wife. Before she died she told the owner of the house that her husband was jealous of everything, although she had never given him cause. The husband later testified that his wife had refused to return to bed with him that night and that he suspected her of adultery because she had some new shoes and stockings that he had not given her. The public prosecutor wrote in his charge that the woman had probably bought the clothes to make the journey, for even poor women had a little money of their own, earned at spinning or given to them by husbands or relatives. The prosecutor stated that murder of a wife was defensible only if the husband caught her in adultery and that public vengeance demanded execution of this man, which required a sentence from the supreme tribunal. . . .

The extraordinary independence of New Mexican women, in full flower during the Republican period, came to an end in 1846 when New Mexico was invaded by United States soldiers, convinced of their own superiority and disdainful of the natives. Very quickly New Mexicans submitted to their conquerors and to many of their foreign ideas. Only fifteen years after the American conquest, the New Mexican woman had all but abandoned her easy, graceful costume and was yielding to the fashionable tyranny of corsets, hoop-skirts, and bonnets. Her *fandangos* were corrupted beyond recognition by strong American whiskey and rough American frontiersmen. Her legal rights upheld in alcalde courts were curtailed in American courts. Her Sunday merriment became a private thing, as foreign priests swept *fandango* music and gaiety out of the churches, and American officials banned other Sabbath activities. As years went by, ethnic discrimination denied her husband political power and jobs, her children were forbidden to speak Spanish in school, and her folk festivals and folk art were scorned. Her way of life was gone. . . .

SUGGESTIONS FOR FURTHER READING

EVELYN BLACKWOOD, "Sexuality and Gender in Certain Native American Tribes: The Case of Cross-Gendered Females," *Signs,* 10 (Autumn 1984), 27–42.

ANNE M. BUTLER, *Daughters of Joy, Sisters of Misery: Prostitutes in the American West, 1865–90* (Urbana: University of Illinois Press, 1985).

JOAN E. CASHIN, *A Family Venture: Men and Women on the Southern Frontier* (New York: Oxford University Press, 1991).

RAYMOND J. DEMALLIE, "Male and Female in Traditional Lakota Culture," in *The Hidden Half: Studies of Plains Indian Women,* ed. Patricia Albers and Beatrice Medicine (Washington, DC: University Press of America, 1983), 237–61.

SARAH DEUTSCH, *No Separate Refuge: Culture, Class and Gender on an Anglo-Hispanic Frontier in the American Southwest, 1880–1940* (New York: Oxford University Press, 1987).

JOHN MACK FARAGHER, *Women and Men on the Overland Trail* (New Haven, CT: Yale University Press, 1979).

DEE GARCEAU, "Nomads, Bunkies, Cross-Dressers, and Family Men: Cowboy Identity and the Gendering of Ranch Work," in *Across the Great Divide: Cultures of Manhood in the American West,* ed. Matthew Basso, Laura McCall, and Dee Garceau (New York: Routledge, 2001), 149–68.

MARION S. GOLDMAN, *Gold Diggers and Silver Miners: Prostitution and Social Life on the Comstock Lode* (Ann Arbor: University of Michigan Press, 1981).

ROBERT L. GRISWOLD, "Anglo Women and Domestic Ideology in the American West in the Nineteenth and Early Twentieth Centuries," in *Western Women: Their Land, Their Lives,* ed. Lillian Schlissel, Vicki L. Ruiz, Janice Monk (Albuquerque: University of New Mexico Press, 1988), 15–33.

RICHARD GRISWOLD DEL CASTILLO, "Patriarchy and the Status of Women in the Late Nineteenth-Century Southwest," in *The Mexican and Mexican American Experience in the 19th Century,* ed. Jaime E. Rodriguez (Tempe, AZ: Bilingual Press, 1989), 85–99.

RAMON A. GUTIERREZ, "Honor Ideology, Marriage Negotiation, and Class-Gender Domination in New Mexico, 1690–1846," *Latin American Perspectives,* 12 (Winter 1985), 81–104.

LUCIE CHENG HIRATA, "Free, Indentured, Enslaved: Chinese Prostitutes in Nineteenth-Century America," *Signs,* 5 (Autumn 1979), 3–29.

ELIZABETH JAMESON, "Imperfect Unions: Class and Gender in Cripple Creek, 1894–1904," *Frontiers,* 1 (Spring 1976), 89–117.

JULIE ROY JEFFREY, *Frontier Women: The Trans-Mississippi West, 1840–1880* (New York: Hill & Wang, 1979).

KAREN J. KEONG, " 'A Distinct and Antagonistic Race': Constructions of Chinese Manhood in the Exclusionist Debates, 1869-1878," in *Across the Great Divide: Cultures of Manhood in the American West*, ed. Matthew Basso, Laura McCall, and Dee Garceau (New York: Routledge, 2001), 131–48.

SABINE LANG, *Men as Women, Women as Men: Changing Gender in Native American Cultures*, trans. John L. Vantine (Austin: University of Texas Press, 1998).

MARY MURPHY, "The Private Lives of Public Women: Prostitution in Butte, Montana, 1878–1917," in *The Woman's West*, ed. Susan Armitage and Elizabeth Jameson (Norman: University of Oklahoma Press, 1987), 193–205.

SANDRA L. MYRES, *Westering Women and the Frontier Experience, 1800–1915* (Albuquerque: University of New Mexico Press, 1982).

PEGGY PASCOE, "Gender Systems in Conflict: The Marriages of Mission-Educated Chinese American Women, 1874–1939," *Journal of Social History*, 22 (Summer 1989), 631–52.

PEGGY PASCOE, *Relations of Rescue: The Search for Female Moral Authority in the American West, 1874–1939* (New York: Oxford University Press, 1990).

PAULA PETRIK, *No Step Backward: Women and Family on the Rocky Mountain Mining Frontier, Helena, Montana, 1865–1900* (Helena: Montana Historical Society, 1987).

MARLA N. POWERS, *Oglala Women: Myth, Ritual, and Reality* (Chicago: University of Chicago Press, 1986).

GLENDA RILEY, *Women and Indians on the Frontier, 1825–1915* (Albuquerque: University of New Mexico Press, 1984).

RUTH ROESSEL, *Women in Navajo Society* (Rough Rock, AZ: Navajo Resource Center, 1981).

MALCOLM J. ROHRBOUGH, *Days of Gold: The California Gold Rush and the American Nation* (Berkeley: University of California Press, 1997).

BENSON TONG, *Unsubmissive Women: Chinese Prostitutes in Nineteenth-Century San Francisco* (Norman: University of Oklahoma Press, 1994).

ROBERT A. TRENNERT, "Educating Indian Girls at Nonreservation Boarding Schools, 1878–1920," *Western Historical Quarterly*, 13 (July 1982), 271–90.

WENDY WALL, "Gender and the 'Citizen Indian,' " in *Writing the Range: Race, Class, and Culture in the Women's West*, ed. Elizabeth Jameson and Susan Armitage (Norman: University of Oklahoma Press, 1997), 202–29.

WALTER L. WILLIAMS, *The Spirit and the Flesh: Sexual Diversity in American Indian Culture* (Boston: Beacon Press, 1986).

GARY WITHERSPOON, "Navajo Social Origins," in *Handbook of North American Indians*, ed. William C. Sturdevant, Vol. 10, *Southwest*, ed. Alfonso Ortiz (Washington, DC: Smithsonian Institution, 1983), 524–35.

JUDY YUNG, *Unbound Feet: A Social History of Chinese Women in San Francisco* (Berkeley: University of California Press, 1995).

CHAPTER NINE

THE NEW WOMAN AND THE NEW MAN AT THE TURN OF THE CENTURY (1890–1920)

MEN, WOMEN, AND THE "CRISIS" IN GENDER IDENTITY

By the 1890s a new style of femininity and masculinity was emerging for men and women in the middle classes. As the century came to an end, more and more women were claiming the right to an education, finding employment in jobs previously held exclusively by men, and demanding the right to vote. An increasing number were campaigning for social reform. In the process, a so-called "New Woman" began to emerge. She was single, well-educated, independent, self-sufficient, and strong-willed. Unwilling to express her femininity by conforming to the demands of the "cult of true womanhood," she seemed to be a strange, new creature. And she received more than her fair share of media attention.

As it became apparent that women were breaking down the barriers that separated the world of men from that of women, definitions of femininity and masculinity began to blur.

Indeed, from the male perspective, it looked as if the world was becoming alarmingly feminized. In Henry James's *The Bostonians*, published in 1886, the male protagonist, Basil Ransom glumly complained, "The whole generation is womanized; the masculine tone is passing out of the world; it's a feminine, nervous, hysterical, chattering, canting age, an age of hollow phrases and false delicacy and exaggerated solicitudes and coddled sensibilities, which, if we don't soon look out, will usher in the reign of mediocrity; of the feeblest and flattest and the most pretentious that has ever been."

Through Ransom, James gave voice to the kind of male insecurity, resentment, and anxiety that accompanied the rise of the New Woman. Male response to this phenomenon was to try to clarify what was manly and what was not. In the process, men began to reformulate how they should express their masculinity and to renegotiate their relationships with women.

Whether, as some historians have suggested, the rise of the New Woman prompted a "crisis" for men is debatable. But what is clear is that at the turn of the century, the question of what constituted manliness and womanliness was the subject of considerable discussion, debate, and self-conscious reflection.

THE DILEMMAS FACING MIDDLE-CLASS MEN AT THE TURN OF THE CENTURY

The rise of the New Woman was only a symptom of a wide variety of fundamental changes in economic, intellectual, political, and social life that were slowly eroding the ability of middle-class men to express their gendered identities in traditional ways. By the 1890s, employment patterns had changed. In 1893, the United States entered a period of depression. The rising unemployment that accompanied the economic downturn exacerbated anxieties about the ability of men to fulfill their gendered roles as breadwinners. On top of that, the growth of big business meant that fewer and fewer of them had the opportunity to run their own companies. They simply did not have access to enough capital to compete with big corporations. The result was that most men could expect to spend their working lives as someone else's employee. Earlier in the nineteenth century success had been defined in terms of a man's economic independence and his ability to compete with others. By the turn of the century, it was increasingly defined in terms of a man's loyalty, efficiency, and respect for authority. Working for a company may have provided men with steady employment, but it made them dependent upon a salary. And as employees, they had little control over their working conditions or the way their companies were being run.

Between 1870 and 1910 the number of white-collar jobs mushroomed. The number of clerical workers, sales people, government employees, technicians and salaried professionals increased from 756,000 to 5.6 million.

While some men were able to rise to powerful and extremely well-paid positions in government or big business, most white-collar workers could realistically expect to spend their working lives in middle management, sitting at their desks and taking orders from others. For them, work became a delicate balance between competing with other salaried employees for recognition and promotion and cooperating with them to promote the interests of their employers.

Added to this situation was the fact that middle-class men faced increased competition from women for access to education and jobs as well as the right to vote. Women had begun taking over jobs as elementary teachers and librarians earlier in the nineteenth century. Now they were taking over office jobs as well. In 1870 only 3 percent of all clerical jobs were held by women. But by 1910, the figure had increased to 35 percent and was still climbing. Women were now working as bookkeepers, accountants, cashiers, stenographers, and typists.

The feminization of office work brought changes in what had been a male work culture. Many women objected, for example, when their male co-workers spit their tobacco juice indiscriminately on the floor or aimed it casually at a nearby spitoon. And they found the use of foul language in their presence offensive. So men were forced to accommodate the presence of women in previously all-male work spaces by changing the way they behaved. In the process, the office became more and more like the home, a place where there was a premium on neatness, cleanliness, and decorous behavior. According to those who were unhappy with such changes, the world outside the home was becoming overly civilized.

Intellectual developments also threatened to undermine the confidence that men had in their own manliness. Journalists and social critics began to complain that "civilization" and evolution as described by men like Charles Darwin and Herbert Spencer were slowly robbing men of their strength and virility. At the same time, social science research was challenging the assumption that the differences between men and women were biologically determined. Darwin's hypothesis that women were less evolved than man had been comforting to those searching for scientific explanations for gender differences. The theory of evolution helped to explain why women were the way they seemed to be—passive, nurturing, physically weaker, and less intelligent than men. But by 1910 Elsie Clews Parsons, a social scientist trained at Columbia, and Jessie Taft, a psychologist from the University of Chicago, were presenting evidence that suggested that what had been assumed to be innate female traits were really the products of socialization. Their work helped to undermine confidence in the idea that gender differences were biologically determined.

To add insult to injury, mass reform movements led primarily, although not exclusively, by women were attacking sources of male power and pleasure. In 1890, the woman suffrage movement established a united front in their attempt to gain the right to vote for women. And women were effectively using their role as mother and protector-of-the-home as well as their claim to moral superiority to carry on campaigns against drinking and prostitution. When it began to look as if they might succeed in their reform efforts, some men began to have second thoughts about the benefits to be derived from the moral leadership of women.

Changes were occurring on the home front as well. As the ideal of companionate marriage gained popular support, the role of husband as patriarch began to decline and a more egalitarian model for married couples emerged. One result of this change was that middle-class men became increasingly dependent upon their wives for emotional support, intimacy, and friendship. At the same time, an increase in leisure time meant that men were able to spend more time at home and take a greater interest in domestic affairs and child rearing. As they did so, however, they became increasingly concerned about the amount of time their sons were spending with women. Mothers and female schoolteachers did little, from their point of view, to encourage little boys to exhibit such manly qualities as aggressiveness and competitiveness. Female influence, they feared, was turning the younger generation into a bunch of sissies. On yet another front, it seemed, women were undermining the manliness of the American male through their feminizing influence.

Free time brought with it other sources of anxiety as well. In the seventeenth and eighteenth centuries, leisure had been associated with sinfulness and laziness or the decadence that accompanied the accumulation of great wealth. After the American Revolution, many believed that idleness posed a threat to the very welfare of the republic. With manliness so traditionally tied to activity and labor, it is not surprising that while normally hardworking, middle-class men were willing to accept a work schedule that was less demanding, they felt some anxiety about the relationship between relaxation and male identity.

The closing of the frontier served as yet another source of concern. For three hundred years, white men had been assured that there was space in the west where they could test their survival skills and manly courage while seeking their fortunes. But by 1890, most of the fertile land in the trans-Mississippi West had been settled. The buffalo herds had been decimated. And the Indians were largely confined to reservations. For all intents and purposes, the frontier was closed. Men who hoped to prove their manliness in that kind of environment would have to find somewhere else to do it.

In short, by 1900 defining what it meant to be a man had become a confusing and anxiety-ridden enterprise. Some were desperately worried about what they perceived to be the feminization of American life. They resented female demands that women be given the same rights and opportunities as men. And their confidence in their ability to maintain their privileged economic, social, and political position in society was eroding. It was not an easy matter, they discovered, to adapt their definitions of masculinity to a whole new set of economic, social, and political realities.

THE EMERGENCE OF A NEW MIDDLE-CLASS MAN

Middle-class men responded to these threats to their sense of manliness in a wide variety of ways. They began celebrating maleness by glorifying such traditionally male traits as competitiveness, aggressiveness, muscularity, and courage. And they also redeemed and romanticized characteristics they had previously considered undesirable, such as primitive savagery, violence, passion, and impulsiveness. At the same time, they disparaged and did what they could to humiliate men who exhibited behavior patterns associated with femininity such as physical weakness, tenderness, dependence, helplessness, emotional sensitivity, and passivity. What had once been considered harmless, romantic friendships between men now became suspect. A whole new category of deviance—homosexuality—was created. Men who exhibited what were considered to be feminine traits or who openly expressed their love for other men were now stigmatized and socially ostracized.

To counteract the feminizing influence of mothers and female teachers, middle-class men founded all-male organizations such as the Boy Scouts. The scout handbook made it abundantly clear what its goals were. "Realizing that manhood, not scholarship, is the first arm of education, we have sought out those pursuits which develop the finest character, the finest physique, and which may be followed out of doors, which in a word, make for manhood." There was no doubt that scouting was intended to turn young boys into "real" men. But participating in scouting also served the gendered interests of scout leaders. By directing strenuous, out-door scouting activities, adult men could validate their own sense of manliness through positions of leadership and responsibility. At the same time, of course, they could be actively involved in the effort to preserve and perpetuate such traditional manly traits as competitiveness, bravery, physical strength, and moral uprightness.

Middle-class, white men also used racism and imperialism to reassure themselves that they were still manly. While it is true that white men from all parts of the country used the rhetoric celebrating Anglo-Saxon racial superiority to enhance their self-image, racist language had particular resonance in the South. Suffering from the shame of having lost the Civil War, the degrading burden of poverty which undermined their ability to support their families, and the humiliation of having to share their political power with ex-slaves, southern white men were desperate to reclaim their manliness. Responding to that impulse, they organized to systematically deny blacks an equal place in southern society. As they gradually gained control over southern state legislatures, they passed legislation that deprived black men of the right to vote or hold office and passed Jim Crow laws that segregated whites and blacks. Because they controlled the court system, they were immune from prosecution when they cheated their black customers, exploited black labor, and raped black women. And they knew that nothing much would happen when they lynched any black man, foolish enough or brave enough to protest what they were doing. By 1900, most southern white men based their manliness on the maintenance of a system of race control that approximated that which had existed under slavery.

Racism also served the interests of men outside the South, but there it was more likely to take the form of support for imperialism. The United States was a late comer to the quest for an overseas empire. Throughout most of the nineteenth century the land that lay west of the Appalachians had provided Americans an outlet for their imperial dreams. But by the 1890s, many were ready to look beyond their borders, compete with the Europeans for markets and sources of raw materials, and confirm their claim to racial superiority by establishing their rule over what they considered to be more "primitive" people.

In pursuit of this goal, the United States declared war on Spain in 1898. The war was short and decisive, lasting for only sixteen weeks. And when it was over, the United States gained possession of Guam and the

Philippines in the Pacific and Puerto Rico in the Caribbean.

The rhetoric used to justify the war reflected the anxieties that plagued American men regarding their claim to manliness. Those who supported the war came from all walks of life, both political parties, and from different regions of the country. But the one thing they had in common was that they all argued that war with Spain would help to "bolster American manhood." The war, they hoped, would return our nation to an earlier stage of our history when strong, aggressive, and courageous republican men fought for their country and republican women reared their sons to become civic-minded, manly heroes. Using traditional gender conventions as a political tool, they implied that anyone who opposed the war or advocated self-restraint in our relationship with Spain was unmanly. Only by successfully engaging in war, they argued, could American men affirm their masculinity and prove that they had not lost their competitive edge. In the name of manly honor, they called upon American men to come forward to prove their manhood through a display of physical strength and stamina, raw courage, and military daring. In response to their challenge, thousands of men volunteered to fight. Indeed, enthusiasm for fighting was so intense that the government had to turn many volunteers away.

Volunteering for service was one thing, but being physically able to survive under combat conditions was quite another. In response to concern that American men lacked strength and vigor, strenuous exercise such as running and body-building became popular as men who spent most of their working day at their desks tried to build up their muscles. Boxing and wrestling became the rage. Interest in pitting one's body and mind against nature meant that there was renewed interest in rowing, camping, hunting, fishing, and mountain climbing. What had once been necessary for survival in the wilderness now became popular forms of recreation. Interest in team sports such as baseball also increased. Participation in rough, contact sports like football

served as a way to exhibit such manly virtues as fearlessness, competitiveness, aggressiveness, and physical prowess and to practice such virtues as cooperativeness, self-discipline, and self-control. Those who did not have the time or talent to excel in organized sports could always watch the game, bond with other men, and express their public support for the exhibition of all kinds of manly virtues.

While they were pursuing activities designed to create and maintain a manly body, middle-class men also focussed on their spiritual lives and carried on a campaign to wrest control of religion away from women and reclaim their position as the moral leaders of their communities. As we have already seen, in the nineteenth century, religion in America was feminized partly because it left men free to pursue their own self-interest in the market place. By the twentieth century two changes had occurred that made this gendered division of labor less satisfactory. First, the world in which men conducted their business had changed. As large corporations took over control of the economy, men had fewer and fewer opportunities to pursue their self-interest by starting their own businesses. And secondly, the uses to which women were putting their piety and claim to moral superiority seemed to be getting out of control. Female efforts in the realm of "social housekeeping" intended to clean up the "mess" that men had made of government and society were perceived as a real threat to male dominance.

Men responded to these changes in a variety of ways. First, they tried to re-create the image of Jesus to emphasize the fact that he was a man. Traditionally Jesus had been portrayed as a gentle young man dressed in a long flowing gown with long, wavy hair and a sad, sweet look on his face. Responding to this feminized image, authors and artists began to portray Jesus as a mature, hearty, virile, muscular carpenter with rough and calloused hands sitting at his workbench holding the tools of his trade. They pictured him as an active and aggressive reformer capable of great anger, who strode into the synagogue and threw out the money changers. At the same time, they reminded their audience that Jesus was a man of considerable charisma—a charming leader, who was able to convince people to do his bidding and within a few short years establish the organizational basis for a major world religion. John D. Rockefeller and Andrew Carnegie had nothing on Jesus Christ, successful entrepreneur.

As a part of their effort to reclaim their control over American religion and moral life, Christian men searched for a suitably manly outlet for their philanthropic impulses. Ministers like Walter Rauschenbush and Washington Gladden provided them with a program of social activism that met their needs. As proponents of what was called the "Social Gospel, " ministers stood in their pulpits and reminded the members of their congregations that affluent Christians who lived lives of ease and privilege should not forget their Christian duty to care for those less fortunate than themselves. They suggested that men should combine activity and aggressiveness with such womanly virtues as social compassion to take an active role in reforming society. The message of those who preached the Social Gospel provided a basis upon which political reformers like the Progressives could build support for limiting the power of trusts, cleaning up politics, improve housing, working conditions, and public education, and eliminating child labor. Together the Social Gospelers and the Progressives transformed reform into a manly endeavor.

The Progressive reform movement was a gendered enterprise. Both men and women participated in it. But the area of trustbusting was an almost exclusively male enterprise. Between the end of the Civil War and the 1890s, the directors of railroads like the Union Pacific and companies like Standard Oil and Carnegie Steel controlled not only the economic life but also the political life of America. By combining themselves into business organizations called trusts, they were able to form monopolies and drive their competitors out of business. They could then charge their customers whatever they liked. Aggressively prosecuting big corporations for violating federal anti-trust legislation became a way for Progressive politicians like Theodore Roosevelt, William Howard Taft, and Woodrow Wilson to confirm their manliness. In pursuit of justice for the "little" guy—the small businessman—Progressives were able to express their gender identities through forceful action and manly courage.

Not all men had the opportunity to exhibit courage or aggressiveness, of course. But even those men who were confined to their desks in Chicago or Boston could vicariously enjoy great adventures and celebrate manly acts of heroism through literature and fantasy. What they could not experience in real life, they could enjoy in an imaginary one. It was no accident that the period saw the rise of the tall tale and the adventure novel, most of which had masculine themes. There was Casey at the bat. There was Paul Bunyan. And there were western heroes like the Virginian, the strong, silent cowboy who killed his enemies and won the heart of a beautiful girl.

Perhaps the most popular and enduring of such heroes was Tarzan of the Apes. Created by Edgar Rice Burroughs in his best-selling novels, Tarzan was a powerful symbol of primitive masculinity. The story of Tarzan clearly resonated with American readers. Orphaned in infancy, Tarzan survives life in an African jungle with the help of a female ape. Under her tutelage he becomes a resourceful, skilled, and fearless hunter. Burroughs describes Tarzan as a perfect specimen of a man, "an embodiment of physical perfection and giant strength." Tarzan's appeal seems to have been that he was able to successfully combine the sensibilities of a white man with the violence and hedonism of a savage. In Tarzan, both the civilized and the primitive could co-exist.

Men at the turn of the century also turned to the home as a place where they could reconstruct their ideas about what was masculine and what was not. Men, who were relatively secure in their white-collar jobs but found life at work uninteresting and even frustrating, found immense satisfaction in reclaiming their responsibilities as attentive parents. They showed a renewed interest in educational issues and spent more time with their children. In the evenings after work or on weekends, they could be seen outside their homes, teaching their sons to play ball or taking them on camping trips or fishing expeditions.

A NEW MAN FOR A NEW CENTURY— THEODORE ROOSEVELT AS THE QUINTESSENTIAL MAN

There was no man at the turn of the century who worked more self-consciously or harder to construct his own manly image than Roosevelt. That was, perhaps, because there was little about his early background that would have made him a likely candidate for "man of the year." He was born in New York City in 1858. His parents were wealthy and socially prominent and were able to give him every advantage. But he was a sickly, pale, near-sighted, small, skinny boy subject to terrifying bouts of asthma. The fact that his nickname was "Teedie" and that he was shy and bookish did not do much to help him establish himself as a so-called "man's man." In an effort to overcome his physical disabilities, he spent much of his early life trying to strengthen his body. After graduating from Harvard in 1880, he married, moved back to New York City, and began to take an interest in local politics. Because he had been protected from ridicule by his family's wealth and social prominence, the issue of his manliness did not really become a problem until he was elected to the state legislature in New York in 1881. When he arrived in Albany to take his seat in January, 1882, the press had a field day with him. They ridiculed his high-pitched voice, his demeanor, and his clothes, and they called him "Jane Dandy" and "Punkin-Lily." Roosevelt knew that as long as his masculinity was impugned, it would be impossible for him to be an effective and influential political figure. So, he began methodically redesigning himself and his image for public consumption.

The first step in his quest for a manly image came when he had the opportunity to spend some time in the Badlands of South Dakota. He could not have been more out of place in that environment—an eastern "dude" in the world of "real" men. Dressed in a hat, a neck scarf, and fringed buckskin jacket with a gun belt around his waist, he learned to ride the range, live outdoors, and hunt wild animals. Combining his flair for self-promotion with his skill in public relations, he wrote about his western exploits and published them in book form. His description of himself and his western adventures had such popular appeal that when he ran for mayor of New York City in 1886, he did so as the "Cowboy of the Dakotas."

Roosevelt's enthusiasm for imperialism also helped give him credibility as a strong, virile, and aggressive man. He was serving as Assistant Secretary of the Navy when President McKinley declared war on Spain in 1898. TR immediately resigned his position, got a commission in the army as a lieutenant colonel, and raised his own cavalry regiment composed of cowboys and frontiersmen with a sprinkling of Ivy League graduates. The press christened them the "Rough Riders" and sent reports of their exploits back to the newspapers in the United States. When Roosevelt and his Rough Riders saw action on Kettle Hill in the battle for the San Juan Heights overlooking Santiago in Cuba, they were front-page news. His reputation as a war hero helped him secure a New York gubernatorial nomination, and he took some of his Rough Riders on the campaign trail with him.

One of Roosevelt's first acts as President of the United States was to order the Justice Department to prosecute the Northern Securities Company, a trust that monopolized much of the American railway system. His aggressive fight to regulate big business earned him a reputation as America's premier trust-buster. As President, he championed legislation designed to reform American politics and society. And his conduct of foreign affairs was characterized by the saying "Speak softly and carry a big stick."

Roosevelt's version of manliness did have a less aggressive side. Roosevelt cultivated an image of himself as a virtuous and loving family man. He did not smoke or swear, and he drank only occasionally and never to excess. He even taught Sunday School. And he particularly enjoyed spending time with his six children. He not only took an interest in their education, he also challenged them to ferocious pillow fights and played with them by getting down on his hands and knees on the floor to play bear. Even the duties of being President of the United States did not diminish his enthusiasm for child play. It was not unusual for him to visit his children before an official dinner and find it necessary to return to his rooms to change his rumpled shirt before he greeted his guests.

By the time he left the Presidency in 1908, there was probably no man who had a greater influence on how white manliness was defined than Theodore Roosevelt. Roosevelt's success in this effort was based not only on his skills in self-promotion but also on his ability to tie together the disparate strands of civilized and primitive manliness into one model. He made virtues out of manly aggression and violence on the battlefield and in the stadium while he sought refuge and pleasure in family life. Through his own exploits, he allowed other men to experience life on the frontier. By example, he demonstrated that men could be loving and sensitive as well as courageous and competitive. He advocated strenuous exercise to minimize the effects of civilization. At the same time, however, he used the rhetoric of racism and civilization to justify American imperialism. He was a man of great intellect as well as a man of action. And his version of the American man was appealing partly because it crossed the lines that separated the men of one social class from another.

A NEW WOMAN FOR A NEW CENTURY

Gender identities tend to be constructed in tandem with each other. Theodore Roosevelt's image of the New Man was constructed as a response to the rise of the New Woman. The image of femininity that she invoked stood in stark contrast with that of the married, middle-class housewife whose world was centered around her home and her church. New Women were women from affluent families who received the best education available at the time. Many had gone to one of the new women's colleges in the East like Vassar, Wellesley, or Smith. They were ambitious, competitive, strong-willed, and determined to make a place for themselves in the world outside the home. Determined to have a useful and personally fulfilling public life, a New Woman earned her own living. She could not yet vote in national elections, but she was politically influential behind the scenes. She and her friends strode confidently into the hallowed halls of state legislatures to lobby male politicians and helped to put together coalitions to influence the passage of legislation on the local, state, and national level. But perhaps the most frightening thing about the New Woman, from her critics' point of view, was that she seemed to be so self-assured and independent. Those who did not marry often found an outlet for their emotional life in their relationships with other women. And those who did marry, tended to marry late and bore fewer children than their mothers and grandmothers.

Jane Addams was as good an example of a New Woman as you could find. Born in a small town in Illinois in 1860, she was the daughter of a successful businessman and politician. She began attending Rockford Seminary for Women in Rockford, Illinois in 1877. Something more than a high school and less than a full-fledged woman's college, Rockford provided the best education available in the Midwest at the time. Addams thoroughly enjoyed both the intellectual life that it provided and the community of bright, young, ambitious women who she found there. It was at Rockford that she developed the kind of leadership skills that would serve her in the years to come.

Like other well-educated young women, Jane hoped that when she graduated she would be able to find a socially useful place for herself outside the home. But as a middle-class woman, her options were severely limited. A woman in her situation was expected to graduate, return home, and prepare herself for marriage. If she failed to attract a husband, she faced the prospect of spending her life living with her relatives and caring for them when they were ill or in need of her services. Jane did not relish the thought of either option and planned to continue her education at Smith College or apply to medical school. But she began to suffer from ill health, which made these options impractical. After her graduation from Rockford in 1881, she essentially lived the life of a bored, semi-invalid spinster.

Her life changed in the spring of 1888. During a tour of Europe, she visited Toynbee Hall, a settlement house in one of the poorest areas of London. It was run by a group of young, well-to-do college-educated men who were devoting themselves to helping the poor. Their example served as an inspiration to her. She returned home and with her best friend Ellen Gates Starr moved to Chicago and set up housekeeping in a dilapidated mansion in a filthy, slum neighborhood.

Jane intended for her home, which she called Hull House, to serve as the place of recreation and a source of social services for the neighborhood. She and Ellen set up clubs, classes in English, nutrition, and household management, a reading room, and a debating society as well as child-care facilities for their neighbors.

Addams was a talented administrator and an effective fund raiser. Eventually, she was able to buy more property in the neighborhood. She turned the saloon next door into a gymnasium and found space to house and feed the increasing number of volunteers who arrived to help her in her work. Most of these "residents" were well-to-do, college graduates who sought alternative ways to carry out their benevolent impulses. With their help, not only did she set up an employment office, a bath facility, and a meeting place for women's labor organizations but she also began lobbying the politicians in City Hall for improved street lighting, garbage collection, sewers, and police protection.

For Addams, the resident community at Hull House became a kind of surrogate family with Ellen Starr serving as her partner in a romantic friendship that in its intensity approximated that which could be found in heterosexual marriage. And as the founder of Hull House, she was a kind of matriarch. Like a mother, ambitious for her children, she encouraged her residents to take on causes of their own. Hull House produced some of the most prominent female Progressive reformers in the country. Julia Lathrop became the first head of the federal Children's Bureau. Florence Kelley led a successful campaign to improve safety for workers in factories. Alice Hamilton went on to become a doctor and founded the field of industrial medicine. And Grace Abbott became the head of the Immigrants' Protective League. They all devoted their lives to improving working conditions and educational opportunities for the working class.

As the years passed, Addams became more and more influential on a national level. She gave lectures all around the country on the subject of world peace and fought against the corruption that characterized local, state, and national politics. As testimony to her prominence in progressive circles, she was invited to second the nomination of Theodore Roosevelt for President at the Progressive Party convention in 1912. In the first decades of the twentieth century, she was one of the most well-known and respected women in America.

A NEW VERSION OF CONVENTIONAL WOMANHOOD

New Women like Jane Addams were clearly exceptional. And while they may have found successfully challenging prevailing gender conventions to be an exhilarating experience, they also found that forging a new definition of womanliness could sometimes be exhausting and lonely.

Addams and others like her provided strong role models for other women eager to believe that a woman could be independent without losing her femininity. Most women in the middle and upper classes, however, did not follow their example. They continued to marry and spend much of their lives in the domestic sphere, keeping house and rearing children, dependent upon their husbands to support them. In that sense they constructed their feminine identities around the same values that had prevailed for centuries.

But just as men had to adjust their definitions of manliness to changing social, economic, and political realities, so did women have to adapt themselves to changes in the meaning of domesticity. By 1920, woman's domestic roles were becoming professionalized. No longer were women expected to rely on an apprenticeship in housekeeping under their mothers and their own maternal instincts to carry out their domestic duties. Now, they were told, they needed specialized skills and scientific knowledge in order manage their households and take care of their children.

In towns and cities across the country, the domestic role of women was increasingly constructed around the idea of woman as consumer. To be a "true woman" one had to be a good shopper, which simply meant that a woman had to make judicious decisions about how to spend her husband's income. Instead of growing and processing food, a housewife could now buy what she needed at the grocers. And instead of sewing clothes for every member of the family, she could select what was most fashionable at the local department store.

Managers of department stores like Marshall Field in Chicago and John Wanamaker in Philadelphia were quick to exploit female buying power by creating a culture of consumption that discouraged thrift and self-denial. Beautifully appointed, these stores offered women a public environment consistent with their social roles. A woman could spend the day shopping and having lunch with her friends in a public space while carrying out her traditional familial responsibilities. Shopping encouraged independent decision-making on the part of women and testified to their economic power within the family.

The context within which a woman performed her housework also changed. For those who could afford it, technology began to relieve the physical burden of housekeeping. Indoor plumbing, stoves, ice boxes, electric power, and washing machines made performing domestic chores easier.

In order to imbue housewives with a sense of their own importance, schools and colleges began to offer courses in domestic "science, " home "economics," and household "engineering." Ladies' magazines and advice manuals began to emphasize the importance of a housewife's managerial skills. She needed to have expertise in time management as well as accounting. She needed to develop a sense of aesthetics in order to tastefully decorate her home. She needed to be familiar with the chemical make-up of fabrics as well as food. And she needed to acquire a rudimentary knowledge of the germ theory, nutrition, and sanitation.

Motherhood also went through a professionalization process. By 1900, many native-born women were limiting the size of their families. That did not mean, however, that they were less likely to construct their femininity around motherhood. Having fewer children simply meant that they were able to focus more attention on each individual child. Child welfare experts began to put pressure on mothers to prepare themselves more completely for fulfilling their maternal role. Specialized skills and knowledge, they said, were required to rear children properly. They argued that mothers needed expertise in child psychology and theories of early childhood development. Not only were ladies' magazines full of helpful hints for mothers, mothers' manuals and maternal organizations like the National Congress of Mothers provided women with an endless stream of information and advice on the subject of child rearing.

With fewer children to care for and less time spent on housekeeping, middle-class women had time to cultivate their public identities. The number of women's organizations concerned with philanthropy, self-improvement, and social reform multiplied by leaps and bounds. All over the country, women joined organizations like the Women's Christian Temperance Union, the Woman's Trade Union League, and their local Woman's Club. In ever increasing numbers, they attended political rallies, voted in school board elections, and campaigned for social and political reform.

In 1890 the two wings of the woman's suffrage movement finally joined forces to form the National American Woman's Suffrage Association. And by 1900 it had a dynamic new leader, Carrie Chapman Catt. In the South, the desire to restore white supremacy with the votes of white women began to undermine male resistance to the idea of women voting. And in the North and West, woman's suffrage became a part of the campaign on the part of Progressives to clean up politics and bring about social reform.

Under the leadership of Catt, the suffragists changed their strategy. Early suffragists like Elizabeth Cady Stanton and Susan B. Anthony had demanded the vote on the grounds that it was an injustice to deny women the same rights as men. By 1900, it was clear that this argument did not resonate with most women. So Catt and Anna Howard Shaw, who succeeded her to the presidency of the NAWSA, developed a strategy that was more congruent with the image that American women had of themselves. Women should have the vote, they argued, not because they were the same as men but because they were different. Their moral nature and nurturing instincts were needed to balance male self-interest and aggression. As one suffrage supporter put it, "Might it not be better for the sex which furnishes nine-tenths of the criminals, to give the sex which furnishes two-thirds of the church members an equal share in the duties and privileges of citizenship?" Women needed to vote, said others, because they were mothers and needed to have the power to protect their homes and their children.

The appeal of this new strategy was evident in the resistance that it provoked. There had been opposition to the idea that women should have the right to vote in national elections ever since the inception of the suffrage movement in 1848. But until the turn of the century it had remained sporadic and largely unorganized. Once the suffragists began to appeal to popularly held ideas about womanhood, however, both male and female anti-suffragists organized themselves and went on the offensive. Among other things, they argued that suffrage would destroy the family by turning wives against husbands and, thus, undermine the very basis of the "republic." And they argued that women were physically, intellectually, and emotionally, incapable of carrying out their civic duties by casting votes in national elections.

Despite the vehemence with which the "antis" opposed woman suffrage, Congress passed a suffrage amendment and the requisite number of states ratified it in 1920. After a campaign that had lasted over seventy years, the political identity of American women as competent adult citizens was confirmed in law. The degree to which they would incorporate their access to political power into their conception about what it meant to be a woman, however, remained to be seen.

MASCULINITY AND FEMININITY IN THE WORKING CLASS

Working-class men and women also had to adjust their definitions of masculinity and femininity to social and economic changes. The quest for manliness on the part of industrial workers took place in a context that was both similar to and different from that of middle-class men. By the time middle-class men had begun to deal with the fact that opportunities to make their fortunes as independent businessmen were quickly disappearing, working-class men had already come to terms with that reality. They had lost their economic independence in the business world early in the nineteenth century when they had found it necessary to give up their artisan status. As wage laborers, they were no longer able to set their own hours or exert much control over their working conditions. And as the century progressed and immigration increased, competition for jobs drove down their wages. Middle-class men who worked for wages could still expect to support their families. But for working-class men, the role of sole provider, which had often been elusive, was becoming increasingly problematical.

For working-class men, a sense of independence, the opportunity to assert themselves, and the chance to regain some control over their working lives seemed to lie in their willingness to unionize. Through collective bargaining, strikes, and boycotts, working men could collectively protest what they believed were efforts on the part of corporations to strip them not only of their livelihood but also of their manhood. The achievements of early unions were negligible. The leaders of big business simply refused to negotiate with their workers and used their seemingly endless financial resources and their influence over government to put down strikes. The first major success on the part of labor came in 1902 when coal miners all over the country went out on strike for higher wages and better working conditions. Faced with the approach of winter and the prospect of no coal for heat and electricity, Theodore Roosevelt forced the mine operators to bargain with their employees. Roosevelt's action marked an early breakthrough for unions.

Union activity did help to enhance the self-esteem of industrial workers and to give them the sense that through collective action they could reclaim some control over their working lives. Union leaders bargained for a family wage which would allow working men to construct their manliness around their role as sole breadwinner and their wives to confine themselves to the domestic sphere instead of having to work for wages in order to supplement the family income. Unionization was the mechanism through which the working class tried to achieve middle-class status and the gender identities that accompanied that sta-

tus. For most, however, that goal would not be realized until the 1950s.

Although some working women belonged to unions, most did not. Yet more and more women were joining the workforce. Between 1880 and 1930 the female labor force grew from 2.6 million to 10.8 million. What made these women different from those who had worked for wages earlier in the century was that many more of them lived away from their families and employers. They were, as historian Joanne Meyerowitz has put it, "women adrift."

A heterogeneous group, these women represented a wide range of racial and ethnic backgrounds and ages. But most of them were single and relatively young migrants, without wealth and with very little if any education, who arrived in places like Chicago by train hoping to find a way to support themselves and enjoy city life. Many found housing in cheap rooming houses where they were able to come and go as they pleased.

Free from the supervision and protection of their families, they tried to construct their femininity around independence. But their job options were limited, their wages were low, and their sometimes desperate economic circumstances meant that self-sufficiency was often beyond their grasp. So they substituted dependence on birth family for dependence on peers with whom they established surrogate families. They shared their meager resources with women like themselves. And it was with these women that they established their own urban subculture with its own definitions of femininity and standards of behavior that often stood in stark contrast to those of women in the middle class.

Like urban, wage-earning women earlier in the century, these working class women turned to the streets to socialize and entertain themselves. With barely enough money to pay for their rooms and food, they depended on the men they met at work, on the streets, or in their boarding houses to pay for an occasional meal or entrance tickets to dance halls and other forms of entertainment. If they were lucky, they could even expect to receive from their male friends small gifts and luxuries as tokens of affection, all of which helped to relieve their poverty. Some repaid such generosity with sexual favors. Others did not. But what seems clear from the evidence available is that their attitudes toward sexuality were much more casual than those of women in the middle class.

Wage-earning women at the turn of the century constructed their ideas about femininity around the competence with which they performed their work, their desire to have fun, their resourcefulness, and their sexuality. Bold and often willful in their desire to express their femininity in their own way, they were a source of considerable frustration for their employers and urban social reformers who did what they could to encourage them to conform to the ideal of middle-class womanhood. Nevertheless, the lives they chose for themselves and the ways they expressed their femininity turned out to have considerable appeal. By the first decades of the twentieth century, the daughters of the middle class were rebelling against social convention and claiming for themselves the kind of freedom that single, wage-earning women had already established for themselves.

GENDER AND THE SPECIAL DILEMMA OF BLACK MEN AND WOMEN

Constructing a masculine ideal for black men at the turn of the century was difficult. After the Civil War, southern black men had taken advantage of opportunities to marry, work for wages, and vote, in order to express their manliness. By 1900 there was a substantial black middle class. Composed of small businessmen, ministers, doctors, lawyers, and newspaper editors, they tried to conform to the manly ideal of the middle class. Generally speaking, they were civic minded, sober, and industrious. But as the century came to a close, they found it impossible to prevent southern whites from passing legislation that slowly eroded the social, economic, and political position of southern men of color. Without economic resources and the support of white politicians and judges, there was very little they could do. Their attempts to protest segregation were futile. And they had no way to resist the economic exploitation that resulted from tenant farming and share cropping or to put an end to the incidents of lynching that became more and more common. Under the pressure of racism, southern black men watched as their claim to manhood was undermined and their human dignity attacked.

There were, of course, those who offered a way of redeeming black manhood. Booker T. Washington, the president of Tuskegee Institute, a vocational school for blacks located in Alabama, deplored the racism that deprived black men of their ability to protect and support their families. But he accepted segregation as the price for the kind of social harmony that would allow blacks to pursue self-help initiatives. He believed that equal rights would come only when blacks could convincingly demonstrate to whites that they were sober, thrifty, law-abiding citizens. He advised black men to work hard, take care of their families, attend church, save their money, and buy property. In the meantime, he told them to be patient and discouraged them from demanding social equality and restitution of their political rights.

W. E. B. DuBois advocated a more active and aggressive approach. A Harvard-educated, middle-class northerner, DuBois found Washington's call for patient submission to racism incompatible with the expression of black manliness. He argued that black men could not call themselves men until they were courageous enough to resist white racism and demand their human rights.

It is unclear exactly what impact either Washington or DuBois had on the way ordinary black men constructed their masculinity. It is clear, however, that some black men found service in the armed forces a way to assert their manhood. Blacks vacillated in their support for the war against Spain. Those who opposed it pointed out that the war was really an effort to subjugate people who whites felt were inferior to them and that if the United States was interested in promoting democracy, its citizens might start at home. But how-ever ambivalent some of the more thoughtful among them were about the war, it provided black men with an opportunity to demon-strate their courage and patriotism, to assert their claim to equal citizenship, to win respect from whites, and reclaim the political identi-ties that were being so systematically eroded in the South. For many of them, participa-tion in war was an exercise in establishing their identity as men and promoting a feeling of self-esteem. Unfortunately, many of them were frustrated in their efforts. In places like Tampa, the main port of embarkation for troops headed for Cuba, they were exposed to every conceivable kind of insult and indig-nity. The owners of restaurants, saloons, and laundries refused to provide them with ser-vice. And at one point white soldiers refused to accept pay from a black officer. The fact that they were armed, gathered together in large numbers, and wore military uniforms which they hoped might provide them with some legal protection made them bold. On June 6, 1898, black soldiers of the 24th and 25th In-fantry responded to the cruel harassment of a two-year-old black child by white volunteers from Ohio by rampaging through the streets of Tampa shooting off their guns and wreck-ing saloons and cafes.

Conditions had not changed much by the time the United States entered World War I in 1917. During the early months of the war, the 24th Infantry Division was stationed in Houston. There they were forced to sit in sep-arate sections on streetcars, in restaurants, and in movie theaters. Frustrated and angry, they responded to the insults and indignities per-petrated on them by the civilian population by rioting.

Despite almost unimaginable provoca-tions, most black soldiers did not defend their manhood by attacking white civilians or their property while they were stationed in the United States. When they were shipped over-seas, they proved their manliness by serving with distinction. Proud of the courage they had exhibited on the battlefield, they returned home to find that conditions in civilian life

had not changed much while they were gone. Whatever they had done during the war to prove their manhood had little impact on the way they were treated. The struggle to redeem black manhood was not yet over.

Black women faced a double burden in their effort to define femininity for themselves. Those in the black middle class expressed their femininity through their roles as wives and mothers. Determined to serve as paragons of respectability, they tried to be virtuous, mod-est, altruistic, and church-going. But race con-sciousness added another dimension to their sense of self. They were deeply aware of the impact that white racism had on blacks and were committed to helping those less fortu-nate than themselves. Dedicated as they were to community uplift, they made no apologies for their intelligence and advanced their edu-cation whenever they had the chance. In those cases where their husbands were denied the right to vote and hold office, they represented the political interests of the black community by demanding access to whatever public ser-vices were available. They made no excuses for their public activities. They may have con-sidered themselves to be proper ladies, but their definition of ladyhood included being bold and courageous social activists.

Ida B. Wells Barnett was one such woman. Born of slave parents shortly after the Civil War, she was first a teacher and then a news-paper editor in Memphis, Tennessee. When three of her closest male friends were lynched by a white mob in 1892, she began a life-long campaign against lynching. She eventually settled in Chicago, married a lawyer, and bore four children. At the same time, she became active in Illinois politics and tried to raise sup-port for national anti-lynching legislation. She failed in this effort, but she continued to ded-icate her life to the struggle for social justice.

SUMMARY

In terms of gender, the turn of the century was not so much a period of crisis as it was a period of confusion as men and women adapted their own gendered identities to changes that were occurring in American social, political, and economic life. As middle-class and working-class women were able to take advantage of new educational and economic opportunities, they found it possible to assert their independence and initiate changes in what was considered feminine. Not all women chose a life that was significantly different from that of their mothers or grandmothers, but an increasing number had the opportunity to do so.

While women were experiencing an expansion in the ways they could express their femininity, some white middle-class men came to believe that their ability to express their masculinity in traditional ways was declining. They found changes in the definitions of femininity disconcerting, at the very least. And for many, any woman who was independent, self-sufficient, and assertive was downright threatening. Such women did not seem to need their support or protection. They seemed to be able to take care of themselves.

Because traditional definitions of manliness depended in part on the degree to which men were able to distinguish themselves from women, they responded by trying to quite self-consciously re-define for themselves what it was that made them manly. They celebrated such characteristics as toughness and aggressiveness—qualities that had traditionally been defined as male. They used their bodies to testify to their masculinity. They assumed responsibility for perpetuating such traditional manly qualities as bravery and competitiveness in their sons through organizations such as the Boy Scouts. Racism had always served white men as a way of justifying their dominance over those they felt were inferior to themselves. At the turn of the century, it simply became more virulent. Men began to change their attitude toward leisure and play, which were now considered manly pursuits. They tried to add a masculine dimension to their churches and to the image of Jesus. And they tried to wrest responsibility for social and political reform from the hands of women by promoting certain types of Progressive leg-

islation. On the home front, they were willing to spend more time and energy on domestic concerns and generally accepted the idea that marriage should be a partnership, but most were not yet willing to give up their positions as senior partner. However much a man might love and respect his wife and the services that she provided for him, he still considered himself the head of the household.

Some white men considered the presence of the assertive New Woman emasculating. But for southern black men, it was racism and a depressed economy that undermined their sense of manliness. Voting restrictions deprived them of their political identities. The pervasive poverty that characterized the South at the turn of the century made it difficult for them to support their families. And the threat of lynching made it dangerous for them to try to protect their loved ones from the humiliating impact of segregation. For the time being, endurance became the central component of southern black manliness.

Industrial workers responded to economic change by taking an increasing interest in collective bargaining as a way to promote their gendered identities. Male workers were most likely to initiate unionization, but female workers were never very far behind. Both searched for ways to control their working conditions and struggled to force their employers to pay them enough money so that they could support themselves and their families. Strikes allowed workers to assert themselves and to feel that they had some way to protest against long hours, low wages, and unsafe working conditions. But it was not until later in the twentieth century that strikes were successful and workers' sense of power was confirmed.

What it meant to be a man and a woman was certainly re-evaluated at the turn of the century. And adjustments in gender roles and relations began to emerge. In the end, independence, courage, and activity were still considered to be quintessential manly virtues. And work was still central to a man's identity. But by 1920 men did not have exclusive claim to those attributes and activities. In 1920, most women still valued such feminine attributes as piety, chastity, and domesticity. But between the working-class woman and the New Woman, female options for self-definition were expanded and sometimes overlapped with those that had always been available to men.

Emerging styles of masculinity and femininity varied depending on race, ethnicity, class, and region. Some of the changes that oc-

curred in gender roles and relations were dramatic. Others were barely noticeable. But what seems clear is that both men and women were aware of the tensions inherent in their desire to re-define what it meant to be manly and womanly and that their attempts to renegotiate their relationship with each other were fraught with discomfort and anxiety on both sides.

Document

Excerpts from Theodore Roosevelt's "The Strenuous Life"

Theodore Roosevelt was an enthusiastic promoter of American imperialism. He and his Rough Riders fought in the Spanish-American War in 1898. And he believed that America's greatness lay in fulfilling her responsibilities to rule her new colonies—Puerto Rico, Guam, Hawaii, and the Philippines. On April 10, 1899 he gave a speech before Chicago's all male Hamilton Club. In that speech he called upon American men to accept the responsibilities inherent in the possession of an empire—to support efforts to build up the navy and reorganize the armed forces. "The army and the navy are the sword and the shield which this nation must carry if she is to do her duty among the nations of the earth," he proclaimed. To fail to do so, he charged, would be cowardly. In the excerpt from his speech that follows, Roosevelt expresses some concern about the ability and willingness of American men and women to do what he thought necessary to fulfill the promise of American greatness.

What kind of manhood and womanhood does he idealize? What anxieties about gender does his speech expose? What might have been the sources of those anxieties?

In speaking to you, men of the greatest city of the West, men of the State which gave to the country Lincoln and Grant, men who

Source: Theodore Roosevelt, *The Strenuous Life: Essays and Addresses* (New York: Century Company, 1902), 1–4, 6–8, 20–21.

preëminently and distinctly embody all that is most American in the American character, I wish to preach, not the doctrine of ignoble ease, but the doctrine of the strenuous life, the life of toil and effort, of labor and strife; to preach that highest form of success which comes, not to the man who desires mere easy peace, but to the man who does not shrink from danger, from hardship, or from bitter toil, and who out of these wins the splendid ultimate triumph.

A life of slothful ease, a life of that peace which springs merely from lack either of desire or of power to strive after great things, is as little worthy of a nation as of an individual. . . . You work yourselves, and you bring up your sons to work. If you are rich and are worth your salt, you will teach your sons that though they may have leisure, it is not to be spent in idleness; for wisely used leisure merely means that those who possess it, being free from the necessity of working for their livelihood, are all the more bound to carry on some kind of non-remunerative work in science, in letters, in art, in exploration, in historical research—work of the type we most need in this country, the successful carrying out of which reflects most honor upon the nation. We do not admire the man of timid peace. We admire the man who embodies victorious effort; the man who never wrongs his neighbor, who is prompt to help a friend, but who has those virile qualities necessary to win in the stern strife of actual life. It is hard to fail, but it is worse never to have tried to succeed. In this life we get nothing save by effort. . . .

In the last analysis a healthy state can exist only when the men and women who make it up lead clean, vigorous, healthy lives; when the children are so trained that they shall endeavor, not to shirk difficulties, but to overcome them; not to seek ease, but to know how to wrest triumph from toil and risk. The man must be glad to do a man's work, to dare and endure and to labor; to keep himself, and to keep those dependent upon him. The woman must be the housewife, the helpmeet of the homemaker, the wise and fearless mother of many healthy children. In one of Daudet's powerful and melancholy books he speaks of "the fear of maternity, the haunting terror of the young wife of the present day." When such words can be truthfully written of a nation, that nation is rotten to the heart's core. When men fear work or fear righteous war, when women fear motherhood, they tremble on the brink of doom; and well it is that they should vanish from the earth, where they are fit subjects for the scorn of all men and women who are themselves strong and brave and high-minded.

As it is with the individual, so it is with the nation. It is a base untruth to say that happy is the nation that has no history. Thrice happy is the nation that has a glorious history. Far better it is to dare mighty things, to win glorious triumphs, even though checkered by failure, than to take rank with those poor spirits who neither enjoy much nor suffer much, because they live in the gray twilight that knows not victory nor defeat. . . .

In 1898 we could not help being brought face to face with the problem of war with Spain. All we could decide was whether we should shrink like cowards from the contest, or enter into it as beseemed a brave and high-spirited people; and, once in, whether failure or success should crown our banners. So it is now. We cannot avoid the responsibilities that confront us in Hawaii, Cuba, Porto Rico, and the Philippines. All we can decide is whether we shall meet them in a way that will redound to the national credit, or whether we shall make of our dealings with these new problems a dark and shameful page in our history. . . . The timid man, the lazy man, the man who distrusts his country, the over-civilized man, who has lost the great fighting, masterful virtues, the ignorant man, and the man of dull mind, whose soul is incapable of feeling the mighty lift that thrills "stern men with empires in their brains"—all these, of course, shrink from seeing the nation undertake its new duties; shrink from seeing us build a navy and an army adequate to our needs; shrink from seeing us do our share of the world's work, by bringing order out of chaos in the great, fair tropic islands from which the valor of our soldiers and sailors has driven the Spanish flag. These are the men who fear the strenuous life, who fear the only national life which is really worth leading. They believe in that cloistered life which saps the hardy virtues in a nation, as it saps them in the individual; or else they are wedded to that base spirit of gain and greed which recognizes in commercialism the be-all and end-all of national life, instead of realizing that, though an indispensable element, it is, after all, but one of the many elements that go to make up true national greatness. No country can long endure if its foundations are not laid deep in the material prosperity which comes from thrift, from business energy and enterprise, from hard, unsparing effort in the fields of industrial activity; but neither was any nation ever yet truly great if it relied upon material prosperity alone. All honor must be paid to the architects of our material prosperity. . . . But our debt is yet greater to the men whose highest type is to be found in a statesman like Lincoln, a soldier like Grant. They showed by their lives that they recognized the law of work, the law of strife; . . . but they recognized that there were yet other and even loftier duties—duties to the nation and duties to the race.

I preach to you, then, my countrymen, that our country calls not for the life of ease but for the life of strenuous endeavor. The twentieth century looms before us big with the fate of many nations. If we stand idly by, if we seek merely swollen, slothful ease and ignoble peace, if we shrink from the hard contests where men must win at hazard of their lives and at the risk of all they hold dear, then the bolder and stronger peoples will pass us by, and will win for themselves the domination of the world. Let us therefore boldly face the life of strife, resolute to do our duty well and manfully; resolute to uphold righteousness by deed and by word; resolute to be both honest and brave, to serve high ideals, yet to use practical methods. Above all, let us shrink from no strife, moral or physical, within or without the nation, provided we are certain that the strife is justified, for it is only through strife, through hard and dangerous endeavor, that we shall ultimately win the goal of true national greatness.

Caroline Ticknor's "The Steel-Engraving Lady and the Gibson Girl"

This short story appeared in a popular monthly literary magazine in 1901. Ensconced in the home, the sedate, quiet, and elegant Steel-Engraving Lady was the symbol of traditional womanhood. The Gibson Girl presented a new and more "modern" image. Dressed in a crisp, white, long-sleeved blouse and a loose, dark skirt with her hair pulled up and away from her face, she was ready for action and adventure.

Source: Caroline Ticknor, "The Steel-Engraving Lady and the Gibson Girl," *The Atlantic Monthly: A Magazine of Literature, Science, Art, and Politics,* LXXXVIII (July 1901), 105–108.

How does this story reflect the anxiety that surrounded changing attitudes toward gender at the turn of the century? What is the attitude of the author toward these two kinds of women? What does she think of the kind of man who each associates with?

The Steel-Engraving Lady sat by the open casement, upon which rested one slender arm. Her drapery sleeve fell back, revealing the alabaster whiteness of her hand and wrist. Her glossy, abundant hair was smoothly drawn over her ears, and one rose nestled in the coil of her dark locks.

Her eyes were dreamy, and her embroidery frame lay idly upon the little stand beside her. An air of quiet repose pervaded the apartment, which, in its decorations, bespoke the lady's industry. Under a glass, upon a gleaming mirror, floated some waxen pond lilies, modeled by her slim fingers. A large elaborate sampler told of her early efforts with her needle, and gorgeous mottoes on the walls suggested the pleasing combination of household ornamentation with Scriptural advice.

Suddenly a heavy step was heard upon the stair. A slight blush mantled the Steel-Engraving Lady's cheek.

"Can that be Reginald?" she murmured.

The door flew open, and on the threshold stood the Gibson Girl.

"Excuse me for dropping in upon you," she said, with a slight nod, tossing a golf club down upon the sofa near by. "You see I've been appointed to write a paper on Extinct Types, and I am anxious to scrape acquaintance with you."

The Steel-Engraving Lady bowed a trifle stiffly. "Won't you be seated?" she said, with dignity.

The Gibson Girl dropped into a low chair, and crossed one knee over the other; then she proceeded to inspect the room, whistling meanwhile a snatch from the last comic opera. She wore a short skirt and heavy square-toed shoes, a mannish collar, cravat, and vest, and a broad-brimmed felt hat tipped jauntily upon one side.

She stared quite fixedly at the fair occupant of the apartment, who could with difficulty conceal her annoyance.

"Dear me! you're just as slender and ethereal as any of your pictures," she remarked speculatively. "You need fresh air and exercise; and see the color of my hands and face beside your own."

The Steel-Engraving Lady glanced at her vis-à-vis, and shrugged her shoulders.

"I like a healthy coat of tan upon a woman," the Gibson Girl announced, in a loud voice. "I never wear a hat throughout the hottest summer weather. The day is past when one deplores a sunburned nose and a few freckles."

"And is a browned and sunburned neck admired in the ballroom?" the other queried. "Perhaps your artists of to-day prefer studies in black and white entirely, and scoff at coloring such as that ivory exhibits?" She pointed to a dainty miniature upon the mantel.

"No wonder you can't walk in those slim, tiny slippers!" the Gibson Girl exclaimed.

"And can you walk in those heavy men's shoes?" the Steel-Engraving Lady questioned. "Methinks my slippers would carry me with greater ease. Are they your own, or have you possibly put on your brother's shoes for an experiment? If they were only hidden beneath an ample length of skirt, they might seem less obtrusive. And is it true you walk the streets in such an abridged petticoat? You surely cannot realize it actually displays six inches of your stockings. I blush to think of any lady upon the street in such a guise."

"Blushing is out of style." The Gibson Girl laughed heartily.

"Nor would it show through such a coat of sunburn," the other suggested archly.

"It very likely seems odd to you," the visitor continued, "who are so far behind the times; but we are so imbued with modern thought that we have done away with all the oversensitiveness and overwhelming modesty in which you are enveloped. We have progressed in every way. When a man approaches, we do not tremble and droop our eyelids, or gaze adoringly while he lays down the law. We meet him on a ground of perfect fellowship, and converse freely on every topic."

The Steel-Engraving Lady caught her breath. "And does he like this method?" she queried.

"Whether he *likes* it or not makes little difference; *he* is no longer the one whose pleasure is to be consulted. The question now is, not 'What does man like?' but 'What does woman prefer?' That is the keynote of modern thought. You see, I've had a liberal education. I can do everything my brothers do; and do it rather better, I fancy. I am an athlete and a college graduate, with a wide, universal outlook. My point of view is free from narrow influences, and quite outside of the home boundaries."

"So I should have imagined by your dress and manner," the Steel-Engraving Lady said, under her breath.

"I am prepared to enter a profession," the visitor announced. "I believe thoroughly in every woman's having a distinct vocation."

The Steel-Engraving Lady gasped. "Doesn't a woman's home furnish her ample employment and occupation?"

"Undoubtedly it keeps her busy," the other said; "but what is she *accomplishing*, shut in, walled up from the world's work and interests? In my profession I shall be brought in contact with universal problems."

"A public character! Perhaps you're going on the stage?"

"Oh no. I'm to become a lawyer."

"Perhaps your home is not a happy one?" the Steel-Engraving Lady said, with much perplexity.

"Indeed it is, but I have little time to stay there."

"Have you no parents?"

"Parents? Why, to be sure; but when a woman is capable of a career, she can't sit down at home just to amuse her parents. Each woman owes a duty to herself, to make the most of her Heaven-given talents. Why, I've a theory for the entire reorganization of our faulty public school system."

"And does it touch upon the influence at home, which is felt in the nursery as well as in the drawing-room?"

"It is outside of all minor considerations," the Gibson Girl went on. "I think we women should do our utmost to purify the world of politics. Could I be content to sit down at home, and be a toy and a mere ornament,"—here she glanced scornfully at her companion,—"when the great public needs my individual aid?"

"And can no woman serve the public at home?" the other said gently. Her voice was very sweet and low. "I have been educated to think that our best service was"—

"To stand and wait," the Gibson Girl broke in. "Ah, but we all know better nowadays. You see the motto 'Heaven helps her who helps herself' suits the 'new woman.' We're not a shy, retiring, uncomplaining generation. We're up to date and up to snuff, and every one of us is self-supporting."

"Dear me!" the Steel-Engraving Lady sighed. "I never realized I had aught to complain of; and why should woman not be *ornamental* as well as useful? Beauty of person and manner and spirit is surely worthy of our attainment."

"It was all well enough in your day, but this is a utilitarian age. We cannot sit down to be admired; we must be 'up and doing;' we must leave 'footprints on the sands of time.'"

The Steel-Engraving Lady glanced speculatively at her companion's shoes. "Ah, but such great big footprints!" she gasped; "they make me shudder. And do your brothers approve of having you so clever that you compete with them in everything, and are there business places enough for you and them?"

"We don't require their approval. Man has been catered to for ages past, while woman was a patient, subservient slave. To-day she assumes her rightful place, and man accepts the lot assigned him. And as for business chances, if there is but one place, and I am smarter than my brother, why, it is fair that I should take it, and let him go without. But tell me," the Gibson Girl said condescendingly, "what did your so-called education consist of?"

"The theory of my education is utterly opposed to yours, I fear," the other answered. "Mine was designed to fit me for my home; yours is calculated to unfit you for yours. You are equipped for contact with the outside world, for competition with your brothers in business; my training merely taught me to make my brother's home a place which he should find a source of pleasure and inspiration. I was taught grace of motion, drilled in a school of manners, made to enter a room properly, and told how to sit gracefully, to modulate my voice, to preside at the table with fitting dignity. In place of your higher education, I had my music and languages and my embroidery frame. I was persuaded there was no worthier ambition than to bring life and joy and beauty into a household, no duty higher than that I owed my parents. Your public aspirations, your independent views, your discontent, are something I cannot understand."

The Steel-Engraving Lady rose from her chair with grace and dignity; she crossed the room, and paused a moment on the threshold, where she bowed with the air of a princess who would dismiss her courtiers; then she was gone.

"She surely is an extinct type!" the Gibson Girl exclaimed. "I realize now what higher education has done toward freeing woman from chains of prejudice. I must be off. I'm due at the golf links at three-fifteen."

When the sun set, the Steel-Engraving Lady might have been seen again seated beside the open casement. Her taper fingers lightly touched the strings of her guitar as she hummed a low lullaby. Once more she heard a step upon the stair, and once again the color mantled her damask cheek, and as she breathed the word "Reginald" a tall and ardent figure came swiftly toward her. He dropped upon one knee, as if to pay due homage to his fair one, and, raising her white hand to his lips, whispered, "My queen, my lady love."

And at this moment the Gibson Girl was seated upon a fence, swinging her heavy boots, while an athletic youth beside her busied himself with filling a corn-cob pipe.

"I say, Joe," he said, with friendly accent, "just you hop down and stand in front of me to keep the wind off, while I light this pipe."

And the sun dropped behind the woods, and the pink afterglow illumined the same old world that it had beautified for countless ages.

Its pink light fell upon the Steel-Engraving Lady as she played gently on her guitar and sang a quaint old ballad, while her fond lover held to his lips the rose that had been twined in her dark locks.

The sunset's glow lighted the Gibson Girl upon her homeward path as she strode on beside the athletic youth, carrying her golf clubs, while he puffed his corn-cob pipe. They stopped at a turn in the road, and he touched his cap, remarking: "I guess I'll leave you here, as I am late to dinner. I'll try to be out at the links to-morrow; but if I don't show up, you'll know I've had a chance to join that hunting trip. Ta-ta!"

And the night breeze sprang up, and murmured: "Hail the new woman,—behold she comes apace! WOMAN, ONCE MAN'S SUPERIOR, NOW HIS EQUAL!"

<u>DOCUMENT</u>

W. E. B. DuBois's
New Year's Resolutions

An African-American intellectual and civil rights advocate, W. E. B. DuBois was born in Great Barrington, Massachusetts. He received a classical, college preparatory education in the local public schools, and in 1886, he enrolled at Fisk University. After two years at Fisk, he transferred to Harvard where he eventually earned a Ph.D. In 1910, he left his teaching position at Atlanta University and became the editor of The Crisis, *the monthly magazine of the NAACP, which served as a platform for him to expose the racism that made black men and women second-class citizens and inhibited their ability to establish their own definitions of femininity and masculinity.*

In his New Year's resolutions, DuBois says that he is determined to "play the man" in the coming year. What did he mean by that? Why does he choose these particular behavior patterns as indications of having achieved manhood?

I AM RESOLVED

I am resolved in this New Year to play the man—to stand straight, look the world squarely in the eye, and walk to my work with no shuffle or slouch.

I am resolved to be satisfied with no treatment which ignores my manhood and my right to be counted as one among men.

I am resolved to be quiet and law abiding, but to refuse to cringe in body or in soul, to resent deliberate insult, and to assert my just rights in the face of wanton aggression.

I am resolved to defend and assert the absolute equality of the Negro race with any and all other human races and its divine right to equal and just treatment.

I am resolved to be ready at all times and in all places to bear witness with pen, voice, money and deed against the horrible crime of lynching, the shame of "Jim Crow" legislation, the injustice of all color discrimination, the wrong of disfranchisement for race or sex, the iniquity of war under any circumstances and the deep damnation of present methods of distributing the world's work and wealth.

I am resolved to defend the poor and the weak of every race and hue, and especially to guard my mother, my wife, my daughter and all my darker sisters from the insults and aggressions of white men and black, with the last strength of my body and the last suffering of my soul.

For all these things, *I am resolved* unflinchingly to stand, and if this resolve cost me pain, poverty, slander and even life itself, I will remember the Word of the Prophet, how he sang:

> *"Though Love repine and Reason chafe,*
> *There came a Voice, without reply,*
> *'Tis man's Perdition to be safe*
> *When for the Truth he ought to die!"*

Source: W. E. B. DuBois, "I Am Resolved," *The Crisis,* 3 (Jan. 1912), 113.

ARTICLE

In Time of War [The Construction of American Manhood in WWI]

Peter G. Filene

World War I began in Europe in 1914 when Britain, France, and Russia declared war on Germany and Austria-Hungary. The United States was able to maintain its neutrality until 1917. But in April of that year, President Woodrow Wilson asked Congress to declare war. This war, he assured his countrymen, would be the "war to end all wars." America, he declared, was fighting to "Save the World for Democracy." The young men who volunteered to fight in Europe were often as idealistic as their President. But many of them were totally unprepared to deal with the reality of war. By 1917 when they arrived on the front, combat had degenerated into trench warfare. Soldiers found that they were as likely to spend their time helplessly trying to dodge rockets and missiles as they hid in their ditches as they were to engage the enemy in hand-to-hand combat. War was much more impersonal than they expected, and they had trouble incorporating that reality into their idea of what it meant to be a man.

According to this excerpt from Peter Filene's Him/Her/Self: Gender and Identities in Modern America, *how did fighting in World War I influence the construction of masculinity in early twentieth-century America? What anxieties about what constituted manliness did it expose?*

"You are going into a big thing: a big war: a big army: standing for a big idea," wrote "Dad" to "Tom" in a letter published as an editorial by the *Ladies' Home Journal*. "But don't forget that the biggest thing about a principle or a battle or an army is a man! And the biggest thing that a war can do is to bring out that man. That's really what you and the other chaps have gone over for: to demonstrate the right kind of manhood, for it is that which weighs in a fight and wins it."

When Congress declared war on Germany in April 1917, the American public responded with almost ferocious zeal. The nation launched a campaign to destroy those Huns who had mutilated Belgian women and children and who sought to crush freedom under their iron heels. It was a venture in which, as President Wilson had so nobly declared and a million publicists repeated, the United States wanted nothing for itself except the rights and happiness of people around the world—a peace without victory. It was a crusade.

This disinterested idealism was sincere. But middle-class American men also wanted some satisfaction for themselves from the war. Basically they envisioned the battlefield as a proving ground where they could enact and repossess the manliness that modern American society had baffled. Beneath the tidal wave of war propaganda issued by the government's Committee on Public Information and its imitators, the theme of manliness protruded again and again during 1917–18.

Source: Peter G. Filene, *Him/Her/Self: Gender Identities in Modern America,* pp. 102–111. Copyright © 1986. Reprinted by permission of the Johns Hopkins Press. Notes omitted.

Nowhere was this more graphic than in the hundreds of enlistment posters, such as the one depicting a gleeful sailor riding a torpedo into the ocean like a cowboy.

Americans entered the Great War to achieve not simply political principles, but psychological reassurance as well. And not simply for the doughboys in actual battle, but also for the citizens on the home front. Indeed, the incessant propaganda that filled newspapers, magazines, auditoriums, and street corners focused primarily on those who were not in uniform. The trenches represented only one part of the war's meaning; the rest of it took place among civilians. As Americans translated the ideals of progressivism to the international sphere, they hoped thereby to restore within the United States their Victorian values of pure, strenuous manhood. . . . But instead, there were rampant materialism, licentious sexuality, and stifled individual opportunity. Now men turned to real war for the virtues that they had failed to find in symbolic substitutes.

The most immediate and tangible consequence of belligerence was rationing. Led by Herbert Hoover's Food Administration, civic leaders and publicists from New York to Keokuk to Seattle implored families to eat meatless meals, to walk instead of driving automobiles, and to patch their pants instead of buying new ones. "Four-minute men" exhorted theater audiences and sidewalk crowds to serve the national cause by buying Liberty Bonds. The rich were urged to volunteer their energy in government jobs and Red Cross work, while giving up servants and limousines. Many people welcomed self-denial. Thrift would be "a fine experience for us," they announced. It would save the American soul from "the leprosy of materialism," end the mad "extravagance and luxury" that had contaminated civilization. In short, according to these writers, the economic sacrifices would produce purification after an era of materialism.

The war was more than an economic emergency; for males over the age of seventeen, it became a matter of sacrificing job or education, an arm, a leg, perhaps life itself. But that

was, for many commentators, precisely its value. Through the crucible of combat a boy would emerge a man. Even as improbable a boy as Neil Leighton, the hero of a *Saturday Evening Post* story entitled "The Feminine Touch." He was the son of an actor, who had died soon after Leighton's birth, and a Fifth Avenue milliner. As a teenager, he worked in his mother's establishment, developed a taste for opera and ballet, and was teased by girls for being a sissy. Finally, he enlisted to fight in France, in order to "show them the sort of man I am!" Ironically, however, he found himself stationed, not as a doughboy in the trenches, but as an assistant in a French doctor's office. In fact, he agreed to take a woman's role in a play being produced by the soldiers. So far so bad for Leighton. But suddenly the Germans invaded during a rehearsal. Disguised in his female costume, Leighton managed to shoot three enemy soldiers with a pistol concealed in a muff. He then proceeded to save the town by discovering the Germans' code for retreat (church bells to be rung three times). By the end of the story, he had won several medals and the love of a French girl, while enduring an arm wound with manly stoicism.

Almost all young boys suffered the anxiety of being considered sissies, and reluctantly or not, they got into fist fights to prove their masculinity. The world war provided a larger arena for the same proof. At least, this is how civilian observers liked to interpret it. To risk one's life for America signified more than patriotic idealism; it defined manly character. When the poet Joyce Kilmer died as he was reconnoitering on a battlefield, a mass-circulation magazine offered this eulogy: "Kilmer was young, only thirty-two, and the scholarly type of man. One did not think of him as a warrior. And yet from the time we entered the war he could think of but one thing—that he must, with his own hands, strike a blow at the Hun. He was a man!"

Manliness included more than physical courage. It included those moral qualities that Victorians had in mind when they spoke of "character." Whoever would save his soul must be willing to lose his life. The Great War became a "crusade" because Americans proclaimed enormous moral consequences for those who went off to fight. Consider Kelsey, the protagonist of a *Saturday Evening Post* story published in 1917. Throughout his life this ship's fireman had wanted only to drink, fight, and earn as much money as he could. If anyone talked about defending freedom and democracy against Germany, he sneered at such sentimentality. "Mr. Nietzsche would have approved of Kelsey," the author remarks. "To look out for number one was his gospel." When a German submarine torpedoed his ship during an Atlantic crossing, however, Kelsey went out of his way to save a woman and child whom he had met previously. On the lifeboat during the icy night he gave them his fur coat. Eventually they reached England, whereupon he donated to the Red Cross a gold-filled purse that he had stolen from a dead passenger. In the end, Kelsey gruffly signed up to fight against the Huns who were killing women, children, and freedom.

He had proved himself "a true man," the Victorians would have said, demonstrating not only strength, but honor as well. Like the heroes of countless wartime stories and essays and sermons, he had vindicated the ideal of manliness that the Beveridges, Roosevelts, Stimsons, and other patriarchs so earnestly espoused. For them the war represented a crusade—more precisely, a chivalric crusade, an adult version of what the Boy Scouts embodied in more artificial terms. And as more and more Americans went into uniform and into battle, as the casualties increased, these civilian commentators were convinced that their hopes were coming true. "The slouching, dissipated, impudent lout who seemed to typify young America has disappeared," a *Washington Post* editorialist announced in 1918. Service to the nation, he said, had molded a youth who was serious, active, courageous, "with the ideals of his country stamped upon his heart." When such men returned home, they would not be content with desk jobs or more education, those unmanly options that prewar America had offered. No, said the narrator in one novel of 1918, "there will be a new movement toward the ever-vanishing frontier, a setting westward in the search for wider ranges, for life in the open air."

Such was the meaning of the Great War as defined by observers at home, interpreting to the American public the bloody events across the ocean. But how did the soldiers themselves understand their experience? Did they see themselves as chivalric knights riding tanks or planes in the name of democracy and manhood? As one might expect, no single generalization holds true for more than 2 million men of diverse backgrounds and temperaments. For some, war was simply another job, one that they took with the same dispassionate attitudes that they had applied to their civilian jobs. Russell G. Pruden, for example, never once, throughout his wartime letters and diaries, betrayed any ideological interpretation or personal feeling beyond compassion and humor. Similarly, several doughboys recounted the ferocious battles of the Argonne without a trace of emotional flourish, merely depicting themselves and their fellows as working stoically to win or at least survive. For others, however, the experience of Woodrow Wilson's war aroused very vivid feelings. "Darling dear this is the most tiresome trip that I have ever taken or ever expect to take again," one soldier wrote en route to France. "Sophia if I could only get back to you and have some of your mothers [sic] regular meals you cannot realize how I would eat." But beyond disgust at sugarless porridge and tainted fish was the pain in his heart. "It seems as fate has dealt us an awful blow, and some times dear, the old tears are bound to come to my eyes, and if I wasn't a man I certainly would cry. If I look at your picture once darling, I look at it thousands of times."

While many never surmounted this sense of personal deprivation, others certainly did. "War is not a pink tea," Arthur Guy Empey conceded in his best-seller *Over the Top*, "but in a worthwhile cause like ours, mud, rats, cooties, shells, wounds, or death itself are far outweighed by the deep sense of satisfaction felt by the man who does his bit." It may have been cliché, but it was a sincere cliché. Some performed their "bit" modestly. "Mother you asked if I dreaded my trip across," Sergeant Thomas Cole wrote home while with the American Expeditionary Force (AEF), "and in ans. I shall say I did not. I feel about this thing as every other true American feels and that is; It is an honour to be here and to fight for such a country as we have." Some tended toward self-grandeur. A young army lieutenant declared in one letter: "You know, I think soldiering makes real men." Alan Seeger, the ill-fated poet, echoed this sentiment with his characteristically romantic flair. "Be sure that I shall play the part well," he wrote to his mother from France, "for I was never in better health nor felt my manhood more keenly."

However breezy or brassy the rhetoric, it expressed genuine emotions. After all, more than 25,000 American men—Empey and Seeger among them—enlisted in the Canadian, British, and French forces before 1917. Their zeal was authentic. Yet it alone does not explain the propelling motives. Which needs in them were seeking the "deep sense of satisfaction" that Empey mentioned? Again, any generalization is presumptuous. But perhaps the example of John Dos Passos is suggestive, in exaggerated form, of what prompted other young combatants.

In August of 1916, months before the United States entered the war, the twenty-year-old Dos Passos wrote to his friend Arthur McComb, "I am dying to get to Belgium & exhaust surplus energy." Almost a year later, still not having reached his destination, Dos Passos expressed the same frustrations, but now specifying their source.

> I think we are all of us a pretty milky lot,—don't you?—with our tea-table convictions and our radicalism that keeps so consistently within the bounds of decorum—Damn it, why couldn't one of us have refused to register [with the draft board] and gone to jail and made a general ass of himself? I should have had more hope for Harvard....
>
> And what are we fit for when they turn us out of Harvard? We're too intelligent to be suc-

cessful businessmen and we haven't the sand or the energy to be anything else.

> Until Widener is blown up and A. Lawrence Lowell assassinated and the Business School destroyed and its site sowed into salt—no good will come out of Cambridge.
>
> It's fortunate I'm going to France as I'll be able to work off my incendiary ideas.

By enlisting in the ambulance corps, Dos Passos finally found release for those "incendiary" feelings that burned so impatiently within him. Writing from a small village in Champagne after experiencing his first air attack, he announced to McComb, "I've not been so happy for months." But from what precisely did this happiness derive? From the violence surrounding him. The war's havoc fed the fire of his aesthetic romanticism. An entry in his notebook, dated August 1917, almost vibrates with passionate delight in the violence.

> But gosh I want to be able to express, later, all of this, all the tragedy and hideous excitement of it. I've seen so very little. I must experience more of it and more—the grey crooked fingers of the dead, the dark look of dirty mangled bodies, their groans and jottings in the ambulances, the vast tomtom of the guns, the ripping tear shells make when they explode, the song of shells outgoing like vast woodcocks—their contented whirr as they near their mark—the twang of fragments like a harp broken in the air and the rattle of stones and mud on your helmet....
>
> In myself I find the nervous reaction to be curious hankering after danger that takes hold of me. When one shell comes I want another, nearer, nearer, I constantly feel the need of the drunken excitement of a good bombardment—I want to throw the dice at every turn with the old roisterer Death ... and through it all I feel more alive than ever before—I have never lived yet.

Dos Passos had come closer than ever before to fulfilling his thwarted energies—and did so in literary rendition of suffering. Between the real violence and his imagery, he found resolution of those "incendiary ideas" that had driven him to France.

"I know these men will return finer, cleaner, straighter men," a Harvard alumnus wrote from a French battlefront. In the light of Dos Passos's attitudes, however, one wonders. Finer and cleaner? Perhaps only because purged of the furious energy that so many adolescents turned against the enemy and, in suicidal heroism, against themselves. For many, especially the fervent romantics like Dos Passos and Seeger, war meant the ultimate test of manliness—at the edge of death. Nothing short of that could satisfy them. "A night attack is a wonderful thing to see . . . ," wrote Charles Nordhoff. "Into the maelstrom of sprouting flames, hissing steel, shattering explosions, insignificant little creatures like you and me will presently run—offering, with sublime courage, their tender bodies to be burned and mangled."

For others, less compelled by the need for total self-definition, war meant physical action and adventure sanctioned in the name of patriotism. And for some, it gave the opportunity to enact a more bluntly physical violence than the aesthetic college men could admit. "I do not mind saying," wrote the author of *Gunner Depew*, "that I was glad whenever I slipped my bayonet into a Turk, and more glad when I saw another one coming." And an infantryman wrote home about killing three Germans: "Why I just couldn't kill them dead enough it seemed like. Believe me it was some fun as well as exciting." Finally, there were those whose feelings were much more prosaic. A private, after being wounded at the Argonne and therefore withdrawn from action, remarked, "I was happy to be hit again, because life in the trenches, plugging through the mud and water up to the waist, sleeping in wet, damp dugouts is unspeakable." This same private would receive the Croix de Guerre for earlier bravery in an Argonne raiding party that had captured forty-one German machine guns and fifty-seven prisoners.

Whether any of these experiences produced "finer" and "cleaner" men is dubious. Yet Americans insisted vehemently that the war purified the young men who took part. War produced not simply stronger, more courageous, more honorable men, but purer men. Indeed, many Americans made it an extension of the purity crusade that the Victorian reformers had been directing for half a century against vice. This was the last dimension of manliness, which Americans hoped to vindicate by means of the war.

And they thought that they had. According to one reporter in 1918, "Our fighting force today is not only the cleanest body of fighting men the world has ever seen, but the cleanest group of young men ever brought together outside a monastery." Others, particularly those working in the social-hygiene movement, made the same boast. Venereal disease among the armed forces, they claimed, had been virtually eradicated. They credited two factors for this achievement. First of all, the American Social Hygiene Association had persuaded the secretary of war to create a Commission on Training Camp Activities that would suppress vice in military camp areas. With the cooperation of other government agencies as well as groups like the Young Mens' Christian Association, the War Department undertook a $4 million campaign to keep prostitutes (and alcohol) away from the recruits, to abolish red-light districts near the camps, to require soldiers to obtain medical examination if they had sexual relations, and to disseminate information on venereal disease. "How much sweeter and cleaner would our home lives be," remarked one lieutenant, "if we were to live like these [army] boys do?"

But prohibition was not the whole reason for this uniformed purity. No, the soldiers themselves rejected sexual temptation; they were clean in body and mind. Or so the American public was told. Even when they came into contact with the proverbially promiscuous French women, these American men remained true to their principles and to their sweethearts back home, doing no more than to stroll with the *mademoiselles*. And again the civilian writers argued that the war itself sublimated the male passions. The hero of Willa Cather's novel *One of Ours*, for example, enlisted after suffering the humiliation of marriage to a woman of stronger will than his own. Thereafter he never again turned to women for erotic satisfaction. Instead, he reasserted his masculinity by embracing battle and making love to war.

That civilians, especially the social hygienists, proclaimed the purity of the chivalric doughboys is not surprising. After decades of service in moral-reform movements, they wanted and needed to believe that Wilson's war was, in all its dimensions, a crusade—a culmination to their tireless efforts and energies. More surprising is the fact that so many soldiers also insisted on this theme. A group of engineers and medical students at the University of Minnesota, for example, drafted a resolution as they enlisted in April 1917: "Aware of the temptations incident to camp life and the moral and social wreckage involved, we covenant together, as college men, to live the clean life and to seek to establish the American uniform as a symbol and guarantee of real manhood." During the next eighteen months, soldiers at the front wrote home with assurances that they had not succumbed to sexual temptation.

What had happened to the notion and practice of "sowing wild oats"? Had the Great War abruptly destroyed an attitude that decades of earnest Victorian moralizing and purity movements had failed to destroy? Hardly. Whatever people believed or professed to believe, the American men who fought during the First World War were not essentially different from those in other wars. According to the reminiscences of a madam operating a New Orleans whorehouse, the war had not at all inspired men to find "true manhood," courageous and celibate. "Every man and boy wanted to have one last fling of screwing," she declared, "before the real war got him. Every farm boy wanted to have one big fuck in a real house before he went off and maybe was killed. . . . The idea of war and

dying makes a man raunchy. . . . I dreamed one night the whole city was sinking into a lake of sperm." From a training camp in Plattsburgh, New York, meanwhile, one soldier estimated that most of his comrades were "unchaste" and that one-half had contracted venereal disease. More precisely, the surgeon general of the army reported a venereal disease rate of 114 per thousand enlisted men in 1917, rising a year later to 150 (as compared to 81 per thousand in 1898).

The vast majority of these patients had contracted the disease in civilian life, before they enlisted. Conditions were better after the men came under army supervision. Not much better, though, and certainly far from the life of a monastery. Strenuous efforts by military officials in France—including prohibitive regulations, propaganda, and medical treatment—kept the loss of manpower among the AEF to a lower rate than in any previous war. Of approximately 2 million fighting men, an average of 18,000 were out of action each day because of venereal disease (as compared to an average of 606 men incapacitated during the Second World War). Nevertheless, 18,000 daily cases constituted a medical problem serious enough that, in mid-1918, the army created a venereal disease detention camp in France. The men of the AEF may indeed have been "cleaner" than previous armies, but they were not monks, either in body or, more important, in mind. "Wandering through dark streets," one lieutenant wrote in his diary. "Ever-present women. So mysterious and seductive in darkness. . . . A fellow's got to hang on to himself here. Not many do." According to one officer's study, 71 percent of the Americans stationed in France engaged in sexual relations.

Obviously the spokesmen of purity were deceived by their own hopes or propaganda. The Victorian crusade for chastity had not abruptly achieved victory in the war to end wars. Soldiers' bodies may have been less contaminated, but not their minds. Nor had the Victorian male dilemma of ambivalence regarding continence and wild oats been resolved; if anything, it had intensified as the gap between public allegations and actual behavior widened still further. The prewar dilemma of manliness persisted—but not entirely. Some of its features had changed because of the war. For one thing, men had at last found, it seemed, an opportunity for the strenuous life that the corporate economy and the vanishing frontier had been steadily stifling. To this extent they could win manliness, even if some of them in the process failed to transcend brutality and sexual vice. Second, the prevailing myth portrayed the warriors as chivalric knights (while the public at home forsook materialism in a patriotic campaign of thrift). Whatever the facts of how the soldiers were behaving, people did not know those facts or refused to believe them. Until the Armistice and even beyond, the American public believed that the crusade for worldwide democracy was also purifying their soldiers and themselves. And many of the doughboys, too, insisted romantically on this interpretation. In war Americans found, for the time being, peace of mind about their national morality, in large part because men were manly again.

ARTICLE

The Appetite as Voice [Women, the Body, and Feminine Identity at the Turn of the Century]

Joan Jacobs Brumberg

At the turn of the century, women were as concerned about their bodies as men. But while their brothers engaged in activities designed to build up their muscles, many young women in the middle and upper classes agonized over their weight. A number of cultural factors contributed to their concern. By 1900 doctors and insurance companies were collaborating to increase public awareness about the hazards of being overweight. Home economists and nutritionists were trying to turn food selection and preparation into a science. And in the second decade of the twentieth century, fashion designers began showing dresses with slim and straight lines. In this excerpt from Fasting Girls: The Emergence of Anorexia Nervosa as a Modern Disease, *Joan Jacobs Brumberg discusses some of the ways that eating habits and the construction of femininity were related.*

Source: Joan Jacobs Brumberg, *Fasting Girls: The Emergence of Anorexia Nervosa as a Modern Disease,* Pp. 171–180, 182, 185–188. Copyright © 1988 by Joan Jacobs Brumberg. Reprinted by permission of George Borchardt, Inc. Notes omitted.

How did ideas about femininity dating back to the Victorian period contribute to concern about body weight at the turn of the century? What role did social class play in attitudes toward food and its relationship to femininity?

In the late nineteenth century, adolescent girls demonstrated an array of health problems that involved eating and appetite disturbances. . . . In effect, there was a wide spectrum of "picky eating" and food refusal, ranging from the normative to the pathological. Anorexia nervosa was the extreme—but it was not altogether alien, given the range of behaviors that doctors saw in adolescent female patients. . . .

The health of young women was definitely influenced by a general female fashion for sickness and debility. The sickly wives and daughters of the bourgeoisie provided the medical profession with a ready clientele. In Victorian society unhappy women (and men) had to employ physical complaints in order to be permitted to take on the privileged "sick role." Because the most prevalent diseases in this period were those that involved "wasting," it is no wonder that becoming thin, through noneating, became a focal symptom. Wasting was in style.

Among women, invalidism and scanty eating commonly accompanied each other. . . .

Adolescent girls simply followed and imitated the behavioral styles of adult women. As a consequence, mothers were urged to take action against their daughters' fondness for wasting and debility. In *Eve's Daughters: or, Common Sense for Maid, Wife, and Mother,* Marion Harland told parents:

Show no charity to the faded frippery of sentiment that prates over romantic sickliness. Inculcate a fine scorn for the desire to exchange her present excellent health for the estate of the pale, drooping, human-flower damsel; the taste that covets the "fascination" of lingering consumption; the "sensation" of early decease induced by the rupture of a blood-vessel over a laced handkerchief held firmly to her lily mouth by agonized parent or distracted lover. All this is bathos and vulgarity . . . Bid her leave such

balderdash to the pretender to ladyhood, the low-minded *parvenu,* who, because foibles are more readily imitated than virtues, and tricks than graces, copies the mistakes of her superiors in breeding and sense, and is persuaded that she has learned "how to do it."

Harland, an American, called the "cultivation of fragility" a "national curse."

Of the conditions that affected girls most frequently, dyspepsia and chlorosis both incorporated peculiar eating and both could be confused with anorexia nervosa. Dyspepsia, a form of chronic indigestion with discomfort after eating, was widespread in middle-class adults and in their daughters. Physicians saw the adolescent dyspeptic frequently; advice writers suggested how she should be managed at home; health reformers used her existence to argue for changes in the American diet; and even novelists considered her enough of a fixture on the domestic scene to include her in their portraits of social life. The dyspeptic had no particular organic problem; her stomach was simply so sensitive that it precluded normal eating. Whereas dyspeptic women could be extremely thin, some, according to doctors' reports, were corpulent. Yet dyspepsia sometimes looked much like anorexia nervosa. For example, a physician described his young dyspeptic patients as persons "who enter upon a strict regimen which they follow only too well. By auto-observation and auto-suggestion, by constantly noticing and classifying their foods, and rejecting all kinds that they think they cannot digest, they finally manage to live on an incredibly small amount."

Chlorosis, a form of anemia named for the greenish tinge that allegedly marked the skin of the patient, was the characteristic malady of the Victorian adolescent girl. Although chlorosis was never precisely defined and differentiated, it was unequivocally regarded as a disease of girlhood rather than boyhood. Its symptoms included lack of energy, shortness of breath, dyspepsia, headaches, and capricious or scanty appetite; sometimes the menses stopped. Chlorotic girls tended to lose some weight as a result of poor eating and aversion to specific foods, particularly meat. (Today iron-deficiency anemia corresponds to the older diagnosis of chlorosis.)

Doctors of the Victorian era fostered the notion that all adolescent girls were potentially chlorotic: "Every girl passes as it were through the outer court of chlorosis in her progress from youth to maturity . . . Perhaps, no girl escapes it altogether." In contrast to anorexia nervosa, treatment for this popular disease was relatively easy: large doses of iron salts and a period of rest at home. As a result, parents were not afraid of chlorosis. In fact, it was accepted as a normal part of adolescent development. Many doctors and families were also fond of tonics to stimulate the appetite, restore the blush to the cheek, and cure latent consumption. "Young Girls Fading Away" was the headline of a well-known advertisement for Dr. William's Pink Pills for Pale People, a medicine aimed at the chlorotic market. A vast amount of patent medicine was sold to families that assumed chlorosis in an adolescent whenever her energy, spirits, or appetite waned. . . .

Taken together, these conditions suggest that young women presented unusual eating and diminished appetite more often than any other group in the population. Apparently, it was relatively normal for a Victorian girl to develop poor appetite and skip her meals, "affect daintiness" and eat only sweets, or express strong food preferences and dislikes. A popular women's magazine told its readership that in adolescence "digestive problems are common, the appetite is fickle, and evidences of poor nourishment abound." Between 1850 and 1900 the most frequent warning issued to parents of girls had to do with forestalling the development of idiosyncracies, irregularities, or strange whims of appetite because these were precursors of disease as well as signs of questionable moral character.

Ideas about female physiology and sexual development underlay the physician's expectations and his clinical treatment. Doctors believed that women were prone to gastric disorders because of the superior sensitivity of the female digestive system. Using the machine metaphor that was popular in describing bodily functions, they likened a man's stomach to a quartz-crushing machine that required coarse, solid food. By contrast, the mechanisms of a woman's stomach could be ruined if fed the same materials. The female digestive apparatus required foods that were soft, light, and liquid. (Dyspepsia in women could result from the choice of inappropriate foods that required considerable chewing and digestion.)

To the physician's mind, a young woman caught up in the process of sexual maturation was subject to vagaries of appetite and peculiar cravings. "The rapid expansion of the passions and the mind often renders the tastes and appetite capricious," wrote a midcentury physician. Therefore, even normal sexual development had the potential to create a disequilibrium that could lead to irregular eating such as the kind reported in dyspepsia and chlorosis. But physicians reported on eating behavior that was far more bizarre. In fact, the adolescent female with "morbid cravings" was a stock figure in the medical and advice literature of the Victorian period. Stories circulated of "craving damsels" who were "trash-eaters, oatmeal-chewers, pipe-chompers, chalk-lickers, wax-nibblers, coal-scratchers, wall-peelers, and gravel-diggers." The clinical literature also provided a list of "foods" that some adolescent girls allegedly craved: chalk, cinders, magnesia, slate pencils, plaster, charcoal, earth, spiders, and bugs. Modern medicine associates iron-deficiency anemia with eating nonnutritive items, such as pica. For the Victorian physician, nonnutritive eating constituted proof of the fact that the adolescent girl was essentially out of control and that the process of sexual maturation could generate voracious and dangerous appetites.

In this context physicians asserted that even normal adolescent girls had a penchant for highly flavored and stimulating foods. A reputable Baltimore physician, for example, described three girlfriends who constantly carried with them boxes of pepper and salt, taking the condiments as if they were snuff. The story was meant to imply that the girls were slaves of their bodily appetites. Throughout the medical and advice literature an active appetite or an appetite for particular foods was used as a trope for dangerous sexuality. Mary Wood-Allen warned young readers that the girl who masturbated "will manifest an unnatural appetite, sometime desiring mustard, pepper, vinegar and spices, cloves, clay, salt, chalk, charcoal, etc."

Because appetite was regarded as a barometer of sexuality, both mothers and daughters were concerned about its expression and its control. It was incumbent upon the mother to train the appetite of the daughter so that it represented only the highest moral and aesthetic sensibilities. A good mother was expected to manage this situation before it escalated into a medical or social problem. . . . Mothers were expected to educate, if not tame, their adolescent daughter's propensity for "sweetmeats, bonbons, and summer drinks" as well as for "stimulating foods such as black pepper and vinegar pickle." "Inflammatory foods" such as condiments and acids, thought to be favored by the tumultuous female adolescent, were strictly prohibited by judicious mothers. Adolescent girls were expressly cautioned against coffee, tea, and chocolate; salted meats and spices; warm bread and pastry; confectionery; nuts and raisins; and, of course, alcohol. These sorts of foods stimulated the sensual rather than the moral nature of the girl.

No food (other than alcohol) caused Victorian women and girls greater moral anxiety than meat. The flesh of animals was considered a heat-producing food that stimulated production of blood and fat as well as passion. Doctors and patients shared a common conception of meat as a food that stimulated sexual development and activity. For example, Lucien Warner, a popular medical writer, suggested that meat eating in adolescence could actually accelerate the development of the breasts and other sex characteristics; at the same time, a restriction on the carnivorous aspects of the diet could moderate premature or rampant sexuality as well as overabundant menstrual flow. "If there is any tendency to precocity in menstruation, or if the system is very robust and plethoric, the supply of meat should be quite limited. If, on the other hand, the girl is of sluggish temperament and the menses are tardy in appearance, the supply of meat should be especially generous." Meat eating in excess was linked to adolescent insanity and to nymphomania. A stimulative diet of meat and condiments was recommended only for those girls whose development of the passions seemed, somehow, "deficient."

By all reports adolescent girls ate very little meat, a practice that certainly contributed to chlorosis or iron-deficiency anemia. In fact, many openly disdained meat without being necessarily committed to the ideological principles of the health reformers who espoused vegetarianism. . . .

When it became necessary to eat meat (say, if prescribed by a doctor), it was an event worthy of note. For many, meat eating was endured for its healing qualities but despised as a moral and aesthetic act. For example, eighteen-year-old Nellie Browne wrote to tell her mother that a delicate classmate [Laura] had, like her own sister Alice, been forced to change her eating habits:

> I am very sorry to hear Alice has been so sick. Tell her she must eat meat if she wishes to get well. Laura eats meat *three* times a day.—She says she cannot go without it.—If Laura *can* eat *meat, I am sure Alice can*. If Laura needs it *three* times a day, Alice needs it *six*. [Italics in original.]

After acknowledging the "common distaste for meat" among his adolescent patients, Clifford Allbutt wrote, "Girls will say the entry of a dish of hot meat into the room makes them feel sick."

The repugnance for fatty animal flesh among Victorian adolescents ultimately had a larger cultural significance. Meat avoidance was tied to cultural notions of sexuality and decorum as well as to medical ideas about the digestive delicacy of the female stomach. Carnality at table was avoided by many who made sexual purity an axiom. Proper women, especially sexually maturing girls, adopted this orientation with the result that meat became taboo. . . . In this milieu food was obviously more than a source of nutrition or a means of curbing hunger; it was an integral part of individual identity. For women in particular, how one ate spoke to issues of basic character.

In Victorian society food and femininity were linked in such a way as to promote restrictive eating among privileged adolescent women. Bourgeois society generated anxieties about food and eating—especially among women. Where food was plentiful and domesticity venerated, eating became a highly charged emotional and social undertaking. Displays of appetite were particularly difficult for young women who understood appetite to be both a sign of sexuality and an indication of lack of self-restraint. Eating was important because food was an analogue of the self. Food choice was a form of self-expression, made according to cultural and social ideas as well as physiological requirements. . . .

Female discomfort with food, as well as with the act of eating, was a pervasive subtext of Victorian popular culture. The naturalness of eating was especially problematic among upwardly mobile, middle-class women who were preoccupied with establishing their own good taste. Food and eating presented obvious difficulties because they implied digestion and defecation, as well as sexuality. A doctor explained that one of his anorexic patients "refused to eat for fear that, during her digestion, her face should grow red and appear less pleasant in the eyes of a professor whose lectures she attended after her meals." A woman who ate inevitably had to urinate and move her bowels. Concern about these bodily indelicacies explains why constipation was incorporated into the ideal of Victorian femininity. . . .

Some women "boasted that the calls of Nature upon them averaged but one or two demands per week."

Food and eating were connected to other unpleasantries that reflected the self-identity of middle-class women. Many women, for good reason, connected food with work and drudgery. Food preparation was a time-consuming and exhausting job in the middle-class household, where families no longer ate from a common soup pot. Instead, meals were served as individual dishes in a sequence of courses. Women of real means and position were able to remove themselves from food preparation almost entirely by turning over the arduous daily work to cooks, bakers, scullery and serving maids, and butlers. Middle-class women, however, could not achieve the same distance from food.

Advice books admonished women "not to be ashamed of the kitchen," but many still sought to separate themselves from both food and the working-class women they hired to do the preparation and cooking. A few women felt the need to make alienation from food a centerpiece of their identity. A young "lady teacher," for example, "regard[ed] it as unbecoming her position to know anything about dinner before the hour for eating arrived . . . [She was] ashamed of domestic work, and graduate[d] her pupils with a similar sense of false propriety." Similarly, in the 1880s in Rochester, New York, a schoolgirl was chastised by her aunt for describing (with relish) in her diary the foods she had eaten during the preceding two weeks.

Food was to be feared because it was connected to gluttony and to physical ugliness. In advice books such as the 1875 *Health Fragments; or, Steps toward a True Life* women were cautioned to be careful about what and how much they ate. Authors George and Susan Everett enjoined: "Coarse, gross, and gluttonous habits of life degrade the physical appearance. You will rarely be disappointed in supposing that a lucid, self-respectful lady is very careful of the food which forms her body and tints her cheeks." Sarah Josepha Hale, the influential editor of *Godey's Lady's Book* and an arbiter of American domestic manners, warned women that it was always vulgar to load the plate.

Careful, abstemious eating was presented as insurance against ugliness and loss of love. Girls in particular were told: "Keep a great watch over your appetite. Don't always take the nicest things you see, but be frugal and plain in your tastes." Young women were told directly that "gross eaters" not only developed thick skin but had prominent blemishes and broken blood vessels on the nose. Gluttony also robbed the eyes of their intensity and caused the lips to thicken, crack, and lose their red color. "The glutton's mouth may remind us of cod-fish—never of kisses." A woman with a rosebud mouth was expected to have an "ethereal appetite." . . .

But Victorian women avoided connections to food for a number of other reasons. The woman who put soul over body was the ideal of Victorian femininity. The genteel woman responded not to the lower senses of taste and smell but to the highest senses—sight and hearing—which were used for moral and aesthetic purposes. One of the most convincing demonstrations of a spiritual orientation was a thin body—that is, a physique that symbolized rejection of all carnal appetites. To be hungry, in any sense, was a social faux pas. Denial became a form of moral certitude and refusal of attractive foods a means for advancing in the moral hierarchy.

Appetite, then, was a barometer of a woman's moral state. Control of eating was eminently desirable, if not necessary. Where control was lacking, young women were subject to derision. "The girl who openly enjoys bread-and-butter, milk, beefsteak and potatoes, and thrives thereby, is the object of many a covert sneer, or even overt jest, even in these sensible days and among sensible people." . . .

By the last decades of the nineteenth century, a thin body symbolized more than just sublimity of mind and purity of soul. Slimness in women was also a sign of social status. This phenomenon, noted by Thorstein Veblen in *The Theory of the Leisure Class*, her-

alded the demise of the traditional view that girth in a woman signaled prosperity in a man. Rather, the reverse was true: a thin, frail woman was a symbol of status and an object of beauty precisely because she was unfit for productive (or reproductive) work. Body image rather than body function became a paramount concern. According to Veblen, a thin woman signified the idle idyll of the leisured classes.

By the turn of the twentieth century, elite society already preferred its women thin and frail as a symbol of their social distance from the working classes. Consequently, women with social aspirations adopted the rule of slenderness and its related dicta about parsimonious appetite and delicate food. Through restrictive eating and restrictive clothing (that is, the corset), women changed their bodies in the name of gentility.

Women of means were the first to diet to constrain their appetite, and they began to do so before the sexual and fashion revolutions of the 1920s and the 1960s. In the 1890s Veblen noted that privileged women "[took] thought to alter their persons, so as to conform more nearly to the instructed taste of the time." In effect, Veblen documented the existence of a critical gender and class imperative born of social stratification. In bourgeois society it became incumbent upon women to control their appetite in order to encode their body with the correct social messages. Appetite became less of a biological drive and more of a social and emotional instrument.

Historical evidence suggests that many women managed their food and their appetite in response to the notion that sturdiness in women implied low status, a lack of gentility, and even vulgarity. Eating less rather than more became a preferred pattern for those who were status conscious. The pressure to be thin in order to appear genteel came from many quarters, including parents. "The mother, also, would look upon the sturdy frame and ruddy cheeks as tokens of vulgarity." Recall that Eva Williams, admitted to London Hospital in 1895 for treatment of anorexia nervosa, told friends that it was her mother who complained about her rotundity.

A controlled appetite and ill health were twin vehicles to elevated womanhood. Advice to parents about the care of adolescent daughters regularly included the observation that young women ate scantily because they denigrated health and fat for their declassé associations. In 1863 Hester Pendleton, an American writer on the role of heredity in human growth, lamented the fact that the natural development of young women was being affected by these popular ideas. "So perverted are the tastes of some persons," Pendleton wrote, "that delicacy of constitution is considered a badge of aristocracy, and daughters would feel themselves deprecated by too robust health." Health in this case meant a sturdy body, a problem for those who cultivated the fashion of refined femininity. One writer felt compelled to assert: "Bodily health is never pertinently termed 'rude.' It is not coarse to eat heartily, sleep well, and to feel the life throbbing joyously in heart and limb." Consequently, to have it insinuated or said that a woman was robust constituted an insult. . . .

In the effort to set themselves apart from plowboys and milkmaids—that is, working and rural youth—middle-class daughters chose to pursue a body configuration that was small, slim, and essentially decorative. By eating only tiny amounts of food, young women could disassociate themselves from sexuality and fecundity and they could achieve an unambiguous class identity. The thin body not only implied asexuality and an elevated social address, it was also an expression of intelligence, sensitivity, and morality. Through control of appetite Victorian girls found a way of expressing a complex of emotional, aesthetic, and class sensibilities.

By 1900 the imperative to be thin was pervasive, particularly among affluent female adolescents. Albutt wrote in 1905, "Many young women, as their frames develop, fall into a panic fear of obesity, and not only cut down on their food, but swallow vinegar and other alleged antidotes to fatness." The phenomenon of adolescent food restriction was so widespread that an advice writer told mothers, "It is a circumstance at once fortunate and notable if [your daughter] does not take the notion into her pulpy brain that a healthy appetite for good substantial food is 'not a bit nice,' 'quite too awfully vulgar you know.' "

Because food was a common resource in the middle-class household, it was available for manipulation. Middle-class girls, rather than boys, turned to food as a symbolic language, because the culture made an important connection between food and femininity and because girls' options for self-expression outside the family were limited by parental concern and social convention. In addition, doctors and parents expected adolescent girls to be finicky and restrictive about their food. Young women searching for an idiom in which to say things about themselves focused on food and the body. Some middle-class girls, then as now, became preoccupied with expressing an ideal of female perfection and moral superiority through denial of appetite. The popularity of food restriction or dieting, even among normal girls, suggests that in bourgeois society appetite was (and is) an important voice in the identity of a woman. In this context anorexia nervosa was born.

SUGGESTIONS FOR FURTHER READING

GAIL BEDERMAN, *Manliness & Civilization: A Cultural History of Gender and Race in the United States, 1880–1917* (Chicago: University of Chicago Press, 1995).

GAIL BEDERMAN, " 'The Women Have Had Charge of the Church Work Long Enough': The Men and Religion Forward Movement of 1911–1912 and the Masculinization of Middle-Class Protestantism," *American Quarterly*, 41 (Sept. 1989), 432–65.

SHIRLEY J. CARLSON, "Black Ideals of Womanhood in the Late Victorian Era," *Journal of Negro History*, LXXVII (Spring 1992), 61–73.

HOWARD P. CHUDACOFF, *The Age of the Bachelor: Creating an American Subculture* (Princeton, NJ: Princeton University Press, 1999).

SUSAN CURTIS, "The Son of Man and God the Father: The Social Gospel and Victorian Masculinity," in *Meanings for Manhood: Constructions of Masculinity in Victorian America*, ed. Mark C. Carnes and Clyde Griffin (Chicago: University of Chicago Press, 1990), 67–78.

ALLEN F. DAVIS, *American Heroine: The Life and Legend of Jane Addams* (New York: Oxford University Press, 1973).

JOE L. DUBBERT, *A Man's Place: Masculinity in Transition* (Englewood Cliffs, NJ: Prentice Hall, 1979).

JOE L. DUBBERT, "Progressivism and the Masculinity Crisis," *Psychoanalytic Review*, 61 (Fall 1974), 443–55.

PETER G. FILENE, *Him/Her/Self: Gender Identities in Modern America*, 3rd ed. (Baltimore, MD: The Johns Hopkins Press, 1998), 6–99.

WILLARD B. GATEWOOD, JR., *Black Americans and the White Man's Burden, 1898–1903* (Urbana: University of Illinois Press, 1975).

GLENDA ELIZABETH GILMORE, *Gender and Jim Crow: Women and the Politics of White Supremacy in North Carolina, 1896–1920* (Chapel Hill: University of North Carolina Press, 1996).

CLYDE GRIFFIN, "Reconstructing Masculinity from the Evangelical Revival to the Waning of Progressivism: A Speculative Thesis," in *Meanings for Manhood: Constructions of Masculinity in Victorian America*, ed. Mark C. Carnes and Clyde Griffin (Chicago: University of Chicago Press, 1990), 183–204.

JEFFREY P. HANTOVER, "The Boy Scouts and the Validation of Masculinity," *Journal of Social Issues*, 34 (1978), 184–95.

KRISTIN L. HOGANSON, *Fighting for American Manhood: How Gender Politics Provoked the Spanish-American and Phillipine-American Wars* (New Haven, CT: Yale University Press, 1998).

JOAN PATERSON KERR, ed., *A Bully Father: Theodore Roosevelt's Letters to His Children* (New York: Random House, 1995).

MICHAEL KIMMEL, *Manhood in America: A Cultural History* (New York: Free Press, 1996), 81–188.

AILEEN S. KRADITOR, *The Ideas of the Woman Suffrage Movement, 1890–1920* (New York: Anchor Books, 1971).

WILLIAM R. LEACH, "Transformations in a Culture of Consumption: Women and Department Stores, 1890–1925," *Journal of American History*, 71 (Sept. 1984), 319–42.

JAMES R. MCGOVERN, "The American Woman's Pre-World War I Freedom in Manners and Morals," *Journal of American History*, 55 (Sept. 1968), 315–33.

JAMES R. MCGOVERN, "David Graham Phillips and the Virility Impulse of the Progressives," *New England Quarterly*, 39 (Sept. 1966), 334–55.

MARGARET MARSH, "Suburban Men and Masculine Domesticity, 1870-1915," *American Quarterly*, 40 (June 1988), 165–86.

ELAINE TYLER MAY, "The Pressure to Provide: Class, Consumerism, and Divorce in Urban America, 1880–1920," *Journal of Social History*, 12 (Winter 1978), 180–93.

JOANNE J. MEYEROWITZ, *Women Adrift: Independent Wage Earners in Chicago, 1880–1930* (Chicago: University of Chicago Press, 1988).

EDMUND MORRIS, *The Rise of Theodore Roosevelt* (New York: Ballantine Books, 1979).

ROBYN MUNCY, "Trustbusting and White Manhood in America, 1898–1914," *American Studies*, 38 (Fall 1997), 21–42.

ROSALIND ROSENBERG, *Beyond Separate Spheres: Intellectual Roots of Modern Feminism* (New Haven, CT: Yale University Press, 1982).

E. Anthony Rotundo, *American Manhood: Transformations in Masculinity from the Revolution to the Modern Era* (New York: Basic Books, 1993), 247–83.

Cynthia Eagle Russett, *Sexual Science: The Victorian Construction of Womanhood* (Cambridge, MA: Harvard University Press, 1989).

Carroll Smith-Rosenberg, "The New Woman as Androgyne: Social Disorder and Gender Crisis, 1870–1936," in *Disorderly Conduct: Visions of Gender in Victorian America,* ed. Carroll Smith-Rosenberg (New York: Oxford University Press, 1985), 245–96.

Susan Strasser, *Never Done: A History of American Housework* (New York: Pantheon, 1982).

Arnaldo Testi, "The Gender of Reform Politics: Theodore Roosevelt and the Culture of Masculinity," *Journal of American History,* 81 (March 1995), 1509–33.

Kim Townsend, *Manhood at Harvard: William James and Others* (New York: W. W. Norton, 1996).

Marjorie Spruill Wheeler, *New Women of the New South: The Leaders of the Woman Suffrage Movement in the Southern States* (New York: Oxford University Press, 1993).

Chapter Ten

Masculinity in the Twentieth Century (1920–1975)

New Men in a New Age

In 1947 claiming the right to be treated like a man in places like Clarenden County, South Carolina, was a particularly complicated matter if the color of your skin was black. Black men had to negotiate their claim to manliness in at least two separate contexts. Achieving a sense of manhood was least problematical within their own black communities. There they could establish reputations for being loving and responsible husbands and fathers, hard workers, property owners, generous neighbors, and devout church members. But most black men did not live in isolated black communities. When they wanted to purchase land, they had to buy it from whites. When they needed to borrow money to start a business or build a home, they had to persuade white bankers to loan it to them. When they needed to buy household furnishings, food, and clothing, they often had to shop in stores owned and operated by white merchants. And when they

wanted to arrange for their children's education, they had to appeal to white superintendents of schools. The real challenge, then, was to establish and preserve a sense of manliness in their relationships with whites. This was not an easy task. In the 1940s segregation and discrimination were an integral part of life in the South, and the masculine identities of white men were tied to their ability to deprive black men of dignity and self-respect as well as the ability to support and defend their families.

Joseph Albert DeLaine was a black man. Known to his friends as J. A., he was very much aware of the connection between race and ideas about what constituted manliness. Born at the turn of the century, he grew up on a farm in Clarenden County, South Carolina. Even as a youth, he was determined to protect the members of his family. When a white boy shoved his sister off the sidewalk in the town of Manning, J. A. shoved him back. Charged with assault, J. A. was sentenced to twenty-five lashes by a white judge. Rather than submit to the humiliation and pain that a white-dominated legal system was determined to impose on him for defending his sister, he ran away to Atlanta. There he found employment and started his education. Eventually, he trained as a minister and earned a teaching certificate. By 1947, he was a married man with three children. He owned a small house on nine acres of land, paid his taxes, and taught school in the county where he had grown up. He also preached the gospel every Sunday at the AME Methodist Church. He sprinkled his sermons with social commentary including an admonition to the men in his congregation to hold their heads high, live honorably, work hard, preserve the peace, and persevere in the face of adversity. A man deeply respected by those who knew him, he became a driving force behind efforts to improve the quality of life for blacks in Clarendon County.

One of the problems he had to deal with was the issue of school buses. White children had access to them. Black children did not. Both white and black parents paid taxes to support the public education system. So Reverend DeLaine and a committee of two others asked the white superintendent of schools to provide school buses for black students. The answer was not long in coming, and it was no. DeLaine wrote to the state superintendent of schools in Columbia and the Attorney General of the United States. Neither was willing to intervene. Eventually he was able to persuade twenty of Clarendon County's black citizens to sign a petition which could be used as the basis for a law suit against the school district. The first name on the list was that of Harry Briggs, the son of a sharecropper and the father of five children, who worked as a gas station attendant in Summerton, South Carolina.

It is hard for those unfamiliar with life in the South at mid-century to appreciate the kind of courage it took for ordinary men like DeLaine and Briggs to do what they did. White reprisals were as predictable as they were swift. The owner of the gas station fired Briggs when he refused to remove his name from the petition. The manager of the motel where his wife worked as a maid told her he no longer needed her services. The bank cut off their credit. Then it was DeLaine's turn. He and his wife both lost their teaching jobs. He received threatening letters, was hauled into court on trumped up charges, and had to stand by helplessly watching while his house burned to the ground. Someone vandalized his church. When shots were fired at him in the middle of the night, he took his shotgun and fired back. He called the police, but they never arrived. Finally, he took his family and fled across the state line. After they left South Carolina, his church went up in flames, and he was charged with felonious assault for having tried to protect himself with a shotgun. Aged 57 and in poor health, he was now a fugitive.

But he had initiated a lawsuit to provide black children with better access to education. Others were determined to pursue that goal. So the case, known officially as *Briggs v. Elliott*, began winding its way through the courts. Combined with a discrimination case from Kansas called *Brown v. the Board of Education of Topeka*, as well as similar cases from Delaware and Virginia, it was eventually heard by the Supreme Court of the United States. When it was all over, school segregation was declared illegal. The year was 1954, and the struggle over implementing the court's decision was about to begin.

J. A. DeLaine paid a high price for proving his manhood. But prove it he did. He had asserted his manly rights and responsibilities as he understood them. He had stepped forward to demand that whites acknowledge his right as a parent to protect the interests of his children. He had insisted that they respect his rights as a property owner and tax payer to the benefits that were to be derived from citizenship. And he forced them to listen to his complaints and was willing to challenge their authority in an effort to receive fair and equitable treatment before the law. When he left South Carolina, he could hold his head high and take comfort in the knowledge that he had conducted himself honorably.

It is not entirely clear whether ideas about what it meant to be a man changed more rapidly or dramatically between the 1920s and the late 1970s than they had in earlier periods. But is seems apparent that men were quite self-consciously attuned to those changes.

Shifts in the definition of manliness were driven by a number of factors. World War I had been a disappointing experience for those whose participation involved the desire to prove their manhood. Fighting in trenches rather than on the open battlefield was an impersonal experience, and men returned from Europe often cynical about the degree to which war could be used as a proving ground for manliness. Behind pride in their efforts to preserve democracy there was the sneaky suspicion that military technology was as responsible for the defeat of the enemy as the courage of individual soldiers.

The prosperity of the 1920s allowed men to explore a variety of possibilities for defining manliness. It was a period in which ambition and acquisitiveness competed with the quest for heroes like Charles Lindbergh, whose exploits could assure men of lesser stature that it was still possible for courage and daring to lead to fame and fortune. After the stock market crash in 1929 however, the exuberance of the twenties gave way to the desperation of trying to cope with the worst economic depression in American history. Unemployment figures sky-rocketed. By 1933, one fourth of the work force was unemployed. During that decade manliness had less to do with expressing one's self and fulfilling one's aspirations than it did with scraping together enough money to pay the rent or desperately trying to hold onto the family farm. Once the United States declared war on Germany and Japan in 1941, men whose self-confidence had been severely damaged during the depression could now risk their lives fighting a "good" war or working in war industries to provide the armed forces with the means to defeat the enemy. During the economic boom that followed the war, men searched for a return to what they considered normalcy—a chance to work and reassume their position as heads of their households.

By the 1960s, an indeterminate number of young, middle-class, college men began rejecting the kind of gender prescriptions that their parents had brought them up to fulfill. Idealistic and full of enthusiasm for social and political reform, they questioned their fathers' definitions of success, rejected the crass commercialism of middle-class life, and tried to expose the hypocrisy of a generation who espoused the doctrine of equality but, in their view, did little or nothing to make it a reality.

Manliness was not a static concept between 1920 and 1975. Prosperity, depression, war, fear of communism, and social reform movements forced many men quite self-consciously to reassess what it meant to be manly. The process was an extremely difficult and painful one. Change did not come easily. But by the 70s, manliness was being defined much less rigidly than it had been before, and men could choose from a wide variety of behavior patterns in their efforts to establish for themselves what it meant to be a man.

WHITE MANHOOD AND THE TRANSITION FROM PROSPERITY TO DEPRESSION

The decade of the 1920s was a period of prosperity for many, but not all, Americans. While farmers and their wives struggled to make ends meet in the twenties, industrial and white-collar workers seemed to be enjoying increased opportunities to assure their positions as breadwinners and to assert their role as heads of their households. Wages were relatively high for skilled laborers. And while many white collar jobs might be boring and dead end, they were relatively secure. Consumerism was the name of the game. More and more wage-earning men with access to credit were able to provide housing for their families that included electricity and indoor plumbing. They had the means to clothe their wives and children in fashionable clothing.

And some even made enough money to buy automobiles.

In the pursuit of self-interest during the twenties, some men equated manliness with defiance of the law. Drinking had long been an important component of the definition of masculinity. In 1919, the ratification of the eighteenth amendment to the U. S. Constitution prohibited the manufacture, sale, or transportation of intoxicating liquors. While drinking was not illegal, access to liquor was cut off. So it was not long before violating prohibition laws became a part of defining manliness, particularly in urban areas where enforcement was weak if not non-existent. Speakeasies sprang up, smuggling proved profitable, and bootleggers abounded. With liquor available, men continued to drink. And gangsters like Al Capone, who made their money through the distribution of liquor and control of gambling and prostitution, became folk heroes in some quarters.

Membership in the second Ku Klux Klan, organized outside Atlanta in 1915, also encouraged men to break the law. Native-born, white men living in urban as well as rural areas attempted to prove their manhood by pledging to preserve white supremacy, to protect the honor and well being of white women, and to do what they could to minimize the social, economic, and political influence of Catholics, Jews, and immigrants. By establishing a siege mentality, Klan leaders promoted the idea that only through violence and intimidation could the power of white, native-born men be maintained.

Prosperity fed the individualism and pursuit of self-interest around which American men constructed their manliness in the 1920s. But when the stock market crashed in 1929, American men had to adjust their ideas about what it meant to be a man to the economic realities of the depression. Thousands of farmers, already besieged by poverty, lost their land to foreclosure and were forced to search for other ways to support their families. The depression had an equally devastating effect on stockholders, small business owners, and wage laborers.

Declaring bankruptcy, being fired from their jobs, and losing their savings when the banks closed were emasculating experiences for many men. It is true that some of them may have viewed their situation as a test of their competitiveness. But as it became clear that their lost jobs could not be replaced, many of the unemployed came to view their position as a shameful one and felt humiliated by their inability to support themselves and their families.

Because of circumstances beyond their control, unemployed men, who had never before had to ask for charity, faced the prospect of becoming dependent upon the benevolence of others. Those who could not pay their mortgages or the rent had to consider giving up their positions as heads of their families and moving in with their relatives. The only other alternative was to live on the streets or move their wives and children into a tar paper shack like the ones that were springing up in shantytowns on the outskirts of towns and cities.

In response to their loss of self-respect, some men committed suicide. Others turned to alcohol, now available because the prohibition amendment had been repealed. Unable to face the fact that they could no longer support their wives and children, still others deserted their families and became hobos roaming the country looking for work. Male unemployment made gender relationships more fragile. Some young couples had to postpone marriage or practice birth control so that wives did not bear children that neither could support. Some men literally hid away in their homes so that they would not have to admit to their friends and neighbors that they no longer had a job. With nothing else to do all day, they were available to help with childcare and housework. When they did so, they imposed themselves on what had traditionally been female space, thus disrupting the kind of separation of spheres that many of them had considered central to the construction of masculinity and femininity.

Some men, used to fulfilling the role of breadwinner, found it necessary to depend upon their wives to support them and their children. In cases where male and female roles were reversed, the relationship between husband and wife often deteriorated. Men expressed their frustration through violence directed at those they loved the most. Women nagged their husbands about their inability to support their family. And the divorce rate soared.

The Roosevelt administration did what it could to relieve the pressures that the depression placed on men. New Deal economic planners were particularly sensitive to the emasculating feeling of helplessness and inadequacy that plagued men who wanted to support their families and found it impossible to do so. By 1935 the government was using its considerable resources to reinforce the idea that manliness should be equated with bread winning by establishing federal work programs, designed both to relieve poverty and to redeem the manhood of the unemployed. Federal agencies like the Works Progress Administration and the Civilian Conservation Corps provided men with jobs building roads, bridges, dams, reservoirs, and public buildings. By subsidizing jobs, the New Deal provided the jobless with honest and respectable ways to support their families.

Living through the depression was a bewildering and frustrating experience for many men because they couldn't figure out what was happening to them or what was expected of them. They had fulfilled all of the obligations that they felt a man should fulfill. They had been hardworking. They had saved their money. They had married. They had bought homes. They tried to be good fathers. They didn't understand where they had failed. And they did not have an alternative model of manliness that might have allowed them to adjust more easily to their new circumstances.

Their anxiety and unease was reflected in popular culture. Cartoonists caught the tenor of the times by creating characters like Dagwood, a well meaning but bumbling anti-hero who lived his life as the hen pecked husband of an efficient and controlling woman named Blondie. Even more revealing of the difficulty that men faced in their efforts to come to con-

sensus about what constituted manliness was the figure of Superman who provided his fans with two completely different models of masculinity. The first was Clark Kent, a handsome and mild-mannered but thoroughly dull, newspaper reporter. The other was the muscle-bound, heroic Superman who was able to leap off tall buildings with a single bound in order to save beautiful young women from fates worse than death and the world from being destroyed by evil forces.

Given the degree to which the depression undermined traditional definitions of manliness, it is not surprising that it was in the 1930s that Lewis Terman, a Stanford behavioral psychologist, and his associate, Catherine Cox Miles, devised a test intended to measure the degree to which American adolescents were acquiring the appropriate gender identities. In this test, children were asked to answer questions about their knowledge, attitudes, and behavior patterns. Their answers were scored as masculine or feminine, and their score was placed along a continuum with masculinity at one end and femininity at the other. The point for boys was to measure the degree to which they had successfully internalized what it meant to be a man. For example, when asked, "Do you rather dislike to take your bath," they were rated at the masculine end of the scale when they responded "yes." This was also true when they replied that they did not keep a diary. Alternatively, they were rated as potentially feminine when they responded that they were interested in their "manner of dress." Young men tested as manly when they preferred reading *Robinson Crusoe* rather than *Rebecca of Sunnybrook Farm* and when they drew ships rather than flowers. In the name of "scientific inquiry," Terman and Cox's test attempted to measure the differences between what was considered feminine and what was considered masculine. In the process, it defined as "normal" or "abnormal" gendered activities and attitudes. In doing so, it reinforced the line dividing men's and women's spheres. By confirming and validating traditional gender conventions, it discouraged attempts to expand or modify generally accepted definitions of masculinity and femininity.

WORLD WAR II, THE COLD WAR, AND THE DEFINITION OF MANLINESS

On December 7, 1941 the Japanese bombed American military installations in and around Pearl Harbor in Hawaii. Within days, the United States was at war with Germany, Italy, and Japan. Unemployment figures fell as men volunteered or were drafted into the various branches of the armed services and others remained behind to fill their jobs. Another war meant another opportunity to emphasize strenuous masculinity, another chance for men to exhibit their courage in defense of their country and families.

Technology was even more important to winning this war than it had been in World War I. It was perhaps for this reason that while millions of American men fought bravely, they did not seem to view their combat experiences in terms of their need to prove that they were men as much as a fulfillment of their manly responsibilities. The Japanese had attacked, and Americans considered it their duty to protect their country and its inhabitants from any further danger and to seek vengeance against those who had perpetrated this atrocity. There was a subtle difference between war as a test of one's manhood and war as retribution against other men, but it was there.

When the war ended in 1945, combat troops returned home. Their willingness to fight and their desire to work to support their families provided a temporary respite from anxiety about what it meant to be a man. World War II veterans wanted to forget the war, settle down to life as civilians, and resume their roles as wage-earners, fathers, and husbands. Returning soldiers looked for employment and proposed to their sweet hearts, not necessarily in that order. The government and civilian employers fired women and minorities so that there would be jobs available for returning vet-

erans. And in 1944 Congress passed the GI Bill, which provided them loans and grants so that they could enroll in school or borrow money to buy a house or start a business. Men embraced the idea of fatherhood after the war, and a "baby boom" ensued. Their virility, eagerness to form households, and success as wage earners all testified to their manhood.

Like the 1920s, the 1950s was an age of prosperity for many men, particularly if they were white. Despite periods of temporary economic recession, even working-class men tended to work fewer hours and make more money. Their role of provider was confirmed. The wages that they earned paid for an expanding range of consumer products that were produced when American industry switched over from war to peacetime production. For many men, particularly those in the middle class, success was defined in terms of materialism—by the year and model of a man's car, the size of his house, the neighborhood where it was located, and the clothes that he and the other members of his family wore.

Manliness was also measured by the shape of a man's body and the size of his waistline. By the late 1950s doctors and dietitians were pleading with men to pay more attention to their eating habits. Obesity, they argued, was feminizing men and rendering them physically incapable of defending their country from the threat of communism. Their campaign continued the emphasis on the male body as a symbol of masculinity that had been evident since the nineteenth century. Concern about the male physique at the turn of the century had emphasized building up the body. Skinny and weak were not good. Theodore Roosevelt had led a national campaign encouraging men to strengthen their bodies through exercise. Now the emphasis was on slimming down the body through self-discipline and nutrition. Being fat, the authorities seemed to be saying, was even worse than being skinny.

During the Cold War, men, whose gendered identity had been bruised and battered by unemployment and then a struggle against the Germans and the Japanese, seem to have been more in search of security and stability than in achievement. Working-class men were increasingly protected by labor contracts that guaranteed them high wages and protected them from losing their jobs. As technology continued to be applied to industry, a workingman's skills in constructing, maintaining, and using machines became more and more important. And while machines were supposed to simplify the production process and make it more efficient, they did not necessarily make an industrial worker's job less physically demanding. Most workers still had to lift, shove, and push in the brutal cold of winter and the sweltering heat of summer. To be successful, many factory workers still needed to be physically strong. Working with machines also took some degree of courage since it could be extremely dangerous. Industrial accidents maimed and killed thousands of workers every year. Under such circumstances, it was no coincidence that knowing how to fix a machine or change a tire became associated with manliness. Nor is it surprising that working men, with time on their hands and skills in handling tools, assumed increasing responsibility for home maintenance and improvement. They claimed space in their homes for their workshops and took pride in their ability to build their own furniture, paint their own houses, and plumb their own bathrooms. The era of "do it yourself" was reborn as men reverted to a philosophy of self-sufficiency as a sign of manliness.

The number of white collar jobs expanded after the war, helping to provide men with a sense of security and stability. Wage earning had always been at the center of men's lives, but some observers saw what they considered to be a new obsession with work. Some men, they charged, found their jobs so absorbing that, despite the pressure to be good husbands and fathers, they neglected their wives and children and took very little time off to enjoy themselves. Definitions of manliness became more rigid in the 1950s and early 1960s as the ambitious tried to work their way up the corporate ladder by demonstrating that they

were cooperative team players who had no intention of challenging the authority of those in positions of power. In the words of social critics, they were "organization men," who were willing to sacrifice their individuality and independence in order to fit in. Conformity was the name of the game. Many traditional gender norms prevailed. Men still expected each other to be emotionally strong, economically successful, politically informed, sexually vibrant, and physically fit.

By the 1960s it became obvious that the industrial economy that had served as the economic basis for defining manliness for about a hundred years was beginning slowly to shift toward one focused on service. As a result of this shift, man's ability to produce marketable goods became less important than his ability to persuade and please. Charm and salesmanship began to replace strength and skill as the characteristics most likely to lead to economic success. This transition was marked by the rise of a whole new generation of ambitious entrepreneurs who saw the opportunity to make names for themselves helping other men adjust their behavior to this new economic reality.

Dale Carnegie was one such entrepreneur. Carnegie was born in 1888 and grew up on a farm near Maryville, Missouri. His family was desperately poor, so he had to struggle to earn a college degree. After he graduated in 1908, he traveled west and worked for a short time as a salesman. In 1912 he began teaching public speaking at the YMCA in New York City. His classes were so popular that he expanded his business and hired substitutes who were willing to use his techniques to conduct classes that he did not have time to teach. Eventually, he began traveling the country making his living giving a speech on "how to win friends and influence people." It was an expanded version of this speech that he published in book form in the middle of the depression. The book was enormously popular. It went through its fifty-seventh printing in 1948. He established what was essentially an advice empire. Appealing to ordinary workers and small businessmen, he sent his representatives to give workshops in cities and small towns all over the country. His message was simple: If a man could master the skills necessary to express himself clearly and persuasively and if he could endear himself to others, he would prosper financially and enjoy a satisfying private life. In other words, he suggested that it was through self-assurance and force of personality rather than formal education, skill, hard work, or even character than a man could achieve success in the workplace and emotionally gratifying relationships with his friends and family.

Carnegie was successful partly because he helped men bridge the gap between work and home. Men were no less torn between the two than had been their forebears. During the 1950s family togetherness was idealized. Since the mid-nineteenth century there had been considerable pressure on men to parent as well as provide. That pressure was particularly intense after the war as many men found it increasingly easy to provide homes for their families. Suburbs mushroomed in the postwar era. Low interest rates, the availability of cheap land, and mass production made homes relatively cheap and widely available. High employment and advances in transportation made suburban homes accessible.

Living in the suburbs meant that many men were geographically if not emotionally separated from their families during the work day, thus making it difficult for them to take an active role in child rearing. Social critics and child rearing experts were particularly concerned about this matter, arguing that a father's presence was necessary for the proper rearing of children in general and sons in particular. In order to intimidate men into assuming more influence in the home, they indulged in a form of mother bashing that included the charge that the overbearing influence of mothers could destroy a boy's ability to make the transition to manhood. The very future of men, they warned, was in jeopardy. Like nineteenth-century child rearing authorities, they urged fathers to spend more time with their children in order to counterbalance the influence of their wives. The editors of *Parents' Magazine,* for example, published ar-

ticles assuring men that they had an important role to play in child rearing. "Father's arms are strong," wrote one of their child rearing experts, "and the child who experiences the security they give him grows up with a warm regard for some of the best qualities of masculinity—tenderness, protection, and strength."

Television, which became widely available in the 1950s and 1960s, also helped to promote ideas about what constituted the ideal in fatherhood. The character of the father in programs such as "Father Knows Best" and "Ozzie and Harriet" provided the model. In both programs, while there was no evidence that the father figure actually worked for a living, it was clear that he was more than an adequate provider. His wife and children lived in a spacious, beautifully decorated home in a safe neighborhood, wore fashionable clothing, and ate plenty of food. He was a sensitive, attentive, companionable, loving husband and father. He was Mr. Fix-it, a man of action when faced with a problem to solve, a man of honor and integrity, and the source of family wisdom. He was in essence a nurturer, and his life was focused on domestic concerns. Yet there was not even the hint of a suggestion that such involvement had a feminizing effect on him.

The high standards of domestic masculinity set by such characters were impossible for most men to meet. Under even the best of circumstances, work interfered with life at home. A man could conscientiously set aside time to play with his children. He could volunteer his time to serve as scoutmaster or baseball coach. He could take his son on camping trips and schedule his work around parent-teacher conferences and appointments with the pediatrician. But in the end, there were simply not enough hours in the day to do what was being demanded of him. As a result, many men found that trying to fulfill their fatherly responsibilities was a frustrating and disappointing experience. It was an enterprise fraught with potential for failure.

Faced with what in many cases were unreasonable expectations, men longed for other ways of expressing their manliness. In order to compensate for feelings of inadequacy, they searched for some sort of new frontier, some place where they could carry out, if only vicariously, their desire for adventure. Popular literature, film, and television could help fulfill a desire for confirmation that there was still a place where men could exhibit courage, strength, and stamina in a hostile environment. But real adventure was hard to come by. The western frontier had been closed since the 1890s. And by the 1960s imperial powers were slowly granting independence to their colonies. It was no longer possible to seek adventure helping to administer a foreign empire. If a man were rich enough, he could try to climb Mt. Everest or to sail around the earth by himself. But most men were not that rich. The opportunities for adventure available to ordinary fellows were few and far between. It was within the context of this reality that interest in space exploration began to emerge. In space, a representative man could pit his strength, stamina, will, and intellect against the forces of nature. By overcoming the law of gravity and hurling himself into the unknown, a man could confirm his manhood and along with it that of all who applauded his efforts.

The motivation for American men to fly into space was in part a by-product of the Cold War. In 1957, the Russians sent the first man-made satellite into space. Four years later, they sent Yuri Gagarin into orbit. All of this was tremendously embarrassing to the Americans, who thought of themselves as technologically and economically superior to the Russians. President John F. Kennedy responded to the Russian challenge by pledging that the United States would win what became popularly known as the "space race." Congress appropriated money for space research and the National Aeronautics and Space Administration (NASA) authorized tests to determine how suited human beings were to stand the stress of space flight. Doctors, psychologists, and scientists at the Lovelace Institute in Albuquerque, New Mexico, tested the stamina of

thirty-one men. Seven emerged as the first American astronauts.

During the same period, however, the Institute also tested 25 women. Among them was Terri Cobb. She had been flying since she was twelve years old and by 1960 had logged 10,000 flight hours. Another was Wally Funk, a flight instructor for the military. Both performed well on the Institute's tests. Among other things, they proved that women required less oxygen per minute relative to weight than the average male astronaut and that when immersed in water and left in total darkness, a women could last longer than a man without lapsing into hallucinations. All in all, their performance suggested that women might be better adapted to space flight than men. But no one in charge of the space program was enthusiastic about allowing women to participate in the effort to send an American into space. Their reluctance had more to do with attitudes toward gender than it did with the abilities or qualifications of the women who wished to participate. Kris Kraft, who eventually became the head of NASA, is reported to have commented retrospectively, "Had we lost a woman in space back then, because we'd put a gal up there rather than a man, we would have been castrated." His attitude was echoed by a NASA spokesman who told a congressional hearing, "The thought of a U. S. space woman makes me sick to my stomach. I'd prefer to send a monkey into space than a bunch of women." So in 1963, testing on women was scrapped, and space remained an all-male frontier until 1983 when Sally Ride became the first American woman in space.

MANLINESS IN THE AGE OF YOUTHFUL REVOLT

In the 1960s, traditional ideas about manhood were challenged by the young and the counter-culture that they created. Interest in supporting civil rights led to criticism of other aspects of American government policy, criticism which eventually focused on American involvement in Vietnam. President John F. Kennedy sent American troops into Southeast Asia in the early 1960s at a time when very few Americans even knew where Vietnam was. By 1968, a few male college students were burning their draft cards and organizing mass demonstrations to protest American military involvement in Indo-China. Unwilling to prove their manliness by fighting in a war that they opposed on ideological grounds, they saw no dishonor in fleeing to the sanctuary of Canada when they received their draft notice or serving time in jail for refusing to show up for the physical examinations that preceded induction into the army. In their eyes it was more courageous to walk up to an armed national guardsman and hang a wreath of flowers around his bayonet than it was to kill people with whom they had no quarrel.

Given the fact that fighting wars has always been seen as a male activity, it is not surprising that both proponents of the war and those who opposed American military action in Southeast Asia used gendered language to discuss it. The government call to fight was intended in part to reinforce masculine values. Government spokesmen feminized the enemy, depicting the Viet Cong as weak and vulnerable and promising that it would be a simple matter to defeat this disorganized, poorly supplied, rag tag, guerrilla army full of soldiers who were afraid to come out of the jungles and into the open and fight like men. They argued that the reason American troops were being sent to Southeast Asia was to protect the world from communism. But they also gendered the war by insisting that part of the job of American ground troops was to protect innocent women and children from the atrocities that usually accompanied war.

As the war dragged on and victory seemed increasingly elusive, those who opposed the war became more vocal. In a gendered rhetoric of their own, they questioned the manliness of America's political and military leaders. Characterizing President Lyndon B. Johnson and his advisors as misguided, weak, and ineffectual, they charged that it was their incompetence and lack of will that was responsible for the casualties that continued to spiral upward. President Johnson countered by characterizing his critics as "nervous Nellies" and implied that they were unmanly cowards.

All in all, the 1970s was a period in which a particularly articulate minority of privileged, angry, and rebellious young men went about quite self-consciously trying to construct a model of manliness that contrasted in significant ways to the one they felt that their fathers had unquestioningly embraced. They viewed their fathers' conformity as a form of weakness and their fathers' willingness to tolerate social injustice and what seemed to them to be their unquestioning deference to authority as evidence of cowardice. As an extension of their protest, they rejected the material symbols of affluence and the pursuit of wealth for its own sake. They rejected hierarchy in favor of egalitarianism. And the strategies that they pursued to achieve social change focused more on common people, whom they hoped to empower, rather than on those in local, state, and federal government, who they claimed were corrupt and out of touch with the principles of true democracy. Instead of quietly making deals in the back rooms of state houses and congress, they organized huge demonstrations and took to the streets to plead the cause of social justice.

At the same time, a homosexual minority began to challenge the cultural convention that equated masculinity with heterosexuality. Arguing that a man's desire for an intimate relationship with another man had no bearing on his claim to manliness, they created a movement devoted to promoting the right of gay men to express their sexual preferences openly without fear of harassment or discrimination.

While all of this was going on, women were continuing to try to redefine their place in American society. By the 1960s, the National

Organization for Women and the Women's Liberation Movement were pushing a feminist agenda that included such things as equal pay for equal work, equal opportunity to compete in the labor market, and equal educational opportunities. As a result of their efforts, women intruded even farther into male work space and demanded that men share even more of their masculine privileges. To make things worse, they publicly criticized men for abusing their power and accused them of being insensitive and emotionally repressed.

Male response to such criticism was mixed. The initial response of some men was bewilderment. Others were furious. They simply proceeded to do everything they could to resist social change and preserve their male prerogatives. Less common, but no less important, was the willingness of some men to follow the feminist lead and reject traditional definitions of masculinity which required that they consistently exhibit such characteristics as strength, emotional stoicism, athleticism, and dominance. They were willing to admit that it was just as manly to cry as it was to swear. They agreed that it was just as manly to co-operate as to compete. They were convinced that fathers could be as nurturing as mothers. They were willing to acknowledge that there was nothing really gendered about the desire to make money. And they welcomed the opportunity to seek support, intimacy, affection, and love with other human beings whether they be male or female. In short, they accepted the idea that men and women should be allowed to express their masculinity and femininity any way they chose. They promoted the idea of gender equality. Some even viewed it as perfectly acceptable for a man to stay home and take care of the house and the kids while his wife went out and made enough money to support the family.

Most men did not organize their lives around these principles. But some did. They participated in what was called the "men's movement," held consciousness raising sessions, and embraced a definition of manliness that was fundamentally different from that of their fathers.

By the mid-1970s the distinctions between the expression of masculinity and the expression of femininity had begun to blur in some quarters. In living rooms, kitchens, bedrooms, and boardrooms all across the country, men and women worked out a new set of gendered relationships in tandem with each other just as their parents and grandparents had done. Participating in this process took courage and single-mindedness. It was difficult for men to give up their social, political, and economic privileges. It was not easy for them to accept women as equals at home and competitors at work. But in the end, ideas about what constituted manliness were much more flexible than they had ever been.

THE CONTINUING STRUGGLE TO REDEEM BLACK MANHOOD

Organized efforts to redeem black manhood in the United States began during the 1920s in the North. A "Great Migration," as it was later called, had begun during World War I as blacks fled the poverty and racial prejudice that characterized their lives in the South. Many traveled north and west by rail, carrying their belongings with them through the bustling, cavernous main halls of train stations in places like Chicago, St. Louis, and Detroit. Most of them settled in ghettoes that comprised cities within cities complete with black schoolteachers, black shopkeepers, and black policemen. But it was in the Harlem section of New York City where many of the most talented congregated. It was there that black musicians, artists, writers, calling themselves "New Negroes," participated in what became known as the Harlem Renaissance. The Harlem Renaissance was an exercise in self-discovery for black artists and intellectuals. And one of the questions they were asking was "What does it mean to be a black man in American society?"

Because the 1920s was a period of general prosperity, many people in New York City had time on their hands and money to spend. And Harlem was a place where their needs and fantasies could be met. Whites from downtown, bored and in search of the exotic, made their way uptown to patronize the art galleries, speakeasies, coffee houses, night clubs, and cabarets that lined the streets of black neighborhoods. There they listened to jazz, ragtime, and dixieland performed by black musicians. They purchased paintings and sculpture created by black artists, and they read novels and poetry written by angry black writers. Harlem in the 1920s was an environment in which introspective black men could critique their position in American society, create and celebrate their own version of black culture, and express their own version of manliness without the inhibiting influence of whites. It was there that they were free to rebel against white cultural conventions, express new ideas, and lead a public campaign against racism. There was no need in Harlem to shuffle as you walked or avoid eye contact with people whose skin was white. In the Harlem of the 1920s, you could hold your head high and express your manliness in relative freedom.

To some degree, of course, the Harlem Renaissance was a rebellion of the intellectual elite. Marcus Garvey, a flamboyant and charismatic immigrant from Jamaica, provided ordinary black men with his own distinctive vision of black manhood. Garvey established the Universal Negro Improvement Association intended to promote economic self-sufficiency and race pride among Afro-Americans. He and his message had tremendous appeal among blacks in all parts of the country. Headquartered in New York City, the UNIA had its own newspaper and became the largest black organization of the day with hundreds of thousands of members. Dressed in an elaborate military uniform, Garvey led parades through the streets of the city in an effort to celebrate black culture. When he spoke at mass meetings, he told his audiences that black men were as good

as white men. His newspaper declined to run ads promoting hair straighteners and cosmetics intended to bleach the skin. And he encouraged black men to work hard, save their money, and set up their own businesses. His organization even loaned some of them the money to do so. In this sense, he promoted values that were similar to those of Booker T. Washington and W. E. B. DuBois. But added to his message of self-help was a call for blacks to separate themselves from white society and develop a sense of black nationalism. Black men, he suggested, did not have to tolerate treatment that demeaned them and took away their manhood. They could escape the impact of white racism, he told them, by returning to Africa. To support the "Back to Africa Movement," he established the Black Star Line, a steamship company intended to facilitate African emigration. Despite his efforts, however, emigration was not really a viable option for most blacks. By the end of the 1920s his steamship company had gone bankrupt and he had been deported for mail fraud. Nevertheless, he left behind a legacy that encouraged African-American sharecroppers in the South as well as emigrants to the North to take pride in their heritage and to hold their heads high.

BLACK MANLINESS DURING DEPRESSION AND WAR

The role of provider had always been problematic for black, working-class men. Discrimination in education, employment, and housing meant that only through great effort and considerable luck could a black man make a place for himself in the black middle class. During the depression, black farmers, sharecroppers, and tenant farmers continued to work the land, deriving their sense of manliness from their ability to at least keep a roof over their children's heads and put food on the table. But in urban areas, the economic crisis of the 1930s put black businesses at risk and meant that employment opportunities for black men, which had always been scarce, became virtually nonexistent. White-dominated labor unions had never been enthusiastic about protecting the interests of black workers and had made it difficult for black men to acquire the skills they needed to compete for well-paying industrial jobs. So when the factories began to close, black men were among the first to face the prospect of unemployment.

Black men had few resources to fall back on. Unless they were in the middle class, their wives were already helping them support their families. And their friends, relatives, and neighbors faced problems similar to theirs. Even more desperate than they had been in the 1920s, these men benefited from the welfare programs of Franklin D. Roosevelt's New Deal. Government subsidized jobs and subsidies for housing helped to fulfill their manly responsibilities as heads of their households.

However helpful New Deal job programs were for helping poor black men sustain their sense of manliness, it was not until the United States entered World War II that job opportunities became widely available to them. Black men, as predisposed as white men to define masculinity in terms of defending their country, volunteered for all branches of the service and participated in both the European and the Pacific theaters of war. But the American military was still segregated. In the navy, for example, black men could serve but were usually relegated to the galleys of ships where they worked as cooks or washed dishes. Not until 1944 was there a warship with a black crew.

Some of those who remained at home found that jobs in heavy industry that had previously been closed to them were now available. Special training programs provided them with skills, and wages in war industries were relatively high. Racial discrimination was still rampant, but because of the need to maintain production, the federal government took steps to assure that workers were treated equitably. Thus, the war and the need for labor made it easier for black men to fulfill their roles as providers and protectors. As a result of their experiences in World War II, many black men became even less willing to accept their status as second-class citizens.

BLACK MANHOOD REDEEMED

The black struggle for civil rights began after the Civil War ended in 1865. Black men in the South, who for the first time in American history had a constitutional right to vote and hold office, tried to use their political power to assure their economic futures and to press their claim to social equality. But their efforts failed. Attempts to rectify the situation never stopped despite the tremendous pressure on the part of whites to deny equality to anyone whose skin was darker than theirs. It was during the period immediately following World War II that the Civil Rights Movement began to gain momentum. Disturbed by the revival of racial disturbances such as the 1943 race riot in Detroit and embarrassed by the record of discrimination that had plagued the armed forces during the war, President Harry Truman issued an executive order in 1948 which banned racial discrimination in the federal government. His initiative prompted the integration of all of the branches of the service. The army was quicker to implement his order than the navy or the air force. Nevertheless, in theory at least, black men would henceforth be given the right to confirm their manliness by defending their country in the same way as white men.

Some black men benefited from the period of prosperity that followed the war. Labor unions, which now had black members, renewed their efforts to gain improvements in wages, hours, and working conditions. Strikes in the steel and automobile industries gave workers a new sense of their own power to control industrial output and influence the economy. And with prosperity came growth in the black middle class. For the first time in their families' histories, some black men were able to express their manhood by buying homes and aspiring to be the sole support of their families and to turn their attention to providing their children with the kind of education they deserved. But others did not reap the benefits of prosperity. Unemployment for black men remained high, and wages for many black workingmen remained low compared to those of whites, which continued to make the economic disparity between white and black obvious.

Backed by a strong middle class, black leaders like Thurgood Marshall took a lead in the effort to destroy the kind of discrimination that limited the ability of black men to pursue the "American dream." With the financial support of the NAACP and the grassroots efforts by men like J. A. DeLaine, he and other lawyers began initiating court cases like *Briggs v. Elliot* and *Brown v. Board of Education*, both intended to end the doctrine of "separate but equal" which had limited access to public facilities in such areas as transportation and education. The first real breakthrough came in 1954 when the U. S. Supreme Court found that school segregation was unconstitutional.

Winning court cases, however, did not end discrimination. White supremacist organizations like White Citizens' Councils blossomed throughout the South as white men again resorted to violence and intimidation in an effort to resist federal court orders and to reassure themselves that they were capable of protecting their interests. White parents withdrew their children from integrated schools. And blacks throughout the South lost their jobs, were denied credit, and were physically attacked because of their willingness to assert their right to equality.

In 1955, Rev. Martin Luther King, Jr., a young Baptist minister in Montgomery, Alabama, helped to organize a black boycott of the city's bus system, a system that required black patrons to sit in the back of the bus and give up their seats to white passengers when the buses were full. King espoused a policy of passive resistance as a way of dealing with manifestations of white racism. Black manliness, he argued, could best be expressed in self-discipline and restraint. His strategy worked. In 1956 the Supreme Court found Alabama's segregation laws unconstitutional, paving the way for the integration of all public facilities in the United States.

Unfortunately, the Civil Rights Movement was not able to maintain either a sense of unity or a dedication to non-violence. The Ku Klux Klan and other white supremacy organizations unleashed a campaign of violence in response to black activism. They bombed churches and the homes of black civil rights leaders, and they murdered civil rights advocates. While all this was going on, civil rights leaders like King began to turn their attention to the impact of racism on urban blacks, many of whom suffered from unemployment and lived in degrading poverty in segregated neighborhoods.

By the late 1960s, the Civil Rights Movement was in the process of fragmenting over policy and strategy. Malcolm X, one of the founders of the Nation of Islam, commonly known as the Black Muslims, posed a challenge to King's leadership by suggesting that blacks were superior to whites and that they should give up on the idea of integration. Echoing the voice of Marcus Garvey, he espoused black pride and black nationalism. Defiantly branding whites as "devils," he encouraged black men to resort to violence if they were attacked.

Meanwhile, Stokely Carmichael, the young leader of the Student Non-violent Coordinating Committee (SNCC), became disenchanted with the philosophy of non-violence and began shifting his allegiance away from King. Less and less enthusiastic about integration, Carmichael called for blacks to join the Black Power Movement in 1966. In order to be free of white influence, he argued, blacks needed to control their own institutions. They needed to establish their own schools and work through the election process to take control of city and county governments. For Carmichael, the redemption of black manhood was dependent upon their establishing independence from white influence. But it was also dependent upon establishing their dominance in gender relationships. His version of masculinity was one that focused on power, authority, and the subjugation of women. Responding to a complaint that women in SNCC were being denied positions of leadership in the organization and were treated by their male colleagues with disrespect, he allegedly remarked, "The only position of women in SNCC is prone."

Civil rights leaders like Malcolm X and Stokely Carmichael blended militancy with black nationalism, a sense that blacks should separate themselves from white society and should value and celebrate their unique history and cultural heritage. For them, being a black man meant being able to take advantage of the benefits to be derived from a free society to support their families, provide their children with an education which celebrated their racial heritage, and exert more control over the economic, political, and social life of their communities in the interests of their race. Their version of black masculinity differed in significant ways from that of middle-class black men who were pushing for integration and who tended to embrace the idea that masculinity, like other social constructions, should have no racial boundaries.

SUMMARY

The shifts in definitions of manliness for middle-class, white men that were evident in the late nineteenth century became increasingly obvious in the twentieth. The Victorians had tried to define manliness by encouraging men to be concerned about their "character." In theory at least, they valued self-control, honor, loyalty, independence, self-sufficiency, a sense of duty, and integrity in a man. Esteem for these qualities had not entirely disappeared by the third quarter of the twentieth century, but a whole new set of characteristics competed with the old ones for transcendence. For some, manliness was equated with a pleasing appearance and charm rather than an upright character, with expressiveness

rather than reserve, with self-indulgence rather than self-control, with youth rather than maturity, and with instant gratification rather than responsible self-denial. Perhaps, most surprising of all, was the fact that by the mid-1970s, the ideal of the "self-made man," a concept that had served as the model for manliness for the better part of three centuries, was being critiqued and re-evaluated. Certainly there were many who still regarded Horatio Alger and those like him as heroes and role models. But there was an increasing awareness of the price that some men paid in their efforts to achieve economic success and the power that was expected to accompany it. It became routine for doctors to warn their ambitious, impatient, competitive, aggressive, highly focused male patients that they were stressed out candidates for heart attacks or strokes and to encourage them to find ways to release the tension that made them perpetually irritable and unable to sustain meaningful relationships with others. These shifts made the search for an understanding of what constituted manliness an increasingly frustrating and isolating experience. Men found that they had to choose a vocation, earn approval from their peers, win the love of at least one woman, support their families, make friends, and fulfill their civic duties without the benefit of clear guidelines.

Typically, they responded in one of three ways. A few men welcomed these challenges to traditional definitions of masculinity. They participated in a men's movement that arose in New York and California and was centered largely in urban areas and college towns. Determined to help each other navigate through the murky waters of changing gender expectations, they encouraged their friends to talk openly about their lives and offered them the opportunity to self-consciously express their dissatisfactions with the pressures that trying to fulfill manly ideals placed on them. They supported efforts to shift the emphasis from self-making to self-realization and to work out a wide variety of manly identities suited to provide each individual with a productive and satisfying life.

Others approached the need to re-evaluate the definition of manliness with less enthusiasm. Reluctant to give up the privileges that traditionally accompanied being a man in American society, they dug in their heels and resisted the demand that they help with child care and housework. They subjected their female co-workers to varying degrees of harassment. And they retreated to their bars and clubs in order to avoid having to face the changing demands that were being made on them. Some even beat their wives and children out of the sheer frustration of not being able to stem the tide of changing expectations.

But most middle-class men simply adapted slowly. When their wives decided to go to work, the difference between them and working-class men with working wives began to blur. Two incomes meant that they could enjoy the benefit of being able to spend more money and not having to be the sole breadwinner. They accepted more child care responsibility as a part of the price that had to be paid for those benefits, so they cooked dinner on Tuesday nights, played poker or went bowling with their friends only one night a week instead of two, and adjusted their work schedule so that they could attend parent-teacher conferences. When their wives were subjected to sexual harassment on their jobs or discovered that they were not getting equal pay for equal work, they began to pay more attention to what was going on in their own work environment. And having supported their sons' participation in Little League, they began to coach their daughters' soccer team. Changes in their gendered behavior patterns and gender ideals were gradual. Sometimes they were self-conscious. Sometimes they

were not. But those men who did change gave up some of the last vestiges of patriarchal authority and power within the family and simply adjusted to the presence of women in the workplace.

The situation for black men was, in some ways, entirely different. They showed much more initiative than white men did in attempting to change the context in which their manhood was expressed. By pressing their claim to equality, they were establishing their claim to manhood in a society that had erected significant barriers to the achievement of that goal. Through the civil rights movement, they tried to establish their right as men to employment opportunities that would allow them to take care of their families, provide them with decent housing, guarantee them access to public facilities like schools, hospitals, restaurants, and hotels, and guarantee them the right to fulfill their manly responsibilities as citizens by voting and holding public office.

By 1975, the power that white, heterosexual men had traditionally wielded in American society was being challenged by both women and men who considered themselves minorities, including those who identified themselves as gay (see Chapter 12). Those in power do not typically give up their power without a struggle. And so a struggle over the definition of masculinity ensued. By the 1980s it was abundantly clear that ideas about manliness were in a state of flux. There was no longer a general consensus about how masculinity should be defined. Manliness could be expressed in a wide variety of ways, and American men could quite self-consciously decide for themselves which definition of masculinity was best suited to them as individuals.

DOCUMENT

Claude McKay's "If We Must Die"

Claude McKay was born in 1890 on a farm in Jamaica. His forebears had been abducted from Madagascar in Africa and sold as slaves. McKay came to the United States in 1912 to study agriculture, intending eventually to return home. Instead, he moved to New York City where he worked at odd jobs in order to support himself as a poet. In the 1920s black artists, writers, and musicians living in and around Harlem in New York City participated in a vibrant and exciting black cultural movement known as the Harlem Renaissance. Known as "New Negroes," they not only celebrated black culture but also exposed the evils of white racism. Claude McKay's poem "If We Must Die" is an example of the kind of literature they produced.

What is the tone of McKay's poetry? How does he think black men should express their manliness?

If we must die, let it not be like hogs
Hunted and penned in an inglorious spot,
While round us bark the mad and hungry dogs,
Making their mock at our accursèd lot.
If we must die, O let us nobly die,

So that our precious blood may not be shed
In vain; then even the monsters we defy
Shall be constrained to honor us though dead!
O kinsmen! we must meet the common foe!
Though far outnumbered let us show us brave,
And for their thousand blows deal one
    deathblow!
What though before us lies the open grave?
Like men we'll face the murderous, cowardly
    pack,
Pressed to the wall, dying, but fighting back!

Source: Claude McKay, *Harlem Shadows: The Poems of Claude McKay* (New York: Harcourt, Brace and Company, 1922), 53.

DOCUMENT

Robert Benchley's "The Vanishing Father"

The Great Depression (1929–1941) had a devastating impact on both economic and social life in America. It was a particularly difficult time for wage-earning men. From the colonial period through the twentieth century, an important component of masculinity had

Source: Robert Benchley, "The Vanishing Father" in *From Bed to Worse, or Comforting Thoughts about the Bison* (New York: Harper & Bros., 1934), 111, 113.

been a man's ability to support his family. Unemployment, therefore, tended to under-mine a man's claim to manliness and to erode his authority over his wife and children. In some cases, when men lost their jobs, gender roles were dramatically reversed. Un-employed men found it necessary to stay home, take care of the children, and assume re-sponsibility for at least part of the cooking and cleaning while their wives went off to work. From their point of view, being a house husband was no laughing matter.

Yet there were writers such as Robert Benchley who were able to relieve some of the tensions and anxieties that they felt through the use of humor. During most of the de-pression, Benchley earned a living as a screen writer. In 1934, he published From Bed to Worse, or Comforting Thoughts about the Bison, *a book of humorous essays in-tended to provide his readers with a temporary escape from the realities of everyday life. "The Vanishing Father" pokes fun at the efforts of men to fulfill their role as fathers.*

According to Benchley, how had men's status as fathers declined in the 1930s? What is it about men that prevented them from fulfilling their roles as good fathers, in his opinion?

It is perhaps a little late in the day to be asking, but whatever became of the old-fashioned Pater Familias, the father who packed a punch? He was one of the bulldog breed, whose word was law, and when he rumbled in to breakfast all the boys and girls, to say nothing of Mumsie, threw themselves up against the wall and saluted. Being a father in those days was a job that called for a West Point training.

Today the entire breed of fathers seems to have gone sissy. They are lucky if they get what the rest of the family gets to eat and, as for personality, they might as well be the man who holds the tray for a magician. And it isn't so much because the rest of the family have got more self-confident (although a certain suspicion of poise has crept into the young folks lately), but the fathers have definitely turned yellow as a class.

The day that fathers stopped wearing sideburns and high-buttoned coats, they began to lose ground. A man in a soft-collared shirt can't expect to rate much respect, especially if the ends of his four-in-hand look like a lasso and he still tries to dress like a junior in college. The custom of carrying gold-headed canes was also a big help to building up a following. The men in the old days weren't afraid to rig themselves up in the regulation father's uniform, even to the extent of a Prince Albert on Sundays, and, as a result, they both looked and felt the part. It is this trying to keep young-looking that has put the father-racket on the rocks.

Along with this fear of looking like a father has come a fear of acting like a father. Fathers today are a craven lot when it comes to appearing in public as a parent. They try to wheel the baby-carriage up side streets and, if they are caught leading a toddler along by the hand, they try to make believe that they are minding the child for some strange woman who has just disappeared. I have even seen a father hurriedly slip a cigar into his son's mouth at the approach of friends, hoping that they will think he is out with a midget business acquaintance.

Martin Luther King, Jr., on Manliness and Passive Resistance

Martin Luther King, Jr., lived in a racist society that discriminated against all Afro-Americans. Compared to many other men of his race, he was relatively privileged. He grew up in a stable, middle-class family and then went to college and to seminary. In the winter of 1955–1956, he helped to organize the Montgomery, Alabama, bus boycott, thus becoming one of the most important leaders of the Civil Rights Movement. King was outraged by the racism and poverty that plagued black people in the United States. But he turned his anger into a positive agent for change by advocating passive resistance as a device for protesting the mistreatment of black men and women. It was this technique that was used to desegregate buses engaged in interstate commerce and public facilities such as lunch counters throughout the South.

In this excerpt from his book Stride Toward Freedom, *King explains his philosophy of nonviolence. It is clear that he is talking to both men and women even though he uses the generic "he." Nevertheless, his words had special resonance for black men.*

What do his comments on passive resistance suggest about his attitudes toward manhood in general and black manhood in particular? How does his conception of manliness compare to that of Booker T. Washington, W. E. B. DuBois, and Claude McKay?

Since the philosophy of nonviolence played such a positive role in the Montgomery Movement, it may be wise to turn to a brief discussion of some basic aspects of this philosophy.

First, it must be emphasized that nonviolent resistance is not a method for cowards; it does resist. If one uses this method because he is afraid or merely because he lacks the instruments of violence, he is not truly nonviolent. This is why Gandhi often said that if cowardice is the only alternative to violence, it is better to fight. He made this statement conscious of the fact that there is always another alternative: no individual or group need submit to any wrong, nor need they use violence to right the wrong; there is the way of nonviolence resistance. This is ultimately the way of the strong man. It is not a method of stagnant passivity. The phrase "passive resistance" often gives the false impression that this is a sort of "do-nothing method" in which the resister quietly and passively accepts evil. But nothing is further from the truth. For while the nonviolent resister is passive in the sense that he is not physically aggressive toward his opponent, his mind and emotions are always active, constantly seeking to persuade his opponent that he is wrong. The method is passive physically, but strongly active spiritually. It is not passive nonresistance to evil, it is active nonviolent resistance to evil.

A second basic fact that characterizes nonviolence is that it does not seek to defeat or humiliate the opponent, but to win his friendship and understanding. The nonviolent resister must often express his protest through noncoöperation or boycotts, but he realizes

Source: Martin Luther King, Jr., "Pilgrimage to Nonviolence," *Stride Toward Freedom: The Montgomery Story* (New York: Harper & Brothers, 1958), 101–104, 106–107. Reprinted by arrangement with the Estate of Martin Luther King, Jr., c/o Writers House as agent for the proprietor New York, NY. Copyright © 1963 Dr. Martin Luther King, Jr., copyright renewed 1991 Corretta Scott King.

that these are not ends themselves; they are merely means to awaken a sense of moral shame in the opponent. The end is redemption and reconciliation. The aftermath of nonviolence is the creation of the beloved community, while the aftermath of violence is tragic bitterness.

A third characteristic of this method is that the attack is directed against forces of evil rather than against persons who happen to be doing the evil. It is evil that the nonviolent resister seeks to defeat, not the persons victimized by evil. If he is opposing racial injustice, the nonviolent resister has the vision to see that the basic tension is not between races. As I like to say to the people in Montgomery: "The tension in this city is not between white people and Negro people. The tension is, at bottom, between justice and injustice, between the forces of light and the forces of darkness. And if there is a victory, it will be a victory not merely for fifty thousand Negroes, but a victory for justice and the forces of light. We are out to defeat injustice and not white persons who may be unjust."

A fourth point that characterizes nonviolent resistance is a willingness to accept suffering without retaliation, to accept blows from the opponent without striking back. "Rivers of blood may have to flow before we gain our freedom, but it must be our blood," Gandhi said to his countrymen. The nonviolent resister is willing to accept violence if necessary, but never to inflict it. He does not seek to dodge jail. If going to jail is necessary, he enters it "as a bridegroom enters the bride's chamber."

One may well ask: "What is the nonviolent resister's justification for this ordeal to which he invites men, for this mass political application of the ancient doctrine of turning the other cheek?" The answer is found in the realization that unearned suffering is redemptive. Suffering, the nonviolent resister realizes, has tremendous educational and transforming possibilities. "Things of fundamental importance to people are not secured by reason alone, but have to be purchased with their suffering," said Gandhi. He continues: "Suffering is infinitely more powerful than the law of the jungle for converting the opponent and opening his ears which are otherwise shut to the voice of reason."

A fifth point concerning nonviolent resistance is that it avoids not only external physical violence but also internal violence of spirit. The nonviolent resister not only refuses to shoot his opponent but he also refuses to hate him. At the center of nonviolence stands the principle of love. The nonviolent resister would contend that in the struggle for human dignity, the oppressed people of the world must not succumb to the temptation of becoming bitter or indulging in hate campaigns. To retaliate in kind would do nothing but intensify the existence of hate in the universe. Along the way of life, someone must have sense enough and morality enough to cut off the chain of hate. This can only be done by projecting the ethic of love to the center of our lives.

In speaking of love at this point, we are not referring to some sentimental or affectionate emotion. It would be nonsense to urge men to love their oppressors in an affectionate sense. Love in this connection means understanding, redemptive good will. . . .

A sixth basic fact about nonviolent resistance is that it is based on the conviction that the universe is on the side of justice. Consequently, the believer in nonviolence has deep faith in the future. This faith is another reason why the nonviolent resister can accept suffering without retaliation. For he knows that in his struggle for justice he has cosmic companionship. It is true that there are devout believers in nonviolence who find it difficult to believe in a personal God. But even these persons believe in the existence of some creative force that works for universal wholeness. Whether we call it an unconscious process, an impersonal Brahman, or a Personal Being of matchless power and infinite love, there is a creative force in this universe that works to bring the disconnected aspects of reality into a harmonious whole.

ARTICLE

The "Flabby American," the Body, and the Cold War

Robert L. Griswold

In the colonial period, most men performed strenuous labor out of doors and tended to take their bodies for granted unless they were injured or became too ill to work. In the commercial economy that developed in the nineteenth century, an increasing number of jobs required more mental than physical effort. This, combined with new confidence that the human body could be controlled, made middle-class men increasingly self-conscious about the relationship between masculinity and the condition of the male body. By 1900 body building came into vogue as a way of reducing anxieties of American men about their masculinity. According to Robert Griswold, concern about the condition of the male body took on a new sense of urgency during the Cold War.

According to the essay reprinted below, what impact did the Cold War have on strengthening the connection between the construction of manliness and physical fitness? What are the long-range implications of the physical fitness campaign for defining both masculinity and femininity in today's society?

John F. Kennedy's "The Soft American," which appeared in the December 26, 1960, issue of *Sports Illustrated*, began the president-elect's campaign to reinstill physical vigor (a favorite Kennedy word) in the American people. He praised the Greeks' conviction that physical excellence and athletic skill were "among the prime foundations of a vigorous state" and then suggested that intellectual ability could not be separated from physical well-being: "But we do know what the Greeks knew: that intelligence and skill can only function at the peak of their capacity when the body is healthy and strong; that hardy spirits and tough minds usually inhabit sound bodies."

Source: Robert L. Griswold, "The 'Flabby American,' the Body, and the Cold War," in *A Shared Experience: Men, Women, and the History of Gender*, ed. Laura McCall and Donald Yacovone (New York: New York University Press, 1998), 323–39. Reprinted by permission of New York University Press. Notes omitted.

Tough minds lodged in tough bodies were now at risk, undermined by America's material success. And the young, the nation's future, seemed imperiled: "A single look at the packed parking lot of the average high school," wrote Kennedy, "will tell us what has happened to the traditional hike to school that helped to build young bodies." Nor were cars alone to blame. Prosperity had reshaped the American body: what had once been "hard" was now "soft," what had once been full of vigor could now scarcely bestir itself from the car seat or the television chair. Modern life itself was the culprit: "The television set, the movies and the myriad conveniences and distractions of modern life all lure our young people away from the strenuous physical activity that is the basis of fitness in youth and in later life." America's destiny, Kennedy feared, was sinking beneath a sea of flab. . . .

How, Kennedy seemed to be asking, could we "pay any price, bear any burden, meet any hardship, support any friend, oppose any foe" if we were too weak to defend freedom? Thus, the fitness crusade of the Kennedy administration focused cultural discourse on the body. A critical look at this effort helps us explore important dimensions of American culture, clarify the body as a cultural symbol, reveal how cultural anxieties are written onto the body, and expose conflicting conceptions of gender. The fitness crusades of the Kennedy and Eisenhower administrations suggest that the body of youth—especially male youth—became the repository for a host of cultural anxieties about Cold War America and men's place within it. The concern for physical fitness, at its core, set about redeeming manhood, reenergizing masculinity, and restoring force, dynamism, and control to males in a culture full of doubts and contradictions about men's future.

I say *manhood* for this reason: although the fitness campaign included both boys and girls, the great preponderance of the discourse focused on boys, and it did so because flabby boys—and ultimately a flabby, defenseless, "womanlike" manhood—was the target of cultural concern. The physical fitness movement arose at a time of great cultural anxiety about the future of American manhood. . . .

The fitness campaign occurred within this context: it was an effort to rescue manhood by rescuing the body, to teach boys, as one theorist put it, to use the body in "forceful and space-occupying ways." Such bodies are crucial to the development of male identity; to learn to be a male is to learn to project a physical presence that speaks of latent power. Promoters of physical fitness hoped to do as much for American boys and, in so doing, to revitalize manhood so that it could better meet the Communist threat to national survival. Cold Wars could not be fought with soft bodies.

The Roots of Softness

Promotion of physical fitness began in the mid-1950s, when John Kelly, a Philadelphia businessman, one-time Olympic sculler, and long-time advocate of physical fitness, learned that in every category the physical fitness of American boys and girls lagged far behind their European counterparts. Kelly, who had been United States Director of Physical Fitness during World War II, brought his concerns to Senator James H. Duff, who, in turn, contacted President Eisenhower. These contacts led to a White House luncheon, out of which came the establishment by presidential proclamation of the President's Council on Youth Fitness and the President's Citizens Advisory Committee on the Fitness of American Youth. By July 1956 the fitness crusade was underway.

In defending the need for a fitness program, authorities explored the causes of the bodily weakness of American youth. Their explanations turned the body itself into a metaphor of American life. Just as American culture once had been disciplined by sacrifice and hard work, so had the body. Now, just as the culture had become morally corrupt and a prisoner of materialism and technology, so too had the body. Americans once had been a group of sturdy pioneers, living the simple life, diligently working in fields and shops in the countryside and in small towns. Sadly, their descendants had become a soft-bodied society of weaklings, living in complex environments, pushing buttons in the glass towers of downtown skyscrapers or sitting mindlessly in front of television sets in the affluence of their suburban homes.

This vision of declension appeared in many places, but none more clearly than in the speeches of Dr. Shane MacCarthy, executive director of Eisenhower's Council on Youth Fitness. MacCarthy had served in the CIA, spoke frequently on juvenile delinquency and the evils of Communism, and, more than anyone else, promoted the fitness movement during the Eisenhower era. In his view, America had moved from a "rugged, primal" society that naturally built muscles to an industrial one where "the tendency is to put first the aspect of ease and soft enjoyment." . . . MacCarthy feared the worst. Labor-saving devices sapped bodily strength that could only be restored by a conscientious, vigorous exercise program. Otherwise, the "self, the person, the individual may well be lost in a mass accumulation of mechanical might."

If technology was the driving force, materialism comprised the visible manifestation of the body's decline. The condition of the body mirrored the condition of the culture. John Friedrich, a Michigan physical educator, decried the flabbiness of Americans and attributed it to materialism run amok. "Living in the lap of luxury and enjoying a state of affluence induced by our high level of prosperity has resulted in a sapping of the vigor of the people of this nation." Worst of all, wrote a New Mexico official, Americans seemed utterly complacent about their situation: "The movies took us away from home, the radio brought us back, and television glued us there," but despite admonitions to exercise, Americans resisted any effort to interfere with the "comfortable and pleasant process of physical deterioration."

The bodies of children were especially vulnerable to material excess. Over-indulgent parents in over-heated homes carted children off to school in over-sized cars, and the results were now mirrored in the over-sized bodies of the young. Whereas schools once worried about "the gangling, underweight child and set up special milk periods for him," now the problem was one of obesity and weakness, of youth who "were overfed, spent too much time watching TV, and seldom walked farther than from their house to the car in the garage." . . .

Morality, Gender, and the Body

Ultimately, the body had been victimized by more than automation, cars, or televisions. Its flabbiness, inability to pull itself over the chin-up bar, and exhaustion at the end of six hundred yards of running signified something more troubling. Written on the bodies of the future adults of America, inscribed on the flaccid muscles and the potbellies of youth, were doubts about American society and its manhood. The body had taken on the sins of the culture; its problems were ultimately moral and reflected profound doubts about the self-indulgent world of postwar consumerism.

A sense that the body's physical decline reflected the country's moral deterioration was widespread. Eisenhower had faced the issue squarely in his State of the Union message in 1960: "A rich nation can for a time, without noticeable damage to itself, pursue a course of self-indulgence, making its single goal the material ease and comfort of its own citizens." But comfort and ease begat "internal moral and spiritual softness," which would lead to economic and political disaster. Such a path repudiated the hard-spirited history of the nation. "America did not become great through softness and self-indulgence," Eisenhower warned. "Her miraculous progress in material achievements flows from other qualities far more worthy and substantial."

Without a commitment to "total fitness," America would continue to drift in a sea of "inactivity, apathy, disuse, erosion, and resultant decay and atrophy." Amid the softness of postwar life, fitness leaders lamented that the "inevitable national diseases of 'do-it-easy-ism' and 'do-nothing-ism' make it difficult for the younger generation to avoid drifting into a state of internal anarchy." This anarchy might well induce the "rebels without a cause" among the middle class and the duck-tailed, hip-swiveling Elvis imitators among the working class to slide into juvenile delinquency and sexual excess: "All will agree," averred MacCarthy, "that well-rounded fitness programs involving mental alertness, moral straightness, and physical keenness can help forestall the sexual impulses from monopolizing and taking priority in the emotional life of the adolescent." . . .

As symbols and carriers of culture, as repositories of taste and preferences, the bodies of the young were fraught with meaning, a message that many in the mid-1950s and early 1960s found deeply troubling. Almost every cultural anxiety of Cold War America had found its way onto the bodies of the young: materialism, conformity, maternal overprotection, parental neglect, government paternalism, moral corruption, and sexual excess had sent the body, now free of the regimentation and discipline of earlier generations, out of control. The result was perilous for social order, manhood, and national security, a point made by Attorney General Robert

F. Kennedy in a speech in January 1961 at the "Coach of the Year Dinner" in Pittsburgh. Since the end of World War II—a war in which "we had proved we had the mental genius, the moral certitude and the physical strength to endure and conquer"—America had been on a precipitous downward moral and physical slide. American prisoners of war in Korea evidenced this decline, as did television quiz show scandals and political, labor, and corporate corruption. Kennedy saw a direct correlation between this moral blight and the rot of the body. "Has there been a connection," he asked, "between the facts that I have just mentioned and our physical fitness?" Indeed there was. Moral decline had brought with it a physical slide, as evidenced by a 40 percent rejection of draftees for moral or physical deficiencies and the fact that American youth lagged far behind European children in physical fitness. To arrest such trends, Kennedy praised the coaches who could "exert a tremendous influence for good in this country. . . . You, who participate in football, who have played well and have trained others to play well, symbolize the needs of the Nation."

Making Bodies Hard

Robert Kennedy's praise of football, the quintessentially male sport, was no accident. Although champions of fitness included girls from the beginning, the cultural discussion focused overwhelmingly on the bodies of boys and young men. Given the doubts about manhood in the postwar years, a rough sport like football helped to establish a hierarchy of competing masculinities that favored the sturdy athlete over his limp-wristed counterpart, the heterosexual linebacker over the homosexual fop. What the celebration of physical prowess ultimately brought was a cultural message that celebrated one kind of masculinity over another. Physical force and toughness were woven together to produce what theorists call "hegemonic masculinity,"

a masculine bearing that projects strength, power, aggressiveness, morality, and superiority while "inferiorizing the other," that is, females and less manly men.

This process of "inferiorizing the other" is clear in the physical fitness crusades. To fitness authorities, sports and exercise had different meanings for girls and boys. For boys, fitness leaders emphasized competition: winning the game, running the fastest, doing the most sit-ups, or joining the elite fitness group in one California high school that entitled students to wear distinctively colored gym shorts. For girls, experts underscored participation, friendship, good health, and sexual attractiveness. Dr. Benjamin Spock, for example, did not oppose exercise for girls but doubted whether they liked competitive athletics. Sports he said, were "really invented by boys, for boys." . . .

Although the fitness crusaders praised everything from calisthenics to bicycling, many authorities hoped that manhood would be reborn on the playing fields of the nation's communities. Sports—"rough sports"—would toughen bodies, teach boys to endure pain, and ultimately redeem masculinity itself. Colliding bodies hardened the flesh and the spirit and could serve as a viable substitute for the ultimate maker of men: "Except for war," Robert Kennedy averred, "there is nothing in American life which trains a boy better for life than football. There is no substitute for athletics—there can be no substitute for football." Even the American Medical Association recognized "that a fractured ankle may leave less of a scar than a personality frustrated by reason of parental timidity over participation in contact sports." Fitness advocates supported contact sports precisely because they involved challenging fear and accepting the inevitability of pain. The chair of the Illinois Athletic Commission, for example, praised boxing for fostering toughness, aggression, and courage among young men. . . . Fitness and athletic competition taught a boy to "disguise or hide his feelings of fear," restrain his impulses, and "reject being 'babied.'" In essence, the fitness movement hoped to remold the male body, to remasculinize it, to restore the strength, resilience, and toughness that had been elided by modernity. So remade, the boy could place his body at the service of his country. After noting the dismal fitness level of American youth, Robert Kennedy told a New York City audience that sports and athletic competition were crucial to the country. They were fun to be sure, but they also built healthy bodies and promoted "stamina, courage, unselfishness and most importantly, perhaps, the will to win." And without the will to win, added Kennedy, "we are lost."

Hard Bodies and Cold Wars

Kennedy's martial rhetoric was not idle after-dinner chit-chat. He, his brother, and a host of others believed and hoped that physical fitness would ready the male body for war. Nothing less than national survival was at stake: the body had become a visible manifestation, a flesh-and-blood repository of national decline and weakness, and to restore the male body's strength and vigor was to restore the nation's power and vitality. America could fulfill its commitment to freedom and secure its national survival only if a vigorous fitness program could first transform the body. If the program succeeded, indulged bodies would be replaced by disciplined bodies that would work with disciplined minds to defend liberty against Communism. . . .

In part, fitness crusaders in the Eisenhower and the Kennedy administrations were driven by the fear that flabby American bodies could not possibly survive if pitted against the rough bodies of Russian and Chinese foes. Shane MacCarthy worried that Americans' love of comfort and ease might make them vulnerable "to subjugation of tougher races, even though these races knew a far lower standard of living." Many commentators voiced similar concerns, including a reporter who warned that Americans "had better become plenty tough too if we are to survive such enemies." Military expert and Pulitzer Prize–winner Hanson W. Baldwin put

the matter even more starkly: "Can American man—after years of protective conditioning—vie with the barbarian who has lived by his wits, his initiative, his brawn? Will he retain the will to fight for his country?" He was not optimistic. American virility had been replaced by a boyhood and manhood enfeebled by "sedentarianism, push buttonitis and indoorism. . . . From all this emerges a picture—not of an American who can lick any two or three enemies, but of a slow-witted, vacuous adolescent with an intellectual interest keyed to comic books and a motivation conspicuous by its absence." Soft-bellied American boys could not stand up to hard-muscled Communist youth, a point made by one medical expert who feared that Americans could either rebuild their bodies or become "spineless physical and moral molluscs" who might as well "give up right now, enjoy a nice farewell dinner, and go home to our easy chairs and T.V. sets." . . .

Military leaders shared these sentiments and voiced ongoing concern about the physical deterioration of young men and the threat this physical corruption posed to the future of the nation. Their opinions were especially important; in linking fitness and freedom, they provided steady support for an aggressive physical fitness program capable of producing fighting men. Colonel Frank J. Kones, director of physical education at the Military Academy, feared that without a fitness program, "our children will certainly become a race of eggheads walking around on bird-legs," an anatomical anxiety shared by Brigadier General S. I. A. Marshall, who told a congressional committee that "we're a nation that has become flabby in the legs" and that physical weakness inevitably brought with it a decline in "moxie." Americans needed courage to fight foes who were, in the words of the surgeon general of the Army, Leonard Heaton, "primitive, rugged, and relatively unaffected by the ease and prosperity in which we live." In the face of such foes, national survival required a high level of fitness.

But it was John and Robert Kennedy who most determinedly drew the connection between the fitness program and the Cold War.

The "muscle gap" and the "missile gap" were central elements in Kennedy's effort to wage the Cold War at a higher level. In the fall of 1961, President Kennedy called on American educators to do their duty in the fitness crusade. The long shadows of America's international commitments now fell across the nation's schools. Kennedy became convinced that administrators and teachers had a vital role to play in preparing the nation to meet obligations that would sorely test the loyalty, stamina, determination, and preparedness of all Americans. He considered his school-based fitness program to be "the decisive force" in equipping young Americans "to serve our nation in its hours of need." Physical strength had spelled the difference for American soldiers in the past and had made the nation "history's mightiest defender of freedom." Strong bodies would defend freedom in the present and ensure America's greatness in the future. "In our own time, in the jungles of Asia and on the borders of Europe, a new group of vigorous young Americans helps to maintain the peace of the world and our security as a nation." . . .

Robert Kennedy sounded the same alarm and assured school physical education teachers of the administration's commitment to fitness. Although science, engineering, and mathematics education needed improvement, such efforts would redound to no one's benefit if American youth lacked the bodily strength to make use of their education. After all, Kennedy made clear, even technological warfare required American soldiers and technicians to walk to the silos to push the buttons: "if we are sick people; if we are people that have difficulty walking two or three blocks to the engineering laboratory, or four or five blocks to the missile launching site, we are not going to be able to meet the great problems that face us in the next ten years."

Robert Kennedy concluded by praising Americans as a "tough, viable, industrious people" who do not "search for a fight" but are "prepared to meet our responsibilities." Seemingly innocuous pull-ups, sit-ups, and sprints in school gym classes the nation over

were the first line of defense in the Cold War. "We cannot afford to be second in anything—certainly not in the matter of physical fitness." Before it was too late, Kennedy urged Americans to adopt a nationwide, systematic program that would stem the physical deterioration of the young, a "program that, in the defense of our freedoms, will enable them to pass any test, any time, any place in the world."

Much like efforts at the turn-of-the-century to resuscitate a floundering manhood, the fitness crusade that began in the 1950s tried to rescue youth, especially male youth, from the sins of immorality and technological excess that were now inscribed on the flabby physiques of America's children. The threat to the body was not inconsequential; the future of manhood and of the nation itself hung in the balance. In a culture struggling with profound changes in race, work, and community, in a society vexed by fears of male homosexuality and women's changing position, the male body and the symbolic weight it carried were matters of grave importance. Bodily strength is the bottom line of male dominance, the ultimate proving ground of manhood, and in the late 1950s and early 1960s that body seemed to be at risk: hence the obsession with restoring its vitality and place as a cultural marker.

Ultimately, even more was at stake. The Cold War profoundly shaped the early years of the fitness campaign. Boys' bodies would be rebuilt not only to reassert the power of men over women and less manly men, but to stand against the threat of the age. On the chinning bar and in athletic competition, boys would learn to be men and men would ultimately learn to be warriors. The body redeemed would be the body at war, and it would not be long until American foreign policy would bear out this truth.

The Body of the Future

The martial rhetoric of the early fitness advocates did not last, but the movement itself did.

The Vietnam War rendered the overheated diction of fitness crusaders both naive and callous. Schoolyard pull-ups were an insufficient and inappropriate preparation for what was happening in Hue and Da Nang. Instead, the message that evolved in the late 1960s and after drew on an alternative discourse— muted though present from the beginning— that equated the fit body with a healthy body that would help individuals realize their full potentials. From this perspective, the body was a source of freedom and pleasure, albeit one distinctively shaped by the formidable powers of a burgeoning consumer culture.

What gave the fitness campaign staying power, in fact, was this early recognition that fitness could be linked to deeply held ideas about individualism, to popular ideas about human potential and self-esteem, and to the twin lures of sexuality and consumption. Kennedy recognized these connections early on and boosted the cultural meaning of strong bodies into the realm of democratic theory and the meaning of civilization itself. Fitness promoted the health and vitality of free people, qualities "essential if each American is to be free to realize fully the potential value of his own capabilities and the pursuit of his individual goals." Healthy and vital bodies, Kennedy concluded, were the sine qua non of individualism, and individualism was the core of American life. "In the final analysis, it is this liberation of the individual to pursue his own ends, subject only to the loose restraints of a free society, which is the ultimate meaning of our civilization."

Even as President Kennedy fused physical fitness with America's traditional commitment to individualism and democracy, others concocted less high flown, more prosaic rationales for fitness. A 1963 pamphlet argued that a fit body enhanced energy, enthusiasm, longevity, and ultimately one's sense of selfhood: "Its primary aim is to help every American realize his full potential by being physically fit." This "full potential" quickly caught the eye of businessmen, media consultants, and moviemakers, who connected fit bodies to leisure opportunities, consumerism,

and sexual allure. Fitness expert Julian Smith believed that the judicious use of free time would enhance "self-expression," and businessman Robert Hoffman urged an audience of parks, education, and recreation leaders to sell fitness to youth as a product to enhance their sense of well-being: "We must convince them [teenagers] that it is the most desirable thing in the world, that they can't live without it, that it is the most important purchase of their entire lives." A fit body, Hoffman implored, must be marketed as a commodity: "We must make them want fitness the way every teenager yearns for a blue convertible or a swimming pool." Packaged properly, fitness would be irresistible: "We must make it beautiful and safe and warm and wonderful."

And so it has become. Business quickly saw the potential marketability and financial profit of fitness. As early as 1959, Athletic Institute President Theodore Banks urged industry to study the youth fitness movement to enhance sales. A year later, the publisher of *Sports Illustrated* praised the fitness campaign for boosting profits: "Thanks to Youth Fitness and the President's council, we have more readers, more editors, more departments." Other corporations quickly answered the call. General Mills, the Milk Industry Foundation, the Bicycle Institute of America, Coca-Cola, Pepsi, U.S. Rubber, and a host of others threw their weight behind fitness. Building bodies would also build sales: young athletes needed Wheaties and milk, and thirsty competitors needed Coke and Pepsi.

It would not be long until fitness became big business, and the fit body a passport to all that American capitalism had to offer. A sign of things to come appeared in a 1960s movie sponsored by the American Dairy Association that equated fitness with improving sex appeal and one's ability to compete with other girls for the attention of boys. Milk drinkers, the movie implied, had a head start on the competition. From here it was a short step to constructing a body that mirrored a highly sexualized consumer culture—a toned, vibrant body that celebrated fashion, cosmetics, sports equipment, travel, and leisure. Fitness opened doors to the good life of cycling, skiing, tennis, golf, backpacking, surfing and, ultimately, to sex.

In the 1970s and beyond, this commercial, eroticized view of the fit body would dominate and the Cold War rhetoric of the Eisenhower and Kennedy years would be consigned to *Rambo* movies and the magazine pages of *Soldier of Fortune*. But the promotion of physical fitness, launched in the 1950s and given a boost by the Kennedy administration in the early 1960s, has had remarkable durability. The bodies of youth, and the cultural anxieties written onto their bodies, continue to fascinate and to trouble. For every person worried that boys are becoming video-addicted drones, there is another extolling the sports prowess of youthful athletes; for every citizen worried that girls are becoming anorexic Kate Moss look-a-likes, there is another convinced that Kerri Strug's Olympic vault exemplifies all that is right and true about American youth. The body remains a key signifier of gender and an important locus of cultural debate. The anxiety about youthful bodies has taken new shape, but we continue to see our aspirations and doubts, our ideas of manhood and womanhood, written on the bodies of the young. The body is, after all, a mirror of our hopes and fears, our needs and desires.

<u>ARTICLE</u>

Hardhats: Construction Workers, Manliness, and the 1970 Pro-War Demonstrations

Joshua B. Freeman

In his article Joshua Freeman turns our attention to the construction of working-class manliness. He argues that construction workers in cities like New York and St. Louis were important symbols of masculinity in late 1960s. Portrayed by the media as aggressive, crude, and sexist, these men became icons of manly American patriotism. In his article, Freeman argues that the working environment of construction workers in the post World War II era was both highly gendered and sexualized. And he maintains that construction workers' particular way of expressing manliness was a relatively new phenomenon.

In what way was the "hardhat" construction of masculinity different from that which had prevailed earlier? According to Freeman, what factors were most important in changing the way working-class men expressed their manliness? Why did the "hardhat" image have such popular appeal as an expression of masculinity in the 1970s, in his opinion?

Source: Joshua B. Freeman, "Hardhats: Construction Workers, Manliness, and the 1970 Pro-war Demonstrations," *Journal of Social History,* 26 (Summer 1993), 725–37. Reprinted by permission. Notes omitted.

When in the spring of 1970 construction workers in New York and St. Louis violently attacked anti-war demonstrators, an image of the "hardhat" was fixed in popular consciousness: journalists, politicians, social scientists, novelists, and moviemakers portrayed building tradesmen as the rudest, crudest, and most sexist of all workers. The stereotyped brawny, flagwaving construction worker became a pivot of national cultural and political debate. For some, hardhats were "real men," more willing than other Americans to defend their country and its values from enemies abroad and political dissidents, racial minorities, and counterculturalists at home. For others, hardhats were ominous figures: politically reactionary, pathologically violent, and deeply misogynist. The general public was ambivalent: by a 40% to 24% plurality those polled indicated more sympathy for the hardhats than for the students they attacked, but 53% disapproved of their use of violence.

The hardhat image was of considerable importance because the construction worker was commonly presented in the mass media, public discourse, and commercial iconography as the archetypical proletarian. Although building tradesmen occasionally had filled that role before, from the 1920s through the 1950s it was the auto worker, associated with the ethos of mass production and modernity, and belonging to a key, pattern-setting union, whom academics, artists, and businessmen generally studied, celebrated, and negotiated with as the leading blue-collar worker. However, as the composition of the work force shifted away from manufacturing, the assembly line lost its glamour, and the influence of the United Automobile Workers diminished, construction workers eclipsed auto workers in emblematic importance. By the 1970s, the hardhat itself became—and still is—the central symbol of American labor, a role earlier filled by the leather apron, the lunch pail, and the worker's cap. Furthermore, construction workers were widely held forth as prime examples of "Middle Americans" (or alternatively, "The Silent Majority"), a vast, vague grouping that was key to conservative designs for political realignment during the Nixon and post-Nixon eras.

The multiple symbolic meanings of the hardhat—both the piece of apparel and the person wearing it—were intensely gendered. The manliness of construction workers was so taken for granted by imagemakers and their audiences that the hardhat was treated as a magical object, conferring masculinity on its wearer. Beer companies, trying to convince men that drinking a particular brand of beer would confirm their manhood, began featuring hardhat-wearing actors in their advertisements, while political candidates, worried that they were perceived as "wimps," donned hardhats and posed near industrial equipment.

While the hardhat identity is universally recognized, it has yet to be seriously investigated. When, why, and how did construction workers come to be associated with aggressive, crude masculinity? Were they significantly different from other workers in this regard, and if so why? And what does the case of construction workers tell us about the changing place and meaning of manliness in the image, self-understanding, and culture of American workers?

At this point, answers to these questions have to be tentative. For one thing, while historians have written extensively about working-class notions of manliness during the nineteenth century, they rarely have addressed how these ideas changed thereafter. For another, in spite of the huge size of the U.S. construction industry and its absolute centrality to the history of organized labor, remarkably little has been written about its social history.

Several of those who have written about construction workers have cautioned against taking too seriously what carpenter-historian Mark Erlich called the "popular stereotype of the narrow-minded hardhat, who loves to drink, swear, and fight." Erlich noted the enormous diversity among construction workers and stressed how much building tradesmen have in common with other workers. Philip Foner argued that "all hard hats were not pro-war" and many who took part in the 1970 hardhat demonstrations "did so because they were compelled to." Such comments point to a general danger: the temptation, given the paucity of sources that describe how workers behaved among themselves or what they thought, to use as a surrogate how they presented themselves to outsiders or how they were represented by others. Sometimes workers' behavior, their self-image, and the popular perception of them coincide, but usually the relationship among the three is more complex.

Even a cautious assessment of the available evidence, however, reveals the world of post-World War II construction workers, especially on large urban projects, as not only remarkably male in composition—even today women make up under 2% of the work force—but also remarkably male in culture and remarkably sexualized. Take its very language. In building trades argot, circa 1970, easy work was "tit work," heavy labor "bull work." Loafing was "fucking the dog," while a very small measurement was a "cunt hair." A tool used to reshape wire was known as the "bull's dick," while calls for diagonal cutters—"dia x" for short—were the occasion for endless jokes about "dykes." Even routine griping came out in sexual terms. One ironworker complained that: "You freeze your balls right up into your belly in the winter and seat 'em down to your knees in the summer."

Of course, earthy, profane language was heard at non-construction worksites as well. Testicles were as central—if in a somewhat different way—to the speech and worldview of left-wing painter and former United Electrical Workers organizer Ralph Fasanella as to Tommy and Chubby De Coco, the conservative construction electricians and "fifty-year-old pussy chasers" in Richard Price's 1976 novel *Bloodbrothers* (made into a movie three years later). But if far from unique, the profanity and sexualization of language among post-World War II construction workers seem extreme. Furthermore, because the public was more likely to see building tradesmen at work than most other blue-collar groups, profanity was more widely associated with hardhats than with

workers in more isolated occupations who might curse mightily among themselves.

Proximity to the public made possible another type of sexually-related construction worker behavior, "watching the windows." This consisted of peering from structures being built into adjacent apartments or hotel rooms to spy on naked women or couples engaged in sex. Often elaborate preparations—bringing binoculars to work, building hiding places or even bleachers—were made to facilitate such voyeurism, which was widespread and almost always a group activity. When live women were unavailable for viewing, pornographic magazines, books, or even movies shown in on-site trailers might substitute. Pasted-up pictures of nude women—"paper pussy"—were virtually a norm in American industry, but peeping as a regular part of work culture was highly unusual.

Still more evidence of the gendered, sexualized nature of construction work comes from the women who entered it after 1978, when the federal government began requiring construction companies and apprenticeship programs to develop affirmative action programs for recruiting female workers. Pioneer building tradeswomen reported over and over again being harassed on the job both sexually and in non-sexual ways meant to drive them away, up to and including serious physical assaults.

The hardhat image, then, perhaps exaggerated the extent to which construction workers were "macho" and different from other workers, but clearly there was something intensely male about the culture of post-World War II construction work. In and of itself this was not new; it was also the case for late nineteenth-century and New Deal-era construction work. What was different was the changing meaning of manliness, to both construction workers and those who observed them.

For the turn-of-the-century skilled construction worker, manliness meant independence, mutuality, and pride in craft. Worksite photographs of early twentieth-century carpenters, for example, show neatly dressed men, wearing derby hats and sometimes white shirts and ties, carefully maintaining an erect, dignified bearing. This self-presentation (even in apparently unposed photographs workers usually were aware of the camera) corresponded to a political construct in which building tradesmen, like other craftsmen, closely linked self-respect, manhood, and citizenship. Reinforcing one another, all three ultimately rested on economic independence, which was seen as the fruit of skill, hard work, sobriety, and organization.

Within this craft tradition, manhood apparently did not have an explicitly sexual meaning. Nick Salvatore, for example, wrote that for Eugene Victor Debs the essential attributes of manhood were "personal honor, industry, and responsibility to one's duties." David Montgomery described the phrase "manly," as used by nineteenth-century craftsmen, as connoting "dignity, respectability, defiant egalitarianism, and patriarchal male supremacy."

These notions of manliness grew out of a gender system and an industrial system in flux. Long-term developments away from the workplace, such as the female suffrage and temperance movements, had profound implications for thinking in all classes about what it meant to be a man. Working-class ideas of manhood and manliness also were affected by changes at work, especially the introduction of new technologies that made venerated skills outmoded, the greater use of female or child labor, and the rise or fall of union power. While the pattern varied from industry to industry, generally it seems that as the nineteenth century drew to a close, physical strength and specific craft skills became less important in working-class male identity, while the ability of a worker to provide for his family became more so. This might explain why photographic portraits of workers posed with symbols of their trade declined in popularity, while those of workers and their families dressed in their finest clothes became favored.

Literary as well as visual evidence suggests that for the late-nineteenth-century craft worker, the concept of manliness was firmly attached and even subsumed to ideas of respectability and domesticity. Skilled workers— including building tradesmen—were not immune from the temptations of drink, gambling, and extra-marital sex. But apparently most sought to temper themselves, to control such impulses, and thereby disassociate themselves from the "rough working-class culture" dominated by less-skilled, more poorly-paid workers. Many found an alternative to plebeian rowdiness in the huge fraternal orders that sprang up all over postbellum America. Typically these joined together skilled artisans and small proprietors around ritualized expressions of male solidarity, promoting a link between manliness, respectability, and economic standing. These groups were racially exclusionary and often nativist. For many native-born white workers, manhood was as much a racial and ethnic category as one of gender: African-Americans and immigrants from many regions were considered incapable of behaving in manly ways.

Construction unions built on, embodied, and promoted the idea of respectable manliness. Many building trades unions called themselves brotherhoods, and like other craft unions borrowed extensively from the fraternal movement. The oath of the Bricklayers was typical in calling on its members to "solemnly and sincerely pledge by my honor as a man that I will not reveal any private business . . . of this union." The International Association of Bridge and Structural Iron Workers, while not hesitant to use explosives against open-shop employers, took it upon itself to promote bourgeois respectability among its members in other regards. One business agent claimed: "The organization has made men [out] of a lot of irresponsible bums. . . . I remember when a bridgeman wearing a white collar couldn't get a job. The foreman would say that he was a dude, who didn't know his trade. It's different now. If a man is well dressed . . . the foreman will size him up and conclude that he is a decent fellow."

This quest for respectability, to dress well, was both an expression of workers' sense of their dignity and an effort to meet middle-class norms, part and parcel of the struggle by workers and unions, as Sidney Hillman once put it, to "establish themselves as a full-fledged part of organized society." It was evident at the top of the labor movement in the pleasure leaders like Samuel Gompers, John Mitchell, and John L. Lewis took in rubbing elbows with the rich while decked out in their finery. At the bottom it could be seen in the jackets and ties unionists so often wore to demonstrations.

The ironworkers in the most famous photographs of construction workers ever taken—those by Lewis W. Hine of the raising of the Empire State Building—did not wear white shirts and ties, but like the turn-of-the-century carpenters they projected a strong sense of dignity and self-possession. While the photographs they appear in are more candid than earlier ones—Hine more deeply penetrated the worksite than previous photographers—their image nonetheless was carefully crafted; Hine frankly wrote that his purpose in making these and the other photographs in his 1932 collection, *Men at Work,* was to win respect for the "men of courage, skill, daring and imagination" who "make . . . and manipulate" the machinery of modern life.

"Constructive heroism"—to use Alan Trachtenberg's characterization of the Empire State Building photographs—was typical of artistic representations of labor during the 1930s, both in North America and Europe. Caught up in a cult of productivity, liberals and leftists worshipped giant industrial enterprises and the men who built and operated them, regardless of their social or economic context. The Soviet White Sea Canal and the American Grand Coulee Dam, the auto plants at River Rouge and Gorky, were all seen as part of the great Faustian drama of man conquering nature.

And man it was. It can hardly be a coincidence that in Hine's pre-World War I photographs, documenting the exploitation of labor, women and children figured prominently, but in his later celebration of work only adult men appear, beautiful men, strong and vigorous, hanging high in the air like Icarus, challenging the gods themselves. Hine's pic-

tures of bare-chested ironworkers, with their hint of eroticism, are informed by "the fetish of masculinity," "the magic of masculinity, muscle and machinery" that Beatrix Campbell argues was embraced by the British left during this same period. In fact, as Eric Hobsbawm has noted, in most of the industrialized world the once-dominant symbol of liberty, revolution, and working-class struggle, the bare-topped female holding banner high, was replaced by the 1930s by its "exact counterpart," "namely a . . . masculine laborer . . . *naked to the waist.*" In the United States that laborer was likely to be a construction worker.

The increased use of a male worker's body to symbolize the working class—and masculinity—may have been a reaction, at least in part, to continuing changes in industrial life and gender relations, including increased mechanization, a further decline of craft labor, the ever-greater dominance of the corporation over the individual, rising female labor force participation, and increased social and political freedom for women. The image of the manly worker, Barbara Melosh argues, "spoke to a [post-World War I] crisis of masculinity experienced by both working-class and middle-class audiences," a crisis made worse by the mass unemployment of the Great Depression. It was as if artists and other imagemakers were trying to bolster a male role in deep peril. Significantly, the workers portrayed by New Deal-sponsored sculptors and muralists tended to be in precisely those occupations hardest hit by unemployment and automation: the building trades, mining, and factory work.

How much the labor imagery of the 1930s corresponded to working-class reality is unclear. The workers in Hine's photographs and in New Deal public art seemed poised between the turn-of-the-century republican craftsman and the socialist-realist worker-hero. The detached, formal bearing and sexual coolness of both archetypes is far removed from the earthiness of the immigrant bricklayers in the best-selling 1939 novel, *Christ in Concrete,* written by Pietro Di Donato, a bricklayer and son of a bricklayer who presumably had a better sense of life at construction sites than most artists.

On and off the job Di Donato's workers were fountains of ribaldry and sexual reference. But this in itself was not a mark of their manhood, for the women in the book were almost as open in their joyful, rustic sexuality. To be a man was to be sexual, but sexuality was seen as an attribute of all healthy, natural beings in the profoundly familial—but not puritanical—outlook of these workers. More than sexuality, craft, strength, and the ability to endure made a man a man. "Look villain," one worker told another on a sharp winter day, "the scaffold planks crack with cold 'neath footstep, the bricks weep with frost, and the wall is swollen crooked. . . . But tell me—what are we Christians, men or not?" Manhood was not respectability; the workers had contempt for the owners of the structures they were building, "soft, white-fingered men who looked like painted mustached women dressed in tailored men's clothes."

The construction workers Di Donato describes are in many ways different from modern ones, but one incident in his novel previews a scene strongly associated with the hardhat image. When a "tall slim girl with dancing ripe breasts" walked past a construction site, one bricklayer "stood up, rolled his sleepy eyes and drawled from loose lips in American, 'Ahhhhbye-bee, you make-a-me seeck . . . uhmnnnnnn bye-bee you make-a-me die-a . . .'." Another "bared his horse teeth and stuttered ecstatically, 'Ma-Ma-Madonna mine, what grapes she has!' Two other workers admonished them for being disrespectful, but they too joined in the watching.

This scene has a number of elements that figure in explanations of post-World War II hardhat behavior. Most obvious is ethnicity. Di Donato's workers are almost all Italian, and some commentators—from sociologists to filmmakers—have strongly associated postwar plebeian vulgarity with Italian-American culture. (Often, as in Jonathan Rieder's *Canarsie* and Woody Allen's *Broadway Danny Rose*, tough, sexually electric, thick-headed Italian provincials are contrasted with wimpy, verbal

Jewish cosmopolitans, in the perpetuation of ahistoric stereotypes.) Without ruling out the possible relevance of ethnicity—it is notable that *Bloodbrothers* also was set in an Italian-American milieu—in the absence of systematic, comparative studies it seems dangerous, and pat, to place too much weight on ethnicity as an explanation for the sexual stance of construction workers, especially given anecdotal evidence that participants in the demonstrations that helped establish the hardhat image came from varied backgrounds.

In explaining construction worker behavior, others have pointed to the peculiar social geography of urban building sites—another element in Di Donato's "girl" watching scene. Such sites are self-enclosed spaces, off-limits to passersby, yet surrounded by, and literally looking out on, well-used public areas. This creates the possibility for spying on, ogling, or verbally harassing nearby women (and men) from within a zone of psychological and physical safety. (Worksite proximity to places where students happened to be demonstrating against the invasion of Cambodia, of course, was one reason why construction workers were at the forefront of pro-war activities.) Protected from outsiders by fences, hardhats, and each other, construction workers have a sense of invulnerability unlike, say, bus drivers or waiters. Sociologist and journeyman electrician Jeffrey W. Riemer further argues that the primitive conditions on construction sites contribute to crude behavior of all kinds, including "urinating in public, farting, wearing dirty clothes daily, excessive profanity, spitting, [and] throwing one's lunch garbage to the wind."

Riemer contends that construction worker job behavior dubbed deviant—including sexually related behavior—is actually quite normal and largely benign. Other workers, he argues, would act similarly if they had the chance. To some extent he undoubtedly is right; physical setting and work organization play a role in what might be called "hardhatism." Other groups of male workers who operate with only loose supervision on the borders between protected private space and busy public space—for example truck drivers—also have been notorious for sexist behavior. But Riemer's tendency to treat the crude behavior he observed as being the result of natural male impulses freed from normal inhibitory structure is naive at best and ahistoric. Unless we believe in a genetic masculinity programmed for such behavioral detail as shouting "Ahhhh bye-bee," we need to look further.

One place to look is at the danger of construction work, a central theme of *Christ in Concrete* and almost all other writing about the building trades. For workers in occupations like mining, police work, and construction, which combine high risk with small team organization, safety and survival depend on the establishment of mutual trust. When the work force in such situations was all male, or virtually so, trust often was built through a decidedly male idiom of physical jousting, sexual boasting, sports talk, and shared sexual activities. This had a particularly strong impact in construction for two reasons. First, in contrast to mining, where work and residential communities heavily overlapped and women played a prominent role in supporting worker struggles, in construction, work and home life were usually quite separate. In fact, many construction workers were semi-itinerant, living long stretches away from their families. Second, because construction jobs were of limited duration, informal work groups had to be continually recreated; workers often found themselves working alongside people they never had met, yet on whom their lives and safety depended. Shared masculine activities—from peeping to whoring to whistling at women—were a way to glue together a work force in an endless process of recombination. In an era when no outward signs generally distinguished gay men from straights, aggressive heterosexual behavior also was a way of ensuring that close male bonding was not seen as evidence of homosexuality. Solidarity, safety, and sexism thus reinforced one another.

In the post-World War II era, as in the more distant past, construction unions actively encouraged a shared sense of manhood—often specifically white manhood—as a mode of worker bonding and solidarity. Apprenticeship programs, through hazing, surveillance, common experience, and the exclusion of women and non-whites, were used to build this collective identity; as much as a process of skills acquisition, apprenticeship was an "initiation into the fraternity of tradesmen." Riemer recalled that while attending apprenticeship classes, he and his fellow trainee electricians pooled work on class exercises, giving them time to engage in "extracurricular activities": "picking up girls in the downtown area, going to . . . taverns, sitting in on court cases . . . , bowling or playing pool, or just going . . . to watch girl students in the student lounge." On the job, apprentices—often called "punks"—faced numerous rites of passage to full occupational manhood, in the process reinforcing the maleness of the trade. Not surprisingly, it was young workers—full of anxieties about their own status—who were the most hostile to women when they began entering the construction trades. Some large construction locals further bolstered male bonding through clubs for particular subgroups of the membership. Usually organized on an ethnic, religious, or neighborhood basis, or consisting of unionists who belonged to the same fraternal order, these groups served social and political functions, helped mediate internal union conflicts, and used fraternalism to tie workers to one another and to the union.

Employers encouraged an intensely male work culture as well, for example by tolerating sexual shenanigans on the job and distributing nude calendars at Christmas. Many believed that male bonding increased the motivation, productivity, and stability of their work force. For this reason, contractors long resisted hiring women; one told an interviewer that "a lot of these guys [construction workers] are ex-service guys. They don't want a woman around—they'll just distract them . . . the guys start competing for their attention or whistling or fighting over them." Also, some employers believed a shared sense of maleness eased antagonisms between workers and themselves (much in the way that the fraternal movement helped bridge the gap between skilled workers and higher social orders).

Ethnicity, worksite ecology, occupational structure, and union tradition, then, all to one degree or another contributed to the hardhat phenomenon. However, they do not explain why it emerged when it did nor the intensity of the hostility some construction workers displayed toward women, homosexuals, and antiwar demonstrators in the late 1960s and early 1970s. What makes that rage particularly puzzling is that it came at the end of a long period when construction workers, by objective measures and their own assessments, had done exceedingly well.

The years between the end of World War II and the early 1970s constituted a golden age for American workers, when earnings, benefits, and living standards rose to unprecedented heights. Construction workers especially prospered; a long building boom, a labor shortage, an astounding unionization rate of over 80 percent, and a sympathetic legal and political environment (including the Davis-Bacon Act and similar state laws), enabled skilled tradesmen to push their hourly wages to the point that the over-paid construction worker became a stock figure in postwar culture.

In an era when studies of workers' attitudes towards their jobs stressed their alienation (in spite of their growing affluence)—the much discussed "blue collar blues"—construction workers were notable for their high level of job satisfaction. Unlike almost everyone else, building tradesmen apparently liked their jobs. In addition to high pay and good benefits, they repeatedly cited the challenge of their work, its variety, and their independence. Equally important was the pride they had in their crafts and in the products of their labor. Often workers would visit buildings they had worked on, sometimes bringing along their families, to admire the tangible product of what they considered their "honest work."

Of course there was nothing inherently masculine about these feelings; in the 1970s

and 1980s building tradeswomen shared them. Yet indirectly, job satisfaction and craft pride contributed to the swaggering masculinity of the hardhats. Many construction workers looked down on other blue-collar workers, especially those on assembly lines, and even more on white-collar workers, who they saw as doing little of social importance. Construction unions reinforced this attitude by remaining aloof from, or even opposing, worker struggles outside their industry.

Not especially interested in upward mobility, postwar construction workers had no particular admiration for those above them in the social hierarchy. Unlike their predecessors, they did not feel the need to create a respectable self-presentation when in the presence of middle-class observers. Rather, they often did the opposite, deliberately flouting middle-class notions of decorum by wearing rough work clothes as a badge of honor, riddling their speech with curses, and harassing women who passed by construction sites. Ironworker Mike Cherry recalled his pleasure at the "weekly dumb show" when his coworkers building a midtown New York skyscraper went to cash their checks, evoking "the uncomprehending, often half-frightened stares of Chase Manhattan's more typical customers as the . . . hoards of construction workers—variously oily, muddy, or dusty and all irrepressibly and vulgarly gregarious—poured in."

While this desire to shock reflected craft pride, fraternity, and a healthy contempt for elites, it also was rooted in the resentment many construction workers felt about their social invisibility. After World War II construction workers no longer needed to seek economic and political power; collectively they already had won it. Yet during these same years construction workers—like other manual workers—virtually disappeared from popular culture, political discourse, even advertising. This was understandably galling to building tradesmen, with their acute sense of their social contributions and accomplishments. Public rowdiness was one way for them to make themselves socially visible. As a strategy, it worked brilliantly with the pro-war hardhat demonstrations.

Social status, however, was not the only cause of construction worker concern. Even during good times, workers in construction never felt completely secure because of the limited duration of their jobs. In the late 1960s, although the economy and construction continued to boom, there were particular reasons for anxiety. Profit rates for American businesses had begun to fall, leading to a drive for higher productivity. In some building trades this meant efforts to standardize tasks and force greater specialization, diminishing needed skill. At the same time, accelerating inflation—a by-product of the Vietnam War—impacted construction in a number of ways. First, it threatened to wipe out wage gains. Second, it led the largest purchasers of new buildings, the major national corporations, to form the Construction Users Anti-Inflation Roundtable (which later became the Business Roundtable) to press for lower construction labor costs. And third, it exposed the industry to unaccustomed political pressure as President Nixon, in September 1969, suspended most federal construction spending as an anti-inflationary measure, insisting that labor and management find a way to control costs before money would be released.

Falling profits, a productivity drive, and inflation on the one hand, and workers made confident by low unemployment, years of prosperity, and powerful unions on the other, led to an increase of strikes of all kinds in the late 1960s, including in the construction industry. In New York, for example, in 1969 there were strikes by steamfitters, sheet metal workers, hoisting engineers, rigging and machinery movers, and construction teamsters. The combination of confidence and anxiety that fed the late 1960s strike wave contributed to the aggressive masculinity associated with the hardhat image. In fact, one of the key groups initiating the New York hardhat demonstrations were elevator constructors, who the previous year had struck for three-and-a-half months, tying up work at dozens of high-rise worksites.

Both anxiety and confidence also could be seen in the sharp, occasionally violent response to efforts to desegregate the construction industry. As a result of sustained pressure by civil rights activists, by 1969 various public agencies were pressing contractors and construction unions—many of which were all white or virtually so—to open their ranks to African-Americans. In September of that year the Nixon Administration announced the Philadelphia Plan, a model program requiring contractors to set specific goals for minority hiring. Many white construction workers opposed such efforts. In some cases immediate self-interest was involved. Suburban and out-of-town workers on big city projects feared losing their jobs to inner-city residents. Also, many building tradesmen wanted to reserve training and job slots for their kin. Other objections were ideological and psychological, ranging from pure and simple racism to workers' belief that their own early struggles—real or imagined—would be rendered meaningless if black workers were given new, supposedly easier ways to enter the industry.

In 1969, in at least two cities, white construction workers held raucous anti-desegregation demonstrations that had many similarities with the better-known pro-war demonstrations the following year. In Pittsburgh some 4,000 white workers rallied against a decision by the mayor to shut down local construction while negotiations were held with black protestors. In Chicago over 2,000 building tradesmen gathered outside a building where a federal hearing was being held on alleged union discrimination, jeering at witnesses, scuffling with police, and rushing Jesse Jackson and his wife as they entered the building. Later, part of the crowd invaded the Chicago *Sun-Times-Daily News* building chanting "we want the truth," while others taunted a group of demonstrators supporting the Chicago 8 anti-war activists, then on trial.

The impressive 1970 mobilization of construction workers in support of U.S. foreign policy thus built on earlier struggles against employers and integration. Some observers believed that the pro-war demonstrations themselves were linked to the issue of racial discrimination. Almost immediately after the New York demonstrations Assistant Secretary of Labor Arthur A. Fletcher suggested that there was "an ulterior motive" for the pro-war marches. "I believe they feel that if they can support the President on this one issue," he said, "they can get inside the White House and be a formidable opponent of the Philadelphia Plan."

Part of the power of the race issue lay in its relationship to workers' sense of self-worth. Craft identity, union membership, and earning power—all established partly by exclusion—were linked in workers' minds to their social position and patriarchal authority. Efforts by non-whites to enter the building trades thus threatened white workers' sense of status as producers, citizens, and men. So did the growing drive by women for legal and social equality. In the late 1960s this threat was not job-related; until the end of the following decade there was no significant push to allow women into the building trades. But it was everywhere else: in the streets, in the media, and, most important, in the home. In 1968, for example, radical feminists received extensive publicity in connection with their protest against the Miss America contest, women were allowed for the first time to serve on juries in Mississippi, and Princeton University tenured its first female professor, to mention just a few headline events. And only days before the 1970 hardhat demonstrations, the Senate, under pressure from women's groups, held the first hearings on the Equal Rights Amendment in twelve years, the prelude to its passage two years later.

Many construction workers saw themselves as surrounded by overly-assertive women and uppity blacks. One plumber commented to sociologist E. E. Le Masters: "I don't mind [women] being equal, but some of them want to run the whole damn show. They're just like niggers—give them an inch and they'll take a mile." Le Masters reported that the construction workers he studied in the early 1970s were deeply frightened by women's liberation.

While these workers did not object to their wives working for wages, which about half did, or having separate social lives, which the men actually preferred, they had no interest in egalitarian marriages. Non-white men imperiled the patriarchal notions of white workers who equated manliness and whiteness, but feminists presented a more direct and serious challenge. When modest desegregation finally did come to the construction industry, white male workers generally accepted non-white male colleagues more easily than female ones.

Just as nineteenth- and early twentieth-century notions of masculinity developed in relation to changing gender roles, the hardhat persona, then, developed against the background of sweeping changes in the place of men and women in the society. The whole structure of patriarchy was seemingly at stake. Exaggerated assertions of masculinity, like those associated with the hardhats, were one reaction. Sometimes they were brutal. When a young, female, New York City official grabbed the jacket of a construction worker about to join three others in pummeling a student, the worker responded: "If you want to be treated like an equal, we'll treat you like one" and proceeded with two other tradesmen to punch the woman, break her glasses, and bruise her ribs so badly that she was taken to the hospital.

If new notions of womanhood were seen as threatening by many construction workers, new notions of manhood were likewise unsettling. On popular music stages, at "be-ins," and on college campuses a new figure appeared in the 1960s, the long-haired young man who explicitly rejected the idea that manhood meant physical strength and aggressiveness. Instead these counter-culturalists linked manhood to such traditionally female notions as sensuality and sensitivity. Even more startling were the growing number of men, particularly after the June 1969 Stonewall Inn riot, who proudly announced their homosexuality. To love other men, they proclaimed, was not to be a sissy—a feminized male—but to be male in the purest form.

Initially these new images of manhood had a particular class content; they were associated with privilege, with those who did not have to labor all day in the heat and cold like hardhats did, with those who were using their class position to dodge the draft and the war in Vietnam (a particularly touchy issue for construction workers, since many were World War II or Korean War veterans and some had sons in the armed forces). It was the combination of class resentment and perceived threat to patriarchal notions of manliness that gave the hardhat demonstrations their explosive character. One tradesman commented about the demonstrations that: "Here were these kids, rich kids, who could go to college, who didn't have to fight, they are telling you your son died in vain. It makes you feel your whole life is shit, just nothing." Tellingly, pro-war construction workers singled out male anti-war protestors with the longest hair for assault and shouted at New York's patrician mayor, John Lindsay—a special target of their wrath—that he was a "faggot."

In the Spring of 1970 a variety of factors—from long-standing characteristics of construction work to recently developed racial, class, cultural, political, and sexual tensions—combined to shape construction worker behavior and spark the hardhat demonstrations. The mass media—newspapers, magazines, television, and movies—then fixed the hardhat image in the public eye. The widespread publicity they gave the hardhats reflected the dramatic nature of the New York and St. Louis events, which were the first substantial physical clashes between groups of civilians over the Vietnam War. But the media also found in the hardhat image a powerful metaphor for the deepening conflicts that had developed during the 1960s over politics, gender roles, and cultural values.

The hardhat image endured in part because it resonated with a crisis of *middle-class* masculinity; during the 1970s, as Peter Biskind and Barbara Ehrenreich have noted, "Safe, tame domesticity faded as a social ideal" while "its traditional antithesis—untamed

machismo" was undermined by the Vietnam experience and resurgent feminism. Anxiety over this dilemma made it safer for middle-class artists and imagemakers to explore the meaning of manhood metaphorically rather than through self-examination. Thus moviemakers, writers, and advertisers became fascinated by the white, ethnic working-class, which was portrayed, for better or for worse, as the last enclave of traditional manliness. In movies like *Bloodbrothers, Saturday Night Fever,* and the multi-part *Rocky* series, to quote Biskind and Ehrenreich again, "the blue-collar world . . . replaced the Old West as the mythical homeland of masculinity." Thus even as the specific political events surrounding the initial prominence of the hardhat receded into the past, the hardhat continued to serve as a symbol of masculinity. At least in this respect the 1970s replicated the 1930s, when the muscular, sensuous, blue-collar male was used to represent the strength, self-confidence, defiance, and virility that many artists and intellectuals yearned for.

The particular historical moment that created the hardhat in all his splendor was a short one. Within a few years the construction boom, along with the rest of the economy, collapsed. Taking advantage of changed economic and political circumstances, a fierce anti-union drive succeeded by the late 1980s in reducing the unionization rate for construction workers to 22 percent, one of the most remarkable reversals of class power in American history. The sense of confidence and well-being that allowed construction workers to snub their noses at what the middle class considered acceptable behavior turned out to rest on shaky economic foundations.

The cultural foundations of the hardhat phenomenon also proved shaky. By the mid-1970s a long-haired young man was more likely to be a construction worker than a college student. Though neither side realized it at first, there was common ground between hardhats and long-haired, middle-class protestors: both rejected bourgeois respectability. But when the American Century came to an end a half-decade after the hardhat demonstrations, the middle-class longhairs could and did run for the shelter of conventional careers and social acceptability. It was not so easy for the young workers who by then had adopted some of their style. So the counterculture made its last stand not among the children of privilege but in the working class. In the process of class migration it lost its expansive, optimistic character—no long-haired construction worker ever thought that the age of Aquarius was dawning—and took on a sullen aspect, a statement of difference and diffidence. Ironically, the longhair became the heir of the hardhat.

While the reality of construction work rapidly changed, the public image of the hardhat remained frozen, with substantial political and social consequences. On May 26, 1970, less than three weeks after the first hardhat march, President Richard Nixon held a carefully orchestrated White House meeting with the leaders of New York Building and Construction Trades Council, at which he accepted a hardhat labelled "Commander in Chief." While delighted to receive support for his invasion of Cambodia at a time when protest against the Vietnam War had reached unprecedented heights, Nixon saw grander possibilities in the hardhats and their image: a vehicle for accelerating the breakup of the already tottering Democratic coalition and for forming a new, conservative, Republican-led electoral bloc that included a substantial number of white workers. Accordingly, the White House launched an intense effort to woo union support, which paid off handsomely when the AFL-CIO remained neutral in the 1972 presidential election.

The hardhat demonstrations and image also helped maintain white, male dominance of construction jobs, just as Arthur Fletcher had predicted. Shortly after the 1972 election, Nixon appointed Peter Brennan, who as president of the New York Building Trades Council had endorsed, promoted, and helped spread the hardhat demonstrations, as his new Secretary of Labor. From this post Brennan successfully choreographed resistance to the desegregation of the construction industry. At the same time, the hardhat image itself may have attracted to construction men seeking a last bastion of white male privilege, fortifying the hostility to outsiders. In the late 1980s, African-Americans and Hispanics each made up only about 7 percent of the construction work force, and women less than 2 percent, with the percentages far lower in many of the skilled trades.

Finally, the hardhat phenomenon reinforced an image of the labor movement as male at the very moment that the work force was becoming more female than ever before. In August 1991 women constituted nearly 46 percent of the civilian labor force, up from 37 percent in August 1970. Studies have shown that in recent years women have had a greater propensity to unionize than men. However, during the 1970s and 1980s many women were put off from joining unions by what one sociologist called the "hardhat imagery of militancy." Furthermore, many unions—especially old-line craft groups—were unreceptive to women and made little effort to recruit them. As a result, the unionization rate of women workers trailed and still trails that of men. A mismatch between image and reality thus contributed to the precipitous decline of the union movement after 1970. Gendering the image of the working class was one piece of a social and political catastrophe whose consequences we are still suffering.

SUGGESTIONS FOR FURTHER READING

BARBARA BAIR, "True Women, Real Men: Gender, Ideology, and Social Roles in the Garvey Movement," in *Gendered Domains: Rethinking Public and Private in Women's History*, ed. Dorothy O. Helly and Susan M. Reverby (Ithaca, NY: Cornell University Press, 1992), 154–66.

JESSE BERRETT, "Feeding the Organization Man: Diet and Masculinity in Post War America," *Journal of Social History,* 30 (Summer 1997), 805–25.

K. A. CUORDILEONE, " 'Politics in an Age of Anxiety': Cold War Political Culture and the Crisis in American Masculinity, 1949–1960," *Journal of American History,* 87 (Sept. 2000), 515–45.

JOE L. DUBBERT, *A Man's Place: Masculinity in Transition* (Upper Saddle River, NJ: Prentice Hall, 1979).

PETER G. FILENE, *Him/Her/Self: Gender Identities in Modern America,* 3rd ed. (Baltimore, MD: The Johns Hopkins University Press, 1998).

STEVEN M. GELBER, "Do-It-Yourself: Constructing, Repairing and Maintaining Domestic Masculinity," *American Quarterly,* 49 (March 1997), 66–112.

ROBERT L. GRISWOLD, *Fatherhood in America: A History* (New York: Basic Books, 1993).

SUSAN JEFFORDS, *The Remasculinization of America: Gender and the Viet Nam War* (Bloomington: Indiana University Press, 1989).

MICHAEL KIMMEL, *Manhood in America: A Cultural History* (New York: Free Press, 1996).

RICHARD KLUGER, *Simple Justice: The History of* Brown v. Board of Education *and Black America's Struggle for Equality* (New York: Vintage Books, 1977).

TOM PENDERGAST, " 'Horatio Alger Doesn't Work Here Any More': Masculinity and American Magazines, 1919–1940," *American Studies,* 38 (Spring 1997), 55–80.

E. ANTHONY ROTUNDO, "Patriarchs and Participants: A Historical Perspective on Fatherhood in the United States," in *Beyond Patriarchy: Essays by Men on Pleasure, Power, and Change,* ed. Michael Kaufman (New York: Oxford University Press, 1987), 64–80.

"She Should Have Gone to the Moon," *Sunday [London] Times Magazine,* Nov. 15, 1998, 38–47.

ROBERT STAPLES, "Masculinity and Race: The Dual Dilemma of Black Men," *Journal of Social Issues,* 34 (Winter 1978), 169–83.

PETER N. STEARNS, *Be a Man! Males in Modern Society,* 2nd ed. (New York: Holmes & Meier, 1990).

JESSICA WEISS, "Making Room for Fathers: Men, Women, and Parenting in the United States, 1945–1980," in *A Shared Experience: Men, Women, and the History of Gender,* ed. Laura McCall and Donald Yacovone (New York: New York University Press, 1998), 349–67.

CHAPTER ELEVEN

FEMININITY IN THE TWENTIETH CENTURY (1920–1975)

THE HOUSEWIFE'S REVOLUTION

Suburban housewives do not in the normal course of events lead social revolutions. Betty Friedan was the exception to the rule. Born in 1921 in Peoria, Illinois of Jewish parents, she studied psychology as an undergraduate at Smith College and then went on to graduate school at the University of California, Berkeley. In 1943, she was awarded a prestigious and lucrative fellowship to continue her graduate work but gave it up to move to New York. There she became a journalist specializing in labor issues.

Friedan claimed that she unthinkingly embraced the cult of domesticity that prevailed in the 1950s and never seriously questioned the idea that her destiny as a woman lay in becoming a wife and mother. Having lost her job after World War II, she married, set up housekeeping with her husband, and bore three children. At the same time, however, she

worked as a free-lance writer selling her articles to mass circulation ladies' magazines such as *Good Housekeeping, Parents' Magazine, Cosmopolitan,* and *Mademoiselle* and supported New Left efforts to promote social justice.

In 1957 she returned to Smith for a class reunion. It was her discussions with former classmates that led her to write what was arguably one of the most socially influential books written in twentieth-century America. *The Feminine Mystique,* published in 1963, was a critique of the way that femininity was defined by the middle class. In it, Friedan argued that attempts on the part of women to fulfill prevailing ideals of femininity resulted in making them prisoners in their own homes. Domesticity, she said, rendered women passive and economically dependent on their husbands. It not only trivialized and demeaned them, it also isolated them from public life, business, and the professions and smothered their intellects. Constructing their femininity around domesticity, she suggested, may have given middle-class women a sense of security and assurance of social respectability, but it also laid the groundwork for destroying a woman's sense of self. Women who constructed their identities around their husbands and children lost touch with who they were. They suffered from what she called a "problem that has no name."

Despite the fact that her tone was angry and strident and her social criticism was sometimes overstated, Friedan's commentary on domesticity resonated with the feelings and experiences of millions of women. She did not reject the wife/housekeeping role for women. She merely claimed that it was not in and of itself very satisfying and called on women to search for other sources of personal fulfillment. Her book freed some women from what Friedan called their "comfortable concentration camp" and encouraged them to search for alternative definitions of true womanhood. It caused others to froth at the mouth in outrage and anger. As a result of the controversy it provoked, it became a best seller.

During the twentieth century, women quite self-consciously constructed for themselves an increasingly wide variety of options for defining femininity and expressing their womanliness. Prosperity's child—the flapper of the 1920s as well as women who performed jobs traditionally held by men during World War II and feminists in the 1960s and 1970s all challenged various conventional attitudes about what it meant to be a woman. Access to education, job opportunities, birth control, and abortion brought changes in the meaning of woman as worker, wife, and mother. During the middle of the twentieth century, more and more women entered the workforce. As a result, femininity was increasingly expressed through a woman's ability to support herself if she was single or contribute to the support of her family if she was married. Her potential for economic independence meant that she did not necessarily need a man to support her. This reality, combined with the liberalization of divorce laws, brought about a significant

shift in gender relations and in the meaning of wifehood. On top of that, increasing access to birth control meant that women were in a stronger position to choose whether or not they wanted to express their womanliness through motherhood.

All of these challenges to traditional ideas about womanhood were, to say the least, socially disruptive. While some women were expanding on the legacy of the middle class "New Woman" or the working class "woman adrift" to challenge traditional ways of expressing their femininity, others either ignored what they were doing or rejected the idea of modifying their conventional ideas about what constituted "true womanhood." Those who were so inclined and could afford to do so preserved the domestic ideal by marrying, bearing children, and devoting their lives to housekeeping and volunteer work. Others who found it necessary to work for wages, looked forward to the day when they could quit their jobs and devote themselves full time to the care of their homes and families. In embracing domesticity, they rejected a definition of femininity that included self-sufficiency and independence.

The period between 1920 and 1975 was a transitional period in which the lines between masculinity and femininity became quite blurred. As the 1970s approached, it became increasingly clear to anyone interested in the issue of gender, that there was no consensus about what was feminine and what was not. Thus, the history of gender in the twentieth century is a history characterized by a conflict between those determined to preserve the domestic ideal and those who were equally determined to challenge it, a conflict that produced considerable anxiety and confusion about what it meant to be a woman.

THE FLAPPER AND HER CHALLENGE TO CONVENTIONAL WOMANHOOD

In the 1920s the flapper rejected many traditional, middle-class definitions of womanhood.

During that decade young, single women who lived in urban areas rebelled against traditional social conventions that restricted their ability to define for themselves what it meant to be a woman. The flapper blurred the distinctions between working-class and middle-class femininity. Typically the daughter of respectable, middle-class parents, she was daring, outrageous, and adventurous. Ignoring the rules of social propriety, the flapper smoked cigarettes and drank in public. She bobbed her hair, wore make-up, and shortened her skirts. She rejected the Victorian idea that women were morally superior to men, flirted shamelessly with men to whom she had not been properly introduced, stayed out until the wee hours of the morning, and asserted her right to express herself sexually. She may have drawn the line at engaging in premarital intercourse, but heavy petting was another story. Willful, capricious, physically active, competitive, and contemptuous of respectability, she demanded access to many of the privileges that men had always enjoyed and, much to the despair of her parents, challenged almost every aspect of the nineteenth-century, middle-class feminine ideal.

The flapper was no social revolutionary, however. Self-absorbed and intent on asserting her own independence, she was completely oblivious to the problems of those outside her own narrow social circle. And while she was determined to have a good time while she was young, she did not reject the idea that a woman should marry and bear children. If she worked for wages, she did so only as a way of supporting her desire for material possessions and the pursuit of pleasure. She was not particularly ambitious nor was she very concerned about breaking down gender barriers in the work force. Perfectly satisfied working as a typist or a sales clerk, she did not fantasize about becoming a bank president. She merely postponed conformity to traditional, middle-class gender conventions until she tired of life in the fast lane and found someone to share her life with. Once she hit her 30s, the woman who once identified herself as a flapper was probably married and indistinguishable from her more conventional middle-class sisters.

The flapper ignored the opportunity to create a political identity for herself. In that way she was similar to most other American women in the 1920s. The hope on the part of suffragists that women would use their right to vote and hold office to feminize politics proved illusive. After the passage of the nineteenth amendment, the woman's suffrage movement splintered. Some suffragists formed the League of Woman Voters, a nonpartisan, public service organization dedicated to the education of the female electorate. Others ran for public office on the state or local level or lobbied for appointments to federal and state government agencies like the Woman's Bureau and the Children's Bureau so that they could influence the formulation of government policies that would address the needs and concerns of women. A distinct minority lobbied for the passage of an equal rights amendment. But the amendment had little support among most women, who did not equate femininity with gender equality.

As it turned out, American women did not vote in large numbers, and when they voted they did not vote as a distinct interest group. Between 1920 and the 1970s, there was no "woman's" vote to speak of. So despite the time and effort that had been expended in order to win equal political rights for women, they did not immediately incorporate participation in politics into their definition of femininity. For women who felt that they were morally superior to most men, politics was suspect, fraught with deal making and corruption. It was a world they did not necessarily seek to enter. And the leaders of the Democratic and Republican parties, who considered politics to be one of the last bastions of male privilege, did nothing to welcome them. Thus, the fact that women now had the ability to define femininity in terms of political activism did not substantially change the character of American politics and did little to undermine the influence of the cult of domesticity.

THE PERSISTENCE OF THE DOMESTIC IDEAL

Despite the fact that in the 1920s an increasing number of married women, including those with children, worked for wages, the domestic ideal persisted. The editors of popular magazines like *McCall's* and *Ladies' Home Journal* continued to support traditional views of women as wife and mother, celebrated domesticity, and were critical of liberated women whom they accused of threatening traditional gender relations. Women who had the opportunity to go to college were much more likely to major in home economics than they were to study mathematics or physics. During the 1920s, women married in large numbers, and they married younger than they had at the turn of the century. Some continued to work after marriage, but most did so out of necessity rather than as a way to express their own individuality. The companionate marriage was the ideal, but responsibility for keeping the romance and friendship alive rested on the shoulders of the wife. To fulfill that responsibility, she was expected to run her household efficiently, uphold certain standards of beauty, defer to her husband's opinions and decisions, and make herself sexually available to him.

Even the second Ku Klux Klan, organized in 1915 and headquartered in Indianapolis, Indiana, did its best to promote traditional definitions of femininity by idealizing women's place in the home and their identities as morally superior, sexually virtuous wives and mothers in need of male protection. A part of their campaign to rid the country of vice was a public acknowledgment that women were victimized by domestic violence, desertion, and all sorts of other socially objectionable male behavior including gambling, drinking, and extra-marital sexual activities. As a matter of policy, members of the Klan pledged themselves to uphold the idea that men should treat their wives with respect and fulfill their marital obligations. Such a commitment was appealing to women who rejected the feminist vision of woman as an independent and self-sufficient individual on the grounds that such

a vision would deprive them of the security and privileges that they were supposed to enjoy as wives and mothers. Thousands joined the Women's Ku Klux Klan and others appealed to male Klan members to resort to vigilante justice to discipline their wayward husbands.

The stock market crash of 1929 and the depression that ensued tended to reinforce traditional gender conventions and the assumption that a woman's place was in the home. As the economic crisis deepened, more and more women were fired from their jobs and found it increasingly difficult to find new ones. Unemployment undermined their ability to take care of themselves and forced many back into a state of economic dependence on the men in their families.

Some women, of course, continued to work for wages. Because employment for women was concentrated in the service sector rather than in sales and heavy industry, they were able to keep jobs as janitors, secretaries, and department store clerks. But their continuing ability to earn wages did not pass without comment when so many men were out of work and unable to fulfill their role as breadwinner. The employment of married women was a particularly controversial issue. Many of those who determined public policy both in the government and in the private sector were convinced that married women who worked outside the home were selfishly depriving unemployed men of their ability to fulfill their manly obligations. As a result, it was not unusual for a bank manager, an office supervisor, or a local school board to fire married women from their jobs in order to make room for men. Government agencies on both the federal and state level followed suit, making it their policy to refuse jobs to the wives of their male employees. The ability of many women to define femininity in terms of their ability to contribute to the financial well being of their families through wage work was thereby lost.

Unemployment forced many working women back into the home. Once there, they found that the depression placed increased importance on women's skills and resourcefulness as housewives. As their household allowances shriveled, their domestic role expanded. The motto of the day was "Use it up, wear it out, make it do, or do without." For farm wives and working-class women, these were not new ideas. But many middle-class women were not used to practicing small economies, particularly if they lived in cities. They did not have gardens in which to grow food. They were not used to darning socks or remaking their children's clothes. In ordinary times, they would not have considered buying day-old bread, gluing broken dishes back together, or using margarine instead of butter. But times were not ordinary, and they found it necessary to express their femininity through their ability to adapt their housewifery skills to the realities of hard times.

Woman's role as the glue that holds the family together was also enhanced during the depression. During these hard economic times, femininity was often defined in terms of the degree to which a woman could exhibit emotional strength and patience. When their husbands came home to tell them that they had lost their jobs, women were expected to ignore their own distress at the news and to provide their spouses with emotional support and encouragement.

They also had to resist the temptation to consider their husbands' daily presence in the household an intrusion. Women with employed husbands were used to being in charge of running the household and caring for the children. Generally speaking, they had little supervision in the conduct of their domestic duties from their gainfully employed husbands, and they made independent decisions about the way they used their time. Housewives may have found their domestic duties exhausting and tedious, but they did not have to share their decision making with anyone else.

Unemployed husbands who spent their time at home had the potential for undermining the kind of independence that their wives enjoyed within the domestic sphere. Like children, they were constantly under foot. And if they were willing to adjust their ideas about

manliness to help with the housework or to assume more responsibility for child care, they often did so grudgingly and inevitably had their own ideas about how to perform those domestic duties. For housewives, sharing domestic responsibilities also meant sharing domestic space and authority, a reality that often placed great strain on female patience as well as marital relationships.

WORLD WAR II AND ITS CHALLENGE TO THE DOMESTIC IDEAL

The Japanese bombed Pearl Harbor in Hawaii on Sunday, December 7, 1941. The next day Congress declared war. Not only did the federal government start to recruit men to fight in the army, but it called upon civilians to do what they could to support the war effort. When war was declared, women were not expected to serve in the military. And while 90 percent of all American women were married, only 15 percent of all married women worked for wages. In 1944 the picture was quite different. There were an unprecedented number of women serving in the armed forces. And for the first time in American history, the number of married women outnumbered single women in the work force. By the end of the war, the parameters of woman's sphere had been significantly expanded and the definition of what constituted femininity had been successfully adjusted to fit the demands of the American war effort.

When war broke out, the government called on women to replace the men who were being inducted into the armed services and to demonstrate their patriotism by accepting jobs in government, business, and industry. Officials in the federal government and business leaders with the collaboration of the media engaged in a highly organized campaign designed to convince women that they would retain their femininity when they took over what had traditionally been defined as manly duties and responsibilities. They emphasized the fact that working in war industries and transportation was only temporary and assured women that when they left their homes and accepted jobs that had traditionally been performed by men, they were not sacrificing their womanliness. Instead they were confirming it by demonstrating their willingness to fulfill their obligations as citizens and by sacrificing themselves in order to support their husbands, fathers, brothers, and boyfriends. Moreover, recruitment advertisements emphasized the gender appropriateness of the work that might be demanded of women and assured middle-class women that their class status would not be threatened if they volunteered for war work. One ad assured potential war workers that "an American homemaker with the strength and ability to run a house and raise a family . . . has the strength and ability to take her place in vital War industry." Others compared the jobs that women were expected to perform to those they performed in their own homes. Spot welding was, according to recruitment films, analogous to sewing; stamping metal was comparable to cutting cookies; and ordering parts from the parts department was like shopping. The work place, according to the promotion materials, was a congenial, social environment. Working in war production would end the isolation of women whose lives were confined to housekeeping. If they engaged in war work, they could enjoy the company of other women on a regular basis.

The result of this recruitment campaign was that women flocked into jobs that had previously been defined as male. Single women were the first to seek jobs made available by the wartime emergency. They became welders, riveters, railroad engineers, machinists, and taxi drivers. By 1943, however, the reserves of single women were pretty much exhausted, and recruiters had to turn to married women in their search for workers who could be trained to perform skilled labor in shipyards, powder plants, and airplane manufacturing facilities. In the name of patriotism, working for wages became a respectable activity for middle class, married women many of whom had children. Public opinion polls told the

story. In 1938, over 80 percent of Americans strongly opposed the idea of married women working. By 1943 over 60 percent approved. The war made paid employment by married women a part of the definition of middle-class femininity.

The gendered nature of military service was also redefined during World War II. There had always been women workers in the military. They served as cooks and laundresses during the American Revolution, and during the Civil War they worked as nurses. A few women served as support staff in World War I. But it wasn't until World War II that they were recruited in large numbers.

Recruiting women posed a serious problem for the military establishment. There was perhaps no subculture in American life that was so clearly defined as masculine as that of the military and no attributes that were so associated with manliness as the kind of aggressiveness, violence, courage, and physical stamina required of the American soldier. Yet it was clear from the very beginning of the war that if the United States and its allies were going to win, they needed women to help them do it. The result was that the federal government adopted an aggressive policy designed to convince women that they should volunteer to serve in auxiliary military units.

In order to incorporate women into the armed services, military leaders had to reconcile the idea of "woman" with the idea of "soldier." Nowhere was the difficulty in accomplishing this task more evident than in the time and effort they spent designing military uniforms for their new recruits. On one hand, they wanted to reassure women that they would not be sacrificing their femininity by becoming soldiers. On the other, they were determined to modify the typical military uniform as little as possible. In order to maintain the aesthetic ideal associated with womanliness, female military personnel wore skirts instead of trousers. But their uniform also included serviceable shoes, jackets made of heavy worsted that looked much like the jackets worn by male recruits, and military-style hats.

The military recruitment campaign also focused on convincing potential recruits that they would be associating with women who were respectable, poised, and charming and did not dwell on the physical demands that were an inherent part of military training. While they admitted that some women would be asked to perform tasks that had traditionally been categorized as male, they argued that feminine attributes such as patience, self-sacrifice, and attention to detail were essential to the war effort. And they assured potential recruits that when the war was over, they would be as desirable as wives as their civilian sisters.

The recruitment efforts of the military were quite successful. Women joined the WAC (army), the WAVES (navy), the WASPS (army air forces), and the SPARS (coast guard). Once they were inducted into service, they were trained for a wide variety of jobs but not to participate in combat. Like generations of women before them, they were allowed to step outside the bounds of what was considered appropriate female roles because the emergency of wartime made it necessary for them to support men in non-traditional ways.

But there were limits to the degree to which the military would sanction any fundamental shift in gender roles and relations. The treatment of women in the military exposed the anxieties of government officials about the degree to which the presence of women might undermine military discipline and exposed their determination to preserve gender differences. So, when it was possible, they assigned women to jobs that were considered typically female jobs. Women worked as secretaries and clerks. They served on laundry detail, cooked food, and cleaned up the mess. They also tried to segregate women from men whenever possible. For example, air force regulations allowed women to fly airplanes but prohibited them from flying in the same cockpit as a man or from carrying male passengers. In conformity with the belief that women were inherently weaker and potentially less competent than men, military authorities both privileged female recruits and discriminated against them. WASP pilots were grounded during their menstrual periods, and female military personnel earned less money than their male colleagues. The presence of women in the military may have been expedient, but those in charge of writing the regulations for the armed forces considered it to be a temporary phenomenon. Despite their desperate need for recruits, they were not interested in creating a permanently welcoming environment for women.

The treatment of working women in the civilian sector was also gendered. Work regulations often reflected traditional assumptions about gender. In Seattle, for example, women whose job it was to deliver telegraphs were not allowed to work at night and were not sent to taverns or potentially disreputable places like second-class hotels or rooming houses. Women guards at Boeing Aircraft were not armed with guns and were instructed to call one of their male colleagues if they found themselves in the position of having to use force. And women at the Puget Sound Naval Yard were hired to drive trucks but not to load cargo into them.

When World War II ended, women had transgressed gender boundaries in every aspect of American life. They had served as heads of their families while their husbands were away, had competently done what had traditionally been considered men's work in heavy industry, and had made a place for themselves in the armed forces. They had stepped into the political vacuum and helped to run towns and cities; they had earned graduate degrees in such male dominated fields as architecture and chemical engineering; and they had successfully run their families' businesses. War had provided them unprecedented opportunities for independent action and decision making.

The degree to which gender roles and identities were blurred during World War II was both dramatic and startling. But in many ways such blurring was a temporary phenomenon fed by the determination of businessmen and government officials to use all of the resources available to them to meet a political and military crisis. There was no intention on the part of those in charge of public policy to support permanent changes in the definitions of femininity. No effort was made, for example, to establish a program that would fund and regulate a nation-wide system of day-care centers in perpetuity so that after the war married women could continue to work knowing that their children were being well cared for. There was no support for the idea that married women should work outside the home on a permanent basis. They were applauded for their patriotism and for the sacrifices they were willing to make during the war, but when the war was over, they were expected to resume their roles as full time wives and mothers. The war may have expanded woman's sphere, but that expansion was temporary. For most Americans, the ideology of domesticity continued to prevail, and the home served as the context within which femininity was defined.

FEMININITY AND THE POST-WAR BACKLASH

As GIs began to return home in 1945, government and business leaders systematically dismissed women from their jobs. The effort to push women out of the workplace was prompted partly by a fear that the effort to switch from a wartime to a peacetime economy would result in a recession. But it was also prompted by a belief that returning veterans had first claim on jobs both as a reward for the sacrifices they had made during the war and because they needed jobs so that they could resume their manly roles as breadwinners and heads of their households. There was no longer any work for highly skilled female welders. And the image of Rosie the Riveter, the icon of the female labor force during the war, disappeared from the front pages of American magazines.

Some women gave up their jobs with nary a whimper. Wartime work had been particularly grueling for married women with children. Factory supervisors often demanded that women work overtime so that government contracts could be filled. Refusing to do so was considered unpatriotic. They were expected to work at least eight hours a day at their jobs and then shop for groceries, clean the house, cook the food, do the laundry, and care for their children. Finding adequate child care was always a source of concern. And there was little time for relaxation or entertainment. For women whose husbands returned from the war ready and willing to support them, the prospect of only having to fulfill their domestic duties was very appealing. Those who were not married welcomed home their boyfriends or fiances. Having postponed their marriage plans because of the war, they now said their vows and set up their households. The birth rate soared, and the cult of domesticity returned with a vengeance. Husbands left for work in the morning while their wives stayed home to care for the children. Fathers returned at night to barbecue in the back yard and coach Little League.

The fifties version of the domestic ideal did not differ much from the nineteenth-century version. Femininity was still defined in terms of wifehood, motherhood, housekeeper, and economic dependence. Virginity before marriage was still considered important. And women were still expected to provide moral leadership for their families. The biggest difference was that in the 1950s, sexual desire was no longer considered a male prerogative. Married women were expected to enjoy engaging in sexual activity with their husbands.

In the nineteenth century, the cult of domesticity had raised some concerns about allowing women to have so much power within the home. Social critics called upon men to mediate this power by spending less time on the job and more time supervising the rearing of their children. At the turn of the century, a new generation of social critics warned that the influence of mothers and female teachers might lead to the feminization of the nation's boys. Anxiety about the impact of woman's domestic influence continued through the 1940s and 1950s. While magazine editors, movie producers, and television script writers were promoting the idea that women should embrace domesticity in order to find personal fulfillment, Philip Wylie, the author of *Generation of Vipers*, warned his readers that women who focused their lives on their husbands and children were dangerous. Because homemaking was not in and of itself an inherently satisfying vocation, he argued, women lived vicariously through their husbands and children thus putting undue pressure on them to succeed whether it be in terms of business, popularity, or sports. These unhappy and unfulfilled women over-protected their sons and made it difficult for them to develop qualities such as independence and self-sufficiency that would allow them to make their own way in the world. Picturing wives as parasites, he charged that they drained their partners not only of their wealth but also of their emotion and virility. According to Wylie, the American housewife was one of the most destructive forces in American society. For American women, it was a case of damned if you do, damned if you don't.

Wylie was not alone in his concern, but his complaints, articulated in 1942, did not in any way stem the tide of domesticity that enveloped the nation after the war. An unfulfilled woman might threaten her children's gendered development and the happiness of her husband. But Wylie's warnings did not seriously undermine the conviction that women were born to fulfill their roles as wives and mothers and that, therefore, they found satisfaction in their domestic duties. It wasn't until 1963 that Betty Friedan successfully burst that bubble.

THE CONTINUING CHALLENGE TO THE CULT OF DOMESTICITY

Despite the fact that millions of women collaborated in the effort to confirm the belief that the domestic sphere was the most appropriate place for a woman to express her femininity, an alternative way of expressing womanliness persisted after the war. Millions of women continued to work for wages. In doing so, they embodied the idea that women could make their own decisions, could earn their own money, and could cope with the physical demands of wage labor.

The post-war attitude toward the working woman could be summarized as follows: There was nothing wrong with a woman working outside the home for wages (1) if the economy was booming and there were plenty of jobs, (2) if she was single, or widowed, or her husband was disabled, (3) if she did not aspire to do what was traditionally considered men's work, (4) if she did not equate work with pursuing a career that might give her both status and independence, and (5) if she continued to perform her traditional domestic duties. As a result of this attitude, the hundreds of thousands of working women who lost relatively lucrative jobs in war industries had to revert back to working at vocations traditionally defined as female, many of which were low-skilled and poorly paid. Back to washing dishes, waiting tables, checking out groceries at the supermarket, cleaning other women's homes, typing, or working as sales clerks or beauticians, these women found themselves in dead-end jobs with little or no chance for advancement.

Many post-World War II workers were married women. Some worked because they had to help provide food, clothing, and shelter for their families. Others were concerned about improving their standard of living. They wanted to live in a bigger house in a better neighborhood. They wanted to send their children to private school rather than public school. In short, they wanted to help their husbands provide the whole family with "the better things in life."

In part, married women who worked for wages were responding to the fact that the post-war economy was plagued by inflation. They and their husbands may have had money in their bank accounts; but immediately after the war, the availability of consumer products was limited. Factories were converting from war production to peacetime production. And that conversion took time. To buy a new car, for example, you could not just walk into a showroom and buy a car even if you were willing to pay in cash. You had to put your name on a list and wait until it was manufactured. With so many people competing to buy so few consumer goods, prices soared. It simply took more money for a man to provide for his family. As a matter of expediency, many married women continued to work so that their families could enjoy a higher standard of living than would have been possible on a single income. They were joined in the work force by a small contingent of exceptionally well-educated women who pursued careers in the professions. Clearly, the expression of womanliness through wage labor was increasing despite the refusal on the part of most Americans to change their belief that a woman's place was in the home.

BLACK WOMANHOOD AND DEFINITIONS OF FEMININITY

There was considerable continuity in the ways in which black women defined their gender identities in the twentieth century. The period between 1920 and 1975 was not very different from the period between 1865 and 1920. Except in the ever growing black middle class, black women continued to work outside the home for wages in order to support themselves or to help their husbands support their children. As they tried to balance their domestic obligations with their need to contribute to their family income, they looked forward to the day when they could devote their time more exclusively to caring for their own families and keeping their own homes. In pursuit of that goal, many black women, who worked as domestic servants, were able to negotiate a change in their conditions of employment. Once required to live as well as work in their employers' homes, they eventually were able to arrange a work schedule that required only that they work during the day, an arrangement that allowed them to combine homemaking with wage earning more effectively.

The marriages of black couples, whether common law or legally sanctioned, continued to be more egalitarian than those of many whites. As wives, black women were much less likely than their white counterparts to unquestioningly defer to their husband's authority. In that sense, independence and a willingness to rely on oneself continued to be an important component of black definitions of womanliness. Those very characteristics, however, could lead to tension between black women and black men, who often considered black women's self-sufficiency and lack of deference to be an inherent challenge to their masculinity.

World War II allowed women to confirm and enhance their tendency to equate femininity with wage earning. Before the war, most black women were confined to working as agricultural workers or as domestic servants. The need for labor during the war meant that for the first time in history, they had access to job training that allowed them to do highly paid, skilled work in heavy industry. Because their feminine identity had traditionally been expressed in part by their ability to earn a living and by pride in their strength and physical stamina, the kind of work that they were expected to perform did not fundamentally threaten their self-images. Unfortunately, after the war, many of them were fired from their well paying jobs and had to return to jobs in such areas as domestic service.

No matter what their social class or economic status, black women had a long tradition of expressing their womanliness through public activism. In the nineteenth century, they had combined benevolence and a desire for self-improvement with efforts to improve living and working conditions in black communities. The nineteenth amendment gave women in the North and West a constitutionally sanctioned political voice. But for a good part of the twentieth century, it made no difference to women living in the South, where blacks were systematically denied the right to vote and hold office.

Black women had long been critical of whites and assertive in their struggle against racism and discrimination. Reticence about discussing these matters publicly had no place in their definition of womanliness. Thus, it is not surprising that they took a leading role in efforts to end segregation and campaign for the right of African Americans to vote and hold office. Rosa Parks of Montgomery, Alabama, was only one in a long line of strong, southern black women who were willing to put their lives at risk to challenge the Jim Crow laws of the South in an effort to promote human equality. A seamstress and church-going Methodist, Parks was a member of the Montgomery NAACP and had a long record of service to the black community when she refused to give up her seat on a Montgomery city bus to a white man in December, 1955. Her personal resistance to segregation led to a black boycott of the municipal bus system. By 1957 segregation as a system of racial control was slowly being dismantled in the South. By that time, Daisy Bates was leading efforts to integrate Little Rock's Central High School in Arkansas. As a result of her leadership and the cooperation of nine black families whose sons and daughters had to walk through screaming mobs to go to school, the Supreme Court issued an order forcing state governments to enforce the school desegregation mandated in *Brown v. Board of Education,* and Congress passed a series of civil rights acts to enforce the court's decision.

Despite the fact that the U.S. Constitution guaranteed African Americans the right to vote, southern blacks had been disenfranchised since the turn of the century. So one of the goals of the Civil Rights movement was to provide them with the right to participate in the political process. Fannie Lou Hamer was a poor, middle-aged sharecropper who lived in the Mississippi Delta when she first became involved in the Civil Rights Movement. For asserting her fundamental right to vote, she and her husband were evicted from the land they had worked for eighteen years. When she continued her activism, she was arrested and savagely beaten until she was covered with blood. But she persisted and helped to form the Mississippi Freedom Democratic

Party in an attempt to break the hold of whites on the Democratic Party in her state.

Neither Parks nor Bates nor Hamer were feminists. They were much more concerned about racism than they were about sexism. But they embodied a version of black femininity that incorporated assertiveness and courage as well as a political consciousness that sprang from hatred of injustice. Black women had never been silent about their opposition to racism and the discrimination that accompanied it, but during the period between 1950 and 1975, their voices were raised in protest to a degree that was unprecedented.

FEMININITY AND HISPANIC WOMANHOOD

It is hard to generalize about concepts of femininity among Hispanic women because as the twentieth century progressed, the diversity of the Spanish-speaking community in the United States increased. In the late nineteenth century, the largest group of Hispanic women in America were Mexican-American most of whom lived in the Southwest. When the United States acquired Puerto Rico in 1898, Spanish-speaking women from that island began to immigrate and settled in and around New York City. And after the Communist takeover in Cuba in 1960, Cuban women fled with their families to south Florida. Meanwhile, immigrants from other areas in the Caribbean as well as South and Central America flocked to the United States in search of political freedom and economic opportunity.

Each group of women came from a distinctive Hispanic culture with its own set of gender constructions. The way they expressed their femininity depended upon such factors as their country of origin, their social class, and where they settled. For example, many Cuban immigrant women were relatively well-educated members of the Cuban middle class whose definition of femininity did not include the need to work for wages. When they arrived in South Florida, after having fled Cuba to escape communism, however, many of them had to forgo the privileged lives that they had formerly enjoyed and found it necessary to work in order to help support their families. The need to work outside the home, however, did not necessarily bring about a permanent change in the degree to which they equated femininity with domesticity. Many of them embraced what Betty Friedan called "the feminine mystique" as a way of recovering their former social status, and as their economic situation improved, they left their jobs and again became full time housewives.

Mexican-Americans in the Southwest expressed their gendered identity in a different context. Their community was an old one bound by traditions that slowly changed in response to Mexican-American migration within the United States and contact with Anglo society. Despite these influences, there was considerable continuity in the way Mexican-American women expressed their femininity. Most continued to construct their gendered identity around the roles of wife and mother. But the persistence of poverty in Mexican-American families made it necessary for many Mexican-American women to work outside the home. Therefore, they were likely to equate femininity with working for wages. The strength of female bonds within the Mexican-American community persisted. Female kin and neighbors continued to provide valued services for each other in such areas as child rearing and health care. The result was that within their own community, Mexican-American women were not likely to value independence and self-reliance. Dependence upon other women remained an important component of the Mexican-American definition of womanliness.

As the century progressed, however, there were important changes in how Mexican-American women defined womanliness. Young women in the 1920s began to assert their independence from their families by challenging the tradition of chaperonage which inhibited their ability to freely associate with members of the opposite sex. Some openly rebelled against the system. Others simply adopted strategies designed to subvert their families' desire to restrict their social activities. Persuading their parents to allow a sympathetic, older brother rather than an elderly aunt to accompany them to a dance, for example, was likely to give them more control over their social life.

Mexican-American women also expanded their definition of femininity to include a public component. As students, farm laborers, cannery workers, and housewives, they participated in activities designed to improve working conditions and the quality of life in Mexican-American neighborhoods. Some helped to organize labor unions and expressed their sensitivity to gender issues by demanding publicly supported childcare services and paid maternity leave. Others led campaigns to get streets paved in their communities and demanded improvement in their access to health-care services. In the context of such reform work, Mexican-American women incorporated such qualities as assertiveness into their definition of womanliness.

SECOND WAVE FEMINISM AND ITS IMPACT ON DEFINITIONS OF FEMININITY

The popularity of *The Feminine Mystique* and the fact that the 1960s was a period of social reform led to the rise of what has been called "second wave feminism" and a self-conscious redefinition on the part of some of what constituted womanliness. Building on the legacy of early feminists like Elizabeth Cady Stanton and Susan B. Anthony, second wave feminists pointed out that women in America were still denied equality with men and called upon them to finish the campaign for woman's rights that had begun in the nineteenth century. They called on women in every walk of life to assert their independence and autonomy and pursue a campaign of self-realization. And they formed organizations like the National Organization for Women in 1966 in order to promote public policies that were gender specific in the sense that they were designed to serve the interests of women. In terms of gender relations,

American society was in the midst of yet another major shift.

There were two sources of second wave feminism. The first, represented by women like Betty Friedan, consisted of white, middle-class, well-educated liberals who were willing to work within the existing social, economic, and political system to gain equality for women. Sometimes called liberal-political feminists, they attempted to place women in positions of power so that they could influence public policy as it related to women's issues. Organizations like the National Organization for Women and the Women's Equity Action League used data documenting systematic discrimination against women at the local, state, and federal levels collected by President Kennedy's Commission on the Status of Women (1963) and the state commissions that came afterward as the basis for promoting the idea of equal pay for equal work. They lobbied for laws against wife abuse, funding for day-care centers, and protection against sexual harassment. Once they had succeeded in promoting the interests of women through legislation, they used their resources to guarantee enforcement of the law through litigation.

The second branch of second wave feminism was called the Woman's Liberation Movement. Its adherents were young, radical reformers who participated in the Civil Rights Movement and protests on college campuses against the war in Vietnam. A part of what was called the "New Left," many of these women were socialists before they were feminists. Intent on social, political, and economic revolution and dedicated to the principle of human equality, they resented being treated with disrespect by their male colleagues when they tried to claim positions of leadership in organizations like Students for a Democratic Society. When their complaints were trivialized and ignored, they began to systematically examine their relationship to male reformers and to protest the unequal position of women in American society. Radical in their ideology, strident in their rhetoric, and sometimes outrageous in their protests, they had caught the attention of the media by the late 1960s. One New York group calling itself WITCH (Women's International Terrorist Conspiracy from Hell), for example, dressed up as witches and put a hex on the New York Stock Exchange. The same group also invaded a bridal fashion show singing, "Here come the slaves / Off to their graves" to the tune of the wedding march. Highly individualistic, suspicious of authority and hierarchy, and often unwilling to form permanent organizations, they focused a great deal of effort on self-education in what they called "consciousness raising sessions," small groups who spent their time critiquing woman's place in American society. Their program of social reform included campaigns against rape, domestic violence, and pornography. They demanded that women have the right to reproductive freedom. And they supported the formation of women's institutions ranging from women's health collectives to women's bookstores. Their efforts prompted women who may not under normal circumstances have been interested in feminist issues to re-evaluate their relationships with men.

Together, the feminists of the 1960s and 1970s accomplished a great deal in their efforts to promote the interests of women. Due in part to feminist demand for equal opportunity in education and employment, Congress passed the Equal Pay Act in 1963 which established the principle of equal pay for equal work. In 1964, Title VII of the Civil Rights Act forbade gender discrimination in employment. Theoretically, the law made it illegal for an employer to refuse to hire a woman to do what had traditionally been a male job. If she was qualified, a woman could become a fireman, a policeman, an electrician, or a plumber. Similarly, qualified men could not be denied jobs as nurses or airline stewardesses because of their gender. Title IX of the Education Amendments Act passed in 1972 guaranteed that women would have the same access to educational opportunities that were available to men. Those opportunities included the right to participate in intercollegiate sports. These laws and the policies that they put into place helped to undermine traditional ideas about gender difference and the social and economic practices that had supported those differences. By 1975, political activity had come into its own as a way for a woman to express her femininity.

During the same period, some women also began to question the way that femininity had traditionally been tied to maternity. Until the 1960s, American women had difficulty trying to control their fertility. In 1873, Congress passed the Comstock Law, which defined information about birth control and abortion as obscene and forbade its distribution through the United States postal service. Without easy access to information about family limitation, many women could do nothing but accept the inevitability of motherhood once they were married. But between 1965 and 1973 all of that changed. In 1965, the U. S. Supreme Court declared that it was legal to distribute birth control information to married couples (*Griswold v. Connecticut*), and in 1973 it legalized abortion in the United States (*Roe v. Wade*). These cases combined with FDA approval of the birth control pill in the early 1960s meant that motherhood was increasingly a matter of choice and that women were free to express their femininity by remaining childless.

The debate over this issue took on various forms. In *The Baby Trap*, for example, Ellen Peck observed that most women were passive about their reproductive lives because, besides believing that they had no control over them, they assumed that motherhood would be an enriching experience, that bearing children would fulfill the natural urge to procreate, and that rearing a family would cement the relationship they had with their husbands. On the contrary, she argued. In her opinion, the desire for children was not an instinct at all but a socially constructed imperative designed to deprive women of what she considered to be a much more pleasant and rewarding lifestyle, one that was devoid of children. Most children were, in her view, not only irritating nuisances but extremely expensive irritating nuisances who were more likely than not to strain marital relationships. For these reasons, she encouraged her readers to resist the call to motherhood. *The Baby Trap*, originally published in 1971, and its companion piece, *Mother's Day Is Over* by Shirley Radl, published in 1973, did not beat around the bush. They were overt attacks on what might be called "the motherhood mystique" and a call to women to reconfigure their ideas about femininity and its relationship to maternity.

The institution of marriage suffered from the same sort of attack during the 1960s and 1970s. Before that period, divorce had not been a real option for married women who had any interest at all in preserving their respectability. In many states it was much more difficult for a woman to get a divorce than it was for a man. That situation changed during the 1970s. As women began to question their status in society, they also questioned their relationships with men. And once they critiqued those relationships, many began to find them intolerable. Some couples tried to adjust to the wife's dissatisfaction by changing their assumptions about how husbands and wives were supposed to relate to each other and how power within the family should be distributed. Some couples signed contracts which laid out what obligations each partner owed each other. Typically, husbands agreed to assume more responsibility for housekeeping and childcare and wives agreed to accept more financial responsibility for the family. More often than not, however, couples who disagreed about their responsibilities toward each other eventually ended up in divorce court. State governments responded to the flood of divorce petitions by streamlining the process, instituting "no fault" divorce in an effort to clear the dockets of their family court systems. The divorce rate soared as millions of women began to assert their independence and reject their obligation to "love, honor, and obey." It is true that many divorced women remarried. But many of them did so hoping that in their new relationship, they would have more influence in determining what their marital obligations would be.

RESISTANCE TO THE FEMINIST VISION

During the late 1960s and early 1970s, both women and the media explored the implications of the feminist vision of gender equality. But while they did so, there were some who simply ignored the debate over woman's roles and the construction of femininity in America society, went about their business, and solved their own personal problems in their own way. On the surface, second wave feminism had little impact on the way they defined themselves as women or the way they related to men.

Others saw the feminist attempts to redefine what it meant to be a woman as threatening and opposed feminist efforts to change the social, economic, and political context in which they expressed their femininity. Many non-wage earning women who had embraced the domestic ideal, had devoted their lives to caring for their families, and whose activities outside the home centered on church work had previously taken little or no interest in debates over public policy as they related specifically to women. But the debates over divorce, abortion, and the Equal Rights Amendment politicized them. Concerned about the rising divorce rate, they were, for example, determined to preserve what they considered to be the benefits they derived from their domestic roles such as a the right to alimony and child custody. They rejected the idea that men and women should be treated as equals and continued to see women as individuals in need of protection. In pursuit of their self-interest, they supported the Right to Life Movement and identified with the Moral Majority, which organized opposition to the ERA and abortion. Their efforts were moderately successful. Under the leadership of conservative Republican Phyllis Schlafly, they organized STOP-ERA and were able to defeat attempts to ratify the Equal Rights Amend-

ment. Working with like-minded legislators and lawyers, they were also able to limit the access of some women to abortion on demand. As a result of their efforts, political action became an integral part of the definition of what it meant to be a "true woman" even among those most concerned with preserving traditional gender roles.

SUMMARY

During the period between 1920 and 1975, American women were buffeted by two main versions of true womanhood. The first was a conservative vision in which the roles of woman as wife and mother were idealized. In this model, femininity was defined in terms of moral superiority, dependence, passivity, domesticity, physical attractiveness, and sexual accessibility in marriage. A woman who accepted these attributes as desirable usually married at a fairly early age, bore children as a natural outcome of marriage, worked for wages outside the home only out of necessity, and spent a great deal of time cooking and cleaning. Her activities outside the home revolved around her church and civic organizations such as the PTA and hospital volunteer associations. In return for her service to her family and community, she expected her husband to support her, protect her, and remain faithful to her and the state to make sure that he did so.

The second model was a feminist version that called upon women to create an alternative vision of true womanhood. The ideal woman using this model made conscious, sometimes unconventional choices about the way she lived. She rejected the idea that women were not men's intellectual equals. Taking advantage of federal legislation guaranteeing equal access to education, she integrated such bastions of male intellectual life as Harvard and Yale. She earned a degree in a field such as engineering or molecular biology and went on to carve out a career for herself in finance, transportation, industry, or academe. She was free to marry or not as she chose because she was perfectly capable of supporting herself. She did not just accept the inevitability of motherhood. She quite self-consciously decided when and if she wanted to become a mother. She did not necessarily reject woman's domestic role, but she set the parameters of its importance in her life. She decided when and under what circumstances she would defer to male authority both at home and in the work place. She was physically active, ambitious, and assertive. And by the late 1970s, she was beginning to understand that she had to accept responsibility for defining her own political interests and then actively support those politicians who were sympathetic to them.

Of course, these visions of true womanhood were only sets of ideals. Like all ideals, they were sometimes impossible to fulfill. It is not at all clear that most American women accepted them as anything more than sets of options some of which were more compatible with their personal circumstances than others. It is unlikely, for example, that a farm wife living in central Illinois would aspire to become a corporate executive. But she might apply for a job in a local bank so that she could afford to divorce her wife-beating husband. And a Catholic, Mexican-American, migrant worker might not reject the idea of marrying, bearing children, and deferring to her husband's authority in family matters, but she might testify before a legislative committee as a part of a campaign to improve working conditions in the lettuce fields of California.

It is important to acknowledge the degree to which factors like age, ethnicity, race, economic and social status, access to education, religion, sexual preference, and geographic location influenced women's attempts to construct their gendered identities. It is also important to recognize that a woman's definition of what constituted femininity was likely to change over time. But the main point is that by the 1970s, women had been able to establish for themselves a wide variety of socially acceptable ways of defining true womanhood. What that meant, of course, was that women had to be much more self-conscious about what it meant to be a woman. And they found that making choices about how they wanted to express their femininity was not always an altogether easy or pleasant process.

Women Trying to Unravel the Mysteries of Motherhood

Since the colonial period, American women have constructed their femininity around childbearing and motherhood. But since "mothering" was neither instinctive nor easy, they often needed help in order to carry out their maternal duties. Before 1800, expectant

Source: Women's Letters to the Children's Bureau, Children's Bureau Records, National Archives, Washington, DC.

mothers and those with small children were most likely to seek advice from their relatives, friends, and neighbors. By the middle of the nineteenth century, child rearing manuals were widely available for those with the money to buy them and the ability to read them. In 1912, the Children's Bureau was established by the federal government to study the condition of children in the United States. In an effort to provide mothers with advice on how to take care of their children, it published two pamphlets, Prenatal Care and Infant Care, and sent them out to anyone who requested them. The staff of the Children's Bureau also responded to letters from women who wrote asking specific questions about carrying out their maternal duties. A number of those letters, written during the 1920s are printed below.

What kinds of issues were the women who wrote these letters concerned about? What do these letters tell us about the relationship between motherhood and the expression of womanliness?

June 14, 1920
Dear Madame

I need advise. I am a farmers wife, do my household duties and a regular field hand too. The mother of 9 children and in family way again. I am quar[re]lsome when tired & fatigued.

When I come in out of the field to prepare dinner my Husband & all the children gets in the kitchen in my way. I quarrel at them for bening in my way. I tell them I will build them a fire if they are cold. I also threaten to move the Stove out on the porch. What shall I do? My Husband wont sympathise with me one bit but talks rough to me. If I get tired & sick of my daily food & crave some simple article, should I have it? I have [helped] make the living for 20 years. Should I be [de]nied of a few simple articles or money either? Does it make a Mother unvirtuous for a man physician to wait on her during confinement? Is it Safe for me to go through it Without aid from any one? Please give me Some advise. There isent any mid wives near us now. I am not friendless but going to you for advise too keep down gossip. Yours.

January 10, 1920
To the Chief of the Children's Bureau

I am writing you for advice. I am a young mother, my baby will be thirteen months old the tenth of this month. He is not weaned yet, he eats from the breast all day and part of the night. This pulls me down & makes me look worn & be tired. I cannot get out of his sight a minute, if he is not crying.

There is no real cause for crying as he is a health child. Has not been sick & under the doctors since birth. I cannot even get out a couple of hours for the pictures.

He has a crib of his own to sleep in but he will not sleep in it. There is no one else at home with me except my husband he is willing to mind the baby while I get out for a couple of hours, but he cries after me so that I am afraid to leave home. Not even to the corner to mail a letter.

I would like to know is it now too late to train him not to cry after me. He has all kinds of toys & yet nothing quiets him but me. Please send me some advice as to how I can wean him & to stop him from clinging to me so. My husband tells me to feed him good & let him cry himself to sleep but this seems very cruel. Please make this letter strictly private, as I am classed a very foolish mother.

March 4, 1920
Dear Mrs. Lathrop,

Would I be intruding too much upon your valuable time if I bring you my personal problems and ask your assistance? I would be greatly indebted to you if you would advise me or send me helpful literature.

I am a *busy* mother of three dear babies—aged 3 years, 20 months and 3 months. I am obliged to do all my work and we have not the conveniences and modern utilities that I wish we could afford. I am up-to-date in the care of my babies, reading and following the best literature on the care of babies. The help I need is in planning my work—a work schedule or something to aid me in the daily routine. I do the very best I can. I am busy all day and all evening but my work is never done—I am tired enough to drop when night comes and in the morning look with dread upon the day ahead of me. I want to play with my babies, I want to have time to love them and laugh with them. I have wanted babies for years and now, when Im so tired and with unfinished work every where I turn, I could scream at their constant prattle. I love them until it hurts and know that, when they are out of their babyhood, I can never forgive myself for not making more of these precious years.

Is there not some way that I can do all these scientific and hygienic duties for babies, keep our house up in proper fashion and still have time to rock and play with my babies? What of all my housework and baby-care could best be left undone? I do not ask time for myself but it would be nice to have a short period during the evening in which to read as I feel that I am growing narrow with no thoughts other than my household.

Thanking you for all the past helps your department has rendered me. Sincerely.

DOCUMENT

Lundberg and Farnham's Critique of the American Housewife

Until World War II, definitions of femininity for middle-class women had been constructed around the fact that while they worked in their homes, they did not work for wages. But during the early months of WWII, an appeal went out to American women to join the work force as their way of contributing to the war effort. Along with working-class women, women from the middle classes responded to that call. For some, it was the first time they had earned their own money and spent their time working with other women. When the war was over, most of them left the work force to make room for returning GIs and again became full time housewives. Some of them found the transition from independence to dependence difficult. It was partly in response to shifts in definitions of femininity following the war that sociologist Ferdinand Lundberg and psychiatrist Marynia Farnham wrote Modern Woman: The Lost Sex.

In the Foreward to their book, Lundberg wrote "The central thesis of this book is that contemporary women in very large numbers are psychologically disordered and that their disorder is having terrible social and personal effects involving men in all departments of their lives as well as women." Such a conclusion, he argued, was substantiated

Source: Ferdinand Lundberg and Marynia F. Farnham, *Modern Woman: The Lost Sex* (New York: Harper and Brothers, 1947), 235–36, 239–41. Notes omitted.

by the clinical research of his co-author. Lundberg and Farnham's analysis of the female condition was not widely accepted partly because it ignored the millions of women who were not neurotic and who found great satisfaction in their domestic lives. Nevertheless, their book illustrates the kinds of anxieties that surfaced concerning the relationship between women and their domestic role after the war.

According to Lundberg and Farnham, what was the source of female neuroses? How was their neuroses gendered? What was the impact of their neuroses on men?

Work that entices women out of their homes and provides them with prestige only at the price of feminine relinquishment, involves a response to masculine strivings. The more importance outside work assumes, the more are the masculine components of the woman's nature enhanced and encouraged. In her home and in her relationship to her children, it is imperative that these strivings be at a minimum and that her femininity be available both for her own satisfaction and for the satisfaction of her children and husband. She is, therefore, in the dangerous position of having to live one part of her life on the masculine level, another on the feminine. It is hardly astonishing that few can do so with success. One of these tendencies must of necessity achieve dominance over the other. The plain fact is that increasingly we are observing the masculinization of women and with it enormously dangerous consequences to the home, the children (if any) dependent on it, and to the ability of the woman, as well as her husband, to obtain sexual gratification.

The effect of this "masculinization" on women is becoming more apparent daily. Their new exertions are making demands on them for qualities wholly opposed to the experience of feminine satisfaction. As the rivals of men, women must, and insensibly do, develop the characteristics of aggression, dominance, independence and power. These are qualities which insure success as co-equals in the world of business, industry and the professions. The distortion of character under pressure of modern attitudes and upbringing is driving women steadily deeper into personal conflict soluble only by psychotherapy. For their need to achieve and accomplish doesn't lessen, in any way, their deeper need

to find satisfactions profoundly feminine. Much as they consciously seek those gratifications of love, sensual release and even motherhood, they are becoming progressively less able unconsciously to accept or achieve them. . . .

It is not only the masculine woman who has met with an unhappy fate in the present situation. There were still many women who succeed in achieving adult life with largely unimpaired feminine strivings, for which home, a husband's love and children are to them the entirely adequate answers. It is their misfortune that they must enter a society in which such attitudes are little appreciated and are attended by many concrete, external penalties. Such women cannot fail to be affected by finding that their traditional activities are held in low esteem and that the woman who voluntarily undertakes them is often deprecated by her more aggressive contemporaries. She may come to believe that her situation is difficult, entailing serious deprivations, as against the more glamorous and exciting life other women seemingly enjoy. She may be set away from the main stream of life, very much in a backwater and fearful lest she lose her ability and talents through disuse and lack of stimulation. She may become sorry for herself and somewhat angered by her situation, gradually developing feelings of discontent and pressure. As her children grow older and require less of her immediate attention, the feelings of loss increase.

Unless she busies herself extensively with the poorly organized and generally unrewarding voluntary civic or cultural activities, she may find herself with much idle time and much frustration on her hands. Her home alone, unless it is a rural one, cannot occupy her whole time and attention because so much in it is now completely prefabricated and automatic. For amusement she is forced to resort either to the radio "soap opera," or to some other equally unrewarding use of leisure such as game playing, movie-going or aimless shopping. She is deprived of her husband's companionship during the long hours of the day when he is away from home and often the evening finds him preoccupied and disinterested in the affairs that concern her. Consequently she must construct her life out of artificial undertakings with no organic functional connection with the realities of her relationships or her interests. In this way she may easily and quickly develop attitudes of discontent and anger injurious to her life adjustment. She may begin to malfunction sexually, her libidinal depths shaken by her ego frustrations.

So it is that society today makes it difficult for a woman to avoid the path leading to discontent and frustration and resultant hostility and destructiveness. Such destructiveness is, unfortunately, not confined in its effects to the woman alone. It reaches into all her relationships and all her functions. As a wife she is not only often ungratified but ungratifying and has, as we have noted, a profoundly disturbing effect upon her husband. Not only does he find himself without the satisfactions of a home directed and cared for by a woman happy in providing affection and devotion, but he is often confronted by circumstances of even more serious import for his own emotional integrity. His wife may be his covert rival, striving to match him in every aspect of their joint undertaking. Instead of supporting and encouraging his manliness and wishes for domination and power, she may thus impose upon him feelings of insufficiency and weakness. Still worse is the effect upon his sexual satisfactions. Where the woman is unable to admit and accept dependence upon her husband as the source of gratification and must carry her rivalry even into the act of love, she will seriously damage his sexual capacity. To be unable to gratify in the sexual act is for a man an intensely humiliating experience; here it is that mastery and domination, the central capacity of the man's sexual nature, must meet acceptance or fail. So it is that by their own character disturbances these women succeed ultimately in depriving themselves of the devotion and power of their husbands and become the instruments of bringing about their own psychic catastrophe.

But no matter how great a woman's masculine strivings, her basic needs make themselves felt and she finds herself facing her fundamental role as wife and mother with a divided mind. Deprived of a rich and creative home in which to find self-expression, she tries desperately to find a compromise. On the one hand she must retain her sources of real instinctual gratification and on the other, find ways of satisfying her need for prestige and esteem. Thus she stands, Janus-faced, drawn in two directions at once, often incapable of ultimate choice and inevitably penalized whatever direction she chooses.

Radical Feminists Reject the Feminine Ideal

The Woman's Liberation Movement was one of two groups who led what has been called "second wave feminism." In the 1960s and 1970s young women, many of them college students involved in the Civil Rights Movement, the anti-war movement, and the student movement, organized consciousness-raising sessions in towns and cities all over the United States. These were meetings where women talked about their status in American society and devised ways of protesting what they perceived to be the subjugation and exploitation of women. One of the practices that angered them was the way that women's bodies were objectified by advertisers and the promoters of events such as the Miss America Pageant. In the fall of 1968, a group of feminists calling themselves the Radical Women of New York published a flyer encouraging women to gather together to demonstrate in Atlantic City against the Miss America Pageant.

What was it about the Miss America Pageant that these feminists specifically objected to? What do their objections tell us about the way they wished femininity to be constructed?

No More Miss America!

August 1968

On September 7th in Atlantic City, the Annual Miss America Pageant will again crown "your ideal." But this year, reality will liberate the contest auction-block in the guise of "genyooine" de-plasticized, breathing women. Women's Liberation Groups, black women, high-school and college women, women's peace groups, women's welfare and social-work groups, women's job-equality groups, pro-birth control and pro-abortion groups—women of every political persuasion—all are invited to join us in a day-long boardwalk-theater event, starting at 1:00 p.m. on the Boardwalk in front of Atlantic City's Convention Hall. We will protest the image of Miss America, an image that oppresses women

Source: "No More Miss America!" Anonymous Flyer, August, 1968.

in every area in which it purports to represent us. There will be: Picket Lines; Guerrilla Theater; Leafleting; Lobbying Visits to the contestants urging our sisters to reject the Pageant Farce and join us; a huge Freedom Trash Can (into which we will throw bras, girdles, curlers, false eyelashes, wigs, and representative issues of *Cosmopolitan, Ladies' Home Journal, Family Circle,* etc.—bring any such woman-garbage you have around the house); we will also announce a Boycott of all those commercial products related to the Pageant, and the day will end with a Women's Liberation rally at midnight when Miss America is crowned on live television. Lots of other surprises are being planned (come and add your own!) but we do not plan heavy disruptive tactics and so do not expect a bad police scene. It should be a groovy day on the Boardwalk in the sun with our sisters. In case of arrests, however, we plan to reject all male authority and demand to be busted by policewomen only. (In Atlantic City, women cops are not permitted to make arrests—dig that!)

Male chauvinist-reactionaries on this issue had best stay away, nor are male liberals welcome in the demonstrations. But sympathetic men can donate money as well as cars and drivers.

Male reporters will be refused interviews. We reject patronizing reportage. *Only newswomen will be recognized.*

The Ten Points We Protest

1. The Degrading Mindless-Boob-Girlie Symbol. The Pageant contestants epitomize the roles we are all forced to play as women. The parade down the runway blares the metaphor of the 4-H Club county fair, where the nervous animals are judged for teeth, fleece, etc., and where the best "specimen" gets the blue ribbon. So are women in our society forced daily to compete for male approval, enslaved by ludicrous "beauty" standards we ourselves are conditioned to take seriously.

2. Racism with Roses. Since its inception in 1921, the Pageant has not had one Black finalist, and this has not been for a lack of test-case contestants. There has never been a Puerto Rican, Alaskan, Hawaiian, or Mexican-American winner. Nor has there ever been a *true* Miss America—an American Indian.

3. Miss America as Military Death Mascot. The highlight of her reign each year is a cheerleader-tour of American troops abroad—last year she went to Vietnam to pep-talk our husbands, fathers, sons and boyfriends into dying and killing with a better spirit. She personifies the "unstained patriotic American womanhood our boys are fighting for." The Living Bra and the Dead Soldier. We refuse to be used as Mascots for Murder.

4. The Consumer Con-Game. Miss America is a walking commercial for the Pageant's sponsors. Wind her up and she plugs your product on promotion tours and TV—all in

an "honest, objective" endorsement. What a shill.

5. Competition Rigged and Unrigged. We deplore the encouragement of an American myth that oppresses men as well as women: the win-or-you're-worthless competitive disease. The "beauty contest" creates only one winner to be "used" and forty-nine losers who are "useless."

6. The Woman as Pop Culture Obsolescent Theme. Spindle, mutilate, and then discard tomorrow. What is so ignored as last year's Miss America? This only reflects the gospel of our society, according to Saint Male: women must be young, juicy, malleable—hence age discrimination and the cult of youth. And we women are brainwashed into believing this ourselves.

7. The Unbeatable Madonna-Whore Combination. Miss America and Playboy's centerfold are sisters over the skin. To win approval, we must be both sexy and wholesome, delicate but able to cope, demure yet titillatingly bitchy. Deviation of any sort brings, we are told, disaster: "You won't get a man!!"

8. The Irrelevant Crown on the Throne of Mediocrity. Miss America represents what women are supposed to be: unoffensive, bland, apolitical. If you are tall, short, over or under what weight The Man prescribes you should be, forget it. Personality, articulateness, intelligence, commitment—unwise. Conformity is the key to the crown—and, by extension, to success in our society.

9. Miss America as Dream Equivalent To—? In this reputedly democratic society, where every little boy supposedly can grow up to be President, what can every little girl hope to grow to be? Miss America. That's where it's at. Real power to control our own lives is restricted to men, while women get patronizing pseudo-power, an ermine cloak and a bunch of flowers; men are judged by their actions, women by their appearance.

10. *Miss America as Big Sister Watching You.* The Pageant exercises Thought Control, attempts to sear the Image onto our minds, to further make women oppressed and men op-pressors; to enslave us all the more in high-heeled, low-status roles; to inculcate false values in young girls; to use women as beasts of buying; to seduce us to prostitute ourselves before our own oppression.

NO MORE MISS AMERICA

ARTICLE

White Women and Klan Violence in the 1920s

Nancy Maclean

In 1915, an organization, calling itself the Ku Klux Klan, was founded on Thanksgiving night when hooded men burned a cross on top of Stone Mountain just outside Atlanta, Georgia. This organization was much larger than the first Klan that had been founded just after the Civil War, and its influence was national rather than regional. There were Klaverns in the South to be sure. But there were also Klan organizations in places like Indianapolis, Denver, and Chicago. The second Klan did not restrict itself to terrorizing Blacks. Determined to protect American institutions from the influence of anyone who was not white and Protestant, it opposed immigration and did what it could to intimidate Catholics and Jews as well as Afro-Americans. Maclean's article focuses on the relationship between women and the Klan in Clarke County, Georgia in the 1920s. Women who lived in and around Athens wrote to the Klan encouraging its members to try to intimidate or punish men who either abused their privileges or neglected to fulfill their obligations.

What do these letters and the action of Klan members in response to them tell us about gender conventions in the 1920s South? Why were Klan members so willing to respond to the letters written by these women?

In July of 1928, Mrs. Bertha Thornton Peghini wrote the Ku Klux Klan of Athens, Georgia a

Source: Nancy Maclean, "White Women and Klan Violence in the 1920s: Agency, Complicity, and the Politics of Women's History," *Gender & History* (Autumn 1921) 285–295. Reprinted by permission. Notes omitted.

desperate fourteen-page appeal for help. The story she told was a saga of psychological torture and physical abuse at the hands of her alcoholic, gambling husband. After she left him for the second time, taking their two children with her, he challenged her petition for divorce with allegations of adultery. The result was a mistrial, leaving Mrs. Peghini with no divorce, no alimony, no funds to fight the suit further, and the prospect of losing her 'two poor innocent children' because of his widely-broadcast slanders. Mrs. Peghini implored the Klan to force her husband to grant her a divorce on the grounds she stipulated. 'Being an American woman I feel that I ought to have Justice,' she concluded. 'If I can't have it from the Courts I know of no other one to go to except your organization, who has it in your power to deal with such cases.'

The organization to which Mrs. Peghini directed her plea was no charity agency but was instead the largest right-wing, paramilitary movement in American history. Capitalizing on anxieties about the pervasive turmoil in social relations in the wake of World War I, the Klan amassed a claimed membership of five million white, Protestant men by 1926. The order's program fused virulent racism, avid nationalism, Protestant fundamentalism, and a backward-looking populism with conservative family and sexual politics. The widespread appeal of these politics among native-born white men made it possible for the Klan, by mid-decade, to dominate the governments of several states and hundreds of towns and counties across the nation. Klansmen enlisted this extraordinary power to secure immunity for their propagandistic, legislative, and sometimes violent attacks on African-Americans, Catholics, Jews, labor radicals, liberals—and white men and women who deviated from the Klan's Victorian moral code. In fact, local 'moral cleanups,' aimed at policing white mores and employing both legal and extra-legal methods, were among its most common and popular crusades.

These anti-vice campaigns, like the Klan's overall program, attracted the sympathies of myriad white, native-born, Protestant women. Although formally excluded from the Klan, which operated as an all-male fraternal order, many such women actively supported it from without. The most ardent built a parallel order for their sex, the Women of the Ku Klux Klan (WKKK), which boasted some one and a half million members by 1926. WKKK members called on the then-common concepts of a higher female morality and a maternal mission in society to claim a distinctive role for themselves in promoting the politics they shared with male Klansmen. Others, including some activists in established organizations like the Women's Christian Temperance Union and local women's clubs, cooperated with the Klan in joint efforts to enforce Prohibition and rid their communities of perceived moral disorder.

This article uses a case study from Athens, Georgia—a small manufacturing and commercial city in the southern Piedmont—to focus on another, little-known aspect of women's relationship to the Klan of the 1920s: the efforts of some to incite Klansmen to vigilante activity. The study draws upon a unique archival collection of internal Klan papers from the Athens chapter, which contains documents that appear not to have survived in any of the other few extant collections: requests from local white women asking the Klan to punish husbands or neighbors for alleged transgressions, including adultery, desertion, wife-beating, gambling, prostitution, and bootlegging. Since such requests were acknowledged by contemporaries to be a common phenomenon, evidence of which the Klan ordinarily destroyed, the appeals from Clarke County—in which Athens is located—no doubt represent only a tiny fraction of the actual cases. Indeed, one official of the order's national headquarters maintained that it 'gets hundreds of letters from women asking that some man they don't like be whipped.' The Georgia state office of the Klan, for its part, reported receiving an average of twenty letters *each week* from women urging the order to threaten or use violence against someone of whose conduct they disapproved.

The surviving Clarke County appeals for vigilantism permit us to examine women's behind-the-scenes initiatives—normally obscured—to defend themselves and their perceived interests in domestic and community conflicts. While women's ability to make the Klan serve their ends suggests the value of gender analysis to the study of right-wing movements, the patterns revealed in these cases also raise troublesome questions for feminist theory and women's history, questions explored at greater length in the conclusion. For if these instances show how even abused, seemingly powerless women were capable of marshalling the limited resources at hand to ameliorate their situations, they also caution us against construing such female agency as in and of itself progressive. In the apt words of historian Barbara Fields:

> Those inclined to romanticize, sentimentalize, or take vicarious comfort in the flowering of cultural forms among the oppressed which challenge their subordination—as if, somehow, what has been lost politically has been regained on a higher (cultural) level—would do well to remember that these autonomous cultural forms need not be gentle, humane, or liberating. Where they develop apart from a continuing challenge, politically articulate and autonomous, to the real structure of power, they are more likely to be fungi than flowers.

Indeed, the history described here illustrates the complexity of women's resistance to male domination. These white women prodded their self-styled protectors into vigilantism, manipulating the contradictions of Klan ideology to compel its adherents to help them achieve their ends. In doing so, they forced a redefinition of acceptable male behavior and thus modified their subordination. Yet they also helped to ensure its perpetuation by aiding a movement determined to ensure the supremacy of white male proprietors in domestic as in public life. Moreover, in seeking to redress their own problems, female petitioners exacerbated the plights of other oppressed groups. The legitimacy these women conferred upon the Klan facilitated its offensives against Blacks, Catholics, labor radicals, and Jews. An examination of paradigmatic instances of, first, vigilantism instigated by women and then vigilantism against women will demonstrate some of the sources and consequences of women's collusion with the Klan.

I

Perhaps the most fascinating—and certainly the most detailed—episode of morals-related vigilantism in Clarke County was the case of the Kenney family. In early March of 1922, five masked men visited the Kenney household, where Frank Kenney lived with his mother and two sisters. They came to warn him about his private conduct. Frank was having an affair with a married woman, Lillie Toole, on whom he spent most of the salary that otherwise would have gone to support his household, and he had a history of violently abusing his twenty-seven-year-old sister Nora. Nora had earlier sought help from a foreman at the textile mill where the siblings worked as operatives to compel her brother to pay the family's rent. Toole's mother had tried the same tactic, asking the foreman to make her daughter return to her lawful husband. The failure of these efforts to dissuade Frank or his mistress precipitated the Klan's first warning.

Frank ignored the warning, and three weeks later, on the night of March 22nd, seven masked men broke into the Kenney home, took Frank from bed and drove him out to the countryside. There, they beat him with rawhide whips and left him to walk, barefoot and bloody, back to his home. Frank's assailants threatened to do worse if he did not allow Nora, whom he had recently thrown out, to return to the household. While Frank's financial neglect of his family, his illicit affair, and his chronic cruelty toward his sister provided the context for the Klan's vigilante assault, it was triggered by a specific incident. When Lillie Toole was visiting Frank one day, she insulted Nora, who retorted that the married woman should go home 'where [she] ought to be.' Frank joined the argument, asserting that since he paid the rent, the couple's actions were none of Nora's business; if anyone should get out, it was her. He then beat her so badly that she needed surgery. Kenney had thereby exploited the privilege of male dominance, using his power not to maintain the household order but to safeguard his own profligate, abusive ways.

Yet if Nora suffered in the Kenney household, she was hardly a passive victim. On the contrary, she held clearly-defined views of her rights and her brother's obligations. She used what little leverage she had to good effect, portraying herself as a martyr in the quest for domestic propriety. While hospitalized she appealed through the press to the public conscience, attributing her suffering to her efforts 'to keep an honest and decent house.' To demonstrate her own piety, Nora described how she prayed to God that Frank would 'stop sinning.' She implied that her challenge to his authority issued from worry that her younger sister would be 'led astray,' particularly since Frank and Mrs. Toole openly displayed their physical attraction.

Nora's agency can be contrasted with her mother's submission. Financially dependent on her son, Mrs. Kenney publicly took his side in the conflict. She apparently felt incapable of opposing the man on whose income she relied—despite her disapproval of the company he kept. After Frank was flogged, Mrs. Kenney even swore out warrants for the arrest of Nora and her boyfriend, accusing them of complicity in the assault. Nora, however, had none of her mother's inhibitions. According to Mrs. Kenney, her daughter had 'come to her saying she had enlisted the services of the Ku Klux Klan, and that they would visit the Kenney house' and discipline both renegade brother and passive mother. Nora thus used the Klan to enhance her bargaining power, and used her moral rectitude as grounds for upstaging her mother's authority.

Other aspects of the case offer further insights into the Klan's vigilante activity against white morals offenders. First, the behavior that led to the flogging stopped Kenney's contemporaries from defending him or condemning his assailants in public. As one sardonic Georgian put it in 1927, 'it is not considered an honor to be whipped by masked men.' Consciousness of his own vulnerability probably dissuaded Kenney from pressing for prosecu-

tion of his Klan assailants. His reticence no doubt increased as he watched the local establishment's handling of the case. Although the authorities originally maintained that the Klan was responsible, within days they began trying to direct blame elsewhere. They reported, for example, that Kenney was flogged 'for paying too much attention to another man's wife,' as if this motive somehow established the Klan's innocence.

By far the most intriguing effort to deflect blame from the Klan, however, was the accusation that a group of mill women were behind the incident. Police officials told the press that 'the women in the Southern mill vicinity have formed a league designed to oust undesirables from the neighborhood.' The officials said that some residents had been driven out 'for no other reasons than their non-employment' and insinuated that these women were 'responsible for Kenney's being taken out and flogged.' Although there is no other direct evidence of this league, certain factors make its existence plausible. First, contemporary studies reported deep divisions between less respectable 'floating' workers and established residents of mill communities. Second, the combination of women's vulnerability to domestic abuse and the sense among at least some that they were entitled to better treatment—a sense perhaps derived from their wage-earning and the support networks created among female co-workers—could have led them to collective efforts to police their neighborhood. Finally, the economic straits of mill families in these years might have led women to try to control the earning capacity of husbands and children by ridding the environment of temptations to vice, bad examples, or cheaper labor.

Nevertheless, even if such a formal female league existed and encouraged the Klan to act, the attempt of the police to pin the flogging on it was a logical absurdity; Kenney was whipped, after all, not by women but by men. In blaming mill women, the authorities in fact displayed both their uneasiness about the willingness of some white women to bypass the state and their fear of the political consequences of criticizing the Klan and thus appearing to side with those against whom it acted. Thus, the Kenney case soon disappeared from the press and never resulted in any indictments—as did another Klan flogging a few months later of a man with chronic 'domestic troubles.' Both men had violated community notions of right. Although some residents may have disapproved of the Klan's methods, no one had the courage to challenge them in public—not even the victims, who grasped the dynamics of the situation too well to pursue legal redress.

By viewing the Kenney case in light of other morals-related vigilantism in the area, we can better understand its meanings. Nora's role in promoting the Klan's violence was by no means unusual. Indeed, local women, more often than men, sought to deploy the Klan as a resource in domestic struggles; almost all of the surviving appeals to the Athens Klan are from women. Some women, for example, called on the Klan to punish abusive men, while others asked it to find husbands who deserted, to drive out prostitutes or bootleggers, or to deter hooligans from disrupting their churches. When established channels failed to satisfy their notions of right, duty, and justice, these women felt justified in bypassing the state to achieve their ends.

Yet despite these initiatives, the appeals themselves suggest the vulnerability of many women in the South of these years. Caught in a period of transition between an older family order that subjugated women but nonetheless afforded them provision for basic needs and some measure of protection, and an emerging one that offered women greater freedom but little security, they were left exposed to the worst of each. No longer could they rely on earlier patterns of community life, in which family, neighbors, and church punished men who failed to meet their familial obligations or grossly abused their power. Nor could such women expect help from the state. Its response to the problems of desertion, non-support, and wife-beating was fines and perhaps jail sentences for the husbands. Either

merely exacerbated the economic plight of dependent women and children who lacked other means of support. Convinced of the futility of the state's methods but determined to remedy their situations, some of the affected white women called upon the Klan.

Their appeals constitute tangible proof of some women's attempts to exercise a measure of control in their intimate lives. By claiming rights for themselves and defining duties incumbent on their partners, they sought to renegotiate the terms of their relationships. In their requests, they articulated a 'moral economy' of their own, exploiting the Klan's ideology of honor and chivalry to achieve their ends. If they had performed their domestic roles well, then, they insisted, they deserved protection when their mates failed to honor the marital contract. They expressed a sense of outrage that they, or those women on whose behalf they wrote, had fulfilled their obligations only to be betrayed by their partners. One woman expressed this clearly, venting her anger at having 'tried very hard to make the best of a bad bargain' in her marriage, to no avail. If the Klan wanted a system of private patriarchy, female petitioners implied, then its 'Knights' had an obligation to protect women wronged by men. Indeed, another woman called on the Klan 'in God's name for help.' 'If ever a woman needed your protection,' it was her neighbor, starved and beaten mercilessly by her unrepentant husband, to whom the writer wanted the Klan to administer 'the last resort in *full.*' These women searched tenaciously for decent treatment and proved adroit in exploiting the limited means at their disposal to gain it.

II

But empathy for their victimization and recognition of their initiative in negotiating the power relations that shaped their lives should not blind us to the wider consequences of their efforts. Lest we be tempted to romanticize their resistance, we would do well to recall the nature of the organization to which they appealed. At the same time as the local Klan served some white women, it also demonstrated, in word and deed, its fidelity to the full spectrum of politics for which the Klan is more commonly known: fierce anti-Catholicism, anti-Semitism, and hostility to labor organizing and radicalism among them. Most dramatically, it employed brutal and systematic terror against Black residents. Klansmen drove whole neighborhoods of African-Americans from their homes, destroyed their churches and schools, confiscated their property, and tortured individuals. The two faces of the Klan were not unconnected: its ideology of chivalry was of a piece with its general reactionary politics.

Some women used this connection to their advantage. We can see this in the case of Mrs. Peghini. She may have had a weak hand, but she knew how to play it. With a curious mixture of cunning and sincerity, Peghini connected her struggle for an equitable divorce to a range of issues in the Klan's program. Not only did she emphasize her history of devotion as a mother and perseverance as a wife, but she also drew attention to other details about her husband, which, if they failed to sway a jury, could at least convince the Klan. While she was 'an American woman,' her estranged husband—as she pointed out over and over again—was an Italian, and a 'devote [sic] Roman Catholic' at that. Indeed, she expressed stupefaction that the jury would 'deal so hard with an American woman and be so lenient [with] a devote [sic] Catholic.' Given the Klan's nativism and anti-Catholicism, Mrs. Peghini's emphasis on these factors was no doubt intentional. Further hoping to strengthen her case, she also alleged that Mr. Peghini had gotten 'very intimate with a colored nurse' hired for the children. Finally, she played to the Klan's populism, noting that her husband had lately acquired property; 'he was able to bring up a good many business men' to support him in court, she said, implying that he had bought a verdict. Similarly, the woman who requested help for her abused neighbor observed that the husband, who de-

prived his wife and child of basic necessities, had 'made [a] lot of money & has good property now.' She also stated that during one of his attacks on his wife, 'a colored hired man came to her relief & pulled him of[f] her,' suggesting that if a Black man had protected this white woman, surely the Klan ought to. By thus feeding the Klan's multiple hatreds, these women encouraged its efforts to maintain dominance over other groups.

The very fact of the appeals from women gave succor to the Klan. Indeed, one local minister and Klan leader evoked them to vindicate the Klan's vigilante methods and silence public opposition. 'Sisters have called me,' he chided critics, 'with tears in their eyes because of brothers who have been led into lives of dissipation . . . mothers weep over wayward sons and daughters, while "Peaceful Athens" sleeps on.' While the Klan used such pleas to convince white non-members of the justice of its cause, Klansmen's own commitment to their movement was no doubt steeled by the effusive praise lavished on them by women to whose aid they had come. 'It seems as tho [sic] you were a band of white robed angels sent from the father above,' wrote one female recipient of their support, while another promised that 'God will bless each and every one.'

Thus sanctified, the Klan turned its force not only against African-Americans, immigrants, and Catholics, against labor unions, radicals and liberals, but also—of more immediate bearing on the topic here—against other women as well. Black and immigrant women were by definition beyond the pale of the Klan's vaunted chivalry. They never enjoyed the 'protection' nominally accorded white women, another reason for Mrs. Peghini to distinguish her native-born background from her immigrant husband's. To the extent that Black women received attention, it was as targets of Klansmen's abuse. One such woman was Mrs. Odessa Peters, the wife of a local Black farmer. Having brutally beaten her husband and driven him from the area, the Klan then cheated the terrified Mrs. Peters out of all of the couple's property. White working-class women fared better, but only so long as they observed a sexual decorum defined by 'respectable' whites, male and female; if they lived outside the control of individual men and acted in ways subversive of the Klan's gender ideology, they too could be subject to its violence.

Indeed, of the surviving written complaints to the Athens Klan, all those not from women were *about* women. One rural man, for example, informed on a widow in his neighborhood whom he summoned the Klan to 'clean out.' Her conduct affronted him on several counts: she drank and sold whiskey, she lured neighborhood men into default on their familial duties, and she flouted the customary sexual division of labor that required female-headed farm households to rely on men for help. A male resident of the Athens mill community where the Kenney family lived complained to the Klan twice about a neighbor named Mary Meade, whom he accused of malicious gossip, and about Meade's daughter, whom he charged with treating her husband 'meaner than a dog.' The writer asked the Klan to discipline the pair, insisting that other neighbors were also 'tired' of the Meade women's orneriness. 'I think,' he concluded, 'your order ought to take hold of all such women and let them know they must behave their selves [sic].' 'You can take sorry men and make good men out of them,' he challenged Klansmen, so 'can you take a Woman and make her do like a White Woman ought to[?]'

Other men also recognized the Klan's value as a tool for disciplining disorderly women. C.W. Hoyt penned a letter to the organization the day after Klansmen paid him a warning visit in 1925. Hoyt sought to absolve himself by redirecting the Klan's zeal. 'I *do* do my best to support my family,' he swore, 'I want to do right, I want to work for and raise my little children [sic], Right is Right.' 'The trouble' was not with him, but 'with [his] wife,' whom he couldn't 'do anything with.' To convince the Klan of his wife's recalcitrance, Hoyt had three male neighbors sign to confirm his claims. Yet another man, W.A. LaCount, called on the Klan to bring back his wayward wife, who had run away with his business partner and

refused to return. In effect, these writers wanted the Klan to exact from their womenfolk deferential, submissive behavior that individual, economic and community pressure could no longer always secure by the 1920s.

For its part, the Klan complied eagerly in the project of these male petitioners. That Klansmen relished the role granted them was evident in their notice to Albert Mobley, a poor farmer in rural Athens. 'We give you fair warning that we have been called upon to make investigation in you and your wives [sic] affairs,' they wrote, admonishing him 'to keep her off [the] streets. . . . You Be ruller [sic] of your home. But treat your wife right. We mean she must respect you and home and children.' As if to emphasize their own regard for mitigating factors, the Klan authors noted that Mobley was 'a hard working man' and that he had 'cut out drinking.' In effect, he had met two of their criteria for appropriate male conduct; if he would only compel his wife to act properly, they promised there would be 'no more said or done.'

The Mobley case illustrated the conservative goals of the Klan's morals-related vigilantism, which sought to fortify the chain of male dominance by mending weak links. The order disciplined men who neglected their obligations and abused their power over women and children, but it also affirmed that power in urging less aggressive men to exert control over unruly women. To the extent that the Klan punished white men, it did so not to promote genuine equality for women, but to suppress conduct that disrupted the smooth functioning of male-dominant households. Sometimes Klan vigilantism, like the warning to Mobley, openly sought to shore up men's authority over their wives. Other times the male supremacist logic appeared more indirectly, as in several episodes in which Klansmen attacked suitors of whom the women's male relatives did not approve. In these cases, the Klan made clear its disregard for individual women's choices and its antipathy to the principle of female autonomy. This violence ritually enacted the order's belief that women's sexuality ought to be subject to the control of men with propriety rights over them. In short, while the white women who appealed to the order may have achieved their own immediate goals, in the process they encouraged a force dedicated to the very hierarchies that put their sex in such exasperating positions.

III

That paradox points to some of the larger implications of the patterns described here. On the one hand, the record of women's collusion with the Klan demonstrates the way gender analysis can enhance, even change, our understanding of movements not usually thought of in these terms. Although historians of the Klan, most of them male, have neglected to explore the meaning of the rich evidence thereof, questions of gender, family, and sexuality were near the center of Klan politics. The Imperial Office that presided over local chapters shrewdly grasped the mobilizing potential of purity campaigns, whether waged with legal or extra-legal tactics. Indeed, national officers instructed local Klans, once chartered, to 'clean up their towns.' Presumably, the Imperial Office thought these clean-ups an excellent way to confirm the value of the Klan to its constituency. In practice, they proved far more effective than its other activities or propaganda in rallying initial support. Contemporaries and scholars alike have tended to concur that, across the nation, such efforts came to be the most popular activities of the second Klan and its most effective recruiting device.

Interestingly, too, as the reluctance of Clarke County residents to come to the defense of the Klan's victims illustrates, the order's efforts to buttress traditional gender roles and family obligations proved the least contested of all its politics. As one North Carolinian opponent of the Klan later explained, much of its support stemmed from a public consensus that 'generally speaking the [white] people that they punished had a whole lot

lacking in their character and they deserved some punishment.' Non-Klan white residents would point to people 'leading these immoral lives, and they've been doing it for ten years and the children out there are suffering and nothing's being done about it. So the Klan did something about it; they put the whip to them.' This acquiescence reveals the extraordinary utility of gender and generational issues in the Klan's bid for hegemony. For once its members' right to police some kinds of deviant behavior was accepted, it was difficult to draw clear lines as to what was within their purview and what was outside it.

How other right-wing movements and conservative causes accrued strength from their ability to tap into anxieties about the future of the family and relations between the sexes merits further exploration. Scholars have noted that such concerns played into campaigns ranging from antebellum pro-slavery, to turn-of-the-century anti-Socialism, to the white Citizen's Councils of the South in the 1950s and '60's, to the anti-busing movement of the 1970s. The exact relationships need to be determined in each specific case and context, but studies of the New Right suggest that gender issues can play an absolutely pivotal role in winning mass support for a wider right-wing agenda.

As women's relationship to the Klan attests, however, the potency of gender issues likely had roots deeper than ideology. It is, in fact, in the nitty-gritty reality of lived experience that the more troubling questions about the Klan's ability to garner a mass following through sexual politics lie. Desertion and wife-beating, for example, were hardly illusory problems; they produced real suffering for many women. Few contemporaries addressed these problems; fewer still offered meaningful, immediate solutions. If this is largely still the case today, it was all the more so in the 1920s when the welfare state was still a thing of the future, particularly in the South, with its deeply ingrained traditions of privatism and limited government. The disparity between men's and women's power in the home, in short, and women's inability to find other means to offset it and get their needs met, enabled the Klan to fill a real vacuum. A straightforward social control interpretation of the Klan's vigilantism cannot address these complexities; a more nuanced understanding is required.

The lines of influence, after all, could run in more than one direction. The history recounted here suggests that the Klan may have found its agenda for the reconstitution of American society modified by its female constituency. Historian Linda Gordon has observed of the origins of state intervention into family life that 'the clients helped to shape the nature of the social control itself.' The same could be said of the white women who appealed to the Klan. Committed as it was to shoring up patriarchal authority in the home, the Klan might never have taken the initiative in punishing wife-beaters. More than a few Klan members, after all, harassed their own estranged wives and neglected financial responsibilities to them and children. Certainly no man, to my knowledge, ever complained to the Klan about wife-beating. It was the affected women themselves who, pressing from behind the scenes, charted for the Klan the dividing line between legitimate male authority and unacceptable abuse—and compelled its members to patrol that border or lose face. These women grasped onto the ambiguity of the Klan's rhetoric of 'home defense,' pulling the tail to wag the dog. 'If you all are for the protection of a community' one rural woman with a philandering husband thus directed the Klan, you should drive out local prostitutes who are taking 'money that poor wives and children really need.' Her use of a conditional sentence structure ('if . . . then') illustrated how women used the Klan's stated goals as leverage for their own demands. Their proficiency in doing so, in turn, helps to make more sense of the Klan's widespread appeal among ordinary whites in these years—notwithstanding its profoundly conservative and anti-working class political agenda. By proffering itself as a resource to non-elite white people enmeshed in gender and generational power struggles and rendering concrete aid to those threatened by the emerging sexual order, the Klan no doubt won both credibility and loyalty.

Yet the fact that it responded to real needs and offered some measure of relief to distressed women and children in no way diminishes the Klan's horror. Quite the contrary, it underscores it. Such protective efforts established a humanizing facade that rendered the Klan the more insidious. This facade, as stated above, won for the order the public sanction it might otherwise have lacked. It seems fair to speculate, moreover, that it enabled members to nurture delusions about their enterprise. The gratitude Klan members received from their female beneficiaries likely had an effect analogous to that of the work of German fascist women. 'While Nazi men brutally murdered their political, racial, and national enemies,' historian Claudia Koonz observed, 'Nazi women organized motherliness so the world would appear normal and virtuous to average German citizens and to the most murderous SS men. . . . gloss[ing] evil with the healthy glow of motherly virtue.' . . .

Suggestions for Further Reading

Karen Anderson, *Changing Woman: A History of Racial Ethnic Women in Modern America* (New York: Oxford University Press, 1996).

Karen Anderson, *Wartime Women: Sex Roles, Family Relations, and the Status of Women during World War II* (Westport, CT: Greenwood Press, 1981).

Barbara Bair, "True Women, Real Men: Gender, Ideology, and Social Roles in the Garvey Movement," in *Gendered Domains: Rethinking Public and Private in Women's History*, ed. Dorothy O. Helly and Susan M. Reverby (Ithaca, NY: Cornell University Press, 1992), 154–66.

KATHLEEN M. BLEE, *Women of the Klan: Racism and Gender in the 1920s* (Berkeley: University of California Press, 1991).

DOROTHY M. BROWN, *Setting a Course: American Women in the 1920s* (Boston: Twayne Publishers, 1987).

D'ANN CAMPBELL, *Women at War with America: Private Lives in a Patriotic Era* (Cambridge, MA: Harvard University Press, 1984).

WILLIAM H. CHAFE, *The Paradox of Change: American Women in the 20th Century* (New York: Oxford University Press, 1991).

NANCY F. COTT, *The Grounding of Modern Feminism* (New Haven, CT: Yale University Press, 1987).

GERALD E. CRITOPH, "The Flapper and Her Critics," in *"Remember the Ladies": New Perspectives on Women in American History,* ed. Carol V. R. George (Syracuse, NY: Syracuse University Press, 1975), 145–60.

PETER G. FILENE, *Him/Her/Self: Gender Identities in Modern America,* 3rd ed. (Baltimore, MD: The Johns Hopkins University Press, 1998).

SUSAN M. HARTMANN, *The Home Front and Beyond: American Women in the 1940s* (Boston: Twayne Publishers, 1982).

MAUREEN HONEY, *Creating Rosie the Riveter: Class, Gender, and Propaganda during World War II* (Amherst, MA: University of Massacusetts Press, 1984).

DANIEL HOROWITZ, *Betty Friedan and the Making of* The Feminine Mystique: *The American Left, the Cold War, and Modern Feminism* (Amherst, MA: University of Massachusetts Press, 1998).

ALICE KESSLER-HARRIS, "Gender Ideology in Historical Reconstruction: A Case Study from the 1930s," *Gender and History,* 1 (Spring 1989), 31–49.

REBECCA E. KLATCH, *Women of the New Right* (Philadelphia, PA: Temple University Press, 1987).

MOLLY LADD-TAYLOR, *Raising a Baby the Government Way: Mother's Letters to the Children's Bureau, 1915–1932* (New Brunswick, NJ: Rutgers University Press, 1986).

BLANCHE LINDEN-WARD AND CAROL HURD GREEN, *American Women in the 1960s: Changing the Future* (New York: Twayne Publishers, 1993).

LEISA D. MEYER, *Creating GI Jane: Sexuality and Power in the Women's Army Corps during World War II* (New York: Columbia University Press, 1996).

JOANNE J. MEYEROWITZ, "Beyond the Feminine Mystique: A Reassessment of Postwar Mass Culture, 1946–1958," *Journal of American History,* 79 (March 1993), 1455–82.

JOANNE J. MEYEROWITZ, ed., *Not June Cleaver: Women and Gender in Postwar America, 1945–1960* (Philadelphia, PA: Temple University Press, 1994).

RUTH MILKMAN, "Redefining 'Women's Work': The Sexual Division of Labor in the Auto Industry during World War II," *Feminist Studies,* 8 (Summer 1982), 336–72.

JESSAMYN NEUHAUS, "The Way to a Man's Heart: Gender Roles, Domestic Ideology, and Cookbooks in the 1950s," *Journal of Social History,* 32 (Spring 1999), 529–55.

VICKI L. RUIZ, *From Out of the Shadows: Mexican Women in Twentieth-Century America* (New York: Oxford University Press, 1998).

WINIFRED D. WANDERSEE, *On the Move: American Women in the 1970s* (Boston: Twayne Publishers, 1988).

SUSAN WARE, *Holding Their Own: American Women in the 1930s* (Boston: Twayne Publishers, 1982).

DEBORAH GRAY WHITE, *Too Heavy a Load: Black Women in Defense of Themselves, 1894–1994* (New York: W. W. Norton, 1999).

KENNETH A. YELLIS, "Prosperity's Child: Some Thoughts on the Flapper," *American Quarterly,* XXI (Spring 1969), 44–64.

CHAPTER TWELVE

GENDER, IDENTITY, AND SEXUALITY (1600–1975)

QUESTIONS OF GENDER/SEXUAL IDENTITY

"Boston Woman Posed as Man with a Wife" read the headlines on the front page of the *New York Times* on the morning of October 1, 1901. It seems that Miss Caroline Hall of Boston had boarded the steamship *Citta di Torino* in Genoa in early September. Calling herself "Mr. Charles Winslow Hall," she was dressed as a man and was accompanied by a woman she referred to as her wife. Early in the voyage, she became ill and retired to her cabin. Hall was apparently suffering from the last stages of tuberculosis. Shortly after the ship arrived in New York, she died. It was the ship's doctor who discovered that Mr. Charles Hall was a woman.

Hall's fellow passengers must have been very surprised. According to the *Times,* Hall had been very convincing as a man. Although slight of build, she had short hair and wore the clothes of a gentleman. She walked and gestured like other men and spoke in a deep,

resonant voice. According to the story, she enjoyed the company of the men on the ship and spent time with them smoking cigars, talking about sports, and drinking brandy in the ship's saloon.

It turns out that Caroline Hall was returning to the United States from Italy. It was there that she met her companion/wife, Giuseppina Boriani. According to the *Times*, Hall had become increasingly convinced "that women were not afforded as many opportunities in the world as men. She was an artist, and in addition was an excellent rifle shot. It was easier for men to get about, she asserted, and after brooding for some time over the disadvantages of being a woman she decided to adopt male attire, and her friend humored her whim." Posing as a man, she was able to compete successfully in several shooting matches. She also traveled freely throughout the country painting. Because people thought she was a man, her movements and activities were in no way inhibited.

Hall's decision to pose as a man raises a number of interesting issues in terms of gender identity. As a crossdresser, she was able to present herself as a man. She found herself privileged and powerful as long as she was able to exhibit male characteristics in terms of appearance and behavior. She could successfully lay claim to public space in the sense that she was free to go unaccompanied wherever she pleased. She was taken seriously as an artist. She could participate in competitive sports. And she could eat, drink, and smoke whatever she liked with whomever she liked. Her charade was made all the more convincing by the fact that she was accompanied by a woman who claimed to be her wife. The collaboration of Giusippina Boriani in validating Hall's disguise made it unlikely that anyone would pause to question Caroline Hall's claim to manliness.

What Hall's story illustrates is how much issues about gender identity have been contested in American society. No doubt the readers of the *Times* found the story of Caroline Hall troubling as well as titillating. But she was, after all, dead by the time they read about her. Her attempt to reformulate her gender identity posed no immediate threat to their gender conventions. The case of Thomasine Hall was, unfortunately, not as benign as that of Caroline Hall because it involved the issue of sexual identity as well as gender identity.

Thomasine Hall was born in England sometime in the late sixteenth or early seventeenth century. Raised as a girl, she wanted to follow her brother into the military. So she cut off her hair, donned men's clothes, called herself Thomas, and became a soldier. Eventually, she left the military, resumed her identity as a woman, and supported herself by doing needlework. When the opportunity to emigrate to the American colonies presented itself, she again adopted a male identity and arrived in Virginia as an indentured laborer in 1627. There she apparently switched back and forth between wearing men's clothes and wearing women's clothes, a practice that caused considerable consternation among the inhabitants of the colony.

In those days, most Virginians were not noted for their piety. Nevertheless, some of them were no doubt at least vaguely aware that there was a Biblical injunction against crossdressing. A passage in Deuterotomy said, "The woman shall not wear that which pertaineth unto man, neither shall a man put on a woman's garment, for all that do so are abominable unto the Lord." So Thomasine/Thomas became the object of an investigation. When asked if she was a man or a woman, she said, "both," justifying her answer on the grounds that although she had an extremity that looked like a small penis, she did not have "the use of the man's part" (she could not achieve erection). She was subjected to a physical examination which revealed that she/he seemed to lack a vagina. The legal authorities did not quite know what to do with this man/woman. But, from their point of view, it was impossible to allow Thomasine/Thomas to maintain her/his double identity. Allowing such gender ambiguity was socially disruptive since there were important gender issues at stake. If Thomasine was declared a man, she would have much more freedom of movement than if she was a woman. Her gender would to some degree determine what kind of work she could be expected to do. As a man, for example, she was unlikely to be expected to cook or sew. Once she had served her time as an indentured servant and was free to marry, her gender would determine whom she might pursue in that regard. Moreover, if she were declared a man, she could own and control property after she married and could be expected to fulfill such civil responsibilities as serving in the militia.

The case of Thomasine/Thomas was complicated because it was not possible to tell with any certainty from an examination of her/his genitals whether she/he was a man or a woman. This phenomenon, called intersexuality, is relatively rare. But the gender and sexual ambiguity that resulted from it was just as disconcerting in colonial society as it is today. So Thomasine's case was sent the House of Burgesses to be resolved. Clearly the members of the House of Burgesses were no more successful than local officials in determining the sex of Thomasine/Thomas. After conducting their own investigation, the court sentenced Thomasine to wear pants but also to wear a female head dress, crosscloth, and apron thus giving her/him a permanently hybrid gender identity. That is all we know of Thomasine/Thomas. She/he makes no other appearance in the historical record.

GENDER AND THE EXPRESSION OF SEXUALITY IN AMERICAN SOCIETY

The cases of Caroline Hall and Thomasine Hall were problematic because both attempted to blur the gender boundaries that helped to order their world. Because of the way they chose to present themselves, observers made certain assumptions about their roles in society and the privileges they could claim as a result of their gender. By dressing as a man, Caroline Hall escaped from the restrictions that would have inhibited her movement, activities, and creativity as a woman. By using the ambiguity of her anatomy to justify switching back and forth between presenting herself as a woman and presenting herself as a man, Thomasine/Thomas was able to claim the right to both male and female privileges. Dressed as a man, she was free to seek adventure and enjoy freedom of movement. Posing as a woman allowed her to make her living as a seamstress, work that may have been more appealing to her than an alternative that required a great deal of physical strength.

While the stories about Caroline Hall and Thomasine Hall tell us a good deal about attitudes toward gender in American society, they tell us little or nothing about how these two individuals expressed themselves sexually. Caroline Hall and Giuseppina Boriani clearly cared for one another. Boriani nursed Hall devotedly during her last bout of illness and, according to the *Times*, remained with the body until Hall's relatives could claim it. But we have no way of knowing if Hall and Boriani had sexual relations with each other. They

may simply have been bound together by mutual affection, the desire for adventure, and the ties of loyal friendship.

We know just as little about the sexual life of Thomasine/Thomas Hall. It seems clear from the testimony that Thomasine/Thomas was aware that she/he was impotent. After all, she/he told the authorities that although she/he had what appeared to be a penis, she/he did not have the use of it. Her/his answer to their questions implies that she/he had tried to use it to perform what she/he considered to be a sexual act and failed. Therefore, she/he must have had some interest in engaging in sexual activity. Unfortunately, we don't know what sort of sexual activity that might have been. Nor do we know whether Thomasine/Thomas chose a man or a woman as her/his partner.

What these stories do suggest is that the relationship between sexual activity and gender is an extremely complex one. They also illustrate how difficult it is to reconstruct the history of gender and its relationship to sexual behavior. Part of the problem, it seems, is that we are unable to agree on just what constitutes a sexual relationship and what meaning to give those relationships and the behavior patterns that accompany them.

WHAT QUALIFIES AS SEXUAL—OR WHAT IS SEX ANYWAY?

To anyone who reads magazines or novels, goes to the movies, or spends their evenings watching television, it is clear that contemporary American society is obsessed with the subject of sex. Our jokes are laced with sexual innuendo. Television programs and films show men and women engaged in sexual activities including sexual intercourse. Sometimes those depictions are more implicit than explicit—nude bodies discreetly covered with sheets, passionate kisses, sounds of heavy breathing and rhythmic movement. But for the viewer with a little imagination, it is clear what kind of activity the directors and actors are trying to suggest is taking place on the screen. Advertisements on the billboards that line our highways, not to mention those that appear in newspapers, in magazines, and on television, frequently contain sexual content of one sort or another even if it is only to suggest that the use of a particular brand of perfume or aftershave is likely to make an individual more sexually desirable.

Despite the volume of sexually explicit material that we are exposed to on any given day, however, we rarely pause to define exactly what constitutes sex. The assumption seems to be that everyone over a certain age knows, more or less, what it is. Yet, "sex" means different things to different people. Some people define sex as penis-vagina intercourse that leads to or is intended to lead to procreation. For others, sexual activity is a form of recreation that has little or nothing to do with procreation. It includes any erotic behavior—kissing, caressing, prolonged eye contact, oral/anal stimulation—that can lead to the attainment of physical pleasure. For some, sex is a way of achieving intimacy with the object of their affection. For others, it is merely a way of asserting their power over their partners. For a few people, sexual activity is a means by which they hope to achieve spiritual transcendence. None of these definitions of sex is mutually exclusive. But the wide variety of meanings attached to sexual activity make it difficult to generalize about the role of sex and its relation to gender in American society.

Whatever the definition of sex, the meaning we give it, or the various ways we express our sexual natures, sexual expression is and always has been an important component of our gendered identities. Throughout western history, for example, one of the prerogatives of being male has been to initiate sexual activity with women. The double standard of sexuality which allows men relative freedom to pursue sexual pleasure and denies that freedom to women has been based partly on a definition of masculinity that includes a man's ability to control female sexuality and

a definition of ideal femininity that precludes the pursuit of men for the specific purpose of engaging in sexual activity.

We know from historical evidence that there have always been a wide variety of options for expressing our sexual impulses. And we know that often those options are gendered. Some societies demand that sexual expression be confined to relationships between men and women who are married to each other. Others are much more relaxed about sexual conduct and allow relatively free expression of sexuality. What we call homosexuality, for example, has a long history in western society. Among Athenian citizens, sexual relations between men were not only tolerated, they were socially acceptable. It was, however, a behavior pattern that was gendered. The wives of Athenian citizens were expected to confine their sexual activity to their husbands.

It is also clear that attitudes towards the expression of sexuality and its relationship to gender change over time. During the colonial period, for example, it was assumed that both men and women were lusty. But by the middle of the nineteenth century, there were those who claimed that respectable, married women had little interest in sexual activity. Such changing parameters for expressing sexuality testify to the degree to which patterns of sexual behavior as well as gendered identities have been socially constructed.

GENDER AND SEXUALITY DURING THE COLONIAL PERIOD

Attitudes towards sexuality during the colonial period were relatively relaxed. Whatever ambivalence the colonists had about pursuing their sexual desires centered on concerns relating to religion and maintaining social order. Most of those who settled the English colonies were Protestants who rejected the idea that sexual desire was inherently sinful. It is true that the Puritan clergy sometimes equated lustfulness with idolatry and expressed concern that the pleasure of participating in sexual activity could distract people from focusing on their love of God. As community leaders, they were also afraid that illicit sexual activity such as fornication or adultery would have a disruptive effect on their attempts to maintain an orderly as well as a Godly society. But the influence of Puritan ministers was confined pretty much to New England. Those who lived in the mid-Atlantic or southern colonies appear to have been less concerned with such issues. And by about 1700, the influence of both Puritanism and its ministers was declining in the Northeast.

In general, no matter where they lived, ordinary colonists considered sexual desire to be natural and desirable, a quality possessed by both men and women. They believed that sexual activity was as essential to good health as it was to a loving and stable marriage. Indeed, they held that a willingness to participate in sexual activity was a duty of both husbands and wives. In the absence of such willingness either could ask the courts to grant them an annulment or a divorce.

Seventeenth-century colonists were also willing to acknowledge the pleasure they received from sexual activity. Indeed, they held that female pleasure was necessary for the conception of a child. However, they drew the line at recreational sex. In their view, the only legitimate purpose for engaging in sexual intercourse was to procreate and the only place where that was appropriate was within marriage. To seek sexual pleasure for any other reason and under any other circumstances was a sin.

Given their economic circumstances, the belief that sexual activity should be devoted to procreation rather than personal pleasure was not surprising. The availability of land and the need for labor meant that children were highly valued, welcome additions to both the family and the community. There was little reason to limit the number of children a woman bore. Infant mortality was high and the need for an extra pair of hands great. The more sons a man had, the more land he could cultivate and the more animals he could raise. The more daughters a woman had, the

more help she had in her efforts to fulfill her domestic obligations. During the colonial period, masculinity and femininity were very much constructed around parenthood, so large families were the rule rather than the exception. Infertility, whether caused by impotence or barrenness, was both an economic disadvantage and a personal misfortune.

It is hard for us to appreciate the degree to which sexual activity was an integral part of everyday life during the colonial period. Most colonists were farmers whose livelihood depended on plant and animal reproduction. By our standards, households were very large, often consisting of husband, wife, children, other family members, visitors, and servants. During the early stages of settlement, few colonists lived in dwellings that accorded them any degree of personal privacy. Indeed, a married couple might sleep not only in the same room but also in the same bed with their children. And when those children grew up and began looking for a husband or a wife, they might be allowed to court in bed as long as they were separated with a bundling pillow or board, which was intended to discourage them from consummating their relationship before they took their wedding vows. Under such circumstances, there was very little, if any, mystery or reticence associated with sexual activity. The result was that young men and women approached their wedding night with a relatively good idea of what was expected of them.

However much the colonists may have been willing to acknowledge sexual passion as a genderless attribute, they were not willing to allow women the same opportunities to express their sexual urges as men. A double standard prevailed. Free, white men had a broader set of parameters within which to conduct their sexual activities than were available to their wives, sisters, and daughters. Indeed, female sexual expression was in some ways suspect since women were believed to be much more emotional and less rational than men and thus less able than men to control their passions. As a result of this attitude, masculinity was equated with a man's ability to control the sexual activity of the women in his family. It was up to him to decide when and under what circumstances female sexual desire could legitimately be expressed. One of the duties of a father was to try to assure that when his daughter married, she was a virgin. And it was a husband's responsibility to make sure his wife confined her sexual activities to the marriage bed. In that sense, then, both women's bodies and their emotions were considered to be the property of the men in their family, and a man's claim to manhood was constructed around his ability to exert power over the sexual expression of those in his household including his indentured servants.

Despite the fact that indentured servants were usually young and almost always single, they were expected to abstain from all sexual activity during their period of servitude, unless, of course, their master wanted to engage in illicit sexual activities with them. In an age when knowledge of birth control was limited and largely ineffective, it is not surprising that female servants were more likely to face punishment for engaging in sexual intercourse than their male counterparts. Typically, a female indentured servant who found herself pregnant faced the prospect of having her term of servitude lengthened in order to compensate her master for the labor that she was unable to perform during pregnancy, childbirth, and lactation. Unless she exposed his identity, her partner could simply go about his business without worrying about the consequences of his actions.

The gendered nature of punishment for illicit sexual activity also took other forms. One of the benefits of the double standard for men was that they were much less likely than women to be prosecuted for adultery and fornication. But the acts of sodomy and rape were gendered male. Colonial law defined sodomy as non-procreative sexual acts between two men, or between a man and an animal (also called "buggery" or "bestiality"), or oral/anal sex between a man and a woman. The colonists considered such acts "unnatural" offenses against God and passed laws making them illegal.

Rape was also a crime with a particularly strong gendered dimension. Certainly rape was a crime against women. But it was also considered to be a crime against men in the sense that women, whether they were wives, daughters, or servants, were virtually the property of men. Thus, it is not surprising that colonial court records in places like Massachusetts suggest that juries (which were all male) were much more likely to convict a man of rape if the victim was a child or married woman. This tendency made it extremely difficult for a single woman of childbearing age to find judicial redress for having been raped.

In contrast to men, women were much more likely to be tried for adultery, fornication, or bastardy. All three "crimes" were at some level evidence of women's rejection of male power and authority. In the sense that the free expression of female sexuality undermined male prerogatives, it also had the potential of undermining their confidence in their manliness. Bastardy (bearing an illegitimate child) was a particularly troubling issue for colonial courts. Inheritance laws were based on the assumption that men preferred to leave their property to their biological offspring rather than the children of their wives' lovers. Under such circumstances, it was important for them to know which of their children was legitimate and which was not. Propertied men, however, were just as concerned about the illegitimate offspring of single women. Magistrates tried to force pregnant women who were unmarried to reveal the identity of their sexual partners so that they could order biological fathers to assume financial responsibility for their illegitimate offspring. If they failed in their efforts, the community had to pay to keep the children until they were old enough to support themselves. Male taxpayers were not enthusiastic about fulfilling these responsibilities and considered that obligation to be an unwelcome drain on their resources.

Punishment for sexual crimes was as gendered as prosecutions. A man convicted of sexual crimes was usually required to pay court fees and fines. A woman was more likely to be whipped. Women, after all, had little access to property and were, therefore, unlikely to have the money to pay for their offenses.

By the eighteenth century, the expression of sexuality on the part of both men and women was carried out in an economic and social context that was changing. Movement westward, the growth of towns and cities, the expansion of commerce, and the development of an increasingly heterogeneous population undermined the ability of male heads of families and male community leaders to monitor the expression of sexuality of those around them. Choices about such matters were increasingly left in the hands of the individual, who now had to accept more responsibility for his or her actions.

Slavery also complicated the sexual landscape in the colonies. By the eighteenth century, slaves, either directly or indirectly imported from Africa, were replacing indentured servants, who had typically been white and of British origin. Like their European counterparts, white colonists considered Africans or those of African descent to be relatively uninhibited sexually. One of the assumptions that white men made about black men was that they were particularly virile. At the same time, white men viewed slave women as passionate and promiscuous.

Colonial legislatures passed laws forbidding sexual relations between blacks and whites, but such laws had little impact on white men, many of whom engaged in sexual relations with black women without fear of reprisal. They constructed their manliness around their ability to exploit what they considered to be the sexual licentiousness of black women, their power to prevent black men from protecting the virtue of their loved ones, and the assumption that they could control the sexual lives of the women in their own families. Added to the personal benefits to be derived from sexual access to female slaves was a widely acknowledged economic benefit. The birth of children to slave women enhanced the wealth of her master. And to the degree that manliness was measured by economic success, it confirmed his claim to manhood.

GENDER AND SEXUALITY IN THE NINETEENTH CENTURY

The rise of an influential middle class in the North in the late-eighteenth and early-nineteenth centuries led to some important changes in how those who wished to establish themselves as respectable and genteel incorporated the expression of sexuality into their definition of masculinity and femininity. Determined to establish standards of behavior that would differentiate them from both the working class and the idle rich, they became very self-conscious and anxious about the way they conducted their sexual lives.

Their anxiety was caused by a number of factors. First, as long as people lived on farms and were a part of tightly knit communities, families, ministers, and legal authorities could try to monitor and regulate sexual behavior. But the growth of towns and cities made it difficult to continue that kind of control. When sons and daughters left the farm to seek employment in the cities, parents lost their ability to regulate what their children did in their free time and to supervise their relationships with members of the opposite gender. The anonymity of city life meant that there was little to discourage sexual experimentation among young people, a situation which, in some cases, led to an increase in prostitution, illegitimate births, and the incidence of venereal disease.

Middle-class anxiety about the expression of sexuality also derived from the development of a consumer culture. Self-control was one of the bases for claiming middle-class respectability in the nineteenth century. Yet economic development brought about the rise of consumerism, which encouraged quite the opposite characteristic. The economic prosperity of those ready to provide goods and services to the burgeoning middle class was dependent upon convincing those who could afford it to spend their money on ease, comfort, and pleasure. Thus, both men and women were caught between the desire to confirm their respectability through self-control and the desire to testify to their affluence through consumption.

Another factor that influenced the attitudes of the middle class toward sexual activity was the changing role of children in the family. In the seventeenth and eighteenth centuries, children were valued in part because of their ability to contribute economically to the well being of the family. In the nineteenth century, middle-class children were essentially a drain on family resources. They had to be fed, housed, clothed, and educated but were not expected to do anything that might help to pay for their upkeep. Indeed, masculinity among middle-class men was defined in terms of being the sole support of one's wife and children. Children were still valued, of course, but their value was increasingly measured in emotional rather than economic terms. During the nineteenth century, middle-class couples began quite self-consciously to regulate their sexual activities, and the birth rate began to fall.

The fact that they lived in homes that were large enough to accord married couples a certain degree of privacy in the conduct of their sexual lives also influenced attitudes toward sexuality in the middle class. Middle-class children slept in their own rooms and could conceivably grow up in complete ignorance of the character of their parents' sexual activities. The claim to gentility was dependent upon conversation patterns in which references to matters of a sexual nature were avoided. In that sense, sex became invisible, an activity that was neither acknowledged nor discussed in polite society.

Both men and women were affected by these changes, but their response was gendered. Throughout the nineteenth century, masculinity continued to be tied to lust, potency, vigor, and aggressive sexual behavior. Men continued to enjoy the benefits of the double standard, which left them relatively free from the fear of being punished for engaging in pre-marital or extra-marital sexual activities. They accepted the responsibility for initiating sexual activities with women and assumed that they had a right to sexual satisfaction. In the middle class, sexual promiscuity for a man was certainly not condoned, but when it occurred it was usually tolerated as

long as it was discreet. Men were willing to refrain from passing judgment on each other as long as they did not flaunt their dalliances. And wives had little recourse other than turning a blind eye to the peccadilloes of their husbands. Most middle-class women were financially dependent upon their husbands, were unlikely to persuade a judge to give them a divorce on the grounds of adultery, and were unwilling to risk losing custody of their children in the process. Divorced women were social pariahs in the nineteenth century. So there was a great deal to lose by publicly exposing a husband's infidelity.

That the double standard prevailed does not, however, mean that men remained secure in their ability or willingness to express themselves sexually. Equating masculinity with the ability to satisfy sexual desire was both an asset and a liability to middle-class men, particularly those who lived in urban areas. Certainly they were interested in preserving the sexual privileges that they enjoyed as a result of their gender, but doing so undermined their belief that a "real" man was also the protector of female virtue. No one who lived in a city like New York or Philadelphia could ignore the fact that women who walked the streets by themselves were more vulnerable to the sexual advances of strange men than those who lived in farming communities. It was increasingly common for women walking alone or riding by themselves on public conveyances to experience some form of what we would call sexual harassment whether in the form of insulting remarks or the threat of physical assault. The assumption seemed to be that an unaccompanied woman was fair game for anyone who wished to pursue her. As cities grew and the century progressed, the streets became the place where sexual commerce was transacted, a place where working girls entertained themselves by flirting with men to whom they had not been properly introduced and prostitutes exchanged access to their bodies for cash. From the middle-class point of view, roaming the streets was not a proper activity for a "lady." Only safely ensconced in her home or holding onto the arm of a male relative or friend could her innocence and sexual safety be ensured and her sexual activities be monitored.

Anxiety about the power of male sexual desire was not just restricted to problems inherent in preserving the virtue of genteel women, however. As the century progressed, health reformers became increasingly concerned about the degree to which sexual activity could undermine a man's ability to compete in the world of business and achieve success. Convinced that the human body possessed a limited amount of energy, they argued that sexual orgasm drew blood and energy away from brain, heart, and lungs, thus depriving ambitious young men of the energy they needed to achieve success. Sylvester Graham, William Alcott, and O. S. Fowler, all nineteenth-century health reform advocates, viewed male orgasm as a source of physical, mental, and social deterioration. In their view, sexual activity in the pursuit of personal pleasure was particularly harmful because it was a waste of energy, which they considered a valuable and irreplaceable resource. Advocating what they considered to be sexual purity for men, they warned their readers that men should remain virgins until they married in their late twenties or early thirties. And they advised married men to initiate sexual intercourse only when they and their wives wanted to conceive a child.

Even more troubling from the point of view of health reformers was the issue of masturbation. Known as "the secret vice," masturbation was believed to pose a threat to both a man's health as well as his claim to manliness. According to O.S. Fowler, any man who indulged in self-stimulation "lays down his nobleness, dignity, honor, and manhood and is no longer bold, resolute, determined, aspiring, dignified, but becomes deprecated, irresolute, . . . tamed."

Anxiety about the connection between femininity and the expression of sexuality took an altogether different form. One of the bases of the middle-class sexual ideology was the belief that female sexual desire was tied to a woman's reproductive function. In contrast to the seventeenth century, the assumption was that women were more moral than men and that they had little interest in the more carnal aspects of life except when it applied to their "natural" desire to become mothers. Thus, the very definition of middle-class femininity was tied to the idea that to be womanly a woman had to be modest and passionless.

Women in the middle class were unlikely to enter marriage with any real understanding of what might be expected of them in terms of sexual expression. They rarely if ever knew very much about their own bodies or the biology of reproduction. Their marriageability was dependent upon their having had no sexual experience. Thus, many brides in the middle class were largely ignorant of what the consummation of a marriage might entail. Given those circumstances, a woman could only respond to the sexual initiatives of her husband and had to depend on him to provide her with sexual knowledge. Once married, a woman's happiness and economic well being was dependent upon the good will of her spouse. Participating in sexual activity was one way to cement the marital relationship, but a woman's willingness to do so was mediated by the fact that in reality she was her husband's sexual property. What she did not give willingly, he might feel justified in taking by force. And if he did so, she had virtually no recourse. There were no laws against marital rape, and divorce was not usually an available option.

Some women, of course, found pleasure in sexual activity. But that pleasure could be yet another source of anxiety. If a woman accepted the idea that women were by "nature" moral and passionless, how was she supposed to understand any tendency that she might have to indulge in sexual fantasies or to crave sexual intercourse? If she consulted a doctor regarding these tendencies, he might diagnose her as suffering from nymphomania. Some in the medical profession viewed everything from flirting and wearing perfume to committing adultery or seeking a divorce as symptoms of this condition. Treatments for nymphomania included removal of the ovaries and female circumcision (excision of the clitoris and/or labia).

If all of that were not enough to inhibit a woman's expression of sexuality, the belief that pregnancy and childbirth were dangerous if not life-threatening processes gave women even more reason to distrust their erotic impulses. Information about birth control was available but the only sure way to prevent conception was abstinence. As a result of these factors, many middle-class women appear to have been somewhat ambivalent about sexual activity and disinclined to equate sexual desire with "true womanhood."

Not all women, of course, felt that kind of ambivalence. In the slave quarters of the South among those without strong religious impulses, attitudes toward sexual activity were relatively relaxed. Because they had only a limited amount of control over their personal lives, there was little reason for slaves to stigmatize a woman who had sexual relations with a man who was not her husband. And since there was no property at stake, there was no reason to censure a woman who engaged in premarital sex. Infidelity and illegitimacy among slaves had little meaning in a society where marriage had no legal significance. And there was little reason for a slave couple to limit the size of their family. The result was that both men and women constructed their gendered identities around the relatively uninhibited expression of sexuality and the parenthood that was likely to accompany it.

The Civil War and Reconstruction did little to change those attitudes among southern blacks. Outside the emerging black middle class, neither reticence about acknowledging sexual desire nor reluctance about expressing it prevailed. Among working-class blacks, erotic desire was not considered shameful. Fertility rates among black women remained high. And children were welcomed even if they were illegitimate.

But military defeat and the abolition of slavery had a profound impact on the relationship between masculinity and femininity and the expression of sexuality in southern white communities. Before the war, white southerners exhibited very little concern about how black men and women expressed their sexuality. Slave owners valued black women who bore many children and viewed black men as so powerless that it rarely occurred to them to worry about the threat that male slaves might pose to the virtue of white women. That is not to say that there were no sexual relationships between white women and black men. But they were not common.

After the war, however, whites were desperate to reassert their supremacy over the black population of the South. White men continued to seek sexual liaisons with black women partly because they felt the need to reassure themselves that losing the war had not left them completely powerless. But they also created the image of black men as sexual predators and constructed their gender identity around their willingness to protect white women from the real or imagined sexual advances of freed slaves. In response to their desire to control the black population, they accused black men of raping or attempting to rape white women. They then mutilated and lynched the accused. White women colluded in these efforts, thus reaffirming definitions of white womanhood built around dependence, passivity, and sexual purity.

The connection between definitions of femininity and sexuality in the white working class was to some degree dependent upon ethnicity and the degree to which parents were able to maintain control over their daughters' social life. First generation immigrant parents in the early nineteenth century, for example, did whatever they could to supervise and control their daughters' access to members of the opposite sex and in that way inhibit the ability of their children to engage in sexual activity. By the end of the nineteenth century, however, more and more young working women were able to achieve some degree of independence from their parents. They lived in boarding houses and after long hours at work took to the streets in search of companionship and entertainment. In an environment in which masculinity was measured in part by a man's ability to treat a young woman to dinner, presents, or entrance tickets to a dance hall or amusement park, femininity was often constructed around a woman's ability to attract such a man. In return for the attention of a generous companion, a woman could show her appreciation in a wide variety of ways ranging from a thank you or peck on the cheek to engaging in sexual intercourse.

GENDER AND UTOPIAN VIEWS OF SEXUALITY IN THE NINETEENTH CENTURY

Middle-class notions concerning gender and its relationship to the expression of sexuality had great influence in the nineteenth century. But a few people formed communities designed to allow a great deal more freedom for men and women to construct their gendered identities around their sexual natures. The rise of the Free Love Movement illustrates the point. Led by Stephen Pearl Andrews and Josiah Warren, free lovers rejected totally the double standard of sexuality, believed that both men and women had sexual desires, and argued that individuals should not only be free to choose their own sexual partners but should also be able to change them whenever they were so inclined. They emphasized the importance of sexual activity as a source of pleasure for both men and women and considered the expression of sexuality integral to the maintenance of good health.

In 1850 they founded a free love commune, called Modern Times, about 40 miles east of New York City. Free lovers who joined their community held that marriage as it existed "was an irrational contract that limited the freedom of the male partner and made the female a virtual slave." Together they instituted a system of informal marriage and divorce. Along with another group of free lovers who settled in Berlin Heights near Cleveland, they carried out a secular experiment in the unrestricted expression of sexuality.

During the same period there were others engaged in attempts to define sexuality as a transcending experience. One such group was the Oneida Perfectionists. Their leader, John Humphrey Noyes, was from a relatively well-to-do family. During a religious revival in 1831, he underwent a conversion experience and dedicated his life to preaching the word of God. He studied theology at both Andover and Yale and eventually convinced himself that the pursuit of godliness could lead to human perfection. In order to pursue that goal, he established a religious commune in Putney, New York, in 1838. In his commune there was no gendered division of labor. Women worked on machines. Men knitted in public and made their own clothes. Social life among the Perfectionists, as they were called, was organized in such a way as to encourage loyalty to the group and love of all members for each other. Noyes convinced his followers that romantic love and monogamous marriage were dysfunctional in the sense that they encouraged exclusive relationships that were often accompanied by jealousy and quarreling. As an alternative, he instituted what he called "complex marriage," a system whereby each member of the community was encouraged to express his or her love for every other member of the community. It should not be assumed, however, that he was countenancing sexual promiscuity. Life in the commune was highly disciplined and sexual relations were strictly controlled. Once they moved from Putney to Oneida, New York, in 1848, the community numbered about 200 adults who with permission could change sexual partners as often as twice a week. By that time sexual activity had been redefined as an expression of godliness among the Perfectionists.

GENDER AND SAME SEX INTIMACY IN THE NINETEENTH CENTURY

If we find it difficult to agree on the meaning of sex and what constitutes sex, we face the same problem in defining what it means to be a homosexual. At what point, for example, does love for a friend become a homosexual relationship? Who determines what that point is? What role does same sex genital contact play in defining a relationship as homosexual? Such questions illustrate the degree to which the boundaries between homosexuality and heterosexuality can be somewhat unclear.

While loving, erotic relationships between men and between women have a very long history, social attitudes toward those relationships have changed over time. Typically, same sex erotic relationships develop in places where men or women live with each other outside the boundaries of the family. Such locations include the military, prisons, boarding schools, or gender segregated boarding houses. Before the end of the nineteenth century in America, there was no word for these relationships other than the word "friend," and there was a great deal of social tolerance for the wide variety of ways that "friends" expressed their love for each other.

The case of Daniel Webster and James Harvey Bingham serves as a case in point. Both attended Dartmouth College and then studied law together, taught school, and served as law clerks. Between the time that they left school and married, they experienced a relationship that was loving, warm, and tender and had a clearly erotic component. After they graduated, Webster wrote to Bingham, "I knew not how closely our feelings were interwoven; had no idea how hard it would be to live apart, when the hope of living together again no longer existed." He missed his best friend desperately and at one point jokingly announced in a letter that what he really wanted was to move in with him. "We will yoke together again;" Webster wrote, "your little bed is just wide enough." In their letters, Webster and Bingham addressed each other as "lovely boy" and "Dearly beloved." It is clear that these two men were emotionally intimate and found in each other a source of great personal happiness. Their letters clearly suggest that their feelings for each other

verged on the erotic, but they do not say anything about whether or not that eroticism took the form of intimate sexual activities.

Other men were more explicit, although again it is difficult to determine the exact character of their physical relationship or the degree of their physical intimacy. In 1863, Theodore Tilton wrote to the Rev. Henry Ward Beecher, "Your private letters are like so many kisses. . . . Send some more! My love multiplies for you everyday." On another occasion he wrote, "I toss you a bushel of flowers and a mouthful of kisses." In another letter he admitted, "I never knew how much I loved you till your absence. I am hungry to look into your eyes." The two men kissed when they met and parted and on one occasion Beecher sat on Tilton's lap discussing the sermon on the Mount.

While these men were quite graphic in their descriptions of their feelings for each other, it is not at all clear that they considered the physical expression of their affection for each other sexual. Nor is it clear that others interpreted those physical expressions in a way that would have defined them as socially inappropriate. It was not until the turn of the century that physical expressions of affection between two men or two women were defined as suspect.

Women also expressed their affection for each other both verbally and physically in the nineteenth century. And there was a similar tolerance for their feelings and behavior. Since most people considered women to be naturally affectionate and emotional, close, intimate relationships between women raised no eyebrows. And few considered women's physical closeness such as holding hands, kissing, or caressing each other in any way objectionable. In a society that held that women were more moral and had less passion than men and where female sexuality was so closely tied to reproduction, it was unlikely that anyone would have considered the possibility that a woman might find sexual pleasure in her relationship with another woman.

The result was that romantic friendships between women flourished in places like women's boarding schools and colleges. Some took the form of what was called "smashing." Smashing was essentially a courting ritual. When a girl felt attracted to another student or teacher, she sent her flowers, candy, little notes on fancy paper, locks of her hair, and other tokens of affection. The object of her attention could respond or not. But if she did respond, they were likely to become intimate friends, spending all of their free time in each other's company, sleeping together, or lying in the same bed talking all night. Such relationships were fraught with petty jealousies and emotional turmoil and often had a negative impact on the health and academic performance of the students involved.

In some cases, same sex relationships among school girls were short lived. But that was not always the case. The relationship between Mary Hallock Foote and Helena Dekay Gilder during the second half of the nineteenth century serves as an illustration. Foote and Gilder became close friends when they were students at the Cooper Union Institution of Design for Women in New York City. As they grew to know each other, their feelings for each other deepened, so that when they were apart, they missed each other desperately. Writing to each other provided a means by which they could sustain their emotional attachment. Molly began letters to Helena with "My Beloved" and in one missive encouraged Helena to "Imagine yourself kissed a dozen times my darling." At one point in their relationship, Molly wrote Helena: "I wanted so to put my arms round my girl of all the girls in the world and tell her . . . I love her as wives do love their husbands, as *friends* who have taken each other for life—and believe in her as I believe in my God. . . . If I didn't love you do you suppose I'd care about anything or have ridiculous notions and panics and behave like an old fool who ought to know better. I'm going to hang on to your skirts. . . . You can't get away from [my] love."

When Helena became engaged, Molly wrote a congratulatory letter to the man that Helena was about to marry, saying, "Do you know sir, that until you came along I believe that she loved me almost as girls love their lovers. *I know I loved her so.* Don't you wonder that I can stand the sight of you?" It remains to be seen what Helena's fiancé made of such sentiments.

Some women, of course, never transferred their romantic feelings to a man. Instead, they chose to live together in what were called "Boston marriages." Conducted quite openly and accepted by respectable society, these partnerships provided women the opportunity to set up housekeeping and share each other's lives on a relatively permanent basis while they pursued their own careers. Boston marriage couples bought property or rented rooms, slept in the same bed, entertained friends and family, and took trips together.

It was only at the turn of the century that same sex relationships among men and women became the focus of social concern. During that period definitions of what constituted womanliness and manliness were in a state of transition. Just as men began to doubt their ability to express their masculinity in traditional ways, it became apparent that women were beginning in ever increasing numbers to transgress gender boundaries by demanding access to what up to that time had been areas of exclusive male privilege. More and more women were enrolling in colleges and universities, seeking access to employment opportunities that would allow them a certain degree of economic independence, and demanding the right to vote.

Added to the distress and anxiety caused by the blurring of gender roles among the general population was the interest that doctors, researchers, and reformers began to take in the expression of human sexuality. Sigmund Freud was among the first to focus attention on the role that sexual desire played in human psychology. Sexologists like Havelock Ellis in England and Richard von Kraft-Ebing in Germany followed his lead by dedicating their professional lives to studying attitudes toward sexual activity and behavior patterns that reflected those attitudes. Under the guise of scientific inquiry, they studied same sex romantic/sexual relationships, defined them as deviant, and labeled men and women who showed a preference for members of their own sex "inverts" or "homosexuals."

SEXUALITY AND GENDER IN THE TWENTIETH CENTURY

By the 1920s, there was a growing acceptance of recreational or non-procreative sexual activity. Belief in female passionlessness had declined. And while self-restraint in matters relating to sexual activity did not totally disappear, there were fewer pressures on both men and women to inhibit themselves in terms of sexual expression or the discussion of it.

At the same time, however, in many circles early twentieth-century attitudes toward gender and sexuality bore considerable resemblance to nineteenth-century attitudes. For many people throughout the period, interest in and pursuit of heterosexual activity was still central to the definition of manliness, and femininity was still equated with sexual innocence. The persistence of these attitudes was, however, taking place in a context in which it was increasingly easy for young men and women to associate with each other and to find the opportunities to explore their sexual feelings and engage in sexual activity. Access to privacy whether it was in the back seat of a car or the balcony of a movie theater encouraged young couples to engage in sexual experimentation. Sometimes they confined themselves to what was known as "petting," activities of a sexual nature that did not include intercourse. Sometimes they did not.

The result was that by the 1970s, adherence to the double standard of sexuality had declined. By that time, no well informed person seriously believed that women lacked sexual desire or that their potential for expressing sexual passion was in any way inferior to that of men. The availability of penicillin which proved effective in treating venereal disease, the distribution of cheap, effective methods of birth control, and access to abortion during the first trimester of pregnancy made it possible for both men and women to engage in recreational sex without being overly worried about conceiving a child or contracting some sort of sexually transmitted disease. In the nineteenth century, married women who for whatever reason could not conceive a child had to resort to adoption. By the 1970s, reproductive technology such as artificial insemination was so advanced that women who equated femininity with maternity could give birth to a child of their own without engaging in sexual intercourse.

Attitudes toward same sex relationships and homosexuality also began to change as the nineteenth century came to a close. Between about 1890 and 1920, intimate relationships between men were increasingly viewed as a betrayal of the masculine ideal. During that period, however, it was effeminacy in appearance and gestures rather than the choice of a sexual partner that was most likely to be viewed with alarm. As long as he was discreet, a conventionally masculine looking man could engage in homosexual activity without attracting much attention or being subject to such epithets as "pansy" or "fairy." Unless they engaged in crossdressing, lesbians and their sexual activities were largely ignored.

Public concern about homosexual activity increased as the twentieth century progressed. The period following World War II was a particularly repressive time for homosexual men and lesbian women. Forced to keep their sexual preferences a secret for fear of reprisals and violence, they created their own subculture. In urban areas, homosexual social life often centered on bars where gay men and lesbian women felt free to act out their particular understanding of gender and its relationship to sexuality.

For example, in working-class lesbian communities such as the one in Buffalo, New York in the 1950s, it was common for one partner to adopt the dress and mannerisms of a man and to assume a privileged position within what was called a butch/femme relationship. A butch cut her hair, wore heavy starched shirts, pants, jackets, and sturdy shoes, and spoke in a low voice. The feminine partner, or femme, wore dresses, high heels, and makeup and assumed a relatively passive, domestic role in the relationship. She expected a butch to help support her, to do what was considered man's work around the house, and to take the lead in initiating sexual activity and provide her with sexual pleasure. But a butch did not expect her to reciprocate. Indeed, while enjoying sex was central to the femme identity it was antithetical to that of the butch, whose sexual gratification was centered on giving rather than receiving sexual pleasure.

The butch/femme gender arrangement was a product of a certain time and place. Most of those who participated in homosexual or lesbian relationships did not court public attention in the 1950s and 1960s. The same cannot be said of some gay men and lesbian women in the 1970s. In 1969, a riot in New York City between the homosexual patrons of a gay bar called the Stonewall Inn, located in Greenwich Village, and the police prompted the founding of what became known as the Gay Rights Movement. A part of a culture of protest, Gay Rights activists openly acknowledged their sexual preferences and demanded social justice for homosexual men and lesbian women, which included the right to serve in the military and freedom from harassment and arrest. Response to their campaign ranged from sympathy to open hostility. Their politicization of the issue of the connection between gender and the expression of sexuality was successful to the extent that by 1976 the list of mental disorders compiled by the American Psychiatric Association no longer included homosexuality and the federal government had lifted its ban on the employment of gays and lesbians. The Gay Rights Movement helped to remove some of the constraints that inhibited the expression of sexuality in the twentieth century and encouraged a great many Americans to explicitly address their own attitudes towards the relationship between gender and sexuality and the role they thought it should play in their own lives and the lives of others.

Not all Americans were comfortable with the liberalization of attitudes towards the expression of sexuality. The persistence of the belief that men should initiate sexual contact and that women should respond continued. Some gendered attitudes and behaviors were hard to change. The conservative Christian Right demanded a return to what they considered the less promiscuous expression of sexuality of a bygone era. Supporting a return to what they called "traditional values," they advocated the continued persecution of homosexuals, bemoaned the increase in teenage pregnancies while they resisted attempts to institute sex education classes in schools, and did what they could to try to limit the right of women to control their bodies by opposing abortion.

SUMMARY

The relationship between gender identity and the way individuals express their sexual nature has always been tied to such factors as race, class, and ethnicity and their relationship to time and place. During the colonial period, the need for labor encouraged the expression of sexual desire on the part of both men and women and made it an important component of definitions of masculinity and femininity. There appears to have been little ambivalence or anxiety about the expression of sexuality, and that which existed centered on concerns relating to upholding morality and the desire for social order. Free whites were free to engage in sexual activity as long as they were married and pursued sexual pleasure within marriage for the purpose of reproduction. Expression of sexual desire on the part of slaves and indentured servants was subject to the control of their masters, who encouraged slaves to reproduce and discouraged indentured servants from becoming sexually involved until they had served their time and were free to marry. But whatever rung in society the colonists occupied, they were inclined to define masculinity in terms of virility and femininity in terms of the ability to bear children.

It was during the late-eighteenth and early-nineteenth centuries that attitudes toward the expression of sexuality and its relationship to gender began to change. The rise of commerce that followed the American Revolution brought about an increase in urbanization in the North and the rise of a large middle class searching for a way to create a distinctive social identity for itself. Their definitions of ideal manhood and womanhood were tied to artificially imposed standards for judging who was genteel and respectable, definitions that established ideal patterns of sexual behavior. While they continued to define masculinity in terms of man's need to express the physical side of his nature, they also expressed concern about the willingness of men to control their sexual desires and activities. Equating manliness with material success, they worried that energy that men needed to make a living for themselves and their families might be squandered on the pursuit of sexual pleasure.

Middle-class ideals of femininity centered on the widely held belief that women, in general, were morally superior to men and were, therefore, capable of controlling their carnal natures. As a result, those in the middle class defined femininity in terms of the degree to which a woman was willing to protect her sexual innocence through self-restraint before marriage and to limit her interest in sexual activity afterwards to the procreation of children.

These ideals, were, of course, both class and race specific. As cities and towns grew and young working people were able to escape the supervision of their parents, they were able to engage in sex for pleasure. Young men could construct their definition of manliness around their ability to persuade young women to engage in sexual activities with them in return for small tokens of affection or a night's dinner or entertainment. When all else failed, they could hire a prostitute to reassure themselves that they were sexually potent. Young working women who lived in boarding houses and spent their leisure hours parading up and down the city streets in provocative clothes had the opportunity to be less inhibited in their expression of sexuality than their middle-class contemporaries.

Attitudes toward gender and sexuality in the nineteenth-century South were compli-cated by the existence of slavery. Before the Civil War, white men defined their manliness in terms of their sexual access to black women and their ability to control the sexual lives of white women. And southern white women defined femininity in terms of sexual innocence before marriage and motherhood after it. Slaves had their own way of integrating sexuality with their gender identities. Neither slave men nor slave women had much reason to be sexually inhibited.

After the Civil War, in response to the shame associated with military defeat and frustration arising from the fact that they were being forced to share political, economic, and social power with their former slaves, some southern white men reconstructed their sense of manliness around their continued ability to engage in sexual relations with black women and protect the virtue of white women from the sexual advances of black men. White women colluded in this effort and in that sense perpetuated the image of southern women as powerless, dependent, and passive. In the black community, the association between gender and sexuality remained very much the same except in the middle class where those struggling to establish reputations for respectability tended to adopt the same sexual mores as those in the white middle class.

During the nineteenth century there were some attempts on the part of utopian reformers to challenge the prevailing middle-class attitudes toward gender and sexuality. But it was not until the twentieth century that the age-old double standard of sexuality began to decline in some circles. To some degree men had always equated manliness with sexual activity whether it was expressed within marriage or not. But many women had been inhibited in this regard. Even the flapper, who symbolized the sexual liberation of women in the 1920s, was not necessarily promiscuous when it came to engaging in sexual intercourse before marriage. Throughout the 1930s, 1940s, and 1950s, the relationship between femininity and sexuality was defined in terms of motherhood rather than in terms of a woman's right to sexual pleasure. But by the late 1970s, all that was changing as some women, freed from fear of pregnancy by the availability of the birth control pill and inspired by feminist demands for equality with men, began to claim the right to sexual gratification for its own sake.

Attitudes toward same sex relationships were also in the process of change. In the nineteenth century, few people expressed concern about loving relationships between men or between women. At the turn of the century, anxiety about how manliness and womanliness should be defined combined with increasing interest on the part of doctors and social scientists in the subject of human sexual expression prompted so-called "sexologists" to conflate gendered behavior (acting manly or womanly), gender identity (seeing oneself as male or female), and sexual object choice (preferring a love relationship with another man or another woman) and to define relationships that had once been perfectly acceptable in polite society as abnormal and deviant. The result was that for a good part of the twentieth century, masculinity and femininity were defined within a social context in which discussion of sexuality was relatively open but the socially acceptable parameters of sexual behavior were much narrower than they had been in the century before.

DOCUMENT

William Acton on Female Passionlessness

During the seventeenth and eighteenth centuries, lustiness was considered a part of the definition of femininity. Naturally, the sexual appetites of American women varied according to the individual, but few would have questioned the idea that women in general had as much sexual desire as men. In fact, there was a long tradition in western culture that viewed women as sexual predators.

That attitude began to change in the nineteenth century as the middle classes attempted to distinguish themselves from what they considered to be the lower orders of society. Along with viewing women as morally superior to most men, there were some in the middle class who believed that genteel and respectable women were largely uninterested in sexual activity except for the purpose of procreation. One of the people who promoted that idea was William Acton, a British doctor with considerable influence in the United States. His pronouncements on female passionlessness promoted a debate over the relationship between femininity and sexuality.

In what ways might equating passionlessness with femininity have served the interests of men? Are there any ways in which it might have served the interests of women as well?

Source: William Acton, *The Functions and Disorders of the Reproductive Organs* (Philadelphia: Lindsay & Blakiston, 1875), 162–64. Notes omitted.

Want of Sexual Feeling in the Female a Cause of Impotence

We have already mentioned lack of sexual feeling in the female as not an uncommon cause of apparent or temporary impotence in the male. There is so much ignorance on the subject, and so many false ideas are current as to women's sexual condition, and are so productive of mischief, that I need offer no apology for giving here a plain statement that most medical men will corroborate.

I have taken pains to obtain and compare abundant evidence on this subject, and the result of my inquiries I may briefly epitomize as follows:—I should say that the majority of women (happily for society) are not very much troubled with sexual feeling of any kind. What men are habitually women are only exceptionally. It is too true, I admit, as the divorce courts show, that there are some few women who have sexual desires so strong that they surpass those of men, and shock public feeling by their consequences. I admit, of course, the existence of sexual excitement terminating even in nymphomania, a form of insanity that those accustomed to visit lunatic asylums must be fully conversant with; but, with these sad exceptions, there can be no doubt that sexual feeling in the female is in the majority of cases in abeyance, and that it requires positive and considerable excitement to be roused at all: and even if roused (which in many instances it never can be) it is very moderate compared with that of the male. Many persons, and particularly young men, form their ideas of women's sensuous feelings from what they notice early in life among loose or, at least, low and vulgar women. There is always a certain number of females who, though not ostensibly in the ranks of prostitutes, make a kind of trade of a pretty face. They are fond of admiration, they like to attract the attention of those immediately above them. Any susceptible boy is easily led to believe, whether he is altogether overcome by the syren or not, that she, and therefore all women, must have at least as strong passions as himself. Such women, however, give a very false idea of the condition of female sexual feeling in general. Association with the loose women of the London streets in casinos and other immoral haunts (who, if they have not sexual feeling, counterfeit it so well that the novice does not suspect but that it is genuine), seems to corroborate such an impression, and as I have stated above, it is from these erroneous notions that so many unmarried men think that the marital duties they will have to undertake are beyond their exhausted strength, and from this reason dread and avoid marriage.

Married men—medical men—or married women themselves would, if appealed to, tell a very different tale, and vindicate female nature from the vile aspersions cast on it by the abandoned conduct and ungoverned lusts of a few of its worst examples.

I am ready to maintain that there are many females who never feel any sexual excitement whatever. Others, again, immediately after each period, do become to a limited degree, capable of experiencing it; but this capacity is often temporary, and may entirely cease until the next menstrual period. Many of the best mothers, wives, and managers of households, know little of or are careless about sexual indulgences. Love of home, of children, and of domestic duties are the only passions they feel.

As a general rule, a modest woman seldom desires any sexual gratification for herself. She submits to her husband's embraces, but principally to gratify him; and, were it not for the desire of maternity, would far rather be relieved from his attentions. No nervous or feeble young man need, therefore, be deterred from marriage by any exaggerated notion of the arduous duties required from him. Let him be well assured, on my authority backed by the opinion of many, that the married woman has no wish to be placed on the footing of a mistress. . . .

Femininity and Lesbianism in the WAVES

During World War II, military policy on the subject of lesbianism was based on the principle of expediency. While military leaders did not condone homosexual behavior within the ranks, they could not afford to dismiss every soldier, male or female, who participated in homosexual activities. The policy of relative toleration changed after the war was over. By 1948, the Republicans were intent upon discrediting the Truman administration and the Cold War with Russia had begun. Newspapers and magazines ran stories warning the general public that there was a hidden "homosexual menace" which was undermining the moral strength of the nation. The message seemed to be that homosexuals posed a threat to national security. As a result of this hysteria, the military engaged in a campaign to rid itself of homosexual men and lesbian women.

During this period, women in the military were particularly vulnerable to accusations that they were lesbians. Isolated together in what could be an incredibly unwelcoming all-male environment, they often turned to each other for emotional support and companionship. Moreover, their very willingness to serve in the armed forces could be viewed as a denial of their feminine natures. It was within this context that the following lectures on the subject of homosexual behavior were given to female naval recruits beginning in 1952.

What do these lectures reveal about attitudes toward female sexuality? What do they say about the feminine ideal in post–World War II America? Is there any difference between this ideal and the one that existed for middle-class women in the nineteenth century?

Excerpts from the Line Officer's Lecture

Good morning/afternoon! I am ————. The officer on my right/left is Dr. ————. The officer on my left/right is Chaplain ————.

Source: "Samples of Standard Indoctrination Lectures," Report of the Board Appointed to Prepare and Submit Recommendations to the Secretary of the Navy for the Revision of Policies, Procedures, and Directives Dealing with Homosexuals, 21 December 1956–15 March 1957, Captain S. H. Crittenden, Jr., Chairman. U.S. Navy Board Report. Vol. A, app. 23 (Washington, DC, 1957).

We would like to speak to you today about a subject with which, very likely, many of you have never been confronted and on which most of you, perhaps, have never heard a formal discussion. The subject is homosexuality. . . . I shall speak to you as a woman officer because there are some things about homosexuality that concern us as women in the service. This presentation is to tell you the facts concerning homosexuality and most important of all, how to avoid becoming involved with homosexuals. . . .

My purpose today is to: (1) warn you that there are homosexuals[;] (2) inform you why the Navy doesn't tolerate homosexuals in the Naval service[;] (3) tell you what can happen if you are foolish enough to commit a homosexual act[;] (4) and most important of all, to show how any one of you may become involved in a homosexual act unless you understand the circumstances under which the homosexual may make an approach to you.

Let us first review the definition of homosexuality. It is sexual gratification of an individual through physical contact with another person of the same sex. A homosexual, then, is one who gratifies her sex desires by being sexually intimate with another woman.

You may ask, how can a young woman who has always led a wholesome life become involved? There are several techniques which may be used by the practicing homosexual to lure you into involvement in a homosexual act.

One of the most commonly used techniques is for the practicing homosexual to use friendship as a means to secure for herself a partner in her homosexual acts. . . . The practicing homosexual may begin her approach to you as a sympathetic, understanding and motherly person. At first she will present the same appearance as many of your friends. She will have many interests in common with you, but as time progresses you will be aware that she is developing this friendship as much as possible along emotional lines. This person may begin to demand all of your time, and to shower you with expensive gifts, and to pay all the expenses when you are out together. Even though you may never have indulged in alcohol, she may initiate you into the "art of social drinking." She may plan activities that will end in parties where heavy drinking is being done. She may plan more and more time for the two of you to be alone . . . late rides in her car, intimate conversations between the two of you, and physical advances such as embraces. As time goes by, she may propose that you take a week-end trip with her to a near-by city, to sightsee or take in a show. This trip will involve sharing a hotel or motel room. When you are alone . . . she orders drinks . . . , and

more and more alcohol is consumed. Then follow the improper physical advances and a homosexual act is committed. . . .

A woman homosexual may use a technique that is opposite to the one of kindliness, protective sympathy, and understanding. Her approach may be signalled by domineering, severely bossy, mentally cruel or bossy conduct toward the individual approached. This technique is to secure the domination of the sought individual, and to gain mastery and control over her. Just how this dominance is secured, whether through timidity or fear does not matter . . . ; it may lead to seduction.

The "Come-on-and-no-risk" approach is still another technique that may be used, and it fits into the battle against boredom. Navy women may be propositioned to indulge, just a little bit, in homosexuality, "because you can have a lot of fun with no after effects." Frankly, what is being said is that you can experience sexual stimulation and sexual satisfaction in a homosexual act without risk of pregnancy. . . .

It is important that you understand the Navy's policy toward homosexuality. The policy of the Navy is quite positive in that all persons found guilty of so much as one single homosexual act while in the Naval service must be eliminated from the service. The "first timer" or experimenter is just as liable to separation as the confirmed homosexual. A woman is not tried for being a homosexual, she is tried for committing a homosexual act. One thing is certain, she is going out of the Navy and fast. Under certain circumstances she will be given an undesirable discharge, commonly called a U.D. It means she has been discharged from the Navy as an undesirable, and her discharge papers will state that it is under conditions other than honorable and without satisfactory service. In certain circumstances she may face trial by General Court-Martial.

Answer these questions for yourselves . . . if you were discharged from the Navy for committing a homosexual act . . . , what kind of a job would you be able to get? The person hiring you would investigate and find out that you were not the type of person who would be a good risk as an employee. Government employment is impossible. You may lose virtually all rights as a veteran under both Federal and State legislation. You would probably be reduced to getting a job of such low level and so undesirable that your employer wouldn't bother to investigate.

What would you tell your family and friends? Or the man you hope someday to marry? Could you tell them that you were discharged from the Navy as an undesirable, or were Court-Martialed for abnormal sex practices? These facts have an unpleasant way of coming out, no matter how much you try to hide them. . . .

If a homosexual makes an approach to you . . . , stay away from her. If you have evidence of homosexual acts report them to the proper authorities. . . .

Remember, the fine friendships between normal, decent women is not the thing I'm referring to today. The many wholesome friendships formed in the Naval service are one of the finest influences in barracks and social life. These friendships are of great value to the Navy woman, both while in the service and in civilian life when she has returned to her home. The annual reunion celebration of Navy women throughout the United States every year gives some concept of the importance of such friendships. It is good for young women coming into the service to use their petty officers as guides and models of service life. Be wise in your choice of friends. Be alert and avoid emotional pitfalls.

Finally, all of us should be very proud to be women serving in the United States Navy, but let us be sure that we retain as much of our basic femininity as possible. We are not competing with the men . . . , we are supplementing and complementing them. We must take pride in the kind of things women do well . . . , that of setting a high standard of conduct by living in accord with the moral beliefs of our society.

May I now present Doctor ————, Medical Corps, U.S. Navy, who will speak to you on the medical aspects of homosexuality.

Excerpts from the Medical Officer's Lecture

The medical officer, particularly one that specializes in psychiatry, is interested in homosexuality as an abnormal form of human behavior. . . .

Generally speaking, homosexual activity is the manifestation of failure on the part of the individual to grow up sexually, which leads to personality disorders in adult life. This is true whether the individual be exclusively homosexual or only a "dabbler." . . . What you have done in your younger and developing life is *not* to be taken as placing you in a position of the person under discussion today, or to be in a position of danger. To draw a comparison, it is not that you wet the bed as a child but do you wet the bed today.

By virtue of the fact that you are now in the Navy, you are considered grown-up and adult behavior is expected of you. If such behavior is not forthcoming, you will be held accountable. . . .

Several common misconceptions exist about homosexuality and it is these misconceptions which lead people into trouble. One such misconception is that it is easy to identify a practicing female homosexual by her masculine mannerisms and characteristics. This is not true. Many practicing female homosexuals are quite feminine in appearance and some are outstandingly so. There are probably more female homosexuals who are completely feminine in appearance than there are female homosexuals who are masculine in appearance.

Another common misconception is that those who engage in homosexuality are safe from acquiring venereal disease. This also is not true, as both gonorrhea and syphilis can be readily contracted through sexual relations with females as well as through sexual relations with males. Reports from various clinics reveal one out of every four male and female patients admitted with syphilis acknowledged homosexual contacts as the source of their infection. Practicing homosexuals are notoriously promiscuous and not very particular in whom they pick up, infected or otherwise.

A third misconception is that homosexuals are born and not made. This idea leads to the beliefs, first, that an individual who is not born a homosexual can participate in homosexual acts without danger and, second, that nothing can be done medically for the confirmed homosexual. Neither of these beliefs is true. Treatment is available for even the confirmed homosexual but this is not an obligation of the Navy Medical Corps. As to the other belief, repeated dabbling in homosexuality in late adolescence as well as in adulthood can and frequently does constitute the making of a homosexual. Some who start as "dabblers" or "experimenters" progress steadily to become exclusively homosexual in their behavior. Experimentation, therefore, aside from being an infringement on social as well as Navy standards, is dangerous in its own right. . . .

May I now present Chaplain ———— who will speak to you on the social, moral and spiritual aspects of homosexuality.

Excerpts from the Chaplain's Lecture

The Chaplain's primary concern with the problem of homosexuality is its relationship to the individual's social, moral and spiritual life. . . .

Homosexuality Destroys a Woman's Social Status and Her Social Future.

I do not feel I have to emphasize to you how delicate a structure is a woman's good name, or how easy it is to tarnish or destroy it.

A single act, or an association, may brand a woman as a sexual pervert. Society allows women more emotional demonstrations in public than it allows men. Women friends may embrace and kiss each other as they meet in public without causing suspicion or starting a whispering campaign. Such displays of emotion and friendship, however, must always be within good taste.

By her conduct a Navy woman may ruin her chances for a happy marriage. Friends should be chosen with great care. Friendships are best when they are carefully formed on the basis of similar ages and interests. . . .

To get entangled with homosexuality means three things: (1) The woman gambles with the possible destruction of her social life and future marriage[;] (2) She will become the target of other homosexuals[;] (3) All normal, decent people who know, or even who strongly suspect the facts will have nothing to do with her. . . .

Playboy *Magazine on the Subject of Gender and Sexual Activity*

In November, 1953, Playboy *hit the news stands with a photograph of Marilyn Monroe on the cover. Edited by Hugh Hefner, it served as the basis for what became an entertainment empire by exploiting the sexual fantasies of American men. Filled with pictures of beautiful women and advertisements for scotch and cigarettes,* Playboy *promoted the pursuit of pleasure as well as the idea of sexual freedom and presented images of what its editorial staff considered to be manly sophistication. Its most noted feature was the "centerfold," a two-page-spread, color photograph of a nude, buxom, young woman which appeared in every monthly edition. The material in* Playboy *was sexually explicit in the sense that sexual issues were discussed quite openly. Besides the centerfold, features published every month during the late 1960s and early 1970s included "The Playboy Advisor" (an advice column), "The Playboy Philosophy" (an essay explaining what the Playboy philosophy was), and "The Playboy Forum" (an interchange of ideas between the readers and the editors).*

Reprinted below are readers' letters to the editors of Playboy. *What do these letters tell us about the relationship between gender and the expression of sexuality in the 1960s?*

To Playboy

What do you do with a girl whom you love and plan to marry but who has got it into her hard little head that the only way to catch a man is not to go to bed with him until the wedding night? She even agreed to our registering at a motel as man and wife "to save money" and I thought I had it made. Then she spent the night in the car! How can I convince her that no matter how much I love her, this is no way to catch me but a darn good way to lose me?

To Playboy

When I met my girl a year and a half ago, she said she was a virgin, and I had no reason to doubt her. As time went on, we became more intimate and our sexual relationship flourished. However, I soon found that she was always one step ahead of me sexually. She was the initiator and aggressor, even suggesting we have intercourse—which we did. I soon began to have doubts concerning her prior claim of virginity. My suspicions eventually came out into the open and we fought constantly before breaking up.

For six miserable months I was a shattered man. We finally made up, but then the pattern of suspicion and accusation began again. We are still going together—indeed we are contemplating marriage. But I still have my doubts and she still denies any intimacies prior to our meeting. Should I give her the engagement ring she's asked for, or should I give her the air?

To Playboy

I have been married for three years and have two daughters. During the first year of our marriage everything went fine, but shortly

Source: Letters to the Editor, *Playboy,* Feb. 1967, p. 29; May 1967, p. 50; Oct. 1966, p. 188; Jan. 1967, p. 46.

after our first daughter was born, a change came over my wife. She became frigid and stopped showing affection toward me, except on rare occasions. Since then, things have gone from bad to worse. I have suggested reconciliation, divorce, separation and everything else I could think of, but she seems uninterested. She wants to stay with me on account of the children, she says.

I have found that after several days of "doing without" I get to a point where a TV commercial is about all it takes to arouse my desires, so later, when we go to bed, I can't sleep, and if I do it's only for a few minutes, and after I wake up I am really worked up.

So what am I going to do?

My wife has mentioned the fact that animals don't do it all the time, only when the female is in heat. I have heard this before; and all I have to say is, if I were to mate with every woman within a quarter of a mile of my home the way a dog does, I would probably work myself to death within a month. Sex without love is nothing to brag about, but I can tell you from experience that it is a little bit better than no sex at all.

To Playboy

I am a graduate student at a large Southern college where for the last six months I have been combining studies with sex by bedding with a young coed whose typing and editing talents have proved invaluable in the preparation of various term papers and reports. Now, however, I find my academic life somewhat confused by the fact that I have become deeply enamored of another girl on campus but cannot dismiss the attentions of my former flame without also endangering my grades on several upcoming written assignments. In particular, I'm concerned about losing the lady's literary services when I'm so close to thesis time and a master's degree. Should I put off my new amatory interests until after the semester or continue to play musical beds and hope that the two women in my life never find out about my cheating ways?

Sex, Smashing, and Storyville in Turn-of-the-Century New Orleans: Reexamining the Continuum of Lesbian Sexuality

Katy Coyle and Nadiene Van Dyke

At the turn of the century, southern white men, like their fathers and grandfathers, reserved for themselves the right to seek sexual satisfaction with whomever they pleased, a right they denied to their wives and daughters. To some degree, they equated masculinity with the ability to control the sexuality of the women around them. In return for respect and chivalrous behavior, they expected the women in their families to be sexually innocent before marriage. They did not have the same expectations of black women or women in the lower classes. In their article, Coyle and Van Dyke explore the role that sexuality played in the construction of both white and black womanhood in New Orleans between 1890 and 1920.

Doyle and Van Dyke describe the sexual behavior of two very different groups of women. In what way did social class and race influence the way they expressed their sexuality? According to Coyle and Van Dyke, what is the relationship between the expression of sexuality and the construction of feminine identity?

In October 1893, the *New Orleans Mascot,* a weekly newspaper that covered activities in the tenderloin district, ran a cover picture depicting two prostitutes lounging together on a couch—one leaning back provocatively, the other on her knees leaning into her consort's breast. The caption proclaimed, "Good God! The Crimes of Sodom and Gomorrah Discounted." Although the sensational headline teased at the subject, it did not record any information about the lives of the several lesbians who lived and worked in

Source: Katy Coyle and Nadiene Van Dyke, "Sex, Smashing, and Storyville in Turn-of-the-Century New Orleans: Reexamining the Continuum of Lesbian Sexuality," in *Carryin' On in the Lesbian and Gay South,* ed. John Howard (New York: New York University Press, 1997), 54–68. Reprinted by permission. Notes omitted.

the brothels of New Orleans's infamous Storyville between the last years of the nineteenth century and the end of World War I.

During this same period, just a few blocks uptown from the red-light district, the first coordinate college in the country, H. Sophie Newcomb College of Tulane University, opened its doors to "white girls and young women." Isolated from the Tulane campus, the college in its earliest years provided an ideal setting for typical Victorian-era female "smashes." Newcomb women, like their Northern counterparts, developed intense homosocial relationships with their classmates, held women-only dances, and wooed their upperclass crushes. . . . They also snuggled in their beds, "big enough for two but made for one," until the early morning hours.

At first glance these two worlds, less than a mile apart, seem antithetical. On the one hand, as archetypal genteel, middle-class white, Victorian women, Newcomb students represented all the innocence and chastity historians attribute to Southern ladies and "romantic friends." The madams and "working girls," on the other hand, provided a mirror image—fallen women, notoriously lewd, predatory and dangerous to both women and men. These women lived on opposite sides of the public/private split, both physically and symbolically. A streetcar ride geographically separated the Downtown red-light district below Canal Street from the respectable Uptown Garden District. This physical separation made concrete the fictional dichotomy between the virgin and the whore, archetypes defined in the South in terms of race and class. For both turn-of-the-century New Orleans society and modern historians, the two worlds were locked in a dialectic dance.

This chapter suggests that race and class shaped perceptions of lesbian sexuality and sexual activity in turn-of-the-century New Orleans. Moreover, race and class affected the way women represented that sexual activity to the public. We assert that both Newcomb students and Storyville prostitutes practiced a fluid range of public and private lesbian sexual behaviors. For both groups of women, however, the privileges and restrictions concomitant with their social stations influenced how they expressed their sexuality and how others perceived their sexuality. Further, an examination of these two groups illuminates a multiplicity of lesbian histories.

In New Orleans, economic affluence alone did not assure class standing. Rather, a complex mosaic of family and racial backgrounds along with financial influence provided entrée to power and status. In fact, New Orleans's red-light market may problematize traditional markers of class construction and maintenance. Successful madams could acquire wealth but could never attain the respectability related to middle-class status. It could also be argued that these madams and prostitutes had intimate access to avenues of power closed to virtuous women, even while they were excluded from the formal institutions of

that power. To problematize their status further, some of these Storyville women made no secret of the fact that they engaged in private sexual relationships with other women.

Within the framework of romantic friendship, white middle-class Newcomb women could never be seen as lesbians, either by their contemporaries or by modern scholars. By virtue of their privilege, they could express their passions publicly through rituals and writings, as well as some degree of physical intimacy, without threatening their social standing. At the same time, to remain protected by the privileges of Southern, white, middle-class womanhood, they had to maintain the public perception of asexuality.

By definition, the historiographical construction of romantic friends has delimited the boundaries of "Victorian" women's relationships. Exceptional evidence of sexual activity is required to overturn persistent assumptions of celibacy intrinsic to romantic friendship. Precisely because questions addressing Newcomb women's sexuality appear to invade their private lives, and because they saw their own sexual activities as private and therefore protected, evidence of explicit lesbian sex is anecdotal.

In contrast, the working-class prostitutes of Storyville, primarily ethnic and racial minorities, could never be viewed as romantic friends. Excluded from the boundaries of Victorian womanhood, they could be seen only in sexual terms. In general, both lesbian historians and women's historians, looking to recover historical identities, have been reluctant to claim prostitutes. Nonetheless, prostitutes provided the historical counteridentity for romantic friendship, and their inclusion expands the historiographical scope of the lesbian continuum. In counterpoint to Newcomb students, Storyville prostitutes not only publicly practiced a wide range of sexual behaviors, they openly acknowledged these behaviors. Because their sexual activity was public, it is accessible to historians. However, prostitutes' personal, affectional relationships remain as hidden from history as romantic friends' sexual activities.

At the intersection of these two worlds stood the prosperous, influential, and highly respectable white men who founded, controlled, and patronized Storyville. Contemporary accounts indicate that the elaborate mansions of the tenderloin district drew the majority of their clients from elite white New Orleans society, many of whom had significant financial interests in the district. In fact, according to jazz great Bunk Johnson, the expensive sporting houses employed "light colored women, . . . strictly for white" clientele. Jelly Roll Morton concurred, stating, "No poor men could even get in these mansions."

In addition, the district's newspapers frequently noted the city fathers' financial and social liaisons with the red-light district. Numerous articles in Storyville papers, such as the *Sunday Sun* and the *Mascot,* as well as in mainstream dailies such as the *New Orleans Item,* connect wealthy, influential men to Storyville. For example, one *Mascot* cartoon, published in the early years of the district, depicts "prostitutes' progress" aided by "the high-toned owners returning from church." Likewise, a 1914 photograph documents an engagement dinner honoring Anna Deubler, niece of Storyville madam Josie Arlington; also in attendance were Gertrude Dix, madam of the brothel at 209–11 Basin Street, Mayor Martin Behrman, former mayor Paul Capdeville, Judge Otero, and State Senator Tom Anderson. Anderson, who owned significant property in the tenderloin, was often referred to as the Mayor of Storyville.

These same men had daughters, wives, and sisters who defined Southern womanhood for the post–Civil War era. Indeed, many of these women comprised the first generation of Newcomb students. The same men who assumed Victorian asexuality for the women of their own class participated in the entire range of sexual activities offered within the red-light district. Studying the intersection of these two worlds provides a lens with which to view the interaction of race, class, gender, and sexuality.

Historians of women have recently examined the interlocking aspects of class, race, and gender, but few have included sexuality in their analysis. In contrast, lesbian history for the Progressive era has focused on the definitional and perceptual shift from romantic friendship to sexual inversion. Because white middle-class romantic friends were the first subjects of study, issues of race and class remain largely unexamined in lesbian history.

Certainly, "smashing" is a much-studied form of female friendship, best documented in women's colleges in the Northeast. Helen Lefkowitz Horowitz found evidence of female crushes at the Seven Sisters colleges just before the turn of the century, although she took no stand about the sexual nature of those relationships. More recently, Lillian Faderman examined college "smashes," "crushes," and "spoons." She maintains they continued through the turn of the century, with "romantic all-women dances" commonly held at Smith and Vassar. While she clearly includes these women within the "lesbian continuum," she minimizes the importance or existence of sexual activity. Only Nancy Sahli has closely studied American women's collegiate romances in "Smashing: Women's Relationships before the Fall." As her title suggests, this model theorized a romantic "golden age" in lesbian history, during which same-sex relationships between women, sexual or not, enjoyed freedom from condemnation. The reluctance to label such relationships as "sexual," as well as use of the standard of "genital contact" to establish the sexual nature of a relationship, imply the desire to maintain the fallacy of women's lack of sexual drive. Such a construction perpetuates phallocentric interpretations of sexuality, assuming sex to be a single vector of analysis.

Like the students of the Northeastern women's colleges, young women at Newcomb College engaged in elaborate courting rituals. Letters, poems, and sentimental cards, intricately decorated, cut into hearts, or pressed with flowers, expressed a student's devotion to her "Lady of Dreams." These flowery, romantic sentiments appeared frequently both throughout the early years of the students' literary magazine, the *Newcomb Arcade,* and in the numerous student and Alumnae Association scrapbooks. Students cherished mementos of these relationships by placing them in scrapbooks, which they saved for years, eventually donating them to the college archives. In doing so, graduates demonstrated the importance of smashing as part of their college experience.

Poetry was one of the most frequent expressions of student crushes, often passionate and sexually suggestive. Poems in verse and rhyme, odes to the graces and beauties of lovers, adorned the pages of both personal correspondence and institutional publications. The 1912 poem "My Lady of Dreams" exemplifies the romantic language and unabashed sentiment of this phenomenon:

> Like the blue of the sea are My Lady's eyes,
> Like a benediction, her face;
> And the sunbeams that touch her hair with light
> But reveal all her gentle grace.
>
> And the song that is on My Lady's lips,
> That she sings in her voice of gold,
> Doth pass to my soul with its message of hope,
> With its meaning manifold.

Drawing on the imagery of the Romantic poets, Newcomb students sanctified their lovers' physical attributes with spiritual meaning and natural perfection. "Fairest of all," this lady's love possessed a "voice of gold," hair touched by "sunbeams," and a face "like a benediction." As yet unrequited, the author's love held promise for the future with a "message of hope, . . . its meaning manifold." Students gave voice to such romantic desires publicly, unselfconsciously confessing their affections in college publications. Such flowery language may well have contributed to the view that smashing was "girlish" and therefore not reflective of sexual desire.

In addition to original works, students claimed suggestive writings from other sources, both ancient and contemporary, as their own. In 1916, for example, Alice Perrin Norton won the student-awarded Arcade translation prize for her version of Catullus's poem "Kisses," in which one woman confesses her love to another:

> My Lesbie, let us live, Lesbia,
>   and love.
> A penny has value far,
>   far above
> The censure of old men
>   in senile decay. . . .
> So kiss me, my Lesbia,
>   a thousand, and then
> A hundred, a thousand, a
>   hundred more, when
> A thousand should follow, a
>   hundred more, dear
> Then so many thousands it will
>   be quite clear
> The reckoning's lost—e'en we
>   the count lose.
> No one upon us, our love
>   to confuse
> Can an evil eye cast, when
>   he shall know
> There were just so many
>   kisses in love's glow.

Although it is doubtful that this student understood the term *lesbia* in the modern sense, the translation obviously describes same-sex sexual activity. The poem describes two women so lost in passion that "e'en we the count lose." Further, no observer to their passion would mistake or condemn the true nature of their love; in fact, the lovers disdain the threatened "censure of old men in senile decay." That this student chose to translate a work that contained explicit lesbian references suggests both a personal interest in the topic and its acceptance in the Newcomb community, indicated by its commendation and publication.

It is clear that students shared the sentiments expressed in this classical poem, because their private writings reveal the explicit nature of their own crushes. The following student-authored scene depicts two women caught in the throes of newly requited passion:

> Scene—on the pier in the moonlight
> *Cate:* How pretty the moon is!
> *Adaline:* Yes it makes me think of you
> *Cate:* Oh why—Adaline
> *Adaline:* Yes, Cate—darling—I've wanted to tell you for so long. I—I—I—

Cate (falling off pier): You need not tell me—
    I know, I know just how you feel. I felt that
    way for a year.
Adaline: Oh, Kate [*sic*]
Curtain, as Adaline swoons in Cate's arms to
    the tune of a loud smack.

This scene, scribbled on the back of a 1919 newspaper and later preserved in a personal scrapbook, was not intended for public consumption. In it Katherine Wilson revealed her private fantasy. In the scene, she presumably saw herself as "Cate," experiencing the fulfillment of her romantic desires.

"The Lad-woman," authored by a "Barnard Bear" and reprinted in the *Newcomb Arcade,* suggests not only a consciousness of sexual roles but the students' awareness of their own ambiguities regarding these roles.

From her eyes peeps a mischievous lad,
    With a heart that is fearless and glad,
Her's the wild throbbing joy of an innocent boy,
    But her mouth is tender and—sad,
    Womanly tender—and sad.

Oh! tell me, dear heart, tell me true:
    Do your eyes or your lips reveal you?
And she laughed and she sighed, and she said,
        neither lied:
    I'm a lad and a woman, too,
    Lad and woman, too.

The author, clearly in love with the "lad-woman," sees the attributes of both the boy and the woman in the object of her affection. The lad-woman's "womanly tender" lips reveal her female nature, while her "mischievous" eyes disclose "the wild throbbing joy of an innocent boy." She readily embraces the duality of her own identity.

During this period, such young women often donned the trappings of the opposite sex, in settings where such behavior was socially sanctioned. For instance, Newcomb women frequently dressed and acted as men at dances and in student plays. Throughout the Progressive era, students held several women-only dances a year at which women in "drag" accompanied their dates in dresses. As late as 1918, the city newspaper printed a picture of an all-women dance held at Newcomb. Half of the young women, attired in formal dress, attended the dance with their "dates," dressed as soldiers.

In fact, pictures offer rare insight into these women's relationships. Two photographs from the early years of the twentieth century document the physical intimacy that some students shared. The first, from Lydia Frotscher's scrapbook, depicts her spacious dormitory room with canopied twin beds pushed together in the middle of the room. The size of the room and the fact that the camera captured the entire space, along with a classmate's recollection that the beds were "big enough for two but made for one," certainly suggests that students slept together. The second photograph . . . provides conclusive evidence that some young women unabashedly cuddled together in bed.

As demonstrated above, students expressed a range of social behavior that included courting, dating, kissing, cuddling, and sleeping together. As numerous historians have concluded, these public demonstrations of affection strongly suggest parallel private sexual activity. However, the realities of late nineteenth- and early twentieth-century mores, as well as the historiographical construction of romantic friendships, have obscured these women's sexuality from view, both then and now. By virtue of their class and racial status, Newcomb students could—in fact, had to—protect any sexual activity within the cloak of privacy.

Constructions of race and class afforded social protection to those Newcomb students who did have sex; privilege placed these women's private sexual lives beyond question. Innocent girls would not engage in sexual activity, and Newcomb student were, by definition, innocent. This tautological reasoning that protected Newcomb students' position of privilege provides the context for viewing the photograph in . . . asexual terms. At the same time, the *Mascot* illustration refers to prostitutes who lacked the protections of race and class privilege. Invoking the horrors of Sodom and Gomorrah, the caption appeals to fears of lesbianism; prostitutes' sexuality and deviance are unquestioned. However, juxtaposed with the 1893 *Mascot* cover, the assertion of sexual activity for some Newcomb middle- and upper-class white women becomes not only thinkable but logical. Placed side by side, but without the benefit of contextual clues, the photo of the two Newcomb women in bed certainly is more suggestive. Storyville prostitutes, by virtue of their working-class, ethnic, and racial minority backgrounds, legitimized genteel womanhood.

In New Orleans, the repeated references to "Octoroons," "Coloreds," "Creoles," "Jews," and "women of all nations" among the Blue Book advertisements highlight the nexus of working-class status and the inherent sexualization of women of color. Cast as the archetypal reflection of the innocence of Southern ladies, prostitutes lacked the protections of privilege, opening even their private sexuality to public scrutiny. Their visibility, however, freed them to acknowledge their sexuality, making their sexual histories more accessible to historians. The spectrum of lesbian activity among prostitutes can be documented through their own words, through decoding Storyville advertisements, and through recollections of Storyville customers. With these sources, we can begin to re-create a range of lesbian sexual activity among Storyville prostitutes: lesbian acts performed for male customers, private lesbian sex, and primary identification with female sexual partners.

Well publicized among the brothels in Storyville, "French houses" advertised a specialty in oral sex and voyeurism. Women pantomimed fellatio in the windows of these houses in order to draw business in from male passersby or from passengers on the Basin Street train. In addition, these establishments, most notably Emma Johnson's French House, provided "erotic circuses" for the viewing pleasure of large audiences.

Advertisements for these houses in the famous "Blue Books," guides to the tenderloin district, used the term *French* with reference to women to suggest sexual exoticism and lesbianism. For example, the advertisement for

Diana and Norma's, in a pre-1912 edition of the Blue Book, queried:

> Why visit the play houses to see the famous parisian model portrayed, when one can see the French damsels, Norma and Diana? Their names have become known on both continents, because everything goes as it will, and those that can not be satisfied there must surely be of a queer nature. Don't fail to see these French models in their many poses.

This advertisement identifies Norma and Diana as "French damsels," whose establishment provided men with the opportunity to purchase oral sex. Further, the admonition that "those that can not be satisfied there must surely be of a queer nature" suggests a connection to homosexual activities. By the second decade of the twentieth century, homosexual men used the term *queer* as a self-descriptor that indicated their homosexual interest. More than one possible interpretation of the above admonition is possible. Perhaps we can assume that, as the only advertisement in the Blue Books that uses the term *queer*, it was a coded message to those interested in watching or participating in lesbian sex. In contrast, it may be taken literally, as a claim that only gay men would not find satisfaction there.

Regardless, the term *French* described only those houses that provided this specialty or women who engaged in it. All of these houses were run by madams known as "notorious" lesbians. According to contemporary accounts, neither Diana nor Norma concealed their lesbianism. In addition, observers of Storyville culture agreed that both Lulu White and Emma Johnson readily acknowledged their preference for women as sexual partners. In her early days, Emma Johnson gained the title "French Emma." The 1906 *Sunday Sun* described her as the "originator of the French studio," claiming that Ms. Johnson had "established a line of business envied by most of the French women . . . The French Studio is crowded with girls of all nations and to those who are looking for a genuine circus

[this] is the place [*sic*]." As the first edition of the Blue Book announced, "Everything goes here."

Emma Johnson's "mammoth sex carnival" was well known for its depravity. The leading exhibitionist show in the tenderloin, the circus included ponies, dogs, and women who "specialized in public display of explicit sexual acts." Notably, the circus employed only one man throughout more than a dozen years of operation. One young female performer recounted her act in the circus:

> I was twelve and Edna had been sendin' me over there nights to be in the circus. . . . There was another kid my age. . . . By this time we were getting a little figure and looked pretty good . . . and neither one of us was afraid to do them things the johns liked. . . . We came on with everything we could think of, includin' the dyke act. . . . We did a dance we had worked out where we jerked ourselves and each other off.

This quote graphically illustrates that there was a significant market for lesbian exhibitions, which French houses recognized and satisfied.

Early jazz musicians such as Jelly Roll Morton performed background music in many of the Storyville bordellos and have provided firsthand accounts of such activities. Jelly Roll, pianist at Emma Johnson's French Studio, reported that "they did a lot of things there that probably couldn't be mentioned, and the irony part of it is that they always picked the youngest and most beautiful girls to do them right before the eyes of everybody." According to these accounts, the "dyke act" was a staple of the nightly circus shows.

In the process of working out the dyke act to perform it for the pleasure of men, prostitutes sometimes incorporated lesbianism into their private sexual lives. "We got to like it so much," the young prostitute quoted above disclosed, "we'd lots of times do it when we was by ourselves." With this admission, she described lesbian activity as part of her personal sexual repertoire. However, this revelation cannot necessarily be taken as evidence that she considered herself either lesbian or bisexual. Although this woman practiced lesbian sex while a prostitute, after the district closed, she married one of her customers and gave birth to four children. According to her recollections, her early lesbian experiences played no significant role in the formation of her identity, sexual or otherwise. In fact, she framed her memory of private lesbian activity within the story of the loss of her virginity, not in reference to her own sexual awakening. Her youth at the time of her Storyville experiences notwithstanding, she provides evidence not only of the range of sexual activity but that sexual activity alone does not necessarily influence the formation of identity.

The dyke act became so popular in Storyville that in addition to Emma Johnson's French Studio and Diana and Norma's French house, "Sapho" House began welcoming clients in 1912. The house's name obviously referred to the Greek poet Sappho, synonymous with lesbianism. Tellingly, unlike most Storyville bordellos, Sapho House did not announce its madam's name in the Blue Book. However, the advertisement used virtually identical wording to the advertisement for Diana and Norma's, suggesting that the two women either ran both houses or were involved in the founding of Sapho House. "Why visit the play houses to see the famous parisian model portrayed, when one can see the French damsel at the Cosmopolitan?" the ad inquired. "Don't fail to see these French models in their many poses."

Presumably, Sapho House catered to clients interested in voyeurism or in a ménage à trois. The presence of Sapho House, dedicated specifically to lesbian sex, unmistakably documents both a social awareness of lesbianism and the market for it among the Storyville clientele. The clients of Sapho House, like those of the other fancy houses, came from the upper echelons of white New Orleans society.

Although men moved easily between the sporting world and polite society in New Orleans without sacrificing their status or reputation, women did not enjoy the same freedom. A woman's class and racial status depended greatly on context. Countless generations of miscegenation and the social upheaval caused by the economic devastation of the Civil War necessitated complex signifiers of status. In fact, city fathers created Storyville as a distinct geographical entity simultaneously to protect respectable women from notoriety and to identify lewd and lascivious women. Josephine Louise Newcomb, the donor of Newcomb College, even expressed explicit concern that the initial site of the college in the Garden District exposed "white girls and young women . . . [to] common boarding houses, filled with baser class [*sic*] of humanity, thus subjecting the girls and young women, to scenes and sights of immoral influences." Once the city had cordoned off the district, administrative fears that a bordello might open next door to the college evaporated.

One example that illustrates that the distinction between respectable women and "notorious" women relied on context took place along the geographical dividing line between Uptown and Downtown. On Sunday afternoons, when they had the afternoon off, prostitutes shopped along fashionable Canal Street. In doing so, they ostentatiously breached the barrier between the sporting world of Storyville and respectable society. Presumably in response to this well-known practice, between 1911 and 1917 Newcomb's "Rules for Student Residence" specifically prohibited the students, even those escorted by chaperons, from "walking on Canal Street on Sunday." In 1918, the year after Storyville was dismantled, Newcomb lifted the restriction.

In a city with fluid racial classifications, where prosperous prostitutes—both heterosexual and lesbian—obtained the accoutrements of the middle class, only context and their enforced separation protected "respectable" women from depravity. In contrast, these same conventions and regulations excluded marginalized women from protection: neither store-bought attire nor "walking Canal Street" provided entrée into respectable society. . . .

In turn-of-the-century New Orleans, race and class significantly shaped the way women represented their sexual activity to the public and provided the context through which the public viewed their sexuality. The above evidence demonstrates that both Newcomb students and Storyville prostitutes practiced a fluid range of lesbian sexual behaviors, from romantic courting rituals to graphic lesbian exhibitions.

The lack of evidence of both sexual activity among romantic friends and of romantic friendship among prostitutes reflects not merely the historical absence of these relationships but the problems inherent in the definition of the terms. The tautological reasoning inherent in the historical and historiographical construction of romantic friendship precludes the broadening either of the range of women included within its boundaries or of the sexual behaviors associated with it. On the one hand, middle-class Victorian white womanhood required the public perception of asexuality. Hence, overturning this stereotype requires explicit evidence of genital contact, resulting in a skeptical reading of the extant sexual evidence. On the other hand, the public perception of prostitutes as fundamentally sexual beings proscribed them from the paradigm of romantic friendship. These same assumptions obscure prostitutes' interior lives, including the affectionate commitment intrinsic to romantic friendships.

In this chapter, we have argued for an expansion of the range of women and activities defined as lesbian. Not only do those women who fall within the rubric of romantic friendship contribute to our understanding of lesbian histories, but so do those women who are excluded from that rubric. Newcomb romantic friends and Storyville prostitutes are historically and historiographically entwined—each illuminates the other.

A<small>RTICLE</small>

"Lost Manhood" Found:
Male Sexual Impotence and Victorian Culture in the United States

Kevin J. Mumford

From the colonial period to the present, the ability to bear a child has stood as testimony to a woman's femininity. But parenthood has been important to men as well. Indeed, men have typically constructed their masculine identities around their sexual potency. Up to this point, most historians of sexuality have been more likely to study the issues of homosexuality or the expression of female sexuality than they have to focus on male heterosexuality. Kevin Mumford's essay attempts to redress the resulting imbalance. In his article, he explores the relationship between manliness and the ability to father a child. In it he suggests that attitudes toward that ability and its relationship to the definition of masculinity have changed over time.

According to Mumford, what was the relationship between manliness and sexual potency in the colonial/preindustrial period? How did attitudes toward that relationship change? What factors were most important in bringing about those changes? How did attitudes toward impotence affect gender relations?

In any given edition of a popular late nineteenth-century tabloid, the *National Police Gazette,* located between boxing results, bizarre crime stories, and revealing photos of showgirls, one could usually find two or three pages of sexual advertising. Alongside advertisements for "rubber safes" and "female illustrations," there were notices addressed to "Sufferers from Nervous Debility, Youthful Indiscretions, [and] Lost Manhood," promising to restore a "nerveless condition to one of renewed vigor." The condition that these products purported to cure was male sexual impotence. Whatever the efficacy of the products, the advertisements themselves offer some intriguing clues about late Victorian understandings of sexual disorders. A survey of comparable texts indicates that both earlier in the preindustrial era and later in the twentieth century the dominant conceptions of impotence substantively differed from the conception that prevailed in Victorian culture. This essay maps the changing conceptions of male impotence and analyzes these conceptual changes within the context of the histories of sexuality and masculinity in the United States. . . .

To explore both the contours of conceptual change and systems of social inequality, this essay analyzes two paradigmatic shifts in impotence discourse, one roughly in the 1830s and another in the 1920s. The first shift occurred in the social context of the separation of sexuality from reproduction, the rise of sexual reform movements, and the elaboration of a new model of sex difference. By the 1830s the dominant understanding of the disorder had evolved from a belief that impotence represented a divine curse of infertility that struck both men and women to the belief that impotence was a predominantly male disorder that impaired sexual performance. By the 1880s, largely in response to modernization, physicians and reformers drew a connection between impotence and "overcivilization" and argued that civilized men, although superior to other groups of men, were particularly susceptible to sexual impotence. It was this contradiction between civilized superiority and sexual vulnerability, I believe, that generated a crisis in late Victorian masculinity. By the 1890s at least some middle-class men proclaimed that, in effect, they had lost their manhood.

The second paradigmatic shift in impotence discourse occurred in the early twentieth century, as sexual scientists helped to replace the Victorian nervous system theory of impotence with what might be called a psychological one. Underlying this shift in scientific theory was a more fundamental transformation of the sex/gender system: sexual standards, gender conventions, and ideals of marriage were redefined in the early twentieth century. Consequently, by the 1920s male sexual impotence was understood as a problem of repressed desire rather than bodily depletion, for which experts prescribed a therapy not of continence but of sexual release. Taken together, these dramatic developments seemed to sophisticated moderns to signal the coming of a sexual revolution. But it might better be characterized as a counterrevolution, for the emergent sex/gender system supported a theory of male impotence that had the dual effect of undermining women's sexual authority and reinforcing inequalities of difference.

In early American society, colonists typically defined impotence as a fertility problem. They organized intimate relations within what John D'Emilio and Estelle Freedman term the "reproductive matrix," a family-centered system that encouraged sexual relations within marriage and treated nonprocreative acts as sins against God (which if committed by men were termed "onanism"). Given that the so-

cially acceptable goal of sexual relations was procreation, it is not surprising that reproductive authorities—clergy, physicians, and midwives—blurred any distinction between sterility and the inability to perform sexually. They tended to conceive of impotence in men as comparable with barrenness in women. One entry in the *Oxford English Dictionary* (under the heading "Impotence") suggests that in discussing impotence, some authorities did not emphasize gender difference, claiming that "impotence may exist in either sex." Speculation about the causes of impotence usually focused on divine providence, rather than on individual physiology. As one authority put it, impotence was "some mysterious interference of heaven."

Sexual norms in early America not only supported this definition of impotence but also linked impotence with diminished manhood. Colonists believed female orgasm was necessary for conception and held husbands responsible for both impregnating and giving erotic pleasure to their wives. A husband who failed at either task would likely be considered impotent, as one colonial court case suggests. Anna Maria Miller petitioned the court of Philadelphia to restrain her husband, George, from forcing them to leave the province. She alleged that her husband had failed to consummate their marriage and that therefore he wanted to leave for "Parts remote and unknown where he may be free from the reproach and scandal of Impotency." The couple had married two years earlier, when Anna believed George to be a "perfect Man." But George had proven to be "impotent in his virility" and "[un]qualified for the Procreation of Children." To verify Anna's claims, an investigative body was convened to discover if George was in fact impotent, which they did by inspecting both his "organs of Seed" and the quality of his erections. They declared that although George had one deformed testicle, he possessed "sufficient Erection and length of penis." Thus George was declared fit to perform his duties as husband, and his reputation as a man was saved.

Over the course of the next century, in response to both cultural and structural developments, the prevailing conception of impotence gradually shifted. A comparison of preindustrial and late Victorian impotence remedies suggests the extent and direction of change. In the preindustrial era, some infertile couples resorted to consuming aphrodisiacs, including red meats or certain seeds and berries, supposedly endowed with fecundity. Others may have purchased specially prepared substances that were advertised in eighteenth-century advice manuals such as *Onania* and *Aristotle's Masterpiece*. The advertisements that appeared there contrasted sharply with those in the *National Police Gazette:* while the former promoted cures for infertility such as "Elixir of Life" and "Prolific Powder," the late nineteenth-century notices emphasized male sexual performance in promoting substances that promised to "cure sexual weakness," "increase desire," and "develop parts." More than a change in marketing strategies for aphrodisiacs, this contrast suggests that between roughly the middle of the eighteenth century and the middle of the nineteenth century, the dominant conception of impotence shifted from predominantly a problem of infertility to a problem of diminished sexual capacity, while the associated construction of masculinity shifted from emphasizing male reproductive duty to emphasizing male sexual self-control.

The origins of this conceptual change (and of the first paradigmatic shift in impotence discourse) can be located in the historical separation of sexuality from reproduction. During the nineteenth century, through abstinence, contraception, and abortion, northern middle-class white couples cut their rate of fertility by half. Simultaneously, northern Protestants revised the sexual traditions of their Puritan forerunners and elaborated a new moral distinction—between sex for reproduction and sex as an expression of specific cultural ideals, such as romantic love or spiritual fulfillment. One effect of this emergent distinction between sexuality and reproduction was the increase in prescriptive literature and popular reform movements that discussed nonprocreative sexual behavior.

From the prominent physician Benjamin Rush to the health reformer Sylvester Graham, early nineteenth-century authorities focused particularly on the theme of male licentiousness, or what Rush characterized as "the wanton dalliance with women." At first glance, however, their work seems to suggest continuity with earlier religious prohibitions of onanism. In his *Medical Inquiries and Observations, Upon the Diseases of the Mind,* for example, Rush characterized all nonprocreative behavior as the "futile attempt of indolence that cheats the intentions of nature and God." But a closer look reveals that these and other writers had combined the traditional moral injunctions against nonreproductive sexual activity with a new concern about the somatic consequences. Rush argued that the "sexual appetite, which was implanted in our natures for the purpose of propagating our species, when excessive, becomes a disease of both the body and the mind." Termed debility, this disease depleted the nervous system, leaving the sufferer vulnerable to a variety of related disorders. In Rush's controversial formulation, debility was caused not only by too little stimulation (as his mentor William Cullen had argued) but also by too much.

As scientists further explored the connection between mental or physical stimulation and somatic disorders, they began to focus on sexually related cases of debility. French physician Claude-François Lallemand combined the theory of debility with the conception of body fluids as limited resources to diagnose the sexual disorder called spermatorrhea. Appearing in the United States in 1853, Lallemand's *A Practical Treatise on the Causes, Symptoms, and Treatment of Spermatorrhoea* reported that masturbation, foreplay, illicit thoughts, and extramarital sexual relations could trigger spermatorrhea, resulting in (among other things) continual and involuntary genital secretions. Medical textbooks and articles included discussion of spermatorrhea, and popular tracts advised young men on how to avoid the disorder. The growth in advice literature probably heightened concern about the loss of bodily fluids among men and helped to make spermatorrhea "a household word."

Thus between roughly 1810 and the 1850s, several prominent physicians and reformers had formulated a new scientific conception of impotence. The writings of Rush, Graham, and Lallemand contributed to the novel theory that licentiousness could diminish the individual's bodily energy. The resulting depletion, they reasoned, induced the state of debility, which in turn adversely affected male sexual performance. Rather than viewing impotence as a curse from heaven that impeded procreation, nineteenth-century authorities promoted the theory that it was predominantly a male disorder, caused by insufficient self-control, that resulted in the inability to perform sexually.

The development of this etiology of impotence corresponded to a growing movement of male youth to the city. The few published tracts reveal that physicians targeted the cohort of young men who in the early nineteenth century had been pushed from rural household economies and pulled toward the urban northeast. In his popular *Young Men's Guide* (1846), for example, William Alcott warned his readership about the disastrous potential of urban vice: "A whole race of young men in our cities, of the present generation, will be ruined." Young, enfranchised, geographically and socially mobile, these men were a powerful symbol of autonomy and potential sexual disorder. Impotence discourse shifted in ways that addressed these symbolic concerns, perhaps reflecting a deeper anxiety among reformers about authority in an era when independent self-made men challenged traditional social hierarchies. But although reformers warned disorderly men about the risks of impotence (and advised them on how to regain their virility), they generally treated disorderly women, whom they termed "fallen," as beyond reform. The fallen woman symbolized a challenge to the cult of domesticity, particularly to the idea that innately pure women were responsible for restraining men's lust. By the 1830s, it was widely believed that lost womanhood—unlike lost manhood—could not be redeemed.

Toward the goal of redemption, reformers and scientists advocated continence, holding up impotence as one extreme consequence of male sexual misconduct. Graham advised young men to restrain from "self-pollution," "illicit commerce between the sexes," and "unnatural commerce with each other." Continent men saved their masculinity through "preserving their bodily chastity" and avoiding "adultery of the mind." Incontinent men were likely to be found wanting in virtually all manly endeavors, especially in the pursuit of profit. According to one physician, "Everyday employment should be . . . a necessity. A man who is lazy . . . is nearly always a licentious man." Moral rectitude, productivity, and self-restraint were the characteristics or behaviors that saved manhood.

The new emphasis on manly chastity reflected not only shifts in scientific thought but also a broader emphasis on the individual, and particularly the body, in antebellum culture. Inspired by the reform activity of the Second Great Awakening, especially by perfectionism, authorities on male sexual health such as Graham argued that "the millennium, the near approach of which is by many so confidently predicted, can never reasonably be expected to arrive until those laws . . . which God has implanted in the physical nature of man are . . . universally known and obeyed." Thus in the burgeoning health reform movement, dietary faddists, water-cure specialists, animal magnetizers, and physical educators focused attention on the disciplining of the body as a route to moral perfection. So too did temperance reformers and antislavery activists (who contrasted southern licentiousness, as exemplified by the incidence of interracial sex, with a northern ideal of self-control). Finally, Charles Rosenberg and Anthony Rotundo each have suggested that the construction of masculinity increasingly emphasized the body: they argue that the eighteenth-century ideal of "publik Usefulness" gradually gave way to a more individualized "physical ideal of manliness."

This analysis of changing conceptions of the body suggests the extent to which gender relations had influenced impotence discourse. The new etiology of impotence was predicated on an emergent model of sex difference that counterpoised the irrational and uncontrollable female body with the rational male body. The new conception imposed certain burdens on men, to be sure, and one tenet of impotence theory held that man's loss of will resulted in a loss of bodily energy and ultimately in his loss of control over erection. But this conception nevertheless presumed that, by virtue of their sex, men possessed the will to exercise that control in the first place. In sharp contrast, women were viewed as driven by, rather than actively controlling, their bodies. As Carroll Smith-Rosenberg has argued, woman was "seen as a higher, more sensitive, more spiritual creature—and as a prisoner of tidal current of an animal and uncontrollable nature." Of the several most significant developments—a new concern with the erotic apart from reproduction, the growth of scientific literature about impotence after 1830, reformers' anxiety about young men in the city—it was the attribution of sexuality and rationality to the male body and of reproduction and irrationality to the female body that decisively shaped the first paradigmatic shift in impotence discourse.

Throughout the nineteenth century, physicians continued to rely on the opposition between male and female bodies to define the etiology of impotence. By the 1870s, however, physicians not only focused on differences between men and women, but discussed class and racial differences among men. At the same time, they also refined the prevailing definition of impotence by shifting the emphasis away from immorality or individual licentiousness and toward external social pressures—that is, overcivilization—as the cause of impotence.

These and other implicit developments in impotence discourse surfaced in the diagnosis of neurasthenia. New York City neurologist George M. Beard popularized the disorder, introducing its general etiology to his colleagues in 1869. Beard connected the increasing number of cases of neurasthenia with what today

we would term modernization; he argued that it resulted from overcivilization—from the "necessity of punctuality," "railway travel," and the "disorderly city." Although some physicians initially expressed skepticism, more agreed that neurasthenia was a serious problem, and Beard's 1881 treatise, *American Nervousness*, became the standard textbook.

Historians have focused more on general neurasthenia than on Beard's subsequent discussion of sexual neurasthenia. He began researching *Sexual Neurasthenia* soon after completing *American Nervousness*; but Beard died in 1882, before the volume was completed. His long-time colleague, A. D. Rockwell, published the book in 1884, which outlined the variety of types of neurasthenia—including cerebral, digestive, and spinal—though it maintained that the sexual type was most prevalent. Like general neurasthenia, sexual neurasthenia stemmed from the depletion of nervous energy, caused by overcivilization and the stifling quality of rationalized culture. To a greater extent than earlier theories of impotence, sexual neurasthenia relied on the conception of the body as a closed-energy system, or what G. J. Barker-Benfield has termed the "spermatic economy." Hence physicians tended to conceive of nervous energy as scarce and finite, in much the same way as a financier might conceive of economic resources in a market economy.

While physicians treated both men and women who suffered from neurasthenia, their formulation of sexual neurasthenia emphasized the difference between male and female bodies. Given that sexual neurasthenia was a disorder of diminished sexual energy, and that most physicians conceived of women more as reproductive than as sexual beings, it is not surprising that they tended to associate diminished sexual energy with the male variety of neurasthenia. Sexual authorities saw the female body as a closed-energy system, much the same as the male body, but they conceptualized the female system as a cycle of fertility, driven by the womb. Beard and other sexual authorities worried about the effects of overcivilization on women; but, again, they primarily focused on women's reproductive capacity, pointing to the deleterious consequences of the civilizing process for the womb and menstrual cycle. Indeed, one best-selling remedy for female disorders, Lydia Pinkham's all-vegetable elixir, promised to counteract overcivilization by fortifying the reproductive organs. In short, although physicians disagreed over whether women possessed sexual urges (engaging in debates rarely conducted about men), they emphasized the importance of the womb to women's psychic and physical health.

While Victorian physicians continued to center sex difference in their definitions of impotence, by the 1880s dramatic social change—the end of slavery and worker-capital conflict—prompted some physicians to discuss racial or class differences. This shift reflected a key trend in late nineteenth-century thought—the rise of evolutionary naturalism. Indeed, social Darwinism (specifically, the doctrines that there exist immutable laws of human development and that a natural hierarchy of groups determined social inequalities) had gained a strong following among nineteenth-century sexual authorities. Beard relied on several aspects of social Darwinism, which he learned about from his "close friend Herbert Spencer," to understand the relationship between society and the etiology of neurasthenia. One connection between Beardian science and Spencerism was the evolutionary concept of arrested development. In this theory individuals or groups developed in stages, becoming more civilized and fit as time passed. At certain stages, however, some groups ceased to evolve—and development was arrested. The consequences of arrested development included criminal behavior, lower intelligence, and diminished inhibitions. Individuals or groups evincing arrested development therefore lacked the capacity to control their impulses, particularly their sexual instincts.

Beard and other sexual scientists employed these evolutionary concepts to explain the incidence of impotence among different groups of men. In brief, they argued that white middle-class men were highly susceptible to sexual neurasthenia, that working-class men were largely immune from the disorder, and that black men represented what might be called hyperpotency. Thus in the late nineteenth century, there emerged at least two primary sexual boundaries—drawn along class and race lines—which, if they wished to avoid both impotence and primitive sexual excess, white middle-class men had to negotiate. By the 1890s these negotiations seemed to require more and more vigilance, leaving some men weak and debilitated, and late Victorians proclaimed they were in the midst of a crisis.

The importance of class in late nineteenth-century definitions of manhood can be seen in Beard's discussion of impotence among common laborers and rural men. In Beard's view, workers were "constitutionally different" from urban professionals, possessing a kind of natural immunity from the enervating influences of civilization. In drawing the distinction between the "highly organized brainworker" and the "muscle worker," Beard classified the latter as "persons who have very strong, old-fashioned constitutions and are rarely or never injured in the nervous system." Robust and constitutionally resistant to overcivilization, the muscle worker was immune from neurasthenia in general and from impotence in particular.

Physicians and reformers incorporated this ideal of artisan virility into their medical practices and reform movements. Beard, for example, treated one sexual neurasthenic, a man who expressed dissatisfaction with his routinized life as an urban professional, by advising him to take more exercise. Thus by selectively following the routines of workers and farmers, this mid-level manager in burgeoning industrial America might defend himself from the deleterious effects of civilization that had drained his nervous resources. For others Beard would more likely prescribe rest, because in certain cases strenuous activity could compound "nervelessness." Most reformers of manhood, however, addressed the problem of a "flaccid bourgeoisie" by promoting physical exercise or manly work. In effect they romanticized the artisan—as a symbol of a bygone era, not only of republican virtue and evangelical morality but also of authentic manhood. It remains difficult to determine how current among middle-class men the artisan ideal had become, or how its popularization influenced workers themselves, but one conclusion can be drawn: in contrast to the discussion of impotence in the 1830s, when authorities emphasized the value of self-control for upwardly mobile men, late nineteenth-century conceptions of impotence emphasized sexual distinctions drawn along class lines. Thus some middle-class men idealized (or parodied) the artisan, even as they became more and more enmeshed in corporate bureaucracies that eroded the autonomy and appropriated the skills of craftsmen.

A comparable contradiction can be seen in the increasing emphasis on racial difference in late nineteenth-century discussions of impotence. In the lexicon of evolutionary science, the black man was termed a reversionary type, who exhibited criminal tendencies, inferior intelligence, and immorality. According to G. Frank Lydston, the supposedly higher rate of perpetration of rape by black men than by white men could be attributed to the fact that "inhibitory influences such as ordinary self-control are more effective in the white than in the Negro race." Lydston explained that "when a race of a low type is subjected to an emotionally intellectual strain, inhibitory or restraining ideas and impulses are affected." The slightest provocation was enough to destroy the Negroes' self-control and bring "the primitive instincts to the surface"—a "reversion manifest in the direction of sexual proclivities."

This racial discourse played a dual role in Victorian culture—as a justification for white domination and as a negative reference for the dominant group—which can be seen in the medical literature about impotence. In Beard's view, for example, "there [was] almost no insanity among Negroes . . . nor [was] there functional nervous disease." Because Beard believed that black people were "not very

much in advance of their African ancestors," he argued that they possessed a "supernatural constitution." Like the muscle worker, the Negro was considered to be immune from general neurasthenia and from impotence in particular. Beard, upon returning from a trip to the Sea Islands, argued that Negroes' "indulgence of passions was severalfold greater, at least, than is the habit of whites." According to Beard, their sexual prowess was such that "if you would find a virgin among them, it is said you must go to the cradle." While physicians advised their patients to emulate the artisan, they emphasized a sharp opposition between black and white male sexuality, holding up the black man as a "bit of barbarism at our door-step" and contrasting his primitive lack of sexual will with "the restraint of the Anglo-Saxon."

In diagnosing the black man as hyperpotent, scientists and reformers stigmatized him as morally inferior by divesting him of sexual self-control. But the stigmatization served ulterior purposes. In mapping hyperpotency on black men and then furthering among white men a regime of continence as its antithesis, scientists and reformers helped to transform sexual self-restraint into a social practice through which middle-class men not only avoided sexual disorders but also distinguished themselves as white. Impotence was a white man's problem; unlike black men (and Victorian women), white men possessed the capacity to exercise enough rational self-control to avoid the disorder.

In the final analysis, the rise of Beardian science represented a complex transitional era in the history of impotence. Older ideas about impotence operated alongside novel theories, reflecting the variety of conceptions of male sexuality that circulated in late nineteenth-century society. One advertisement in an 1893 edition of the *National Police Gazette* pitched a remedy, "Brown's capsules," that targeted the antebellum disorder of spermatorrhea by "stopping drains within 48 hours," while another pitched a cure for neurasthenia that purported to "restore perfect vigor and Nerve force to small Shrunken and Weak Sexual

Organs." The etiology of neurasthenia itself reflected sexual scientific thought in transition. Thus Beardian science can be seen as the fullest development of the antebellum theory of debility—or, perhaps as persuasively, as the harbinger of the second major transformation of impotence discourse in the twentieth century. Beard had identified a contradiction implicit in Victorian impotence discourse that would come to be seen as the root of the modern sexual crisis: the rise of civilization was inevitable and widely believed to be a sign of progress, and yet the civilizing process engendered deleterious sexual consequences for the civilized man. By the 1890s some civilized men sounded the alarm of a crisis in masculinity.

Several historians have analyzed the content of these proclamations and have argued that the crisis reflected men's response to the first wave of New Womanism, which symbolized middle-class women's increasing encroachment into traditionally male spheres of power, such as higher education and the professions. But my analysis of shifts in impotence discourse suggests a sexual—more than a gender—crisis. By the late nineteenth century, the regime of male continence had become part and parcel of late Victorian respectability. But middle-class men's achievement of civilized self-restraint seemed to signify more their social superiority than their attainment of manhood. Moreover, the advertising pitches for impotence remedies suggest that a new standard of male sexuality—"giant strength and power," "enlarged organs," and "sexual power"—was gradually emerging and becoming more and more central to constructions of masculinity. Yet white middle-class men (at least the men who visited their doctors for sexual advice or sent away for impotence cures) were less and less confident about their ability to rise to the new standard. Just beneath the surface of Victorian civility lurked, I believe, the fear that respectable middle-class men were assiduously conserving their sexual energy but losing their manhood. . . .

As impotence research and therapy continued, however, medical opinion on the causes of impotence began to change. The shift re-

flected trends within and outside of science. A new conception of disease filtered through the still nascent medical profession, transforming scientific research methods in particular and health care in general. Concomitantly, some physicians rejected the concept of neurasthenia because it was predicated on what seemed an unscientific theory of nervous exhaustion. Additionally, as psychologists followed physicians in cultivating a culture of professionalism, they too studied the problem of sexual impotence, shifting the object of scientific enquiry from nervous systems to psyches. Finally, these developments in medical theory and practices coincided with two broad shifts—one in capitalism, from producerism to consumerism, and another in gender ideology, from separate and incommensurable spheres to overlapping compatibility. By the 1920s a fully developed psychological theory of impotence had overtaken the theory of neurasthenia. Sexual experts increasingly stressed repressed desire instead of the depletion of bodily resources; accordingly, they were more likely to prescribe therapies of sexual release, rather than restraint, while some psychologists went so far as to argue that restraint itself caused impotence. . . .

As they reevaluated the tenets of civilized morality, sexual authorities sparked debates about sexuality across several academic disciplines. Criminologists concerned with the sexual basis of crime reversed the Victorian formula that nonprocreative activity led to mental exhaustion and argued instead that "sexual excesses are usually the result, rather than the cause, of nervous disorder." The New Psychologists, Progressive-era behaviorists, adopted a similar view of male sexuality; they saw human behavior as guided by a cluster of inherited but nonetheless malleable impulses, one of the most powerful of which was the sexual impulse. In addition, many sexologists expressed the view that innate instincts or drives determined sexual behavior. As John Burnham has argued, by the 1920s "whatever the author's ethical social stance or the psychological theory, the sexual instinct was admitted to be general, inherited, and human as well as animal."

Sexual authorities now argued that, theoretically, male sexual desire was powerful and abundant but among civilized men the sexual instinct had been damaged by years of internalized repression. Hence experts who treated impotence replaced therapies designed to restore sexual energy with therapies designed to lift inhibitions. Physicians experimented with a variety of aphrodisiacs to draw out sexual desire, including "canine semen" and "cannabis indica [marijuana]." In one particular case, in which the physician had "reached the end of his therapeutic rope," none of the usual treatments had proven effective. The situation was serious because, according to the physician, the patient was "becoming a wild-eyed paranoiac." Finally, in a last-ditch effort to cure the impotent man, the physician inquired whether the patient knew of a "voluptuously developed girl, young and good looking and of sufficient elastic morality," who "would of necessity be highly magnetic." The physician proposed that the patient and the woman spend the night together, on a bed "positioned precisely two feet from the wall," though they were to be separated by a thick glass partition, ensuring that "the treatment was to be platonically moral." The impotent man was instructed to keep a diary detailing the effects of electrical exchange. But the notebook was "utterly forgotten," apparently because the patient "had no time for clerical work." According to the physician, "the patient turned up at my office the next morning with his former lacklusterless eyes beaming like two shiny jet beads, a flushed nose and an expansive smile." As it turned out, the patient "had within ten minutes after the initiation of the treatment thrown all stipulation and technical direction to the four winds and undertaken his own cure."

Whatever its rate of success, the new therapy reflected a decisive shift in impotence theory from emphasizing the male nervous system to emphasizing the object of male desire, a shift that can be seen in medical discussions of homosexuality and impotence. Before about 1910, authorities on impotence avoided the issue of sex perversion; when they did discuss the relationship between impotence and homosexuality, their analyses seem confused. Beard argued that cases of perversion were "very much more frequent than supposed," which he had learned from observing homosexuals in New York City. He attributed perversion to men who suffered from extreme nervelessness and who had lost their "attributes of virility": "Their genital organs atrophy . . . their body loses its force and energy and at last they come to a condition where they partake of feminine costume, and assimilate to women." But on the whole Beard strained to link bodily depletion with homosexuality, largely because he was working with an undeveloped psychological concept of perversion that was incongruous with his general theory of nervelessness. By the 1920s, however, some psychologists devoted large sections of their books to answering the question, "Why is the homosexual impotent with women?" Stekel identified two general cases of homosexual impotence. The first case concerned the "passive ones," the feminine homosexual, whom Stekel contrasted with "the 'active ones' who overcome the inhibitions and evinced their potency through all sorts of homosexual acts." The second, and more common, case concerned the latent homosexual, who was impotent because of sexual inhibitions: he could not admit his homosexual tendency, but he was terrified by "his lack of interest in the opposite sex." In either case, some physicians argued that internalized inhibitions and anxiety about the object of sexual desire caused male impotence.

One solution both to the particular case of homosexual impotence and to the general problem of male inhibitions was to refortify the sexual aim toward women by encouraging wives and girlfriends to become more sexually responsive. Increasingly, physicians not only treated impotent husbands but also counseled wives on how to be more sensitive to their spouse's sexual problems. B. S. Talmey reported the case of one patient, a thirty-five-year-old professional man, "burdened with many responsibilities" and "happily married," who complained that he was unable to achieve an erection. He did report, however, that he experienced "healthy erections" while asleep. Talmey advised the wife to "watch her husband and if she notices a strong erection in his sleep, she should suddenly wake him and cause him to effect conjugation." Talmey also advised that, in every way possible, the wife should humor her husband, "Mr. X," who claimed that "he found conjunction was only possible if his wife was attired in Tyrolean peasant costume and assumed the same posture as his pretty dairy maid years ago had taken when she first taught him the arts of Venus." In another case, Stekel advised a wife to fulfill her husband's sexual fantasies—which required that during intercourse "she had to treat him like a dog and call him Caro." In short, the burden of male impotence seemed to be shifting to women.

Of the growing number of experts who studied marital relations and male impotence, perhaps none was as influential as Dr. William Robinson, president of more than ten medical societies and chief of genitourinary surgery at Bronx Hospital. Robinson published fifteen books dealing with sexual matters; his *Sexual Impotence,* published in 1912, went through thirteen editions. In contrasting Victorian with modern approaches to sexual disorders, Robinson argued that the "older doctors" had overlooked the role of women in exacerbating, and in some instances causing, male sexual impotence. He employed the term "frigidity" to describe the sexually unresponsive wife. Found primarily among the middle class, the frigid woman had "absolutely no desire and no pleasure." According to Robinson, "a man is to them an indifferent object." An early formulation of frigidity classified it as a pathological disorder: "With the cases of sexual perversion may be classed those women in whom such intensely modest ideas have been acquired by education that the sexual act not only gives no pleasure, but actually gives rise to feelings of disgust." Other expressed the view that, rather than a discrete malady, frigidity was symptomatic of a more serious disorder, prevalent among women who were "probably in most cases homosexual."

Although they contested the precise meaning of frigidity, sexual experts agreed that sexually repressed women increased the incidence of sexual impotence in men. As one expert commented, "Sanctimonious frigidity will not call out his virility." Robinson, however, conceded that "the woman's virginal reserve attracts men"; but he advised wives that they "must not continue this reserve throughout [their] entire married life." Yet even as they criticized women for failing to elicit sexual responses from their husbands, male experts instructed wives to modify their sexual behavior in subtle and particular ways. Further research on frigidity may reveal that these women, whom physicians classified as ill, were in fact clinging to the earlier ideal of passionlessness as a way to resist both sexually demanding husbands and increasingly powerful sexual scientists.

Whether or not they were actually resisting remains to be seen, but clearly women were being held to a new standard of sexuality. Throughout the nineteenth century, many physicians had pronounced women to be devoid of sexual feeling, providing their social roles as paragons of virtue with a measure of scientific legitimacy. Within the Victorian sex/gender system, through voluntary motherhood and maintenance of the purity ideal, women could claim the authority to restrain male lust, both within and outside the home. By the 1920s this was dramatically changing. The New Woman—liberated, citizen, worker—openly flirted with men in public and displayed an erotic sensibility. As Christina Simmons has argued, modern "women were supposed to desire and enjoy sexual relations but they were considered less lustful than men."

As experts manipulated the ideology of passionlessness, they helped to revise the Victorian conception of the successful marriage. Psychologists and physicians not only encouraged wives to become more erotically stimulating, but in some cases they advised husbands of unresponsive wives to take drastic steps to overcome their impotence and even advocated adultery. One physician, for example, said that there was "but one cure in cases of this class [in which the wife was frigid] and that is for the husband to set aside all mores and social and marital restrictions and have his sexual needs ministered to." Another suggested to his patient that he "locate a young woman, possessed of strong desires for sexual gratification." Although exceptional, such cases illustrate the extent to which experts, and presumably some married couples, increasingly judged marital success by a new model of companionate marriage that emphasized sexual fulfillment.

Scientific revision of sexual standards, gender conventions, and marriage occurred within the context of a popular debate over a new modern morality. As working-class and middle-class women entered the public sphere in increasing numbers, as immigrants and African-Americans formed subcultures that included distinctive sexual values, and as an emergent youth culture experimented with premarital sex in the context of dating, sophisticated moderns declared a sexual revolution. They encouraged display of the erotic and of sexual expression and emphasized the appeal of sexual "others." Modern impotence discourse corresponded with the revolution, encouraging male sexual release and highlighting sexual satisfaction as an important part of middle-class marriage. But the new view of impotence also shifted the balance of power in gender relations. By sexualizing women and stigmatizing those who resisted as frigid, and by then making performance of this normative sex role critical not only to a good marriage but also to male sexual health, modern impotence discourse could serve to legitimate men's sexual claims on women. . . .

Suggestions for Further Reading

Ben Barker-Benfield, "The Spermatic Economy: A Nineteenth Century View of Sexuality," *Feminist Studies*, I (Summer 1972), 45–74.

Allan Berube, *Coming Out Under Fire: The History of Gay Men and Women in World War Two* (New York: Free Press, 1990).

Allen Berube and John D'Emilio, "The Military and Lesbians During the McCarthy Years," *Signs*, 9 (Summer 1984), 759–75.

Kathleen Brown, " 'Changed . . . into the fashion of man': The Politics of Sexual Difference in a Seventeenth-Century Anglo-American Settlement," *Journal of the History of Sexuality*, 6 (Oct. 1995), 171–93.

George Chauncey, "Christian Brotherhood or Sexual Perversion? Homosexual Identities and the Construction of Sexual Boundaries in the World War I Era," *Journal of Social History*, 19 (Winter 1985), 189–211.

George Chauncey, *Gay New York: Gender, Urban Culture, and the Making of the Gay Male World, 1890–1940* (New York: Basic Books, 1994).

Nancy F. Cott, "Passionlessness: An Interpretation of Victorian Sexual Ideology, 1790–1850," *Signs*, 4 (Winter 1978), 219–36.

Carl N. Degler, "What Ought to Be and What Was: Women's Sexuality in the Nineteenth Century," *American Historical Review*, 79 (Dec. 1974), 1467–90.

John D'Emilio, *Sexual Politics, Sexual Communities: The Making of a Homosexual Minority in the United States, 1940-1970* (Chicago: University of Chicago Press, 1983).

John D'Emilio and Estelle B. Freedman, *Intimate Matters: A History of Sexuality in America* (New York: Harper & Row, 1988).

Lillian Faderman, *Odd Girls and Twilight Lovers: A History of Lesbian Life in Twentieth Century America* (New York: Columbia University Press, 1991).

Lawrence Foster, *Religion and Sexuality: The Shakers, the Mormons, and the Oneida Community* (Urbana: University of Illinois Press, 1984).

THOMAS A. FOSTER, "Deficient Husbands: Manhood, Sexual Incapacity, and Male Marital Sexuality in Seventeenth-Century New England," *William and Mary Quarterly*, 3rd ser., LVI (Oct. 1999), 723–44.

RICHARD GODBEER, " 'The Cry of Sodom': Discourse, Intercourse, and Desire in Colonial New England," *William and Mary Quarterly*, 3rd Ser., LII (April 1995), 259–86.

MICHAEL GORDON, "From an Unfortunate Necessity to a Cult of Mutual Orgasm: Sex in American Marital Education Literature, 1830–1940," *Studies in the Sociology of Sex*, ed. James M. Henslin (New York: Appleton-Crofts, 1971), 53–77.

CAROL GRONEMAN, "Nymphomania: The Historical Construction of Female Sexuality," *Signs*, 19 (Winter 1994), 337–67.

KAREN V. HANSEN, " 'No *Kisses* Like Youres': An Erotic Friendship between Two African-American Women during the Mid-Nineteenth Century," *Gender and History*, 7 (Aug. 1995), 153–82.

ELIZABETH LAPOVSKY KENNEDY AND MADELINE D. DAVIS, *Boots of Leather, Slippers of Gold: The History of a Lesbian Community* (New York: Routledge, 1993).

MARGARET MARSH AND WANDA RONNER, *The Empty Cradle: Infertility in America from Colonial Times to the Present* (Baltimore, MD: The Johns Hopkins University Press, 1996).

JOANNE MEYEROWITZ, "Sexual Geography and Gender Economy: The Furnished Room Districts of Chicago, 1890–1930," *Gender and History*, 2 (Autumn 1990), 274–96.

EDMUND S. MORGAN, "The Puritans and Sex," *New England Quarterly*, 15 (Dec. 1942), 591–607.

ROBERT F. OAKS, " 'Things Fearful to Name': Sodomy and Buggery in Seventeenth-Century New England," *Journal of Social History*, 12 (Winter 1978), 268–81.

KATHY PEISS, " 'Charity Girls' and City Pleasures: Historical Notes on Working-Class Sexuality, 1880–1920," in Ann Snitow, Christine Stansell, and Sharon Thompson, eds., *Powers of Desire: The Politics of Sexuality* (New York: Monthly Review Press, 1983), 74–87.

DONNA PENN, "The Meanings of Lesbianism in Post-War America," *Gender and History*, 3 (Summer 1991), 190–203.

CHARLES E. ROSENBERG, "Sexuality, Class, and Role in 19th-Century America," *American Quarterly*, XXV (May 1973), 131–53.

ELLEN K. ROTHMAN, "Sex and Self-Control: Middle-Class Courtship in America, 1770–1870," *Journal of Social History*, 15 (Spring 1982), 409–25.

E. ANTHONY ROTUNDO, "Romantic Friendship: Male Intimacy and Middle-Class Youth in the Northern United States, 1800–1900," *Journal of Social History*, 23 (Fall 1989), 1–25.

NANCY SAHLI, "Smashing: Women's Relationships Before the Fall," *Chrysalis*, 8 (Summer 1979), 17–27.

CHRISTINA SIMMONS, "Modern Sexuality and the Myth of Victorian Repression," in *Passion and Power: Sexuality in History*, ed. Kathy Peiss and Christina Simmons (Philadelphia: Temple University Press, 1989), 157–77.

CARROLL SMITH-ROSENBERG, "The Female World of Love and Ritual: Relations between Women in Nineteenth-Century America," *Signs*, 1 (Autumn 1975), 1–29.

CAROL Z. STEARNS AND PETER N. STEARNS, "Victorian Sexuality: Can Historians Do Better?" *Journal of Social History*, 18 (Summer 1985), 625–34.

KATHLEEN VERDUIN, " 'Our Cursed Natures': Sexuality and the Puritan Conscience," *New England Quarterly*, 56 (June 1983), 220–37.

CHAPTER THIRTEEN

GENDER AND SPORT (1600–1975)

BABE AND THE QUESTION OF GENDER

There was no doubt in anyone's mind that she was a great athlete, perhaps the greatest female athlete of all time. She was, after all, an Olympian. She could run, she could jump, she could throw. She could play basketball and baseball. In fact, she could play almost any game. And when asked if there was any game she did not play, her answer was "dolls." In that answer lay the problem. Her problem was that there were some who were not sure that Mildred Ella (Babe) Didrickson was really a woman. Those who publicly speculated about this matter tended to be sports reporters, and they were not known for their subtlety.

Babe Didrickson rose to fame in the 1930s, an age when sports were male-dominated and conventional feminine ideals did not include such attributes as fierce competitiveness and physical prowess. The fact that she came from the wrong side of the tracks didn't help matters. Born in 1911, the daughter of Norwegian

immigrants, she grew up in Beaumont, a bustling shipping port in Texas. As a child, she preferred lifting barbells to helping her mother with the housework. Her youth was spent in a poor, white, southern environment that allowed girls a great deal of physical freedom. Since she was not expected to become a southern belle, her activities were not subject to a great deal of supervision, and no one was overly concerned about her appearance. She was quick witted, opinionated, and outspoken. Her humor was bawdy, and her language crude. She wore her hair short, she was oblivious to the demands of fashion, and she reveled in the use and exhibition of her body. When she exercised, her body exuded sweat. It was not ladylike "dew." It was not even perspiration. It was just plain, ordinary, slimy, smelly sweat. Fearless, streetwise, tough, and energetic, she played golf, tennis, and basketball in high school. She was so good at baseball that she was recruited to work for an insurance company in Dallas so that she could play on their team, the Golden Cyclones. In 1932 at the Los Angeles Olympics, she won two gold medals, one in javelin and another in the 80 meter hurdles. A week later, at the age of 19, she turned professional. Rejecting the idea that femininity was tied to dependence, she became self-supporting and economically independent. It wasn't her goal as a young woman to get married and have children. It was to try to be the best athlete in the world.

Didrickson's success as an athlete, her ability to compete and win, was to some degree dependent upon her gender ambiguity. In an age in which the ideal woman was supposed to be vain about her appearance, modest in her demeanor, physically weak, and uninterested in anything other than her home and family, Didrickson created a public gender identity for herself that one biographer claims "personified a stereotypical Norwegian 'masculine imperative.' " As a successful athlete, she was, as much as any man, courageous, self-centered, strong, self-disciplined, competitive, and resourceful. At the same time, however, she felt compelled to reassure her fans that she was indeed a woman and not just an androgynous freak. So she bragged about the time she had won a prize for her sewing at the state fair, and she assured one reporter that she liked to dance even more than she liked to compete. Increasingly sensitive to the need to promote herself in a way that testified to her femininity, she gradually adopted traditional standards of middle-class beauty. She painted her fingernails, got her hair styled, and applied make-up to her face. And she gave up track and field for the more feminine and genteel game of golf.

It was while she was playing in a golf tournament in Los Angeles in 1938 that she met George Zaharias, a 300-pound, professional wrestler known as the "Crying Greek from Cripple Creek." Her relationship with George bolstered her campaign to promote her image as a "normal" woman. The media circus that enveloped their courtship ended when they married later that year. But she remained in the sports spotlight. She was news because she was a prominent sports figure; she was news because she was exotic; she was news because

she nurtured her relationship with reporters. She knew that the public had a short attention span and that she could not afford to fade into obscurity because of a lack of the kind of publicity that sports reporters could provide. So she gave them something to write about, and they considered her metamorphosis from Amazon to doting wife to be newsworthy. She fed their need for stories by alluding to the pleasure she got from having sex with her husband, allowing them to photograph her in the kitchen wearing a shirtwaist dress and an apron, and openly fretting about her hair and make-up. Her performance was convincing. In 1947 *Life Magazine* ran the following headline: "Babe is a Lady Now: The World's Most Amazing Athlete Has Learned to Wear Nylons and Cook for Her Huge Husband."

Babe Didrikson Zaharias faced a serious dilemma as an extraordinarily talented female athlete because she transgressed gender boundaries. In a society in which sport served as a major vehicle for defining and reinforcing gender differences, Babe crossed the line between what was considered female and what was considered male. The kind of attributes that were necessary for her to compete and win were culturally defined as male attributes. And many of the attributes that were often used to measure a woman's claim to femininity were of no use to her at all on the playing field.

In the early stages of her career, there was almost nothing about her that testified to her femininity. The press made a great deal of appearance—her thin lips, her "door-stop" jaw, and her muscular physique. When she was so unladylike as to exhibit her anger in public, they referred to her "Viking capacity for beserk rage." She commercialized her body and its abilities by going professional. And she immodestly created a persona that was not only public but also newsworthy.

Conscious that her propensity to transgress gender norms had its limits in terms her ability to earn a living, she did what she could to balance her fame as a superb athlete with reassuring gestures that would testify to her womanliness. In that sense, she quite self-consciously created a gender identity for herself that allowed her to pursue activities that gave her great satisfaction and at the same time helped to exempt her from the negative publicity that was likely to accompany those pursuits. Her ability to balance these two goals provided a model for other women whose natural athletic abilities and competitive spirit propelled them into the national spotlight. Her successes on the playing field challenged conventional wisdom about woman's "natural" physical inferiority to man. She helped to pave the way toward the expansion of the concept of femininity to include the idealization of female athleticism. And while she did not pose for Nike ads and her face did not appear on boxes of Wheaties, she led the way for other women to claim a share of the profits to be derived from the commercialization of sport. The long campaign to assure that the terms "professional athlete" and "womanly" were not mutually exclusive had begun in earnest.

THE EMERGENCE OF THE SPORTSMAN

The preconditions that usually serve as the basis for the rise of sports did not really exist in the early colonial period. Practical considerations combined with what some have called the Protestant "work ethic" left little time for people to relax. Merely to survive in the colonies was a time-consuming enterprise, requiring a tremendous amount of physical effort not to mention a good deal of luck. The men and women who were most successful in the colonies were those for whom bodily exercise was a normal part of every day life. Work was considered a calling from God. So from early childhood onward, men and women were expected to work, and much of that work required a great deal of strength, stamina, and physical exertion. The development of muscles was a prerequisite for success on the part of both men and women. While men did much of their heavy work outside, women performed similarly strenuous tasks in the house when they were not tending

to their duties in the barnyard or garden or helping in the fields. Although Sunday was generally set aside as a day of rest, the amount of rest to be enjoyed was extremely limited for everyone. Besides the fact that food still needed to be prepared and animals cared for, Sunday was supposed to be reserved for the expression of piety and dedicated to spiritual reflection, not a day intended for the pursuit of pleasure or recreation.

Idleness was considered a sin in seventeenth-century colonial society. That did not mean, however, that leisure and amusement were necessarily frowned upon. Colonial leaders were willing to acknowledge that all work and no play did more than make "Jack a dull boy." They were convinced that unrelieved work led to an unbalanced life and that a certain amount of leisure was necessary to refresh the body and mind in order to serve God and carry out His work on earth. Their only concern was that the pursuit of leisure be enjoyed in moderation and that leisure activities not degenerate into social disorder. Their idea of sport was any activity that was as useful as it was enjoyable. In short, recreation should not be a waste of time or result in the waste of valuable resources. Hunting, fowling, and fishing conformed to that criteria because they put food on the table and helped rid the countryside of pests and predators. Contests of skill, strength, and stamina such as foot races were perfectly acceptable as long as they did not involve betting or result in such injury as might prevent a man from supporting his family.

As a result of such circumstances and attitudes, there was not a very clear distinction between work and leisure in the early period of colonial settlement. Activities that might qualify as sports were activities that allowed participants to practice practical skills that served them in real life. When they occurred, shooting contests, horse races, and boat races were usually spontaneous events. There may or may not have been spectators present. And there were no generally understood and accepted set of rules.

By the mid-eighteenth century, however, the influence of Calvinism was slowly declining and the accumulation of wealth allowed some men more leisure time than others. Successful farmers and businessmen, who were able to hire laborers or purchase slaves, found themselves less and less engaged in physical labor and more and more concerned with the management of their estates and businesses. For the economically privileged, physical labor was no longer considered a particularly ennobling form of exercise. Nor did wealthy men continue to believe that it was essential for the development of a man's good character. With more time on their hands and less opportunity to assert their manliness by demonstrating their bodily strength on a regular basis, they turned their attention to sporting activities. The "sportsman" became an integral part of the gentlemanly ideal. Organizing and playing games such as cricket, challenging a friend to a fencing match, or breeding and racing horses gave wealthy men an alternative way to exhibit their physical prowess and courage as well as an opportunity to flaunt their exemption from the need to spend most of their time engaged in physical labor. For the leisured gentleman, participation in sport became something of a self-conscious performance and as well as a pleasant diversion.

While their social betters were training their racehorses and organizing cricket matches, tradesmen and apprentices, slaves and farm laborers and the women with whom they associated participated in a wide variety of leisure activities. Among respectable workers, sports tended to involve activities that both men and women could participate in such as fishing, sledding, boating, horseback riding, and throwing balled stockings. The less reputable spent their leisure time challenging each other to boxing matches or watching blood sports such as cock fights and bear baiting. One particularly bloody and gruesome sport was gander pulling. Organizers greased the neck of a goose and tied it upside down from the limb of a tree or a rope strung between two trees. Contestants rode their horses at a gallop toward the hapless goose and tried to pull its neck off. The winner got to take

the decapitated bird home for supper. Such events, sometimes organized by enterprising tavern keepers, were often rowdy affairs, characterized by gambling, drunkenness, and brawling.

Women tended to be less involved in sport than men. Their domestic responsibilities left them little time to amuse themselves. Indeed, the development of sport was to some degree dependent upon the leisure that men derived from the labor that women performed. Upper-class women with time on their hands could cultivate skills in such activities as horseback riding, which was considered both useful (as a form of transportation) and femininely graceful. But while galloping across an open field and skillfully jumping a very high fence or wide stream might not pose a threat to a woman's claim to femininity, competing in a public horse race did. As a result, even the most accomplished female equestrian was expected to confine herself to the role of spectator at horse races. There she was welcomed in part because male organizers considered women to be moral arbiters whose presence at races and athletic contests as spectators might discourage social disorder. If she were truly daring and unconventional, she and her female friends might sponsor a "purse" or prize to offer to the gentleman who won. But the relationship between womanliness and engaging in sporting activities was a tenuous one.

By the mid-eighteenth century, then, work and sport had evolved into separate activities. Such activities were as class specific as they were gendered. The result was that sport evolved into a platform where leisured men could publicly exhibit their manliness by competing with each other.

TAKE ME OUT TO THE BALLGAME

The nineteenth century was a period of transition in attitudes toward sport and its relationship to gender. As late as the 1820s, there was little interest in organized sporting activities.

In the new republic where self-restraint and virtue were idealized, economic abundance and the leisure that often accompanied it were considered to be potentially corrupting influences. It was the age of "self-making," a time when ambitious, God-fearing, hardworking men had little time to engage in unproductive activity. During the early nineteenth century, the influential, family-centered, middle class remained ambivalent about the merits of recreation and sport and, like their colonial predecessors, considered it a waste of energy and resources. Their gendered identities were constructed around work and family, not leisure.

But attitudes toward sport were changing. Horse and harness racing were organized in places like NYC in the 1820s, and by mid-century there were a host of cricket, rowing, racquet, yachting, and shooting clubs in cities like New York and Philadelphia. Those who were most likely to participate in such sporting activities were members of male bachelor subcultures, a brotherhood of pleasure seekers, some of whom lived in the South but most of whom lived in the rapidly developing urban centers of the Northeast. There artisans, day laborers, Irish immigrants, and young libertines with too much money and time on their hands joined together for fun and friendship, spending their time thinking up ways to display their sense of honor and physical prowess. Their favorite pastimes tended to be blood and gambling sports, many of which were as illegal as they were brutish.

By the 1870s, the middle class had come to embrace the connection between masculinity and sport. What were once spontaneous, rural pastimes became organized, commercialized, urban spectacles. A wide variety of factors contributed to the rise of sports enthusiasm. Between the 1820s and the late nineteenth century, work patterns changed. In an agrarian economy, the workday began at dawn and did not usually end until dusk. But work for industrial and office workers was measured by the clock. And while the workday was still long, a great many people were able to reserve for themselves a few hours to pursue leisure activities. Eventually, work was divided by class. While many men performed jobs that required strength and stamina, an increasing number of men spent their day sitting behind their desks. Their working lives were relatively sedentary, a situation that alarmed doctors and social critics. During this period, the ability of employers to supervise the private lives of their employees also declined. Before the advent of industrialization, master craftsmen usually supervised the work of their apprentices and journeymen. They lived together, worked together, drank together, and played together. But factories were not organized so that managers could supervise the free time of their workers. Working-class men and women created a subculture of their own, a culture in which they indulged in their freedom to do as they pleased after they had put in a full day of work. The middle class responded to this situation by looking for ways to save the working class from dissipation. Sport seemed to offer them a way to provide their social inferiors with a wholesome alternative to drinking, gambling, and fornication.

The growth of cities also contributed to the rise of sport. Urbanization was, in part, a product of increased immigration. Determined to preserve what they considered to be "the American way of life," native-born Americans searched for effective and speedy ways to assimilate the foreigners in their midst. The concentration of population that characterized city life brought with it serious public health problems. In an effort to ameliorate those problems, city councils set aside money not only for sewers but also for open spaces like Central Park in New York City, where urban dwellers could escape from their cramped and unhealthy neighborhoods and enjoy the benefits to be derived from fresh air and exercise.

Industrialization, accompanied by a rise in the standard of living, encouraged a demand for increased goods and services including new forms of entertainment. Improved transportation made it possible for urban dwellers to travel longer distances in pursuit of pleasure. And advances in communication technology such as the invention of the telegraph and the rise of the penny press meant that information regarding sporting events was now widely and cheaply available.

It was the support of the middle class that made commercial sport a reality. In response to the social problems that accompanied urbanization and industrialization, middle-class men spearheaded the drive to develop leisure time activities that were congruent with their value system. Not able to prove their manhood by working at physically demanding jobs, they created a world where they could participate in physically demanding sport. But they were not interested in just any sport. What they wanted was "clean" sport by which they meant sport that provided men with outdoor physical exercise that would help to socialize the immigrants, control the behavior of the lower classes, promote good physical health, help workers relieve emotional stress and mental fatigue, establish and preserve high moral standards, and build character.

What they came up with is what historians have called "Muscular Christianity." Widely promoted by organizations like the YMCA, the idea was that men should seek physical, mental, and spiritual harmony through work, moral uprightness, and perfection of their bodies. This ideology held that participation in sports was a way to promote a whole range of manly characteristics such as self-confidence and determination, competitiveness and courage. Athletic contents were intended to teach boys and men to be tough physically and mentally, to obey authority, and to be loyal to their team. By encouraging restrained physical violence, some sports also prompted the development of such manly characteristics as self-control and stoicism in the face of physical pain. All in all, interest in and participation in sports was viewed as a way to fend off charges that American men were being feminized.

It was within this context that baseball become popular. Originally a child's game, baseball became the quintessential man's game

after the first baseball club, the Knickerbockers, was organized in 1845 in New York. A sport originally intended for middle-class gentlemen, it became the sport of choice for urban craftsmen and shopkeepers as well since it required very little equipment and could be played on any space available. After the Civil War, businessmen organized company baseball teams and gave the men who worked for them time off to compete with other teams because they were convinced that participating in baseball would help to instill in their employees such qualities as sobriety, virtue, and an appreciation of the value of hard work. By the 1880s there were thousands of amateur baseball leagues. So many people either played baseball or watched baseball games that by 1900 sportswriters viewed the sport as nothing less than a national pastime.

THE MORAL EQUIVALENT OF WAR

At the turn of the twentieth century, ideas about what constituted manliness were in a state of flux. As more and more men became wage laborers instead of small businessmen, opportunities to express one's manliness through independence shrank. That combined with what some historians have called the increasing feminization of American culture led many to believe that American society was becoming overly civilized and that one of the hazards of that civilization process was a decline in manliness.

One response to this so-called "masculinity crisis" was an increasing emphasis on the body and its development. Men were encouraged to participate in vigorous physical activity to ward off their predisposition to feminization. Theodore Roosevelt led the charge to redeem American manhood through physical exercise and participation in competitive sport. Partly through his influence, amateur boxing became respectable. Boxing, he claimed, was a "vigorous manly pastime, one of those pastimes which have a distinct moral and physical value, because they encourage such essential virtues as courage, hardihood, endurance, and self-control."

Football became popular during this period for much the same reason. Introduced in the 1870s and 1880s as a derivation of soccer and rugby, football appealed to young men interested in violent, strenuous yet presumably "gentlemanly" sport. In the sense that it taught martial skills such as courage and obedience to command, without having to endure the terror of war, it was in the words of author William James the "moral equivalent of war." At first football was played by college boys who attended elite institutions like Yale and Harvard, but it soon spread to midwestern colleges. Compared to football today, its nineteenth-century version was extremely brutal and dangerous. Players were expected to attack each other straight on en masse, there was very little opportunity to pass the ball to divert the opposition, and the use of deceptive strategy was unknown. Players wore no padding or other protective gear. The number of players injured playing this form of football was enormous, and deaths were not unknown. For some, it was its very violence that made football the most manly of sports. The game, in the words of one editor, "is a mimic battle-field, on which the players must reconnoiter, skirmish, advance, attack, and retreat in good order." A football player, he argued, had to "meet emergencies with coolness and judgment under trying circumstances; be trustworthy, observant, vigilant," as well as courageous and strong. Football became a socially sanctioned male outlet for violence and aggression, a ritualized substitute for war. On Saturday afternoons in fair weather and foul, two groups of men, designating each other as "the enemy," set out to prove their manhood by risking life and limb on a playing field to do battle while hundreds of others vicariously shared their experience by cheering them on from the sidelines. Win or lose, both participants and spectators emerged from such experiences convinced that they had done what they could to confirm their manhood.

By the turn of the century, sport had become an increasingly important vehicle through which American men could construct their gendered identities. Those interested in doing so (and not everyone was) used sport to confirm and refine their definitions of what constituted manliness. In playing fields across the nation, they met individually or as part of a team to publicly test their skill and stamina, their courage and competitiveness.

SPORT, ETHNICITY, AND MANLINESS

Immigrants to the United States brought with them a wide variety of attitudes toward sport. Participating in track and field events appears to have been popular among the Scots. In the early nineteenth century, interest in physical fitness in Germany led to the development of a public health movement organized around gymnastics. When they were able, German immigrants to the United States built gymnasia in their neighborhoods. These facilities often served as community centers, providing German-Americans with a way to preserve their culture as well as the opportunity to promote physical fitness and sound morals.

But the kind of sporting heritage that the Scots and Germans brought with them was almost completely lacking among eastern European, Jewish immigrants who began arriving in the United States after the Civil War. While this group of immigrants appreciated the degree to which care of the body was necessary for the preservation of good health, their leisure time tended to revolve around the kind of intellectual and spiritual activities that were an integral part of Jewish life. Often desperately poor, they had to work hard to make ends meet and had little time for leisure. The result was that most of them did not equate interest in sports with manhood.

The same cannot be said, however, of their children. Intent on assimilating as quickly as possible into American life, second-generation Jews showed considerably more interest in sports than had their fathers' generation. As children, they played games like stickball in the streets of the city or participated in organized sporting activities like baseball or basketball sponsored by social settlements and organizations such as the Young Men's Hebrew Association. Settlement house workers such as the German-Jewish director of the Henry Street Settlement in New York City, Lillian Wald, were convinced that the gym was "a manhood factory" whose purpose was to build both muscles and character. Through participation in sport, she hoped that Jewish boys would develop a healthy sense of competition as well as courage, self-discipline, and self-respect.

Jewish girls were not barred from settlement house gyms, but the kinds of sports that they were encouraged to engage in were those that were intended to preserve their femininity as well as their health. Gymnastics and dancing were acceptable activities partly because they provided opportunities to engage in vigorous exercise in a non-competitive environment and partly because they did not divert a girl's attention away from her family responsibilities and, therefore, helped to preserve Jewish definitions of womanliness.

Interest in and participation in sport became one of the ways that young Jewish men could testify to their Americanness and try to counter negative and often anti-Semitic stereotypes that characterized them as inherently weak physically. Two examples illustrate strategies that Jewish sports figures used to try to construct a masculine ideal that incorporated both American and Jewish values. Nat Holman was a Jewish basketball superstar in the 1920s. He played for the New York Celtics and coached basketball for City College of New York, whose student population was predominantly Jewish. At the same time, however, he earned a reputation as a man of intellect because of his love of the theater and his high regard for such playwrights as Ibsen and Moliere.

Like Holman, Hank Greenberg was a man of impressive physical stature. Six feet four inches tall and weighing 210 pounds, Greenberg was one of the most highly regarded baseball players in the major leagues during the 1930s and 1940s. Having led the Detroit Tigers into the World Series four times, he became the first Jew to earn a place in the Baseball Hall of Fame. His talent, competitiveness, and success as a ball player combined with his enlistment in the air force in 1941 stood as a mute challenge to those who saw Jewish men as weak and effeminate.

But success as an athlete did not diminish his commitment to his religion or his pride in his ethnicity. He created a flurry in the press in 1934 when he threatened to miss a game against the Boston Red Sox in order to celebrate the Jewish New Year. In the end, he played the game, but ten years later, he spent Yom Kippur in the synagogue worshipping with the rest of the congregation rather than play a game against the Yankees. To those in the Jewish community who were interested in sport, Greenberg was a hero because, like Holman, he had created a version of manliness congruent with both American and Jewish values. One reporter, Bud Shaver, wrote in the Detroit *Jewish Chronicle*, "His fine intelligence, independence of thought, courage and his driving ambition have won him the respect and admiration of his teammates, baseball writers, and the fans at large." It was particularly gratifying to Shaver that Greenberg seemed to feel and acknowledge "his responsibility as a representative of the Jews in the field of a great national sport." The Jewish people, he declared, "could have no finer representative."

Some Gentiles concurred in this assessment as the following poem published by the Detroit *Free Press* illustrates:

"The Irish didn't like it when they heard of
    Greenberg's fame
For they thought a good first baseman should
    possess an Irish name;
And the Murphys and Mulrooneys said they
    never dreamed they'd see
A Jewish boy from Bronxville out where Casey
    used to be. . . .
In July the Irish wondered where he'd ever
    learned to play.
"He makes me think of Casey!" old man
    Murphy dared to say;

And with fifty-seven doubles and a score of
   homers made
The respect they had for Greenberg was being
   openly displayed.
But upon the Jewish New Year when Hank
   Greenberg came to bat
And made two home runs off pitcher
   Rhodes—They cheered like mad for that
Come Yom Kippur—holy fast day world wide
   over to the Jew, And Hank Greenberg
To his teaching and the old tradition true,
Spent the day among his people and he didn't
   come to play.
Said Murphy to Mulrooney, "We shall lose the
   game today!
We shall miss him in the infield and shall miss
   him at the bat.
But he's true to his religion—and I honor him
   for that."

Jewish athletes like Nat Holman and Hank
Greenberg used sport not only as a way of
pursuing their own version of the American
dream but also as a way to redefine what it
meant to be a Jewish man. In the process, they
devised a way to serve the interests of the Jewish community and preserve important components of Jewish culture without sacrificing
their claim to American manhood.

Sport, Race, and Manliness

There is perhaps no sporting event that testifies with as much eloquence to the role of
racism in the construction of manliness in
America as the Jack Johnson/Jim Jeffries fight
that took place in Reno, Nevada, on July 4,
1910. Jack Johnson was the first African American world heavyweight boxing champion.
Jim Jeffries was his white challenger. The
stakes were high. But it was not just money
they were fighting over. It was the definition of what it meant to be a man. In 1910 a
black man was champion and reigned as the
strongest man in the world. For those who
considered whiteness to be a prerequisite for
manhood, that situation was simply intolerable. So Jim Jeffries, the man who was considered most likely to defeat Jackson in the ring,
was called upon to vindicate "Anglo-Saxon
manhood."

Jeffries was a reluctant challenger. He had
won the heavyweight title in 1899. But between his championship victory and his re-
tirement in 1905, he had simply refused to
fight a "Negro." In 1910, however, Jeffries was
convinced that white manhood had to be redeemed and that he was the man to do it. "I
am going into this fight for the sole purpose
of proving that a white man is better than a
negro," he is reputed to have said. The press
labeled him the "Hope of the White Race."
Jackson was called the "Negroes' Deliverer."
This fight was more than a prize-fight. It was
a fight to determine which race could produce
the most virile specimen of manhood. And
Jack Johnson retained his title. The symbol of
white manhood was humiliated. Black men
could hold their heads high.

Today it is difficult to appreciate the degree
to which black athletes had to struggle to earn
the right to construct their manhood around
their participation in sports. Athletes like Magic
Johnson and Michael Jordan are powerful cultural symbols. Physically imposing, immensely
talented, and economically successful, they
are perceived as models of manliness in white
and black communities alike. But they are very
much products of their time and place. Had
they been born one hundred years earlier, they
would have had virtually no chance to earn
reputations as national athletic heroes.

Before slavery was abolished in the United
States, slave owners were willing to exhibit
their slaves as athletes. But riding a winning
thoroughbred or fighting with one's fists was
not so much about establishing standards for
judging black manhood as it was about being
put on display at the whim of one's master.
However willing or unwilling male slaves were
to participate in athletic events organized by
whites, they were in no position to do so freely.
Their participation in sporting events testified
as much to their masters' sense of competitiveness and sportsmanship as it did to their own.

Freedom that followed the Civil War did
not improve matters much. Only in horse racing and prize fighting did blacks have much

opportunity to compete against whites. Segregation established in the 1890s meant that they had to form their own leagues if they wanted to participate in sport. It was not until the 1940s, that Jackie Robinson desegregated major league baseball when he was hired to play for the Brooklyn Dodgers.

From a sports promoter's point of view, Robinson was an ideal candidate for the job. He played ball well enough to win acceptance among whites. And promoters hoped that the fact that he was black might encourage African American baseball fans to spend their money to see him play in the white leagues. He was educated at UCLA where he played a wide variety of sports including football, basketball, golf, and track. And he was an active Methodist who abstained from both liquor and cigarettes. The only problem was that he had a temper and was likely to use it when faced with the racial slurs that were sure to come his way as the only black player in major league baseball.

The price he had to pay for playing for the Dodgers was to promise that he would control himself when he was verbally attacked and subjected to discrimination. Temporarily willing to accommodate the dictates of Jim Crow, he took separate transportation to the games and he ate his meals on the bus. He remained silent when he was publicly insulted and called a "damned nigger." Through it all, he suffered from headaches and depression. After three years of being "kept in his place," he broke his self-imposed code of silence and asserted his right to say what he thought.

Like all black athletes, Robinson carried into professional sports a double burden. The first was to make a living for himself by successfully fulfilling his contractual obligations to be the best baseball player he could possibly be. The second was to serve as a model of black manhood. A man of great physical strength and immense talent, he also was a man of great courage, dignity, and determination. The kind of self-restraint that he demonstrated during his major league career would have warmed the heart of those nineteenth-century, white, middle-class sports enthusiasts who had looked to sports as a way of instilling such a virtue in American men.

PARTICIPATION IN SPORT AND THE FEMININE IDEAL

"[W]e have a peculiar antipathy to ladies in gigs; . . . we nauseate all skating in the feminine gender; and . . . we have an extraordinary aversion to ladies riding to hounds. . . . We would not marry a downright, thoroughgoing, hurdle jumping, racing pace, fox hunting lady, if she had the planet, Jupiter, for her portion [dowry]," declared a male contributor to the *New York Sporting Magazine* in 1834. In his opinion, participating in sport did nothing to enhance a woman's femininity or desirability as a mate. Women who dared to transgress on this male territory were literally out of bounds.

Because sport was by definition a male activity, because manliness was measured by its distinctiveness from womanliness, and because that distinction was one of the pillars upon which society was based, it is not surprising that once women managed to find the time to take an interest in sports, their interest was met with a great deal of consternation and resistance. The entry of women into the realm of male sports blurred the lines between masculinity and femininity and expanded the definition of what it meant to be a "true woman."

Resistance to female athleticism took two forms. The first was ideological; the other was practical. Ideas about the human body and the nature of women in general (and genteel and refined women in particular) played a significant role in discouraging female participation in sporting activities. According to nineteenth-century conventional wisdom, the body was a mechanism blessed with a limited amount of energy. Thus, energy spent in one sort of activity deprived the body of that needed to engage in another sort of activity. The secret to success and a long and healthy life, then, was to budget one's energy. This theory, combined with the belief that a woman's body was both inferior to and more complex than a man's, led doctors, educators, and even politicians to conclude that participation in sports would inhibit a woman's ability to bear children.

Added to these concerns was the desire to uphold a middle-class feminine ideal that viewed women as modest, obedient, physically delicate, and unassertive. It was an age that viewed women as most feminine when they remained in their homes, sheltered from public gaze. Such a feminine ideal precluded participation in most rigorous, competitive, athletic activity. That did not mean that women were excluded completely from sporting activities, only that certain sports were set aside as ones most conducive for preserving a woman's femininity. Sports such as archery, croquet, tennis, and golf were deemed acceptable for genteel, middle- and upper-class women because the way they were played provided the participant with moderate exercise intended to develop muscle tone, grace, and physical vigor but did not require extreme physical exertion, courage, or highly developed skills. Such sports weren't considered particularly competitive, didn't involve vigorous exercise, didn't induce sweat, and didn't require much strength. Under such circumstances, playing tennis meant gently lobbing the ball over the net so that it was easy to return rather than smashing it to the other side of the court. In the nineteenth century, participation in sports, like playing the piano or dabbling in art, was acceptable for women as long as it was not taken too seriously. Occasionally playing croquet or tennis was a good form of mild exercise and a respectable way to encounter and enjoy the company of young men in the out of doors.

Added to a cultural ideology that discouraged female participation in sport were practices that inhibited the development of athletic skills in women and discouraged them from developing a passion for sport. Parents and teachers, for example, encouraged boys to use their bodies freely, to cover space, to take risks, and to play outdoors. Girls were discouraged from participating in such activities. Instead, while their brothers rushed outside to play a game of ball, they were encouraged to remain quietly sedentary, to read books, play with their dolls, or practice the piano. Girls were expected to protect their bodies and use them in socially prescribed ways designed to establish and preserve their femininity. Excessive physical activity was considered socially unacceptable. On a practical level what that meant was that little effort was spent trying to interest women in sport or to provide them with the training necessary to excel in competitive sporting activities. And until the second half of the nineteenth century, there was almost no one who was willing to invest in facilities that would provide women the space to develop their individual athletic talents.

Women's clothing was another significant impediment to their participation in sport. Designed to testify to their femininity, women's clothes made it impossible for them to move about freely. Tightly laced corsets essentially disabled a woman by pressing against her lungs, preventing her from breathing normally. And until the 1920s, fashionable dresses with long skirts combined with petticoats, hoops, or bustles compelled her to carry around yard upon yard of heavy fabric. Field hockey players, for example, were expected to dash across the playing field wearing ankle-length, long-sleeved dresses with petticoats.

Once women asserted their right to participate in sports, the rules that were imposed on their play tended to minimize physical exertion as well as to discourage competition and the desire to meet athletic standards established by and for men. The baseball diamond for women's baseball, for example, was smaller than the one used by men. Female tennis tournaments were reduced from three sets out of five to two sets out of three. Basketball rules for women, adopted in 1899, discouraged physical contact and prevented female players from playing full court. According to the regulations, the court was divided into three zones, two forwards were confined to playing under one basket, two guards confined to playing under the other, and a center played in the middle. None of the players were allowed to bounce the ball more than three consecutive times, they couldn't hold the ball for longer than three seconds, and they could not be so unladylike as to grab the ball from another player. When female athletic teams met for intercollegiate play, they were often mixed, part of one team playing on the same side as part of another in order to inhibit competitiveness. Physical educators, college administrators, and sports promoters were determined that if women were going to participate in sports, every effort should be made to prevent them from exhausting themselves or jarring their reproductive organs unnecessarily.

These factors served to inhibit women's interest in sports and to prevent them from incorporating love of sport into the way femininity was defined. At the same time, however, concern about the state of public health, the rise of women's colleges, the development of a corporate welfare system, the increasing importance of sport as entertainment as well as recreation, improvements in sport technology, and the passage of federal gender equity legislation laid the groundwork for creating a place for athleticism in the definition of what it meant to be an American woman.

By the second half of the nineteenth century, concern about public health and the falling birth rate among white, native-born, middle-class women prompted doctors, educators, social critics, and public officials to call upon women as well as men to exercise in the fresh air in an effort strengthen their bodies. Fearful of what they called "race suicide," they searched for ways to assure that white, native-born Americans would continue to maintain their economic and social power. One response to those concerns was efforts to provide respectable and genteel women with activities that would prepare their bodies to tolerate the strains believed to accompany childbirth.

The establishment of women's colleges also contributed to the rise of women's sport. Administrators at women's colleges were determined to provide women with educational opportunities that were comparable to those provided by such male institutions like Harvard, Yale, and Princeton. Dedicated to proving that rigorous intellectual activity did not have a negative effect on a woman's health or ability to bear children, they went to great lengths to provide female students with good wholesome food and the time to engage in vigorous exercise. They built athletic facilities for their students and hired physical educators to run athletic programs. Students in these schools came from some of the most socially prominent families in the United States. Self-assured, used to doing what they pleased, and eager to play the kind of games that their brothers were allowed to play, they took advantage of the privacy provided by the ivy-covered walls of their colleges to form baseball and basketball teams. As early as 1866, Vassar College had two baseball clubs. Smith College was not far behind. By the late nineteenth century, sports teams from women's colleges were competing against each other.

It was the corporate welfare system that provided working-class women with the opportunity to engage in organized sports. As labor began to organize in the late nineteenth century, some corporate managers tried to stem the tide of unionization by providing their workers with a wide variety of benefits such as recreational facilities. They authorized the organization of corporate teams and encouraged their employees to participate in competitions. Babe Didrickson was one of the beneficiaries of that practice. She trained with coaches hired by the company and was paid well for her participation.

Such opportunities to play on company-sponsored teams and compete against other athletes were appealing to working-class women who were athletically inclined. They were not overburdened by the same kind of gender stereotypes that inhibited their middle-class sisters from participating in sport. No one viewed them as weak, passive, or physically delicate. They did not necessarily aspire to be "ladies," nor did they necessarily hold the genteel, middle-class feminine ideal in high regard.

In the spirit of P. T. Barnum, entrepreneurial sports promoters were quick to take advantage of such willingness. An integral part of the growing, commercial entertainment industry, they organized exhibitions for all-female teams called the "Blondes" and "Brunettes," who traveled the country in the 1870s playing baseball. The attraction, of course, was the novelty of such competitions. No one thought of the members of either team as men. They were simply women trying to play a man's game. At the turn of the century, teams called the "Bloomer Girls" toured the country, challenging local men's teams. Their performances were burlesques. Occasionally a man, trying to disguise himself as a woman, would don a wig and take his place on the pitcher's mound or in the outfield.

The tradition of female exhibition games eventually evolved into the formation of the All American Girls' Baseball League in 1943 during World War II. In the absence of male athletes, the resistance to female participation in sports declined. Women were allowed to ride as jockeys and work as caddies as well as coach and umpire. It was in this environment that Philip K. Wrigley, owner of the Chicago Cubs and the Wrigley Chewing Gum Company, came up with a plan to provide a suitable substitute for men's professional baseball. He hired talented female ball players and organized teams in Racine and Kenosha, Wisconsin, Rockford, Illinois, and South Bend, Indiana, who played each other to the delight of enthusiastic crowds. His players were professionals in every sense of the word. They played ball full time, earned relatively high wages, and were held to high standards of athletic performance. But they were also expected to conform to equally high standards of middle-class feminine behavior and appearance. They were expected to wear conventionally feminine clothes when not playing ball. Slacks and shorts were allowed only at casual social events like picnics, on the buses that transported them from place to place, and at the beach. Team owners hired charm teachers to teach them how to conduct themselves properly. They were forbidden to wear short hair or to smoke or drink in public. Where they lived, who they associated with, and where they went in their free time were all monitored by their chaperones.

Improvement in sport technology also had an important influence on promoting women's interest in sport. The development of the bicycle is a case in point. Some sports historians maintain that the bicycle did more to engage women in health-related exercise than any other single activity. Because of the way that bicycles were originally designed, with a huge wheel in the front and a very small one in the back, bicycle riding was intended as a man's sport. It took a refined sense of balance as well as considerable skill to maneuver the unwieldy contraption along bumpy roads and byways. But once the size of the wheels was equalized, brakes were installed, and the surface of roads was improved, bicycle riding became relatively safe. The result was that by the 1890s, cycling was all the rage among women, who challenged conventional definitions of femininity by immodestly splitting and shortening their skirts so that they could ride astride the seat of a bicycle.

Given the power of middle-class gender norms, it is not surprising that there were those who opposed the idea of women riding bicycles. As more and more women took to the sidewalks and streets, social critics warned that enthusiasm for cycling might encourage women to neglect their children, their husbands, and their domestic duties. Doctors and sexologists worried about the role of cycling in increasing women's awareness of their bodies. Concerned about what they considered to be the deleterious effect of masturbation, they suggested that bicycle riding gave women the opportunity to engage surreptitiously in genital stimulation as they sat upon their bicycle seats. Others were concerned about the impact of bicycle riding on the preservation of feminine virtue. After all, they warned, riding bicycles gave women unprecedented physical mobility. The activity allowed women to wander far from home, thus making them vulnerable to the advances of strange men who might entice them into secluded spots and seduce or rape them.

Women's participation in sport blurred the lines between public and private by creating public spaces where women could exhibit their skills and their bodies. But no factor had quite the impact on equating femininity with athleticism as the passage of Title IX. A part of the Educational Amendments Act of 1972, Title IX provided for gender equity in education. "No person in the United States shall, on the basis of sex, be excluded from participation in, be denied the benefits of or be subjected to discrimination under any education program or activity receiving federal financial assistance," it read. Since most schools received federal funding of some sort, its potential impact on school-sponsored sports programs was enormous.

Male coaches and athletic directors did not respond to the passage of this law immediately, partly because it took the Office for Civil Rights and the Department of Health, Education, and Welfare three years to issue guidelines designed to enforce compliance. And once they issued their guidelines, they gave high schools, colleges, and universities another three years to redesign their programs to accommodate the presence of substantially more women in the gym and on the athletic field.

The process of redistributing resources to accommodate the desire of women to participate in school sports was a painful one. Male athletes cried foul when some athletic directors cut men's sports programs and diverted money from their budgets to support women's athletic activities. But as a result of federal legislation, the kinds of facilities and support available to female athletes were vastly improved, and the number of women participating in athletic competitions mushroomed.

Race as well as class determined the impact that these changes had on women. Unless they aspired to middle-class status, African American women were not constrained by the same set of gender conventions that affected a great many white women. They neither defined their femininity in terms of physical weakness nor were they inclined to tie their gender identities to activities and attributes that were separate and distinct from those possessed by men. Black women created an ideal of womanhood rooted in circumstances that forced them to be physically strong, active, wage earners who were dedicated to community and family. And since there was little pressure on them to inhibit their physical activity, they were relatively free to use their bodies as they saw fit.

But while their race may have freed them to participate in sports, the fact that they were black meant that their opportunities were severely limited. Most young black women did not live in a world that encouraged them to excel in anything, let alone excel in sports. Once they were old enough to work for wages, there was not much leisure in their lives. And the kind of athletic facilities available to them were virtually non-existent. Only the most talented, determined, and well-connected were able to pursue an interest in sport.

The case of Althea Gibson is a case in point. The daughter of a sharecropper, Gibson was born in South Carolina but grew up in New York City's Harlem. She preferred playing basketball and paddle tennis to going to school. Her father taught her how to box so that she could protect herself on the city's streets. Gibson was an immensely talented athlete, but if it hadn't been for men and women in the black middle class who were willing to sponsor her, she would never have been able to develop the skills that made her a champion tennis player. They recommended her for membership in the Cosmopolitan Tennis Club, paid for her lessons, entered her in tennis tournaments, and paid her expenses. They encouraged her to go to college, taught her how to dress, how to behave, and how to present herself as a lady. You had to be "polite," she remembered, but you could still, "play like a tiger and beat the liver and lights out of the ball."

Gibson integrated the game of tennis at Forest Hills in 1950 and won the women's singles championship at Wimbledon in 1957. In 1963 she became a professional golfer. She competed in an age that was, for the moment, more self-conscious about race than it was about gender. The Civil Rights Movement was in full swing in the late 1950s and early 1960s. For those interested in sport, Gibson in some ways served as a genderless symbol for what African Americans could accomplish once they were no longer subjected to discrimination based on the color of their skin. Given that context, Gibson was in a relatively good position to establish her own definition of what was feminine and what was not.

SPORTS AND THE CAUSE OF EQUAL RIGHTS

The kind of discrimination that black athletes faced in the 1960s was humiliating. There were some places in the United States where they could not stay in the same hotels as their white teammates. And when integrated, northern college and university teams played segregated, southern schools, black athletes were expected to sit on the bench because of the concern that their participation might offend the social sensibilities of their southern opponents. By 1968, there were athletes who were determined to put an end to that sort of treatment. One of the platforms for their protest was the Olympic Games held in Mexico City. Some Afro-American athletes, determined both to preserve their self-esteem and to register their protest against racism, boycotted the games. Others decided to take a more confrontational approach. As they stood on the platform wearing their medals around their necks, two runners, Tommie Smith and John Carlos, raised their arms and clenched their fists as the American national anthem was being played. Sports writers and television announcers roundly denounced their gesture of defiance. The two champions were suspended from the Olympic team, asked to leave Mexico, and banished from amateur competition for the rest of their lives. The promising professional careers that they had hoped for never really materialized. Like rebellious slaves such as Frederick Douglass in the nineteenth century and civil rights activists such as J. A. DeLaine in the twentieth, Smith and Carlos, found that the

consequences for participating in public social protest, no matter how justified, could be severe for African American men. However much they may have enjoyed watching black Americans win international sporting events, many white Americans were not yet ready to accept assertiveness and expressions of black pride and self-respect as legitimate components of the definition of black manhood.

Women, like Blacks, used athletic competition as a way to try to promote the cause of equal rights as well as to expand the way femininity was conceptualized in America. In 1973, fifty-five year old Bobby Riggs, a former Wimbledon champion and a pre-eminent sports entertainer and hustler, publicly asserted that female tennis players were in every way inferior to male tennis players. A self-confessed male chauvinist, he bragged that he could easily defeat any one of the high profile female professional tennis champions who played on the circuit. On Mother's Day, Margaret Court took up the challenge and lost to Bobby Riggs, 6–2, 6–1. It was at that point that Billie Jean King, a tennis champion in her own right, agreed to play Riggs.

The so-called "Battle of the Sexes" took place in Houston's Astrodome in September. The event was pure show biz from beginning to end and steeped in gendered symbolism. King, wearing a white dress that glittered with rhinestones, was carried into the stadium like Cleopatra on a litter carried by heavily muscled, bare-chested men. Riggs arrived in a Chinese rickshaw pulled by what has been described as a "gaggle of young women known as 'Bobby's Bosom Buddies.'" Riggs presented King with a huge caramel sucker as a gesture of good will. She presented him with a pig sporting a pink bow. Then they got down to business. Billie Jean King defeated Bobby Riggs in the first three sets, 6–4, 6–3, 6–3 as over 40,000,000 people around the world looked on. King was proud of her victory. Of it she said, "I had shown thousands of people who had never taken an interest in women's sports that women were skillful, entertaining, and capable of coming through

in the clutch." She was convinced that her victory had helped to expand the range of characteristics that contributed to the womanly ideal.

SUMMARY

Women were not absent from sport between the colonial period and the twentieth century. But for much of that period, their presence was marginal. From the seventeenth century on, participation in sport served as a means of defining what constituted manliness and reinforcing gender differences, differences that Americans in every rank of society considered essential for maintaining social order. For most of American history, sport was an almost exclusively male activity. Whether it was a bucolic pasture full of sweet smelling grass and wild flowers in the seventeenth and eighteenth century, a bustling city street where children playing stick ball had to dodge carts and horses in the nineteenth century, or a gigantic domed stadium filled with thousands of screaming fans in the twentieth century, the athletic field has served as a place where masculinity could be defined, achieved, and publicly displayed. It was there that a boy, whether he be native born or of immigrant stock, could learn to be a specific kind of American man.

It was the influential middle class who established sport as a means by which manhood could be earned. As a result of their efforts, participation in sports has come to be valued as one of the most important ways for a man to acquire those qualities necessary to fulfill his role as breadwinner and citizen. Competing on the playing field is supposed to teach men how to compete in business. And in the absence of war, sporting activities provide them with an environment in which violence and aggressiveness are socially sanctioned. Male resistance to female participation in athletic competition stands as testimony to the importance of sport as a gender marker in American society. Men have not only used sport as a way of differentiating themselves from women but also as a way of confirming traditional patterns of male domination and privilege and bolstering the ideology of male physical and mental superiority.

Building a relationship between sports and femininity is still a work in progress. The entry of women into the male-dominated world of sport in the late-nineteenth and early-twentieth centuries was unnerving in the sense that it forced people to reconsider what they believed to be manly and womanly qualities. It also forced them to question the degree to which gender differences were socially constructed or naturally imposed. For most of American history, femininity and the possession of athletic prowess have been mutually exclusive since physical competence was an important marker of masculinity rather than femininity as far as the influential middle and upper classes were concerned. So when women insisted on participating in male dominated sports, they transgressed gender boundaries, and, in doing so, they threatened male power.

In American society, gender transgression is often accompanied by discomfort, fear, and anxiety on the part of both men and women. When it comes to sports, such feelings have expressed themselves in at least two ways. The first was an attempt on the part of sportsmen and women to marginalize men who were not athletically gifted or who preferred to spend their time and hard-earned money doing something other than sitting in a grandstand in ninety-degree weather watching other men play ball. They may have agreed that competitiveness, endurance, self-discipline, determination, persistence, and courage were important indicators of manliness, but their lack of interest in sports led them to construct their masculine ideal around participation in other activities.

The second response was to define participation in sporting activities as unfeminine. It was such a response that made it so difficult for women like Babe Didrickson to pursue their love of sport. While male athletes could concentrate on improving their athletic skills and prowess and establishing lucrative careers for themselves in competitive sports, Didrickson was distracted by the need to persuade sports reporters and her fans that despite the fact that she was a superb athlete she was still a woman.

In this post-Title IX era, sport as a gender marker has lost some, but not all, of its power. While interest in sport remains a masculine imperative for some, female athletes have successfully established physicality and athleticism as an acceptable part of the feminine ideal. For an increasingly wide range of people, firm muscles and a healthy body combined with quick thinking, physical grace, and precision of movement have become genderless characteristics, widely admired in men and women alike.

DOCUMENT

American Manliness and the College Regatta

Prior to the mid-nineteenth century, intercollegiate athletic competitions were unknown. But an ambitious, imaginative, and entrepreneurial railroad superintendent came up with a scheme that would change all that. Intent on selling passenger tickets on his railroad and encouraging tourists to come to New Hampshire, he promoted a boat race between Harvard and Yale which was to take place on New Hampshire's Lake Winnipesaukee on August 3, 1852. In return for an afternoon of rowing, he offered to defray all of the expenses of the participants and to pay for a two week vacation for each of them.

A sense of wounded nationalism spurred even more interest in rowing. Offended by a remark made by an American correspondent in England who alleged that American men were physically inferior to British men, a Harvard student organized another contest in 1859. On July 26, from 15,000 to 20,000 spectators gathered on the shores of a lake near Worcester, Massachusetts to watch teams representing Harvard, Yale, Brown, and Trinity compete. Rowing had become a spectator sport, and the New York Herald *devoted three and one-half columns on its front page to the contest.*

The article that is reprinted below refers to that race. According the reporter, what is the value of sports activities and contests like the one he describes? In his opinion, what is the relationship between sports and manliness?

Source: "The College Regatta Yesterday—Progress of American Sports," *New York Herald,* July 27, 1859.

THE COLLEGE REGATTA YESTERDAY—PROGRESS OF ATHLETIC SPORTS.—It was remarked by an English journal some time ago, that the men of America were becoming physically degenerate very rapidly. The absence of those athletic and muscle-developing sports so common among the youth of England undoubtedly tended to reduce our young men to effeminacy; but a great revolution has taken place in this respect. Within a few years we have made wonderful progress in the cultivation of manly exercises. Yachting, rowing, cricket and base ball are now the universal diversions of the youth in the country. Clubs for the encouragement of all these amusements exist almost everywhere, and we shall have in the rising generation a muscular developement which may shame our British friends. Our yachtsmen are beginning to take long sea stretches, in place of the fresh water dabbling to which they used to confine themselves. Almost every level green sward around New York has its party of base ball players and cricketers, and every river and harbor its rowing matches. So great has the passion for rowing become that the colleges have taken it up and formed rowing clubs, like those at Eton and other English colleges. We are led to these reflections mainly by the fact that a splendid rowing regatta came off yesterday at Worcester, Massachusetts, between the boat clubs of Yale and Trinity Colleges, and Harvard and Brown Universities, the prizes for which were furnished by the city. This affair met with so much *éclat* that the banks were shut and business suspended during the day. The description and result of this novel regatta we give in another column. . . .

If these athletic exercises are persevered in our young men will all become gymnasts, and we shall have material in this country for such a volunteer army as the world never saw before. The games of cricket and base ball may be said to be the rival games of England and America, the latter being peculiar to this country; and of the two we think it is the better game for developing the muscles and improving the conformation of the chest and body generally, for the reason that while cricket is played a good deal on the stoop, and with the head downwards, in base ball the head is mostly erect, the face turned upwards, and the stroke made with uplifted arms and a consequent expansion of the chest. Next to swimming, which is the finest exercise in the world—all the muscles being brought into full play, while the body is extended with a graceful curve, and the head elevated to its natural position—we think base ball is the best exercise. Rowing, too, has the peculiar advantage of bringing every muscle into action, from the fingers to the very toes, at the same time that the motion of the arms is an exercise for the chest, like that of the dumb bell.

A great cricket match is to come off at Hoboken during the first or second week in September, between eleven English and twenty-two American players. In alluding to this game, our Canadian neighbor, the Montreal *Advertiser,* remarks that the American players are "English by birth," and, in the same spirit which evoked the comment of the English journal referred to, complacently adds:— "Nobody supposes that native Americans can play cricket, or any other game requiring muscular force, agility and endurance." We were under the impression that some games requiring all these qualities were pretty well played at Bunker Hill and Chippewa, and if our neighbor would pay a visit to the Central Park when its ball ground is in good order, we promise him that he will see a little more of it there among our base ball clubs.

Another manly and healthful exercise, we are glad to perceive, is becoming very popular—that is horse riding. Most of our young men who can afford it keep good riding horses, and inspiriting exercise in the saddle is fast superseding the less useful one in the wagon or the sulkey. In a year or two we shall have a display of horse flesh and horsemanship in the Central Park that no city in the world need blush for.

Let us go ahead with our athletic sports, for when we have tough muscles and broad chests we will want no doctors.

Femininity Transformed:
Women Play Baseball

During World War II, professional baseball fell on hard times. Both major and minor league club owners lost their players either to the armed services or to jobs in war industries and were unable to recruit others. In their desperation, they called upon women to fill the athletic void. In 1942, thirty-two amateur women's softball teams banded together to form the International Girls' Major League. The next year Philip K. Wrigley, the owner of the Chicago Cubs and the President of Wrigley Chewing Gum Company, formed the All-American Girls Professional Softball (soon to be changed to "baseball") League. The problem that the promoters of both leagues faced was how to reconcile prevailing notions regarding what constituted femininity with the obvious athleticism of their female players. The article reprinted below exposes the kind of ambivalence and anxiety that observers experienced when women transgressed gender boundaries and played baseball for money in public.

How does Yoder express his ambivalence? In what way did promoters accommodate prevailing ideas about "true womanhood" when they presented their female players to the public? How is Yoder's article gendered? In other words, in what way would his article have been different if he had been reporting on male ball players? How does what Yoder describes fit in with the changes in ideas about femininity prompted by participation in World War II?

New Orleans blew into Chicago one day this summer with a thirteen-game winning streak, the hottest pitcher who ever lost a bobby pin, and the reputation of being the best outfit the new International Girls' Major League has seen yet. For the opening cataclysm, New Orleans was playing a Chicago club that was no better than it should be, a team that had no chance at all and was a cinch to lose its middy. It was a night when there was nothing much doing around town, and the professional gamblers decided to look in on the contest and win a few dollars on the favorites. They bet 5 to 1 on New Orleans, whereupon the underdogs began playing like champions and the Louisiana wonder girls folded up as if by magic. The gamblers went away muttering that the man who trusts a woman ballplayer has holes in his head.

It was the first time the girls' league had attracted attention from big-city gamblers to any important extent. It may also be the last. For it seems agreed that the league's greatest charm is one the gamblers overlooked—the fact that the girls' remarkable dexterity is matched only by their remarkable unpredictability.

New Orleans should have won hands down, for they are supposed to be the Yankees of the league, a rough and raffish crowd that ought to take the pennant this year, when the annual tournament is held in Detroit in mid-September. Though they didn't win, nevertheless it's a club that will serve as an introduction to the whole phenomenon, for New Orleans has such girls as Nina Korgan and the Misses Savona, and it is still news to most people that there are such girls. They typify a new set of career girls—the closest thing to professional ballplayers the female sex has yet produced.

Source: Robert M. Yoder, "Miss Casey at the Bat," *Saturday Evening Post,* 215 (Aug. 22, 1942), pp. 16–17, 48–49.

It would be ungallant to call them professionals, for their athletic purity is watched over every minute by the Amateur Softball Association. But it would be equally ungallant to say the girls dally around like amateurs, for they live and play like professionals. Although this is the first year they have had a league, the individual clubs have been going strong for some time. Last year they did so well that thirty-two of the more ambitious teams formed the new circuit. Frequently they draw bigger crowds than the National or American league teams. Four of the top Chicago girls' teams played to 234,000 cash customers last year.

Why thousands will pay good money to see girls play softball is a question that fills conservative baseball fans with helpless disgust. The best theory is simply that the girls are getting extremely good, and that they are wonderfully erratic. They have learned every trick and every mannerism of masculine big leaguers, on top of which they have mastered every error.

"They'll be seven runs ahead," says one observer, "and then blow up completely. They'll look like world beaters for six games and go to pieces in the seventh. Nothing wrong; they just get flighty. One minute they'll play the coolest, smartest ball you ever saw, and the next, they'll pull the biggest bonehead of the season. But they know the game and I think they play harder than men. They are in there to win every minute, and there are none of the lulls you see in big-time baseball when one team has the other on the hip. Nobody ever stalls in this league and anything can happen."

Right now, New Orleans is doped to win the national championship, and Nina Korgan is the league's most-talked-of star. Miss Korgan is a lofty, twenty-six-year-old right-hander generally hailed as the best pitcher in the business. She has black hair, the rangy build of a basketball center, and an upshoot that gives the girls fits. It comes in low, about the garters, and leaps right up toward the batter's swan-like throat—a fact the girls find disconcerting in the extreme. After four years of hard practice, Miss Korgan can make this break

either in or out, and it is probably the best ball she has. . . .

The Bob Feller of the ladies' league stands five feet, eleven inches tall and, slim as she looks in uniform, is 180 pounds of solid girl. The league is full of six-footers, although height isn't as characteristic as durability and tensile strength. These are good, substantial girls, and it is muscle, not fat, although there is a broth of a girl playing for St. Louis who weighs around 225. Not all the girls are Amazons, and the statistics show they are not so big as the uniforms make them look, averaging, for the stars, around 135. There is even an occasional peewee, like Shirley Jamison, shortfielder on the Garden City Maids, of Chicago, who stands only four feet eleven. When the great Korgan has to pitch to Shirley, she all but kneels, sinking one knee to the ground as if teaching babykins to catch the pretty red ball. . . .

The Gentle Razzberry

The Misses Savona, also of New Orleans, are, respectively, Miss Frieda, at third, and Miss Olympia, who can play any position, but usually obliges behind the bat, where she grabs a hot foul tip as happily as a child catching fireflies. Olympia runs bases like a man, slides like a man and catches like a man. If she could spit, she could go with Brooklyn. The fans dispute over which of the Savona girls is the more talented. Miss Olympia, although built like a football halfback, looks frail compared to Miss Frieda, who handles third base as though born there. Both are iron women, and had the flighty little genes produced a Luigi and Giovanni instead of an Olympia and Frieda, the name "Savona" might be as well known as "DiMaggio." . . .

Most of the top teams in the girls' league are sponsored by factories or breweries. Nina and the Savonas, for instance, play under the bright gonfalon of the Jax Beer Company; their team is called the Jax. On the scale the girls are operating these days, it costs a lot of money to maintain them, and the Jax are reputed to cost their sponsor from $15,000 to $20,000 a year. On the other hand, a team that can draw fifty to ninety thousand paid admissions in the course of a season, as some of the Chicago teams do, goes quite a way toward being self-supporting.

Most of the girls have jobs with the sponsoring company, which can offer them work without putting any smirch on the girls' amateur standing, and it is reasonable to suppose that the stars find very good jobs indeed. If employed, they have to work at it, or the Amateur Softball Association would kick them out. But there is no rule saying that a pitcher can't get more money for typing than an ordinary typist does. The stars probably can count on forty to sixty dollars a week, which, though it doesn't make them rich, is not sweatshop pay. . . .

The girls play nine innings and use a team of ten players, standard in softball. The extra player is a shortfielder, or spare shortstop, who works wherever she is needed, usually in short right or short left field. Their coaches are usually old-time baseball players—a fact which helps explain where the girls get so much style. The diamond is in miniature, less than half the size of a baseball layout. Men play softball with sixty feet between bases, but the girls' diamond is a full size smaller than that—just forty feet from base to base. The pitcher stands only thirty-five feet from home plate, as against forty-three feet in masculine softball.

Diamonds and Satin

Most of the girls on the bigger teams could operate handily on a man-sized diamond. On the midget one, they can play a highly strenuous brand of ball. That is one thing that lends speed to their games—the diamond is small, but the girls are big.

The girls play in regular baseball pants, sometimes wool, sometimes satin, but usually wear a satin blouse over the regular jersey. . . .

There are girls' teams that wear shorts, but not the top teams. They play too strenuous a game for bare legs. The A. S. A. frowns on shorts, anyway, lest sex rear its pretty head and convert this vigorous outdoor exercise into a leg show. Teams like the Jax or the St. Louis Rangers are bundled up in baseball breeches and thick socks to a degree that makes grandmother's bathing suit look daring.

Decked in these manly accouterments, and whipping the ball around the bases with an easy overhand snap, the girls manage to look very competent indeed, and there are those who argue that some of them are as good as men ever will be. It's an argument that won't be settled, for the A. S. A. won't approve of mixed games, and even if it would, the A. A. U. would put its foot down. It is the inflexible rule that there cannot be coeducational or intersex athletics wherever there might be what is elegantly called "body contact." Every now and then, one of the Army softball teams hurls a defi at one of the outstanding girls' clubs, but while they would be nicely matched for size, the girls can only shake a muscular head and say "No." The A. S. A. is a stern mother and its only concession is that soldiers can watch while one girls' team plays another. The strapping Miss Korgan, incidentally, doesn't hold with the idea that the girls are as good as men. If they'd switch batteries, she says, it would be an even contest, but not unless they did. "Men are faster and can stand more abuse" is the way she looks at it. . . .

There are nights when the girls knock the ball all over the park, and there are nights when they can't hit for sour apples. Every now and then one of them steps up and raps out a home run, but, on the other hand, there are girls whose batting averages are dainty enough for Little Eva. You will find batting averages of .091, for instance, or .083—the latter meaning that the lady got one hit in twelve times up. Others bat as high as .450. But it seems agreed that hitting is the girls' weakest department. . . .

"Why, they play just like men!" is the common remark from first-time spectators, who are always surprised to see how far the girls have come along and how professional they look. The batter will have a stance, and frequently a build, that would do for Babe Herman. The catcher stands there with fist in mitt, looking as much at home in mask and chest protector as most girls do in an apron. And the pitcher has the pitcher's act down pat. She will wear a reflective squint that needs only a cud of Plowboy to pass for big-league stuff. The late Arthur Brisbane, who was always urging American womanhood to go out and get muscle-bound for the betterment of the race, would note with approval that the frailest creature on the field frequently is that undeveloped shrimp, the male umpire.

Batter Up!

But if our myopic friend were down close enough to hear the conversation, he would find that these huskies don't play like men and don't sound like men. Most of the heckling that goes on is gay badinage about fellas. . . .

Nor do they play exactly like men. If they did, they wouldn't get the crowds they do. What interests the customers is the fact that the girls play as women are expected to. You can see all kinds of ball playing, even in the same inning, even from the same girl. When they are good, they are very, very good, and when they are bad, it's murder.

Like Casey of the Mudville nine, there is pride in their bearing and a smile on their face, and no stranger in the crowd can doubt that this is Miss Casey at the bat. But as happened in Casey's case, you can't be sure what will come next.

In this league, the players carry bandannas, but wear rings. In this league, the losers sometimes go back to their hotel and cry like babies. In this league, they play half the time like Dead End kids and then develop sudden streaks of daintiness that would do for Sweet Alice. This is a league where the batter will stride up to the plate, fan out miserably, walk back to the dugout and remark loudly, "She hasn't got a thing! I'm just not hitting today!"

When Nina Korgan was pitching for Tulsa last year, there was a slight girl with New Orleans who could hit anything Korgan had to offer, even if Korgan was fanning everyone else.

"How was it you could always get a hit?" Korgan asked her after joining the Jax.

"To me," was the sisterly response, "you don't have anything on the ball."

They may occasionally play like men, and occasionally even look like men, but beneath that satin perspiration shirt there beats a feminine heart.

ARTICLE

Baseball and the Reconstitution of American Masculinity, 1880–1920

Michael S. Kimmel

Some historians have identified what they call a "crisis" in the attitude of men toward the construction of masculinity at the turn of the twentieth century. Michael Kimmel is one of them. In his article on the connection between baseball and the construction of manhood in the twentieth century, he argues that involvement in sports in general and baseball in particular helped to bolster the confidence of American men that they were "real" men during an age in which great effort was being spent trying to turn them into "docile and disciplined" laborers.

    What does he identify as significant threats to manliness during the period between 1880 and 1920? How did baseball help to modify those threats for both players and spectators? What role did class play in this process? Was baseball unique in this regard, or do you think it should be considered a metaphor or symbol for all sports?

Baseball is sport as American pastoral: More, perhaps, than any other sport, baseball evokes that nostalgic longing, those warm recollections of boyhood innocence, the balmy warmth of country air, the continuity of generations. More than this, baseball is a metaphor for America, "the very symbol, the outward and visible expression of the drive and push and rush and struggle of the raging, tearing, booming 19th century," as Mark Twain wrote in 1889.

Baseball expresses the contradictions that lie at the heart of American culture. The ball park itself is a bucolic patch of green nestled in a burgeoning urban landscape. The relaxation of an afternoon spent languidly in the bleacher sun is a sharp counterpoint to the ex-cruciating tension that hangs on every pitch. Carefully calculated strategies (like hit and run or the double steal) executed with drill-like precision contrast with the spontaneous enthusiasm of the great catch. The players' cold professionalism at the bargaining table is antithetical to their boyish exuberance on the field.

And baseball is about remaining a boy and becoming a man. Like other sports, baseball fuses work and play, transforming play into work and work into play, thus smoothing the transition from boyhood to manhood. Play as work generates adult responsibility and discipline; work as play allows one to enjoy the economic necessity of working. Some studies suggest that men who are successful as boyhood athletes become more successful in business than those who were not successful child athletes. Contemporary high-tech corporations have introduced team sports among managers on the premise that such teamwork will increase productivity.

But unlike other sports, baseball inspires a literary eloquence that is unmatched, perhaps

Source: Reprinted, by permission, M. S. Kimmel, 1990, "Baseball and the Reconstitution of American Masculinity, 1880–1920," in *Sport, Men, and the Gender Order: Critical Feminist Perspectives*, edited by M. A. Messner and D. F. Sabo (Champaign, IL: Human Kinetics), 55–65. Notes omitted.

because baseball is so delicately poised between boyhood and manhood. No other sport has produced a Roger Angell or a Donald Hall; interestingly, each explores the link between baseball and family memory. Angell writes that, for him, "going through baseball record books and picture books is like opening a family album stuffed with old letters, wedding invitations, tattered newspaper clippings, graduation programs, and curled up darkening snapshots," so that for writer and fan, baseball players "seem like members of our family, or like trusted friends." And Hall underscores how baseball "connects American males with each other, not only through bleacher friendships and neighbor loyalties, not only through barroom fights, but, most importantly, through generations." He continues:

> Baseball is fathers and sons. Football is brothers beating each other up in the backyard, violent and superficial. Baseball is the generations, looping backward forever with a million apparitions of sticks and balls, cricket and rounders, and the game the Iroquois played in Connecticut before the English came. Baseball is fathers and sons playing catch, lazy and murderous, wild and controlled, the profound archaic song of birth, growth, age, and death. This diamond encloses what we are.

In this essay, I will examine one of the ways in which this diamond encloses what we are by looking at the historical links between baseball and masculinity in the United States. By focusing on the rise of baseball at the turn of the century, I will develop two themes. First, I will look at the ways in which the rise of organized participatory sports was offered as a corrective to a perceived erosion of traditional masculinity in the late 19th century. Second, I shall explore the rise of mass-level spectator sports as part of the shift in America from a culture of production to a culture of consumption. I will argue that baseball—as participatory and spectator sport—was one of the chief institutional vehicles by which masculinity was reconstituted and by which Americans accommodated themselves to shifting structural relations. By specifying the terms on which sports reconstituted American masculinity, I shall link participation and spectatorship and explore how baseball provided an institutional nexus by which turn-of-the-century men recreated a manhood that could be experienced as personally powerful while it simultaneously facilitated the emergence of a docile and disciplined labor force. The lyrical eloquence that baseball above other sports inspires derives, in part, from the sport's centrality in the effort to reconstitute American masculinity at the turn of the century.

Forces

The early 19th century provided a fertile environment for an expansive American manhood. Geographic expansion combined with rapid industrial and urban growth to fuel a virile optimism about social possibilities. The Jacksonian assault against "effete" European bankers and the frighteningly "primitive" Native American population grounded identity in a "securely achieved manhood." But by midcentury, the male establishment began to waver as social and economic changes began to erode the foundations of traditional American masculinity. Westward expansion came to an abrupt end at the Pacific coast, and rapid industrialization radically altered men's relationships to their work. The independent artisan, the autonomous small farmer, and the small shopkeeper were everywhere disappearing. Before the Civil War, almost 9 of every 10 American men were farmers or self-employed businessmen; by 1870, that figure had dropped to 2 out of 3, and by 1910, less than 1 out of 3 American men were as economically autonomous. Increased mechanization and the routinization of labor accompanied rapid industrialization; individual workers were increasingly divorced from control over the labor process as well as dispossessed of ownership.

Simultaneously, social changes further eroded American men's identities. In the burgeoning cities, white men felt increasingly threatened by waves of immigrants. In 1870, for example, of the nearly 1 million people who lived in New York City, 4 out of every 9 were foreign-born. And the rise of the women's movement in the late 19th century spelled the beginning of the end for men's monopoly over the ballot box, the college classroom, and the professional school. The appearance of the "new woman"—single, upwardly mobile, sexually active, professionally ambitious, and feminist—also seemed to exacerbate men's insecurity and malaise.

The Crisis of Masculinity

The crisis of masculinity in the late 19th century emerged from these structural and social changes, as "the familiar routes to manhood were either washed out or road-blocked"; men

> were jolted by changes in the economic and so-cial order which made them perceive that their superior position in the gender order and their supposedly "natural" male roles and preroga-tives were not somehow rooted in the human condition, that they were instead the result of a complex set of relationships subject to change and decay.

The perceived crisis of masculinity was not a generic crisis, experienced by all men in similar ways. It was essentially a crisis of mid-dle-class white masculinity, a crisis in the dominant paradigm of masculinity that was perceived as threatened by the simultaneous erosion of traditional structural foundations (e.g., economic autonomy and the frontier), new gains for women, and the tremendous in-fusion of nonwhite immigrants into the major industrial cities. It was a crisis of economic control, a struggle against larger units of cap-ital that eroded work-place autonomy and new workers (immigrants and women), who were seen as displacing traditional American men. And it was also a political crisis, pitting the traditional small town and rural white middle-class masculinity against new con-tenders for political incorporation. It was a crisis, in this sense, of gender hegemony, of

whether or not the traditional white middle-class version of masculinity would continue to prevail over both women and nonwhite men. And therefore, to understand how base-ball articulated with these various dimensions of crisis in hegemonic masculinity, we will need to draw on analyses of the relations among various social classes, the relations be-tween whites and nonwhites, and the rela-tions between women and men.

Responses to the Crisis of Masculinity

Men's responses to the turn-of-the-century crisis of masculinity varied tremendously, es-pecially given the simultaneity of the forces that seemed to be affecting middle-class white men. Some (comprising the antifeminist re-sponse) gave vent to an angry backlash against the forces that were perceived as threatening men, whereas others (comprising the profem-inist response) embraced feminist principles as the grounds for a reconstitution of a new masculinity. A third response sought to revi-talize masculinity, to return the vitality and strength that had been slowly draining from American men. This masculinist response was not as anti-female as it was pro-male, attacking the enervation of American manhood and de-veloping those interpersonal and institutional mechanisms by which masculinity could be retrieved. Often the masculinist response was articulated with an anti-modernist rejection of the city as evil den of corruption, where healthy country men were thought to be trans-formed into effete dandies and where hordes of unwashed immigrants threatened the racial purity of the nation. "Get your children into the country," one real estate advertisement for Wilmington, Delaware, urged potential buy-ers in 1905. "The cities murder children. The hot pavements, the dust, the noise, are fatal in many cases and harmful always. The history of successful men is nearly always the history of country boys." Surely the anti-urban senti-ments that composed part of the masculinist response were also fueled by a nativist racism that saw the cities as the breeders of an immi-grant threat.

The masculinist effort to stem the tide of feminization of American manhood included the development of the YMCA and the Boy Scouts, in which young boys could experience the remedial effects of the wilderness away from the feminizing clutches of mothers and teachers. If consumer society had "turned robust manly, self-reliant boyhood into a lot of flat chested cigarette smokers with shaky nerves and doubtful vitality," as Chief Scout Ernest Thompson Seton had it, then the Boy Scouts could "counter the forces of feminization and maintain traditional manhood."

The masculinist effort also included the Muscular Christianity Movement, in which, through texts like Thomas Hughes's *The Manliness of Christ* (1880) and Carl Case's *The Masculine in Religion* (1906), the image of Jesus was transformed from a beatific, delicate, soft-spoken champion of the poor into a muscle-bound he-man whose message encouraged the strong to dominate the weak. Jesus was no "dough-faced lick-spittle proposition," proclaimed itinerant evangelist Billy Sunday, but "the greatest scrapper who ever lived." A former professional baseball player turned country preacher, Sunday drew enormous crowds to his fiery sermons, in which he preached against institutionalized Protestantism. "Lord save us from off-handed, flabby cheeked, brittle boned, weak-kneed, thin-skinned, pliable, plastic, spineless, effeminate, ossified three-karat Christianity," Sunday preached. Masculinism also promoted a revived martial idealism and found a new hero in Theodore Roosevelt, because "the greatest danger that a long period of profound peace offers to a nation is that of [creating] effeminate tendencies in young men."

And masculinism also found institutional expression in the sports craze that swept the nation in the last decade of the century. The first tennis court in the United States was built in Boston in 1876, and the first basketball court was built in 1891. The American Bowling Congress was founded in 1895 and the Amateur Athletic Union established in 1890. Sports offered a counter to the "prosy mediocrity of the latter-day industrial scheme of life," as economist/sociologist Thorstein Veblen wrote. Sports revitalized American manhood while they simultaneously "had taken the place of the frontier . . . as the outlet through which the pressure of urban populations was eased."

Nowhere was this more evident than in the rapid rise of baseball, both as a participatory sport and as a spectator sport. Baseball became one of the central mechanisms by which masculinity was reconstituted at the turn of the century, as well as one of the vehicles by which the various classes, races, and ethnic groups that were thrown together into the urban melting pot accommodated themselves to industrial class society and developed the temperaments that facilitated the transition to a consumer culture.

Playing

In the late 19th century, America went "sports crazy." The nation had never been as preoccupied with physical health and exercise, and across the country Americans flocked to health spas, consumed enormous quantities of potions and elixirs (like the 63 imported and 42 domestic bottled waters advertised by one firm in 1900), lifted weights, listened to health reformers extol the tonic virtues of country air and bland high-fiber diets, raced through urban parks on bicycles, and tried their hands at tennis, golf, boxing, cricket, and baseball. The search for individual physical perfection indicated a hopelessness about the possibilities of social transformation and pointed to the intimately linked fears of the enervation of the culture and individual lethargy and failure of nerve.

Development of Body and Character Through Sport

Sports were heralded as character building, and health reformers promised that athletic activity would not only make young men physically healthier but would instill moral virtues as well. Sports were cast as a central element in the fight against femininization; sports made boys into men. In countless advice books that counseled concerned parents about proper methods of child rearing, sports were invariably linked with the acquisition of appropriate gender-role behavior for males. Sports were necessary, according to physician D. A. Sargent, to "counteract the enervating tendency of the times and to improve the health, strength, and vigor of our youth," because sports provided the best kind of "general exercise for the body, and develop courage, manliness, and self-control." Sports aided youth in "the struggle for manliness," wrote G. Walter Fiske in *Boy Life and Self-Government.*

Manhood required proof, and sports provided a "place where manhood was earned," not as "part of any ceremonial rite de passage but through the visible demonstration of achievement." Such demonstration was particularly important, because lurking beneath the fear of feminization was the fear of the effeminate—the fear of homosexuality—which had emerged in visible subcultures in urban centers. In England, for example, one newspaper championed athletics for substituting the "feats of man for the 'freak of the fop,' hardiness for effeminacy, and dexterity for luxurious indolence."

Some were less sanguine about sports' curative values. Thorstein Veblen's blistering critique of the nascent consumer culture suggested that organized sports are an illusory panacea. For the individual man, athletics are no sign of virtue, because "the temperament which inclines men to [sports] is essentially a boyish temperament. The addiction to sports therefore in a peculiar degree marks an arrested development of the man's moral nature." And culturally, Veblen continued, sports may be an evolutionary throwback, as they "afford an exercise for dexterity and for the emulative ferocity and astuteness characteristic of predatory life."

Most commentators saw sports as the arena in which men could achieve physical manhood but also believed that organized sports would instill important moral values. Here, especially, the masculinist response to the crisis of masculinity resonated with the anti-urban sentiments of those who feared modern industrial society. Sports could rescue American boys from the "haunts of dissipation" that seduced them in the cities—the taverns, gambling parlors, and brothels, according to the *Brooklyn Eagle.* Youth needs recreation, the *New York Herald* claimed, and "if they can't get it healthily and morally, they will seek it unhealthily and immorally at night, in drink saloons or at the gambling tables, and from these dissipations to those of a lower depth, the gradation is easy."

The Link to Baseball

And what was true of sports in general was particularly true of baseball. Theodore Roosevelt listed baseball in his list of "the true sports for a manly race" (along with running, rowing, football, boxing, wrestling, shooting, riding, and mountain climbing). Just as horse racing had resulted in better horse breeding, health advocate Edward Marshall claimed in 1910, so baseball "resulted in improvement in man breeding." "No boy can grow to a perfectly normal manhood today without the benefits of at least a small amount of baseball experience and practice," wrote William McKeever in his popular advice manual, *Training the Boy.*

The values that baseball called into play were important to the man and central to the nation. The baseball player was "no thug trained to brutality like the prize fighter," noted baseball pioneer Albert G. Spalding, nor was he a "half-developed little creature like a jockey"; rather, he was an exemplar of distinctly "native" American virtues, which Spalding alliteratively enumerated in *America's National Game;* "American Courage, Confidence, Combativeness; American Dash, Discipline, Determination; American Energy, Eagerness, Enthusiasm; American Pluck, Persistence, Performance; American Spirit, Sagacity, Success; American Vim, Vigor, Virility."

Such values were not only American but Christian, replacing the desiccated values of a dissolute life with the healthy vitality of

American manhood. Moral reformer Henry Chadwick saw baseball as a "remedy for the many evils resulting from the immoral associations boys and young men of our cities are apt to become connected with" and therefore deserving "the endorsement of every clergyman in the country." McKeever added that "baseball may be conducted as a clean and uplifting game such as people of true moral refinement may patronize without doing any violence to conscience." Baseball was good for the bodies and for the souls of men; it was imperative for the health and moral fiber of the body social. From pulpits and advice manuals, the virtues of baseball were sounded. As M. L. Adelman notes, baseball

> took manliness beyond a mere demonstration of physical prowess and linked it to virtues such as courage, fortitude, discipline, and so on. The argument concluded that if ball games called these virtues into play—as in fact they were critical to doing well at such sports—then ball playing was obviously one way of demonstrating manhood.

One central feature of the values that were instilled by playing baseball was that they appeared on the surface to stress autonomy and aggressive independence, but they simultaneously reinforced obedience, self-sacrifice, discipline, and a rigid hierarchy. This was equally true with other boys' liberation movements designed to counter the feminization of the culture. The Boy Scouts instilled a "quest for disciplined vitality," in which scouts were taught, according to founder Lord Baden-Powell, to work hard, sacrifice, and be obedient to their fellow countrymen and the king. The results of this and other efforts were noted with glee by Octavia Hill, the celebrated English social reformer, in the 1880s:

> There is no organization which I have found influence so powerfully for good the boys in such a neighborhood. The cadets learn the duty and dignity of obedience; they get a sense of corporate life and of civic duty; they learn to honour the power of endurance and effort; and they come into contact with manly and devoted offi-

cers. . . . These ideals are in marked contrast with the listless self-indulgence, the pert self-assertion, the selfishness and want of reverence which are so characteristic of the life in the low district.

For the boys learning to play baseball, these values were also underscored. Surely the team came first, and one always obeyed one's coaches and manager. What Veblen claimed about football is equally true about baseball:

> The culture . . . gives a product of exotic ferocity and cunning. It is a rehabilitation of the early barbarian temperament, together with a suppression of those details of temperament which, as seen from the standpoint of the social and economic exigencies, are the redeeming features of the savage character.
> The physical vigour acquired in the training for athletic games—so far as the training may be said to have this effect—is of advantage both to the individual and to the collectivity, in that, other things being equal, it conduces to economic serviceability.

Sports reproduced those character traits required by industrial capitalism, and participation in sports by working-class youths was hailed as a mechanism of insuring obedience to authority and acceptance of hierarchy. If the masculinity on the baseball field was exuberant, fiercely competitive, and wildly aggressive, it was so only in a controlled and orderly arena, closely supervised by powerful adults. As such the masculinity reconstituted on the baseball field also facilitated a docility and obedience to authority that would serve the maintenance of the emerging industrial capitalist order.

Watching

Just as on the field, so in the stands: Baseball as a spectator sport facilitated an accommodation to industrial capitalism as a leisure-time diversion for the urban lower-middle and working classes. Ball parks were located in the city and admission fees were low, so that "attendance at baseball games was more broadly based than at other spectator sports."

The Crafting of a National Pastime

Baseball did not spring to such popularity overnight, as restorer of both individual virility and national vitality; its emergence as the "national pastime" was deliberately crafted. In fact, in the early half of the 19th century, cricket was hailed for its capacity to instill manly virtues in its players. "Whoever started these boys to practice the game deserves great credit—it is manly, healthy, invigorating exercise and ought to be attended more or less at all schools," waxed the *New York Herald*. In 1868, the *Brooklyn Eagle* informed potential spectators of a cricket match that they were about to see a "manly game." Baseball was regarded, in fact, as less than fully manly; one letter to the editor of a newspaper contended that

> You know very well that a man who makes a business of playing ball is not a man to be relied upon in a match where great interests are centered, or on which large amounts of money is pending.

By the late 19th century, the relationship between baseball and cricket had been reversed. The man who played cricket, Albert Spalding warned, regarded his match as a chance "to drink afternoon tea, flirt, gossip, smoke [and] take a whiskey and soda at the customary hour."

How can we explain such a change? In part, the shift from cricket to baseball can be understood by the changing class and regional composition of baseball's players and observers. Whereas earlier in the century baseball had been the domain of upper-middle-class men, by the end of the century it was played almost exclusively by lower-middle-class men. Similarly, the rise of mass spectator sports—the erection of the urban stadium, the professionalization of teams and leagues, and the salaries of players—dramatically changed the class composition of the baseball fan. The values

that were thought to be instilled by playing baseball were now thought to be instilled by watching baseball. And values of discipline, self-control, and sacrifice for the team and an acceptance of hierarchy were central to the accommodation of a rapidly developing working class to the new industrial order.

It was during this period of dramatic economic expansion in the late 19th century that baseball "conquered" America. In the first few decades following the Civil War, the baseball diamond was standardized, teams and leagues organized, rules refined, game schedules instituted, and grand tours undertaken by professional baseball teams. And though the earliest baseball teams, like the New York Knickerbockers, were made up of wealthy men, baseball was soon played by small-town lower-middle-class men and watched by their urban counterparts.

The urban baseball park was one of the new important locations for social life in the burgeoning late-19th-century city. Like the vaudeville theater, the department store, and the urban park, the stadium provided a world of abundance and fantasy, of excitement and diversion, all carefully circumscribed by the logic of urban capitalism. Here the pain and alienation of the urban industrial working life was soothed; the routine dull grayness of the urban landscape was broken up by these manicured patches of green. As Barth writes, the baseball park was a constructed imitation of a pastoral setting in the city, in which identification with one's professional team provided a feeling of community with anonymous neighbors; the ball park was a rural haven of shared sentiments in the midst of the alienating city.

Baseball as Fantasy and Democracy

If masculinity had earlier been based on economic autonomy, geographic mobility, and success in a competitive hierarchy, baseball—among the other new social institutions of the turn of the century—allowed the reconstitution of those elements in a controlled and contained location. On the field, baseball promoted values essential to traditional masculinity: courage, initiative, self-control, competitive drive, physical fitness. In the stands, the geographic frontier of the midcentury was replaced by the outfield fences and by the mental frontiers between rival cities. (What we lose in reality we recreate in fantasy, as a Freudian axiom might have it.)

Baseball was fantasy and diversion. "Men anxious to be distracted from their arduous daily routines provided a natural market for the product of the new industry." And baseball was viewed by boosters as a potential safety valve, allowing the release of potential aggression in a healthy, socially acceptable way; it was a "method of gaining momentary relief from the strain of an intolerable burden, and at the same time finding a harmless outlet for pent-up emotions" which otherwise "might discharge themselves in a dangerous way." For the fan, baseball was, Bruce noted, catharsis.

Like the frontier, the baseball park was also celebrated as democratic. The experience of spectatorship, baseball's boosters claimed, was a great social leveler:

> The spectator at a ball game is no longer a statesman, lawyer, broker, doctor, merchant, or artisan, but just plain every-day man, with a heart full of fraternity and good will to all his fellow men—except perhaps the umpire. The oftener he sits in grand stand or "bleachers," the broader, kindlier, better man and citizen he must tend to become.

"The genius of our institutions is democratic," Albert Spalding gushed. "Baseball is a democratic game."

Such mythic egalitarianism, however, ignored the power relationships that made American democracy possible. For the experience of incorporation into community was based on exclusion: the exclusion of nonwhite men and the exclusion of women. The ball park was a "haven in a heartless world" for white lower-middle-class men, and the community and solidarity they found there, however based on exclusion, facilitated their accommodation to their positions in class society. Professional spectator sports maintained the "rigid gender division and chauvinist masculine identity" as well as the strict separation between whites and nonwhites that provided some of the main cultural supports of class domination. While providing the illusion of equality and offering organized leisure-time distraction, as well as by shaping working-class masculinity as constituted by its superiority over women, baseball helped white working-class men accommodate themselves to the emergent order.

Reproducing

Baseball, as participatory sport and as spectator sport, served to reconstitute a masculinity whose social foundations had been steadily eroding; in so doing, baseball served to facilitate the reproduction of a society based upon gender, racial, and class hierarchies. For it was not just masculinity that was reconstituted through sports but a particular kind of masculinity—white and middle-class—that was elaborated. And part of the mechanisms of that elaboration was the use of white middle-class masculinity to maintain the social hierarchies between whites and nonwhites (including all ethnic immigrants to the cities), between upper classes and working classes, and between men and women.

These mechanisms were developed in the last 2 decades of the 19th century and the first 2 decades of the 20th century. In 1919, this world was shaken during the world series scandal that involved the infamous Chicago "Black Sox," who had apparently "fixed" the series. The scandal captivated American men, and a certain innocence was lost. Commercialism had "come to dominate the sporting quality of sports"; heroes were venal and the pristine pastoral was exposed as corrupt, part of the emergent corporate order and not the alternative to it that people had imagined. But by then it was too late: The corporate order had triumphed and would face little organized opposition from a mobilized and unified working class. The reconstituted masculinity that was encouraged by baseball had replaced traditional definitions of masculinity and was fully accommodated to a new capitalist order. The geographic frontier where masculinity was demonstrated was replaced by the outfield fence; men's workplace autonomy and control were replaced, in part, by watching a solitary batter squaring off against an opposing pitcher. What had been lost in real experience could be reconstituted through fantasy.

The baseball diamond, as I have argued in this essay, became more than a verdant patch of pastoral nostalgia; it was a contested terrain. The contestants were invisible to both participant and spectator and quite separate from the game being played or watched. Baseball was a contest between class cultures, in which the hegemony of middle-class culture was reinforced and the emerging industrial urban working class was tamed by consumerism and disciplined by the American values promoted in the game. It was a contest between races, in which the exclusion of nonwhites and non-European immigrants from participation was reflected in the bleachers, as racial discrimination further assuaged the white working class. And it was a contest between women and men, in which newly mobile women were excluded from equal participation (and most often from spectatorship); the gender hierarchy was maintained by assuming that those traits that made for athletic excellence were also those traits that made for exemplary citizenship. The masculinity reconstituted on the ball field or in the bleachers was a masculinity that reinforced the unequal distribution of power based on class, race, and gender. In that sense, also, baseball was truly an American game. And if we continue, as I do, to love both playing and watching baseball, we will deepen an ambivalent love, which, like the love of family or country to which baseball is so intimately linked, binds us to a place of both comfort and cruelty.

ARTICLE

From the "Muscle Moll" to the "Butch" Ballplayer: Mannishness, Lesbianism, and Homophobia in U. S. Women's Sport

Susan K. Cahn

Until the late nineteenth century, the construction of ideal femininity did not typically include an athletic prowess component. This combined with the fact that participation in sport was one of the prerogatives of being male meant that when women intruded into

Source: Susan K. Cahn "From 'Muscle Moll' to the 'Butch' Ballplayer: Manishness, Lesbianism, and Homophobia in U. S. Women's Sport," *Feminist Studies* Vol. 19, No. 2 (Summer 1993), pp. 343–364. Copyright © 1993 by Feminist Studies, Inc. Reprinted by permission of the publisher. Notes omitted.

the male world of sport, their willingness to both participate and compete undermined their claim to womanliness in the eyes of many Americans. Because they crossed gendered boundaries, they risked having their claim to femininity questioned. Susan Cahn explains why this happened and argues that during the 1930s concern about "mannish" female athletes began to change.

In what way did attitudes toward female athletes change? Why did they change? What role did race play in these changing attitudes? What insights did Cahn's interviews with female athletes bring to the issue of female athleticism and sexuality?

In 1934, *Literary Digest* subtitled an article on women's sports, "Will the Playing Fields One Day Be Ruled by Amazons?" The author, Fred Witner, answered the question affirmatively and concluded that as an "inevitable consequence" of sport's masculinizing effect, "girls trained in physical education to-day may find it more difficult to attract the most worthy fathers for their children." The image of women athletes as mannish, failed heterosexuals represents a thinly veiled reference to lesbianism in sport. At times, the homosexual allusion has been indisputable, as in a journalist's description of the great athlete Babe Didrikson as a "Sapphic, Broddingnagian woman" or in television comedian Arsenio Hall's more recent witticism, "If we can put a man on the moon, why can't we get one on Martina Navratilova?" More frequently, however, popular commentary on lesbians in sport has taken the form of indirect references, surfacing through denials and refutations rather than open acknowledgment. When in 1955 an *Ebony* magazine article on African American track stars insisted that "off track, girls are entirely feminine. Most of them like boys, dances, club affairs," the reporter answered the implicit but unspoken charge that athletes, especially Black women in a "manly" sport, were masculine manhaters, or lesbians.

The figure of the mannish lesbian athlete has acted as a powerful but unarticulated "bogey woman" of sport, forming a silent foil for more positive, corrective images that attempt to rehabilitate the image of women athletes and resolve the cultural contradiction between athletic prowess and femininity. As a stereotyped figure in U.S. society, the lesbian athlete forms part of everyday cultural knowledge. Yet historians have paid scant attention to the connection between female sexuality and sport. This essay explores the historical relationship between lesbianism and sport by tracing the development of the stereotyped "mannish lesbian athlete" and examining its relation to the lived experience of mid-twentieth-century lesbian athletes.

I argue that fears of mannish female sexuality in sport initially centered on the prospect of unbridled heterosexual desire. By the 1930s, however, female athletic mannishness began to connote heterosexual failure, usually couched in terms of unattractiveness to men, but also suggesting the possible absence of heterosexual interest. In the years following World War II, the stereotype of the lesbian athlete emerged full blown. The extreme homophobia and the gender conservatism of the postwar era created a context in which longstanding linkages among mannishness, female homosexuality, and athletics cohered around the figure of the mannish lesbian athlete. Paradoxically, the association between masculinity, lesbianism, and sport had a positive outcome for some women. The very cultural matrix that produced the pejorative image also created possibilities for lesbian affirmation. Sport provided social and psychic space for some lesbians to validate themselves and to build a collective culture. Thus, the lesbian athlete was not only a figure of discourse but a living product of women's sexual struggle and cultural innovation.

Amazons, Muscle Molls, and the Question of Sexual (Im)Mortality

The athletic woman sparked interest and controversy in the early decades of the twentieth century. In the United States and other Western societies, sport functioned as a male preserve, an all-male domain in which men not only played games together but also demonstrated and affirmed their manhood. The "maleness" of sport derived from a gender ideology which labeled aggression, physicality, competitive spirit, and athletic skill as masculine attributes necessary for achieving true manliness. This notion found unquestioned support in the dualistic, polarized concepts of gender which prevailed in Victorian America. However, by the turn of the century, women had begun to challenge Victorian gender arrangements, breaking down barriers to female participation in previously male arenas of public work, politics, and urban nightlife. Some of these "New Women" sought entry into the world of athletics as well. On college campuses students enjoyed a wide range of intramural sports through newly formed Women's Athletic Associations. Off-campus women took up games like golf, tennis, basketball, swimming, and occasionally even wrestling, car racing, or boxing. As challengers to one of the defining arenas of manhood, skilled female athletes became symbols of the broader march of womanhood out of the Victorian domestic sphere into once prohibited male realms.

The woman athlete represented both the appealing and threatening aspects of modern womanhood. In a positive light, she captured the exuberant spirit, physical vigor, and brazenness of the New Woman. The University of Minnesota student newspaper proclaimed in 1904 that the athletic girl was the "truest type of All-American coed." Several years later, *Harper's Bazaar* labeled the unsportive girl as "not strictly up to date," and *Good Housekeeping* noted that the "tomboy" had come to symbolize "a new type of American girl, new not only physically, but mentally and morally."

Yet, women athletes invoked condemnation as often as praise. Critics ranged from physicians and physical educators to sportswriters, male athletic officials, and casual observers. In their view, strenuous athletic pursuits endangered women and threatened the stability of society. They maintained that women athletes would become manlike, adopting masculine dress, talk, and mannerisms. In addition, they contended, too much exercise would damage female reproductive capacity. And worse yet, the excitement of sport would cause women to lose control, conjuring up images of frenzied, distraught co-eds on the verge of moral, physical, and emotional breakdown. These fears collapsed into an all-encompassing concept of "mannishness," a term signifying female masculinity.

The public debate over the merits of women's athletic participation remained lively throughout the 1910s and 1920s. Implicit in the dispute over "mannishness" was a longstanding disagreement over the effect of women's athletic activities on their sexuality. Controversy centered around two issues—damage to female reproductive capacity and the unleashing of heterosexual passion. Medical experts and exercise specialists disagreed among themselves about the effects of athletic activity on women's reproductive cycles and organs. Some claimed that athletic training interfered with menstruation and caused reproductive organs to harden or atrophy; others insisted that rigorous exercise endowed women with strength and energy which would make them more fit for bearing and rearing children. Similarly, experts vehemently debated whether competition unleashed nonprocreative, erotic desires identified with male sexuality and unrespectable women, or, conversely, whether invigorating sport enhanced a woman's feminine charm and sexual appeal, channeling sexual energy into wholesome activity.

Conflicting opinion on sexual matters followed closely along the lines of a larger dispute which divided the world of women's sport into warring camps. Beginning in the 1910s, female physical educators and male sport promoters squared off in a decades-long struggle over the appropriate nature of female competition and the right to govern women's athletics. The conflict was a complicated one, involving competing class and gender interests played out in organizational as well as philosophical battles. It was extremely important in shaping women's sports for more than fifty years. Although historians of sport have examined the broad parameters of the conflict, they have paid less attention to the competing sexual perspectives advanced by each side. . . .

On all sides of the debate, however, the controversy about sport and female sexuality presumed heterosexuality. Neither critics nor supporters suggested that "masculine" athleticism might indicate or induce same-sex love. When experts warned of the amazonian athlete's possible sexual transgressions, they linked the physical release of sport with a loss of heterosexual *control*, not of *inclination*. The most frequently used derogatory term for women athletes was "Muscle Moll." In its only other usages, the word "moll" referred to either the female lovers of male gangsters or to prostitutes. Both represented disreputable, heterosexually deviant womanhood.

By contrast, medical studies of sexual "deviance" from the late nineteenth and early twentieth centuries quite clearly linked "mannishness" to lesbianism, and in at least two cases explicitly connected female homosexuality with boyish athleticism. It is curious then that in answering charges against the mannish Muscle Moll, educators and sport promoters of this period did not refer to or deny lesbianism. However, the "mannish lesbian" made little sense in the heterosocial milieu of popular sports. Promoters encouraged mixed audiences for women's athletic events, often combining them with men's games, postgame dances and musical entertainment, or even beauty contests. The image of the athlete as beauty queen and the commercial atmosphere that characterized much of working-class sport ensured that the sexual debate surrounding the modern female athlete would focus on her heterosexual charm, daring, or disrepute. The homosocial environment of women's physical education left educators more vulnerable to insinuations that their profession was populated by "mannish" types who preferred the love of women. However, the feminine respectability and decorum cultivated by the profession provided an initial shield from associations with either the mannish lesbian or her more familiar counterpart, the heterosexual Muscle Moll.

The Muscle Moll as Heterosexual Failure: Emerging Lesbian Stereotypes

In the 1930s, however, the heterosexual understanding of the mannish "amazon" began to give way to a new interpretation which educators and promoters could not long ignore. To the familiar charge that female athletes resembled men, critics added the newer accusation that sport-induced mannishness disqualified them as candidates for heterosexual romance. In 1930, an *American Mercury* medical reporter decried the decline of romantic love, pinning the blame on women who entered sport, business, and politics. He claimed that such women "act like men, talk like men, and think like men." The author explained that "women have come closer and closer to men's level," and, consequently, "the purple allure of distance has vamoosed." Four years later, the *Ladies Home Journal* printed a "Manual on the More or Less Subtle Art of Getting a Man" which listed vitality, gaiety, vivacity, and good sportsmanship—qualities typically associated with women athletes and formerly linked to the athletic flapper's heterosexual appeal—as "the very qualities that are likely to make him consider anything but marriage." Although the charges didn't exclusively focus on athletes, they implied that female athleticism was contrary to heterosexual appeal, which appeared to rest on women's difference from and deference to men.

The concern with heterosexual appeal reflected broader sexual transformations in U.S. society. Historians of sexuality have examined the multiple forces which reshaped gender and sexual relations in the first few decades of the twentieth century. Victorian sexual codes crumbled under pressure from an assertive, boldly sexual working-class youth culture, a women's movement which defied prohibitions against public female activism, and the growth of a new pleasure-oriented consumer economy. In the wake of these changes, modern ideals of womanhood embraced an overtly erotic heterosexual sensibility. At the same time, medical fascination with sexual "deviance" created a growing awareness of lesbianism, now understood as a form of congenital or psychological pathology. The medicalization of homosexuality in combination with an antifeminist backlash in the 1920s against female autonomy and power contributed to a more fully articulated taboo against lesbianism. The modern heterosexual woman stood in stark opposition to her threatening sexual counterpart, the "mannish" lesbian.

By the late 1920s and early 1930s, with a modern lesbian taboo and an eroticized definition of heterosexual femininity in place, the assertive, muscular female competitor roused increasing suspicion. It was at this moment that both subtle and direct references to the lesbian athlete emerged in physical education and popular sport. Uncensored discussions of intimate female companionship and harmless athletic "crushes" disappear from the record, pushed underground by the increasingly hostile tone of public discourse about female sexuality and athleticism. Fueled by the gender antagonisms and anxieties of the Depression, the public began scrutinizing women athletes—known for their appropriation of masculine games and styles—for signs of deviance. Where earlier references to "amazons" had signaled heterosexual ardor, journalists now used the term to mean unattractive, failed heterosexuals. . . .

The Butch Ballplayer: Midcentury Stereotypes of the Lesbian Athlete

Tentatively voiced in the 1930s, these accusations became harsher and more explicit under the impact of wartime changes in gender and sexuality and the subsequent panic over the "homosexual menace." In a post-World War II climate markedly hostile to nontraditional women and lesbians, women in physical education and in working-class popular sports became convenient targets of homophobic indictment.

World War II opened up significant economic and social possibilities for gay men and women. Embryonic prewar homosexual subcultures blossomed during the war and spread across the midcentury urban landscape. Bars, nightclubs, public cruising spots, and informal social networks facilitated the development of gay and lesbian enclaves. But the permissive atmosphere did not survive the war's end. Waving the banner of Cold War political and social conservatism, government leaders acted at the federal, state, and local levels to purge gays and lesbians from government and military posts, to initiate legal investigations and prosecutions of gay individuals and institutions, and to encourage local police crackdowns on gay bars and street life. The perceived need to safeguard national security and to reestablish social order in the wake of wartime disruption sparked a "homosexual panic" which promoted the fear, loathing, and persecution of homosexuals.

Lesbians suffered condemnation for their violation of gender as well as sexual codes. The tremendous emphasis on family, domesticity, and "traditional" femininity in the late 1940s and 1950s reflected postwar anxieties about the reconsolidation of a gender order shaken by two decades of depression and war. As symbols of women's refusal to conform, lesbians endured intense scrutiny by experts who regularly focused on their subjects' presumed masculinity. Sexologists attributed lesbianism to masculine tendencies and freedoms encouraged by the war, linking it to a general collapsing of gender distinctions which, in their view, destabilized marital and family relations.

Lesbians remained shadowy figures to most Americans, but women athletes—noted for their masculine bodies, interests, and attributes—were visible representatives of the gender inversion often associated with homosexuality. Physical education majors, formerly accused of being unappealing to men, were increasingly charged with being uninterested in them as well. . . .

Constant attempts to shore up the heterosexual reputation of athletes can be read as evidence that the longstanding reputation of female athletes as mannish women had become a covert reference to lesbianism. By mid-century, a fundamental reorientation of sexual meanings fused notions of femininity, female eroticism, and heterosexual attractiveness into a single ideal. Mannishness, once primarily a sign of gender crossing, assumed a specifically lesbian-sexual connotation. In the wake of this change, the strong cultural association between sport and masculinity made women's athletics ripe for emerging lesbian stereotypes. This meaning of athletic mannishness raises further questions. What impact did the stereotype have on women's sport? And was the image merely an erroneous stereotype, or did lesbians in fact form a significant presence in sport?

Sport and the Heterosexual Imperative

The image of the mannish lesbian athlete had a direct effect on women competitors, on strategies of athletic organizations, and on the overall popularity of women's sport. The lesbian stereotype exerted pressure on athletes to demonstrate their femininity and heterosexuality, viewed as one and the same. Many women adopted an apologetic stance toward their athletic skill. Even as they competed to win, they made sure to display outward signs of femininity in dress and demeanor. They took special care in contact with the media to reveal "feminine" hobbies like cooking and sewing, to mention current boyfriends, and to discuss future marriage plans.

Leaders of women's sport took the same approach at the institutional level. In answer to portrayals of physical education majors and teachers as social rejects and prudes, physical educators revised their philosophy to place heterosexuality at the center of professional objectives. . . .

Curricular changes implemented between the mid-1930s and mid-1950s institutionalized the new philosophy. In a paper on postwar objectives, Mildred A. Schaeffer explained that physical education classes should help women "develop an interest in school dances and mixers and a desire to voluntarily attend them." To this end, administrators revised coursework to emphasize beauty and social charm over rigorous exercise and health. They exchanged old rationales of fitness and fun for promises of trimmer waistlines, slimmer hips, and prettier complexions. At Radcliffe, for example, faculty redesigned health classes to include "advice on dress, carriage, hair, skin, voice, or any factor that would tend to improve personal appearance and thus contribute to social and economic success." Intramural programs replaced interclass basketball tournaments and weekend campouts for women with mixed-sex "co-recreational" activities like bowling, volleyball, and "fun nights" of ping-pong and shuffleboard. Some departments also added co-educational classes to foster "broader, keener, more sympathetic understanding of the opposite sex." Department heads cracked down on "mannish" students and faculty, issuing warnings against "casual styles" which might "lead us back into some dangerous channels." They implemented dress codes which forbade slacks and men's shirts or socks, adding as well a ban on "boyish hair cuts" and unshaven legs.

Popular sport promoters adopted similar tactics. Martialing sexual data like they were athletic statistics, a 1954 AAU poll sought to sway a skeptical public with numerical proof of heterosexuality—the fact that 91 percent of former female athletes surveyed had married. Publicity for the midwestern All-American Girls Baseball League included statistics on the number of married players in the league. . . .

Behind the scenes, teams passed dress and conduct codes. For example, the All-American Girls Baseball League prohibited players from wearing men's clothing or getting "severe" haircuts. That this was an attempt to secure the heterosexual image of athletes was made even clearer when league officials announced that AAGBL policy prohibited the recruitment of "freaks" and "Amazons."

In the end, the strategic emphasis on heterosexuality and the suppression of "mannishness" did little to alter the image of women in sport. The stereotype of the mannish lesbian athlete grew out of the persistent commonsense equation of sport with masculinity. Opponents of women's sport reinforced this belief when they denigrated women's athletic efforts and ridiculed skilled athletes as "grotesque," "mannish," or "unnatural." Leaders of women's sport unwittingly contributed to the same set of ideas when they began to orient their programs around the new feminine heterosexual ideal. As physical education policies and media campaigns worked to suppress lesbianism and marginalize athletes who didn't conform to dominant standards of femininity, sport officials embedded heterosexism into the institutional and ideological framework of sport. The effect extended beyond sport to the wider culture, where the figure of the mannish lesbian athlete announced that competitiveness, strength, independence, aggression, and physical intimacy among women fell outside the bounds of womanhood. As a symbol of female deviance, she served as a powerful reminder to all women to tow the line of heterosexuality and femininity or risk falling into a despised category of mannish (not-women) women.

Beyond the Stereotype: "Mannish" Athletes and Lesbian Subculture

. . . [But] was the mannish lesbian athlete merely a figure of homophobic imagination, or was there in fact a strong lesbian presence in sport? When the All-American Girls Baseball League adamantly specified, "*Always appear in*

feminine attire . . . MASCULINE HAIR STYLING? SHOES? COATS? SHIRTS? SOCKS, T-SHIRTS ARE BARRED AT ALL TIMES," and when physical education departments threatened to expel students for overly masculine appearance, were administrators merely responding to external pressure? Or were they cracking down on women who may have indeed enjoyed the feel and look of a tough swagger, a short haircut, and men's clothing? And if so, did mannishness among athletes correspond to lesbianism, as the stereotype suggested? In spite of the public stigmatization, some women may have found the activities, attributes, and emotions of sport conducive to lesbian self-expression and community formation.

As part of a larger investigation of women's athletic experience, I conducted oral histories with women who played competitive amateur, semiprofessional, and professional sports between 1930 and 1970. The interviews included only six openly lesbian narrators and thirty-six other women who either declared their heterosexuality or left their identity unstated. Although the sample is too small to stand as a representative study, the interviews offered a rich source of information about popular sexual theories, the association of lesbianism with sport, and lesbian experience in sport. The oral histories and scattered other sources indicate that sport, particularly softball, provided an important site for the development of lesbian subculture and identity in the United States. Gay and straight informants alike confirmed the lesbian presence in popular sport and physical education. Their testimony suggests that from at least the 1940s on, sport provided space for lesbian activity and social networks and served as a path into lesbian culture for young lesbians coming out and searching for companions and community.

Lesbian athletes explained that sport had been integral to their search for sexual identity and lesbian companionship. Ann Maguire, a softball player, physical education major, and top amateur bowler from New England, recalled that as a teenager in the late 1950s,

I had been trying to figure out who I was and couldn't put a name to it. I mean it was very—no gay groups, no literature, no characters on "Dynasty"—I mean there was just nothing at that time. And trying to put a name to it. . . . I went to a bowling tournament, met two women there [and] for some reason something clicked and it clicked in a way that I was not totally aware of.

She introduced herself to the women, who later invited her to a gay bar. Maguire described her experience at age seventeen:

I was being served and I was totally fascinated by the fact that, oh god, here I am being served and I'm not twenty-one. And it didn't occur to me until after a while when I relaxed and started realizing that I was at a gay bar. I just became fascinated. . . . And I was back there the next night. . . . I really felt a sense of knowing who I was and feeling very happy. Very happy that I had been able to through some miracle put this into place.

Loraine Sumner, a physical education teacher who for several decades also played, coached, and refereed sports in the Boston area, recalled: "We didn't have anybody to talk to. We figured it out for ourselves you know." In sport she found others like herself, estimating that as many as 75 percent of the women she played with were lesbian. In such a setting Sumner put a name to her own feelings and found others to support her: "There was a lot of bonding, there's a lot of unity. You've got that closeness." For these women, sport provided a point of entry into lesbian culture.

The question arises of whether lesbians simply congregated in athletic settings or whether a sports environment could actually "create" or "produce" lesbians. Some women fit the first scenario, describing how, in their struggle to accept and make sense out of lesbian desire, sport offered a kind of home that put feelings and identities into place. For other women, it appears that the lesbian presence in sport encouraged them to explore or act on feelings that they might not have had or responded to in other settings. Midwestern baseball player Nora Cross remembered that "it was my first exposure to gay people. . . . I was pursued by the one I was rooming with, that's how I found out." She got involved with her roommate and lived "a gay lifestyle" as long as she stayed in sport. Dorothy Ferguson Key also noticed that sport changed some women, recalling that "there were girls that came in the league like this . . . yeah, gay," but that at other times "a girl come in, and I mean they just change. . . . When they've been in a year they're completely changed. . . . They lived together."

The athletic setting provided public space for lesbian sociability without naming it as such or excluding women who were not lesbians. This environment could facilitate the coming-out process, allowing women who were unsure about or just beginning to explore their sexual identity to socialize with gay and straight women without having to make immediate decisions or declarations. Gradually and primarily through unspoken communication, lesbians in sport recognized each other and created social networks. Gloria Wilson, who played softball in a mid-sized midwestern city, described her entry into lesbian social circles as a gradual process in which older lesbians slowly opened up their world to her and she grew more sure of her own identity and place in the group.

A lot was assumed. And I don't think they felt comfortable with me talking until they knew me better. Then I think more was revealed. And we had little beer gatherings after a game at somebody's house. So then it was even more clear who was doing what when. And then I felt more comfortable too, fitting in, talking about my relationship too—and exploring more of the lesbian lifestyle, I guess.

. . . In an era when women did not dare announce their lesbianism in public, the social world of popular sport allowed women to find each other as teammates, friends, and lovers. . . .

[But] if athletics provided a public arena and social activity in which lesbians could recognize and affirm each other, what exactly was it that they recognized? This is where the issue of mannishness arises. Women athletes consistently explained the lesbian reputation of sport by reference to the mannishness of some athletes. Nebraska softball player Jessie Steinkuhler suggested that the lesbian image of sportswomen came from the fact that "they tried to act like a man, you know the way they walked, the way they talked and the things they did." . . .

These comments could merely indicate the pervasiveness of the masculine reputation of athletes and lesbians. However, lesbian narrators also suggested connections, although more complicated and nuanced, between athletics, lesbianism, and the "mannish" or "butchy" style which some lesbians manifested. None reported any doubt about their own gender identification as girls and women, but they indicated that they had often felt uncomfortable with the activities and attributes associated with the female gender. They preferred boyish clothes and activities to the conventional styles and manners of femininity. . . .

Several spoke of their own attraction to styles deemed masculine by the dominant culture and their relief upon finding athletic comrades who shared this sensibility. Josephine D'Angelo recalled that as a lesbian participating in sport, "you brought your culture with you. You brought your arm swinging . . . , the swagger, the way you tilted or cocked your head or whatever. You brought that with you." She explained that this style was acceptable in sports: "First thing you did was to kind of imitate the boys because you know, you're not supposed to throw like a girl." Although her rejection of femininity made her conspicuous in other settings, D'Angelo found that in sport "it was overlooked, see. You weren't different than the other kids. . . . Same likeness, people of a kind."

These athletes were clearly women playing women's sports. But in the gender system of U.S. society, the skills, movements, clothing, and competition of sport were laden with impressions of masculinity. Lesbianism too crossed over the bounds of acceptable femininity. Consequently, sport could relocate girls or women with lesbian identities or feelings in an alternative nexus of gender meanings, allowing them to "be themselves"—or to express their gender and sexuality in an unconventional way. This applied to heterosexual women as well, many of whom also described themselves as "tomboys" attracted to boyish games and styles. As an activity that incorporated prescribed "masculine" physical activity into a way of being in the female body, athletics provided a social space and practice for reorganizing conventional meanings of embodied masculinity and femininity. *All* women in sport gained access to activities and expressive styles labeled masculine by the dominant culture. However, because lesbians were excluded from a concept of "real womanhood" defined around heterosexual appeal and desire, sport formed a milieu in which they could redefine womanhood on their own terms. . . .

However, the connections among lesbianism, masculinity, and sport require qualification. Many lesbians in and out of sport did not adopt "masculine" markers. And even among those who did, narrators indicated that butch styles did not occlude more traditionally "feminine" qualities of affection and tenderness valued by women athletes. Sport allowed women to combine activities and attributes perceived as masculine with more conventionally feminine qualities of friendship, cooperation, nurturance, and affection. Lesbians particularly benefited from this gender configuration, finding that in the athletic setting, qualities otherwise viewed as manifestations of homosexual deviance were understood as inherent, positive aspects of sport. Aggressiveness, toughness, passionate intensity, expanded use of motion and space, strength, and competitiveness contributed to athletic excellence. With such qualities defined as athletic attributes rather than psychological abnormalities, the culture of sport permitted lesbians to express the full range of their gendered sensibilities while sidestepping the stigma of psychological deviance. For these reasons, athletics, in the words of Josephine D'Angelo, formed a "comforting" and "comfortable" place.

Yet lesbians found sport hospitable only under certain conditions. Societal hostility toward homosexuality made lesbianism unspeakable in any realm of culture, but the sexual suspicions that surrounded sport made athletics an especially dangerous place in which to speak out. Physical educators and sport officials vigilantly guarded against signs of "mannishness," and teams occasionally expelled women who wore their hair in a "boyish bob" or engaged in obvious lesbian relationships. Consequently, gay athletes avoided naming or verbally acknowledging their sexuality. Loraine Sumner explained that "you never talked about it. . . . You never saw anything in public amongst the group of us. But you knew right darn well that this one was going with that one. But yet it just wasn't a topic of conversation. Never." Instead, lesbian athletes signaled their identity through dress, posture, and look, reserving spoken communication for private gatherings among women who were acknowledged and accepted members of concealed communities.

Although in hindsight the underground nature of midcentury lesbian communities may seem extremely repressive, it may also have had a positive side. Unlike the bars where women's very presence declared their status as sexual outlaws, in sport athletes could enjoy the public company of lesbians while retaining their membership in local communities where neighbors, kin, and coworkers respected and sometimes even celebrated their athletic abilities. The unacknowledged, indefinite presence of lesbians in sport may have allowed for a wider range of lesbian experience and identity than is currently acknowledged in most scholarship. For women who did not identify as lesbian but were sexually drawn to other women, sport provided a venue in which they could express their desires without necessarily having articulated their feelings regarding their sexual identity. It is possible that even as they started "going around" with other women, some athletes may have participated in lesbian sexual relationships and friendship networks without ever privately or publicly claiming a lesbian identity. My evidence supports only speculative conclusions but suggests that the culture of sport provided social space for some women to create clearly delineated lesbian identities and communities, at the same time allowing other women to move along the fringes of this world, operating across sexual and community lines without a firmly differentiated lesbian identity. . . .

Women in sport experienced a contradictory array of heterosexual imperatives and homosexual possibilities. The fact that women athletes disrupted a critical domain of male power and privilege made sport a strategic site for shoring up existing gender and sexual hierarchies. The image of the mannish lesbian confirmed both the masculinity of sport and its association with female deviance. Lesbian athletes could not publicly claim their identity without risking expulsion, ostracism, and loss of athletic activities and social networks that had become crucial to their lives. Effectively silenced, their image was conveyed to the dominant culture primarily as a negative stereotype in which the mannish lesbian athlete represented the unfeminine "other," the line beyond which "normal" women must not cross.

The paradox of women's sport history is that the mannish athlete was not only a figure of homophobic discourse but also a human actor engaged in sexual innovation and struggle. Lesbian athletes used the social and psychic space of sport to create a collective culture and affirmative identity. The pride, pleasure, companionship, and dignity lesbians found in the athletic world helped them survive in a hostile society. The challenge posed by their collective existence and their creative reconstruction of womanhood formed a precondition for more overt, political challenges to lesbian oppression which have occurred largely outside the realm of sport.

SUGGESTIONS FOR FURTHER READING

MELVIN L. ADELMAN, *A Sporting Time: New York City and the Rise of Modern Athletics, 1820–70* (Urbana: University of Illinois Press, 1986).

GAIL BEDERMAN, "Remaking Manhood through Race and 'Civilization,' " in *Manliness & Civilization: A Cultural History of Gender and Race in the United States, 1880–1917* (Chicago: University of Chicago Press, 1995), 1–44.

GAI INGHAM BERLAGE, *Women in Baseball: The Forgotten History* (Westport, CT: Praeger, 1994).

SUSAN K. CAHN, *Coming on Strong: Gender and Sexuality in Twentieth-Century Women's Sport* (Cambridge, MA: Harvard University Press, 1994).

SUSAN E. CAYLEFF, *Babe: The Life and Legend of Babe Didrikson Zaharias* (Urbana: University of Illinois Press, 1995).

GEORGE EISEN, "Sport, Recreation, and Gender: Jewish Immigrant Women in Turn-of-the-Century America (1880–1920)," *Journal of Sport History*, 18 (Spring 1991), 103–120.

ELLEN W. GERBER, JAN FELSHIN, PEARL BERLIN, WANEEN WYRICK, "Historical Survey," *The American Woman in Sport* (Reading, MA: Addison-Wesley Publishing, 1974), 3–47.

ALTHEA GIBSON, *I Always Wanted to Be Somebody*, ed. Ed Fitzgerald (New York: Harper & Row, 1958).

ELLIOTT J. GORN, *The Manly Art: Bare-Knuckle Prize Fighting in America* (Ithaca, NY: Cornell University Press, 1986).

HARVEY GREEN, *Fit for America: Health, Fitness, Sport, and American Society* (New York: Pantheon, 1986).

OTHELLO HARRIS, "Muhammad Ali and the Revolt of the Black Athlete," in *Muhammad Ali: The People's Champ*, ed. Elliott J. Gorn (Urbana: University of Illinois Press, 1995), 54–69.

PETER LEVINE, *Ellis Island to Ebbets Field: Sport and the American Jewish Experience* (New York: Oxford University Press, 1992).

RITA LIBERTI, " 'We Were Ladies, We Just Played Basketball Like Boys': African American Womanhood and Competitive Basketball at Bennett College, 1928–1942," *Journal of Sport History*, 26 (Fall 1999), 567–84.

MICHAEL A. MESSNER, "Sport, Men, and Gender," *Power at Play: Sports and the Problem of Masculinity* (Boston: Beacon Press, 1992), 7–23.

DONALD J. MROZEK, "The 'Amazon' and the American 'Lady': Sexual Fears of Women as Athletes," in *From "Fair Sex" to Feminism: Sport and the Socialization of Women in the Industrial and Post-Industrial Eras*, ed. J. A. Mangan and Roberta J. Park (London: Frank Cass, 1987), 282–98.

S. W. POPE, ed., *The New American Sport History: Recent Approaches and Perspectives* (Urbana: University of Illinois Press, 1997).

BENJAMIN G. RADER, *American Sports: From the Age of Folk Games to the Age of Televised Sports*, 4th ed. (Upper Saddle River, NJ: Prentice Hall, 1999).

STEVEN A. RIESS, "Sport and the Redefinition of American Middle-Class Masculinity," *International Journal of the History of Sport*, 8 (May 1991), 5–27.

STEVEN A. RIESS, *Touching Base: Professional Baseball and American Culture in the Progressive Era* (Westport, CT: Greenwood Press, 1980).

DEBRA SHATTUCK, "Playing a Man's Game: Women and Baseball in the United States, 1866–1954," *Baseball History*, 2 (Westport, CT: Meckler Books, 1989), 57–77.

NANCY L. STRUNA, "The Formalizing of Sport and the Formation of an Elite: The Chesapeake Gentry, 1650–1720s," *Journal of Sport History*, 13 (Winter 1986), 212–34.

NANCY L. STRUNA, "Gender and Sporting Practice in Early America, 1750–1810," *Journal of Sport History*, 18 (Spring 1991), 10–30.

NANCY L. STRUNA, " 'Good Wives' and 'Gardeners', Spinners and 'Fearless Riders': Middle- and Upper-Rank Women in the Early American Sporting Culture," in *From "Fair Sex" to Feminism: Sport and the Socialization of Women in the Industrial and Post-Industrial Eras,* ed. J. A. Mangan and Roberta J. Park (London: Frank Cass, 1987), 235–55.

NANCY L. STRUNA, *People of Prowess: Sport, Leisure, and Labor in Early Anglo-America* (Urbana: University of Illinois Press, 1996).

NANCY L. STRUNA, "Sport and Society in Early America," *International Journal of the History of Sport,* 5 (Dec. 1988), 292–311.

STEPHANIE L. TWIN, "Introduction," *Out of the Bleachers: Writings on Women and Sport* (Old Westbury, NY and New York: Feminist Press and McGraw Hill, 1979), xv–xli.

DAVID WHITSON, "Sport in the Social Construction of Masculinity," in *Sport, Men and the Gender Order: Critical Feminist Perspectives,* ed. Michael A. Messner and Donald F. Sabo (Champaign, IL: Human Kinetics Books, 1990), 19–29.

PATRICIA VERTINSKY, "Exercise, Physical Capability, and the Eternally Wounded Woman in Late Ninteenth Century North America," *Journal of Sport History,* 14 (Spring 1987), 7–27.

CHAPTER FOURTEEN

GENDER AND VIOLENCE
(1600–1975)

GENDER AND THE QUESTION OF VIOLENCE

In the spring of 1908, the good citizens of LaPorte, Indiana must have been saying, "Who'd have thought it?" The idea that someone they actually knew might have been what one newspaper called the "most fiendish murderess of the age" would take some getting used to. But with the evidence continuing to mount, that did indeed, seem to be the case. It looked more and more as if Belle Gunness, the attractive and propertied widow of a local farmer and the mother of three small children, had not been what she appeared to be.

LaPorte was the kind of small, midwestern town where people thought they knew each other and did not hesitate to take an interest in their neighbors' business. As far as they were concerned, Gunness had been a good wife, a competent housekeeper, and a loving mother who did her best to feed, clothe, and shelter her children after her husband's death. As much as any other woman in town she more

or less conformed to the prescriptions of "true womanhood." She not only took her domestic responsibilities seriously but was believed to be virtuous, kind, and charitable, a paragon of conventional middle-class womanhood, a good neighbor, and, by all accounts, a respectable citizen.

By the middle of May, however, the authorities were not only convinced that Belle Gunness had murdered and then decapitated and buried two women and nine men but also speculated that she had poisoned her children and then had committed suicide by setting fire to her house and burning it down. In any case, they found eleven decapitated and dismembered bodies buried in pits in her farm yard and the incinerated bodies of a woman and three children in the cellar. The evidence pointed directly to her as the perpetrator of these heinous crimes. Among other things, it turned out that she had enticed an undetermined number of men to her farm by advertising for a husband in Norwegian newspapers in places like South Dakota. When men in search of land to farm and a woman to look after them responded to her ad, she encouraged them to come to Indiana to meet her and to bring all of their money and belongings with them. After they arrived, the authorities charged that she poisoned them, hacked them to pieces, threw their heads, torsos, and appendages into hastily dug shallow graves, sprinkled quicklime on them, and then covered them up with dirt and garbage. The theory was that by the middle of April, she realized that she was about to be found out. So on April 27, she went into town to settle her affairs and purchase some kerosene. She then returned home, poisoned her children, and either committed suicide by burning herself and the bodies of her children to a crisp or she placed an unidentified female body in the cellar, set fire to the house, and made her escape.

Americans were not used to having to deal with serial killers, let alone female serial killers. But they did tend to think of violence in gendered terms. Given prevailing definitions of manliness at the time, they were prone to view the participation in acts of violence as a male rather than a female activity. By reputation, men, in general, were considered more likely to engage in behavior patterns that were immoral, intemperate, and physically combative than women. It was not that the good people of LaPorte or anywhere else condoned male aggression. It was just that when the peace and tranquility of their communities were disrupted by acts of violence, they weren't surprised when those who were involved were male.

Prevailing attitudes toward what constituted middle-class femininity made it inconceivable that a respectable woman could have systematically planned and carried out fourteen heartless and brutal murders. This sort of woman was supposed to be a paragon of moral rectitude. She was supposed to be the very embodiment of self-discipline, self-sacrifice, and passivity. Thus, it was not easy for either the citizens of LaPorte or those across the country who took an interest in the case to reconcile their view of woman's "nature" with the

overwhelming evidence that implicated Belle Gunness in these atrocious crimes. Unwilling or unable to adjust their definition of womanliness to acknowledge that women had as much potential to behave as violently as men, they proceeded to create a wide variety of extremely imaginative explanations intended to help them understand what had happened. Their efforts testify to the power that gender conventions had on the public imagination in the early twentieth century.

One response to the allegation that Gunness was a mass murderer was to admit that she was probably guilty but should not be held responsible for her crimes. No sane woman, some argued, could have done such a thing. Others speculated that she was in league with the devil, who had given her the supernatural powers to perform such dastardly deeds.

The *New York Times* took another tack. It hypothesized that Guiness was not a mad or victimized housewife but an entrepreneurial businesswoman who simply charged the medical students in her neighborhood for burying the cadavers that they used in their studies. Still another theory held that she was really Kate Bender, a woman whose family was suspected of killing tired and hungry travelers who sought shelter and a good meal in their roadside home in southeastern Kansas. The Benders had fled the law, and, as far as anyone knew, Kate was still at large.

There were, of course, those who were absolutely convinced that Belle had, indeed, murdered her suitors and her children. But they felt compelled to explain her behavior in terms of gender ambiguity. Gunness, they argued was either a failed woman or some sort of man. Once they gave it some thought, they realized that the hard working and competent woman they had once admired was really too ambitious, greedy, willful, and controlling to be considered really feminine. In fact, they decided that her "shrewd business head" was decidedly masculine. Originally many of her neighbors had considered her to be a good looking women. But some of them now decided that she actually looked more like a man. Indeed, they remembered that she even occasionally dressed like one, sometimes wearing a large leather belt around her waist and striding through farm sales wearing a sealskin coat and hat. Belle Gunness was, of course, either dead or missing and could do nothing to defend herself or protect her claim to femininity. But responses to her alleged crimes illustrate how hard it was for the general public to associate violence with womanliness in the early twentieth century.

Violence in one form or another has been endemic in American society. The colonists had to contend with their fair share of it. Among other things, they massacred Native Americans and were massacred by them. Politically motivated violence characterized their revolt against British rule. Those who opposed the Revolution found that remaining loyal to George III could be extremely dangerous. Some unfortunate Loyalists were tarred and feathered by revolutionary vigilantes calling themselves the Sons of Liberty. Tarring and feathering was a particularly painful and humiliating form of mob violence. The practice involved capturing the victim, beating him, stripping him of his clothes, and then pouring very hot pitch over his naked body and sprinkling it with feathers. When the ritual punishment was over, removing the tar meant removing skin already blistered by the intense heat.

The Revolution was followed by more riots as well as family feuds, slave uprisings, assassinations, duels, gunfights, lynchings, rapes, murders, and assaults. Violence not only continued to be an integral part of American life but also was gendered male. When women were discovered to be the perpetrators of violence, it was considered a shocking anomaly.

We have already considered some of the forms that violence has taken in America. In chapter 6 you read about the cultural imperatives that forced some men to defend their honor by dueling. In chapter 8, you read an article that discussed the connection between vigilantism and the struggle to define femininity on the frontier. In this chapter we will consider the gendered nature of the violence that has plagued the relationship between whites and blacks as well as the connection between gender conventions and domestic violence, murder, and rape.

THE GENDERED NATURE OF INTERRACIAL VIOLENCE

Before the Civil War, most conflicts between white and black Americans took place within a power structure that pitted slaves against their masters and mistresses. The history of African-American slavery in the United States contains a litany of horror stories in which whites assaulted and even killed blacks. When they could, blacks sometimes responded in kind.

Take the case of Celia, the slave of Robert Newsom, a yeoman farmer who lived in Calloway County, Missouri. When Newsom took his family from Virginia to Missouri sometime between 1819 and 1822, he owned no slaves. But his land was fertile, he was hardworking, and he was able to accumulate enough money to buy some field hands to help him with his chores.

In 1849 his wife died. While Newsom had two daughters, Virginia and Mary, who were perfectly capable of running his household, they did not provide him with the sexual services he appears to have wanted. So in 1850, Newsom took his wagon into the next county and bought a fourteen-year-old female slave named Celia. On their way back to his farm, he raped her.

Although it is impossible to know how common it was for a master to rape a female slave, it is clear that it occurred often enough for it to have been widely acknowledged, if not entirely condoned, in the antebellum South. Whether or not they sexually assaulted their female slaves, many slave-owning men never doubted their right to do so. They considered it one of the prerogatives associated with being male.

Newsom continued to demand access to Celia's body for the next five years. During that time, she bore two children. In 1855, however, Celia apparently fell in love with a man named George, one of Newsom's bondsmen. This relationship complicated her situation. She found herself caught between two men, each of whom to some degree defined his manliness in terms of his right to her body. Not surprisingly, George objected to Newsom's relationship with Celia. But his position as a slave prevented him from fulfilling his manly responsibility to protect Celia from Newsom's unwanted attentions. So instead of confronting Newsom directly, he insisted that Celia take the initiative and end the liaison.

When she tried to do this, Newsom made it clear that he would return that evening to claim his rights as her master. It was Saturday, June 23, 1855. At about ten that evening, he left his house and entered Celia's cabin. When he advanced toward her, she killed him by beating him over the head with a large stick she had hidden by the hearth. Desperate to get rid of the corpse, she then folded up Newsom's body and wedged it into the fireplace. She stayed up all night. As Newsom's flesh burned off his bones, she removed the remains from the fireplace. She crushed the smaller bones with a rock and threw them back into the ashes. The larger ones she hid underneath the floor. By dawn, her grisly work was finished, and she went to bed. Later that day, she offered Newsom's grandson two dozen walnuts to clean out her fireplace. Unsuspectingly, he took his grandfather's ashes and spread them along the path that led to the stables. Just before Christmas, Celia was hanged for the murder of her master.

The conviction of Celia was predictable. No all-white, male jury in the antebellum South would have considered the killing of a man like Newsom to be justifiable homicide. They did not consider sexual virtue to be an important component of the definition of black womanhood. And they did not recognize the sexual abuse of a female slave to be a crime.

Southern manhood was constructed in a culture that distributed power between men and women unequally. In the case of Newsom, this inequity not only placed Celia in

danger but also discouraged his daughters from doing anything to protect her. Given the proximity of Celia's cabin to their house, it seems inconceivable that they did not know what was going on between their father and their servant. Yet they appear to have been unable or unwilling to do anything about it. Femininity in southern slave-owning families was constructed around passivity, economic dependence, and a woman's willingness to ignore the immoral or antisocial behavior of the men in their families in order to maintain peace in their households. Since Newsom controlled all of his family's resources, his daughters had to depend on his good will to assure that they would continue to live in material comfort. Under the circumstances, it would have been surprising if they had publicly expressed moral outrage at his behavior.

It was unusual for slaves to resort to physical violence on Southern plantations. But slave owners were always at least subliminally aware that it was possible and did what they could to prevent it. Of particular concern to them was not so much an isolated act of violence on the part of an individual slave but the possibility that slaves might join together to organize a rebellion.

Experience demonstrated that slaves were perfectly capable of rebelling. The Stono Rebellion in South Carolina in 1739 was followed by efforts on the part of Gabriel Prosser in Henrico County, Virginia to foment a slave revolt in 1800. It is unclear how many slaves expected to participate, but estimates ran as high as one thousand. Twenty-two years later, Denmark Vesey tried to organize a revolt in Charleston. It failed to materialize, but the same cannot be said of the Turner Rebellion which erupted in Southampton County, Virginia in August, 1831. Convinced that violence was the only way to end slavery and gain his freedom, Turner believed that God called him to lead other slaves in armed revolt. Before he was captured, over fifty white men, women, and children lay dead.

Organized slave rebellions like Turner's were gendered affairs. There is no evidence that any of the slaves who armed themselves and took part in them were female. This is not entirely surprising since men experienced some aspects of slavery differently from women. For example, male slaves tended to have more geographic mobility than female slaves. Masters were much more likely to give men passes to run errands or deliver messages than they were to give them to women. Male slaves were also likely to have more discretionary time than women, whose days were spent first working for their masters and then keeping their own households and taking care of their children. How male slaves spent their free time varied. Some hunted and fished while others socialized with each other in the slave quarters. But having that discretionary time gave them the opportunity to contemplate and organize rebellions.

It seems reasonable to assume that one of the reasons that men were willing to participate in slave revolts was that rebellion provided them an opportunity to claim their manhood. Whatever one might think of their methods, participating in armed revolt against what they had to have known were terrible odds required a remarkable display of manly courage. It also testified to their determination to assert their own will and to act independently in pursuit of what they perceived to be their own interests. During their murderous rampage through the peaceful Virginia countryside, Turner and his followers claimed for themselves the prerogatives that white slave-owning men regarded as exclusively theirs—the right to commit capricious acts of violence against those who, in this case, were caught by surprise and, thus, helpless to resist.

After the Civil War, yet another manifestation of interracial violence plagued the South. Faced with political disenfranchisement following the war, whites had to contend with the poverty that accompanied military defeat and the social adjustments that followed in the wake of emancipation. In need of labor to work their farms and plantations, they searched for ways to control the black population. Their methods for doing so varied, but one of the most violent was lynching, the ritual murder of black men and women by angry mobs of whites.

Between 1882 and 1946 about 5000 blacks were lynched in the former Confederacy. Southern white men, ever suspicious of state authority, had a long tradition of seeking personal justice when they believed their rights abridged or their honor insulted. They shot each other in duels and gouged each other's eyes out rather than make formal complaints or sue each other in courts. Lynching, a form of vigilantism which typically took place in areas where regular law enforcement was weak or nonexistent, was just another manifestation of the sort of personal justice that southern whites tended to rely on to seek retribution for real or imagined insult or injury.

A form of terrorism, lynching was a useful tool for re-establishing and helping to maintain white men's control over ex-slaves. It was not only intimidating to the victims, it was intimidating to those who could do nothing but stand by and watch. There was no sure way to protect one's self against lynching. The kinds of accusations that whites used as a justification for their actions were often completely arbitrary, and the action of the lynch mob was capricious. Author Richard Wright, recalling life in the South during his youth, wrote "The things that influenced my conduct as a Negro did not have to happen to me directly. . . . Indeed, the white brutality that I had not seen was a more effective control of my behavior than that which I knew. The actual experience would have let me see the realistic outlines of what was really happening, but as long as it remained something terrible and yet remote, something whose horror and blood might descend upon me at any moment, I was compelled to give my entire imagination over to it."

White excuses for lynching blacks varied. Many had gendered dimensions. Hardworking, church-going black men who, in an effort to conform to middle-class standards of manliness, accumulated property thereby gaining the sense of independence and self-sufficiency that property ownership bestowed, were often the targets of the mob. But more often than not, victims of lynching were men who wittingly or unwittingly transgressed white imposed standards of interracial social etiquette, standards that demanded that black men assume a deferential, if not obsequious, demeanor in their dealings with whites. Incidents of lynching in the South were often directly tied to assumptions about black male sexual aggressiveness and white female innocence and sexual vulnerability. Merely looking directly at a white women on the street might result in a black man being hung or burned alive.

Lynch mobs were made up of rich and poor, the obscure and socially prominent, tenant farmers as well as merchants and ministers. For the most part, the vigilantes were male. That did not mean, however, that women remained uninvolved. In some cases, they made the accusations that led to lynching. In others, they participated as observers, caught up in the same hysterical enthusiasm for blood sacrifice as the men who actually threw the hangman's rope over the tree and used a knife to disembowl or castrate their unfortunate victim.

Both the charge of rape and practice of lynching allowed white men to reassert and maintain their dominance in southern society and thereby preserve their sense of manliness. Lynchings, theoretically carried out to protect the honor and sexual virtue of idealized white womanhood, reinforced the idea that whatever opportunities the Civil War and its aftermath had given women to demonstrate their economic competence and assert their independence, they were still in need of male protection. The price they were expected to pay for that protection was high. In return for the assurance that white men would commit murder to defend them, they were expected to subordinate themselves to male authority. It also meant that women were likely to internalize the idea that they were inherently weak and incapable of taking care of themselves. One practical effect of constructing womanhood around those characteristics was to reinforce the idea that a woman's place was

in the home where she could be sheltered from harm. Another was to undermine a woman's ability to control her own sex life and to place that control in the hands of men. As long as blacks could be victimized by the threat of lynching, the position of the southern patriarch was secure and the social space allowed to southern women was limited.

It should not be assumed from the above discussion that interracial violence occurred only in the South. During the period just following World War I, racial antagonisms in urban areas in the North exploded into large-scale race riots. Between 1916 and 1919, southern blacks, deprived of education and employment opportunities, segregated and disenfranchised, began to leave the South. In northern cities, they could find jobs, wages were high, and politicians competed for their votes. There they hoped to reclaim their manhood. Black men saw northern cities as places where they could assert their independence. They hoped that by working for wages for northern employers, they could fulfill their obligation to provide their families with some degree of comfort and financial security. And by registering to vote, they hoped to avail themselves of the responsibilities and privileges of male citizenship.

As a result of this so-called "Great Migration," southern blacks poured into the cities like Chicago. Not surprisingly, the Windy City's white working-class men did not welcome these new arrivals. Considering blacks intellectually inferior to whites, lacking in moral and civic virtue, and shiftless, they resented the fact that they had to compete with them for jobs and housing not to mention political influence, all of which were critical to establishing their own claim to manhood.

It did not take long for racial tensions to begin mounting. As long as America was fighting a world war, there were plenty of jobs to go around. But the ethnic immigrant population who lived in the tenement districts around Chicago's stockyards was unwilling to share their housing with blacks or to socialize with them. Blacks who wandered into white neighborhoods did so at their own risk, and those who escaped without black eyes and bruises were lucky.

When the war ended, competition for jobs increased. And the continuing emigration of southern blacks put a strain on housing stock as black neighborhoods began to bulge at the seams. On July 27, 1919, the tension between Chicago's white and black working population came to a head when five black boys, swimming in Lake Michigan, floated past the imaginary boundary that separated their beach from that patronized by whites. When their presence was discovered, a man started throwing stones at them. He hit one of the boys on the head. The dazed swimmer slowly sank beneath the surface of the water and drowned.

What followed was, according to the *Chicago Defender,* Chicago's leading black newspaper, "a carnival of death." Pent-up racial hatred exploded. Whites attacked blacks. Blacks responded in kind. For many of the victims, it was a matter of being in the wrong place at the wrong time. The *Defender* reported, for example, that a young black woman carrying a baby was trying to board a streetcar when the white mob spotted her. They "seized her, beat her, slashed her body into ribbons and beat the baby's brains out against a telegraph pole. Not satisfied with this, one rioter severed her breasts, and a white youngster bore them aloft on a pole, triumphantly, while a crowd hooted gleefully." Much the same thing occurred the next day when an Italian peddler made the mistake of turning his horse and wagon onto 36th Street. Awaiting him was an angry mob of about 4000 blacks, who began by throwing stones at him and ended by dragging him from his wagon and stabbing him to death. Although both victims met the same ultimate fate, there was a gendered difference in the way the mob treated their bodies. Chicago's white rioters, like their southern brethren, clearly defined black womanhood in sexual terms. Geographic location does not appear to have inhibited white men from believing that their gender and race gave them the right to exploit the body of a black woman

for their own pleasure and to publicly display their power to possess her.

After almost a week of pitched battles between whites and blacks resulting in vast numbers of assaults, looting, and arson, peace returned to the city. When it was all over, 23 blacks and 15 whites were dead, over five hundred people had been injured, and about a thousand had no place to live.

It is difficult to determine who participated in the mobs that ruled the streets of Chicago during the 1919 race riot. Those who reported specific acts of violence were more likely to identify the gender of the victims than they were the gender of those who attacked them. It seems likely that most of those who initiated the attacks on property and their fellow citizens were male. Given the extent of the violence and what we know about mob psychology, it is also reasonable to assume that the kind of women, who were used to life on the streets where boldness, public display of anger, and aggressive behavior were not necessarily considered unfeminine, also participated in the mob's violence.

THE GENDERED NATURE OF DOMESTIC VIOLENCE

The home has been the site of violence ever since the colonial period. A number of factors have encouraged this situation. American society was founded on the principles that respect for male authority was fundamental to the maintenance of social order and that the male head of household had the right to compel obedience from those who lived under his roof. As a result, manliness was constructed in part around a man's ability to discipline the members of his household for disruptive or disorderly behavior, willfulness, or lack of deference. A man who, for whatever reason, was unable or unwilling to fulfill that obligation found himself unmanned in the eyes of his friends and neighbors.

Secondly, manliness has typically been defined in terms of physicality. From the colonial period through the present, physical strength and the ability to use it to express frustration or anger has been incorporated into the definition of what it meant to be a man. It is true that men with refined sensibilities made an effort to minimize the opportunities for abusing this male privilege by defining manhood in terms of self-control and rational decision making. But not all men followed their lead. The result was that in working-class neighborhoods as well as those in the South and on the frontier, many men defined masculinity in terms of physical prowess and the willingness to use it in the pursuit of self-interest.

At the same time, prevailing definitions of femininity that characterized women as weak, passive, and dependent made it difficult for women to protect themselves against being abused. Women who understood that their relative lack of economic and political power left them dependent upon the good will of men and who internalized that powerlessness had little to gain by trying to physically defend themselves or running away. If placating their husbands did not work, their only recourse was to file charges against them. In that case, they simply transferred responsibility for their safety to policemen, prosecuting attorneys, judges, and all-male juries by appealing to their obligation to protect "the weaker sex." Even if a battered woman was willing to follow through with the prosecution of her batterer, she found that her ability to convince a jury that the beatings that he had inflicted were unjustified depended upon her ability to prove that she conformed in every way to her community's ideas about what constituted model womanhood. Only those who were able to convincingly present themselves as defenseless and undeserving of abuse were likely to see their abusers convicted. A woman who fought back or neglected her domestic duties by running away could not count on a judicial system run by men to provide them with much protection. Thus, complementary gender ideals combined with the unequal distribution of power between men and women helped to create an environment in which domestic abuse could occur.

Ideas about family privacy simply complicated the situation. The belief that "a man's home was his castle" carried with it the assumption that what he did in his own home was no one else's business. So if he decided to beat his wife or children, he could safely assume that in all probability no one would interfere.

Concern about domestic violence has waxed and waned over time. And consensus about what constituted inappropriate or unwarranted use of force as a way of disciplining family members has been difficult to achieve. For example, colonial New Englanders were theoretically opposed to wife beating. Community leaders considered a man who abused his wife to be an embarrassment. A wife beater, in their view, broke Divine law and dishonored God. They were perfectly willing to admit that there were unruly women who needed to be disciplined. But they suspected that the husband was not the right person to do it. In any case, they considered wife beating both antisocial and disruptive to the peace of their communities.

Despite the fact that they had reservations about wife beating, however, they did not necessarily consider it a crime. Indeed, they permitted it within certain limits because they believed that an orderly household was necessary for an orderly society. The limits varied depending on the community, but conventional wisdom held that a man could beat his wife as a form of discipline if he used a stick no bigger than his thumb. If he observed this social convention, an abusive husband was unlikely to be called to account for his behavior unless he killed his wife in the process.

In the nineteenth century, states like Tennessee, Massachusetts, and New Mexico passed laws against wife beating. But male legislators were vague about what constituted inappropriate physical abuse, and punishment for the crime was rare because male juries were unwilling to impose high fines on or imprison abusers.

Complicating attempts to reduce incidents of domestic violence was the fact that attitudes toward this particular form of violence and what should be done about it were often class specific. Men continued to have the power to abuse their wives and children. But the context in which they did so depended upon where they lived and what social class they belonged to. By the 1850s in the urban North, for example, men in the middle and upper classes were beginning to idealize the home as a place of peace and harmony and marriage as an intimate partnership based on love, companionship, and mutual respect. These attitudes combined with the belief that a "real man" could control and rule his family without resorting to force meant that wife beating came to be regarded as unmanly among those who lived in some degree of economic comfort.

That did not mean, of course, that middle- and upper-class men did not beat their wives. It only meant that in their social circle it was unacceptable to do so. The power of public opinion, however, did not do much to inhibit men of means, who felt provoked beyond endurance by their wives nagging, inadequate housekeeping, extravagance, or unwillingness to engage in sex on demand, from taking out their frustrations and anger on their defenseless spouses. When they did so, they were rarely called to account for their abusive behavior. Such men beat their wives with impunity because they could do so in the privacy of their homes and could count on the fact that their victims were not likely to report what they had done. They understood as well as their wives that in order to maintain their social status, both of them had to conform at least outwardly to class expectations. So only the most desperate of middle- and upper-class victims were tempted to expose the fact that they were being physically abused. In doing so, they had to admit, first, that they had not used good judgment in choosing their spouse and, second, that they were incapable of fulfilling their womanly obligation to maintain the peace and tranquility of their households and preserve the love and affection of their husbands. Shame and fear of social humiliation combined with economic dependence meant that "ladies" were more likely than not to bear victimization in silence in order to maintain their claim to womanliness and to keep up the appearance of gentility and respectability.

While some working men, like their middle-class counterparts, valued domestic harmony and avoided using their male prerogatives to brutalize their wives and children, not all did. The working class was dubbed the "working class" partly because some wage workers were unable or unwilling to conform to middle-class standards of behavior. As a result, they developed their own set of gender ideals. In some ways emasculated by wage labor that left them relatively poor and powerless, there were some working class men who considered it fundamental to their definition of manliness and necessary for the maintenance of their self-esteem to discipline their wives and children by force if they thought it necessary. For them, physical strength, male dominance, and the right to pursue pleasure where and when they wished comprised the essence of manliness. If, for example, a married man decided to spend his earnings buying drinks for himself and his friends at the local tavern, he considered it his right to do so. If his wife complained, she did so at her own peril. Police and court records indicate that wife abuse often stemmed from the struggle over who would control the economic resources in working-class households. In places like New York City, wife battering was most likely to occur on Thursdays, the day before payday when there was no money in the house to by food or fuel. It was on Thursday night that wives were most likely to berate their husbands for being inadequate providers and to be beaten as a result.

The fact that it was difficult in working-class neighborhoods to keep abuse a secret meant that it was possible for working-class women to hope that her friends and neighbors might interfere in domestic quarrels and prevent abuse from occurring. Blacks and poor whites in the South, for example, often spent as much of their time out of doors as inside their cabins. And the presence of friends and neighbors was an integral part of their daily life. They left their doors and windows open, and they never knew who was going to walk through the door unannounced. Under such circumstances, it was hard to keep incidents of domestic violence a secret. Neighbors and kin were not likely to be totally ignorant of what was going on and had the opportunity to form an opinion concerning whether or not a man was abusing his power within the family. What little evidence exists seems to suggest that if they felt that the victim was generally well behaved and had faithfully performed her duties as a wife and mother, they might offer her shelter, threaten the abuser with retribution, or even resort to violence themselves to physically punish him for his abusive behavior.

Working people living in city tenements responded to wife and child abuse in much the same way. It was hard for them to ignore the screams of women and children who were being abused. Tenements were crowded, their walls were thin, and women shared information about their lives and those of their neighbors as they sat on their stoops and watched their children play in the streets. When a man and woman quarreled, their neighbors generally knew what the fight was about. And if a man was beating the members of his family, the whole neighborhood knew that too. But as in the case of those who lived in rural areas, what neighbors were willing to do about it depended upon the degree to which battering victims were able to convince them that their conformity to gender expectations gave them claim to protection.

The creation of social services agencies in the early twentieth century went a long way toward exposing the prevalence of domestic violence. But gender constructions were slow to change, and battering has continued despite the best efforts of social reformers to end it.

Battering is not the only form of violence that took place in American households. Historians have paid very little attention to the crime of incest and its relationship to gender. What literature exists indicates, however, that it was almost exclusively a male crime di-rected at female relatives. That this should have been the case is not particularly surprising. First, manliness in American culture has often been defined in terms of sexual prowess and conquest. Secondly, conflicting definitions of what it means to be a "good" girl left young female family members vulnerable to the sexual advances of their male relatives. On one hand, being a "good girl" meant being sexually naïve and chaste. On the other, being "good" meant being obedient and deferential to the men in their families. No matter how they responded to the advances of their predatory male relatives, incest victims found it impossible to live up to what was expected of them since they could not maintain their chastity without disobeying their fathers, uncles, cousins, or brothers.

From the colonial period to the present in the United States, incest was always recognized as an abuse of power within in the family. But while Americans may have been horrified when cases of incest were brought to their attention, they found it difficult to clearly articulate and define what they considered to be the limits of male privilege and power over their female kin.

Before the Civil War, northerners were apparently more concerned about doing this than southerners. That was perhaps because southerners placed extremely high value on family autonomy, they often lived great distances from each other, and the line between appropriate and inappropriate expressions of sexuality within the family was complicated by a relatively relaxed attitude on the part of the southern elite toward first-cousin marriages. In the planter class, the desire to concentrate property within the family and maintain kin solidarity meant that it was not unusual for a planter's son to marry his first cousin. The result was that the socially prominent, including legislators and jurists who wrote and enforced the law, did not necessarily regard sexual liaisons between close relatives as undesirable. That is not to say that clear cases of father/daughter incest were considered less offensive in the South than they were in the North. Southerners and northerners alike considered incest to be a crime reflecting bestial behavior that, in the words of one Texas jurist, reduced "man from his boastful superiority of a moral, rational being, to a level with brutal creation." Nevertheless, in the nineteenth century at least, there appear to have been different standards for judging whether or not sexual connections were incestuous under the law. In general, southern courts demanded both evidence of the use of physical force on the part of the perpetrator and corroboration from an outside witness to convict a man of incest. Since family members were often reluctant to testify in incest trials and wives were prohibited by law from testifying against their husbands, incest convictions were difficult to obtain. Northern courts were much more likely than those in the South to accept a female child's word that incest had occurred and to take into consideration the influence of psychological coercion. Nevertheless, incest remained a secret vice well into the twentieth century, a crime that was rarely prosecuted and even more rarely punished.

THE GENDERED NATURE OF MURDER AND RAPE

The way Americans have constructed gender has had an important influence on our attitudes toward murder. Throughout American history, men have been more likely than women to commit murder and to be convicted of the crime. It is not that women are less capable of killing another human being than men are. It is simply that definitions of femininity that equate being a woman with being warm, loving, nurturing, weak, and unaggressive have apparently both inhibited women from acting on an impulse to kill and discouraged juries from convicting them when they do.

Ideas about what constitutes manliness have not protected men in the same way. In places where masculinity was defined in terms of aggression, competition, and concern

for personal honor, incidents of interpersonal violence were everyday events. Such was the case in the working-class neighborhoods of New York City in the nineteenth century. Take the murder of William Poole, for example. On the night of February 24, 1855 John Morrissey, a prize fighter, sat drinking with his friends in a working-class barroom called Stanwix Hall located in the Bowery when William Poole entered the saloon. There was no love lost between the two men. So it is not surprising that Morrissey, drunk and looking for a fight, approached Poole, argued with him, and eventually called him "a cowardly son of a bitch." Poole responded in kind, calling his antagonist a "damned liar." Then he threatened Morrissey with a gun. Someone in the crowd passed a second gun to Morrissey, but before they could kill each other, the police arrived and took them down to the station house.

Both of them were released from custody later that night. Morrissey went home, but Poole returned to Stanwix Hall to resume his drinking. It was there that Morrissey's friends found him. After exchanging insults, they pulled guns on each other and in the scuffle that followed Poole was killed and four others were wounded.

Barroom brawls in places like the Bowery were common. The only thing that distinguishes this one from the others is that it was more deadly than most. Men like Morrissey and Poole constructed their manliness in a working-class culture that valued characteristics that were likely to lead to violent behavior, injury, and death. Theirs was a rough and tumble world, where physical prowess and personal courage were highly regarded among men. They lived in an unpleasant, even dangerous environment, where accidents killed and maimed, disease disfigured and incapacitated, and hunger, poverty, and desperation were common. In their world, manliness was defined in terms of an individual's ability to face cruelty, pain, and death with a certain amount of stoicism. The need to earn the esteem of other men meant that a man in this environment had to be willing to respond both verbally and physically to real or perceived insult or face public humiliation. Unlike many middle- and upper-class men who typically defined masculinity in terms of self-control, rational decision making, and a sense of social responsibility, there was a segment of the working class who judged men by their willingness to spontaneously put their life on the line for their friends. Unconcerned that outsiders might view them as bullies and ruffians, they lived in an intensely masculine world where loyalty, defiance of authority, and willingness to fight were the measures of a man.

Life in the city was no less dangerous for women. On April 10, 1836, Helen Jewett was found murdered in her bed in a brothel on Thomas Street in lower Manhattan. The daughter of a poor shoemaker from a village in Maine, she had been making her living as a prostitute ever since she arrived in the city at the age of seventeen.

One of her regular clients was Richard P. Robinson, the outwardly respectable, nineteen-year-old son of a Connecticut legislator. A clerk, he, like many other young working men in the city, lived a double life defined by two very distinct versions of masculinity. His employer, Joseph Hoxie, an eminently respectable merchant with offices in Maiden Lane, expected him be hard working, sober, and honest. In the male world of business, a man's reputation was built upon his willingness to delay personal gratification and live a life of moral rectitude. But when young clerks like Robinson left their offices for the day, they were free to indulge themselves by roaming the streets of the city in pursuit of pleasure. Many young capitalists-in-training like Robinson in cities like New York lived together in boarding houses free from adult supervision and spent their leisure time in theaters, restaurants, brothels, and bars where they drank, quarreled, and flirted with the women they met on the streets.

Robinson appears to have been the last person to see Jewett alive, so when the authorities found evidence that connected him to the crime, they indicted him for murder. Particu-larly damning were a series of letters that Jewett and Robinson wrote to one another. They revealed that the relationship between the two had been an extremely troubled one, characterized by manipulations, deceptions, and jealousies on both sides.

Robinson was tried in June. But despite the testimony of prostitutes who implicated him in the crime, a jury of twelve men found him not guilty. The acquittal had as much to do with assumptions about class and gender as it did with the evidence. Throughout the investigation, Robinson played the role of the wrongly accused gentleman. It was impossible for him to deny that he had spent his free time and a considerable amount of money associating with a prostitute. The excuse presumably was that he was a fun-loving and virile young man, not yet in a financial position to propose marriage to and set up a household with a respectable young woman. Alone in the city with no one to protect him from temptation and profligacy, he was not alone in his waywardness. The city was full of such young men.

The all-male jury was apparently willing to disregard Robinson's youthful indiscretions. But they were not willing to ignore the moral lapses of the prostitutes who testified against him. The prevailing assumption among these respectable citizens of New York was that a woman's willingness to sell sexual services rendered her unreliable as a witness. The jury was willing to discount the eye-witness testimony of what they considered to be disreputable women in favor of the rather vague testimony of Robinson's sexually promiscuous friends and acquaintances. In the end, it was the double standard of sexuality which privileged men rather than the burden of evidence that helps to explain the acquittal of Robinson.

Concern about the expression of sexuality also influenced popular attitudes toward gender and rape. If court records accurately reflect incidence of rape, it appears that the crime was rare in places like colonial New England. It is unclear why this was so. One explanation is that women simply didn't report rapes to the authorities. Another is that the social organization of New England towns discouraged men from assaulting women sexually. New Englanders lived in small, tightly knit communities. Adults were able to closely supervise the activities of young women. And the kind of privacy which might protect a man engaged in sexual assault was virtually nonexistent.

Other factors that may have played a role in discouraging women from accusing men of rape have more to do with class and gender conventions. The belief that being male brought with it certain prerogatives may have given men of wealth and influence the assurance that they had the right to demand sexual services from women whose social status was inferior to their own. Women, taught from birth to defer to men, may not have defined forced sex as rape, particularly if the rapist was a man of some social standing and authority. This, combined with the relatively relaxed attitudes toward the expression of sexuality during the colonial period, may have led female victims of rape to doubt that all-male juries would believe that they had not welcomed the sexual advances of the men they accused of assaulting them. The prevailing assumption at the time was that women like men had healthy sexual appetites. That meant that only clear evidence of resistance could convince an all-male jury that the woman was telling the truth when she claimed to have been raped.

The growth of cities after the American Revolution encouraged an increase in the incidence of rape. And changing attitudes toward gender and female sexuality made the successful prosecution of rapists even more difficult beginning in the late eighteenth century. The case of Henry Bedlow of New York City illustrates the point. Bedlow, a notorious libertine and man about town, raped Lanah Sawyer, a seamstress and the daughter of a sea captain in 1793. Despite the evidence against him, he was acquitted by an all-male jury in less than fifteen minutes.

The case is significant because it illustrates the degree to which the practical, every day definition of rape was shaped by shifting and contradictory, often class-based attitudes toward male prerogatives and responsibilities and the expression of sexuality. For most of American history, men have been caught between two sets of expectations in terms of their relationship with women. On one hand, their claim to manhood was based on their ability to protect them. On the other, their virility was measured by their success in pursuing and dominating women. There were also two prevailing and quite conflicting ideas about the sexual "nature" of women. One viewed them as lusty, and the other that held that they had little if any interest in sex at all. During the colonial period, it was assumed that most women welcomed sexual encounters. By the nineteenth century, conventional wisdom had it that middle- and upper-class women were much more inhibited in their expression of sexuality than their less privileged sisters.

This attitude combined with the life style of middle- and upper-class women meant that they were much less likely to be the victims of rape than working-class women. Their dress and bearing, both of which were intended to testify to their social position and inaccessibility, discouraged any man with whom they were unacquainted from approaching them. They also spent much of their time in their homes and hesitated to appear in public unaccompanied. Working-class women were much more vulnerable to the unwelcome sexual advances of men. They spent most of their waking hours on the streets, working, shopping, and socializing. And assumptions about their lack of sexual inhibitions made them fair game for any man who was willing to approach them.

Successful prosecutions for rape were rare throughout the nineteenth and early twentieth centuries. It was not difficult for middle-class women who claimed to have been sexually assaulted to present themselves as physically weak and morally upright because juries expected them to have those qualities. It was much more problematic for a working-class woman to convince a jury that she was the victim of rape. Out of necessity, she often associated with strangers. And her ability to survive on the streets, on the job, and in the tenements required her to be self-reliant and assertive. Indeed, having successfully fought off an attacker in an attempted rape simply confirmed in the eyes of some that she was capable of taking care of herself. The result was that a working-class woman, often assumed by virtue of her class to be at the very least flirtatious if not sexually promiscuous, had a difficult time convincing juries she had not welcomed the attentions of the accused.

In the late 1960s and 1970s feminists began a campaign intended to challenge those gender conventions that had been used to shift the blame from rapists to the victims of rape. It was partly through their efforts that sexually aggressive men were increasingly held responsible for their behavior.

Summary

From the colonial period to the present, American men have been more likely than American women to engage in acts of violence and to be held accountable for their violent behavior. What that means is that in American society, violence has been gendered male. A variety of factors contributed to this fact. First, masculinity has often been defined in terms of aggression, competition, physical prowess, and sexual conquest. Second, throughout most of American history, white manhood has been defined in terms of racial dominance. And, third, during the same period, definitions of femininity have idealized women as loving, passive, and weak and therefore, unlikely to behave violently. The result has been that men who engage in violent behavior in some ways confirm their manliness, and women who do so abdicate their claim to femininity.

Class considerations and attitudes toward the expression of sexuality have only complicated this picture. For example, men who wished to be considered respectable and genteel were held to standards of manly behavior that privileged cooperation, self-restraint, and rational decision-making over physical aggression. Their efforts to conform to such standards meant that it was unlikely that they would participate in acts of violence. Working-class women who defined femininity in terms of assertiveness and the freedom to express their sexuality when and where they wished were more likely than their middle-class sisters not only to engage in violent behavior but to be the victims of it.

As a result of these circumstances, relations between whites and blacks as well as men and women have been plagued by violence. In the South both before and after the Civil War, white men defined masculinity in terms of the power they had over blacks and their obligation to protect the honor of their wives and daughters. Their efforts to exert their power and fulfill their obligations resulted in incidents of rape and murder. In the twentieth-century North, the determination of white men to preserve their exclusive claim to manliness in terms of economic opportunity and political power sometimes resulted in race riots like the one that took place in Chicago in 1919.

The home has also been the site of violence throughout American history. Typically, though not always, domestic violence has been perpetrated by men. There were various reasons for this. Law and social practice have traditionally upheld men's right to rule their families and to discipline their wives, children, and servants. The construction of manliness around the idea of physicality reinforced their belief that they could use force to compel obedience from those in their households. And the regard for privacy meant that men had the space to inflict their will on their dependents and the assurance that outsiders were not likely to interfere. The construction of femininity around the principles of dependence and passivity inhibited the ability of women to protect themselves from the abuse of men. These factors combined with the reluctance or inability of legislators and judges to agree on what constituted the inappropriate or unwarranted use of force has meant that until recently little has been done to expose the prevalence of domestic violence and identify effective strategies to end it.

Because of the unequal distribution of power between men and women and the way that masculinity has been constructed, women have been more likely than men to be victimized by the kind of violence described in this chapter. Gender prescriptions have had an important influence on public attitudes toward female victims of male abuse. Women who are most likely to garner the sympathy of others in cases of domestic violence or rape are those who are able to demonstrate that they generally conformed to standards of womanhood that made their victimization unacceptable. Obedient wives who did their best to fulfill their domestic obligations were much more likely than those who did not to convince all-male juries that the beatings that they endured at the hands of their husbands were unwarranted. And a woman who charged a man with rape was much more likely to see him convicted if she could demonstrate that she did not welcome his attentions and had been careful to preserve her chastity.

DOCUMENT

The Ku Klux Klan and Violence During Reconstruction

After the Civil War, many northerners emigrated to the former confederate states in order to "reconstruct" the South. There they served as agents of the Freedman's Bureau, helped to run Republican dominated state governments, and worked to establish schools for newly freed slaves. A. P. Huggins was among them. At the time of his testimony before a special committee established by Congress to investigate Klan violence in the South, he was a tax collector and superintendent of schools for Monroe County, Mississippi.

Men like Huggins were very unpopular among southern whites, many of whom resented their presence and had no interest in doing anything to improve the lives of ex-slaves. So members of the Ku Klux Klan did what they could to drive them out. What follows is a description of the treatment Huggins received at the hands of the Klan. The interviewer is Luke Potter Poland, the chairman of the Joint Select Committee and a member of the U.S. House of Representatives from Vermont.

What assumptions did Huggins make about southern gender conventions? What role did ideas about honor, integrity, and manliness play in the confrontation between Huggins and the Klan members?

Source: Excerpts from the testimony of A. P. Huggins before the Joint Select Committee to Inquire into the Condition of Affairs in the Late Insurrectionary States, Mississippi, Vol. I (Washington, DC: Government Printing Office, 1872), 271–73.

Question. State the transaction fully; begin and give us the whole of it.

Answer. I was warned during the day of the 9th that the Ku-Klux had been riding the night before for me. . . . A colored man . . . asked me to go out of the country, for they knew that the Ku-Klux would get me if they could. I laughed at their fears, and had no idea that they would attack a United States officer. . . . at 9 o'clock that night I was in bed at Mr. Ross's house. At 10 o'clock I was awakened by a loud call out of doors upon Mr. Ross for "the man who was in the house." I stepped to my window, which was on the ground floor, and saw that the premises were completely covered with men dressed in white; I knew then I was with the Ku-Klux. . . . I opened the door myself, and stood where I could see them. I asked them if it was me they wanted, and what they wanted of me. They answered that their business was with me altogether; that they were Ku-Klux, or the law-makers of that country, and that they wanted to talk with me. . . . They said that as I was in their power, like all other men, I must obey and come out. I told them that I did not recognize their power over me, and that under no circumstances would I venture out; . . . I told them, then, that if I could do anything to hasten their departure, to get them away from the house, I would do so, as the family was scared; that if they had any warnings to give me I would hear them, and then do just as I chose about obeying them. They answered that they could not do that, that it was against the rules of their camp to give their warnings in the presence of women and children. I told them that that being the case, it was useless to argue any further, that I would not go out. I then stepped inside and shut my door. They then became very furious, and ordered Mr. Ross to bring me out; told him that he was as much under their orders as I was; that he must understand that they made the laws there, and that he must obey them as well as myself. . . . I saw them light a fire, as I supposed for the purpose of kindling a fire at the house, and they went on the other side of the house out of my sight; I cannot say what they did there.

Question. You saw the light?

Answer. I saw the light of the fire they kindled. Mr. Ross came to me then and asked me to leave the house; said that his family was frightened; that his wife was in spasms; that his children were terribly frightened; and he asked me to leave the house for his family's sake. I told him to quiet his family's fears, that I would certainly save his house, that I would not let them go to that extent. . . . I then stepped to the door again, and opened it, and asked them if they would make me any promise. They said they merely wanted to talk with me. I asked them what promises or pledges they would make; they said they would pledge me that I should not be injured in any way at all; that they would not only pledge me that, but they would pledge Mr. Ross. . . . I asked them to give their pledges to Mr. Ross and to give me assurances that I would not be injured. They said, "Not a hair of your head shall be injured; we are now as anxious as you are to get through this business, and let the fears on the part of the family cease." I had not much confidence in their promises and assurances; I knew what kind of men they were. . . .

Question. Were all in the yard, or were more outside? . . .

Answer. There were one hundred and twenty in the crowd altogether, as I numbered them. The gate was closed, and I went down to the fence. . . . When I got down to the fence I asked the chief if he would now state my little bit of warning, that I wanted to hear it and be gone. He said the decree of the camp was that I should leave the county within ten days, and leave the State; that I could not stay there. He then gave me the decree, pronounced it out in a very pompous manner. . . .

He told me that the rule of the camp was, first, to give the warning; second, to enforce obedience to their laws by whipping; third, to kill by the Klan altogether; and, fourth, if that was not done, and if the one who was warned still refused to obey, then they were sworn to kill him, either privately, by assassination, or otherwise. I was then warned again that I would have to go, that I could not stay there, that there was no such thing as getting around one of their decrees; that if I undertook to stay there I certainly should die. They repeated again that I could not live there under any circumstances; they gave me ten days to go away.... One of them said, "Well, sir, what do you say to our warning? Will you leave?" I told them I should leave Monroe County at my pleasure, and not until I got ready....

Question. Was Mr. Ross along?

Answer. He was along; he went with me. He said, "Remember your promise; you must not do anything to harm the man at all; your promise is out."... They ordered me to take off my coat, which I refused to do; they then took it off by force. After that they asked if I consented to leave, and I still refused.... They then showed me a rope with a noose, and said that was for such as myself who were stubborn; that if I did not consent to leave I should die, that dead men told no tales. At this time I saw a man coming from toward the horses; ... he had a stirrup-strap some inch and a quarter in width, and at least an eighth of an inch thick; it was very stout leather; the stirrup was a wooden one. As he came up he threw down the wooden stirrup and came on toward me, and I saw that he was intending to hit me with the strap, that that was the weapon they intended to use first. He came on, and without further ceremony at all—I was in my shirt sleeves—he struck me two blows, calling out, "One, two," and said, "Now, boys, count." They counted every lash they gave me. The first man gave me ten blows himself, standing on my left side, striking over my left arm and on my back; the next one gave me five blows. Then a fresh hand took it and gave me ten blows; that made twenty-five. They then stopped, and asked me again if I would leave the county. I still refused, and told them that now they had commenced they could go just as far as they pleased; that all had been done that I cared for; that I would as soon die then as to take what I had taken. They continued to strike their blows on my back in the same way until they had reached fifty. None of them struck more than ten blows, some of them only three, and some as low as two. They said they all wanted to get a chance at me; that I was stubborn, and just such a man as they liked to pound. When they had struck me fifty blows they stopped again and asked me if I would leave; I told them I would not. Then one of the strongest and most burly in the crowd took the strap himself and gave me twenty-five blows without stopping; that made seventy-five; I heard them say, "Seventy-five." At that time my strength gave way entirely; I grew dizzy and cold; I asked for my coat; that is the last I remember for several minutes....

A Murder Case in 1880s Pittsburgh

William Donaldson was a printer living in a working-class neighborhood in Pittsburgh in the 1880s. He had been courting a young woman that a newspaper reporter identified on July 25 as Annie Stippy and then on July 30 as Annie Stippich. On the evening of July 24, Donaldson called at Annie's home and asked that she accompany him next door to a house that her father was having built so that they could have a private conversation. There they had a quarrel, and he shot her. She died a few days later. Reprinted below are excerpts from two articles that appeared in a local Pittsburgh newspaper describing the incident.

What role did ideas about gender play in the reporter's description of Donaldson and Stippy/Stippich and their relationship? What role did ideas about gender play in her apparent murder?

Cupid's Bullets

Romance reached a bloody denouement out in the Fourteenth ward last night. It was among quiet and respectable people which made it all the more sad. Everybody knew that the tall and manly William Donaldson was the lover of pretty little Annie Stippy. For four or five years past they have been constantly in each other's company. The neighborhood came to look upon them as really betrothed, and there was that respect shown to them that is usually the lot of a plighted couple in a friendly world. To all appearances they were writing their story of love without blurring a line or tearing a page. He is now 22 years of age and lives with his parents on Ann street, between Seneca and Madison streets. Sober and industrious, he earned his living as a printer at the job office of Murdock & Kerr, on Ninth street. He is said to be an unusually

intelligent compositor. She is the daughter of Mr. John Stippy, a middle-aged German, rather well off in financial respects. Scarcely 20 years old, she is a pretty-faced girl, sunny-tempered and becoming in deportment.

The Shooting

Mr. Donaldson spent most of his evenings with Miss Stippy. The lady's home is on Forbes street immediately in front of Mr. Donaldson's house. On an adjoining lot Mr. Stippy is having a new house erected. It was in this unoccupied and partly finished building that the couple happened to be last evening about 8 o'clock. While the people in the locality were sitting out on their doorsteps they heard a loud pistol shot in the house. Then Miss Stippy came running out screaming that she was wounded. She ran into her own home and dropped upon the lounge in the sitting-room. Her parents and sisters gathered about her and the next moment Donaldson himself dashed into the apartment, pushed them away and fell on his knees at the wounded girl's side. He was crying softly. Within a few moments more Constable Robert McAdams, who had heard the shooting, entered the

Source: Excerpts from "Cupid's Bullets: Wm. Donaldson Shoots His Betrothed," *Pittsburgh Commercial Gazette,* July 25, 1884 and "Her Secret: Miss Stippich's Death Brings a Revelation," *Pittsburgh Commercial Gazette,* July 30, 1884.

house, and taking everything in at a glance placed McDonald [sic] under arrest. The young man refused to leave his wounded sweetheart, and for a few moments it looked as though he would offer resistance. But he was finally induced to accompany the officer to the Fourteenth ward police station, where he is at present confined. He claimed that the shooting was accidental, repeating time after time, "I didn't go to do it." This was all he would say to the officer.

What Is Said About It

Dr. Christy was called in. He found the bullet had entered at the right hip and penetrated the bowels. It was an extremely dangerous wound, and he deemed it inexpedient to probe for the ball. The revolver used was a 32 or 38-calibre Smith & Wesson. One chamber in the weapon remained filled after the shooting. The doctor forbid any conversation with the patient. The order was unnecessary, because she would absolutely say nothing. She was silent while under the doctor's care, and volunteered not even a word of information to her parents. At midnight she was resting easy with no immediate prospect of death, although the outcome is very questionable.

The father of the girl appeared before Alderman Jones and made information against Donaldson charging him with felonious shooting.

While Donaldson claims the affair to have been accidental, street rumors said otherwise. One of these reports was to the effect that while in the unoccupied building he asked Miss Stippy to marry him, she refused firmly but friendly and he deliberately shot her. Still another intimation was that they are already married. Chief of Police Braun said he had been informed that it was intentional. Still, there is nothing in their previous intercourse to warrant such a belief, as both had always seemed to be perfectly congenial and happy together and the parents never knew them to have quarreled. . . .

Her Secret

Miss Annie Stippich died yesterday at 8 o'clock A.M. Her death tore away the heavy veil of mystery that hung about her betrothal to William Donaldson and his shooting her. Although she passed into eternity with a terrible and unsuspected secret locked up in her heart, it was revealed to the world one hour after her demise by the attending physician who had discovered it two days before. While he was administering to her wants on Sunday night she was unconsciously delivered of a child, a three months' fetus, her injuries having caused premature birth. She died without knowledge of the fact. Dr. Christie took it, and, telling no living soul except the girl's brother, kept it until her death and then informed the Coroner. The parents and members of both families, with the exception of the young brother, were ignorant of the fact until late yesterday afternoon. In all that Miss Stippich said about the tragedy and her relations with Mr. Donaldson she breathed no word or hint that gave rise to the slightest suspicion of an undue intimacy existing with him or any others.

The Girl's Story

Her second statement, taken by 'Squire Jones as a dying deposition, has now been given to the public. It is as follows:

Personally appeared before me, an alderman in and for said city, Annie Stippich, and, at her home, who being duly sworn according to law, doth depose and say: In last February, he, Donaldson, took me by the throat, but he left me go after. He did this in an angry manner, and he did this because I did not stop at his house. Some time afterward he grabbed me by the throat, and would have grabbed me again the second time if Miss Fehl had not interfered. Then he said, "If I do anything I will go through with it." He came after me once since with a knife, and I ran to his mother's house, and she interfered with him and blamed him. He told her to mind her own business. He accused me of not being true to him. The last time he pulled a revolver out of his pocket I asked him what he meant, and he said he would show what he meant, and said: "I want to put an end to this." "Oh, Willie! what do you mean?" and I tried to get the revolver from him and he would not give it to me. Then he walked off. I was shot, but I did not see him shooting; but I guess he wanted to shoot me. Once before this, some time last winter, he was going to shoot me, but I did not see the revolver then; but afterwards he acknowledged he did have a revolver that night that I am speaking about. That's all.

A partial inquest was held by Coroner Dressler during the day. Mr. N. Stippich, father of the deceased, was the first witness sworn. He did not see the shooting and could only tell about the excitement that followed. He said Donaldson had been keeping company with his daughter for three or four years and had been engaged to her two years. He had taken her to a picnic on the Monday before the shooting. Mr. Stippich never knew of any quarreling between them. . . .

The Confidential Friend

The most important testimony was given by Miss Tennie Fehl, the confidante of the deceased. She said: I was intimately acquainted with Annie Stippich. I know William Donaldson kept company with her for more than three years. Have known them to quarrel. One evening in February Annie and I were going down street; Donaldson was standing at Madison and Tustin streets; I spoke to him; he responded, but did not speak to Annie. He grabbed her by the throat and she said: "Willie, what is the matter with you?" He let her go, and he went with us to Schenk's, on Tustin street. Annie asked him and I asked him what he raised the fuss on the street for, but he did not answer. He only looked at us. I was afraid to leave Annie with him. I then asked him again, and he said nothing was the matter. He promised me that he would not hurt Annie. I left Annie and him together.

When she came to bed she told me Willie was only fooling. She afterward said he was mad because Annie would not go to his house. Another evening Annie and Willie and myself were at Schenk's. We were talking about a young German fellow, and Willie did not like him. I went upstairs, and in a few minutes Annie called me down. Willie had her by the throat. I released her, and he said there was nothing the matter only that she was causing him deep thinking. He was very jealous of her. He told me that it was all over and that he would not hurt her; but he would have grabbed her by the throat again if I had not interfered. I did not see a revolver on any of these occasions. The last evening we were waiting for a band to come out and serenade. It was 12 o'clock, but Donaldson was still there.

Good Advice

When Annie came up stairs I said, "Drop him;" but she made no reply. She never made any complaint against him. When he promised not to hurt her, he said: "When I go to do a thing I go through with it." One evening Annie and Willie were standing on Schenk's porch. He wanted Annie to leave the house. He said he would rather she would not stay, as she didn't have to work. I asked him to say what he had against me; he did not reply. Annie told me that Willie got mad one night and chased her with a knife into his mother's house. He never told me that he would harm Annie, but he was very jealous. He seemed to think that Annie and I were together too much, and that I put mischief into her head. I believe that Annie was afraid to drop him and afraid to marry him. She told me she was afraid, for fear something would happen. I have seen him have a revolver. During the past three months they seemed to be more pleasant. I had stopped visiting, because I thought they would get along better. She told me lately that Willie had insulted her, but he did not say anything about it. . . .

"Gouge and Bite, Pull Hair and Scratch": The Social Significance of Fighting in the Southern Backcountry

Elliott J. Gorn

Preserving one's public reputation was central to southern ideas about manliness in the eighteenth and early nineteenth centuries. Southern gentlemen preserved their sense of honor through such rituals as dueling. Men living in the southern backcountry did not respond to real or imagined insults by challenging each other to duels. Instead they engaged in a particularly savage form of hand-to-hand combat. In his article "Gouge and Bite, Pull Hair and Scratch," Elliott Gorn describes the practice of rough-and-tumble fighting among southern backwoodsmen and explains how that ritual contributed to their manly self-esteem and sense of autonomy.

What was gendered about the events and attitudes that prompted "fist battles" among men living in the southern backcountry? What was it about backcountry culture that encouraged this particular form of male behavior? What does the response of Northerners to eye gouging and other forms of interpersonal violence among backcountry men say about their definition of manliness?

"I would advise you when You do fight Not to act like Tygers and Bears as these Virginians do—Biting one anothers Lips and Noses off, and *gowging* [sic] one another—that is, thrusting out one anothers Eyes, and kicking one another on the Cods, to the Great damage of many a Poor Woman." Thus, Charles Woodmason, an itinerant Anglican minister born of English gentry stock, described the brutal form of combat he found in the Virginia backcountry shortly before the American Revolution. Although historians are more likely to study people thinking, governing, worshiping, or working, how men fight—who

Source: Elliott J. Gorn, " 'Gouge and Bite, Pull Hair and Scratch': The Social Significance of Fighting in the Southern Backcountry," *The American Historical Review,* 90 (Feb. 1985), 18–27, 33–43. Reprinted by permission. Notes omitted.

participates, who observes, which rules are followed, what is at stake, what tactics are allowed—reveals much about past cultures and societies.

The evolution of southern backwoods brawling from the late eighteenth century through the antebellum era can be reconstructed from oral traditions and travelers' accounts. As in most cultural history, broad patterns and uneven trends rather than specific dates mark the way. The sources are often problematic and must be used with care; some speculation is required. But the lives of common people cannot be ignored merely because they leave few records. "To feel for a feller's eyestrings and make him tell the news" was not just mayhem but an act freighted with significance for both social and cultural history.

As early as 1735, boxing was "much in fashion" in parts of Chesapeake Bay, and forty years later a visitor from the North declared that, along with dancing, fiddling, small swords, and card playing, it was an essential skill for all young Virginia gentlemen. The term "boxing," however, did not necessarily refer to the comparatively tame style of bare-knuckle fighting familiar to eighteenth-century Englishmen. In 1746, four deaths prompted the governor of North Carolina to ask for legislation against "the barbarous and inhuman manner of boxing which so much prevails among the lower sort of people." The colonial assembly responded by making it a felony "to cut out the Tongue or pull out the eyes of the King's Liege People." Five years later the assembly added slitting, biting, and cutting off noses to the list of offenses. Virginia passed similar legislation in 1748 and revised these statutes in 1772 explicitly to discourage men from "gouging, plucking, or putting out an eye, biting or kicking or stomping upon" quiet peaceable citizens. By 1786 South Carolina had made premeditated mayhem a capital offense, defining the crime as severing another's bodily parts.

Laws notwithstanding, the carnage continued. Philip Vickers Fithian, a New Jerseyite serving as tutor for an aristocratic Virginia family, confided to his journal on September 3, 1774:

> By appointment is to be fought this Day near Mr. *Lanes* two fist Battles between four young Fellows. The Cause of the battles I have not yet known; I suppose either that they are lovers, and one has in Jest or reality some way supplanted the other; or has in a merry hour called him a *Lubber* or a *thick-Skull*, or a *Buckskin*, or a *Scotsman*, or perhaps one has mislaid the other's hat, or knocked a peach out of his Hand, or offered him a dram without wiping the mouth of the Bottle; all these, and ten thousand more quite as trifling and ridiculous are thought and accepted as just Causes of immediate Quarrels, in which every diabolical Stratagem for Mastery is allowed and practiced.

The "trifling and ridiculous" reasons for these fights had an unreal quality for the matter-of-fact Yankee. Not assaults on persons or prop-erty but slights, insults, and thoughtless gestures set young southerners against each other. To call a man a "buckskin," for example, was to accuse him of the poverty associated with leather clothing, while the epithet "Scotsman" tied him to the low-caste Scots-Irish who settled the southern highlands. Fithian could not understand how such trivial offenses caused the bloody battles. But his incomprehension turned to rage when he realized that spectators attended these "odious and filthy amusements" and that the fighters allayed their spontaneous passions in order to fix convenient dates and places, which allowed time for rumors to spread and crowds to gather. The Yankee concluded that only devils, prostitutes, or monkeys could sire creatures so unfit for human society.

Descriptions of these "fist battles," as Fithian called them, indicate that they generally began like English prize fights. Two men, surrounded by onlookers, parried blows until one was knocked or thrown down. But there the similarity ceased. Whereas "Broughton's Rules" of the English ring specified that a round ended when either antagonist fell, southern bruisers only began fighting at this point. Enclosed not inside a formal ring—the "magic circle" defining a special place with its own norms of conduct—but within whatever space the spectators left vacant, fighters battled each other until one called enough or was unable to continue. Combatants boasted, howled, and cursed. As words gave way to action, they tripped and threw, gouged and butted, scratched and choked each other. "But what is worse than all," Isaac Weld observed, "these wretches in their combat endeavor to their utmost to tear out each other's testicles."

Around the beginning of the nineteenth century, men sought original labels for their brutal style of fighting. "Rough-and-tumble" or simply "gouging" gradually replaced "boxing" as the name for these contests. Before two bruisers attacked each other, spectators might demand whether they proposed to fight fair—according to Broughton's Rules—or rough-and-tumble. Honor dictated that all techniques be permitted. Except for a ban on weapons, most men chose to fight "no holts barred," doing what they wished to each other without interference, until one gave up or was incapacitated.

The emphasis on maximum disfigurement, on severing bodily parts, made this fighting style unique. Amid the general mayhem, however, gouging out an opponent's eye became the sine qua non of rough-and-tumble fighting, much like the knockout punch in modern boxing. The best gougers, of course, were adept at other fighting skills. Some allegedly filed their teeth to bite off an enemy's appendages more efficiently. Still, liberating an eyeball quickly became a fighter's surest route to victory and his most prestigious accomplishment. To this end, celebrated heroes fired their fingernails hard, honed them sharp, and oiled them slick. " 'You have come off badly this time, I doubt?' " declared an alarmed passerby on seeing the piteous condition of a renowned fighter. " 'Have I,' says he triumphantly, shewing from his pocket at the same time an eye, which he had extracted during the combat, and preserved for a trophy."

As the new style of fighting evolved, its geographical distribution changed. Leadership quickly passed from the southern seaboard to upcountry counties and the western frontier. Although examples could be found throughout the South, rough-and-tumbling was best suited to the backwoods, where hunting, herding, and semisubsistence agriculture predominated over market-oriented, staple crop production. Thus, the settlers of western Carolina, Kentucky, and Tennessee, as well as upland Mississippi, Alabama, and Georgia, became especially known for their pugnacity.

The social base of rough-and-tumbling also shifted with the passage of time. Although brawling was always considered a vice of the "lower sort," eighteenth-century Tidewater gentlemen sometimes found themselves in brutal fights. These combats grew out of challenges to men's honor—to their status in patriarchal, kin-based, small-scale communities—and were woven into the very fabric of daily life. Rhys Isaac has observed that the Virginia gentry set the tone for a fiercely competitive style of living. Although they valued hierarchy, individual status was never permanently fixed, so men frantically sought to assert their prowess—by grand boasts over tavern gaming tables laden with money, by whipping and tripping each other's horses in violent quarter-races, by wagering one-half year's earnings on the flash of a fighting cock's gaff. Great planters and small shared an ethos that extolled courage bordering on foolhardiness and cherished magnificent, if irrational, displays of largess.

Piety, hard work, and steady habits had their adherents, but in this society aggressive self-assertion and manly pride were the real marks of status. Even the gentry's vaunted hospitality demonstrated a family's community standing, so conviviality itself became a vehicle for rivalry and emulation. Rich and poor might revel together during "public times," but gentry patronage of sports and festivities kept the focus of power clear. Above all, brutal recreations toughened men for a violent social life in which the exploitation of labor, the specter of poverty, and a fierce struggle for status were daily realities.

During the final decades of the eighteenth century, however, individuals like Fithian's young gentlemen became less inclined to engage in rough-and-tumbling. Many in the planter class now wanted to distinguish themselves from social inferiors more by genteel manners, gracious living, and paternal prestige than by patriarchal prowess. They sought alternatives to brawling and found them by imitating the English aristocracy. A few gentlemen took boxing lessons from professors of pugilism or attended sparring exhibitions given by touring exponents of the manly art. More important, dueling gradually replaced hand-to-hand combat. The code of honor offered a genteel, though deadly, way to settle personal disputes while demonstrating one's elevated status. Ceremony distinguished antiseptic duels from lower-class brawls. Cool restraint and customary decorum proved a man's ability to shed blood while remaining emotionally detached, to act as mercilessly as the poor whites but to do so with chilling gentility.

Slowly, then, rough-and-tumble fighting found specific locus in both human and geographical landscapes. We can watch men grapple with the transition. When an attempt at a formal duel aborted, Savannah politician Robert Watkins and United States Senator James Jackson resorted to gouging. Jackson bit Watson's finger to save his eye. Similarly, when "a low fellow who pretends to gentility" insulted a distinguished doctor, the gentleman responded with a proper challenge. "He had scarcely uttered these words, before the other flew at him, and in an instant turned his eye out of the socket, and while it hung upon his cheek, the fellow was barbarous enough to endeavor to pluck it entirely out." By the new century, such ambiguity had lessened, as rough-and-tumble fighting was relegated to individuals in backwoods settlements. For the next several decades, eye-gouging matches were focal events in the culture of lower-class males who still relished the wild ways of old.

"I saw more than one man who wanted an eye, and ascertained that I was now in the region of 'gouging,' " reported young Timothy Flint, a Harvard educated, Presbyterian minister bound for Louisiana missionary work in 1816. His spirits buckled as his party turned down the Mississippi from the Ohio Valley. Enterprising farmers gave way to slothful and vulgar folk whom Flint considered barely civilized. Only vicious fighting and disgusting accounts of battles past disturbed their inertia. Residents assured him that the "blackguards" excluded gentlemen from gouging matches. Flint was therefore perplexed when told that a barbarous-looking man was the "best" in one settlement, until he learned that best in this context meant not the most moral, prosperous, or pious but the local champion who had whipped all the rest, the man most dexterous at extracting eyes.

Because rough-and-tumble fighting declined in settled areas, some of the most valuable accounts were written by visitors who penetrated the backcountry. Travel literature was quite popular during America's infancy, and many profit-minded authors undoubtedly wrote with their audience's expectations in mind. Images of heroic frontiersmen, of crude but unencumbered natural men, enthralled both writers and readers. Some who toured the new republic in the decades following the Revolution had strong prejudices against America's democratic pretensions. English travelers in particular doubted that the upstart nation—in which the lower class shouted its equality and the upper class was unable or unwilling to exercise proper authority—could survive. Ironically, backcountry fighting became a symbol for both those who inflated and those who punctured America's expansive national ego.

Frontier braggarts enjoyed fulfilling visitors' expectations of backwoods depravity, pumping listeners full of gruesome legends. Their narratives projected a satisfying, if grotesque, image of the American rustic as a fearless, barbaric, larger-than-life democrat. But they also gave Englishmen the satisfaction of seeing their former countrymen run wild in the wilderness. Gouging matches offered a perfect metaphor for the Hobbesian war of all against all, of men tearing each other apart once institutional restraints evaporated, of a heart of darkness beating in the New World. As they made their way from the northern port towns to the southern countryside, or down the Ohio to southwestern waterways, observers concluded that geographical and moral descent went hand in hand. Brutal fights dramatically confirmed their belief that evil lurked in the deep shadows of America's sunny democratic landscape.

And yet, it would be a mistake to dismiss all travelers' accounts of backwoods fighting as fictions born of prejudice. Many sojourners who were sober and careful observers of America left detailed reports of rough-and-tumbles. Aware of the tradition of frontier boasting, they distinguished apocryphal stories from personal observation, wild tales from eye-witness accounts. Although gouging matches became a sort of literary convention, many travelers compiled credible descriptions of backwoods violence. . . .

Thomas Ashe explored the territory around Wheeling, Virginia. A passage, dated April 1806, from his *Travels in America* gives us a detailed picture of gouging's social context. Ashe expounded on Wheeling's potential to become a center of trade for the Ohio and upper Mississippi valleys, noting that geography made the town a natural rival of Pittsburgh. Yet Wheeling lagged in "worthy commercial pursuits, and industrious and moral dealings." Ashe attributed this backwardness to the town's frontier ways which attracted men who specialized in drinking, plundering Indian property, racing horses, and watching cockfights. A Wheeling Quaker assured Ashe that mores were changing, that the underworld element was about to be driven out. Soon, the godly would gain control of the local government, enforce strict observance of the Sabbath, and outlaw vice. Ashe was sympathetic but doubtful. In Wheeling, only heightened violence and debauchery distinguished Sunday from the rest of the week. The citizens' willingness to close up shop and neglect business on the slightest pretext made it a questionable residence for any respectable group of men, let alone a society of Quakers.

To convey the rough texture of Wheeling life, Ashe described a gouging match. Two men drinking at a public house argued over the merits of their respective horses. Wagers made, they galloped off to the race course. "Two thirds of the population followed:—blacksmiths, shipwrights, all left work: the town appeared a desert. The stores were shut. I asked a proprietor, why the warehouses did not remain open? He told me all good was done for the day: that the people would remain on the ground till night, and many stay till the following morning." Determined to witness an event deemed so important that the entire town went on holiday, Ashe headed for the track. He missed the initial heat but arrived in time to watch the crowd raise the stakes to induce a rematch. Six horses competed, and spectators bet a small fortune, but the results were inconclusive. Umpires' opinions were given and rejected. Heated words, then fists flew. Soon, the melee narrowed to two individuals, a Virginian and a Kentuckian. Because fights were common in such situations, everyone knew the proper procedures, and the combatants quickly decided to "tear and rend" one another—to rough-and-tumble—rather than "fight fair." Ashe elaborated: "You startle at the words tear and rend, and again do not understand me. You have heard these terms, I allow, applied to beasts of prey and to carnivorous animals; and your humanity cannot conceive them applicable to man: It nevertheless is so, and the fact will not permit me the use of any less expressive term."

The battle began—size and power on the Kentuckian's side, science, and craft on the Virginian's. They exchanged cautious throws and blows, when suddenly the Virginian lunged at his opponent with a panther's ferocity. The crowd roared its approval as the fight reached its violent denouement:

> The shock received by the Kentuckyan, and the want of breath, brought him instantly to the ground. The Virginian never lost his hold; like those bats of the South who never quit the subject on which they fasten till they taste blood, he kept his knees in his enemy's body; fixing his claws in his hair, and his thumbs on his eyes, gave them an instantaneous start from their sockets. The sufferer roared aloud, but uttered no complaint. The citizens again shouted with joy. Doubts were no longer entertained and bets of three to one were offered on the Virginian.

But the fight continued. The Kentuckian grabbed his smaller opponent and held him in a tight bear hug, forcing the Virginian to relinquish his facial grip. Over and over the two rolled, until, getting the Virginian under him, the big man "snapt off his nose so close to his face that no manner of projection remained." The Virginian quickly recovered, seized the Kentuckian's lower lip in his teeth, and ripped it down over his enemy's chin. This was enough: "The Kentuckyan at length *gave out,* on which the people carried off the victor, and he preferring a triumph to a doctor, who came to cicatrize his face, suffered himself to be chaired round the ground as the champion of the times, and the first *rougher-and-tumbler.* The poor wretch, whose eyes were started from their spheres, and whose lip refused its office, returned to the town, to hide his impotence, and get his countenance repaired." The citizens refreshed themselves with whiskey and biscuits, then resumed their races.

Ashe's Quaker friend reported that such spontaneous races occurred two or three times a week and that the annual fall and spring meets lasted fourteen uninterrupted days, "aided by the licentious and profligate of all the neighboring states." As for rough-and-tumbles, the Quaker saw no hope of suppressing them. Few nights passed without such fights; few mornings failed to reveal a new citizen with mutilated features. It was a regional taste, unrestrained by law or authority, an inevitable part of life on the left bank of the Ohio. . . .

Foreign travelers might exaggerate and backwoods storytellers embellish, but the most neglected fact about eye-gouging matches is their actuality. Circuit Court Judge Aedamus Burke barely contained his astonishment while presiding in South Carolina's upcountry: "Before God, gentlemen of the jury, I never saw such a thing before in the world. There is a plaintiff with an eye out! A juror with an eye out! And two witnesses with an eye out!" If the "ringtailed roarers" did not actually breakfast on stewed Yankee, washed down with spike nails and epsom salts, court records from Sumner County, Arkansas, did describe assault victims with the words "nose was bit." The gamest "gamecock of the wilderness" never really moved steamboat engines by grinning at them, but Reuben Cheek did receive a three-year sentence to the Tennessee penitentiary for gouging out William Maxey's eye. Most backcountrymen went to the grave with their faces intact, just as most of the southern gentry never fought a duel. But as an extreme version of the common tendency toward brawling, street fighting, and seeking personal vengeance,

rough-and-tumbling gives us insight into the deep values and assumptions—the *mentalité*—of backwoods life.

Observers often accused rough-and-tumblers of fighting like animals. But eye gouging was not instinctive behavior, the human equivalent of two rams vying for dominance. Animals fight to attain specific objectives, such as food, sexual priority, or territory. Precisely where to draw the line between human aggression as a genetically programmed response or as a product of social and cultural learning remains a hotly debated issue. Nevertheless, it would be difficult to make a case for eye gouging as a genetic imperative, coded behavior to maximize individual or species survival. Although rough-and-tumble fighting appears primitive and anarchic to modern eyes, there can be little doubt that its origins, rituals, techniques, and goals were emphatically conditioned by environment; gouging was learned behavior. Humanistic social science more than sociobiology holds the keys to understanding this phenomenon.

What can we conclude about the culture and society that nourished rough-and-tumble fighting? The best place to begin is with the material base of life and the nature of daily work. Gamblers, hunters, herders, roustabouts, rivermen, and yeomen farmers were the sorts of persons usually associated with gouging. Such hallmarks of modernity as large-scale production, complex division of labor, and regular work rhythms were alien to their lives. Recent studies have stressed the premodern character of the southern uplands through most of the antebellum period. Even while cotton production boomed and trade expanded, a relatively small number of planters owned the best lands and most slaves, so huge parts of the South remained outside the flow of international markets or staple crop agriculture. Thus, backcountry whites commonly found themselves locked into a semisubsistent pattern of living. Growing crops for home consumption, supplementing food supplies with abundant game, allowing small herds to fatten in the woods, spending scarce money for essential staples, and bartering goods for the services of part-time or itinerant trades people, the upland folk lived in an intensely local, kin-based society. Rural hamlets, impassable roads, and provincial isolation—not growing towns, internal improvements, or international commerce—characterized the backcountry.

Even men whose livelihoods depended on expanding markets often continued their rough, premodern ways. Characteristic of life on a Mississippi barge, for example, were long periods of idleness shattered by intense anxiety, as deadly snags, shoals, and storms approached. Running aground on a sandbar meant backbreaking labor to maneuver a thirty-ton vessel out of trouble. Boredom weighed as heavily as danger, so tale telling, singing, drinking, and gambling filled the empty hours. Once goods were taken on in New Orleans, the men began the thousand-mile return journey against the current. Before steam power replaced muscle, bad food and whiskey fueled the gangs who day after day, exposed to wind and water, poled the river bottoms or strained at the cordelling ropes until their vessel reached the tributaries of the Missouri or the Ohio. Hunters, trappers, herdsmen, subsistence farmers, and other backwoodsmen faced different but equally taxing hardships, and those who endured prided themselves on their strength and daring, their stamina, cunning, and ferocity.

Such men played as lustily as they worked, counterpointing bouts of intense labor with strenuous leisure. What travelers mistook for laziness was a refusal to work and save with compulsive regularity. "I have seen nothing in human form so profligate as they are," James Flint wrote of the boatmen he met around 1820. "Accomplished in depravity, their habits and education seem to comprehend every vice. They make few pretensions to moral character; and their swearing is excessive and perfectly disgusting. Although earning good wages, they are in the most abject poverty; many of them being without anything like clean or comfortable clothing." A generation later, Mark Twain vividly remembered those who manned the great timber and coal rafts glid-ing past his boyhood home in Hannibal, Missouri: "Rude, uneducated, brave, suffering terrific hardships with sailorlike stoicism; heavy drinkers, course frolickers in moral sties like the Natchez-under-the-hill of that day, heavy fighters, reckless fellows, every one, elephantinely jolly, foul witted, profane; prodigal of their money, bankrupt at the end of the trip, fond of barbaric finery, prodigious braggarts; yet, in the main, honest, trustworthy, faithful to promises and duty, and often picaresquely magnanimous." Details might change, but penury, loose morality, and lack of steady habits endured.

Boatmen, hunters, and herdsmen were often separated from wives and children for long periods. More important, backcountry couples lacked the emotionally intense experience of the bourgeois family. They spent much of their time apart and found companionship with members of their own sex. The frontier town or crossroads tavern brought males together in surrogate brotherhoods, where rough men paid little deference to the civilizing role of women and the moral uplift of the domestic family. On the margins of a booming, modernizing society, they shared an intensely communal yet fiercely competitive way of life. Thus, where work was least rationalized and specialized, domesticity weakest, legal institutions primitive, and the market economy feeble, rough-and-tumble fighting found fertile soil.

Just as the economy of the southern backcountry remained locally oriented, the rough-and-tumblers were local heroes, renowned in their communities. There was no professionalization here. Men fought for informal village and county titles; the red feather in the champion's cap was pay enough because it marked him as first among his peers. Paralleling the primitive division of labor in backwoods society, boundaries between entertainment and daily life, between spectators and participants, were not sharply drawn. "Bully of the Hill" Ab Gaines from the Big Hatchie Country, Neil Brown of Totty's Bend, Vernon's William Holt, and Smithfield's Jim Willis—all of them were renowned Tennessee fighters, local heroes in their day. Legendary champions were real individuals, tested gang leaders who attained their status by being the meanest, toughest, and most ruthless fighters, who faced disfigurement and never backed down. Challenges were ever present; yesterday's spectator was today's champion, today's champion tomorrow's invalid.

Given the lives these men led, a world view that embraced fearlessness made sense. Hunters, trappers, Indian fighters, and herdsmen who knew the smell of warm blood on their hands refused to sentimentalize an environment filled with threatening forces. It was not that backwoodsmen lived in constant danger but that violence was unpredictable. Recreations like cockfighting deadened men to cruelty, and the gratuitous savagery of gouging matches reinforced the daily truth that life was brutal, guided only by the logic of superior nerve, power, and cunning. With families emotionally or physically distant and civil institutions weak, a man's role in the all-male society was defined less by his ability as a breadwinner than by his ferocity. The touchstone of masculinity was unflinching toughness, not chivalry, duty, or piety. Violent sports, heavy drinking, and impulsive pleasure seeking were appropriate for men whose lives were hard, whose futures were unpredictable, and whose opportunities were limited. Gouging champions were group leaders because they embodied the basic values of their peers. The successful rough-and-tumbler proved his manhood by asserting his dominance and rendering his opponent "impotent," as Thomas Ashe put it. And the loser, though literally or symbolically castrated, demonstrated his mettle and maintained his honor.

Here we begin to understand the travelers' refrain about plain folk degradation. Setting out from northern ports, whose inhabitants were increasingly possessed by visions of godly perfection and material progress, they found southern upcountry people slothful and backward. Ashe's Quaker friend in Wheeling, Virginia, made the point. For Quakers and northern evangelicals, labor was a means of moral self-testing, and earthly success was a sign of God's grace, so hard work and steady habits became acts of piety. But not only Yankees endorsed sober restraint. A growing number of southern evangelicals also embraced a life of decorous self-control, rejecting the hedonistic and self-assertive values of old. During the late eighteenth century, as Rhys Isaac has observed, many plain folk disavowed the hegemonic gentry culture of conspicuous display and found individual worth, group pride, and transcendent meaning in religious revivals. By the antebellum era, new evangelical waves washed over class lines as rich and poor alike forswore such sins as drinking, gambling, cursing, fornication, horse racing, and dancing. But conversion was far from universal, and, for many in backcountry settlements like Wheeling, the evangelical idiom remained a foreign tongue. Men worked hard to feed themselves and their kin, to acquire goods and status, but they lacked the calling to prove their godliness through rigid morality. Salvation and self-denial were culturally less compelling values, and the barriers against leisure and self-gratification were lower here than among the converted.

Moreover, primitive markets and the semi-subsistence basis of upcountry life limited men's dependence on goods produced by others and allowed them to maintain the irregular work rhythms of a precapitalist economy. The material base of backwoods life was ill suited to social transformation, and the cultural traditions of the past offered alternatives to rigid new ideals. Closing up shop in mid-week for a fight or horse race had always been perfectly acceptable, because men labored so that they might indulge the joys of the flesh. Neither a compulsive need to save time and money nor an obsession with progress haunted people's imaginations. The backcountry folk who lacked a bourgeois or Protestant sense of duty were little disturbed by exhibitions of human passions and were resigned to violence as part of daily life. Thus, the relative dearth of capitalistic values (such as delayed gratification and accumulation), the absence of a strict work ethic, and a cultural tradition that winked at lapses in moral rigor limited society's demands for sober self control.

Not just unconverted poor whites but also large numbers of the slave-holding gentry still lent their prestige to a regional style that favored conspicuous displays of leisure. As C. Vann Woodward has pointed out, early observers, such as Robert Beverley and William Byrd, as well as modern-day commentators, have described a distinctly "southern ethic" in American history. Whether judged positively as leisure or negatively as laziness, the southern sensibility valued free time and rejected work as the consuming goal of life. Slavery reinforced this tendency, for how could labor be an unmitigated virtue if so much of it was performed by despised black bondsmen? When southerners did esteem commerce and enterprise, it was less because piling up wealth contained religious or moral value than because productivity facilitated the leisure ethos. Southerners could therefore work hard without placing labor at the center of their ethical universe. In important ways, then, the upland folk culture reflected a larger regional style.

Thus, the values, ideas, and institutions that rapidly transformed the North into a modern capitalist society came late to the South. Indeed, conspicuous display, heavy drinking, moral casualness, and love of games and sports had deep roots in much of Western culture. . . . We must take care not to interpret the southern ethic as unique or aberrant. The compulsions to subordinate leisure to productivity, to divide work and play into separate compartmentalized realms, and to improve each bright and shining hour were the novel ideas. The southern ethic anticipated human evil, tolerated ethical lapses, and accepted the finitude of man in contrast to the new style that demanded unprecedented moral rectitude and internalized self-restraint.

The American South also shared with large parts of the Old World a taste for violence and personal vengence. . . . Emotions were freely ex-

pressed: jollity and laughter suddenly gave way to belligerence; guilt and penitence coexisted with hate; cruelty always lurked nearby. . . .

Despite enormous cultural differences, inhabitants of the southern uplands exhibited characteristics of their forebears in the Old World. The Scots-Irish brought their reputation for ferocity to the backcountry, but English migrants, too, had a thirst for violence. Central authority was weak, and men reserved the right to settle differences for themselves. Vengeance was part of daily life. Drunken hilarity, good fellowship, and high spirits, especially at crossroads taverns, suddenly turned to violence. Traveler after traveler remarked on how forthright and friendly but quick to anger the backcountry people were. Like their European ancestors, they had not yet internalized the modern world's demand for tight emotional self-control.

Above all, the ancient concept of honor helps explain this shared proclivity for violence. According to the sociologist Peter Berger, modern men have difficulty taking seriously the idea of honor. American jurisprudence, for example, offers legal recourse for slander and libel because they involve material damages. But insult—publicly smearing a man's good name and besmirching his honor—implies no palpable injury and so does not exist in the eyes of the law. Honor is an intensely social concept, resting on reputation, community standing, and the esteem of kin and compatriots. To possess honor requires acknowledgment from others; it cannot exist in solitary conscience. Modern man, Berger has argued, is more responsive to dignity—the belief that personal worth inheres equally in each individual, regardless of his status in society. Dignity frees the evangelical to confront God alone, the capitalist to make contracts without customary encumbrances, and the reformer to uplift the lowly. Naked and alone man has dignity; extolled by peers and covered with ribbons, he has honor. . . .

Bertram Wyatt-Brown has argued that this Old World ideal is the key to understanding southern history. Across boundaries of time, geography, and social class, the South was knit together by a primal concept of male valor, part of the ancient heritage of Indo-European folk cultures. Honor demanded clan loyalty, hospitality, protection of women, and defense of patriarchal prerogatives. Honorable men guarded their reputations, bristled at insults, and, where necessary, sought personal vindication through bloodshed. The culture of honor thrived in hierarchical rural communities like the American South and grew out of a fatalistic world view, which assumed that pain and suffering were man's fate. It accounts for the pervasive violence that marked relationships between southerners and explains their insistence on vengeance and their rejection of legal redress in settling quarrels. Honor tied personal identity to public fulfillment of social roles. Neither bourgeois self-control nor internalized conscience determined status; judgment by one's fellows was the wellspring of community standing.

In this light, the seemingly trivial causes for brawls enumerated as early as Fithian's time—name calling, subtle ridicule, breaches of decorum, displays of poor manners—make sense. If a man's good name was his most important possession, then any slight cut him deeply. "Having words" precipitated fights because words brought shame and undermined a man's sense of self. Symbolic acts, such as buying a round of drinks, conferred honor on all, while refusing to share a bottle implied some inequality in social status. Honor inhered not only in individuals but also in kin and peers; when members of two cliques had words, their tested leaders or several men from each side fought to uphold group prestige. Inheritors of primal honor, the southern plain folk were quick to take offense, and any perceived affront forced a man either to devalue himself or to strike back violently and avenge the wrong.

The concept of male honor takes us a long way toward understanding the meaning of eye-gouging matches. But backwoods people did not simply acquire some primordial notion without modifying it. Definitions of honorable behavior have always varied enormously across cultures. The southern upcountry fostered a particular style of honor, which grew out of the contradiction between equality and hierarchy. Honorific societies tend to be sharply stratified. Honor is apportioned according to rank, and men fight to maintain personal standing within their social categories. Because black chattel slavery was the basis for the southern hierarchy, slave owners had the most wealth and honor, while other whites scrambled for a bit of each, and bondsmen were permanently impoverished and dishonored. Here was a source of tension for the plain folk. Men of honor shared freedom and equality; those denied honor were implicitly less than equal—perilously close to a slave-like condition. But in the eyes of the gentry, poor whites as well as blacks were outside the circle of honor, so both groups were subordinate. Thus, a herdsman's insult failed to shame a planter since the two men were not on the same social level. Without a threat to the gentleman's honor, there was no need for a duel; horsewhipping the insolent fellow sufficed.

Southern plain folk, then, were caught in a social contradiction. Society taught all white men to consider themselves equals, encouraged them to compete for power and status, yet threatened them from below with the specter of servitude and from above with insistence on obedience to rank and authority. Cut off from upperclass tests of honor, backcountry people adopted their own. A rough-and-tumble was more than a poor man's duel, a botched version of genteel combat. Plain folk chose not to ape the dispassionate, antiseptic, gentry style but to invert it. While the gentleman's code of honor insisted on cool restraint, eye gougers gloried in unvarnished brutality. In contrast to duelists' aloof silence, backwoods fighters screamed defiance to the world. As their own unique rites of honor, rough-and-tumble matches allowed backcountry men to shout their equality at each other. And eye-gouging fights also dispelled any stigma of servility. Ritual boasts, soaring oaths, outrageous ferocity, unflinching bloodiness—all proved a man's freedom.

Where the slave acted obsequiously, the backwoodsman resisted the slightest affront; where human chattels accepted blows and never raised a hand, plain folk celebrated violence; where blacks could not jeopardize their value as property, poor whites proved their autonomy by risking bodily parts. Symbolically reaffirming their claims to honor, gouging matches helped resolve painful uncertainties arising out of the ambiguous place of plain folk in the southern social structure.

Backwoods fighting reminds us of man's capacity for cruelty and is an excellent corrective to romanticizing premodern life. But a close look also keeps us from drawing facile conclusions about innate human aggressiveness. Eye gouging represented neither the "real" human animal emerging on the frontier, nor nature acting through man in a Darwinian struggle for survival, nor anarchic disorder and communal breakdown. Rather, rough-and-tumble fighting was ritualized behavior—a product of specific cultural assumptions. Men drink together, tongues loosen, a simmering old rivalry begins to boil; insult is given, offense taken, ritual boasts commence; the fight begins, mettle is tested, blood redeems honor, and equilibrium is restored. Eye gouging was the poor and middling whites' own version of a historical southern tendency to consider personal violence socially useful—indeed, ethically essential.

Rough-and-tumble fighting emerged from the confluence of economic conditions, social relationships, and culture in the southern backcountry. Primitive markets and the semi-subsistence basis of life threw men back on close ties to kin and community. Violence and poverty were part of daily existence, so endurance, even callousness, became functional values. Loyal to their localities, their occupations, and each other, men came together and found release from life's hardships in strong drink, tall talk, rude practical jokes, and cruel sports. They craved one another's recognition but rejected genteel, pious, or bourgeois values, awarding esteem on the basis of their own traditional standards. The glue that held men together was an intensely competitive status system in which the most prodigious drinker or strongest arm wrestler, the best tale teller, fiddle player, or log roller, the most daring gambler, original liar, skilled hunter, outrageous swearer, or accurate marksman was accorded respect by the others. Reputation was everything, and scars were badges of honor. Rough-and-tumble fighting demonstrated unflinching willingness to inflict pain while risking mutilation—all to defend one's standing among peers—and became a central expression of the all-male subculture.

Eye gouging continued long after the antebellum period. As the market economy absorbed new parts of the backcountry, however, the way of life that supported rough-and-tumbling waned. Certainly by mid-century the number of incidents declined, precisely when expanding international demand brought ever more upcountry acres into staple production. Towns, schools, churches, revivals, and families gradually overtook the backwoods. In a slow and uneven process, keelboats gave way to steamers, then railroads; squatters, to cash crop farmers; hunters and trappers, to preachers. The plain folk code of honor was far from dead, but emergent social institutions engendered a moral ethos that warred against the old ways. For many individuals, the justifications for personal violence grew stricter, and mayhem became unacceptable. . . .

"The Deftness of Her Sex": Innocence, Guilt, and Gender in the Trial of Lizzie Borden

Catherine Ross Nickerson

At some point or other, children hear it. "Lizzie Borden took an axe/And gave her mother forty whacks/When she saw what she had done/She gave her father forty-one." On the morning of August 4, 1892 Andrew J. Borden, a wealthy businessman living in Fall River, Massachusetts, left for work as usual and then returned to take a mid-morning nap around 10:30. He didn't know it, but his wife was already dead when he lay down on the couch in the parlor. She was killed between 9 and 9:30 when someone attacked her with an axe. Andrew never woke up from his nap. Sometime between 11 and 11:15, he too was killed. His daughter Lizzie was eventually arrested and tried for both murders. The jury took only a few minutes to acquit her. In the article reprinted below, Catherine Ross Nickerson argues that prevailing gender conventions made it difficult if not impossible for an all-male jury to convict Lizzie.

What kind of evidence does she present to substantiate her argument? In what ways did Andrew Borden conform to prevailing attitudes toward manliness? How did attitudes toward femininity shape public attitudes toward the crime and the accused?

Something terrible and mysterious happened one August morning in Fall River, Massachusetts, in 1892. Andrew Borden, one of the wealthiest men in town, was found murdered in the sitting room of his own home, and minutes later the body of his wife was found upstairs in the spare bedroom. Both had been killed by multiple blows to the head, face, and neck with an axe. The only others known to be in and around the house that morning were Lizzie Borden, Andrew's thirty-two-year-old unmarried daughter, and Bridget Sullivan, the family's Irish housemaid. The people of Fall River were horrified and fascinated by the news of the murders; their excitement only increased when Lizzie was arrested one week later. The story of the murder of the respectable, elderly couple in the middle of day in their own home quickly became national news.

What exactly happened in that house on that day has been a matter of speculation and debate since the discovery of the bodies. Though Lizzie was acquitted of all charges at her trial, she was never fully exonerated in the public imagination, and she remains, to most people, the most famous murderess in American history. There is a voluminous literature about the Borden murders; much of it is the work of people who become fascinated with the case as an intricate puzzle of opportunity,

Source: Catherine Ross Nickerson, " 'The Deftness of Her Sex': Innocence, Guilt, and Gender in the Trial of Lizzie Borden," in *Lethal Imagination: Violence and Brutality in American History*, ed. Michael A. Bellesiles (New York: New York University Press, 1999), pp. 261–277. Reprinted by permission. Notes omitted.

motive, and physical evidence and who attempt to settle the question of Lizzie's guilt or innocence by reconstructing the crime in minute, even obsessive detail. There are also more imaginative treatments of the Borden case in fiction, poetry, drama, dance, opera, and film; Lizzie has been used as a symbol of Victorian repression, of female madness, of rebellion against patriarchy, and even of mystery or uncertainty itself.

We can trace much of this collective compulsion to retell and reconstruct the crime to the fact that Lizzie did not testify at her trial and that a jury acquitted her in the face of strong evidence of guilt; both the absence of the defendant's own testimony and the irresolution of a "not guilty" verdict invite alternate versions of the story and speculation about what "really happened." However, the verdict itself is, for a student of history, as interesting as the question of whether she actually committed murder. How and why she escaped conviction is a matter of culture more than of simple logic, and her acquittal reveals a good deal about the tensions surrounding changing expectations of middle-class women's behavior at the turn into the twentieth century. To contemplate the trial of Lizzie Borden, then, is to encounter both a fascinating legal case and a vivid, concentrated picture of the complexity of gender ideology in the past. This essay argues that Lizzie Borden, who seemed to present a perfect image of genteel Christian womanhood, could not have been convicted in that place and at that moment in time. The first section will sketch the known facts of the case, including Lizzie's own explanation of what happened that day in interviews and in testimony she provided at the coroner's inquest. The second section analyzes the arguments of the defense and the prosecution at the trial and the way in which their rhetoric resonated with the most powerful and pervasive ideas about men, women, and morality at the end of the nineteenth century. . . .

In the 1893 trial of Lizzie Borden, the main cultural ideas in dispute were those having to do with definitions and interpretations of male and female nature and behavior. Lizzie Borden was accused, tried, and acquitted in light of one of the largest social questions of the day: What is a woman capable of? Indeed, both the prosecution and the defense presented arguments about the possibility of a genteel woman slaughtering her parents and about the responsibilities of the all-male jury in determining her fate that reiterated and drew upon the conflicts over gender roles that shaped the culture of the decades surrounding the turn of the century. In politics, the struggle for female suffrage continued to meet active resistance to the idea that women could be rational, responsible voters; in the realm of business, reformers worked to open the doors of all occupations and professions to women and split over the question of whether women workers required special treatment such as shorter hours; in medicine, newly prominent theories of women's health argued that almost any disease of the mind or body might be attributed to problems of the reproductive system or the failure to marry and bear children.

The crimes in Fall River obviously and urgently needed explanation not only because they were so violent, but also because that violence was itself so stunningly at odds with the ideal of protective and dutiful tenderness that was supposed to govern women's behavior within the family circle. The trial, then, was animated and intensified by the ways in which the crimes resonated with the most widespread social problems and fears of its time. The idea that the defendant was a genuine lady was central to the prosecutor's case and to the defense's arguments, and it was surely important to the process by which the jury weighed the evidence and declared the accused "not guilty." To say that Lizzie Borden got off because she was a woman is both to miss the point entirely and to hit the nail right on the head.

Lizzie Borden offered contradictory and sometimes cryptic testimony about the events of the day of the murders, though she always maintained that she was entirely innocent. In response to police questions at the scene and at the coroner's inquest (in those days a formal procedure to rule a death a homicide), she told of a rather desultory round of activities at home that morning. She awoke and came downstairs after her father, stepmother, and a visiting uncle had eaten their breakfasts. Her uncle and father left to go about their separate business errands; her stepmother assigned the maid, Bridget, to wash the outsides of the windows and began herself to dust and straighten the house.

In the hours between about 8:45 and 10:45, Lizzie put away some clean laundry, did a little mending, read an old magazine, and prepared to iron a few handkerchiefs on the dining room table, according to her testimony. Her father returned home shortly after 10:30, and she described helping him settle in for a nap on the sitting room sofa, removing his shoes and suit jacket and offering to adjust the window for his comfort. Then, while waiting for her irons to reheat on the stove, she said she went out to the barn behind the house to look for a piece of screen to repair a door, or a piece of tin to wedge her bedroom window screen more tightly into the frame, or some lead to make sinkers for a fishing trip in the future—the details varied from telling to telling. In the barn she paused to eat three pears from the tree in the yard and to look out the window. On one occasion she said that she had heard a groan or a scraping noise coming from the house; later she swore that she had heard nothing.

When she returned to the house after some period of time (maybe ten minutes, maybe thirty), she discovered the kitchen door wide open and her father where she had left him, bleeding profusely from ten gashes in his skull and face. She ran to the back staircase, called Bridget down from her attic room, and sent her to fetch Dr. Bowen, who lived across the street. The woman who lived next door heard the commotion and came over, saw Andrew's body, and asked someone at the livery stable on their block to call the police (that call came in at 11:15), then returned to the house to sit with Lizzie. The doctor arrived shortly thereafter and pronounced Andrew Borden dead.

People began to ask after Abby Borden; Lizzie said that her stepmother had received a note from a sick friend and had gone to call on her, though, on second thought, she was sure she had heard her stepmother return home. The next-door neighbor and Bridget went upstairs to look for her. They found Abby Borden's body on the floor of the guest bedroom, where she had been changing the pillowcases. She had been dead, the coroner later concluded, for approximately ninety minutes before her husband was killed. She had, like her husband, been murdered by multiple blows to the head and neck, though all nineteen of them had come from behind.

One of the first questions anyone asked Lizzie was "Where were you when it happened?" Her failure to provide a satisfactory answer was the main reason that she became a suspect in the case. To believe Lizzie's tale of ignorance and innocence, one needed to allow an intruder to slip into the house undetected, to murder Abby so quietly that neither Lizzie nor Bridget heard a sound (not even the sound of Abby's two-hundred-pound body falling on the second floor). The intruder would then have had to hide for at least an hour in the house or on the grounds, to murder Andrew Borden in the same remarkably silent manner, and finally to escape unnoticed before any alarm was raised. This series of events seemed particularly implausible, given the peculiar design of the Borden house and the customs of its inhabitants. The Borden house was unexpectedly small and comfortless for the family of a man of Andrew Borden's great wealth; it did not have running water above the first floor and was not connected to the city gas line. The house was long and narrow and divided into small rooms that opened onto one another, without connecting hallways. With three women (and then two women) moving about doing housework, where would there be a safe place to hide in those walk-through rooms, or a safe place to wield an axe without hallways to muffle sounds?

The plan for the second floor was especially awkward. Lizzie's bedroom could be entered from off the front staircase landing, but it also opened onto her elder sister Emma's bedroom and her parents' bedroom. For as long as anyone could remember, the door that communicated between the parents' bedroom and Lizzie's had been kept locked on both sides, an arrangement that split the second floor front, with the guest room and the daughters' rooms, from the second floor rear, with the elder Bordens' room. Andrew and Abby Borden's bedroom could be entered only by the back staircase (which continued up to the maid's attic room), and they further insured their privacy by keeping the door to that room locked at all times.

Locked doors were something of a point in the daily life of the Borden household. Not only did Andrew keep his bedroom locked, he also had installed three locks on the front door. From the testimony of Bridget and Lizzie, it is clear that all the inmates of the house were also careful to keep the cellar and kitchen doors locked when not in use. Despite their diligence, someone broke into the elder Bordens' bedroom about a year before the murders and stole jewelry and cash stored there; the custom of keeping the master bedroom key on the mantelpiece may have been a typically tight-lipped way for the parents to let Lizzie know that they suspected her of the theft. With all this locking of exterior and interior doors, a stranger would not only have had difficulty getting into the house, he or she would have had trouble moving about once inside, and would have faced obstacles in fleeing the house.

The case against Lizzie Borden was entirely circumstantial, built on the fact that she was at home, and driven by police suspicions about the way she answered questions and the way she behaved in the days following the discovery of the crimes. There were immediate problems with her stories. Though she declared that she had last seen her stepmother when Abby received that note calling her to someone's sickbed, no such note was ever found, and no one came forward to say that he or she had sent a message to the house. Police also wondered why Lizzie would want to go into, let alone linger in, the loft of a barn at midday during an August heat wave. One of the most suggestive actions Lizzie took was to destroy one of her dresses three days after the murders. She tore up the dress and burned it in the kitchen stove in the presence of her sister Emma and their friend Alice Russell.

Russell was troubled enough by the incident to approach the authorities with the information a few months after the murders; her last-minute testimony persuaded a previously indecisive grand jury to indict Lizzie Borden for the murders of her parents. Lizzie asserted that the dress had been ruined the previous spring when she brushed against wet brown paint inside the house, that she had worn it for some weeks after to do housework, and that she had burned the dress that morning because her sister complained that it was dirty and taking up space in their closet. At trial, the defense offered the observations of a dressmaker and Emma Borden to corroborate Lizzie's story. Lizzie's wardrobe was an important issue throughout the case. When the police asked her, days after the murders, to give them the clothes she had been wearing that morning, she furnished a blouse and skirt of blue silk and linen fabric. The dress she burned was also blue; there is contradictory testimony about what she was wearing when the first witnesses came on the scene, but it seems likely that she was not wearing the same dress that she furnished to the police.

Then there was the matter of the poisonings. In the two days before the murders, the Bordens and their maid had suffered from an acute intestinal illness; there was something about the circumstances that drove Abby across the street to Dr. Bowen's house, stating that the family was being poisoned. Lizzie had also said the family was under attack; the night before the murders, she visited Alice Russell and told of a "something hanging over me that I cannot throw off" and her fear that her father had enemies who might burn the house down around them. "I am afraid sometimes that somebody will do something to [Father]; he is so discourteous to people," she said. She made rather wild assertions that the milk was being poisoned, or perhaps the bread from the baker. She related an anecdote about overhearing an argument between a prospective tenant and her father, a story she later told at the coroner's inquest. The authorities were extremely skeptical about these presentiments of disaster, especially after their investigation revealed that Lizzie had attempted to buy prussic acid, a highly concentrated poison, the day before the murders (though that evidence was excluded at her trial).

Apart from her circumstantial position and the improbability of her stories, there was little hard evidence against Lizzie Borden. Bridget Sullivan insisted she had neither heard nor seen anything that suggested Lizzie's guilt. She testified that she had been washing the outside of the windows for much of the morning, and that she was taking a nap on the third floor between the time that Andrew Borden arrived and the time that Lizzie called her downstairs with the words "Come down quick; Father's dead; somebody came in and killed him." One witness, passing by the house, testified that he saw Lizzie walking from the barn to the house at around the time she said she had been doing so, and a few people testified to seeing various suspicious strangers near the Borden house that morning or in the environs of the city soon after the murders. Though there were several hatchets in the house, none was positively proven to be the murder weapon (one that looked suspicious tested negative for blood residue in a forensic laboratory). The witnesses who had seen her immediately after the bodies were discovered all said that they had seen no blood on her clothing, skin, or hair. Police, friends, and neighbors who had seen her at that time concurred that she appeared calm and self-possessed, though one person said she saw tears in Lizzie's eyes. The questions of how Lizzie might have washed the blood off her body, concealed any bloodstained cloth-

ing, and hidden or thoroughly washed an axe in the very short period of time she had while Bridget was taking her nap—about ten or fifteen minutes—raise substantial doubts about her guilt, or her exclusive guilt. One reason for the enduring fascination of the case is the way in which the implausibility of her tale of an intruder is so evenly matched by the implausibility of the prosecutor's tale of a daughter who murders her parents suddenly and violently and appears fifteen minutes later looking normal in every way.

Lizzie was arrested one week after the crimes, and imprisoned in the jail in nearby Taunton, Massachusetts. As early as the day of the murders, the press began to point the finger of suspicion toward her; the *Boston Advertiser* reported in its evening edition that the police were focusing their investigations on "persons within the family circle," specifically Lizzie and her uncle John Morse (who was eliminated as a suspect in the first twenty-four hours). The more circumspect *Fall River Herald* waited thirty-six hours before gently suggesting that since "Mr. Borden's daughters were ladies who had always conducted themselves so that the breath of scandal could never reach them," the pattern of evidence at the Borden home would soon bring the police "face to face with embarrassing difficulties." That tension between the obvious need to consider Lizzie a suspect on the strength of the evidence and the impossibility of considering a woman of her social stature as an axe murderer made the story especially fascinating, since it interwove questions of logic with questions of culture and lived experience. In general, papers in and close to Fall River tended to highlight the suspicion against Lizzie; the more distant New York papers tended to underline carefully the indeterminancy of the case against her, perhaps because the locally delectable irony of a Borden being arrested for a violent crime was less germane to the interest of the story elsewhere. Upon Lizzie's arrest, some newspapers expressed surprise and even outrage. One editorialized that given the brutality, depravity, and "devilish malignity" of the murders, "to believe that it could have been committed by a physically weak woman, whose entire life has been one of refined influences, of Christian profession and work, of filial devotion, of modesty and self-abnegation, is to set aside as of no value all that experience and observation have taught us."

The coverage of the case quickly proved to be in and of itself a contentious matter, especially when it came to gender politics. Two days after the murders, one woman reporter for the *Boston Herald* began an article about Lizzie's good character by asserting that "it is the men who have, since the murder, been accorded the space" to present Lizzie's character and personality; "a woman's opinion of a woman is a consideration Lizzie Borden has not yet been allowed." While Lizzie was in jail awaiting trial, she received a public vote of confidence from her fellow members of the local chapter of the national alcohol reform movement, the Women's Christian Temperance Union (WCTU), and had her case presented sympathetically in the journal of the American Woman Suffrage Association by famous women's rights advocates Mary Livermore and Lucy Stone. Livermore, suffragist and author of a book arguing for women's employment entitled *What Shall We Do with Our Daughters?*, interviewed Lizzie in jail and came away impressed with her innocence. She stressed Lizzie's sensitivity, declaring that the press's negative depictions of her unfeeling "stolidity" were "absurd. You can see that she feels her position very keenly." Livermore reinterpretated Lizzie's cool manner for her readers, suggesting that it was actually the outward show of gentility and good breeding: her Lizzie exclaims, "[W]hat would they have me to? Howl? Go into hysterics? . . . I am trying hard to keep calm and self-controlled until I shall be proved innocent."

Another jailhouse interview by a female reporter came to similar conclusions: it presented a sentimental vignette about Lizzie kissing her father's corpse after it was carefully prepared by the undertaker and allowed Lizzie to respond to specific allegations in the press, particularly the mistrust of her detached, inexpressive demeanor. Her Lizzie explains, "I have tried very hard to be brave and womanly through it all." This last article provoked a condescending response from the *Fall River Globe*, one of the newspapers most certain of Lizzie's guilt. In an editorial, the *Globe* mocked the "flap-doodle, gush, idiotic drivel, misrepresentations, and in some instances, anarchic nonsense, which is being promulgated by women newspaper correspondents, WCTU conventions, and other female agencies." Although it is not true that support for Lizzie split on simple gender lines, with men accusing and women defending, it is clear that the question of Lizzie's guilt or innocence was very much caught up in the rhetoric about women's distinctive moral style that surrounded the suffrage and temperance movements.

Overall, Lizzie did not suffer too badly at the hands of the press and seemed to learn that reporters would be reassured of her innocence if they saw overt signs of conventional upper-middle-class femininity in her attitude and behavior. The press, in other words, rewarded her for performing (deliberately or unconsciously) the role of the beset maiden in a style it could understand. She fainted at several strategic moments in the trial, leaned visibly on the arm of the minister who escorted her into the courtroom each day, and reverted to wearing deep mourning for the trial. She was besieged by the press after the murders, but she rarely gave interviews before or during her trial, and never afterward. She showed what we might now call "media savvy" when she employed a private detective from the Pinkerton agency only days after the murders. His charge seems to have been more in the area of public relations than forensic investigation, for the *New York Herald* reported that "Mr. Hanscom's time is chiefly spent about the Mellen house [presumably a tavern] in affable conversation with the newspaper men in whose affections he has made great progress" and suggested that he is the source of at least one of the rumors of strange men lurking about the Borden property on the day of the murders.

Given the public thirst for information about the Borden murders, it is not surprising that the *Boston Globe* was hoodwinked by an enterprising writer into printing a highly sensational account of life in the Borden household later that fall. The utterly groundless tale had Lizzie pregnant and described a violent row between Lizzie and Andrew the night before the murders, in which Andrew threatened to disown her if she did not name the man who had got her "in trouble"—a man who the article's author indicated was none other than Lizzie's uncle John Morse. This story reads like the seediest type of late-Victorian melodrama, and is interesting only for the way it plays out in sensational terms the period's concerns with paternal authority and daughterly dependence in the threat of disinheritance and banishment. In a cynical inversion, it also twists the ideals of domestic intimacy and intensity into a plot of incest. Ultimately, even this story did not damage Lizzie too greatly; the *Boston Globe* was embarrassed into the position of thereafter defending the woman it had so blatantly abused, and the incident on the whole bolstered arguments that she was being mistreated. During the trial, press accounts were almost uniformly straightforward and, as time wore on, convinced that Lizzie would be acquitted (especially after her damaging inquest testimony was excluded). We can trace, over time, a general movement from quick accusation to belief that conviction was unjustified or impossible as reporters considered the tension between Lizzie's social status (well-bred lady) and her forensic status (prime suspect).

However, the trial itself was vigorously argued, and demonstrated, even more clearly than the newspapers, how deeply the mystery of the Borden murders resonated with cultural questions about women's nature. At the trial, which began ten months after the murders, there was much to say, of course, about the physical condition of the crime scenes, the timetable of events, the results of the autopsies of the victims, and other details of the murder, but the real focus of attention was on the character of the defendant—in both senses of the term. Both the prosecution and the defense offered interpretations of her moral character, and they wanted to present her as a knowable type or character in familiar cultural narratives. As we might expect, the two versions of Lizzie's character were diametrically opposed, but each was drafted from the "fund of social knowledge" that constituted Victorian culture's view of women. This focus on character is not unusual in a popular trial. Hariman calls it a "generic constraint" of the phenomenon, one that "amplifies both the dramatic nature of the trial . . . and [the trial's] rhetorical disposition, for character (in the classical vocabulary, *ethos*) is one of the three basic modes of proof." Hariman argues that characters serve to focus the abstractions of the ideas and social issues being adjudicated in a trial, so that, for example, "communism became the Rosenbergs" in the popular imagination. That association works in both directions; in the Lizzie Borden case, as Kathryn Jacob puts it, "not only a particular woman, but the entire Victorian conception of womanhood, was on trial for its life."

Because Lizzie was accused of murdering her father and stepmother, it is perhaps not surprising that the most consistent element in the various characterizations was her status as a daughter, despite her fully adult age of thirty-two years. Alexander Woollcott, a professional wag of the time, dubbed her a "self-made orphan," a joke that cuts right to the heart of the matter. Now fatherless and motherless in any case, the question was whether Lizzie had entered that state by chance or by design, and whether she was deserving of public sympathy or of the death penalty.

Her lead defense attorney, Andrew Jennings, made much of her vulnerable position as an unmarried, unparented woman. He made her out to be the pitiable victim of a police force unable to solve the crime, and he made it clear that she was undeserving of their suspicion. Her past life made that task easy. Lizzie was the real thing, a lady by virtue of her old New England name and Anglo-Saxon ancestry, her father's wealth, and her own personal style. Lizzie's public life before the trial was a long list of good works and worthy undertakings: she was a member of the most fashionable and influential Congregational church in Fall River and taught Sunday school there to Chinese immigrant children. She served as secretary and treasurer of the church's Christian Endeavour Society, and helped serve holiday dinners for the impoverished newsboys of the city. She joined the Fruit and Flower Mission to the city hospital and eventually had a place on its board, and she was elected secretary of the Fall River chapter of the WCTU. She lived a model life for a single woman of her day; she seemed to know her place in the social hierarchy and seemed to want to make herself "useful," in the terminology of her class. Because genteel women did not work unless they fell on hard times—and only then at a few professions, like teaching—a slate of church-associated charity work was the fitting occupation for an unmarried gentlewoman like Lizzie Borden.

She had, as part and parcel of this ladylike style, lived her life as a dependent of her father. In his opening argument, Jennings cast himself and the jury as the protectors of this young woman in distress, the enforcers of the sheltering "circle of the presumption of . . . her innocence" that the law inscribes around a defendant, the replacements for the father she had lost. In his closing argument, her other attorney, George Robinson, also lingered on this idea, pointing out that in the special oath reserved for capital cases, the jurors had accepted responsibility for the defendant as being in their "charge."

Robinson painted a picture of the relationship between father and daughter meant to make the accusation of patricide seem not just cynical, but unspeakable. He focused the jury's attention on a ring Lizzie had given to Andrew, "a man that wore nothing in the way of ornament, of jewelry, but one ring, and that ring was Lizzie's." The ring, even at that mo-

ment on Andrew's hand as he lay in his casket, "stands as the pledge of plighted faith and love, that typifies and symbolizes the dearest relation that is ever created in life . . . the bond of union between the father and the daughter." In a deft rhetorical move, Robinson offered this proof of Andrew's devotion to his daughter as an argument for Lizzie's innocence, declaring, "No man should be heard to say that she murdered the man that so loved her." Though, as historian Ann Jones points out, this portrait of father-daughter devotion takes on a troubling tint in our post-Freudian age, it drew forcefully from the mainstream emotional vocabulary of the Victorian era. The culture of the middle and upper classes of the nineteenth century was in many ways defined by its intense longing for tender, harmonious, and demonstrative relationships within the family circle. As life in the world of advancing industrialization and accelerating capitalism came to seem more rough, competitive, amoral, and alienating, the domestic sphere became increasingly the province of women, who were charged with making the home a serene refuge, redolent of beauty and goodness, for their husbands, fathers, brothers, and sons. The symbolic reading of the ring may sound forced to our ears, but it would have sounded more natural, even reassuring, to the all-male jury, most of whom were property-owning, middle-class fathers more than fifty years of age.

Although the wearing of the ring proved nothing in a legal sense, it gave the jury something to count as physical evidence of the tenderness they were already educated to expect of a woman and of the charming displays of enduring affection that they might have wished from their own daughters. Robinson wanted the jurors to juxtapose this portrait of Lizzie's tender expressiveness with the brutality of the murders:

> The terror of those scenes no language can portray. The horrors of the moment we can all fail to describe. And so we are challenged at once, at the outset, to find someone that is equal to the enormity, whose heart is blackened with de-

pravity, whose whole life is a tissue of crime, whose past is a prophecy of the present. A maniac or a fiend, we say. Not a man in his senses and with his heart right, but one of those abnormal productions that the Deity creates or suffers, a lunatic or a devil.

Robinson's fundamental argument for her innocence was that "such acts as those are morally and physically impossible for this young woman defendant," and he demanded that jurors call on their Victorian common sense about the strength of family ties: "To foully murder the stepmother and then go straight away and slay her own father is a wreck of human morals." By expressing outrage at the accusation of patricide, Jennings and Robinson not only reassured the jurors that all was right with their view of the world, they also allowed the jurors to cast themselves in the pleasant role of a manly guardian of womanly honor.

The prosecution also focused on Lizzie's career as a dependent daughter, but to very different effect. In District Attorney Hosea Knowlton's version of the crimes, the motive for the murders lay in exactly those family relationships that Jennings and Robinson presented in such hushed tones. They offered, through the testimony of neighbors, servants, and even a reluctant Emma Borden, a starkly different picture of life in the Borden household.

Knowlton's theory was that Lizzie was driven to murder by a combination of greed and a deep hatred of her stepmother. Andrew Borden was a very wealthy man, but a notorious miser. He was born into the poorer branch of the successful Bordens in the Fall River area, and began his working life as an undertaker. He was known as a shrewd businessman, and he was disliked for it. In Fall River, the story circulated that Andrew Borden had, in those early years, bought a batch of undersized coffins at a cut rate, then severed the legs of his corpses to make them fit. Borden also owned a good deal of real estate, which he managed for a profit. Later, as Fall River reached the peak of its industrial boom, water rights that he had inherited brought him great wealth. He built a large building in the business district, which he named for himself, and he sat on the boards of several local banks and textile mills. His estate, at his death, was worth about $300,000, several million in today's money.

Yet, the Borden home was not on the fashionable hill where others of Andrew Borden's wealth and standing lived, nor did it boast the standard comforts of the urban middle-class home of the period. One of the few light notes in this grisly case is the revelation of the habits of frugality in the Borden kitchen and dining room: in the days before they died, the elder Bordens had interrupted a steady progress of leftovers through a leg of mutton (so steady that they even served mutton broth for breakfast on the day of the murders) only to consume reheated swordfish, suggesting that they had iron wills if not iron stomachs. Andrew Borden did not believe in waste and he did not, it seems fair to speculate, believe in comfort or pleasure either.

The defense, in trying to minimize the portrait of Andrew Borden as a despot who might provoke murderous rebellion, spoke to the jury of middle-aged men in the language of the older generation: Andrew Borden was an admirably old-fashioned man resisting the general trend toward spending instead of saving, of indulging in conspicuous consumption instead of building a solid financial foundation. In any case, how fully Borden's parsimony extended to his relationships with his daughters is unclear. Some people reported that Lizzie was deeply distressed by her inability to buy the sort of clothes that she wanted or to entertain her social peers at her home. Others said that she had her father wrapped around her little finger and that, to the chagrin of his second wife, he gave her whatever she wanted. In any case, her desire to participate in the capitalist elite's patterns of consumption seems to have been a source of friction within the Borden household.

As in many families, in the Borden household disputes over money were conflated with struggles for power; long-standing resentments between the two generations had come to a crisis point in the five years preceding the murder. Lizzie's sister Emma, though ten years older, was a close ally in a divided household. Their mother had died when Emma was twelve and Lizzie was two years old, their father remarried two years later, and the girls never accepted Abby in the role of mother nor, it seems, brought her to any place in their affections. At the trial, the prosecution made much of Lizzie's "unkindly feeling" toward her stepmother. A policeman testified that while interviewing Lizzie only hours after the murders, he was corrected sharply when he referred to Abby as "your mother." A seamstress testified that about five months before the murders, her use of the term "Mother" for Abby had likewise provoked an angry rebuke; Lizzie said that her stepmother was a "mean, good-for-nothing thing. . . . I don't have much to do with her; I stay in my room most of the time. . . . [W]e don't eat with them if we can help it." Both Bridget Sullivan and Emma Borden also testified that the daughters avoided eating meals with their parents, and that they had understood the front part of the upstairs, including their bedrooms and the guest room, to be their portion of the house. Even though Emma was testifying in her sister's defense, she could not completely gloss over the frigidity in the relations between stepmother and stepdaughters. To the question "Were relations between you and Mrs. Borden cordial?" she answered, "I don't know what you mean by cordial. We always spoke." Emma had always addressed her stepmother as "Abby"; Lizzie, who had called Abby "Mother" in her childhood, took up addressing her as "Mrs. Borden" after a serious family quarrel that occurred five years before the murder.

That dispute, which brought simmering resentments to a rolling boil, centered on Andrew's real estate holdings. Emma and Lizzie Borden became highly agitated when they learned that Andrew helped Abby's half sister, Sarah Whitehead, by buying up a piece of property in which she had held a partial share, and giving Abby the deed. Emma and Lizzie demanded an equal consideration, and as a result their father deeded to them a rental property, formerly their grandfather's house, in Fall River. The defense tried to argue that Lizzie had such personal wealth (about $5,000) that she would never have thought of killing her father for his money. The prosecution suggested that the attacks might have been precipitated by talk about making a will. No will was ever found. There has been some rather imaginative speculation, at the time of the murders and in more recent accounts, that Lizzie burned a will that named Abby Borden as chief beneficiary. It is important, legally, that Abby Borden was killed before her husband; had she survived him even briefly, at least a third of his estate would have gone to *her* heirs. In the end, Emma and Lizzie (after the latter was acquitted) inherited their father's entire fortune.

The conflicts and anxieties of this family connected in many ways to larger historical conflicts and anxieties in the New England of the late nineteenth century. The daughters' worry over the dispersal of their father's fortune echoes, on a smaller scale, the general distress over the decline of Fall River's cotton textile industry after the Civil War, and the narrowing prospect of family fortunes made at midcentury enduring through future generations. Their apparent greed was also connected to their social status and experience in more gender-specific ways. Emma and Lizzie were New England spinsters at a time of growing concern over spinsterhood and the problem of women with "nothing to do." As middle-class women, their main chance at social standing was married motherhood, but their father's refusal to take his rightful residential place in the stratified society of Fall River, with its attendant refusal to fund the courtship rituals of dinner parties and dances, must have undermined their marriageability. Had Emma and Lizzie been sons, they would have been able to enter their father's businesses, taking some corner of his empire to make their own fortunes. As it was, the only way their father's money could come to them was in the form of gifts, including the ultimate gift of inheritance. As daughters, they had no way to earn the family money or the freedom it stood for; as the daughters of a miser, they could not enjoy the wealth that he had accrued.

Knowlton saw in this pressurized family situation a motive for murder, and he thought the jury, cognizant of the social problem of the "superfluous" woman, would see it, too. Like the defense attorneys, the prosecutors focused on Lizzie's character as the key to understanding the truth of the murders. But if Jennings and Robinson relied on the ideological, socially constructed category of womanliness as an a priori argument for Lizzie Borden's virtue and innocence, the prosecutors in the case exposed the cultural double of female virtue, which is secret and irrational vice. As Nina Auerbach has explained, Victorian culture understood the "lunatic or devil," "fiend or maniac" (Robinson's description of the murderer) to be not entirely the opposite of virtuous womanhood but something more like a shadow or even a corollary of it.

Robinson, in his closing argument for the defense, argued for the reliability of appearance. He pointed out that "to find her guilty you must believe her to be a fiend! Does she look it?" And he insisted that the jurors could believe their own eyes: "As she sat here these long weary days and moved in and out before you, have you seen anything that shows the lack of human feeling and womanly bearing?" Robinson, in effect, contended that social knowledge is simple and straightforward: we know what we know because people and things are as they appear.

District Attorney Knowlton offered a more complicated reading of Lizzie's demeanor and history in his closing argument. He acknowledged that the prisoner was the social peer of the jurors and judge, calling her "of the rank of lady, the equal of your wife and mine." His goal, however, was to suggest that Lizzie Borden's respectable, Christian appearance was deceptive. Knowlton asserted, drawing on the

strongest cultural fears about the female body and female wickedness, that "time and time again have we been grieved to learn, pained to find, that those set up to teach us the correct way of life have been found themselves to be as foul as hell inside."

Knowlton used the principles of trickery, treachery, and unpredictability to articulate a theory of female criminality: "If [women] lack in strength and coarseness and vigor, they make up for it in cunning, in dispatch, in celerity, in ferocity. If their loves are stronger and more enduring than those of men, their hates are more undying, more unyielding, more persistent." And continuing to work his arguments around inversions of the cultural principles that assigned women to the realm of ornament and sentiment, Knowlton offered this way for the jurors to estrange themselves from the accused and to dismiss the evidentiary questions raised by the defense: "How could she have avoided the spattering of her dress with blood if she was the author of these crimes? I cannot answer it. You cannot answer it. You are neither murderers nor women. You have neither the craft of the assassin nor the cunning and deftness of the sex."

Knowlton's rhetoric indicates the ease with which Victorian ideology could be made to produce doubles, inversions, and shadows of its most sacred truths about gender and class. Even as it contradicted the defense portrait of natural feminine docility and devotion, this picture of womanhood was equally expressive of the social knowledge clustered around gender in the late nineteenth century. Although women were, in Knowlton's words, the "sex that all high-minded men revere, that all generous men love, that all wise men acknowledge their indebtedness to," Victorian wisdom had it that when women went bad, they went very bad indeed. Insanity was the usual form and symptom of women's deviance in Victorian literature and art, and one of the most important figures for the period is, as Sandra Gilbert and Susan Gubar have shown, the "madwoman in the attic." Like Bertha Rochester in Charlotte Brontë's Jane

Eyre, the madwoman rebels against being shut away in the interior of the house and becomes a symbol for the anger that is so utterly unacceptable in the demeanor of the genteel lady.

The prosecution's closing argument drew directly on this cultural mythology. Knowlton focused on Andrew Borden's murder, calling it the "far sadder tragedy" of the two murders, for he hypothesized that Lizzie killed her stepmother first in a rage and killed her father out of the cold realization that he would know the truth about his wife's death no matter what she said in protest. He dramatized for the jury an imagined encounter between father and daughter just before the murder in which Andrew confronts Lizzie about the murder of his wife. In Knowlton's wording, Andrew Borden takes on mythological stature as "Nemesis," the punisher of the proud and the insolent, and historical significance as "that just old man of the stern Puritan stock" (stock, Knowlton reminded the jurors, that they shared with the victim). Lizzie became nothing less than the madwoman escaped from her attic: "[S]he came down those stairs [from the room where she had killed Abby] . . . transformed from the daughter, transformed from the ties of affection, to the most consummate criminal we have read of in all our history or works of fiction."

Knowlton worked to show Lizzie as a woman—or madwoman—of sufficient evil and cunning to plot and commit parricide between visits to hospital wards and the preparation of Sunday school lesson plans. Such a character is difficult to believe in and uncomfortable to contemplate, so Knowlton made sure to include more mundane demonstrations of a bad nature. Unkind to her stepmother, selfish in her desire for luxury, willful in her actions—if Knowlton's murderess were in a novel of the period, she would quickly be brought to grief or to heel. It is an understatement to say that the prosecutor's strategy was complex and that his arguments were contradictory; what is consistent in them is a desire to consign female criminality to a female realm of the irrational, the emotional, the unknowable.

In the end, normative domestic ideology prevailed; jurors rejected the commonwealth's case against this moneyed female defendant. They did not even deliberate but produced a unanimous "not guilty" vote on the first ballot (then, they later revealed, cooled their heels in the jury room for an hour so as not to seem hasty). By continually reminding the members of the all-male jury that they were in a paternal relationship with Lizzie Borden, by depicting her as a young woman bereft of her own father's protection, by allowing them to see her as a grateful and devoted daughter to her father, and by trading on the cultural currency of class types, Jennings and Robinson successfully argued for acquittal. A story of parricide within a wealthy household was, apparently, not a story that the justices and jurors, themselves middle-class fathers and heads of households, wished to hear. They would rather, it seems, see Lizzie as the angel hovering solicitously over the parlor sofa where her father prepared for a nap than as the madwoman descending the staircase with an axe to bash his head in and claim her inheritance. The defense allowed them to feel comfortably masculine and comfortable with their sense of what women are capable of doing.

Lizzie left the courthouse and went back to the family home with her sister. She and her sister soon used part of their inheritance to buy a comfortable, elegantly decorated home in a fashionable neighborhood of Fall River. Until 1905, the two sisters, neither of whom ever married or began a career, lived together there. They had a serious quarrel—the nature of which they kept to themselves—and Emma moved to New Hampshire, leaving Lizzie to live in the new house, attended by four servants, until her death in 1927. Though Lizzie was acquitted, she never lived down the accusations against her, and she was shunned by most of polite Fall River society, even the congregation of the church to which she had belonged before the trial. Anecdotes about her life after the murders include fits of violent rage and shoplifting. Others who knew her said that she was an extremely generous person, who put several young men through college and lent her automobile for the pleasure of shut-ins and the elderly. Upon her death, which preceded Emma's by only days, she left the bulk of her fortune to the Animal Rescue League and made generous provisions for her servants, for impecunious friends, and for the perpetual upkeep of the family cemetery plot. She lies there together with her sisters, her mother, her father, and her stepmother. No one else was ever tried for the murders.

For us, looking back from a distance of one hundred years at this case about which so much has been argued, imagined, and interpolated, there is still reason to ponder this notorious parricide and acquittal. A crime that becomes national or even regional news has to present something extraordinary and puzzling—the viciousness of the attack, the extreme innocence of the victim, the hitherto unblemished public life of the person accused of the murder. For the purposes of historical study, however, what seems deviant and exceptional actually sheds light on what is normative and typical. Indeed, for a case of murder to move into the public eye, and from there into the popular imagination, it must resonate with the old and new mythologies, anxieties, and conflicts of the culture.

The Borden murders became important, and remain important, because so many of the things that seem particular to the case were also expressive of larger economic and social questions at issue in that historical period in New England. Moreover, study of the trial reveals the process by which a community collectively struggles over and puts into narrative an act of unexpected violence. In the Borden case, that process revealed the paradoxes and contradictions in Victorian wisdom about woman's nature, and yet reaffirmed the power of appearances, of "common sense," of middle-class platitudes about daughterly devotion and feminine morality. Lizzie beat the charges against her not just because she was a woman but more precisely because she was a lady in all the ways that her historical moment demanded. As many pointed out at the time and in the century since, had Lizzie been a poor woman or a man of almost any class, the murder would have had a different meaning within the culture and the trial might well have had a different outcome. The Borden case tells us that although the power of conventionality is at any time formidable, each era actively negotiates what common sense about violence will consist of and to whom it will offer relief.

SUGGESTIONS FOR FURTHER READING

MARYBETH HAMILTON ARNOLD, " 'The Life of a Citizen in the Hands of a Woman': Sexual Assault in New York City, 1790–1820," in *Passion and Power: Sexuality in History,* ed. Kathy Peiss and Christina Simmons (Philadelphia: Temple University Press, 1989), 35–56.

PETER BARDAGLIO, " 'An Outrage upon Nature': Incest and the Law in the Nineteenth-Century South," in *In Joy and in Sorrow: Women, Family, and Marriage in the Victorian South, 1830–1900,* ed. Carol Bleser (New York: Oxford University Press, 1991), 32–51.

GAIL BEDERMAN, " 'The White Man's Civilization on Trial': Ida B. Wells, Representations of Lynching, and Northern Middle-Class Manhood," in *Manliness & Civilization: A Cultural History of Gender and Race in the United States, 1880–1917* (Chicago: University of Chicago Press, 1995), 45–76.

DICKSON D. BRUCE, JR., *Violence and Culture in the Antebellum South* (Austin: University of Texas Press, 1979).

PATRICIA CLINE COHEN, *The Murder of Helen Jewett: The Life and Death of a Prostitute in Nineteenth-Century New York* (New York: Vintage Books, 1999).

PATRICIA CLINE COHEN, "Unregulated Youth: Masculinity and Murder in the 1830s City," *Radical History Review,* 52 (Winter 1992), 33–52.

BETSY DOWNEY, "Battered Pioneers: Jules Sandoz and the Physical Abuse of Wives on the American Frontier," *Great Plains Quarterly*, 12 (Winter 1992), 31–49.

LAURA F. EDWARDS, "Sexual Violence, Gender, Reconstruction, and the Extension of Patriarchy in Granville County, North Carolina," *North Carolina Historical Review*, LXVIII (July 1991), 237–60.

LAURA F. EDWARDS, "Women and Domestic Violence in Nineteenth-Century North Carolina," in *Lethal Imagination: Violence and Brutality in American History*, ed. Michael A. Bellesiles (New York: New York University Press, 1999), 114–36.

LINDA GORDON, *Heroes of Their Own Lives: The Politics and History of Family Violence, Boston, 1880–1960* (New York: Viking/Penguin, 1988).

LINDA GORDON, "A Right Not to Be Beaten: The Agency of Battered Women, 1880–1960," in *Gendered Domains: Rethinking Public and Private in Women's History*, ed. Dorothy O. Helly and Susan M. Reverby (Ithaca, NY: Cornell University Press, 1992), 228–43.

ELLIOTT J. GORN, " 'Good-Bye Boys, I Die a True American': Homicide, Nativism, and Working-Class Culture in Antebellum New York City," *Journal of American History*, 74 (Sept. 1987), 388–410.

PAMELA HAAG, "The 'Ill-Use of a Wife': Patterns of Working-Class Violence in Domestic and Public New York City, 1860–1880," *Journal of Social History*, 25 (Spring 1992), 447–77.

JACQUELYN DOWD HALL, " 'The Mind That Burns in Each Body': Women, Rape, and Racial Violence," in *Powers of Desire: The Politics of Sexuality*, ed. Ann Snitow, Christine Stansell, and Sharon Thompson (New York: Monthly Review Press, 1983), 328–49.

JACQUELYN DOWD HALL, "A Strange and Bitter Fruit," in *Revolt Against Chivalry: Jessie Daniel Ames and the Women's Campaign Against Lynching* (New York: Columbia University Press, 1993), 129–57.

KAREN HALTTUNEN, " 'Domestic Differences': Competing Narratives of Womanhood in the Murder Trial of Lucretia Chapman," in *The Culture of Sentiment: Race, Gender, and Sentimentality in Nineteenth-Century America*, ed. Shirley Samuels (New York: Oxford University Press, 1992), 39–57.

PAULA K. HINTON, " 'The Unspeakable Mrs. Gunness': The Deviant Woman in Early-Twentieth-Century America," in *Lethal Imagination: Violence and Brutality in American History*, ed. Michael A. Bellesiles (New York : New York University Press, 1999), 326–51.

BARBARA S. LINDEMANN, " 'To Ravish and Carnally Know': Rape in Eighteenth-Century Massachusetts," *Signs*, 10 (Autumn 1984), 63–82.

ANN M. LITTLE, " 'She Would Bump His Mouldy Britch': Authority, Masculinity, and the Harried Husbands of New Haven Colony, 1638–1670," in *Lethal Imagination: Violence and Brutality in American History*, ed. Michael A. Bellesiles (New York: New York University Press, 1999), 42–66.

MELTON A. MCLAURIN, *Celia, A Slave* (New York: Avon, 1991).

JEROME NADELHOFT, "Wife Torture: A Known Phenomenon in Nineteenth-Century America," *Journal of American Culture*, 10 (Fall 1987), 39–59.

MARY E. ODEM, "Cultural Representations and Social Contexts of Rape in the Early Twentieth Century," in *Lethal Imagination: Violence and Brutality in American History*, ed. Michael A. Bellesiles (New York: New York University Press, 1999), 352–70.

DAVID PETERSON DEL MAR, *What Trouble I Have Seen: A History of Violence Against Wives* (Cambridge, MA: Harvard University Press, 1996).

ELIZABETH PLECK, *Domestic Tyranny: The Making of Social Policy Against Family Violence from Colonial Times to the Present* (New York: Oxford University Press, 1987).

ELIZABETH PLECK, "Wife-Beating in Nineteenth-Century America," *Victimology*, 4 (1979), 60–74.

WILLIAM M. TUTTLE, JR., *Race Riot: Chicago in the Red Summer of 1919* (Urbana: University of Illinois Press, 1996).

CHAPTER FIFTEEN

GENDER AND WORK
(1600–1975)

THE GENDERED NATURE OF LABOR

In 1849, just a year after she and Lucretia Mott helped to organize the first woman's rights convention in Seneca Falls, New York, Elizabeth Cady Stanton decided to do what she could to encourage the young, single women of her acquaintance to "strike out some new path to wealth and distinction beside[s] the needle, & marriage as a necessity." Several young women in need of work came to her for advice and assistance. She encouraged two of them to move to Buffalo, New York to open a school. But the aspirations of Elizabeth McClintock and Anna Southwick were less conventional. They declared that they wanted to become silk merchants, a vocation they hoped would provide them the opportunity to travel throughout the world in search of fine fabric to sell to fashionable women all along the East Coast.

Stanton sought employment for them at E. M. Davis & Co., a fabric import business with offices in Philadelphia and New York.

The owner of the company, Edward Davis, was Lucretia Mott's son-in-law. As a Quaker interested in social reform, he, in theory at least, was committed to the idea of human equality. So Stanton wrote to Mott and asked if she would intercede with Davis to arrange employment for the two young women.

Mott did as Stanton asked. And Davis responded to his mother-in-law's request a few weeks later. He reported that he had contacted his office in New York, asking that they consider the proposal, and had called a staff meeting in Philadelphia in order to discuss it with his own employees. The staff of the New York office replied almost immediately by letter. "We are *heart, soul,* & body in favor of advancing woman at least to the status of self dependence," they assured Davis. And they declared that they had no reservations whatsoever about the "common sense" of the young women in question or about their possession of the kind of good "taste" and aesthetic sensibilities that were necessary in the fabric import business. Experience had shown, they willingly conceded, that "in almost every instance where they have opportunity, [women] make first rate salesmen." Having said that, however, they refused to take a position on whether Davis should hire McClintock and Southwick. In their letter, they wrote, "We have not the courage to say *no* nor will we take the responsibility of saying *yes.*"

Davis got much the same response from his employees in Philadelphia. None of the men in his firm objected in *principle* to hiring female clerks. But predictably most thought hiring McClintock and Southwick unwise and inexpedient. Their objections focused on four issues. The first was that the presence of women in their office might hurt their business. While they regretted the kind of "absurd prejudice" and "senseless objections" that some might have toward the employment of women, they were afraid that if they were bold enough to hire McClintock and Southwick, their customers might decide to take their business elsewhere. They did not believe the company had sufficient capital reserves to withstand such a boycott. One even went so far as to estimate that it might take a reserve of a half million dollars to protect it against financial loss. Their second concern centered on the degree to which the female "delicacy" of the two young women might be compromised by their daily contact with men, who they implied were by their very nature coarse and unrefined. They also expressed concern about the kind of sexual tension that they might have to endure if they were forced to work in close proximity to women to whom they were unrelated. At the very least, they feared that the presence of women in their office and warehouse would prove a distraction to them. Their final reservation was that the young women in question might be unwilling to perform the duties that were demanded of a clerk. Clerking, they pointed out, was not really a very glamorous job. Indeed, it involved performing all sorts of menial tasks such as running to the bank and sweeping out the store, opening crates, and carrying around large bolts of fabric. Given the background of

the young ladies involved, they were afraid McClintock and Southwick would find such tasks demeaning and might use their "femaleness" as an excuse to avoid the more onerous and tedious aspects of the job. In essence, they felt that female clerks might, in some instances, be more of a hindrance than a help.

In the end, Davis decided not to hire the two young applicants. His reasoning ran something like this. He believed that people should be hired "in every department of business in which they were qualified." But in this case, the young women in question did not have the necessary qualifications. They had no training whatever in the import business. And they did not have any capital to invest to compensate for their lack of training. Therefore, he advised them that if they were serious about working in the fabric business, they should first seek employment in a retail dry goods store. As one of the Davis employees put it, "In one year spent in a fancy retail store you would learn more of fabrick, styles, combinations etc. than in 5 years with us and that would begin to prepare you for our part of the trade. Only in two ways can you attain it, either by gradually working up to it, gathering capital as you progress, or by entering some House whose vast means would enable it to raise you *at once* to position not as a humiliating gratuity to you, but as the beginning of the payment of that immense debt which man owes to woman."

Davis's decision seems to have ended the matter. No more letters about the subject of female employment in the fabric import business flowed between Seneca Falls and Philadelphia. And it does not appear as if Elizabeth McClintock and her friend Anna Southwick took Davis's advice to seek employment in a retail dry goods store.

The story of McClintock and Southwick's effort to pursue an unconventional career as importers raises a number of issues about the gendered nature of work in the United States. First, it illustrates the ways in which the gendered division of work was dependent upon the context in which it was performed. That is to say that there was nothing about the duties that the male clerks at Davis and Co. were expected to perform that was inherently masculine except that, in a business office, they were performed by men. Running errands, sweeping the floor, arranging for the transportation of crates, and opening them when they arrived did not require great intellectual or physical effort. Indeed, women performed that kind of work in their homes. Yet the male staff of Davis & Co. could not imagine women like McClintock and Southwick willingly doing that kind of work outside the home.

Secondly, it illustrates the role that social class bias played in discussions about women and their place in the paid work force. It was unlikely that anyone in Davis's office or elsewhere would have considered a female slave or working-class woman incapable or unwilling to do the kind of work expected of a clerk. But a different set of standards was applied to women like McClintock and Southwick, both of whom came from middle-class families. A middle-class woman risked her claim to gentility and respectability when she sought employment outside the home. It was her social status as much as her gender that limited her economic opportunities. Employers like Davis were quite aware that they could not expect well-bred young ladies like McClintock and Southwick to run errands unaccompanied through the streets of the city. No gentlemanly businessman would intentionally expose women in their employment to the stares and potentially insulting behavior of sometimes quite disreputable men who crowded the offices, streets, warehouses, and docks of Philadelphia's business district.

The story of McClintock and Southwick also illustrates the ways in which the distribution of economic assets was gendered in America. It is not clear whether or not Davis expected his male clerks to have retail experience before he hired them. But it seems perfectly clear that if they did not, he was willing to allow them to compensate for their lack of experience by providing him with investment capital in return for the training they expected to receive. In other words, men in possession of capital, whether in the form of money or practical business experience, were expected

to use it to further their careers. The same expectation did not apply to respectable, middle-class women. First of all, they were not expected to have the kind of capital that would be useful in business. If in the unlikely event they actually had money of their own, however, they were not expected to manage it themselves or to use it to pursue careers outside the home. In polite society, young women with money were considered good marriage prospects not potential business partners. That situation remained the case until well into the twentieth century.

Attitudes toward work and the way it was gendered changed as the American economy shifted from agriculture to commerce and then to industry. As those changes occurred, new questions arose concerning such issues as who should work, where they should work, how work should be performed, and how the rewards and benefits of labor should be distributed. Since ideas about gender were central to the understanding of how society operated, it is not surprising that they should have had a significant influence on the resolution of these issues. The result was that while men and women continued to spend most of their waking hours doing work, the way they experienced their working lives was often very different.

Two observations are in order before we proceed. Labor history is blessed with a vast literature. Until relatively recently, however, most labor historians were more concerned about the status of working men and the rise of unions than they were about issues of gender. That is not to say that they ignored gender completely. They simply assumed that breadwinning was so central to what it meant to be a man in American culture that they did not bother to discuss or analyze the relationship between masculinity and work. Not until the 1970s, when women's historians began documenting the ways in which women's economic lives were limited because of their gender, did interest in the relationship between labor and gender really surface. The result is that there is a great deal more literature on how ideas about femininity affected women's working lives than about how ideas about masculinity affected those of men.

The second issue concerns the kinds of labor we will consider in this chapter. Because American men and women have always spent most of their lives working, the number of activities that they have engaged in is endless. Given the space available here, it would be impossible to consider all of them. Therefore, I will confine our discussion about gender to its impact on various forms of work including farm work, housework, manufacturing, office work, and the practice of law.

THE GENDERED NATURE OF FARM LABOR

To make one's living on a farm required the labor of both men and women. Farm couples tended to think of themselves as an economic and social unit and their work as a shared experience. The result was that masculinity and femininity were defined in terms that bore a close relationship to each other. House work and field work, the care of animals and the care of children were well integrated. The farm was the workplace, and the home was part of the farm.

Whether it was carried out by slaves, hired laborers, or farmers themselves, farm work was divided by gender. Generally speaking, men were responsible for the crops, construction and maintenance of the farm buildings, caring for farm machinery, and providing fuel for heating and cooking. Women were responsible for childcare, cleaning, cooking, and sewing as well as tending to the dairy, poultry, and vegetable garden. But ideas about the gendered nature of such work were not rigid. Men tended vegetables, women helped put in the hay, and both did whatever was necessary to put up a fence, build a barn, or save a crop threatened by rain or insects. Transgressing gender boundaries was common and unselfconscious as the case of Brigham Nims illustrates.

Brigham Nims was a white farmer who lived near Roxbury, New Hampshire in the mid-nineteenth century. He supplemented the income he derived from farming by teaching school and by working periodically as a clerk, as a tailor, as a blacksmith, as a carpenter, and as a stone splitter in a quarry. It was not unusual for farmers, particularly in the more settled parts of the country, to try to supplement the income they got from growing crops and raising livestock by engaging in other kinds of work. Farming was a seasonal activity. And farms in the Northeast were often too small or too infertile to support a large household. Thus, men who took their breadwinning responsibilities seriously, often engaged in other moneymaking activities.

All of jobs that provided Nims with income were viewed as masculine. They required a variety of attributes including strength, stamina, and the kind of education or skills not typically available to most women. But, we know from his diary that Nims also regularly did work that was gendered female. "Work[ed] about home," he wrote in 1845. "Helped put in a quilt and worked it." In other entries he mentioned mending, washing, and ironing clothes, cleaning the house, paring apples and stewing them to make applesauce, and knitting.

It is tempting to view Nims' willingness to engage in such activities as an aberration. Yet he did what would conventionally be called "woman's work" all his life. He seems to have been more involved in domestic affairs when he was young and single and his father ran the farm. But he continued to cook and sew even after his father died and he inherited the land. And when he eventually married, he helped his wife with the laundry and shared in her childcare responsibilities. Moreover, he wrote about his domestic activities quite matter-of-factly and appears not to have given a second thought to the gendered implications of his behavior. Given the tone of his diary entries, it doesn't seem likely that he lost any sleep over the possibility that quilting, cooking, and ironing might emasculate him.

Nims may have been more directly involved in housework than most men, but his willingness to help out in the home illustrates the degree of flexibility inherent in the way gender norms could be defined in farming families. To succeed as farmers, a man and woman had to be partners, each bearing responsibility for the way the farm was run as a whole. A farm household had to produce most of the goods and provide most of the services needed for family members to live comfortably. As a result, the boundaries between what men did and what women did were flexible. It is true that the partnership of husband and wife under the law was an unequal one. Typically a man held title to the land, was viewed as the final authority in all family matters, and had the right to make unilateral decisions about what labor needed to be performed and by whom. But a man with the poor judgment to abuse his power and authority might have to contend with a reluctant, resentful, and even hostile labor force. In the end, it was in his best interest to be as much help to his wife as she was to him.

THE GENDERED NATURE OF DOMESTIC LABOR

There is to this day no field of endeavor as compatible with the definition of femininity as domesticity. Yet not only has woman's domestic role changed over time but the significance attached to it has also shifted. Seventeenth- and eighteenth-century homes were sites of production as well as of maintenance. Whether they lived on farms, plantations, or in the small towns that dotted the landscape, housewives were in charge of household manufacturing as well as of cooking, cleaning, and childcare. While they didn't work for wages, they contributed substantially to the economic well being of their families. They made their own cloth, candles, and soap, bartered for goods they couldn't produce for themselves, and processed dairy products to sell on the open market. A part of their definition of what was feminine focused on the work they did in their homes, work that was both visible and highly valued.

Industrialization and urbanization had a dramatic influence on the way a woman ran her household, the way that her work was perceived, the value that was attached to it, and the way she defined herself as a woman. Industrialization slowly removed manufacturing and food processing from the home, making it increasingly possible for a woman to purchase the goods and services she needed to run her household efficiently. Urbanization provided a context in which those goods and services could be concentrated and, thus, made widely available. So by 1890 an urban housewife with the means to do so could purchase gas and electricity and have plumbing installed in her bathroom and kitchen instead of spending her time and energy hauling wood and water into the house. And instead of making clothes for herself and her family, she could shop for them in department stores. Technology took some, though not all, of the drudgery out of being a housewife and mother. And those who could afford to take advantage of it began to construct their feminine identities around the leisure that it provided them. In the process, housewife as consumer began to replace housewife as producer.

Less and less the site of the production of tangible goods, the nineteenth-century middle-class home increasingly became a space dedicated to the maintenance and nurture of husbands and children. Idealized in fiction and poetry, the home was the place where a woman could carry out her God-given destiny by responsibly providing her loved ones with a haven from the hostile and morally corrupt outside world. Catharine Beecher and her sister, Harriet Beecher Stowe, were on the forefront of efforts to convince women that the home was a quintessentially female space and that fulfilling their domestic duties was an ideal way to demonstrate their womanliness. In their *The American Woman's Home* published in 1869, the Beecher sisters argued that housewifery required a wide variety of skills and a great deal of expertise in such areas as health care, architecture, time management, and nutrition. They also pointed out that woman's claim to moral superiority required that she dedicate her life to monitoring her husband's behavior and supervising the moral education of her children. A middle-class woman's femininity was measured by her willingness to undertake such responsibilities without pay and perform her domestic duties with little or no apparent effort.

In an age when work was increasingly defined in terms of making money, housework performed gratuitously by housewives began to lose its definition as an economically significant activity. The result was that its economic value to the family was increasingly ignored. No monetary value was given to beating rugs or dusting furniture. No one bothered to consider how much money a woman saved by scrubbing her own floors, sewing her own clothes, darning her husband's socks, or buying day-old bread and pastries. Baking cookies for one's children was defined in terms of love and affection rather than in terms of work. And the actual physical and mental labor involved in housekeeping was virtually ignored.

There were those, of course, who continued to consider housework "work" and who understood its value in monetary terms. A slave-owning plantation mistress would have readily admitted that a hardworking and docile servant was worth her weight in gold. And the amount of money that a well-trained cook or lady's maid could bring on the auction block testified to the value of the work that she did. The ability and willingness to work as a domestic servant in another woman's household also provided free women, whether they were black or white, with a way to support themselves and contribute to the income of their families.

By the beginning of the twentieth century, then, the degree to which housekeeping was equated with work depended upon whether those who performed that work were compensated in money and where that work was carried out. Generally speaking, while housework was considered a woman's responsibility, if it was carried out by her in her own home

it wasn't really considered work. If it was carried out in another woman's house it was.

The arrangements surrounding the employment of servants set the parameters within which a woman who worked as a domestic constructed her feminine identity. Despite the fact that she earned money for her work, equating her womanliness with independence and self-sufficiency was problematical. As long as she worked as a live-in servant in someone else's household, her employers determined where she slept, what, when, and where she ate, whom she spent time with, what duties she performed, when and how she performed them, and how much time she had to herself. The conditions of her employment in some ways reduced her to something approximating a state of dependence.

Despite these circumstances, women who earned their livings as domestic servants did have ways of preserving their sense of self-respect, although the way they did so changed over time. In the seventeenth century, for example, it was common for parents, particularly in the North, to send their daughters off to live with friends or relatives in order to learn the art of housekeeping. A young woman working in another woman's home under such arrangements was not really considered a servant, and her tenure was always considered a temporary one. Even a women who worked for another woman for pay often maintained her sense of self worth and independence by thinking of herself as merely "helping out." Despite the fact that they were paid wages, so-called "helps" tended to view their work as doing a "favor" for a neighbor rather than as being employed by her. They typically worked "with" rather than "for" the mistress of the house and could go home anytime they wanted.

As time passed, however, domestic servants began to replace "helps." Unlike "helps," servants were completely dependent upon the wages that they earned and did not have homes to return to if they became dissatisfied with their working conditions. Sometimes they worked side by side with their mistresses scrubbing floors and doing the laundry, but often they did the work while the lady of the house merely supervised it. They were paid employees, but they were also outsiders who could lay no claim to the kind of consideration that might be given to a friend, relative, or neighbor.

Despite the fact that their circumstances made it difficult to avoid being economically and sexually exploited, domestic workers were able to carve out for themselves areas in which they could make independent decisions about their lives. Given the fact that there was a huge demand for domestic labor in the nineteenth and twentieth centuries, well-trained servants with references could choose their employers. They could also decide for themselves what conditions they would tolerate in the work place, how well and how quickly they would perform their duties, what wages they would accept for doing so, and whether they would live in or live out. Quitting, or the threat of it, was their ultimate weapon in their struggle to equalize their relationship with their employers.

The proponents of home economics attempted to systematize housework at the turn of the century, and housewives continued to complain that it was simply impossible to get good "help." But generally speaking, as long the washing was done, food was on the table, and the house was kept relatively neat and clean, most people didn't give housekeeping or its gendered nature another thought. All that changed in the 1970s when second-wave feminists began to argue that there was nothing inherently feminine about cooking, cleaning, and doing the laundry and that men should assume more responsibility for the maintenance of their households. They pointed out that housekeeping did have significant economic value, and demanded that domesticity be given the respect that it would have had if a housewife were paid for her services. And they challenged men to start doing more around the house than changing light bulbs and fixing leaky faucets. They saw no reason why men should consider scrubbing the floors, doing the dishes, and feeding the baby emasculating. As far as

they were concerned, it was all a matter of expanding the definition of what constituted manliness. To substantiate their argument, they pointed out that traditional female jobs such as cooking were perfectly acceptable manly pursuits when there was money to be made and status to be enjoyed. Publicly acclaimed male chefs, they observed, did not have an identity crisis every time they walked around the kitchen with a spoon in their hands.

One result of the discussion about the gendered nature of domestic work and the fact that more and more women were entering the work force and could not devote much time to housekeeping was that some men did start helping with housework and childcare. But while it was no longer considered emasculating to help keep the household running smoothly, men did not generally accept primary responsibility for cooking the food, cleaning the house, doing the laundry, and buying the groceries. "Househusbands" were few and far between. Nevertheless, domesticity was beginning to lose its exclusive association with femininity and to become more gender neutral.

THE GENDERED NATURE OF WORK IN MANUFACTURING, FOOD PROCESSING, AND THE NEEDLE TRADES

The changes that occurred in the work place asa result of the industrial revolution were gradual changes. The production of manufactured goods originally began on farms. Then it shifted to what was called the "putting out system" where entrepreneurial businessmen provided raw materials to men and women who continued to produce things like cloth in their homes. And, finally, manufacturing shifted to mills and factories. As that happened, workers began to migrate from the countryside to the towns, hand production shifted to machine production, small industries grew into large ones, and workers' relationships with their supervisors became less personal.

A wide combination of variables determined what those changes meant for workers and how they affected prevailing definitions of masculinity and femininity. Gender was an important factor in determining how workers responded to industrialization, but age, marital status, where a person worked, and concern about social status were also important. A single, young man, for example, had a great deal more choice over where he worked, how long he worked, for whom he worked, and how he spent his wages and free time than did a mature, married man who was working to support his family. A wife and mother who found it necessary to engage in paid employment was faced with the problem of balancing her domestic duties and child care responsibilities with her need to earn money, a problem that most married men did not have to worry about. And a single, young woman who worked for wages in her home under the watchful eye of her parents was not as likely to define femininity in terms of independence or self-sufficiency as a young woman who moved away from home, found a job, and lived in a boarding house.

The case of New England shoemakers illustrates how marital status, gender, and geographic location affected the way men and women experienced work. Shoemaking was originally a custom business. Cobblers were artisans who worked in or near their homes. Typically a shoemaker cut out the upper part of the shoe, gave it to his wife to sew or "bind" in her spare time, and then fitted the completed "upper" to the sole, sewed them together, attached a heel, and sold it to the person who had ordered it. As the American economy expanded and demand for shoes increased, it became impossible for local cobblers to meet the demand. After the sewing machine was adapted so that it could stitch leather, business entrepreneurs built shoe factories and began to hire skilled cobblers to cut the leather and fit the shoes and young, single women to sew the uppers by machine. There was a period of time, then, when shoemaking took place both in the home and in the factory. Some women worked in the factories under

the supervision of shop stewards. Others worked in their homes under the supervision of their husbands. As a result, the wives of shoemakers continued to think of their domestic shoemaking activities as an integral part of their household economies and of themselves as extensions of their shoemaking husbands. Under such circumstances, it was difficult for them to develop a sense of themselves as workers with their own set of interests. Young women who worked in factories were much more likely to develop ideas that separated them from their families, particularly if they lived in boardinghouses, spent the money that they earned on themselves instead of sending it home to their parents, and worked with men to whom they were unrelated. Their circumstances meant that they were more likely to develop a sense of community with other female workers and to engage in union activities in an effort to improve their wages and working conditions.

Gender also influenced the ways in which shoemakers went about constructing their class identity. Men had to deal with the class implications of the shift from artisan labor to factory labor. As artisans, they had once constructed their class identity around their knowledge and skill and their independence as small businessmen as well as their ability to provide for their families. When master shoemakers took jobs as factory workers, their independence was drastically curtailed. Someone else set their hours and supervised their work. And the skill that they needed to do the work required of them was not comparable to that which had allowed them to earn livings as cobblers. At the same time, however, men normally earned more money than women who were employed in shoe factories, not necessarily because they were more skilled but because it was assumed that they had a family to support. Men also had more opportunities to move from working on the shop floor into management. In the end, no matter what their work assignment, their ability to support their families confirmed their claim to respectability as well as manliness.

Female shoemakers faced a quite different problem relating to their class identity. At one time a woman whose labor was strenuous and visible was considered both feminine and respectable. However, as the social influence of the middle class increased, standards for judging femininity changed. Because they held unpaid domestic labor in higher regard than paid labor in shops and factories, the relationship between femininity and respectability came to be defined in terms of a woman's dependence on a man to support her rather than on her ability to support herself. The challenge for working-class women, then, was to establish their respectability within the parameters established by the middle class despite their obvious need to work for a living. They had some help in trying to solve what was to some degree a public relations problem. Newspapers like the *Reporter* in Lynn, Massachusetts described stitching girls as perfectly willing and able to conform to middle-class standards of gentility. It pictured the girls who worked in Lynn shoe factories as enterprising, energetic, well educated, and well behaved and assured its readers that working in factories did not inhibit their interest in culture. When they attended lectures and concerts, they arrived, it said, fashionably dressed and knew how to comport themselves.

It is difficult to determine how accurate the *Reporter* was in its description of the female shoemakers of Lynn. But its editor's sensitivity to prevailing middle class definitions of femininity clearly provided the standards by which he judged them.

Another way that ideas about gender influenced the work of men and women in manufacturing was in the way the owners and supervisors in factories gendered both work opportunities and the work that was to be performed. Generally speaking, full-time work that required a great deal of physical strength, stamina, and skill was defined as man's work. And part-time work, work that was not particularly strenuous, or work that did not require much skill was defined as woman's work. Take the food processing industry in California, for example. Food processing is typically seasonal work, and, therefore, many of the job opportunities available in the canning

business are part time. For a variety of reasons such seasonal work appealed to women of Mexican extraction whose families' economic circumstances made it necessary for them to work at least for part of the year for wages. In less desperate circumstances, permanent paid labor would have been problematical for these women. Manliness in their communities was defined in terms of a man's ability to support his wife and children, and femininity was constructed around domesticity and the maintenance of kin networks. So in order to uphold and reinforce traditional gender conventions, Mexican women who took seasonal jobs in canning factories often justified their work as a temporary measure and spoke of the money that they earned as supplementary income even when they knew it was critical for the survival of their families.

The work they did in those factories and the compensation they received was also gendered. Employers organized the work that was to be done according to their assumptions about gender. For example, a "cutter" in the preparation department was expected to have such feminine characteristics as dexterity, a sense of rhythm, and good eye-hand coordination. Men were usually employed as "sweepers" because the job was viewed as being physically demanding. And while female cannery workers were paid according to the amount of food they processed per day, men were typically paid by the day, week, or month.

Jobs in manufacturing were not always divided by gender. Sometimes whole industries were dominated by either male or female workers. Making cigars, for example, was originally a home industry dominated by women. Shortly before the Civil War, however, highly skilled Dutch, English, and German immigrant men gradually displaced female cigar makers. They settled in eastern cities, set up small craft shops, and began earning their living as independent artisans.

Like the production of many other commodities, cigar making eventually moved from shops to factories. When that happened, male cigar makers devised strategies intended to preserve their sense of independence and self-esteem. Used to setting their own hours, for example, they resisted the attempts of their employers to tell them when they were going to work. The flexibility of their work schedule had traditionally been based on the fact that their income was tied to the number of cigars they were able to produce. So they accepted piece rates instead of hourly rates. The result was that those with the greatest skill and speed could work a relatively short day and still make a decent living.

Despite the fact that they now worked in factories instead of their own shops, they also developed a wide variety of techniques designed to preserve their manly self-respect and dignity. One was to refuse to perform what they considered to be menial jobs. As they saw it, they were being paid to roll tobacco, not carry it around. So when they sat at their work and saw that their supplies of tobacco were running low, they simply expected some one else to get them some more. It was also traditional for cigar makers to wear their very best clothes as they walked to and from work or when they went to pick up their pay check. Their choice of clothing was a quite self-conscious attempt to assert their pride in the skills that they had and the money that they made.

Between the Civil War until about 1900 the world of the cigar maker was a man's world. But around the turn of the century, cigar manufacturers began to hire young, single, immigrant women to work in their factories. Because they were women, they were considered more docile, reliable, and less likely to show up for work in a state of intoxication. Compared to most male cigar makers, they were largely unskilled and, therefore, formed a cheap labor pool. As a result, the cigar industry once more began to shift from one that was gendered male to one that was gendered female.

Not all manufacturing moved in this direction, however. Some went from being female dominated to male dominated. Such was the case in dressmaking. Dressmaking was considered woman's work for a number of reasons. First of all, sewing and dressmaking were domestic skills that daughters learned from their mothers. Therefore, despite the fact that most dressmakers actually learned their trade in dressmaking shops rather than under the supervision of their mothers, the work that they did fit easily into what was accepted as "woman's work." And then, of course, there was the matter of propriety. When a women went to her dressmaker, she had to stand, sometimes for hours, in a relative state of undress while her body was measured and the garments fitted. Prevailing standards of female modesty made it inconceivable that such measuring and fitting should be carried out by a man. So as long as ladies' wear was custom made, there was no place for men in the ladies' fashion industry.

Dressmaking had great appeal to women who found it necessary to find a way to support themselves. It was a highly skilled and potentially lucrative trade. It required a great deal of business acumen as well as creativity to succeed as a dressmaker. And it was one form of employment that allowed a woman to work with valuable raw materials and to associate with women in the middle and upper classes on a regular basis. For all of these reasons, dressmakers considered themselves to be a notch above that of most working women.

By the end of the nineteenth century, however, the role of female professionals in the dressmaking trade was declining. New technology in the form of pattern making provided men with an entre into the clothing industry. And the introduction of paper patterns like the ones introduced by Ebenezer Butterick and James McCall were turning dressmaking into an amateur enterprise. "I went a few days ago . . . to get a dress made," wrote one woman, "but the dressmaker could not make it at once, and I don't like to wait, so I came home, looked over the many patterns [available] . . . and with aid of those . . . have cut and fitted my dress." While pattern makers were undermining the dressmaker's market and making her skills increasingly irrelevant, other men were investing capital in factories where ready-to-wear garments were produced and in department stores where such garments could be displayed and sold. Stores like Macy's in New York, Marshall Fields in Chicago, and Filene's in Boston had an advantage over small dress shops in the sense that they could provide a woman in need of a dress with a huge selection of incrementally sized garments that she could buy off the rack and take home with her. As the dressmaker's share of the market began to shrink, many went out of business. Others found employment working in male owned and operated department stores as alterations ladies. And still others simply went to work in garment factories. There, as was the case in other areas of manufacturing, production of clothing was divided by gender. Men typically designed the clothes, cut the cloth, and worked on garments that required extensive tailoring while women were relegated to straight sewing and finish work. All of this was justified in terms of gender difference. Women's "delicate constitution," according to a 1911 Department of Labor report, prevented them from performing the "strenuous" task of handling the construction of a man's suit coat. In other areas of the garment industry, their delicate touch, nimble fingers, and concern for cleanliness were seen as being particularly important for work on light, easily soiled fabrics such as those used in the production of underwear. Such division of labor reflected prevailing attitudes about the qualities that men and women brought to the job.

However their work was divided and their identities as workers were constructed, both men and women participated in union activities. The nineteenth-century shoemakers had their Daughters of St. Crispin and their Knights of St. Crispin. The twentieth-century Mexican cannery workers had their United Cannery, Agricultural, Packing, and Allied Workers of America. And the cigar makers had their Cigar Makers' International Union. Participation in union affairs gave both men and women the opportunity to challenge the power and authority of their employers. It gave them the opportunity to assert their independence, display their organizational talents and leadership skills, exert more control over their working lives, and represent their own interests.

But union organizing also exposed the tensions that existed between male and female workers. When men and women worked together in the same industry, men tended to dominate union leadership. Because they viewed women as competitors, they did little to encourage women to organize or to challenge the way that employers used gender to determine who did what work and how work was compensated. The result was that men were typically better trained to perform skilled jobs and were paid more for their work than women were. Union demands for a family wage undercut the identity of women as industrial workers by asserting that a woman's place was really in the home and that employers should pay men enough so that their wives and daughters would not have to help them support their families. Such claims helped to perpetuate the subordination of women by ignoring their breadwinning role. As long as both management and male union leaders agreed that labor should be divided by gender and that men should be paid more than women for the work that they did, women were in a relatively weak position to improve their situation. The belief that women were fundamentally domestic beings who worked only for pin money or who were only unskilled, temporary workers who had no real commitment to their jobs and who could easily be replaced made it difficult for union negotiators to convince employers that they should provide their female employees with such gender specific benefits as paid maternity leave, child care facilities, or flexible hours. It was not until the rise of second wave feminism in the late 1960s and early 1970s that gendered labor issues such as these received any sort of widespread public attention.

THE GENDERED NATURE OF CLERICAL WORK

Office work, like many other kinds of paid labor, was originally gendered male. Before the Civil War, businessmen and lawyers employed young men, whose penmanship was legible, to make copies of letters and business documents and male bookkeepers to keep track of their profits and losses. They hired errand boys to deliver messages and keep the office clean. And they took on apprentices known as clerks, who were essentially "jacks of all trades." The point of their employment was to provide them with a business education so that they could make their way in the world. So clerks did whatever was asked of them hoping that in the process they could save enough money and accumulate enough knowledge to go into business for themselves.

A labor crisis brought on by the Civil War and the rise of corporations that followed changed forever the way that business offices were run. The amount of paper work involved in conducting the war or running a corporation was immense, and the face-to-face relationships that had characterized the conduct of business in early times began to disappear. No longer was business done on a handshake. A legal contract was drawn up. No longer were orders for supplies given orally to the friendly merchant down the street. Now an order form had to be filled out. And no longer were letters written by hand. The invention of the typewriter and the development of stenography brought a dramatic change to the way government and business correspondence was handled.

The need for large numbers of new employees during the war and in the years that followed led to the what was essentially the feminization of office work. As men marched off to war and left their jobs in law firms, businesses, and government offices, women were hired to replace them. The first to hire women to work for the federal government was U. S. Treasurer Francis Spinner, who desperately needed workers to trim, sort, and package newly printed money. The experiment proved such a success that other government bureaucracies began hiring women. The circumstances of these new employees varied, but most of them were white, middle class, literate, and des-

perate for work. Some had lost their husbands in the war and needed to make money to support their children. Others, for one reason or another, could not depend on their families to support them. Whatever their reason for seeking employment, they provided a readily available pool of relatively inexpensive labor in a time of national crisis.

The expansion of business after the Civil War meant that opportunities for women to do office work continued. On a practical level there was very little resistance to their employment. Typing was a relatively new job, so skills in typing had not yet been gendered. Since middle-class women were often trained to play the piano, it was simply assumed that women had the kind of manual dexterity necessary to become good typists. Newly minted business schools that seemed to be popping up everywhere were perfectly willing to admit any woman who was willing to pay tuition and enroll. And business opportunities were expanding so rapidly that many men simply moved from clerical work into higher paying positions in management which brought with them more status and authority.

So women took lessons in typing, filing, and shorthand and then sought employment as filing clerks and secretaries. Clerical work paid more than most other jobs open to women, and compared to many other types of female employment, carried more status. It was considered more desirable than factory work or domestic work because the working environment was cleaner, the hours were shorter, the work was not seasonal, and there was always the remote possibility of promotion.

That women were able to find jobs as clerks, receptionists, and secretaries did not mean however, that there was no resistance to their employment. Predictably, there were those who maintained that a woman's place was in the home rather than the office and that "woman's nature" was incompatible with office work. They argued that God intended women to marry not to pursue business careers and that exposing women to the "dog eat dog" competition the characterized the business world would destroy their moral sensibilities and undermine those qualities that made them most womanly. Women in offices were likely to become, as they put it, "cynical, severe, and falsely independent." And they asserted that the female temperament was incompatible with office work. One writer, for example, warned employers against hiring female reception clerks. "Nine out of ten girls are temperamental," he complained. "On one day they are likely to flirt with every male visitor. On another day they are likely to be flippant. On still another they are likely to be unduly sarcastic." Another claimed that biology rendered women unsuitable for office jobs, saying, "The loss of the services of women employees for several days each month is a serious problem where salaries are paid regularly and the 'docking' system for absences is not in practice. The fact that women are less strong, less agile, less enduring under continued mental strain than men, makes it evident that women in contest with men must be granted something more than a fair field and unrestricted competition."

The problem, then, was to provide a justification for female office employment that reconciled prevailing notions of femininity with the demands of the work. The solution was to redefine clerical work as an occupation consistent with what were viewed as "innately" feminine qualities. So punctuality, diligence, discretion, accuracy, neatness, and reliability were gendered female. And office space was feminized in order to accommodate the presence of women. Spittoons disappeared and the use of profanity was discouraged. Offices became bastions of orderliness. The skills that were needed to succeed in this environment were defined as women's skills as well. And some even claimed that working in an office was the best preparation a woman could have for marriage and keeping house. After all, they argued, it introduced a woman to the world of men and familiarized her with the stresses and strains that men had to endure day after day. And it provided her with an appreciation of the importance of industry, econ-

omy, and self-discipline, attributes that were essential to the smooth running of a home.

As time passed, it became clear that female clerical workers could not expect much opportunity to advance to jobs that paid more money and carried more responsibility and power. Generally speaking, most employers assumed that the women who worked in their offices were merely marking time until they married and that their commitment to their jobs was not comparable to that of men. As a result, the typing pool became a female ghetto. And even when the passage of the Equal Pay Act of 1963 and Title VII of the Civil Rights Act (1964) made it illegal to deny women equal access to employment opportunities, women continued to face an uphill battle to make their way in the world of business. No matter how talented they were, the so-called "glass ceiling" stood between them and the CEO's office.

THE LAW AS A GENDERED PROFESSION

Of all of the professions in America, practicing law has been most closely associated with masculinity. The demonstration of manly qualities and the preservation of male power and privilege was and, to some degree still is, central to its values and culture.

The practice of law was not a full time occupation until after the American Revolution. In the early national period, a young man received his legal training through apprenticeship to a practicing lawyer. He spent a year or more reading the other man's law books and watching him practice law. When he had gained the necessary knowledge and expertise to set up his own practice, his mentor took him before a judge and recommended him for membership in "the bar." After that, he was free to set up his own office and compete with other lawyers for clients.

Because the United States was largely rural during this time, lawyers and judges went to the people rather than the other way around. They left their homes, and rode together through the countryside, stopping to provide legal services or try cases wherever they came up. On any given day, a lawyer might a draw up a real estate contract in the morning and defend a murderer in the afternoon. Their legal brotherhood was based on shared interests and activities. Together, they set up their temporary courts in schools, churches, and taverns when there wasn't a courthouse available. And after a hard day at work, they slept together, ate together, and drank together in roadside inns and taverns. In the process, they developed a standard of conduct which they believed distinguished them, as lawyers, from ordinary men. They considered such characteristics as sociability, courageousness, competitiveness, fearlessness, practicality, trustworthiness, and the ability to argue persuasively to be virtues in their particular line of work. And the man who possessed such characteristics could command the respect of his peers. Because the legal community was such a tightly knit one, a young man's success as a lawyer depended on his conformity to these masculine values.

Industrial expansion and the rise of corporations changed both the practice of law and the definition of what it meant to be a good lawyer. One of the ways that some lawyers adjusted to those changes was to forgo general practice and to specialize in some particular aspect of the law. Some practiced criminal law, some practiced real estate law, some practiced patent law, and some practiced probate law. Whatever kind of law they chose to concentrate on, they continued to be free agents in the sense that they chose their own cases and did their own billing. But those who became corporate lawyers did not have the same kind of control over their professional lives. Their job was to represent the interests of the corporation, which was not necessarily the same thing as serving the interests of justice. As employees, they were paid a salary, they could no longer choose their own cases, and their role began to shift from that of advocate to that of counselor. In some cases, they were asked to devise techniques that would enable corporate executives to subvert the law rather than to uphold it. Because the company's interests and the corporate lawyers' interests were so closely intertwined, many came to view them as exceptionally well paid hired hands.

The way that legal education was delivered also changed during the nineteenth century. Where once an aspiring lawyer learned his craft through what was essentially an apprenticeship system, he now went to school. Harvard was one of the first schools to establish a law school. Yale and the University of Virginia were not far behind. But it was not until the 1870s and 1880s that getting legal training in a school rather than in a lawyer's office became the preferred way for a man to enter the legal profession. It was during that period that the case law method of teaching law was introduced. As students sat at their desks in their classrooms, their professors fired one question after another at them, expecting them not only to be familiar with a large body of legal knowledge but to have informed opinions about cases which had established important legal precedents. The classroom atmosphere was highly competitive and adversarial. Sometimes, it was even downright hostile. The case law method was considered to be a manly approach to the law because its promoters thought it would foster such characteristics as toughmindedness, self-confidence, and argumentativeness. Turning the classroom into a battlefield simply reinforced the belief that the practice of law was a particularly virile profession.

It was at this point, in the late nineteenth century, that women began to demand the right to become lawyers. The first challenge that faced them, of course, was how to get the kind of education they needed to do so. Most of the top law schools refused to admit women, and those who did gain admission to the less prestigious schools had to pursue their education in what can only be described as a hostile environment. So the easiest way to learn enough law to be admitted to the bar was to revert back to the apprenticeship system. All that was necessary was to find a sympathetic lawyer who was willing to provide the necessary training. Typically, the most sympathetic were fathers and husbands.

Once they had completed their training, aspiring female lawyers had to petition for admission to the bar. And when judges consistently refused to grant their petitions, they filed lawsuits in the courts. The first to do so was Myra Bradwell, of Illinois. Most of the judges to whom they appealed seemed to be of one mind on the matter of female lawyers. Women, they declared in decision after decision, were unfit to practice law because their "natural" sensibilities, purity, and delicacy made them incapable of representing the interests of their clients in a courtroom. Judicial arguments against admitting women to the bar ran the gamut from the assertion that women lacked the physical stamina to spend their days in the courtroom to the claim that they lacked the intellect and toughmindedness necessary for the practice of law. According to both federal and state judges, women should be spared from having to come into contact with the baser elements of society. In any case, they maintained that women lacked the self-confidence, not to mention the ambition, aggressiveness, and competitiveness to be good lawyers. Unable to convince judges that they should be admitted to the bar, women who were determined to practice law turned to the state legislatures and lobbied for the passage of laws allowing them to do so. By the mid-twentieth century, women could practice in every state in the union.

Admission to the bar did not, however, end the problems that a woman faced if she wanted to earn her living as a lawyer. Female lawyers could never escape from the problem of trying to maintain their femininity while they attempted to conform to the gender expectations inherent in the practice of law. The fact was that they were women who were expected to behave like men. But if they behaved like men, they might no longer be considered women. As lawyers, they were expected to be aggressive and rational. As women, they were expected to be retiring, passive, emotional,

and nurturing. The practice of law forced women out of the drawing room and exposed them to the sordid world of deception and misrepresentation. And it required that they relate to men in ways that were, to say the least, unconventional.

The result of all this was that aspiring female lawyers tended to be quite self-conscious about their behavior, demeanor, and aspirations. When they were eventually admitted to law school classes, for example, they had to decide whether to participate actively in class discussions or sit quietly in class, act like ladies, and defer to the opinions of male students. Once they had completed their education and had been admitted to the bar, they had to consider the gendered implications of their choice of specialty. Should they become trial lawyers and spend their days arguing their cases in civil and criminal court? Or would it be easier to preserve their sense of femininity if they confined their practice to "office work" such as drawing up wills, arbitrating family disputes, filing motions, or preparing deeds and contracts where skills in negotiation, mediation, and problem solving were more important than competitiveness and argumentation. Because benevolence was considered woman's work in some circles, some female lawyers agonized over the issue of whether they should devote their professional lives to helping the poor and unfortunate or whether they should practice law for profit and self-aggrandizement like most of the male lawyers they knew. Some even felt compelled to sacrifice marriage and children in order to pursue a law career. If they did not, they feared that they would be unable to compete with their male colleagues.

Perhaps one of the most symbolically gendered decisions that a female lawyer had to make was what she should wear when she appeared in court. How could she appear to be competent and professional without completely sacrificing her respectability and femininity? Most women solved this problem by wearing dark, well-tailored suits. To those suits they often added a bit of lace or velvet or a pin on their lapel, something to remind those who saw them that despite their choice of profession they were still women.

But the matter of whether or not to wear a hat in court was an issue in the early years. When they left their homes, "ladies" were not considered fully dressed unless there was a hat on their head. Men also wore hats, of course. But etiquette demanded that they remove their hats when they entered a building. So female lawyers had a problem. If they removed their hat, they undermined their claim to respectability. But if they didn't, they reminded both judge and jury of gender issues that were totally irrelevant to the cases they were arguing. In the absence of generally acknowledged rules of propriety to guide them, they were left to their own resources. Some continued to wear their hats. Others left them in the coatroom lined up along side those of the men. In short, women who wanted to practice law had to make decisions regarding their personal and professional lives that men did not have to worry about.

Female lawyers not only had to make gendered decisions about the way they practiced law, they also faced tensions in the court room that derived from the fact that they were women trying to work with men. Few male judges and lawyers welcomed women into their ranks, and many openly opposed their presence. Male trial lawyers made no bones about the degree of discomfort they felt when they had to argue against female lawyers in the courtroom. They complained that when opposing counsel was a woman, her presence inhibited their ability to represent the interests of their clients. Here both class and gender came into play. They pointed out that while one might disagree with a women in polite society, it was considered totally improper for a gentleman to launch into a full scale verbal attack on a lady. To put it into the words of one trial lawyer, having a female as his opponent undermined his "manly right to attack."

The prevalence of such gender issues meant that even after the official barriers preventing women from practicing law crumbled, unofficial barriers remained. Until the 1970s, while highly qualified women could get into law school, they had difficulty getting into the most prestigious ones. When the opportunities arose to clerk for a judge, they were unlikely to be considered. After they passed the bar, they couldn't get interviews with big law firms, let alone job offers. And through it all, they continued to face the problem of reconciling their identities as lawyers with their identities as women in a culture where people continued to believe that men and women were fundamentally different and that there was no place for women in the practice of law.

SUMMARY

Culturally constructed ideas about masculinity and femininity have had a profound impact on how Americans have experienced work. It has determined what economic opportunities are open to them, how jobs are defined, how much money they earn, whether their work is considered skilled and unskilled, and how they are treated in the work place as well as how their work is evaluated and by whom.

Labor has been divided by gender ever since the colonial period. Just as there were jobs that were considered women's jobs and others that were considered men's jobs on the farm, so was labor divided by gender in commerce and industry. Gender conventions were so strong in American society, for example, that manufacturers typically included or excluded women from various aspects of the manufacturing process on the basis on their preconceived notions about what constituted masculinity and femininity. Women were systematically excluded from heavy industries such as mining, oil drilling, or steel and automobile production, not necessarily because they were incapable of doing the job but because such jobs were considered to be male jobs requiring the kind of skills and strength that only men were believed to have. The fact that during periods of emergency, such as World War I and World War II, gender restrictions were lifted and women proved that they could drill for oil and manufacture steel illustrates the artificiality of the reasons for their exclusion. Even within industries that employed both men and women, women were typically relegated to those jobs that theoretically required little strength and were designated as low skilled and low paying. Thus, women sewed garments together but were not typically employed to cut the fabric from which they were made.

The same can be said for work in such areas as public service. It was partly because women were considered benevolent by "nature," that they dominated the field of social work. Women were encouraged to go into nursing and elementary school teaching because they were considered to be innately nurturing. And because preserving morality, setting standards of good taste, and promoting culture were considered to be an integral part of being female, women could find jobs as librarians whose responsibility it was to promote an appreciation of literature and to safeguard community morals by monitoring the reading patterns of its citizens.

Gendering work in this way was not consistent, however. Ideas about woman's nature could just as easily exclude her from pursuing a specific line of work. A woman's alleged law-abiding nature, for example, did not qualify her to work on a police force. It was simply deemed inconsistent with prevailing definitions of femininity to expect a woman to investigate crime, frequent disreputable neighborhoods, and stalk known criminals. The same thing could be said about the practice of law. Like policemen, the gender identity of male lawyers depended in part on their ability to maintain the exclusiveness of their male fraternity. So like policemen, they defined the characteristics most likely to lead to success in male terms and denied that women had the characteristics necessary to succeed.

While it is true, then, that labor has typically been gendered, the way it is gendered has changed over time. Work defined as male in one era may be defined as female in another and vice versa. In the nineteenth century, for example, cigar making and office work shifted from being male vocations to being female ones. During the same period, men began to claim the dressmaking and retailing business for themselves.

It is clear from the evidence available, that men have systematically done their best to try to limit the occupational choices and economic opportunities of women. They have done so for a wide variety of reasons not the least of which has been their need to protect and preserve that part of their manhood that requires that they adequately support their families. The gender imperative that equates manliness with breadwinning has remained consistent over time. It applied as much to our Puritan forefathers as it does to men today.

It should also be pointed out, however, that the unequal distribution of work opportunities has been and still is more than just a gender issue. It has had class and race implications as well. Whether they were male or female, middle- and upper-class, native-born whites have benefited from the way that work and the wages to be derived from it have typically been distributed in America.

The Problem with Lady Clerks

When the Civil War began in 1861, the federal bureaucracy was small. The demands of the war made it necessary for the various departments of the executive branch to expand at the very time when young men, who had traditionally been employed as clerks, were joining the armed forces. In response to the need for labor, the treasury department began hiring women. As the war progressed more and more relatively well-educated, middle-class women in need of employment were able to find jobs working in other branches of the federal bureaucracy.

In November, 1865 the New York Times *republished an article from the* Washington Chronicle *discussing the issue of women working as government clerks. According to the unnamed Washington writer, what problems arose when women began working as clerks? What was it about drawing room behavior that she found objectionable when it was displayed in an office setting? In what way did she think that ideas about gender and class influenced the behavior of female clerks?*

THE LADY CLERKS IN THE DEPARTMENTS.—It would seem that the employment of women as clerks in the government departments at Washington has proved a failure. In the Department of the Interior, the dismissal of all the female clerks is being effected as rapidly as possible, and it is understood that the Treasury Department, which employs the largest number of any, is about to adopt the same course. The services of women, instead of being more economical than those of men, are found to be more expensive. Individually their wages may be less, but, in the aggregate, they accomplish less labor than an equal number of men. It is alleged in Washington that the mania for extravagant dress is one of the principal drawbacks to the efficiency of the women at their duties in the departments. A writer in the Washington *Chronicle*—herself, we judge, a departmental clerk—comments severely upon this, remarking:

"The employment of women in the government departments *is an experiment*. It has not, thus far, been so complete a success as its friends could wish, and may possibly yet be pronounced a failure. The fault is chiefly all on our side of the house. Women persevere in carrying the drawing-room to the office. Unless this mistake can be corrected, the experiment must fail. A fixed rule of good breeding excludes the shop from the parlor. A man who lugs his business, habitually, into his social hours is always a bore; and what should we think of one who went to his counting or consulting room in the ball-dress of the previous evening? It would certainly be better for humanity that all of this class of government employee should starve at home than that they should corrupt public morals, and we lower the national standard of womanly delicacy by recognizing their right to fill the honorable positions many of them occupy. I know that some, perhaps a majority, of these dress thus from misapprehending the situation. They fail to see the distinction between business and social life, and so drag the drawing-room with them, with its coquetries, on to and into the office."

If this is the only matter to be complained of in the premises, the lady clerks can very easily and quickly work a reform in it, and thus retain themselves in an occupation so well adapted to their capacities.

Source: "The Lady Clerks in the Departments," *New York Times,* November 10, 1865.

DOCUMENT

Should Women Be Recruited to Work in America's Factories?

During the period immediately following the American Revolution, Alexander Hamilton, who was serving as George Washington's Secretary of the Treasury, wrote that "women and children are rendered more useful" by employing them in manufacturing than "they would otherwise be." This was particularly true, he believed, because he was convinced that the economic well being of the United States was dependent on the development of manufacturing rather than agriculture and because he believed that machines were beginning to replace the need for manual labor. Not everyone, however, agreed with that point of view.

The document reprinted below is an excerpt from a speech delivered by William Sylvis. Sylvis was a skilled iron worker who worked in a foundry near Philadelphia in the 1850s. Concerned about the exploitation of working men by factory owners and managers, he joined a union in 1857. A little over ten years later he had worked his way up the ranks and had become the President of the National Labor Union. In the excerpt from a speech he delivered in Buffalo, New York in 1864, he explains his position on the subject of female wage labor in American industry.

What is his position? What assumptions about the construction of femininity does he make? What factors might explain why he disagreed with Hamilton on whether or not women should be employed as factory workers?

The subject of female labor is one that demands our attention and most earnest consideration. There are many reasons why females should not labor outside of the domestic circle. Being forced into the field, the factory, and the workshop, (and they do not go there from choice, but because necessity compels them,) they come in direct competition with men in the great field of labor; and being compelled of necessity, from their defenceless condition, to work for low wages, they exercise a vast influence over the price of labor in almost every department. If they received the same wages that men do for similar work, this objection would in a great measure disappear. But there is another reason, founded upon moral principle and common humanity, far above and beyond this, why they should not be thus employed. Woman was created and intended to be man's companion, not his slave. Endowed as she is with all her loveliness and powers to please, she exercises an almost unlimited influence over the more stern and unbending disposition of man's nature. If there are reasons why man should be educated, there are many more and stronger reasons why woman should receive the soundest and most practical mental and moral training. She was created to be the presiding deity of the home circle, the instructor of our children, to guide the tottering footsteps of tender infancy in the paths of rectitude and virtue, to smooth down the wrinkles of our perverse nature, to weep over our shortcomings, and make us glad in the days of

Source: William H. Sylvis, "Address Delivered at Buffalo, N. Y., January, 1864," in *The Life, Speeches, Labors, and Essays of William H. Sylvis,* ed. James C. Sylvis (Philadelphia: Claxton, Remsen & Haffelfinger, 1872), 119–121.

adversity, to counsel, comfort, and console us in our declining years.

> "Woman's warm heart and gentle hand, in God's eternal plan,
> Were formed to soften, soothe, refine, exalt, and comfort man."

Who is there among us that does not know and has not felt the powerful influence of a good and noble woman? one in whom, after the busy toil and care of the day are past, we can confide our little secrets and consult upon the great issues of life. These, sir, are my views upon this question. This I believe to be the true and divine mission of woman, this her proper sphere; and those men who would and do turn her from it are the worst enemies of our race, the Shylocks of the age, the robbers of woman's virtue; they make commerce of the blood and tears of helpless women, and merchandise of souls. In the poverty, wretchedness, and utter ruin of their helpless victims, they see nothing but an accumulating pile of gold. In the weeping and wailing of the distressed, they hear nothing but a "metallic ring." To the abolition of this wrong imposed upon the tender sex should be devoted every attribute of our nature, every impulse of our heart, and every energy and ability with which we are endowed.

ARTICLE

Gender, Self, and Work in the Life Insurance Industry, 1880–1930

Angel Kwolek-Folland

In her essay, Kwolek-Folland describes how prevailing ideas about gender influenced the development of the insurance industry and discusses how gender ideologies affected the way it was run. She argues that anxieties about gender were reflected in the metaphors that corporate executives used to regulate their relationship with both their customers and their employees. She also analyzes the gendered implications of the way that space was allocated in insurance offices as well as the way that those who worked in the insurance industry dressed.

How was work in the life insurance industry gendered? How did gender affect the way men and women in the insurance industry related to each other? What role did rhetoric, space allocation, and clothing play in delineating gender in this industry? How were they used to challenge the power structure of insurance companies? Why were they used in this way?

In 1924 Glover Hastings, superintendent of agencies for the New England Mutual Life Insurance Company, described life insurance to an agents' training class as "the standing together . . . of hosts of manly men to defend each other's homes from the enemy that shoots on the sly and in the dark." Such metaphors of manhood and womanhood were common in the life insurance field, as workers at all levels in the industry addressed the changing nature of their work at the turn of the century.

The uses of gendered language to describe work and work relations stemmed from at least two interrelated sources. First, executives and workers in life insurance drew on gender metaphors as a primary way to delineate difference. Enlisting the late-nineteenth-century vocabulary of separate spheres, which used dualistic gender terms and relationships drawn from biology to describe nonbiological phenomena, workers and executives expressed their culture's specific obsession with categories of maleness and femaleness as signifiers of difference. Second, the changing demography of the office work force challenged the male-defined and -populated nineteenth-century workplace. Between about 1880 and 1930, young, white, middle- and working-class women entered the formerly all-male world of business in the United States as clerks, typists, bookkeepers, secretaries, and stenographers. In 1870 women made up only 2.5 percent of the clerical labor force; by 1930, 52.5 percent of all clerical workers were women. By the 1880s, life insurance employed more women workers than any other area of the private service sector.

Workers in the insurance industry expressed gender in multiple voices. Executives and managers used images of manhood and womanhood to explain and legitimate their product and production process to the public and to workers. In the process they articulated

a theory of work relations in gendered terms. Workers explicated their own alternative conceptions of the meaning of work through gender. Both explanations infused discussions about the meaning of work in life insurance with powerful cultural and intensely personal meanings. Conceptions of manhood and womanhood defined the meaning of work, the experience of workers, and the limits and possibilities of institutional organization. Men and women in the life insurance industry used gendered metaphors and images to express their understanding of the relationship between personal and institutional definitions of the work experience.

Life insurance is a service industry in its product, its reliance on corporate structure, and its often genuine (and fiscally sound) concern with the health and welfare of its clients and employees. From its commercial origins in the 1840s to the early twentieth century, life insurance changed from a maligned and publicly suspect operation to a well-regulated and respectable business. During that process, the industry in some cases anticipated much that was to take place within the American business community generally. The evolution of status, wage, and gender distinctions between workers, of the corporate bureaucracy and division of labor which were typical of business growth in the late nineteenth century, became noticeable in the life insurance industry by the 1880s.

Life insurance executives looking for ways to make their business appealing found gender imagery both a "natural" and a useful tool. Although any business relies to some extent on reputation, good customer relations are critical in life insurance. The industry "manufactures" and sells financial security, basing its operations on complex and precise computations, accurate and thorough record keeping, and financial investing. The intangible nature of its product and the all but invisible process of production make the public's goodwill of paramount importance. By 1900, life insurance executives had articulated a philosophy of service which justified their product. In their public pronouncements regarding the social purpose of life insurance and in the symbols they attached to their companies, executives incorporated gender in a philosophy I have called "corporate motherhood." Because of their emphasis on security and family protection and their concern with creating a positive public image, life insurance executives perhaps tended more than most to think of their mandate in social terms. Nevertheless, social legitimacy was particularly important in life insurance, which fought an uphill battle for public acceptance until the early twentieth century.

Executives had two interconnected purposes in mind when they used images of motherhood and family: first, to calm the fears of the public and stimulate sales; and second, to encourage a paternalistic relationship with employees. Both Metropolitan Life and New England Life executives repeatedly referred to their companies as "families." This emphasis initially came from the roots of the business in the family partnerships of the 1840s and 1850s. It became increasingly metaphorical, however, as companies grew and altered their organizational and recruiting structures. By the 1920s, Metropolitan Life's "family of 40,000" described an ideal of harmonious public and employee relations, not reality.

Symbols of womanhood emphasized the security of the industry, enhancing its persona by inferring that a company's relationship with the public was that of a mother with her children. Company logos, advertising, and descriptions stressed the nurturing and protective aspects of life insurance with images of domestic womanhood. Metropolitan Life and the Equitable both used the symbol of a mother to suggest the protection and care they offered. In 1859 Equitable adopted as its logo a vignette of an allegorical female figure with shield and spear protecting a mother holding a child in her arms. This vignette varied slightly over time, modifying but not abandoning the symbolic connection between the company and motherhood. In an advertising theme of 1900, a portrait of mother and child, titled "The Equitable Mother," referred to the security of families insured by the company. The New England used a picture of Priscilla Alden at her spinning wheel to illustrate the company in 1886. Between 1908 and 1954, this image appeared on life insurance policies and some promotional items. This was both a localized symbol of colonial antecedents and a larger invocation of Victorian associations of home, hearth, and domesticity. The ideology of corporate motherhood and its attendant symbols marked a major departure from the notion that business was a public, male arena driven by men and masculine values.

The symbols of corporate motherhood also tied a company's product to its production process, articulating an ideal of employee relations. The industry's vision of companies as mothers to the public harmonized with descriptions of the maternal relationship between companies and their employees. In an address of 1920 titled "Mother Metropolitan," company president Haley Fiske told a gathering of sales agents that the Metropolitan was a mother to both its clients and its employees. Referring to his audience as "my dear boys," Fiske said, "If Mother is this great Company, and if these millions of people [clients] are her children, then you are the elder brothers," whose job it was to become part of the client's "family circle," to become their "confidante and advisor." Fiske patterned his vision of corporate motherhood and service on that of the ideal middle-class Victorian woman: a nurturing and concerned figure, intrinsically benevolent and forgiving. Within the corporate family, male sales agents were eldest sons, carrying the ideal of service to the consumer/child.

In addition to these symbolic references to motherhood and family, Metropolitan Life, Equitable, Aetna Life, and New England Life all provided benefits to their employees to convince them that the companies were concerned about their welfare. By the 1890s, these companies sponsored employee lunchrooms, rest and recreation facilities, and sports events.

This package was formalized in the years just before World War I. In the mid-teens, for example, Metropolitan Life created a Welfare Department, headed by Mrs. Gean Cunningham Snyder, to oversee the health and job satisfaction of the company's female employees. Metropolitan hoped through this device to "increase the efficiency and happiness of its employees." The Welfare Department's mandate clearly grew out of the need to undermine worker discontent. Initially, however, it was based on the gender-specific belief that female employees required special maternal protection and guidance when they were far from home and family and so prey to a variety of temptations. Metropolitan developed the concept of corporate motherhood further around 1921, with the creation of the position of "house mother," whose duties were "indicated by her title":

> She is glad to consult with women Clerks as to their relations with their associates and superiors in the office, their domestic affairs, and their personal worries. She will willingly advise them in regard to any difficulties in or out of the office, or their residences and surroundings. Women Clerks who do not live with near relatives may feel free to ask her advice about boarding-places or living accommodations.

The house mother extended corporate motherhood to men as well. The company stressed that while the house mother "is expected, primarily to be of assistance to the women Clerks, . . . yet she is only too glad to advise with any men Clerks to whom she can be of help." In fact, the welfare idiom often took on clearly gendered tones. Athletic facilities at Metropolitan Life, for example, were open to both men and women, as were courses in "self-improvement." For women only, however, Metropolitan Life provided sewing rooms and instructors so that women workers could make their own clothing. Higher wages would have enabled them to buy clothing, but wages would not have expressed so directly the company's message of benevolent motherhood. The rhetorical uses of such symbols as motherhood and family also found expression in the physical spaces of life insurance offices, reinforcing the gendered environment of work relations. Designers and executives recreated the images and ambience of home within the office. They suggested domestic environments by the sizes of rooms (individual offices were smaller than areas where the "family" gathered together), residential fixtures and furniture, and decorative elements. Metropolitan Life's executive library and dining room in the 1890s repeated design elements common to Victorian domestic appointments: mantel clocks, candelabra, framed wall mirrors, a bearskin rug. The executive offices of New England Life's Milk Street building from the 1920s to 1941 were arranged like well-appointed parlors or libraries, with table lamps, leather couches, fireplaces, paintings, books, carpets, and display cabinets. Thus an essentially domestic environment was replicated within the public confines of the office. These "private" spaces within a "public" place reinforced the personalized overtones of the terms *home office* and *family*. The emphasis on domesticity in these decorative details focused on and used cultural assumptions about gender which physically explicated gender differences as status differences, and vice versa.

Office spaces and decoration reinforced not only public corporate status but notions about private, individual gender. Highly articulated private offices set those who possessed them apart from other workers, and in very visible ways emphasized the individualism and masculinity of their occupants. The fact that all of their occupants were men generated crucial repercussions for the significance of gender in business. First, it pulled the male role as husband and father—as domestic family member—directly into the workplace by recreating a private space within a public arena. Thus the private side of a man could be expressed in his public workplace. As one author put it: "He brings his whole life to his office now, where before he left part of it at home, for there was no place for it in his commercial existence. His office is now *his* office, where before he seemed merely to be occupying a space apportioned to him." Second, the private office designed to express a man's domestic side, his essential self as opposed to his commercial self, represented a form of property ownership and thus a traditional proof of manhood. This was especially critical in the corporate setting of a service industry such as life insurance. Corporate organization generally muted individual choice and autonomy, a phenomenon heightened by the feminized persona of a life insurance corporation. The implication was that men without private offices were not only lower in status within the company, they were also less manly as individuals. The private office, arrayed in its domestic symbolism and watched over by female secretaries or "office wives," thus was a mark of manhood as well as status.

Gendered imagery had a decided instrumental influence on how companies presented their product to the public and explained their relation to their employees. Life insurance rhetoric combined a feminized vision of the production process as a benevolent and nurturing spiritual force with imagery that stressed the familial nature of corporate relations and the company as a mother both to employees and to clients. Gendered images painted the inherently unstable and threatening picture of unregulated masculine business with a stable and nonthreatening gloss of motherhood and fatherhood, of women and men within the family serving their public children. This use of gender metaphors drew its emotive power from the specific tensions of the nineteenth-century gender dichotomy. Much as woman's task within the middle-class family was to tame the competitive and chaotic urges of men, so the mother company guided and stabilized the public. The public face of life insurance, in other words, conflated the separate worlds of Victorian manhood and womanhood, pulling privatized images of home and family into the public world and using that imagery to legitimize both a product and a production process.

Gender metaphors had the advantage of being both expandable and mutable, highly specific and personal. The use of gendered terms and metaphors in the insurance industry in the United States at the turn of the twentieth century converted Victorian social ideals of manhood and womanhood into models for a corporate work ethic. The industry's image of business as a family relationship integrated public and private social gender roles. In the process, the industry used beliefs about manhood and womanhood to legitimate both its product and its production process. From the managerial perspective, the use of gender to describe work relations suggested that corporate work was based on a natural hierarchy of the sexes rather than on an economic structure or the needs of managerial capitalism. Corporate motherhood defused and confused the reality of structural paternalism: womanhood had a symbolic existence that masked the hierarchical realities of corporate organization. Corporate work was thus experienced in an ideological context that blurred personal and public definitions of gender in the interests of organizational efficiency.

Both men and women workers accepted and used the same natural and corporate definitions of manhood and womanhood to explicate status, to express a commitment or lack of it to labor, and to assert a sense of self in relation to others in the workplace. Gendered language provided a way for workers to describe their experiences and understand the meaning of labor within their lives as a whole. It also functioned to conflate the distinctions between an individual's experiences as a worker and as a private person, and to this extent reinforced the corporate uses of gendered images.

Although economic and demographic factors were the basis for the changing nature of labor in life insurance from 1870 to 1930, some managers and workers in the industry held women in particular and womanhood in general responsible for men's subordination to the new bureaucratic structures. Women were, after all, one of the most visible signs of the changed business environment. In 1933 an Equitable clerk, Charles H. Vanse, contrasted the environment at Equitable to what it had been in the 1890s: "Now-a-days one is surrounded by an ocean of permanent waves and one's requests (not orders) are received with a smile while one's vocabulary has been refined to such an extent that 'Oh Well' is about as near as one can come except that the 'Old Timers' occasionally relapse into the old version." Vanse remembered the predominantly male office as a place of action. He attributed the politeness, refinement, and enforced cheerfulness he described to the presence of women; women had altered the vigorous, independent masculine office relations beyond recognition. Further, such changes in vocabulary and attitude affected not only the experience of work but the behavior of male managers and executives outside the workplace. In Vanse's account and others, the feminized character of office labor seemed to be a direct result of the feminization of the workplace. The newly "civilized" worker had lost his manhood in the gendered office. The presence of women altered both the social behaviors of the workplace and the association of work with manliness. The experience of office manhood thus took on new and disturbing implications.

Management theorists echoed Vanse's fears. For some, women's presence in offices raised the issue of dependency, and the dangers of that dependency for males. In 1932 one management educator, George Frederick, argued that American executives and managers had become "paralyzed" and "petulant" because they had turned so much of their work over to women. Such dependency was an offense not against corporate order but against nature. "After all, there is something a bit silly in seeing a husky man in an office chair so helpless that there isn't a paper . . . or a utensil he knows how to lay hold upon, without asking a frail little woman on the other side of the room to go get it for him." He likened this businessman to a "spoiled child" whose mother had to pick up after him. The dependency Frederick observed stemmed from the stratification of office work and the job specialization of the corporate structure. Workers under managerial capitalism did not control or participate in the entire process of production, only in

parts of it. Frederick, however, like Vanse, described such fragmentation as a relationship between men and women, as the result of a gender system rather than economic or organizational imperatives.

The expression of the fragmentation, dichotomy, and subordination of office work in gendered metaphors seems to have been typical office rhetoric by at least the 1920s. Observations made by women workers about men in offices echoed the infantile image of the business manager or executive. Many secretaries who responded to a survey conducted by the Bureau of Vocational Information (BVI) in 1925 complained about the irrationality of male demands in the workplace. They referred to men as "temperamental," "difficult to work for," moody, and "disagreeable." By the 1920s, the image of childlike men had become a part of the popular image of male office workers. In 1928 a former secretary, Grace Robinson, lamented that "the man one works for has, more than likely, a healthy, well nourished temper that all its life has been permitted to cavort about naked, untrammeled, and undisciplined." Women as well as men, workers as well as theorists, described their dissatisfaction with fragmentation and lack of control as a function of gender relationships rather than job, position, or corporate structure.

Life insurance executives encouraged the view that all workers, male and female, were dependents in a system of benevolent familial alliances. Both the specialized ideology of corporate motherhood and the structural paternalism it legitimized stressed the childlike nature of workers, voicing the notion that male as well as female corporate employees were undisciplined dependents. Corporate motherhood addressed the issue of dependency by lumping men and women together, asserting the commingling of prescribed male and female behavior, and describing an employee who was loyal and obedient regardless of sex. Yet deep-rooted cultural assumptions of male dominance and female subordination could not be overridden so easily. In fact, the implicit challenge to the gender hierarchy posed by the image of corporate motherhood gave the issue of subordination a highly personal cast.

Descriptions of the childlike and subservient qualities of male office workers linked men to stereotyped images of women, suggesting that the childlike male was emasculated. This idea placed men at the same subordinate level as women and threatened to upset the finely balanced power structures of both the gender dichotomy and corporate status. Male workers tried to shape office gender relations in ways that would emphasize male dominance. Several former secretaries in the BVI survey observed that employers preferred to hire women who did not have college educations because such workers would be less independent and self-assured. One respondent noted that "there is not a little prejudice . . . against the college girl; she's less easily blind folded and men don't like to be 'seen through.' " Another claimed that "some of the men in the concern like to have high school graduates; enjoy the feeling of superiority over their secretaries."

This apparent preference for employees who were female and who were younger and less well educated than their bosses seems to have been borne out in reality. The youth of female office workers was both a subject of comment and a demographic fact throughout the period. Photographs of the Metropolitan Life office staff taken in the 1890s suggest a predominantly young female work force. So prevalent were young women office workers in insurance, in fact, that the term *girl* was shorthand for *clerical worker*. In 1915 Metropolitan Life reported that the average age of its male clerks was 31, that of female clerks 27. A respondent to the BVI survey noted that

One [employment] agency has said that they find it hard to place a young woman in secretarial work when she attains the age of thirty or thirty-five. . . . The advertisements in the papers seem to bear that statement out. . . . Whereas when I started out I was turned away for lack of

experience, today I notice the advertisement calls especially for the inexperienced.

The youthfulness of female insurance workers stemmed in part from the ideological and economic attractions of office work to young, never-married women. The best-paid and most prestigious of positions open to young women, office jobs also were surrounded by a mythology that emphasized the highly personal, even intimate nature of male-female relations in the office. The "office wife," popular literature claimed, could marry the boss and become his real wife. Age played an important role in this mythology, and pointed to its deeper social and sexual meanings. Commonly held notions of appropriate age and gender relations paired an older man with a younger woman. The idea of a young male boss employing an older female secretary upset both the traditional age hierarchy and notions of male dominance. The proper role for an older woman—mother—precluded sexuality or sexual attraction in the boss-secretary relationship. This idea divested such a relationship of its power via marriage imagery (the "wedding" and thus transcendence of two status levels or power levels, the office wife and the corporate family man) and of its potent sexual tensions as well.

The evolution of corporate bureaucracy in life insurance associated gender traits with particular jobs; and gender divisions described the hierarchy of positions within a corporation, replicating differences of status. Thus the people in the lower positions within a business were associated with a wide array of feminine qualities, those in the upper reaches with masculine qualities. A woman manager was expected to adopt masculine business behaviors and beliefs; a male secretary, attributes increasingly defined as feminine. For a woman to display features or attitudes of dominance—age, position, or behavior—undermined both the status hierarchy and the gender system. As we have seen, however, men often attributed their own perceived subordination to the presence of women. Crucial components of male self-definition, in other words, hinged on the meanings womanhood assumed in the corporate context. This uncanny reversal of the hierarchy ascribed to women levels of control and dominance which their definition as subordinates denied.

This inversion of power suggests that patriarchal attitudes and structures in the life insurance industry applied as much to men as to women workers. On the one hand, the attitudes of top managers and executives included the sense that all employees were boys and girls under the care of watchful and protective parents: the executive father and the mother company. Insurance work involved some degree of subordination and inequality for both men and women. Yet experience bore out the organizational presumption of female inferiority. By 1930, notions of appropriate work for men and women, the promotional hierarchy of life insurance corporations, even company buildings created a job segregation by gender and separate promotional tracks, status levels, and pay scales for male and female workers. Thus in life insurance, as in other industries, women did not enjoy the opportunities for advancement open to men. As the role reversal evident in men's sense of dependency illustrates, however, male workers also experienced powerlessness within the corporation. What seems to have been operative in corporate work experience was the increasing degree to which descriptions of gender acted as descriptions of labor relationships, and the concurrent importance of gender roles to ideas about the self.

Women insurance sales agents and managers created definitions of their work which simultaneously drew on and undermined masculine and corporate imperatives. The problems and possibilities of their arguments reveal the complex relations between the genders of work and the self in life insurance offices. Women agents and managers participated in the male world of sales and management even as they asserted a female role in business. They usurped the language of man-

agement and sales to describe their work, and consciously departed from male values. In particular, female agents and managers claimed their superiority to men as *workers*, arguing for the recognition of natural female skills in the life insurance workplace.

The life insurance product, as opposed to the producing company itself, was couched in masculine terms. Companies emphasized life insurance sales as a masculine calling, much like the clergy or the law. At the instrumental level, sales pitches aimed life insurance primarily at male breadwinners and played on the desire for what one historian has called "economic immortality." Life insurance removed death from the feminized regions of sentimentality and placed it in the masculinized realm of rationalism. The industry demonstrated that death could be tabulated, categorized, predicted, and given a cash value through actuarial tables and statistics. As a product, then, life insurance aimed predominantly, although not exclusively, at men.

The meaning of saleswork in life insurance, however, was open to interpretation, and sales literature stressed a complicated mixture of behaviors for agents and managers. Sales demanded competitiveness but also cooperation; agents needed to be enthusiastic but rational; they had to be both self-effacing and aggressive servants of society and their company. The life insurance product and customer also were problematic. Clients were both recalcitrant enemies and grateful beneficiaries; life insurance was both a monetary exchange and social stewardship. Above all, life insurance sales was a "manly calling." It is in the context of these contested and masculinized meanings that women sales agents defined their work.

Women agents, aware of the gendered basis of their employment, requisitioned gender relations and images to legitimate their work. Newsletters printed by women's agencies, for example, used gender to position the agencies within the larger corporate structure. In 1903 Florence Shaal's Equitable agency began to publish a newsletter for agents titled *The Little Sister to the Equitable News*, calling attention to its derivative and gendered relation to the company's newsletter. Marie Little's agency published the *Little Upstart* from 1916 to 1918, using the manager's name as a pun for the position of her agency within the company (and perhaps to take the menace out of *upstart*). As the titles of these journals imply, they borrowed their rationale for existence from the house journals for agents published by Equitable and other companies. Their main purpose, like that of the company journals, was to encourage sales, create solidarity within the agency, and instruct agents on sales technique and attitude. At the same time, however, the women's newsletters acknowledged their diminutive stature and derivative nature. Drawing on the analogy of the company as a family, their titles stressed their childlike, subordinate, and nonthreatening stature.

The *Little Upstart* consciously tried to set the women's agency apart from male agencies. One early issue asserted ascribed female qualities against the masculine tradition of the house papers: "We rather glory in our sauciness and impudence and pride ourselves upon the jewel of our inconsistency, and we snap our fingers at precedent and tradition. We want to have a sweetish number [of the newsletter] bubbling over with sentiment and have deliberately planned it." The use of such terms as *sauciness, impudence,* and *inconsistency* and the implication that sentiment was an appropriate management tool cut two ways. On the one hand, they recognized common beliefs about women's nature and behavior: women were childish and inconsistent. Thus the writer laid claim to an accepted, if arguable, image of womanhood. On the other, she inverted the implications of that image by suggesting that these were business strengths rather than womanly weaknesses. *Sauciness* and *impudence* could be translated in the male language of management as *fighting spirit* and *aggressiveness*. The behavior was generic to sales, but it was expressed in a very different way. Sauciness and impudence were *not* behaviors prescribed for such female corporate workers as typists, or for managers of either gender.

This validation of female assertiveness usurped male-centered definitions of aggressive sales behavior. The use of *sauciness* and *impudence* in this context recognized women's minority position in management and sales; but it also accommodated aggression into the canon of female business behavior. It turned impudence into an element of a female success ethic, legitimizing it as a female version of male aggression. The writer set female agents apart from male and other female workers without stepping beyond the bounds of acceptable female behavior. At the same time, however, she challenged masculinized definitions of management's role and turned female weaknesses into work skills commensurate with those of men.

We can see a similar assertion of female values at the expense of male and corporate codes of behavior in the issue of office clothing for agents. Office clothing illustrates women workers' use of alternative primary structures of self-definition which undermined official power structures and replaced them with alternative possibilities. Women's office dress emphasized sexuality, suggesting that women workers were not wholly committed to their labor in ways management wanted. Popular women's magazines and company journals and newsletters contributed to this impression by suggesting in words and pictures that the female office worker was dressing to attract a husband. Clothing styles were an aspect of female office behavior that management consistently found particularly offensive. The business educator and theorist Edward Kilduff expressed it best:

> The secretary should realize that a business employer silently criticizes the secretary who wears clothing more suited for social affairs than for office work . . . Some women secretaries do not seem to realize that it is a business mistake to wear their "party" clothes to the office, that it is not in keeping with the general scheme of a business office to be "dressed up."

This sort of admonition had been common from the time women began to work in offices. In one of the earliest advice books to prospective women office workers in 1898, Ruth Ashmore counseled women to purchase sensible, dark clothing. She claimed that wearing fancy dress at work suggested to employers that a woman was more interested in parties and the social whirl than in earning a living.

Male business clothing had developed by the 1890s into a kind of uniform that was also worn outside the office by middle-class men. The middle-class male's subdued dark suit asserted his commitment to his job, and carried the implication that office work was an essential component of his self-image in and out of the workplace. Early office clothing for women essentially was a simplified version of middle-class, daytime domestic attire—a dark skirt and a white or dark long-sleeved blouse. Such clothing was not a uniform associated with office work in the same way as a male's dark suit. Significantly, however, it was closer symbolically to male office attire than female dress after about 1915.

Gradually female workers did develop a "uniform" for office wear, and it was precisely this uniform that managers found so disconcerting. By the 1920s, women's office wear was the same as their leisure wear and implied—certainly to management—that women office workers were not wholly committed to their job. Elaborate hair styles, jewelry, perfume, light sandals, and dresses of soft, colorful fabrics told management that women office workers had not sold their entire consciousness to the demands of the typewriter or Dictaphone. In addition, such clothing stressed differences between male and female, accenting femininity and sexuality and reinforcing the gender dichotomy. On one hand, of course, leisure clothing underscored female subordination and the perception that women's primary interest lay in marriage rather than in office work. On the other, it placed women outside the structure of business: it acted as an assertion of self and womanhood which challenged business values, the divisions of status and dominance, and even manhood. Management certainly viewed women's office attire from both these perspectives, seeing such clothing as a statement of female distance from the commitments of corporate labor and as a badge of the feminized office—a reminder of the explosive potential of sexuality and of management's ultimate inability to control the social construction of a worker's gendered self.

In the *Upstart*'s attention to women's fashion, its admonitions to dress "appropriately" and "sensibly," the newsletter echoed prescriptions leveled by management at clerical workers, secretaries, and other managers. Like male-oriented management journals, the *Upstart* proffered constant advice about dressing for saleswork. One article cautioned that "Little Agents should always wear smartly tailored suits," because tailored suits placed their wearers on a businesslike plane and were closer to male office attire. They made women sales agents conform with male managerial definitions of proper business clothing. Further, such requests urged women agents to identify themselves with their careers by projecting an image of commitment and serious intent.

However, the newsletter's comments on dress also alluded to interests at variance with corporate business aims. In keeping with its contrary agenda, clothing columns in the *Upstart* came under such headings as "Flivel and Drivel." Unlike advice to male agents, *Upstart* articles focused on fashion as often as on practicality and business image. And they indicate that some women agents avoided the tailored suit. Under the title "Who's Who in Bankruptcy," the editor mentioned that "Marie Smith is sporting a charming new blue crepe de chine frock, all bespangled with beads, most handsome and expensive." Such comments recognized that women sales agents had a distinct interest in clothing and fashion at odds with the practical matters of life insurance sales, and suggested that female agents shared something of the perspective of other women office workers.

The political quality of women's language and behavior grew out of a problem of self-definition: How could one remain a woman in a man's world? This question underlay much of women's work experience in offices, and female sales agents and managers addressed it in a variety of ways. Aware of their outsider status, women agents used humor to assert difference and to mask or deflect dissatisfaction and criticism. The language and tone of the *Upstart,* for example, sometimes poked fun at the rituals of life insurance sales, rituals that largely excluded women. One article commented that many items in the *Upstart* might seem "hackneyed to the seasoned agent. . . . [But] we hope our blasé readers will kindly remember that few of our agents have had the educational advantages of the conventions, and of listening to the wiseacres air their knowledge at these assemblies." Here the newsletter suggested the pomposity and exclusivity of the male management style. This type of attack on the agent conventions was unprecedented in the house journals. While it may have been the unspoken opinion of some agents, it never appeared in print.

The issue of deviance was particularly important to women agents because it touched on the intimate relation between individual and social gender. The mingling of notions about gender and the labor experience among office workers becomes clearer in the context of women workers' distinctions between their role and that of men. Women sometimes denied their subordinate position at work by asserting their superiority to male workers, using gender awareness to conflate the organizational hierarchy, stand it on its head, and deny its relevance to their sense of women's role. To avoid the perception that they were out of place, women managers and agents could infuse their work with culturally prescribed feminine values, using assumptions about women's nature to assert female superiority and difference. On the one hand, they spoke and acted as outsiders, not bound by company prescriptions, flaunting their deviance from the corporate structure. On the other hand, they claimed that women's approach to sales and management was superior to that of salesmen and male managers,

that they were more appropriate insiders than men in this industry. Marie Little, speaking before a class on "Business Today" held at the New York University School of Commerce in 1915, asserted this perceived difference between male and female life insurance agents. Little explained that a woman agent was more appropriate to the business. Life insurance was inherently not " 'a man's world,' . . . for most insurance is for women. Woman is the homemaker, the true instinct of her is home. Who then should be better able to sell insurance [than] women who know the needs of the home? . . . Woman in the insurance field finds her true vocation." Little claimed that women were more committed than men to the higher ideals of life insurance and the client's welfare because of intrinsic female qualities. She asserted that male agents were more interested in making a sale than in telling the truth; women were "more conscientious than men and, therefore, that very fact will make their statements more conscientious."

For all their assertions of difference, women agents still faced the fact that saleswork required certain generic, male-defined behaviors. One of the primary attributes of the male sales agent was competitiveness. Both the *Upstart* and the *Little Sister* urged competition among women agents, but the language varied from that of the male-oriented journals, which often used agricultural metaphors to explain the role of male sales agents. Customers were viewed as fertile fields for the right man—the ambitious, energetic, enthusiastic man who worked hard. As an article in the house journal for Equitable, *Items for Agents,* put it in 1909, life insurance "lies as an immense farm before you; every possible implement for working it is furnished by the Society. It is up to you to sow the seed and gather the crop."

A short piece in the *Upstart* titled "Her Garden" implied a smaller and more intimate field of endeavor. In a larger sense, however, the garden was the "Laboratory of Life." This metaphor echoes the industry philosophy that life insurance sales was a noble calling of benefit to all humanity, but stresses its particular

suitability as a career for women. The article used the symbolic meanings of various flowers and herbs to describe the qualities needed by agents. These characteristics were identical to those of salesmen generally—ambition, enthusiasm, loyalty—but included others foreign to the vocabulary of male management: "Violets for Modesty; and Mignonette to make you sweet. . . . We will need lots of Red Clover for Industry, and Oh, I pray that my Hollyhocks will grow for in garden language they mean Ambition. Over here, I shall plant White Crysanthemums [sic] for Truth and Shamrocks for Loyalty." Striving for modesty and sweetness were not part of the male canon of management; in fact, while male managers stressed teamwork and sympathy, male cooperation and sensitivity had as their ultimate goal a conquered rather than a coaxed customer. Modesty and sweetness, though were important components of cultural womanhood, projected as specifically female elements of business success.

One issue of the *Upstart* devoted entirely to the career of the agency manager Florence Shaal made clear the differences between male and female approaches to management and sales success. One author claimed that Shaal was "the good comrade of her women, ready to give of her very best to help and encourage them; rejoicing in their successes and sympathizing in their failures and discouragements as though they were her own." Other encomiums to Mrs. Shaal in this issue stressed this same sense of female solidarity and an almost inherent lack of competitiveness. While male managers admonished that all leadership included this personalized empathy with subordinates, the female agents whose articles appeared in the *Upstart* added the distinct notion that such personalism was a feminine trait and the mark of a female management style that set women apart from men.

The distinctions female agents made between manly and womanly job attributes is clearly revealed in the different behaviors ascribed to "business girls" and "business women." Women office workers, after the ad-vent of female professionalism around 1900 to at least 1930, stressed the feminine qualities of the business or office girl and the masculine qualities of the business woman. The heroine of a *Saturday Evening Post* story of 1915 had ambitions to be a business woman, the owner of her own advertising agency. In contrast to the office girls she saw around her, she aspired to a "career." Office girls were clock watchers, uncommitted labor, destined forever to be low-paid subordinates. Their relations to their work described by respondents to the BVI survey also reveal this distinction between "girls" and "women" in business. One woman, a former secretary, commented that "I really feel that the business world rubs the bloom from a woman." Another emphasized that secretarial work "tends to make a business woman of her, thereby tending to detract sweet feminine qualities." Thus business women were more like men in their attachment to their work and their allegiance to business values.

In their assertion of the distinctions between male and female managers, *Upstart* writers addressed this issue of gender deviance directly. They emphasized that Mrs. Shaal, though a manager, had retained her womanhood: "A business woman has been defined by other men besides Shakespeare as 'a woman impudent and mannish grown,' but such a description does not apply to Mrs. Shaal. Dainty, refined, with a magnetic charm of manner, . . . she has had such a brilliantly successful career, and yet has lost nothing of her womanly grace and charm." In affirming Shaal's essential femininity, the author denied that management positions necessarily turned women into men. Marie Little addressed the issue of deviance this way: "I think it only fair to remind you that tradition says all life insurance agents are bores. In that case, however, I never found yet a woman agent that was a bore. It seems that that quality is enjoyed by the men alone, and we will let them have it." Little's comment reassured her listeners that to become an agent or manager did not mean that a woman had to become like a man.

Further, she suggested that female agents were not bound up in the self-definitions business promoted for women, but approached sales on their own terms. The goal of female life insurance managers and agents, in other words, was to retain social definitions of womanhood and use those attributes as a means of engaging the work commitment of other women. One way to accomplish this feat—to be a manager without being manly—was to choose a profession not at odds with cultural definitions of woman's place. Advocates saw life insurance sales, like other evolving "women's professions" such as teaching, nursing, and social work, as uniquely suited to women because it called forth and used so-called natural aspects of womanhood. Thus, in the life insurance industry, women could become managers and sales agents without having to adopt male business values. Rather, they could emphasize feminine traits, such as modesty and sweetness. Further, they could draw parallels between such masculine characteristics as aggression and such feminine ones as impudence. In that way work could be an expression of the female self rather than a negation of womanhood. By simultaneously presenting themselves as antagonists to corporate norms—as outsiders—and asserting their close match to the industry's rhetoric of social service—as insiders—they could carve out a female space within a male world.

In the life insurance industry, work could be defined and expressed by an individual's commitment to gender. A woman who wished to escape the deadening aspects of office work, to step outside the time and space of wage labor and into management or sales, had to adopt male business values and behaviors defined as male—to become *like* a man. A woman who became a manager surrendered her female self; a man who did so fulfilled his masculine self. The issue for women agents and managers was not simply political or economic equality of opportunity and experience; it was whether an individual chose a position of strength or one of weakness within an economic and social system shaped by powerful cultural assumptions regarding the gendered self.

Social and individual gender in the office were composed of images and expectations that reinforced and delineated each other. This process was based, ultimately, on the explanations of experience, on the symbols, images, and metaphors available to connect the abstract qualities of hierarchy, status, and power relationships to the specific experiences of managing people, selling insurance, and typing reports. The discussions about manhood and womanhood, the concern with gender deviance, the gendered uses of space and bodily expression fused the economic and social concerns of the life insurance corporation to the individual concerns of workers. The social constructions of gender expressed in the life insurance industry fitted within and informed both the experience of work and the underlying economic and organizational structures of the corporate work system.

To the extent that definitions of gender behavior were caught up in the experience of work in life insurance, they both legitimized and challenged the power relationships of the corporate labor system. Both men and women in the industry accepted and used a dichotomy of gender to explicate status, to express a commitment or lack of it to labor, and to assert a sense of self in relation to others. The gender analogies of life insurance allowed workers to express a crucial aspect of their personal lives—who they were as men or women—in their work. Glover Hastings and Marie Little, among others, meshed both personal and corporate understandings of gender to explicate their sense of what their work meant. By using gender, workers could draw on a common language and reshape it, describing and defining their work in ways that reinforced rather than undermined their sense of womanhood and manhood.

That workers made their accommodation in gendered terms was in part a response to the structural inequities of the corporation—to the fact that wages, hiring, and status were segregated by sex. In addition, life insurance workers shared the images articulated by executives for other purposes. Executives, after all, used gender symbols precisely because they provided a vocabulary common both to the public and to workers, an Esperanto that bridged differences of class or motivation. Personal concepts of gender, however, imposed constraints and created possibilities that also shaped the institutional system. Managers seldom were able to impose their own dress codes or make actual the corporate family. The social gender system of the life insurance workplace was a product of the way such institutional and personal visions and imperatives were resolved.

SUGGESTIONS FOR FURTHER READING

CINDY SONDIK ARON, *Ladies and Gentlemen of the Civil Service: Middle-Class Workers in Victorian America* (New York: Oxford University Press, 1987).

MARY H. BLEWETT, "Masculinity and Mobility: The Dilemma of Lancashire Weavers and Spinners in Late-Nineteenth-Century Fall River, Massachusetts," in *Meanings for Manhood: Constructions of Masculinity in Victorian America,* ed. Mark C. Carnes and Clyde Griffin (Chicago: Chicago University Press, 1990), 164–77.

MARY H. BLEWETT, *Men, Women, and Work: Class, Gender, and Protest in the New England Shoe Industry, 1780–1910* (Urbana: University of Illinois Press, 1988).

JEANNE BOYDSTON, *Home and Work: Housework, Wages, and the Ideology of Labor in the Early Republic* (New York: Oxford University Press, 1990).

ELIZABETH CLARK-LEWIS, *Living In, Living Out: African American Domestics in Washington, DC, 1910–1940* (Washington, DC: Smithsonian Institution Press, 1994).

PATRICIA A. COOPER, *Once a Cigar Maker: Men, Women, and Work Culture in American Cigar Factories, 1900–1919* (Urbana: University of Illinois Press, 1987).

MELISSA DABAKIS, "Gendered Labor: Norman Rockwell's *Rosie the Riveter* and the Discourses of Wartime Womanhood," in *Gender and American History Since 1890,* ed. Barbara Melosh (London: Routledge, 1993), 182–204.

MARGERY W. DAVIES, *Woman's Place Is at the Typewriter: Office Work and Office Workers, 1870–1930* (Philadelphia: Temple University Press, 1982).

ILEEN A. DEVAULT, *Sons and Daughters of Labor: Class and Clerical Work in Turn-of-the Century Pittsburgh* (Ithaca, NY: Cornell University Press, 1990).

VIRGINIA G. DRACHMAN, *Sisters in Law: Women Lawyers in Modern American History* (Cambridge, MA: Harvard University Press, 1998).

THOMAS DUBLIN, *Transforming Women's Work: New England Lives in the Industrial Revolution* (Ithaca, NY: Cornell University Press, 1994).

THOMAS DUBLIN, *Women at Work: The Transformation of Work and Community in Lowell, Massachusetts, 1826–1860* (New York: Columbia University Press, 1979).

FAYE E. DUDDEN, *Serving Women: Household Service in Nineteenth-Century America* (Middletown, CT: Wesleyan University Press, 1983).

LISA M. FINE, *The Souls of the Skyscraper: Female Clerical Workers in Chicago, 1870–1930* (Philadelphia: Temple University Press, 1990).

WENDY GAMBER, *The Female Economy: The Millinery and Dressmaking Trades, 1860–1930* (Urbana: University of Illinois Press, 1997).

SUSAN A. GLENN, *Daughters of the Shtetl: Life and Labor in the Immigrant Generation* (Ithaca, NY: Cornell University Press, 1990).

MICHAEL GROSSBERG, "Institutionalizing Masculinity: The Law as a Masculine Profession," in *Meanings for Manhood: Constructions of Masculinity in Victorian America*, ed. Mark C. Carnes and Clyde Griffin (Chicago: University of Chicago Press, 1990), 133–51.

KAREN V. HANSEN, " 'Helped Put in a Quilt': Men's Work and Male Intimacy in Nineteenth-Century New England," in *The Social Construction of Gender*, ed. Judith Lorber and Susan A. Farrell (Newbury Park, CA: Sage Publications, 1991), 83–103.

TERA W. HUNTER, *To 'Joy My Freedom: Southern Black Women's Lives and Labors after the Civil War* (Cambridge, MA: Harvard University Press, 1997).

DAVID M. KATZMAN, *Seven Days a Week: Women and Domestic Service in Industrializing America* (New York: Oxford University Press, 1978).

ANGEL KWOLEK-FOLLAND, *Engendering Business: Men and Women in the Corporate Office, 1870–1930* (Baltimore, MD: Johns Hopkins University Press, 1994).

NANCY GREY OSTERUD, " 'She Helped Me Hay It as Good as a Man': Relations among Women and Men in an Agricultural Community," in *"To Toil the Livelong Day": America's Women at Work, 1780–1980*, ed. Carol Groneman and Mary Beth Norton (Ithaca, NY: Cornell University Press, 1987), 87–97.

VICKI L. RUIZ, *Cannery Women, Cannery Lives: Mexican Women, Unionization, and the California Food Processing Industry, 1930–1950* (Albuquerque: University of New Mexico Press, 1987).

CAROLE TURBIN, *Working Women of Collar City: Gender, Class, and Community in Troy, New York, 1864–86* (Urbana: University of Illinois Press, 1992).